Lecture Notes in Computer Science 5821

Commenced Publication in 1973
Founding and Former Series Editors:
Gerhard Goos, Juris Hartmanis, and Jan van Leeuwen

T0180858

Zhihua Cai   Zhenhua Li   Zhuo Kang
Yong Liu (Eds.)

Advances in Computation and Intelligence

4th International Symposium, ISICA 2009
Huangshi, China, October 23-25, 2009
Proceedings

 Springer

Volume Editors

Zhihua Cai
Faculty of Computer Science, China University of Geosciences, Wuhan, China
E-mail: zhcai@cug.edu.cn

Zhenhua Li
School of Computer Science, China University of Geosciences, Wuhan, China
E-mail: zhli@cug.edu.cn

Zhuo Kang
Computation Center, Wuhan University, Wuhan, China
E-mail: kang_whu@yahoo.com

Yong Liu
School of Computer Science and Engineering, The University of Aizu, Japan
E-mail: yliu@u-aizu.ac.jp

Library of Congress Control Number: 2009936008

CR Subject Classification (1998): I.2, I.2.6, I.5.1, F.1, I.6, J.1

LNCS Sublibrary: SL 1 – Theoretical Computer Science and General Issues

ISSN   0302-9743
ISBN-10   3-642-04842-0 Springer Berlin Heidelberg New York
ISBN-13   978-3-642-04842-5 Springer Berlin Heidelberg New York

springer.com

© Springer-Verlag Berlin Heidelberg 2009
Printed in Germany

Typesetting: Camera-ready by author, data conversion by Scientific Publishing Services, Chennai, India
Printed on acid-free paper   SPIN: 12772599   06/3180   5 4 3 2 1 0

Preface

Volumes of LNCS 5821 and CCIS 51 are the proceedings of the 4th International Symposium on Intelligence Computation and Applications (ISICA 2009) held in Huangshi, China, October 23–25, 2009. These two volumes are in memory of Prof. Lishan Kang, the ISICA 2009 Honorary General Chair, who was a leading figure in the fields of domain decomposition methods and computational intelligence.

ISICA 2009 successfully attracted over 300 submissions. Through rigorous reviews, 58 high-quality papers were included in LNCS 5821, while the other 54 papers were collected in CCIS 51. ISICA conferences are one of the first series of international conferences on computational intelligence that combine elements of learning, adaptation, evolution and fuzzy logic to create programs as alternative solutions to artificial intelligence. The last three ISICA proceedings have been accepted in the Index to Scientific and Technical Proceedings (ISTP) and/or Engineering Information (EI).

Following the success of the past three ISICA events, ISICA 2009 made good progress in the analysis and design of newly developed methods in the field of computational intelligence. ISICA 2009 featured the most up-to-date research in analysis and theory of evolutionary algorithms, neural network architectures and learning, fuzzy logic and control, predictive modeling for robust classification, swarm intelligence, evolutionary system design, evolutionary image analysis and signal processing, and computational intelligence in engineering design. ISICA 2009 provided a venue to foster technical exchanges, renew everlasting friendships, and establish new connections.

On behalf of the Organizing Committee, we would like to thank warmly the sponsors, China University of Geosciences and Hubei Normal University, who helped in one way or another to achieve our goals for the conference. We wish to express our appreciation to Springer for publishing the proceedings of ISICA 2009. We also wish to acknowledge the dedication and commitment of the LNCS and CCIS editorial staff. We would like to thank the authors for submitting their work, as well as the Program Committee members and reviewers for their enthusiasm, time and expertise. The invaluable help of active members from the Organizing Committee, including Jiaoe Jiang, Dajun Rong, Hao Zhang and Xiaowen Jin, in setting up and maintaining the online submission systems, assigning the papers to the reviewers, and preparing the camera-ready version of the proceedings is highly appreciated. We would like to thank them personally for helping make ISICA 2009 a success.

October 2009

Zhihua Cai
Zhenhua Li
Zhuo Kang
Yong Liu

Organization

ISICA 2009 was organized by the School of Computer Science, China University of Geosciences, and Hubei Normal University, and sponsored by China University of Geosciences.

Honorary General Chair

Lishan Kang   China University of Geosciences, China

General Co-chairs

Huiming Tang   China University of Geosciences, China
Boshan Chen   Hubei Normal University, China

Program Co-chairs

Zhihua Cai   China University of Geosciences, China
Shudong Shi   Hubei Normal University, China
Yong Liu   University of Aizu, Japan

Publication Chair

Zhenhua Li   China University of Geosciences, China

Program Committee

Mehdi Hosseinzadeh Aghdam	University of Tabriz, Iran
M. Amiri	Allameh Tabatabaee University, Iran
Sujeevan Aseervatham	University of Grenoble, France
Jeremy Bolton	University of Florida, USA
Hua Cao	Mississippi State University, USA
Jiangtao Cao	University of Portsmouth, UK
Cheng-Hsiung Chiang	Hsuan Chuang University, Taiwan, China
Alessandro Ghio	University of Genova, Italy
Erik D. Goodman	Michigan State University, USA
Peng Guo	University of Science and Technology of China, China
A.S. Hadi	University of Baghdad, Iraq
Fei He	City University of Hong Kong, China
Katsuhiro Honda	Osaka Prefecture University, Japan

Yutana Jewajinda	National Electronics and Computer Technology Center, Bangkok, Thailand
He Jiang	Dalian University of Technology, China
Heli Koskimaki	University of Oulu, Oulu, Finland
Takio Kurita	Neuroscience Research Institute National Institute of Advanced Industrial Science and Technology, Japan
Juan Luis J. Laredo	University of Granada, Spain
Bi Li	Guangdong University of Foreign Studies, China
Yow Tzu Lim	University of York, UK
Xiaojun Lu	University of Electronic Science and Technology of China, China
Wenjian Luo	China Science and Technology University, China
Alejandro Flores Méndez	LaSalle University, Mexico
J.I. Serrano	Universidad de Cantabria, Spain
A.K.M. Khaled	The University of Melbourne, Australia
Ahsan Talukder	
H.R. Tizhoosh	University of Waterloo, Canada
Massimiliano Vasile	University of Glasgow, UK
Jun Wang	The Chinese University of Hong Kong, China
Yuxuan Wang	Nanjing University of Posts & Telecom, China
Hongjie Xing	Hebei University, China
Jifeng Xuan	Dalian University of Technology, China
Harry Zhang	University of New Brunswick, Canada

Local Arrangements Chair

Yadong Liu	China University of Geosciences, China

Secretariat

Jiaoe Jiang	China University of Geosciences, China
Dajun Rong	China University of Geosciences, China
Hao Zhang	China University of Geosciences, China
Xiaowen Jin	China University of Geosciences, China

Sponsoring Institutions

China University of Geosciences, Wuhan,China

Table of Contents

Section I: Analysis of Genetic Algorithms

Section II: Computational Intelligence in Engineer Design

Section III: Optimization and Learning

Section IV: Representations and Operators

Section V: Robust Classification

Section VI: Statistical Learning

Section VII: Swarm Intelligence

Section VIII: System Design

A Novel Online Test-Sheet Composition Approach Using Genetic Algorithm

Fengrui Wang[1], Wenhong Wang[2], Quanke Pan[2], and Fengchao Zuo[2]

[1] School of Media and Communications Technology, Liaocheng University, Liaocheng, China
[2] School of Computer Science, Liaocheng University, China
wfrsd@126.com, wwhem@126.com, panquanke@lcu.edu.cn

Abstract. In e-learning environment, online testing system can help to evaluate students' learning status precisely. To meet the users' multiple assessment requirements, a new test-sheet composition model was put forward. Based on the proposed model, a genetic algorithm with effective coding strategy and problem characteristic mutation operation were designed to generate high quality test-sheet in online testing systems. The proposed algorithm was tested using a series of item banks with different scales. Superiority of the proposed algorithm is demonstrated by comparing it with the genetic algorithm with binary coding strategy.

1 Introduction

In e-learning environment, online testing can help to evaluate student's learning status effectively during the learning process without time and place limitation. In order to perform online testing successfully, high quality test-sheets must be constructed in short time from item banks using certain test-sheet composition algorithm [1, 2].

In general, online test-sheet constructing runs through three steps. First, according to the learning process of students, user (teacher or student) can set the relevant parameters of a test sheet, such as total score, number of test items, difficulty degree and expected testing time of the test-sheet by a web browser. Then, test-sheet composition algorithm selects proper test items from the item bank automatically according to the user's multiple criteria. Finally, the obtained test-sheet is displayed in the user's interface. In practical applications, effective test-sheet composition algorithms play a key role in developing online testing systems [2, 3].

Most of the existing online testing systems compose a test-sheet using manual or random test item selecting algorithms [4,5,6]. Such algorithms are inefficient and usually can't the meet multiple assessment requirements simultaneously. Recently, many researches have been done to provide a more systematic approach for optimal test-sheet design. In these studies, computer-aided test-sheet composition problem was modeled as an optimization problem to maximize (or minimize) some objective function with multiple assessment requirements [7, 8].

Usually, the number of candidate test items in the item bank is large, and the number of feasible combinations to form a test-sheet thus grows exponentially. So the search for optimal solutions under multiple criteria has been proven to be

Z. Cai et al. (Eds.): ISICA 2009, LNCS 5821, pp. 1–10, 2009.

computationally demanding and time-consuming. To overcome this limitation, a number of heuristic approaches, such as genetic [5], immune [6], abductive learning machine [8], Tabu [9], particle swarm [10], and so on have been proposed to facilitate finding solutions as close to optimal as possible in a reasonable computation time. However, if the scale of the item bank is large, the time to construct a test-sheet by these approaches may become very long. In addition, according to the study [11], web user's tolerable waiting time should be kept below 8 seconds. Therefore, new methods must be proposed to generate high quality test sheet in online testing systems.

As a method of computational intelligence, genetic algorithm (GA) has the ability of avoiding the local search and can increase the probability of finding the global best. It has been successfully applied to solve difficult optimization tasks in various domains of science and technology [12,13,14].This paper presented a new approach based on GA for solving test-sheet composition problem in online testing environment. There are three contributions of this paper. First, a model that formulates the online test-sheet composition (OTSC) problem under multiple assessment considerations was proposed. Second, an OTSC algorithm based on GA was put forward. Third, an effective float-point number coding strategy and problem characteristic mutation solution were designed, which can reduce the algorithm's execution time extremely even if the scale of the item bank is large. Superiority of the proposed algorithm is demonstrated by comparing it with GA with binary coding strategy.

2 Problem Model

In this section, we propose a model that formulates the OTSC problem under multiple assessment considerations. With regard to each test item, this model maintains five assessment considerations, which are discrimination degree, difficulty degree, answering time, score and type. Assuming that the given item bank $B = \{Q_1, Q_2, ..., Q_m\}$ consists of m items, p items of them maybe selected to compose a test-sheet, which is a subset of B. The model aims at optimizing the discrimination degree of the test-sheet under multiple constraints. The variables used in the formulated model are defined as follows:

(1) x_i, $i = 1, 2, ..., m$, is decision variables, where m is the number of candidate test items in the item bank. The value of x_i denotes whether test item i is selected or not.

(2) dis_i, $i = 1, 2, ..., m$, degree of discrimination of test item i.

(3) dif_i, $i = 1, 2, ..., m$, degree of difficulty of test item i.

(4) t_i, $i = 1, 2, ..., m$, time needed for answering test item i.

(5) p_i, $i = 1, 2, ..., m$, score of test item i.

(6) $type_i$, $i = 1, 2, ..., m$, type of test item i.

(7) ts, total score of the test-sheet.

(8) $upper_{dif}$, upper bound on the test-sheet difficulty degree.

(9) $lower_{dif}$, lower bound on the test-sheet difficulty degree.

(10) $upper_t$, upper bound on the testing time.

(11) $lower_t$, lower bound on the testing time.

(12) test item type collection $\{T_1, T_2, ..., T_j, ..., T_k\}$, T_j, $j=1,2,...,k$, denotes a kind of test item type, for instance multiple choice, fill-in-the-blank and so on.

(13) tp_j, $j=1,2,...,k$, total score of test item type T_j of each test-sheet.

(14) mi, the maximum test item number of the test sheet.

The formulated models of OTSC problem are defined as follows:

Objective function:

$$Maximize \ Z(x = x_1, x_2, ..., x_m) = \frac{\sum_{i=1}^{m} dis_i x_i}{\sum_{i=1}^{m} x_i}$$

Subject to:

$$ts - \sum_{i=1}^{m} p_i x_i = 0 \tag{1}$$

$$\frac{\sum_{i=1}^{m} dif_i x_i}{\sum_{i=1}^{m} x_i} - lower_{dif} \geq 0 \tag{2}$$

$$upper_{dif} - \frac{\sum_{i=1}^{m} dif_i x_i}{\sum_{i=1}^{m} x_i} \geq 0 \tag{3}$$

$$\sum_{i=1}^{m} t_i x_i - lower_t \geq 0 \tag{4}$$

$$upper_t - \sum_{i=1}^{m} t_i x_i \geq 0 \tag{5}$$

$$tp_j - \sum_{i=1}^{m} p_i x_i y_i = 0, \ j=1,2,...,k \ , \ if \ type_i = T_j \ , \ y_i=1 \ , \ else \ y_i=0 \tag{6}$$

$$\sum_{i=1}^{m} x_i <= mi \tag{7}$$

The objective of this model is to select some test items from the item bank, so that the discrimination degree of the generated test sheet is maximized. Objective function $Z(x)$ represents average discrimination degree of all the selected test items, which is also termed as the discrimination degree of the test-sheet. Constraint (1) indicates that total score of the selected test items must equal to the value of ts. Constraint (2) and (3), respectively specify the lower and upper limits on the difficulty degree of the test sheet. The lower and upper limits on the testing time are set in constraint (4) and (5) respectively. Constraints (6) explain the relationship between the total score of each test item type and variable tp_j. Constraints (7) assure the number of selected test items must no more than mi.

3   Online Test-Sheet Composition Algorithm

GA is an intelligent parallel search algorithm invented by John Holland (1975), which is inspired by the mechanics of natural selection and natural genetics [12]. In GA, a population of potential solutions, termed as chromosomes (individuals), is evolved over successive generations using a set of genetic operators called selection, crossover and mutation operation. First of all, based on some criteria, every chromosome is assigned a fitness value, and then a selection operation is applied to choose relatively good chromosome as part of the reproduction process. In the reproduction process, new individuals are created using crossover and mutation operation. The details of each step are described in the following.

3.1   Improved Coding Strategy and Population Initialization

Similar with the natural selection, GA also needs a population to evolve. The population $P_G = \{x_{i,G} \mid i = 1, 2, ..., NP\}$ of G generation of GA consists of NP D-dimensional chromosomes (individuals). Vector $x_{i,G} = (x_{1i,G}, x_{2i,G}, ..., x_{ki,G}, ..., x_{mi,G})$ is called chromosomes and each chromosome represents a potential solution of the optimization task. A fitness value is then calculated related to how well each chromosome solves the problem.

To represent the solutions of the test-sheet composition problem, effective population coding strategy must be designed. In most of the existing algorithms [2,3,5], binary coding strategies are adopted, in which each chromosome $x_{i,G}$ represent a test-sheet and the dimension of $x_{i,G}$ is equal to the number of test items of the item bank. More precisely, the element $x_{ki,G}$ of $x_{i,G}$ is used to denote the test item k. If $x_{ki,G}$ equal to 1, it means that the test item k is selected as a candidate of the test-sheet. Otherwise, test item k is not selected. Although this strategy is simple and easy to understand, when the scale of the item bank is large, the length of individual $x_{i,G}$ becomes very long. As a result, it may consume much time to construct an effective test-sheet.

To cope with the limitation of binary coding strategy, we proposed a floating-point number coding strategy (FNCS). In FNCS, the dimension of $x_{i,G}$ is equal to the maximum number of test item used to construct a test-sheet, we can calculate this number by $min\ (mi, upper_t/minTime)$, where variable $upper_t$ denotes the upper bound on the expected test-sheet answering time, and variable $minTime$ denotes the minimize test item finishing time of the item bank. Different from the binary coding strategy, the value of $x_{ki,G}$ is in the range of $[0, 1]$ in FNCS and it may be valid or invalid. If the value of $x_{ki,G}$ is in $[0, 1/m+1]$, which means $x_{ki,G}$ does not represent any test item, where variable m denote the total test item number included in the item bank. When $x_{ki,G}$ is in $(1/m+1, 1]$, it's value is valid and it represent a test item that will be selected as one of the number of the test-sheet. By equation (8), we can calculate the specific test item l that $x_{ki,G}$ denotes.

$$l{=}t, \text{ if } x_{ki,G} \in \left(\frac{t}{m+1}, \frac{t+1}{m+1} \right], \quad t=1,2,...,m \qquad (8)$$

The initial population is chosen randomly. More precisely, the individual $x_{i,G}$ is a floating-point number vector and $x_{ki,1}$ equal to $rand_k[0,1]$, for $i=1,2,...,NP$; $k=1,2,...,min\ (mi, upper_i/minTime)$, where $rand_k[0,1]$ is a function to produce the kth random number with outcome $\in [0,1]$.

3.2 Selection Operation

According to the roulette wheel selection scheme, a subset of chromosomes was selected from the population P_G to generate the offspring. The probability of a chromosome being selected is directly propitional to its fitness value. Therefore the bigger fitness value a chromosome has the more copies it will have in the reproduction process.

3.3 Crossover Operation

Crossover operation blends the genetic information between chromosomes to explore the search space. When a pair of individuals has been selected for mating, crossover operation occurs with probability CR, and the individuals remain the same with probability $1-CR$, where variable CR is a constant $\in [0,1]$ derived from the results of a series of preliminary experiments. In either event, two offspring are produced.

The crossover operation used in this paper is one-cut-point method. In this method, we select one cut points randomly and exchanging the right parts of two parents to generate offspring. Thus, the crossover operation is a simple, yet powerful, way of exchanging information and creating new solutions.

3.4 Problem Characteristic Mutation Operation

Following crossover operation, mutation serves to maintain diversity in the population. In this work, the mutation operation is designed according to the character of the OTSC problem. It involves changing some genes in the chromosome based on user defined mutation probability parameter MP. The pseudo-code of the proposed mutation operation solution is given as follows.

```
FOR each individual x in current population

    FOR each dimension j of x

        GENERATE a random number r1∈[0,1];

        IF ( r1 < MP )

            SET x[j] = 0;

            SELECT a number h in {1,2,...,min (mi, upper₁/minTime)}
            randomly;

            GENERATE a random number r2∈[0,1];

            SET x[h] = r2;

        END IF

    END FOR

END FOR
```

By this strategy, each individual of current population is mutated by setting some genes to 0 or rand[0,1]. The strategy of setting genes to 0 is used to explore the proper number of test items, where as by setting genes to rand[0,1], more optimal test item can be found from item banks.

3.5 Stopping Criterion

The GA optimization is combined with operations mentioned above and repeats the evolution process until it reaches the predefined terminated conditions.

4 Simulation Experiments and Evaluation

To evaluate the performance of proposed algorithm, a series of simulation experiments were conducted with the execution times and solution quality of the two competing approaches recorded: GA with FNCS (fGA) and GA with binary coding strategy (bGA). The algorithms are implemented in Java language using Microsoft Windows XP on a PC with Intel Pentium3 1.07GHz CPU, 376MB RAM.

4.1 Dataset and Test-Sheet Requirements

To perform simulation studies, five item banks with the number of candidate test items ranging from 600 to 5000 were constructed. All the item banks have the same table structure. The features of each item bank are shown in table 1.

  In our experiment, the parameters of each test sheet were set as follows: (1) According to the testing time used in practical online testing, the lower and upper bounds of testing time were set 30 to 60, 60 to 90 and 90 to 120 minutes respectively. (2) The

Table 1. Features of the item banks

Item-bank scale	Average difficulty	Average discrimination	Average finished time (Minute)	Total test item type's number
600	0.546	0.571	2.405	5
1200	0.547	0.586	2.378	5
2000	0.552	0.579	2.399	5
4000	0.552	0.577	2.419	5
5000	0.547	0.583	2.441	5

test item types in each test-sheet include multiple choice question (MCQ), brief answer question (BAQ) and essays question (EQ). (3) The values of other variables were set the same as table 2.

Table 2. Value of each test-sheet parameter

Initial parameters of the test sheet	Value
Total Percent	100
Upper bound of the difficulty	0.4
Lower bound of the difficulty	0.6
Score of MCQ	30
Score of BAQ	30
Score of EQ	40
Maximum Item number	100

The algorithm's parameters are set based on the result of some preliminary experiments that are carried out to observe the behavior of algorithm in different parameter setting. The parameters of the two competing algorithms are summarized in table 3.

Table 3. Value of algorithm parameters

Parameter	fGA.	bGA
CP	0.9	0.9
MP	0.0045	0.005
NP	10	5

To compare the performance of all algorithms under the same condition, we use the discrimination degree of the test-sheet and computation time as the stop condition of all algorithms. In the simulation experiment, all algorithms stopped when the discrimination degree of the generated test-sheet was bigger than the average discrimination degree of the item bank or they had run 10 minutes.

Three criteria were employed to evaluate the performance of the competing algorithms: (1) Execution time reflects the efficiency of the algorithm in searching for the optimal solution. (2) The success ratio (SR), which indicates the robustness of the algorithm, is the ratio of number of successful runs to that of total runs. (3) Search quality denotes the discrimination degree of the best individual in a run. According to practical online testing requirements, a run is considered to be successful if it stops after it have run not more than 6 seconds, and at the same time the discrimination degree of the generated test-sheet is bigger than the average discrimination degree of the item bank. In this investigation, a high efficiency algorithm is characterized by shorter execution time, high success ratio and search quality.

4.2   Results and Discussion

For the three online testing time ranges 30 to 60, 60 to 90 and 90 to 120 minutes, each algorithm run 50 times for each test item bank. Results of different algorithm on each online testing time range are presented in table 4, 5 and 6. In these tables, Best, Bad, Avg and Std respectively represent minimum value, maximum value, average value and standard deviation of execution time on average. Ad and SR respectively denotes the average search quality and average success ratio calculated from the 50 runs. "--" means no feasible solutions were found when the algorithm had run 10 minutes.

Table 4. Experimental results of online testing time range 30-60 minutes

Scale of item bank	fGA						bGA					
	Execution time (Second)				AD	SR	Execution time (Second)				AD	SR
	Best	Bad	Avg	Std			Best	Bad	Avg	Std		
600	1.10	5.25	2.79	1.41	0.67	100%	4.98	24.42	11.22	3.74	0.63	2%
1200	0.49	3.21	1.72	0.54	0.61	100%	83.31	193.13	137.80	37.36	0.61	0%
2000	0.46	2.27	1.03	0.38	0.61	100%	708.9	--	--	--	--	0%
4000	0.42	1.33	0.88	0.21	0.62	100%	--	--	--	--	--	0%
5000	0.48	1.95	0.98	0.33	0.62	100%	--	--	--	--	--	0%

Table 5. Experimental results of online testing time range 60-90 minutes

Scale of item bank	fGA						bGA					
	Execution time second)				AD	SR	Execution time (second)				AD	SR
	Best	Bad	Avg	Std			Best	Bad	Avg	Std		
600	0.27	2.00	0.73	0.39	0.66	100%	0.89	7.52	3.19	0.89	0.64	92%
1200	0.31	2.47	0.62	0.31	0.62	100%	20.99	53.28	33.71	10.21	0.61	0%
2000	0.20	0.84	0.45	0.16	0.63	100%	361.89	--	--	--	--	0%
4000	0.22	0.97	0.50	0.17	0.65	100%	--	--	--	--	--	0%
5000	0.22	1.24	0.47	0.17	0.63	100%	--	--	--	--	--	0%

Table 6. Experimental results of online testing time range 90-120 minutes

Scale of item bank	fGA						bGA					
	Execution time (second)				AD	SR	Execution time (second)				AD	SR
	Best	Bad	Avg	Std			Best	Bad	Avg	Std		
600	0.13	1.19	0.40	0.22	0.65	100%	0.83	5.14	1.72	0.93	0.66	100%
1200	0.14	0.69	0.33	0.12	0.62	100%	14.47	28.28	18.81	4.05	0.62	0%
2000	0.12	0.70	0.28	0.11	0.63	100%	361.89	--	--	--	--	0%
4000	0.20	0.69	0.34	0.11	0.63	100%	--	--	--	--	--	0%
5000	0.20	0.70	0.35	0.12	0.64	100%	--	--	--	--	--	0%

For the three online testing time ranges and each item bank, it can be seen from table 4, 5 and 6 that fGA can find optimal solutions in very short computational time, in average no more than 3 seconds and the success ratio are all 100%. Even when the number of test items of the item bank increase to 5000, the execution time of fGA for three testing time ranges only need 0.98, 0.47 0.35 second in average to find the best solution. Furthermore, the standard deviations of the execution time are all very small and the average search qualities are very stable. The robustness, high efficiency and quality of fGA in term of success ratio, execution time and search quality are implied in these statistics. Unfortunately, for the three online testing time ranges, bGA can only obtain 2%, 92% and 100% success ratio for the smallest item bank 600, the success rate of bGA on other large scale item banks are equal to zero. When the scale of the item bank increases, the computational complexity of the OTSC problem becomes extremely high for the reason of it's binary coding strategy. It becomes very unlikely for bGA to find optimal solutions in no more than 8 seconds, which can't meet the online testing needs. These results stimulate the need for design of heuristic algorithms, which can solve the OTSC problem effectively and efficiently.

5 Conclusion

This paper proposed a GA with effective floating-point number coding strategy to solve the OTSC problem in e-learning environments. To evaluate the performance of the proposed algorithm, several experiments were conducted to compare the execution time, success ratio and the solution quality of two approaches on five item banks. Experimental results show that high quality test-sheets for online testing can be obtained in a much shorter time by employing our proposed approach. The proposed method is relatively simple, easy to implement and suitable to use in actual online evaluation systems in the future work.

Acknowledgements. This paper is partially supported by National Natural Science Foundation of China (Grant No. 60874075) and the Key Educational and Scientific Project of Shandong Province "the Eleventh-Five-Year-Plan" (Grant NO.115GZ8).

References

1. Peng, C., Anbo, M., Chunhua, Z.: Particle Swarm Optimization in Multi-agent System for the Intelligent Generation of Test Papers. In: Proceedings of 2008, IEEE World Congress on Evolutionary Computation, pp. 2158–2162. IEEE Press, NewYork (2008)
2. Cheng, S.C., Lin, Y.-T., Huang, Y.-M.: Dynamic Question Generation System for Web-based Testing using Particle Swarm Optimization. Expert Systems with Applications 36(1), 616–624 (2009)
3. Gwo-Jen Huang, A.: Test Sheet Generating Algorithm for Multiple Assessment Requirements. IEEE Transactions on Education 46(3), 329–337 (2003)
4. Huang, G.-J., Chu, H.-C., Yin, P.-Y., Lin, J.-Y.: An Innovative Parallel Test Sheet Composition Approach to Meet Multiple Assessment Criteria for National Tests. Computer & Education 51(3), 1058–1072 (2008)
5. Huang, G.J., Lin, B.M.T., Tseng, H.-H., Lin, T.s.-l.: On the Development of a Computer-assisted Testing System with Genetic Test Sheet Generating Approach. IEEE Transactions on Systems, Man and Cybernetics 35(4), 590–594 (2005)
6. Lee, C.-L., Huang, C.-H., Lin, C.-J.: Test Sheet Composition using Immune Algorithm for E-learning Application. In: Okuno, H.G., Ali, M. (eds.) IEA/AIE 2007. LNCS (LNAI), vol. 4570, pp. 823–833. Springer, Heidelberg (2007)
7. Huwang, G.-J., Lin, B.M.T., Lin, T.-L.: An Effective Approach for Test Sheet Composition with Large-scale Item Banks. Computer & Education 46(2), 122–139 (2006)
8. Efaly, E.-s.M., Abdel-Aal, R.E.: Construction and Analysis of Educational Tests using Abductive Machine Learning. Computer & Education 51(1), 1–16 (2008)
9. Huang, G.-J., Yin, P.-Y., Yeh, S.-H.: A Tabu Search Approach to Generating Test Sheets for Multiple Assessment Criteria. IEEE Transactions on Education 49(1), 88–97 (2006)
10. Yin, P.-Y., Chang, K.-C., Hwang, G.-J., Hwang, G.-H., Chan, Y.: A Particle Swarm Optimization Approach to Composing Serial Test Sheets for Multiple Assessment Criteria. Educational Technology & Society 9(3), 3–15 (2006)
11. Galletta, D.F., Henry, R., McCoy, S., Polak, P.: Web Site Delays: How Tolerant are Users. Journal of the Association for Information Systems 5(1), 1–28 (2004)
12. Holland, J.H.: Adaptation in Natural and Artificial System. University of Michigan Press, USA (1975)
13. Tseng, L.-Y., Lin, Y.-T.: A Hybrid Genetic Local Search Algorithm for the Permutation Flowshop Scheduling Problem. European Journal of Operational Research 198, 84–92 (2009)
14. Matta, M.E.: A Genetic Algorithm for the Proportionate Multiprocessor Open Shop. Computers & Operations Research 36, 2601–2618 (2009)

A Route System Based on Genetic Algorithm
for Coarse-Grain Reconfigurable Architecture

Yan Guo[1], Sanyou Zeng[1], Lishan Kang[1],
Gang Liu[1], Nannan Hu[1], and Kuo Zhao[2]

[1] School of Computer, China University of Geosciences,
Wuhan, 430074, China
[2] Hebei Youth Administrative Cadres College,
Hebei, 050031, China
guoyanwuhan@yahoo.com.cn, sanyou-zeng@263.net,
kang_whu@yahoo.com, lg0061408@yahoo.com.cn, cughnn@163.com,
nextrrrcuo@163.com

Abstract. It is a often hard to find a feasible and optimum route because the routing resources are constrained in coarse-grain RA (CGRA) and several functions are often defined in same one element of RA. In this paper, a proposed propriety-based path encoding genetic algorithm is applied for the routing problem of CGRA. By mapping Fast Fourier Transform of the butterfly computation to CTaiJi that is a newly developed CGRA, the proposed GA shows good ability to find the good solution.

Keywords: Coarse-grain reconfigurable architecture; resources-constrained multi-pair shortest path problem in directed graphs; Genetic algorithm; Multi-pair path encoding.

1 Introduction

It is well known that Reconfigurable Architecture (RA) is a bridge between the flexibility of software and performance achievable in hardware. Based on the width of data-path, RA can be divided into two parts: one is fine-grain RA where the typical production is FPGA (field programmable gate array); another is coarse-grain RA (CGRA) whose width of data-path is larger than fine-grain RA. Contrary to FPGA, the routing resources of CGRA are limited. So, it is important to design a good route system to find a feasible routing for the whole compile-synthesis system.

Routing problem (RP) for RA is the process of deciding exactly which routing resources will be used to carry signals from where they are generated to where they are used. Because CGRA has prefabricated routing resources, the router must consider the congestion of signals in a channel and make sure that no more routes are made through the same channel.

By now, there are mainly three routing methods for RP of CGRA [4]. The first method is shortest-path. It is to find the shortest path of every signal in turn, once the shortest path of a signal is found, this path is deleted from the connected graph and begin to find next signal. Therefore, the routing effect of every signal has much relation to the start sequence. The second method is pathfinder. This

Z. Cai et al. (Eds.): ISICA 2009, LNCS 5821, pp. 11–17, 2009.

method firstly finds the shortest path of every signal and then checks if there are congestions on edges of the connected graph. If there are congestions, the weight of the edge on which congestions occur is increased. Repeat above steps, until there are no congestions on edges of the connected graph. This method is very sensitive to parameter. The third method is ant colony. The ant colony approach adds the ability of smell for ant by optimal trail and ordinary trail of pheromone trails. Whenever an ant finds an optimal path, it gives out optimal trail value, whereas it gives out ordinary trail value. Further more, optimal trail value is always larger than that of ordinal.

In the paper, we apply a priority-based encoding genetic approach to solve the routing problem of CGRA. We need to build an effective chromosome representation. How to encode a path in a network is also critical for developing a GA application to RP problems, it is not easy to find out a nature representation. Special difficulty arises from a path contains variable number of nodes and the maximal number is N-1 for an N node network, and a random sequence of edges usually does not correspond to a path.

The mathematics model for route-problem is introduced in the second part of paper. The route-problem can be transformed to resources-constrained multi-pair shortest path problem in directed graphs by model properly changed. The third part is mainly about the genetic algorithm. The effort of GA for routing is compared with that of pathfinder in the last part.

2 Mathematics Model of CGRA Routing Problem

CGRA is a network structure composed of lots of processing elements (PEs). Processing elements array (PEA) is the least macro-module that can run lonely to finish a task in CTaiJi[3], a highly scalar and flexible 16bits coarse grained RC architecture with the applications that are commonly addressed in multimedia applications (like image or video processing. In CTaiJi PEA is a mesh of PEs (made up of 4×4 PEs) connected by a bidirectional data buses, as illustrated in Fig. 1.

After the function of PEs is determined, the employed PEs needs to be connected by unused lines. The routing problem is the process of determining how to connect PEs. There are some requirements about the process: the length sum of line should as short as possible and the congestion should not occur (i.e., the same line should not be used more than once).

If PE is represented as a node and the line between PEs is represented as a directed edge, the PEA network is regard as a directed graph G in Fig.2.

Let $G= (V , E)$ be a directed graph. $V=\{1, 2, 3,......,n\}$ is the set of nodes, $E=\{< i, j> \mid i, j \in V$ and $\text{Path}(i, j)\}$ is the set of edges(arcs). There are m pair startpoints and end-points , denoted as $vs_1, vs_2, vs_3...vs_m$, $vd_1, vd_2, vd_3...vd_m \in V$. Let L_i represents the path from vs_i to vd_i ($i= 1, 2,...m$, $m \leq n \times (n-1)$, n is PEs total number.), it is a directed chain composed of lots of directed edges connected end to end.

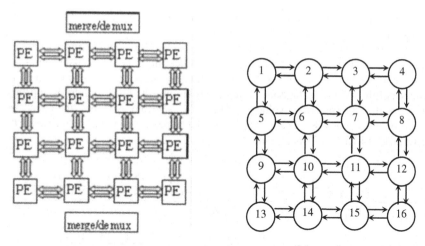

Fig. 1. PEA organization   **Fig. 2.** A directed graph with 16 nodes and 48 edges

The routing problem can be transformed to a resources-constrained multi-pair shortest path problem in G as follows:

$$L = \min \ (\sum_{i=1}^{m} \frac{Length(L_i)}{EDGES} + \sum_{i=1}^{m} IsDisconnected(L_i)) \cdot \tag{1}$$

$$\text{s.t.} \quad \forall i, j \in [1..m], \ L_i \cap L_j = \phi \quad (i \neq j) \tag{2}$$

Where *Length* (L_i) is a function calculating the path length of *Li*. *EDGES* is the edge total number in the graph, i.e. *EDGES* = 48 in Fig. 2. *IsDisconnected* (*Li*) is the connectivity of L_i.

$$IsDisconnected(L_i) = \begin{cases} 0, & \text{if } L_i \text{ is a valid path from } v_{s_i} \text{ to } v_{d_i} \\ 1, & \text{if } L_i \text{ is a invalid path from } v_{s_i} \text{ to } v_{d_i} \end{cases} \cdot \tag{3}$$

Constraints (2) is necessary for routing problem because it imply that no congestion occurs (the same line should not be used more than once).

3 Genetic Algorithm for Routing Problem

In the past, many encoding techniques have been used for path representations in solving the routing problem using GA. The priority-based encoding genetic algorithm is a very effective method proposed by Professor Gen as early as 1998[1], [2], where some guiding information about the nodes that constitute the path are used to represent the path. The guiding information used in that work is the priorities of various nodes in the network. During the initialization phase of GA, these priorities are assigned randomly. The path is generated by sequential node appending procedure beginning with the source node and terminating at the destination node. At each step of path construction from a chromosome, there are usually several nodes available for consideration and the one with the highest priority is added into path and the process is repeated until the destination node is reached.

Fig. 3(a) illustrates this encoding scheme, C1, C2... Cn are the priority values of nodes 1, 2. . . n. Fig. 3(b) shows an example of encoding scheme for path representation in the 16-node network of Fig. 2. The path construction starting from node 4 is performed as follows. From the node adjacency relations, the node with highest priority, i.e., node 3 (priority value = 12), is selected to be included in path, out of the nodes 8. These steps will be repeated until a complete path {4,3,2,1,5,9,13,14,15,16,12} is obtained.

1	2	3	4	5	6	7	8	9	10	11	12	13	14	15	16
C1	C2	C3	C4	C5	C6	C7	C8	C9	C10	C11	C12	C13	C14	C15	C16

(a) Encoding scheme

1	2	3	4	5	6	7	8	9	10	11	12	13	14	15	16
14	13	12	15	5	2	1	8	10	3	6	4	16	7	9	11

(b) The decoding procedure leads to a valid path: 4→3→2→1→5→ 9→13→14→15→ 16→12

Fig. 3. Priority-based encoding scheme for the network of Fig. 2

We design the genetic algorithm for the above model by the idea of the priority-based encoding. Let A be the $n \times n$ adjacent matrix given by

$$a_{ij} = \begin{cases} 1, & \text{if } <i, j> \in E \\ 0, & \text{otherwise} \end{cases} . \tag{3}$$

Suppose there is a partial path under growing. Let $V_p \subseteq V$ be the set of nodes exiting in the partial path. Let t be the terminal node of the partial path. i is the pair number variable. DA is the dynamic adjacent matrix. Let ES be the eligible edge set without forming a cycle in the partial path. V_m is the nodes list in m paths listed ordinarily in corresponding path.

The proposed modifications in the path growth procedure is :

Step 1: (initialization) $DA \leftarrow A$, $i \leftarrow 1$, $V_m \leftarrow \phi$.

step 2: (a path growth initialization) Let $V_p \leftarrow \{v_{si}\}$, $t \leftarrow v_{si}$.

Step 3: (termination test) if $t = v_{di}$, go to step 8; otherwise, continue.

Step 4: (eligible edge set)Make the edge set ES according to dynamic adjacent matrix DA.

Step 5: (pendant node test) If $ES = \phi$, let $t \leftarrow v_{di}$, $V_p \leftarrow V_p \cup v_{di}$. Go to step 8; otherwise, continue.

Step 6: (path extending) if $v_{di} \in ES$, let $t \leftarrow v_{di}$, $V_p \leftarrow V_p \cup v_{di}$. Go to step 8; otherwise,

select t' from $V - V_p$ subject to $<t, t'> \in ES$ with the highest priority. $V_p \leftarrow V_p \cup t'$.

Step 7: (dynamic adjacent matrix update) Let $DA_{tt'} \leftarrow 0$. $t \leftarrow t'$.Go to step 3.

Step 8: (complete a path) $V_m \leftarrow V_m \cup V_p$.

Step 9: (pair index update)$i \leftarrow i + 1$.

Step 10: if $i \leq m$, go to step 2; otherwise, Return the complete path V_m.
The position-based crossover operator and swap mutation operator [1],[2] are employed in the genetic algorithm.

4 Numerical Example

Because there are no standard routing test programs for CGRA, the net lists of Fast Fourier Transform of the butterfly computation in equation 4 is mapped onto CGRA.

$$
\begin{aligned}
A &= a + W \times b = (a_{re} + a_{im}) + ((W_{re} \times b_{re} - W_{im} \times b_{im}) + (W_{re} \times b_{im} + W_{im} \times b_{re})_{im}) \\
B &= a - W \times b = (a_{re} + a_{im}) - ((W_{re} \times b_{re} - W_{im} \times b_{im}) + (W_{re} \times b_{im} + W_{im} \times b_{re})_{im})
\end{aligned}
\tag{4}
$$

The calculation of topography between input data, output data and operators in Fig. 4 is employed. The location of input, output and ten operators is shown in Fig. 5 on CGRA; the routing problem of eleven pairs of start points and terminal points as shown in Table 1 should be implemented corresponding.

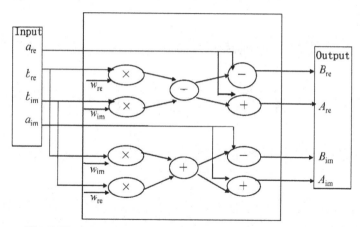

Fig. 4. The calculation of topography of two-point FFT algorithm

Table 1. Eleven pairs of start points and terminal points in the graph of Fig. 2

Source node	Destination node
4	3
1	5
2	6
3	7
1	2
5	6
2	3
6	7
3	2
7	4
7	1

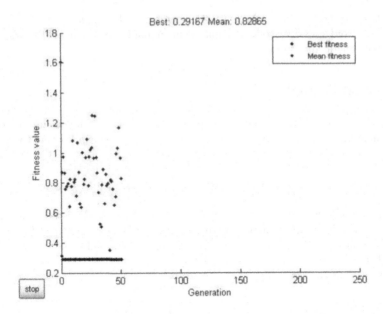

Fig. 5. Evolutionary process

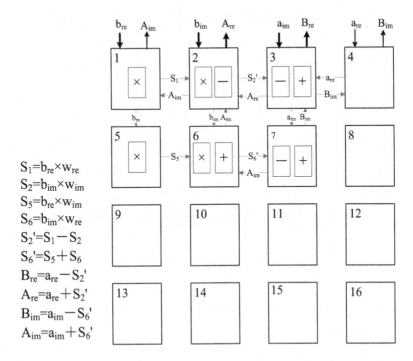

$S_1 = b_{re} \times w_{re}$
$S_2 = b_{im} \times w_{im}$
$S_5 = b_{re} \times w_{im}$
$S_6 = b_{im} \times w_{re}$
$S_2' = S_1 - S_2$
$S_6' = S_5 + S_6$
$B_{re} = a_{re} - S_2'$
$A_{re} = a_{re} + S_2'$
$B_{im} = a_{im} - S_6'$
$A_{im} = a_{im} + S_6'$

Fig. 6. The mapping result of Fast Fourier Transform of the butterfly computation on the CGAR

Fig.5 illustrates the evolutionary process of routing sets. The evolutionary environment is set as the follows: population size is 20, maximum generation is 250, crossover ratio is 0.8 and mutation ration is 0.2. Roulette selection is employed. The elite individual number is 2. The algorithm stops if there is no improvement in the objective function for 20 seconds. The algorithm runs until the cumulative change in the fitness function value over 20 seconds is less than 1e-10. The algorithm stops if there is no improvement in the objective function for 50 consecutive generations.

Genetic algorithm running on the end result is the best route individual is {6, 15, 14, 10, 12, 9, 11, 2, 1, 13, 8, 3, 4, 7, 16, 5}. Fig. 6 illustrates the mapping results of Fast Fourier Transform of the butterfly computation on the CGAR. The path construction starting from node 4 is performed as follows. From the node adjacency relations, the node with highest priority, i.e., node 3 (priority value = 14), is selected to be included in path, out of the nodes 8 (priority value = 2). These steps will be repeated until a complete path {{4, 3}; {1, 5}; {2, 6};{3, 7};{1, 2};{5, 6};{2, 3};{6, 7};{3, 2};{7, 3, 4};{7, 6, 2, 1}} is obtained.

5 Conclusions

The improved priority-based path encoding genetic algorithm for routing problem of CGRA is effective and has stronger ability of searching optimum path than pathfinder. This algorithm is very fit to CGRA whose resources are not too much.

References

1. Gen, M., Cheng, R., Wang, D.: Genetic algorithms for solving shortest path problems. Evolutionary Computation. In: IEEE International Conference on Volume Issue, April 13-16, 1997, pp. 401–406 (1997)
2. Cheng, R., Gen, M.: Apriority based encoding and shortest path problem. Ashikaga Institute of Technology (1998)
3. Liguo, S., Yuxian, J.: CTaiJi——a new coarse grain re-configurable computing platform. Microelectronics and computer (September 2005)
4. Liguo, S., Yuxian, J.: A Route System Based on Ant Colony for Coarse-Grain Reconfigurable Architecture. In: Jiao, L., Wang, L., Gao, X.-b., Liu, J., Wu, F. (eds.) ICNC 2006. LNCS, vol. 4222, pp. 215–221. Springer, Heidelberg (2006)

Building Trade System by Genetic Algorithm

Hua Jiang[1,2] and Lishan Kang[1]

[1] Computer School, Wuhan University, Wuhan, Hubei, China
jianghua_whu@163.com
[2] Computer Center, Wuhan University, Wuhan, Hubei, China

Abstract. This paper employs a genetic algorithm to evolve an optimized stock market prediction system. The prediction based on a range of technical indicators generates signals to indicate the price movement. The performance of the system is analyzed and compared to market movements as represented by its index. Also investment funds run by professional traders are selected to establish a relative measure of success. The results show that the evolved system outperforms the index and funds in different market environments.

Keywords: Genetic Algorithm. Market Prediction.

1 Introduction

This document discusses how to use genetic algorithm to predict the tendency of stock market index. Many papers has researched this problem by evolutionary computation. Some research uses GP or GEP to evolve a function to fit stock trade data[1]. But the evolved functions are often helpless in trade decision process just because stock market is a dynamic system. In some other papers every individual in population were trained to trade as traders in financial markets[2]. This kind system evolves an agent population which uses technical indicators for getting trading decision system. But the profit is not only based on the good prediction but also is affected by trade system and trade strategy. In this paper, we propose new criterion, the validity of prediction, to evaluate individuals in population. The elites in population can make more correct predictions than the others during a period of time. It is important to real-life trade that the trader can predict stock price movements.

Genetic algorithm was proposed by J. Holland in 1979[3]. It is an iterative and stochastic process that operates on a set of individuals (population) which represents a potential solution to the problem being solved. The iterative process will not come to stop until the optimal individual is present. In our system every individual studies how to predicate the direction of movement of stock prices in evolve progress by everyday trading information and technical indicators, such as MACD, KDJ, MA, RSI etc.

2 Genetic Algorithm for Predicting the Stock Market

2.1 Genome Structure

Every individual in the population calculates the probability of trend up and down using trade data, such as open price, close price, highest and lowest price, volume,

Z. Cai et al. (Eds.): ISICA 2009, LNCS 5821, pp. 18–23, 2009.

etc, and the technical indicators, such as moving average (MA), moving average convergence divergence (MACD), relative strength index (RSL), Stochastics (KDJ). Further more, it can not predict trend of stock price by only one day's data. It must observe data from a period of times and make relevant prediction according the short, middle and long term change of stock prices. So we define the structure of the genome as blew:

Table 1. Genome Structure

Gene	Technical Indicator	Time Scale	Time Duration	Weighting
A	MA	5-250	5-250	0.1-0.3
B	MACD	1-30	7-75	0.1-0.3
C	KDJ	1-30	7-75	0.1-0.3
D	RSI	1-30	7-75	0.1-0.3
E	Volume	1-30	1	0.1-0.3
F	Open price	1-30	1	0.05-0.2
G	Close price	1-30	1	0.05-0.2
H	Highest price	1-30	1	0.05-0.2
I	Lowest price	1-30	1	0.05-0.2

The genome composed of several genes. In each gene we defined time duration in which one technical indicator should be traced. And each technical indicator's weight in the decision was also defined. The weighting will be adjusted during the evolve progress.

2.2 Genetic Algorithm

In predicting process each individual analyzes a period time financial data from market using these technical indicators. Each technical indicator gives signal of rise, down of stock price according analysis theory[4]. Different analysis time scales were used to calculate these technical indicators. Some indicators using everyday trade data to generate signal and some others use week data. Thus the individuals can analysis the tendency of stock price movement in long, middle and short term. In this way the disturbance from noise in trade market was avoided. It makes predication more accurate.

In the evolve process the best individual will be selected and survive to the next generation. The remaining normal majority will be replaced by offspring. The genome is an integer string, with Table 1 providing an overview of each genes meaning. The mutation operation changes the time duration, time scale and weight. The crossover operation exchanges two allele genes between two individuals. The successful prediction ratio is adopted as fitness.

2.3 Historical Market Data

In this paper we use real-life stock market data to train and test the population. We select HuShen 300 index, which is an index listing the 300 selected companies registered in Shanghai Stock Exchange and Shenzhen Stock Exchange in China market.

3 Training and Testing

3.1 Training

For getting better predicting ability we trained the population in three stages. Three stages are booming market, depression market and general market which covers up and down. In each stage training was stopped when performance appeared to have reached a plateau and then the best 20% population was kept into subsequent stage. The training data was showed in Table 2.

Table 2. Training Data

	Stage1	Stage2	Stage3
Training days	338	113	477
Training period	2005-12-1 to 2007-4-25	2008-5-15 to 2008-10-29	2007-3-8 to 2009-2-19

The period of stage 1 could be described as a general boom environment where the HuShen 300 index appreciated 115.8%. In this period there is a dip and congestion area. The period of stage 2 could be described as a general depression where the HuShen 300 index depreciated 58.2%. In this period the stock market declined but rallied sometimes. The two kinds of training data can help the population to get the knowledge about determinative influence of the long term tendency. The period of stage 3 includes rising market, downward plunge of the stock market and reversal market. We hope the individuals can learn the characters of the market where direction of price movement stops and heads in the opposite direction.

3.2 Testing

To analysis the population's ability of prediction, test data from different market environments was selected following the similar pattern as for training, with different time spans and general market environments being used in each set.

Table 3. Testing Data

	Test1	Test2	Test3
Training days	137	142	134
Training period	2007-3-19 to 2007-10-9	2008-1-23 to 2008-8-20	2008-8-28 to 2009-3-20

In table 4 best performance refers to the best individual's performance and average performance to the whole population average.

In Test 1 the test data came from the period similar with training stage 1. This period could be described as a boom environment where the HuShen 300 index

Table 4. Performance in Test

	Test 1	Test 2	Test 3
Best performance	72%	74%	79%
Average performance	65%	63%	70%

appreciated 118.0%. The HuShen 300 index rallies to record high in this period and boom continuously. In test 2, the period could be described as general depression similar with training stage2. The HuShen 300 index depreciated 2175.45 points, 46.2%. In these two tests we got good results. The best individuals achieved above 70% success of prediction. In test 3 the result is not good as in the first two test. The best individual got only 60% prediction success rate and average achievement is just 56%. That means many individuals could not make effective prediction. In this period there is great change in stock markets. The HuShen 300 index turned up after long time depression.

4 Analysis

Correct predicting is important for trading but only predict success ratio could not indicate the system is good intuitively. As mentioned above, the profit is not depended on the predict success ratio but also on the strategy of using capital. Just because there is not ETF fund associated with HuShen 300 index in financial market, so we supposed the index is a security and the value of the index was the price of this security to simulate trading. Now we select the best individual in the population to simulate the trader. It purchases the security with its all capital when it predicts the index will rise and sell out all its security when it thinks the index will fall. We calculated the profits in the test periods and compared with selected funds in real-life market and Hushen 300 index. We selected two funds which are Bosera Select Fund(050004) and Harvest Select Fund(070010). These two funds use HuShen 300 index as basis to calculate the rate of return so that they are suitable for compare.

Table 5. Index and Test Performance Comparison

	Test 1	Test 2	Test 3
Best performance	86%	-5%	14%
HuShen 300 index	118%	-46%	2%
Bosera Select(050004)	51%	-19%	-1%
Harvest Select(070010)	65%	-16%	-2%

After the conversion the best individual's profits are listed in Table 5. In period of Test 1, in the boom market environment the individual got good return and outperformed HuShen 300 index. The individual performed better than the two funds. It should be noticed that the two funds were managed by professional traders and they adopted good strategy to use their capital. This point made the two funds take advantage. In the period of Test 2 the market environment was described depression and the Hushen 300 index depreciated 46.2%. The individual and the two funds did not perform well. But when the individual lost 5%, at the same period the two funds depreciated 19% and 16%. The two funds performed badly because they are limited by the policy from China Securities Regulatory Commission that funds must kept their stock position at certain level. It made the funds depreciated passively. The best individual was supposed to sell out securities when the price was expected to fall. So it avoided losing and even gained profit in the rally.

In the period of test 3 the best individual performed as well as in the first two test. It made us feel some surprise because in this period the direction of price movement stops and heads in the opposite direction and the market environment was more complicated. Even professional traders were hard to judge the tendency of the price movement and thus got heavy loss. After analysis we found that the technical indicators in long term analysis helped the individual to judge the tendency correctly when the price movement turned it direction. It is hard to predict the change of the tendency by the signals from those technical indicators in short term analysis. In the third training stage the population got the knowledge about the change of the long term tendency of the stock market, so that the individual made the correct choices in the test 3 and outperformed the two funds and HuShen 300 index. The two selected funds hesitated in this period and did not catch the chance.

From the result of test it is important that the population can study to use long term analysis and short term analysis together to analyze the tendency of stock price. We observed the first 20 elites of the population in which the ratio of weights of the long term analyzing and short term analyzing is almost 1:1. On the contrary, the ratios in normal individuals are far from 1:1. It indicates that they use only long term analyzing or short term analyzing. Thus they did not perform as well as the elites.

Further more, we observed that the weights of some technical indicators were almost zero. That means it is useless in predication in evolve process. Maybe we should study how to use these technical indicators more efficiently.

5 Conclusion

The best individual of the population outperformed the index. However, it could be argued that there is still significant space for improvement.

There several factors that could be considered to improve the system. Because the HuShen 300 index is a new born index so that training data sets are not adequate. More training data should be adopted to train the population to learn more knowledge about the market. The technical indicators should be analyzed in more depth to increase the successful prediction ratio. Furthermore a greater range of learning methods should be induced to train the population to predict better.

References

1. Liao Yong.: Time Series Prediction in Stock-Price Index and Stock-Price Based on Gene-ExPression Programming. Master's Dissertation. Sichuan University. Sichuan. China
2. Schoreels, C., Logan, B., Garibaldi, J.M.: Agent based genetic algorithm employing financial technical analysis for making trading decisions using historical equity market data. In: Proc. of the IEEE/WIC/ACM Int'l Conf. on Intelligent Agent Technology (IAT 2004), Beijing. China, pp. 421–424 (2004)
3. Holland, J.H.: Adaptation in Natural and Artificial Systems: An Introductory Analysis with Applications to Biology, Control, and Artificial Intelligence, 2nd edn. MIT Press, Cambridge (1992)
4. Achelis, S.B.: Technical Analysis from A to Z. McGraw-Hill Trade (2000)

Implementation of Parallel Genetic Algorithm Based on CUDA

Sifa Zhang and Zhenming He

Abstract. Genetic Algorithm (GA) is a powerful tool for science computing, while Parallel Genetic Algorithm (PGA) further promotes the performance of computing. However, the traditional parallel computing environment is very difficult to set up, much less the price. This gives rise to the appearance of moving dense computing to graphics hardware, which is inexpensive and more powerful. The paper presents a hierarchical parallel genetic algorithm, implemented by NVIDIA's Compute Unified Device Architecture (CUDA). Mixed with master-slave parallelization method and multiple-demes parallelization method, this algorithm has contributed to better utilization of threads and high-speed shared memory in CUDA.

Keywords: Genetic Algorithm, Parallel Genetic Algorithm, CUDA.

1 Introduction

Genetic Algorithms is a powerful tool that has been used to solve a lot of difficult problems. As the computer hardware developing and the scale of unsolved scientific problem increasing, the traditional serial genetic algorithm can't satisfy the requirement of application any more, like performance and scalability. In the recently 20 years, a large amount of researchers have studied varied PGAs.

Although PGAs has been developed for years, most implementations of PGAs need dozen of computers, memory, high-speed network, etc. which, without exception, are fairly expensive and difficult to manage. The most important disadvantage is that there is no possible to set up such an academic communication platform for ordinary researchers and students. This situation was not changed till the appearance of NVIDIA's Compute Unified Device Architecture (CUDA), a general-purpose parallel architecture with a new parallel programming model and instruction set architecture, which is introduced by NVIDIA in November 2006.

This paper focuses on the special architecture of CUDA, and explores to design suitable parallel genetic algorithm architecture to maximize the performance of genetic algorithm based on CUDA.

2 Classification of Parallel Genetic Algorithms

The first parallel computing architecture showed up around 1950s, John Holland tried to simulate the evolution of natural population with a parallel architecture. Although the hardware and software were not that flexible, the conception of parallelization constantly developed in the later year.

Z. Cai et al. (Eds.): ISICA 2009, LNCS 5821, pp. 24–30, 2009.
© Springer-Verlag Berlin Heidelberg 2009

Not until the recent 20 years, researchers have proposed lots of parallel genetic algorithm architectures:

(1) Master-slave GAs;
(2) Multiple-demes GAs (Corse-grained GAs);
(3) Fine-grained GAs;
(4) Hierarchical GAs.

Master-slave GAs, we also know as Global PGAs, which consisted of one single population, but evaluation of fitness and/or the application of genetic operators are distributed among several processors (Fig.1). The advantage of this PGAs is, obviously, barely need to communication during natural selection, crossover, and mutation, guaranteeing the efficiency of this algorithm. It can be implemented efficiently on shared-memory and distributed-memory computers.

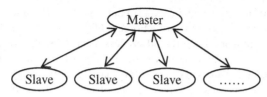

Fig. 1. Master-slave GAs

Multi-demes PGAs is also called multiple-population PGAs, which is the most popular parallel method. Such algorithms assume that several subpopulations (demes) evolve in parallel and demes are relatively isolated. It has two important characteristics: (1) relatively large subpopulations, (2) migration, which allows each subpopulation exchange individuals. Such a PGAs leaves us three issues: (1) find a migration rate that makes isolated demes behave like a single panmictic population, (2) find a suitable communication topology to increase the number of mixture and not increase too much communication cost, (3) find a optimal number of demes that maximizes quality of solution. There are two popular migrate models: island model and stepping-stone model. The manners of communication between each subpopulation like the Fig.2 shows. Double arrows represent communication topology and circles represent isolated subpopulation.

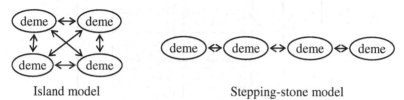

Island model   Stepping-stone model

Fig. 2. Migration Models

Fine-grained PGAs is suited for massively parallel computers, which have only one population, but it is has a spatial structure that limits the interactions between individuals. An individual can only compete and mate with its neighbors, but since the neighborhoods overlap good solutions may disseminate across the entire population.

Finally, a few researchers have tried to combine two or more parallel methods to parallelize GAs, producing hierarchical parallel GAs. Hierarchical implementations can reduce the execution time more than any of their components alone. The speed-up of hierarchical PGAs is product of speed-up of one PGAs at higher level and speed-up of another PGAs at lower level. Decrease faults of one PGAs by combining other PGAs which doesn't have such faults. And this has become a current trend, mixing multiple parallel methods to further improve the performance of PGAs.

3 Architecture of CUDA

The rapid increase in the performance of graphics hardware, coupled with recent improvements in its programmability, have made graphics hardware a compelling platform for computationally demanding tasks in a wide variety of application domains. The graphics hardware we used in experiment has a Nvidia GeForce 8 graphics-processor architecture. This particular GeForce 8 GPU has 128 thread processors, also known as stream processors. Each thread processor has a single-precision Float Point Unit (FPU) and 1,024 registers, 32 bits wide. Each cluster of eight thread processors has 16KB of shared local memory supporting parallel data accesses. The maximum number of concurrent threads is 12,288. And, of course, it could be much more in high-end graphics products. Not only GPU is inexpensive and powerful, but also research on general purpose genetic programming on graphics processing units (GP GP GPU) is becoming more and more attractive to researchers. Nvidia, Microsoft, SIS, and so on, are also promoting the development of graphics hardware.

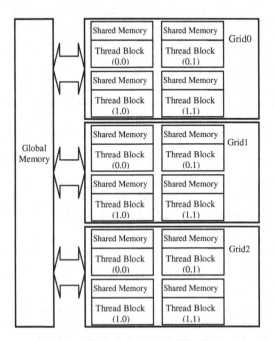

Fig. 3. Architecture of CUDA

CUDA is a platform for massively parallel high-performance computing on the company's powerful GPUs. At its cores are three key abstractions – a hierarchy of thread groups, shared memories, and barrier synchronization – that are simply exposed to the programmer as a minimal set of language extensions. These abstractions provide fine-grained data parallelism and thread parallelism, nested within coarse-grained data parallelism and task parallelism.

Thread, also known as stream, is basic unit of manipulating data in CUDA, which is a 3-component vector, so that threads can be identified using a one-dimensional, two-dimensional, or three-dimensional index, forming a one-dimensional, two-dimensional, or three-dimensional thread block, which also can access concurrently block's share memory. Those multi-dimensional blocks are organized into one-dimensional or two-dimensional grids, each block can be identified by one-dimensional or two-dimensional index, and all grids share one global memory. The whole architecture shows in Fig.3.

Each thread within the block can be identified by a multi-dimension index accessible within the kernel through the built-in *threadIdx* variable, and each block identified by the build-in *blockIdx* variable, the dimension of the thread block is accessible through the build-in *blockDim*. Take a three-dimension thread block for example, we may define the object function of each thread as:

$$thread(x, y, z) = \begin{cases} x = blockIdx.x * blockDim.x + threadIdx.x \\ y = blockIdx.y * blockDim.y + threadIdx.y \\ z = blockIdx.z * blockDim.z + threadIdx.z \end{cases}$$

Now we can identify each thread, just as we conveyed above, each thread within a block shared a high-speed shared memory, but how fast it is exactly? We copied a certain amount of data between CPU to GPU, GPU to CPU, and GPU to GPU. The result shows in Table.1, which represented the speed of communication between GPUs are much faster than it between CPUs. And this is what we need to explore for speeding up.

Table 1. Bandwidth of different memory communication (8400M GS)

Host to Device	Device to Host	Device to Device
1207.2 MB/s	1263.4 MB/s	2400.9 MB/s

High-speed communication between threads and multi-level shared memory contribute the development of parallel genetic algorithms base on CUDA.

4 Implementation of Hierarchical PGAs

The issue we intend to explore is find a suitable parallel genetic algorithms model, maximizing the performance base on the characteristics of CUDA, which means we have to run genetic operations and evaluation the fitness, which could be parallelized, in GPU thread, and share GPU memory instead of system memory as much as possible.

Traditional master-slave GAs cannot satisfy the requirement of performance, because of it only distribute population to each slave, and after each evaluation done each thread has to update the global memory. Considering the relative lower speed of global memory and global memory I/O conflict, frequent read/write global memory is not acceptable. But in a single thread block, which all threads shared with a high-speed shared memory, master-slave model seems available. We divided block shared memory into n parts, (n depends on the number of blocks within each grid), which is a series of continuous addresses for convenience. It means each block can access/write subpopulation independently, that is absolutely we have to do in parallelization.

Although fine-grained GAs is suitable for multi-core processor computer, it only allows one population, and the limited interaction between individuals. Those are not quite match with the structure of thread in CUDA. However, grids separate each block like isolated subpopulation, according to Grosso's conclusion in 1985, who conveyed that the quality of solution found after convergence was worse in the isolated case than in the single population, so we imports migration between blocks in order to improve quality of solution. Meanwhile, Petty Leuze and Grefenstette's paper concluded, which was published in 1987, high level of communication leads the same quality as serial GA with a single large panmictic population. Anyhow, high connectivity always comes with high communication cost, no matter in grids or a computer cluster, which is because of high-speed network cannot satisfy the requirement of high connectivity. Since there is a high-speed shared memory in each thread block, the communication cost is much less than traditional network.

After analyzing the special architecture of CUDA, we proposed a Hierarchical PGAs, which is a product of multi-demes PGAs at higher level and master-slave PGAs at lower level. The architecture of this hierarchical PGAs shows in Fig.4.

The step of hierarchical PGAs:

(1) CPU initializes a single large panmictic population in global memory;
(2) Distribute subpopulation to each shared memory of thread block;
(3) Each thread block starts evolution independently;
(4) Tournament selection, crossover, mutation, evaluation of fitness;
(5) Each block exchanges best individuals using island model;
(6) Each grid exchanges best individuals using stepping stone model;
(6) Update global memory with new individuals;
(7) If objective function not satisfied, go to (2).

The model of migration between blocks is neighbor migration, take thread block(x,y) as central subpopulation for example, it exchanged best individuals with eight neighbors: thread block(x-1,y-1), thread block(x-1,y), thread block(x-1,y+1), thread block(x,y-1), thread block(x,y+1), thread block(x+1,y-1), thread block(x+1,y), thread block(x+1,y+1). Considering the convenient thread block index mechanism, the implementation of migration seems to be relatively easy. Gird exchanging works much similar with block's, which just uses stepping stone model.

In this algorithm, CPU are in charge of initialize populations and distributing them to each thread block's shared memory, then, all GPU threads within each block received a memory address, pointed to their respective subpopulation. Each thread block runs a single genetic algorithm independently, including natural selection, crossover, mutation and evaluation of fitness. After those genetic operations, new data of individuals updates each block's shared memory, which is quite similar with the model of master-slave GAs. Next, migration between blocks followed, exchanging

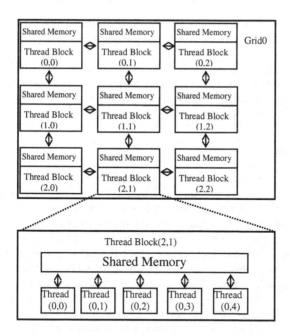

Fig. 4. Architecture of Parallel Genetic base CUDA

```
CPU thread{
    initialize thread block;
    initialize grid;
    initialize population;
    distribute population to block shared memory;
    invoke GPU method;
}

GPU kernel0{
    access respective subpopulation;
    genetic operation(selection,crossover,mutation,evalution);
    update shared memory with new individuals;
}

GPU kernel1{
    while (function condition){
        exchange best individuals with neighbors;
        invoke kernel0;
    }
}
```

Fig. 5. Hierarchical GA mixed with master-slave GAs and Multi-Demes Gas

best individuals to their neighbors (Fig.5). Even if the communication cost increased during migration, high-speed shared memory in each thread block keeps it minimized, much less than the cost of high-speed network.

For a further improvement, we stored several variables, like time of evolution, migration rate, migration interval, and so on, which won't alter during evolution phase and needs to access frequently, in constant memory of CUDA, of which the speed is faster than global memory.

5 Conclusion

The unique thread hierarchy and memory hierarchy of CUDA overcome the effect of the increasing connectivity accompanied by increasing communication cost, and I/O concurrency conflict, therefore, improving the performance of parallelization. This Hierarchical PGAs makes best use of those advantages of CUDA, and regards CUDA as a new generation powerful parallel genetic algorithm tool by experiments. Furthermore, the accessible architecture of CUDA provokes researchers to focus on algorithm itself, not other factors, like delay of network and other peripheries. For developers, one challenge of CUDA is analyzing their algorithms and data to find the optimal numbers of threads and blocks that will keep the GPU fully utilized. Factors include the size of the global data set, the maximum amount of local data that blocks of threads can share, the number of thread processors in the GPU, and the sizes of the on-chip local memories. In summary, Graphics Processor Unit's advantages of high-speed, unique compute architecture, easy implementation, inexpensive, will make evolution computing become increasing common.

References

1. Cantú-Paz, E.: A Survey of Parallel Genetic Algorithms (1998)
2. Owens, J.D., Luebke, D., Govindaraju, N.: A Survey of General-Purpose Computation on Graphics Hardware,STAR – State of The Art Report (2007)
3. Cantú-Paz, E.: Migration Policies Selection Pressure and Parallel Evolutionary Algorithms, IlliGAL Report No.99015, (June 1999)
4. Ali Ismail, M.: Parallel Genetic Algorithms-Master Slave Paradigm Approach Using MPI, E-Tech (2004)
5. Wilkinson, B., Allen, M.: Parallel Programming Techniques and Applications Using Networked workstations and Parallel Computers, 2nd edn. (2006)
6. Lin, C., Snyder, L.: Principles of Parallel Programming (2008)
7. Pettey, C.B., Leuze, M.R., Grefenstette, J.J.: A parallel genetic algorithm. In: Proc. of the Second International Conference on Genetic Algorithms, pp. 155–161 (1987)
8. Tanese, R.: Distributed genetic algorithms. In: Proc. of the Third International Conference on Genetic Algorithms, pp. 434–439. Morgan Kaufmann, San Mateo (1989)
9. Golub, M., Budin, L.: An Asynchronous Model of Global Parallel Genetic Algorithms. In: Second ICSC Symposium on Engineering of Intelligent Systems (2000)
10. Halfhill, T.R.: Parallel Processing with CUDA (Janauary 2000), http://www.mdronline.com
11. NVIDIA, NVIDIA CUDA^{TM} Programming Guide, (December 2008)
12. NVIDIA, NVIDIA CUDA Compute Unified Device Architecture Reference Manual, (November 2008)

Moitf GibbsGA: Sampling Transcription Factor Binding Sites Coupled with PSFM Optimization by GA

Lifang Liu[1,2] and Licheng Jiao[2]

[1] School of Computer Science and Technology, Xidian University, Xi'an 710071, China
[2] Institute of Intelligent Information Processing, Xidian University, Xi`an 710071, China
liulifang@tom.com

Abstract. Identification of transcription factor binding sites (TFBSs) or motifs plays an important role in deciphering the mechanisms of gene regulation. Although many experimental and computational methods have been developed, finding TFBSs remains a challenging problem. We propose and develop a novel sampling based motif finding method coupled with PSFM optimization by genetic algorithm, which we call Motif GibbsGA. One significant feature of Motif GibbsGA is the combination of Gibbs sampling and PSFM optimization by genetic algorithm. Based on position-specific frequency matrix (PSFM) motif model, a greedy strategy for choosing the initial parameters of PSFM is employed. Then a Gibbs sampler is built with respect to PSFM model. During the sampling process, PSFM is improved via a genetic algorithm. A postprocessing with adaptive adding and removing is used to handle general cases with arbitrary numbers of instances per sequence. We test our method on the benchmark dataset compiled by Tompa et al. for assessing computational tools that predict TFBSs. The performance of Motif GibbsGA on the data set compares well to, and in many cases exceeds, the performance of existing tools. This is in part attributed to the significant role played by the genetic algorithm which has improved PSFM.

1 Introduction

In the post-genomic era, identifying regulatory elements is an important step to understanding the mechanisms of gene regulation. Over the past few years, there are many computational tools that identify TFBSs as the sub-sequences, or motifs, common to a set of sequences. The difference from each other chiefly in their definition of what constitutes a motif, what constitutes statistical overrepresentation of a motif and the method used to find statistically overrepresented motifs.

Nearly all motif discovery algorithms fall into three general classes: pattern-based, profile-based and combinatorial. In profile-based algorithms, a motif is usually modeled by a $4 \times W$ position-specific frequency matrix (PSFM), where W is the motif's size in base pairs, so that each column of the PSFM represents the distribution of the 4nt at the corresponding position in the motif. One way of the PSFM estimating can be through standard statistical learning theory methods, such as maximum-likelihood estimation (e.g. MEME [1], The Improbizer [2]), the Markov chain Monte Carlo algorithms (e.g. AlignACE [3], BioProspector [4], MotifSampler [5], GLAM [6],

Z. Cai et al. (Eds.): ISICA 2009, LNCS 5821, pp. 31–39, 2009.

DSMC [7]), greedy search (e.g. Consensus [8]), and genetic algorithms (e.g. GAME [9], GALF-P [10]). Another way of finding shared motifs is to compile a library of motifs which previously characterized or randomized, and assess whether any of these motifs are statistically over-represented in the sequences (e.g. Clover [11], SOM-BRERO [12]). Library-based method has declared improved performance. However the existing tools are still not effective for discovering motifs [13,14]. For example, as shown in paper [13]'s evaluation, even the best performing algorithm has sensitivity <9% and precision <30%. To deal with this issue, a class of algorithms called ensemble methods has been proposed (e.g. MotifVoter [15]). Though the existing ensemble methods overall perform better than stand-alone motif finders, the improvement gained is not substantial.

In this work, we present the Motif GibbsGA approach - a novel *de novo* motif identification approach inspired by Leping Li *et al.* (2007) [16]. Motif GibbsGA is based on Gibbs sampling coupled with PSFM optimization by genetic algorithm. Based on position position-specific frequency (PSFM) motif model, a greedy strategy for choosing the initial parameters of PSFM is employed. Then a Gibbs sampler is build with respect to PSFM model. During the sampling process, PSFM is improved via a genetic algorithm. A post-processing with adaptive adding and removing is used to handle general cases with arbitrary numbers of instances per sequence. We test Motif GibbsGA on the benchmark dataset compiled by Tompa *et al.* (2005) for assessing computational tools that predict TFBSs. The performance of Motif GibbsGA on this data set compares well to, and in many cases exceeds, the performance of existing tools.

2 Materials and Methods

2.1 Basic Matrix Models

By far the most common representation of a motif is a position-specific frequency matrix (PSFM) θ_W of length W. Each entry in this matrix gives the probability $p_{b,j}$ of finding a given base b at position j in the binding site, such that $\sum_{i=1}^{|\Sigma|} p_{i,j} = 1$, Σ is a finite alphabet. For a motif instances (substring) $s=(s_1,s_2,...,s_W)$ of length W in a sequence, the probability Q_s of x given the motif model θ_W is

$$Q_s = P(s_1 \cdots s_W \mid \theta_W) = \prod_{i=1}^{i=W} p_{s_i,i} \tag{1}$$

Except for the motif instances, the remainder of the sequences is classified as non-sites, where each base is generated according to a specific background model. The 0-order background model is $B_0 =[q_{A,0},q_{C,0},q_{G,0},q_{T,0}]$,   this means that each base is drawn independently from a single discrete distribution. The m-order background model is B_m, this means that the probability of finding a certain nucleotide in a sequence depends on the m previous nucleotides in the sequence. For a segment s in a sequence, the probability P_s of segment s being generated by the background model B_m is given by

$$P_s = P(s_1 \cdots s_W \mid B_m) = \prod_{i=1}^{W} P(s_i \mid s_{i-1}, \cdots, s_{i-m}) \tag{2}$$

Corresponding to PSFM, the position weight matrix (PWM) is defined as M_W, each entry in PWM is $m_{b,j} = \ln(p_{b,j} / q_{b,0})$. Given a segment s, the match score of M_W on s is defined as

$$Score_s = \sum_{i=1}^{W} m_{s_i, i} \tag{3}$$

In order to ranking the various motifs found by Motif GibbsGA, the P value of an information content is calculated. The P value is the probability of obtaining an information content greater than or equal to the observed value, given the number of sequences in the alignment and its width. We use the method described in MEME to calculating the P value of information content. The information content of the sequence alignment is defined as

$$I = \sum_{j=1}^{W} \sum_{i=1}^{|\Sigma|} p_{i,j} \ln(p_{i,j} / q_{i,0}) \tag{4}$$

In what follows, we will show an efficient method (Motif GibbsGA) for discovering motifs based the above-mentioned models.

2.2 Greedy Search for Choosing Starting Point

The free parameters for a motif model based on PSFM are the motif length W and the entries in PSFM. One might try using randomly chosen letter frequency matrices as starting points. In this paper, a greedy search strategy is used to choose more intelligent ones.

Since each W-letter segment in the search space may be a candidate of a motif, so we first build a precompiled library of motifs represented by PSFMs, which are constructed from one of the input sequences selected randomly. Each W-letter segment of the selected sequence is associated with a position-specific frequency matrix θ, which constructed as equation (5).

$$\theta = \left[p_{i,j} \right], \text{where } p_{i,j} = \begin{cases} \lambda & \text{if } a_{i,j} = \alpha_i \\ \dfrac{(1-\lambda)}{(|\Sigma|-1)} & \text{otherwise.} \end{cases} \tag{5}$$

Where $\alpha_i \in \Sigma, \lambda > 1/|\Sigma|$, then a PWM $m_{i,j} = \ln(p_{i,j} / q_{i,0})$ is also defined. Next each W-letter segment in the search space is matched to one of the motifs in the library based on the match score's P value. A W-letter segment is matched to one of the motifs with the smallest match score's P value. Following Bailey, and Gribskov (1998) [17], we obtain the match score's P value by calculating the cumulative density function. Let $M^{(k)}(x)$ be the match score probability density function for the motif

PWM matrix if it consisted of only its first k columns, then the density for the matrix consisting of the first $k+1$ columns is

$$M^{(k+1)}(x) = \sum_{j=1}^{|\Sigma|} M^{(k)}(x - m_{j,k+1}) q_{j,0} \tag{6}$$

To start the induction, set $M^{(0)}(0) = 1$ and $M^{(0)}(x) = 0$ for $x>0$. After W iterations, $M^{(W)}(x)$ contains the probability density for matching the motif with a random W-letter segment, from which the P value of the match score of a motif M_W on segment s is

$$P(Score_s) = \sum_{x \geq Score_s} M^{(W)}(x). \tag{7}$$

Finally every W-letter segments have matched to a motif in the library, but only one of the alignment matrices, which has the smallest P value of an information content, is saved as the start point.

2.3   Site Sampler

Every possible segment of width W within a sequence is considered as a possible instance of the motif. Site sampler finds one occurrence per sequence of the motif in the dataset. Based on the probabilities P_s and Q_s, the weight $A_s = Q_s / P_s$ is assigned to segment s, and with each segment within a sequence so weighted. Thus, a motif instance can be randomly drawn from all possible segments with probability proportional to A_x. The implementation of our site sampler algorithm is based on the original Gibbs sampling algorithm previously described by Lawrence *et al.* [18]. The terminating condition of our site sampler is either after a user-specified maximum number of iterations (by default *500*) or until the change in θ_W (Euclidean distance) falls below a user-specified threshold (by default 10^{-6}).

2.4   PSFM Optimization by Genetic Algorithm

PSFM optimization is applied during the site sampling process, and substantially increased the sensitivity/specificity of a poorly estimated PSFM, and further improved the quality of a good PSFM. We use a genetic algorithm inspired by Leping Li *et al.* (2007) [16] for PSFM optimization. The method is described as follows.

1.   Initialization: We made 100 'clones' of the starting PSFM, which estimated by site sampler, to form a 'population'. Different population sizes can be used.

2.   Mutation: All except the raw PSFM were subject to mutation. For each PSFM to be mutated, n (the number of columns subject to mutation) was randomly generated from the following distribution, $P(n = k) = 1/2^k, k = 2, \cdots, W$, and $P(n = 1) = 1 - \sum_{k=2}^{W} 1/2^k$. Next, n columns were randomly selected with equal probability for the W columns. For each column chosen, one of the four bases was then randomly selected and a small value, d, was added to or subtracted from $p_{i,j}$ with equal probability. Mutation was performed

independently for each selected column. After mutation, we set negative values to 0 and standardized each column. We typically set the value of d to 0.05 for the first 100 iterations of site sampler and to 0.02 for the remaining iterations of site sampler. Convert all the PSFMs to PWMs.

3. Substring assignment: After mutation, a W-letter segment in the search space is matched to a PWM if and only if their match score's P value little than the threshold P_{th} (such as 10^{-3} or 10^{-4}).

4. Fitness evaluation: The P value of the information content is used as the fitness score. The alignment matrix with the smallest P value is kept down for the remainder of site sampler iterations.

2.5 The Description of Motif GibbsGA

Site sampler finds one occurrence per sequence of the motif in the dataset. To further extend Motif GibbsGA, we use a simple scan procedure to extract additional motif sites within a set of sequences. Site sampler obtained an optimum PWM_{opt}. Start from this PWM_{opt} configuration, our scan algorithm cycles through all remaining potential motif sites, and selects any additional sites that give the statistical significance of the match score (the threshold P value, P_{th}, is given by user). In other word, if $P(Score_s)$ is the P value of the match score of a motif M_W on segment s, then we accept this addition if and only if $P(Score_s)<P_{th}$.

In order to finding more than one motif in a set of sequences, Motif GibbsGA uses an iterative-masking approach: the binding sites of a discovered motif are masked out of the sequence dataset and then Motif GibbsGA is re-applied to this masked dataset to find additional motifs. The pseudo-code of Motif GibbGA is shown in Tab.1.

Table 1. Pseudo-code of Motif GibbsGA

Procedure Motif GibbsGA
Begin
  S: dataset of sequences; W_{min}: the minimum width of the motif; W_{max}: the maximum width of the motif; W_{step}: increase step for motif width.
For $W= W_{min}$ to W_{max} by W_{step} Do

  Greedy search for choosing starting point (θ_W) from dataset S;

  While ($t < Iteration_{max}$ and $Euclidean\ distance$ (θ_W^t, θ_W^{t-1}) $< 10^{-6}$) Do

    Run site sampler;
    If ($t \% 20 = = 0$)
      PSFM optimization by genetic algorithm;
    End If
  End While
  Extract additional motif sites if and only if $P(Score_s)<P_{th}$.
  Print the motif instances, calculate the P value of the information content;
  "Erase" occurrences of best motif found above;
End For
End

3 Results

The datasets are available as a benchmark at the assessment web site http://bio.cs.washington.edu/assessment/.

These datasets comprised of eukaryotic binding sites belonging to 52 transcription factors representing four different species, 6 belonging to fly, 26 belonging to human, 12 belonging to mouse and 8 belonging to yeast. The binding sites of each transcription factor were presented in three different background models, 'real', 'generic', and 'Markov'. For each of the different type of background model, the known positions of the binding sites were kept unchanged. Four additional datasets of type 'Markov' containing no planted binding sites were included as negative controls. Using these datasets Tompa *et al.* evaluated the performance of 13 different computational tools for *de novo* prediction of regulatory elements. We evaluated Motif GibbsGA on these datasets according to the performance measures described in Tompa *et al.* and compared it to the 13 tools evaluated in that paper. The comparative results of this evaluation are described below.

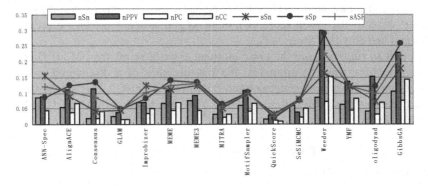

Fig. 1. Combined measures of correctness over all 56 data sets

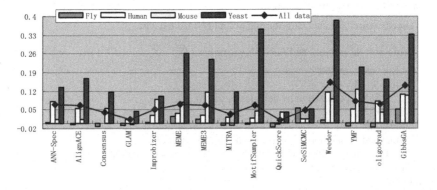

Fig. 2. Correlation coefficient (nCC) by species

For Motif GibbsGA, we set $W_{min}=6$, $W_{max}=12$, $W_{step}=1$, $Iteration_{max}=1000$ and $P_{th}=10^{-4}$, use the 3-order background model. Fig. 1 shows the comparative results for the seven statistics, nucleotide-level sensitivity (nSn), nucleotide-level positive predictive value ($nPPV$), nucleotide-level performance coefficient (nPC), nucleotide-level correlation coefficient (nCC), site-level sensitivity (sSn), site-level positive predictive value ($sPPV$) and site-level average site performance ($sASP$), which summarized over all 56 datasets, regardless of species or background model. The Motif GibbsGA outperforms the other tools in all indicators except for Weeder. Fig. 2 gives the breakdown of the performance, high-lighted by the correlation coefficient, nCC, of each tool on the datasets of the different species (regardless of the background model). Fig. 2 shows that Motif GibbsGA does better than most of the other tools in all species. Fig. 3 breaks down the datasets according to the different background models, 'real', 'generic' and 'Markov' (regardless of the species). Motif GibbsGA performs better than most of the other tools in prediction motifs in all the three background models.

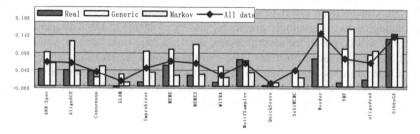

Fig. 3. Correlation coefficient (nCC) by data set type

From Fig. 1-3, we can see that Motif GibbsGA does better than all the other Gibbs or Gibbs-like based method (ANN-Sped, AlignACE, GLAM, MotifSampler and SeSiMCME), this is in part attributed to the significant role played by the genetic algorithm that improved PSFM. Gibbs sampling is a heuristic search algorithm, the performances of this method are subject to potential suboptimal solutions in the search space. One way to tackle this problem is to import stronger global optimization techniques, such as genetic algorithms and others. In order to see the effect of genetic algorithm, we delete the PSFM optimization step, and run the program on the same datasets. Fig. 4 gives the result, and compared to that of Motif GibbsGA.

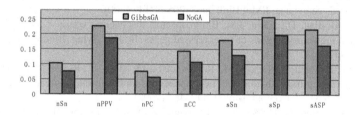

Fig. 4. Comparison of using or not using genetic algorithm

4 Discussion

We have developed a novel *de novo* motif identification approach based on Gibbs sampling coupled with PSFM optimization by genetic algorithm, which we implemented in our software Motif GibbsGA. We test Motif GibbsGA on the benchmark dataset compiled by Tompa *et al.* (2005) for assessing computational tools that predict TFBSs. The performance of Motif GibbsGA on this data set compares well to, and in many cases exceeds, the performance of existing tools. From the result, we can see that here are considerable differences in results from these different programs, which is due to the existence of a large number of possible solutions. Optimization algorithms such as ANN-Sped, AlignACE, GLAM, MotifSampler, SeSiMCME and MEME can locally optimize their motif discovery results, but the inherent multimodality of the solution space restricts these local optimization procedures from exploring many different solutions. The Motif GibbGA framework allows a greater flexibility of movement around the solution space by applying an evolutionary process to an entire population of possible solutions.

Despite considerable effort to date, it remains a complex challenge for computational biologists to convincingly predict regulatory elements in DNA sequences. Further efforts will be put in for several issues, the most important ones of which are the correlation between motif positions [19], motif positional information [20] and synergistic relationships between transcription factors [21]. As the complexity of these models increased, the need for sophisticated algorithms for finding optimal solutions to these models will become increasingly important.

Acknowledgements

This work was supported by the NNSF of China under Grant Nos.60705004.

Reference

[1] Bailey, T.L., Elkan, C.: Unsupervised learning of multiple motifs in biopolymers using expectation maximization. Machine Learning 21, 51–80 (1995)

[2] Ao, W., Gaudet, J., Kent, W.J., Muttumu, S., Mango, S.E.: Environmentally induced foregut remodeling by PHA-4/FoxA and DAF-12/NHR. Science 305, 1743–1746 (2004)

[3] Hughes, J.D., Estep, P.W., Tavazoie, S., Church, G.M.: Computational identification of cis-regulatory elements associated with functionally coherent groups of genes in Saccharomyeds cerevisiae. J.Mol.Biol. 296, 1205–1214 (2000)

[4] Liu, X., Brutlag, D.L., Liu, J.S.: BioProspector: discovering conserved DNA motifs in upstream regulatory regions of co-expressed genes. In: Pac. Symp. Biocomput. vol. 6, pp. 127–138 (2001)

[5] Thijs, G., Marchal, K., Lescot, M., Rombauts, S., De Moor, B., Rouze, P., Moreau, Y.: A Gibbs sampling methods to detect overrepresented motifs in the upstream regions of co-expressed genes. J. Comput. Biol. 9, 447–464 (2002)

[6] Frith, M.C., Hansen, U., Spouge, J.L., Weng, Z.: Finding functional sequence elements by multiple local alignment. Nucleic Acids Research 32, 189–200 (2004)

[7] Liang, K.C., Wang, X.D., Anastassiou, D.: A profile-based deterministic sequential Monte Carlo algorithm for motif discovery. Bioinformatics 24, 46–55 (2008)

[8] Hertz, G., Stormo, G.: Identifying DNA and protein patterns with statistically significant alignments of multiple sequences. Bioinformatics 15, 563–577 (1999)

[9] Wei., Z., Jensen, S.T.: GAME: detecting cis-regulatory elements using a genetic algorithm. Bioinformatics 22, 1577–1584 (2006)

[10] Chan, T.M., Leung, K.S., Lee, K.H.: TFBS identification based on genetic algorithm with combined representations and adapbive post-processing. Bioinformatics 24, 341–349 (2008)

[11] Frith., M.C., Fu., Y., Yu, L., et al.: Detection of functional DNA motifs via statistical over-representation. Nucleic Acids Research 32, 1372–1381 (2004)

[12] Mahony, S., Hendrix, D., Golden, A., Smith, T.J., Rokhsar, D.S.: Transcription factor binding site identification using the self-organizing map. Bioinformatics 21, 1807–1814 (2005)

[13] Tompa, M., Li, N., Bailey, T.L., Chruch, G.M., De Moor, B., Eskin, E.: Assessing computational tools for the discovery of transcription factor binding sites. Nature Biotechnology 23, 137–144 (2005)

[14] Hu, J., Li, B., Kihara, D.: Limitations and potentials of current motif discovery algorithms. Nucleic Acids Research 33, 4899–4913 (2005)

[15] Wijaya., E., Yiu., S.-M., Son, N.T., et al.: MotifVoter: a novel ensemble method for fine-grained integration of generic motif finders. Bioinformatics 24, 2288–2295 (2008)

[16] Li., L., Liang., Y., Bass., R.L.: GAPWM: a genetic algorithm method for optimizing a position weight matrix. Bioinformatics 23, 1188–1194 (2007)

[17] Bailey, T.L., Gribskov, M.: Combining evidence using p-values: application to sequence homology searches. Bioinformatics 14, 48–54 (1998)

[18] Lawrence, C.E., Altschul, S.F., Bogouski, M.S., Liu, J.S., Neuwald, A.F., Wooten, J.C.: Detecting Subtle Sequence Signals: A Gibbs Sampling Strategy for Multiple Alignment. Science 262, 208–214 (1993)

[19] da Fonseca., P.G.S., Gautier, C., Guimaraes, K.S., Sagot, M.-F.: Efficient representation and P-value computation for high-order Markov motifs. Bioinformatics 24, i160–i166 (2008)

[20] Casimiro1, A.C., Vinga, S., Freitas, A.T., Oliveira, A.L.: An analysis of the positional distribution of DNA motifs in promoter regions and its biological relevance. BMC Bioinformatics 9, 89 (2008)

[21] Shen, L., Liu, J., Wang, W.: GBNet: Deciphering regulatory rules in the co-regulated genes using a Gibbs sampler enhanced Bayesian network approach. BMC Bioinformatics 9, 395 (2008)

Network Model and Optimization of Medical Waste Reverse Logistics by Improved Genetic Algorithm

Lihong Shi, Houming Fan, Pingquan Gao, and Hanyu Zhang

Transportation Management College, Dalian Maritime University, 116026 Dalian,
Liaoning Province, China

Abstract. The medical waste management is of great importance because of the
potential environmental hazards and public health risks. Manufacturers have to
collect the medical waste and control its recovery or disposal. Medical waste
recovery, which encompasses reusing, remanufacturing and materials recycling,
requires a specially structured reverse logistics network in order to collect the
medical waste efficiently. This paper presents a Mixed Integer Linear Programming model with minimizing costs for medical waste reverse logistics
networks. The total costs for reverse logistics include transportation cost, fixed
cost of opening the collecting centers and processing centers and operation cost
at these facilities over finite planning horizons. An improved genetic algorithm
method with a hybrid encoding rule is used to solve the proposed model. The
efficiency and practicability of the proposed model is validated by an application to an illustrative example dealing with medical waste returned from some
hospitals to a given manufacture.

Keywords: genetic algorithm, medical waste, mixed integer linear programming, reverse logistics network.

1 Introduction

In the past few years, there has been an increase in public concern about the management of healthcare waste on a global basis[1]. Medical waste refers to any waste generated from the health care industry such as hospitals and medical laboratories. It
includes anatomical waste, pathological waste, infectious waste, hazardous waste, and
other waste[2]. In China, generation of medical waste from the healthcare industry
has rapidly increased over the past decade. Although medical waste represents a small
portion of the total solid waste stream, such waste must be handled with care because
of the potentially infectious and hazardous materials contained in it. Improper disposal of medical waste may pose a significant risk to human health and the environment. Many investigations and studies have suggested that many proper waste management procedures are still not being well implemented[3,4,5].

Nowadays, some studies have focused on the practicability of applying the concept
of reverse logistics to the medical waste management, which may greatly improve the
efficiency of medical waste management and reduce the negative influence it may
impose on the environment. Here reverse logistics is referred to as the process of
logistics management involved in planning, managing, and controlling the flow of

Z. Cai et al. (Eds.): ISICA 2009, LNCS 5821, pp. 40–52, 2009.

medical waste for either reuse or final disposal of waste. The traditional measures, such as: waste processing technologies, used for the treatment of hazardous wastes are inadequate for integrating medical waste management, collection, storage, distribution and transportation activities into comprehensive, reverse logistics operating strategies. Consequently, the efficient design of a medical waste recovery network is one of the challenging issues in the recently emerged field of reverse logistics.

Only recently, reverse logistics has become a topic of research concern. Much of the previous work[6,7,8] has been exploratory, emphasizing the need and importance of reverse logistics issues. General frameworks have been provided. Now, researchers have considered the use of quantitative techniques to various issues related to reverse logistics network design. Louwers, Bert, Edo, Frans, and Simme Douwe[9] have presented a facility location-allocation model for the collection, reprocessing and redistribution of carpet waste to determine the locations and capacities of the regional recovery centers to minimize investment, processing, and transportation costs. Bloemhof-Ruward[10] have examined the distribution issues such as location of collection points in a reverse logistic system. De Koster, de Brito, and van de Vendel[11] have investigated the factors contributing to RL network decisions by considering inbound and outbound flows, the transport routes, the return volume, choice of receiving warehouse and the market location for returned products. Listes [12] has proposed a generic stochastic model for the design of networks comprising both supply and return channels, organized in a closed loop system. Beamon and Fernandes[13]have developed an integer programming model for a four echelon reverse supply chain by assuming infinite storage capacities and same holding costs for recovered and new products. Santoso, Ahmed, Goetschalckx, and Shapiro[14] have proposed a stochastic programming model and solution algorithm for solving supply chain network design problems of a realistic scale. Listes and Dekker[15] have conducted a the case study of recycling sand from demolition waste by using stochastic approach. Hu, Sheu, and Huang[16] have presented a cost-minimization model for a multi-time-step, multi-type hazardous-waste reverse logistics system. Salema[17] has proposed a strategic and tactical model for the design and planning of supply chains with reverse flows.

In this paper, the results and methodologies of all above researches are studied in the development of a more suitable model for a reverse logistics network handling medical waste returns. The mathematical model considers the supply of returned waste through the medical materials producers themselves, that means the returning process dose not include a third party collector. This paper is organized as follows. In Section 2 we define the problem, and in section 3 we propose a mixed integer programming model[18,19,20] of reverse logistics network for the returned medical waste. Section 4 focuses on solving the proposed mathematical model by an improved genetic algorithm and conducting a numerical test to illustrate the application of the method for the optimization problem. Finally, some avenues of future research are discussed in Section 5 which concludes the paper.

2   Problem Definition

The medical waste reverse logistics network in this study is shown in Fig.1. The hospitals and final factories have been fixed. We need to discuss the location problem of

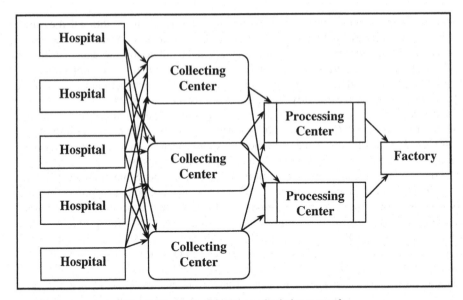

Fig. 1. Medical waste reverse logistics network

collecting centers and processing centers, involving problems such as transportation, fixed cost, operation costs and so on. In the network, there are I collecting centers, and J processing centers. Medical waste is transported from hospitals to colleting centers. Through some segregation and collection in the collecting centers, the medical waste is again transported from collecting centers to processing centers, where it will be completely disinfected, disassembled, remanufactured or disposed. Finally, the reused medical materials were shipped to the final factory for sales. Considering the public wants these waste processing facilities as few as possible, the medical waste reverse logistics network for medical materials producers is consisting of four type nodes: hospital nodes, the collecting centers nodes, the processing centers nodes, the final factories nodes.

The medical waste reverse logistics network design problem can be described as follows: given the potential locations and the capacities of the collecting centers and processing centers, the total amounts of each kind of the medical waste generated by each hospital, the cost structures for transportation, operation and other fixed costs associated with the medical waste, the model we formulate should find out which potential collecting centers and processing centers should be opened and how the medical waste flows should be delivered so that reverse logistics network can achieve the minimum total costs. In summary, the decision belongs to typical location-allocation problem, therefore the vehicle routing problem is not deeply considered.

3 Model Formulation

Prior to developing the mixed-integer programming model for medical waste reverse logistics network design, we made the following underlying assumptions and simplifications: (1)the given medical materials producer has only one factory in this area, and this factory has decided to adopt the self-supporting reverse logistics mode; (2)the medical waste which has been processed by all processing centers will be transported to the factory, that means this recycling supply chain is a closed loop considering both forward and reverse logistics; (3)the mounts of medical waste generated from each hospital are independent; (4) the cost structures for transportation, operation and other fixed cost are known for dealing with the multiple types of medial wastes, especially, the operation costs include all the storage cost and other costs for the management of the medical waste; (5)the discarding ratios of medical waste in all collecting centers are the same, and the processing centers likewise; (7)the capacity of the given factory is limitless.

3.1 Sets

$H = \{1, 2, \ldots, H\}$, set of hospitals where the medical wastes are generated

$I = \{1, 2, \ldots, I\}$, set of possible collecting centers

$J = \{1, 2, \ldots, J\}$, set of possible processing centers

$M = \{1, 2, \ldots, M\}$, set of medical waste types.

3.2 Decision Variables

X_{him} : amount shipped from hospital h to collecting center i for waste m;

Y_{ijm} : amount shipped from collecting center i to processing center j for waste m;

G_{jm} : amount shipped from processing center j to the factory for waste m;

$P_i = \begin{cases} 1, & \text{if colleting center i is open;} \\ 0, & \text{otherwise} \end{cases}$;

$Q_j = \begin{cases} 1, & \text{if processing center j is open;} \\ 0, & \text{otherwise} \end{cases}$;

3.3 Parameters

H : the number of hospitals which are the customers of the given medical materials producer;

$I_{\max}$: the maximum number of potential colleting centers;

$J_{\max}$: the maximum number of potential processing centers;

M : the number of the medical waste types;

A_{hm} : the amount of medical waste m from hospital h;

I_i^f : the fixed costs of building or capacity enlargement of colleting center i;

J_j^f : the fixed costs of building or capacity enlargement of processing center j;

G^f : the fixed costs of capacity enlargement of the given factory;

I^o_{im} : the unit operation cost of medical waste m in collcting center i;

J^o_{jm} : the unit operation cost of medical waste m in processing center j;

G^t_m : the unit operation cost of medical waste m in the given factory;

I^t_{im} : the unit transportation cost of medical waste m from hospital h to collecting center i;

J^t_{jm} : the unit transportation cost of medical waste m collecting center i to processing center j;

G^t_{jm} : the unit transportation cost of medical waste m processing center j to the given medical waste producer;

I^c_{im} : the maximum capacity of collecting center i for medical waste m;

J^c_{jm} : the maximum capacity of processing center j for medical waste m;

I^c_i : the maximum capacity of collecting center i;

J^c_j : the maximum capacity of processing center j;

α_m : the discarding ratio of medical waste m in collecting centers;

β_m : the discarding ratio of medical waste m in processing centers;

3.4 Mathematical Formulation

Subject to:

$$\sum_{i=1}^{I} X_{him} = A_{hm} \; (h = 1, 2, \ldots H \;; m = 1, 2, \ldots, M) \tag{1}$$

$$(1 - \alpha_m)\sum_{h=1}^{H} X_{him} = \sum_{j=1}^{J} Y_{ijm} \; (i = 1, 2, \ldots I; m = 1, 2, \ldots, M) \tag{2}$$

$$(1 - \beta_m)\sum_{i=1}^{I}\sum_{j=1}^{J} Y_{ijm} = \sum_{j=1}^{J} T_{jm} \; (m = 1, 2, \ldots, M) \tag{3}$$

$$\sum_{h=1}^{H}\sum_{m=1}^{M} X_{him} \leq I^c_i P_i \quad (i = 1, 2, \ldots I) \tag{4}$$

$$\sum_{h=1}^{H} X_{him} \leq I^c_{im} P_i \quad (i = 1, 2, \ldots I; m = 1, 2, \ldots, M) \tag{5}$$

$$\sum_{i=1}^{I} \sum_{m=1}^{M} Y_{ijm} \le J_j^c Q_j \qquad (j=1,2,\dots J) \tag{6}$$

$$\sum_{i=1}^{I} Y_{ijm} \le J_{jm}^c Q_j \qquad (j=1,2,\dots J; m=1,2,\dots,M) \tag{7}$$

$$\sum_{i=1}^{I} P_i \le I_{\max} \tag{8}$$

$$\sum_{j=1}^{J} Q_j \le J_{\max} \tag{9}$$

$$X_{him} \ge 0; Y_{ijm} \ge 0 \tag{10}$$

$$P_i \in \{0,1\}; Q_j \in \{0,1\} \tag{11}$$

Minimize:

$$
\begin{aligned}
f(X) = & \sum_{i=1}^{I} I_i^f P_i + \sum_{j=1}^{J} J_j^f Q_j + G^f \\
& + \sum_{h=1}^{H} \sum_{i=1}^{I} \sum_{m=1}^{M} (I_{im}^t + I_{im}^o (1-\alpha_m)) X_{him} \\
& + \sum_{i=1}^{I} \sum_{j=1}^{J} \sum_{m=1}^{M} (J_{jm}^t + J_{jm}^o (1-\beta_m)) Y_{ijm} \\
& + \sum_{j=1}^{J} \sum_{m=1}^{M} (G_{jm}^t + G_m^o) G_{jm}
\end{aligned} \tag{12}
$$

The objective function (1) minimizes total reverse logistics costs comprised of transportation, operation, and other fixed costs for opening nodes. Constraints (2) to (4) guarantee the balance of medical waste in hospitals, collecting centers, processing centers, and the factory accordingly. Constraint (5) insures that the total volume of waste shipped to each colleting center cannot exceed the capacity of the colleting center i serving them. Constraint (6) insures that the volume of waste m shipped to each colleting center cannot exceed the capacity of the center serving it. Constraint (7) insures that the total volume of waste shipped to each processing center cannot exceed the capacity of the processing center j serving them. Constraint (8) insures that the volume of waste m shipped to each processing center cannot exceed the capacity of the center serving it. Constraints (9) and (10) limit the number of the opening collecting centers and processing centers. Constraint(11) assures the non-negativity of decision variables X_{him} and Y_{ijm}. Constraint (12) assures the binary integrality of decision variables P_i and Q_j.

The model we develop belongs to the class of NP-hard problems. In this paper, we design an improved genetic algorithm to solve this crisp model.

4 Model Application and Results

In general, a genetic algorithm is referred to as a stochastic solution search procedure that is designed to solve combinatorial problems using the concept of evolutionary computation imitating the natural selection and biological reproduction of animal species[21,22]. Fig.2 demonstrates the steps of this approach.

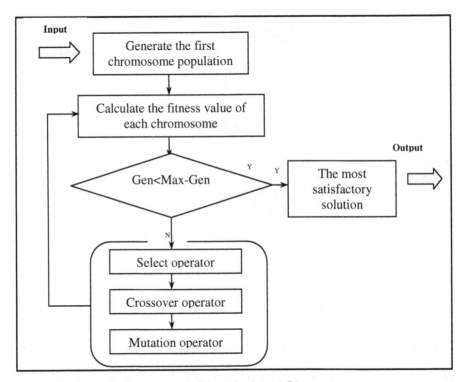

Fig. 2. Steps of proposed GA

4.1 Encoding

The design of a suitable chromosome is the first step for a successful GA implementation because it applies probabilistic transition rule on each chromosome to create a population of chromosomes, representing a good candidate solution. Distinctly, X_{him}, Y_{ijm}, G_{jm} are numerical value variables while P_i and Q_j are logical value variables. This paper adopts a hybrid encoding rule which combines both binary and floating encoding to represent the chromosome. Each chromosome developed is based on

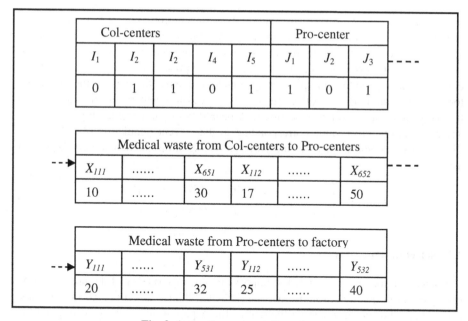

Col-centers					Pro-center			
I_1	I_2	I_2	I_4	I_5	J_1	J_2	J_3	----
0	1	1	0	1	1	0	1	

Medical waste from Col-centers to Pro-centers					
X_{111}	......	X_{651}	X_{112}	......	X_{652}
10	......	30	17	......	50

Medical waste from Pro-centers to factory					
Y_{111}	......	Y_{531}	Y_{112}	......	Y_{532}
20	......	32	25	......	40

Fig. 3. A genetic representation scheme

single dimensional array which consists of binary values, representing decision variables related to initial hospitals, collecting centers, processing centers, and floating point values, representing amount shipped from hospital h to collecting center i, from collecting center i to processing center j, and from processing center j to the factory for waste m.

The representation of a chromosome in this paper is illustrated in Fig.3 above. The chromosome has six hospitals, five potential collecting centers, three processing centers and one final factory. Thus, each chromosome is represented by a (5+3+6*5+5*3) array, where the first (5+3) genes represent whether the center is opened(=1) or closed(=0); the following (6*5) genes represent the returned medical waste from six hospitals to five collecting centers; the last (5*3) genes represent the returned medical waste from five collecting centers to three processing centers. Obviously, every gene is not isolated, that means if a colleting center or processing center is not selected as the opening center(P_i/Q_j =0), there will be no returned medical waste shipped to it(X_{him}/Y_{ijm}=0).

4.2 Evaluation

Evaluation aims to associate each individual with a fitness value so that it can reflect the fitness for an individual. This evaluation process is intended to compare one individual with other individuals in the population. The choice of fitness function is also very critical because it has to accurately measure the desirability of the features described by the chromosome. The function should be computationally efficient since it is used many times to evaluate each and every solution. The penalty function is needed when some potential solutions in a population turn out to be infeasible[23], such as exceeding the capacity limit of some collecting centers or processing centers. To elaborate, the original objective function is comprised of various costs-the fixed cost of collecting centers and processing centers, the expansion cost of the given factory, the operation cost of collecting centers, processing centers and the factory and the transportation cost in reverse flows. A penalty value is considerably larger than any possible objective value corresponding to the current population of individuals. The penalty function(*Fitness*) in the proposed algorithm is mathematically expressed as:

$$Fitness = \begin{cases} C_{max} - f(X), & if \quad f(X) < C_{max} ; \\ 0, & if \quad f(X) \geq C_{max} \end{cases} \tag{13}$$

4.3 Selection Operator

The selection operator is intended to improve the average quality of the population by giving the high-quality chromosomes, i.e., a better chance to get copied into the nest generation. The selection can be thought as the exploitation for the GA to guide the evolutionary process when we regard the genetic operation as the exploration for the search in solution space. We employ roulette wheel selection strategy as a selection mechanism. In roulette wheel selection mechanism, the individuals on each generation are selected for survival into the next generation according to a probability value proportional to the ratio of individual fitness over total population fitness; this means that average quality of the population by giving the high-quality chromosomes a better chance to get copied into the next generation. Also the elitist method is employed to preserve the best chromosome for the next generation.

4.4 Crossover Operator

Crossover is the main genetic operator. It operates on two parents (chromosomes) at a time and generates offspring by combining both chromosomes' features. The crossover is done to explore new solution space and crossover operator corresponds to exchanging parts of strings between selected parents. The crossover probability indicates how often a crossover will be performed. There are several types of crossovers, including single-point crossover, multi-point crossover, and uniform crossover. In this paper, we use the one-point crossover. For each individual in the population, generate a random number rand()$\in$[0,1). If $p_c \geq$rand(), where p_c holds for the given probability of crossover, choose another individual randomly from the population and let these individuals be parent individuals. After determining the crossover point by a random number, generate offspring individuals by changing sub-individuals after the crossover point of one parent individual for that of the other. Carry out the procedure above from for all individuals in the population.

4.5 Mutation Operator

Mutation is a background operator which produces spontaneous random changes in various chromosomes. Similar to crossover, mutation is done to prevent the premature convergence and explores new solution space. However, unlike crossover, mutation is usually done by modifying gene within a chromosome. Several mutation operators have been proposed for permutation representation, such as inversion, insertion, displacement, and reciprocal exchange mutation. The type of mutation varies depending on the encoding as well as the crossover. We also investigate the effects of two different mutation operators on the performance of GA. Inversion mutation is used for this paper. Inversion mutation selects two positions within a chromosome at random and then inverts the substring between these two positions.

4.6 Numerical Test

To demonstrate how the model works and to verify its usefulness, the model is applied to a numerical test. In the test, there are six hospitals and one final factory. The potential collecting centers and processing centers are I_1, I_2, I_3, I_4, I_5 and J_1, J_2, J_3. There are two kinds of medical waste(for example sharp waste and tissues waste) generated from each hospitals, 70,95,60,80,55 for waste I and 40,75,45,55,20 for waste II. The discarding ratios of medical waste I and II in collecting centers are respectively 0.8 and 0.7, while in the processing centers, the discarding ratios for waste I and IIare the same, 0.8, The transportation and operation cost are both related with the amount and types of medical waste. The data are showed in Table 1-4. As to the genetic algorithm parameters, these parameters are: population size=200; maximum number of generations=500; crossover rate = 0.9; mutation rate = 0.05.

Table 1. Related Parameters of the factory, collecting centers and processing centers (Yuan, Yuan/Ton, Ton)

Costs		Factory	Collecting centers					Processing centers		
			1	2	3	4	5	1	2	3
Fixed cost		50000	8500	10000	15000	12000	10000	40000	45000	50000
Opera-tion cost	Waste I	8	7	5	5	6	4	9	7	5
	Waste II	6	3	3	1.5	2.5	3	7	5	4
Capac-ity	Waste I	-	100	150	150	130	120	200	250	300
	Waste II	-	80	120	150	150	100	120	170	220
Maximum capacity		-	160	260	280	260	200	300	400	500

Table 2. The unit transportation cost from hospitals to collecting centers(Yuan)

Hospitals / Collecting centers		1	2	3	4	5	6	1
Waste I	1	5	3	6	7	4	3	
	2	10	5	4	1	3	9	
	3	8	4	5	10	6	7	
	4	7	5	3	12	9	6	
	5	6.5	10	9	6	5	10	
Waste II	1	7	8	10	12	5.5	8	
	2	9	8.5	8.5	11	8	12	
	3	10	3	6	8	7	8	
	4	10	6	5	9	10	9	
	5	13	6.5	7	10	8	10	

Table 3. The unit transportation cost from collecting centers to processing centers(Yuan)

Collecting centers / Processing center		1	2	3	4	5
Waste I	1	4	6.5	6.5	7.5	5
	2	5	5	4	3	4
	3	2	7	5.5	8	4
Waste II	1	6	7	8	10	5
	2	7	8	6.5	8	7
	3	5	5	5	8	6

Table 4. The unit transportation cost from processing centers to the factory(Yuan)

Processing centers / Waste	1	2	3
Waste I	6	3	5
Waste II	1	5	7

Fig. 4 shows the best fitness values at each generation. The fitness value at the 300th generation was gradually reduced to a comparatively steady level around 136500. The purpose of using the genetic algorithm is not to get the accurately best result, but to figure out an acceptable solution with high efficiency. The satisfactory solution we get is 134029. Because of the limitation of the space, some results are omitted.

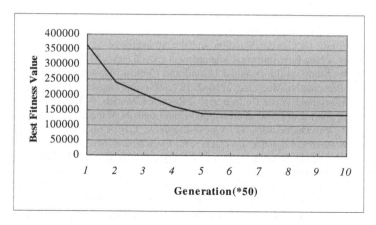

Fig. 4. Fitness value curve of Genetic Algorithm

5   Conclusions and Future Works

In this paper, we have discussed the medical waste reverse logistics network design problem from the medical materials producers' perspective. We have established a mixed integer programming model to minimize the total costs while operating the reverse logistics network and used an improved genetic algorithm to get an acceptable solution with high efficiency. Compared to early literature on reverse logistics, this paper has attempted to apply the basic theories of reverse logistics to improve the rationality and efficiency of the medical waste returning process and also did some work to optimize the whole returning network. The proposed model is successful in designing reverse logistics network for medical waste while considering multi-type waste flows with four nodes(initial hospitals, colleting centers, processing centers and final factories). Experimental result shows that proposed approach has better synthetic performance in both the computation speed and optimality in medical waste reverse logistics model. In the future research, it is possible to investigate the performance of the medical waste reverse logistics network including real-data. Maybe, we can also discuss other heuristic algorithms combined with GA to solve the mixed integer linear programming model in the further study.

Acknowledgments.   The author would like to gratefully acknowledge the assistance of professors from the Dalian Maritime University for their useful suggestions and helps.

References

1. Shinee, E., Gombojav, E., Nishimura, A., Hamajima, N., Ito, K.: Healthcare Waste Management in the Capital city of Mongolia. Waste management 28, 435–444 (2008)
2. Baveja, G., Muralidhar, S., Aggarwal, P.: Medical Waste Management – An Overview. Hospital Today, 485–486 (2000)

3. Liu, C.-b.: Current Situation of Disposing Medical Waste and Developing Method in China. China Environmental Management, 37–38 (2003) (in Chinese)
4. Geng, R.: Study on Current Situation and the Strategies of Medical Waste Disposal in Jiaozuo City. China Environmental Management special issue, 57–58 (2006) (in Chinese)
5. Wang, Y.-h.: Study on the Potential Hazard and Control Measures of Medical Waste in Nanchang. Preventative Medicine, 2216–2218 (2008) (in Chinese)
6. Jahre, M.: Household Waste Collection as a Reverse Channel - A Theoretical Perspective. International Journal of Physical Distribution and Logistics Management, 39–55 (1995)
7. Beullens, P., Van Oudheusden, D., Van Wassenhove, L.N.: Collection and Vehicle Routing Issues in Reverse Logistics. In: Dekker, R., Fleischmann, M., Inderfurth, K., Van Wassenhove, L.N. (eds.) Reverse logistics: Quantitative Models for Closed-Loop Supply Chains. Springer, Berlin (2003)
8. Carter, C., Ellram, L.: Reverse Logistics:A Review of the Literature and Framework for Future Investigation. Journal of Business Logistics, 85–102 (1998)
9. Louwers, D., Bert, K.J., Edo, P., Frans, S., Simme, D., Flapper., P.: A Facility Location Allocation Model for Reusing Carpet Materials. Computers & Industrial Engineering, 855–869 (1999)
10. Bloemhof Ruwaard, J., Fleischmann, M., Nunen., J.: Reviewing Distribution Issues in Reverse Logistics. In: Speranza, M., Stohly, P. (eds.) New Trends in Distribution Logistics. Springer, NewYork (1999)
11. De Koster, R.B.M., De Brito, M.P., Van de Vendel M.A.: Return Handling: An Exploratory Study with Nine Retailer Warehouses. International Journal of Retail and Distribution Management, 407-421 (2002)
12. Listes, O.: A Decomposition Approach to a Stochastic Model for Supply and Return Network Design. Econometric Institute Reports EI (2002)
13. Beamon, B.A., Fernandes, C.: Supply-Chain Network Configuration for Product Recovery. Production Planning and Control, 270–281 (2004)
14. Santoso, T., Ahmed, S., Goetschalckx, M., Shapiro, A.: A Stochastic Programming Approach for Supply Chain Network Design under Uncertainty. European Journal of Operational Research, 96–115 (2005)
15. Listes, O., Dekker, R.: Stochastic Approaches for Product Recovery Network Ddesign: A Case Study. Econometric Institute Report EI (2001)
16. Hu, T.-L., Sheu, J.-B., Huang, K.-H.: A Reverse Logistics Cost Minimization Model for the Treatment of Hazardous Wastes. Transportation Research Part E, 457–473 (2002)
17. Salema, M.I., Barbosa, A.P., Novais, A.Q.: A Strategic and Tactical Model for Closed-Loop Supply Chains. In: EURO Winter Institute on Location and Logistics, Estoril, Portugal, pp. 361–386 (2007)
18. Zhang, L.Y., Zhang, H.F., Wang, Z.P.: An Improved Model of Mixed Integer Programming for Reverse Logistics Network Planning. Industrial Engineering Journal, 90–94 (2006)(in chinese)
19. Zhao, X.Y., Peng., P.: An Optimization Model with Fuzzy Linear Programming for E-waste Recycling Network Planning,[J]. Industrial Engineering Journal, 62–66 (2007) (in Chinese)
20. Pati, R., Vrat, P., Kumar., P.: A Goal Programming Model for Paper Recycling System, Omega (2006)
21. Goldberg, D.E.: Genetic Algorithms in Search, Optimization and Machine Learning. Addison-Wesley, Reading (1989)
22. Gen, M., Cheng, R.: Genetic Algorithms and Engineering Optimizations. Wiley, New York (2000)
23. Ko, H.J., Evans, G.W.: A Genetic Algorithm-Based Heuristic for the Dynamic Integrated Forward/Reverse Logistics Network for 3PLs. Computers & Operations Research, 346–366 (2007)

SGEGC: A Selfish Gene Theory Based Optimization Method by Exchanging Genetic Components

Cheng Yang, Yuanxiang Li, and Zhiyi Lin

State Key Lab of Software Engineering, Wuhan University,
Wuhan 430072, P.R. China

Abstract. In this paper, a new algorithm named SGEGC was proposed. Inspired by selfish gene theory, SGEGC uses a vector of survival rate to model the condition distribution, which serves as a virtual population that is used to generate new individuals. While the present Estimation of Distribution Algorithms (EDAs) require much time to learn the complex relationships among variables, SGEGC employs an approach that exchanges the relevant genetic components. Experimental results show that the proposed approach is more efficient in convergent reliability and convergent velocity in comparison with BMDA, COMIT and MIMIC in the test functions.

Keywords: Estimation of Distribution Algorithms, Selfish Gene Theory, Nonlinearity Check.

1 Introduction

A number of new evolutionary algorithms that construct probabilistic models of potential solutions to explore the search space have been proposed. These algorithms, named Estimation of Distribution Algorithms(EDAs)[11,17], have shown well performance mainly because of the ability that explicitly detects the linkage relationship among variables as well as the free from adjusting various parameters, such as crossover and mutation probability, population size and selection method. While genetic algorithms(GAs) inspired by the Darwin's natural select theory which acts on populations or organisms , these novel approaches put evolution in a microscopic perspective, where the fundamental unit of evolution is gene, rather than individual.

The core of EDAs is the probabilistic model. There are diverse techniques to estimate and sample the probability distribution used in a wide range of EDAs which are proved to be more effective in different optimization problems than GAs. While CGA[9] and UDMA [10] work under the assumption that variables are independent, MIMIC[5] uses a chain model of probability distribution to estimate the pairwise conditional probabilities to present the interaction between two variables and COMIT [3,4] establishes a tree structure to do the same job. BOA [13] and FDA [12]uses Bayesian Network to model the distribution of solution space. And there are more EDAs can be found [1,2,14,16,18,19].

Z. Cai et al. (Eds.): ISICA 2009, LNCS 5821, pp. 53–62, 2009.

Effective though they are, the heritability of gene is almost overlooked. Consequently, as the number of variables increases and linkage of the variables become more complex, EDAs require much time in the learning process of interaction among variables. The performance of EDAs can be improved. First, genetic algorithms based binary encoding system map only one bit to a gene; a gene, however, is genetically defined as the basic unit of heredity in living organism. Genetic component is proposed as a terminology which represent a cluster of sequential or jumping 'genes', when tight linkage among a set of variables are taken into account. Once correct gene components are identified, genetic optimization can use this extra information to search building block candidates and mix them to find an optimal solution. On the other hand, what the conventional EDAs neglect is the information interaction which plays a predominant role in GAs as crossover or recombination among different individuals. EDAs use a more macroscopic linkage information , without implicit heritability of genes, to determine conditional probability model, then the sampling procedure is conduct to generate individuals for next selection and estimation.

The purpose of the paper is to further study the EDAs based on the perspective of Selfish Gene Theory and promoted genetic components. we propose a new approach to detect the nonlinearity of gene as well as a novel algorithm named SGEGC to solve optimization problems. It works on three individuals and dynamically exchanges the information of the best two individuals according to the similar gene components which have been explored before and then conducts sampling procedure to generate individuals by the probability or conditional probability. This progress continued until terminal criteria are met.

The present paper is organized as follows: Next section presents the general ideas by introducing selfish gene theory, section 3 details the SGEGC approach. In Section 4, experimental results and analysis of MIMIC , COMIT, BMDA and SGEGC are described. Section 5 summarizes the paper.

2   Inspiration from Selfish Gene Theory

In 1989, R. Dawkins presented a point of view on the evolution [15]. The term selfish gene serves as a way of expressing the gene-centered view of evolution, which holds that evolution is best viewed as acting on genes and that selection at the level of organisms , populations or even species almost never overrides selection based on genes. This theory implicates that adaptations are the phenotypic effects of genes to maximize their representation in the future generations by increasing the frequency of those alleles whose phenotypic effects successfully promote their own propagation. There are several method base on selfish gene theory[8,7,6].

From the methodological review of Selfish Gene Theory, this paper focus on two distinctive aspects. First, according to Selfish Gene Theory, organisms or populations are not important because the struggling for existence occurs among competing genes on which the selection acts through differential survival ability. There is no concept of population, yet a vector $p = (p_1, p_2, \cdots, p_n)$ serves as virtual population, where n identifies its number of gens and p_i indicates the survival rate of the ith gene, by which individual would be generated. Therefore, during the evolution process, the solutions evolve on the basis of the survival rate p_i rather than explicit individuals, which means less space complexity. If taken genetic component into consideration, the survival vector P would be extend to a set $M = (P_1, P_2, \cdots, P_m)$, where m denotes the number of genetic component and $P_i = (p_{i,1}, p_{i,2}, p_{i,j-1}, \cdots, p_{i,n-1})$ indicates the conditional probability chain of nonlinear loci, $p_{i,j}$ is the survival rate of locus j, under the condition that the survival is $p_{i,j-1}$.

Another point of view is that there is not much of struggle because the genes usually win without a fight, which implicates the traditional selection in genetic algorithms is not important. According to Selfish Gene Theory, the only motive power is survival competition between two differential genetic carrier. Two individuals selected from the pool of virtual population represented by the frequency parameters. Then these parameters are update by the statistics that indicate which genes will survival in the race and which pairs or groups are together incline to birth a better solution. The contention is that the genes that get passed on are the ones whose consequences serve their own implicit interests, not necessarily those of the organism. As long as genetic components are correctly detected this simple competition can be expanded by interaction among good individuals, this extending brings importance to detecting genetic components.

3   SGEGC: A Selfish Gene Theory Based Optimization Method by Exchanging Genetic Components

3.1   The General Description of SGEGC

As mentioned above, selfish gene theory emphasizes the struggle among genes rather that individual. It is clear that competition plays a key role in evolution of algorithm; however, cooperation is of importance too. In order to improve the performance of the optimization, a new SGEGC algorithm which is based on the cooperation among selfish genes is proposed. The proposed method is focused on utilizing the true inheritable structure which stands for the basic nonlinear linkage group.

1. Initialization
2. Generate three individuals
3. Conduct Nonlinearity Check if necessary
4. Rank the three individuals
5. Choose the best two $gBEST$ and $gMOD$,
6. If there are more than one group then execute the following procedure
   (a) If the fitness of $gBEST$ and $gMOD$ are quite similar then reverse all the bit of $gMOD$
   (b) Cross over the selected group to generate 2 other individuals $D1$, $D2$
   (c) $D = MAX(D1, D1)$

(d) If ($D > gBEST$) then $gBEST = D$

(e) Else go to (a) , repeat until inner termination conditions are met

7. For each loci recalculate the probability of survival

8. Reward $gBEST$ and Punishment the worst individual $gWORST$ individuals.

9. If the termination conditions have not been satisfied than go to 2.

3.2   Nonlinearity Check in SGEGC

The statistic independent detecting and other similar methods cannot be applied to detect the genetic components because they are too broad to find such microstructures. For example, if the selected predominated individuals are all the same, such as 1s, statistic independent approach only imply that all those loci are correlative. In order to dig up the gene components, methodology should be performed in terms of phenotype or fitness effect. Taking the linear property of encoded string into account, as depicted in Fig.1, we worked on the assumption that a pair loci both belong to a gene component if they cause a nonlinear effect in the overall fitness function corresponding to the perturbation on a string, that is if the change of fitness on two loci i and j cannot be consistent to the mutation of loci on string, i and j are in a genetic component. It is necessary to check nonlinearity for all possible strings under certain context.

Consider a string $s = s_1 s_2 s_3 \cdots s_l$, S denotes the set of all s_i in s, supposed that two variables x_i and x_j satisfy linear property, the function can be write as:

$$f(s) = g(s|s \in S - \{s_i, s_j\}) + g_i(s_i) + g_j(s_j) = e \cdot (g, f_i(s_i), f_j(s_j))^T \quad (1)$$

where $e = (1, 1, 1)$. For every pair of loci (s_i, s_j) can perturbations as $(0, 0)$, $(0, 1)$, $(1, 0)$, $(1, 1)$ which cause fitness changes.

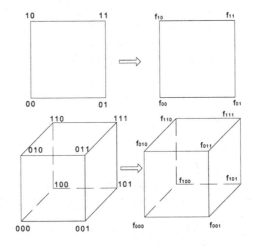

Fig. 1. Linearity

$$\begin{aligned}
f_{00} &= f(s_1 \cdots s_{i=0} \cdots s_{j=0} \cdots s_l) = e \cdot (g, f_i(0), f_j(0))^T = e \cdot \overline{f}_{00} \\
f_{01} &= f(s_1 \cdots s_{i=0} \cdots s_{j=1} \cdots s_l) = e \cdot (g, f_i(0), f_j(1))^T = e \cdot \overline{f}_{01} \\
f_{10} &= f(s_1 \cdots s_{i=1} \cdots s_{j=0} \cdots s_l) = e \cdot (g, f_i(1), f_j(0))^T = e \cdot \overline{f}_{10} \\
f_{11} &= f(s_1 \cdots s_{i=1} \cdots s_{j=1} \cdots s_l) = e \cdot (g, f_i(1), f_j(1))^T = e \cdot \overline{f}_{11}
\end{aligned} \tag{2}$$

Two results can be induced to form a rectangular correlated to perturbations of loci pairs. First, the midpoints of the line segments $\overline{f}_{00}\overline{f}_{11}$ and $\overline{f}_{01}\overline{f}_{10}$ should be same , that is point $\frac{\overline{f}_{00}+\overline{f}_{11}}{2}$ and $\frac{\overline{f}_{01}+\overline{f}_{10}}{2}$ are the same point. The following equation which is promoted as $\overline{f}_{ij}$ is unknown.

$$\frac{f_{11} + f_{00}}{2} = \frac{f_{01} + f_{10}}{2} \tag{3}$$

let $P(x)$ denotes the first condition.

The second condition is that the lengths of diagonal lines should be equal, that is:

$$\left\| \overline{f}_{11}, \overline{f}_{00} \right\|_n = \left\| \overline{f}_{10}, \overline{f}_{10} \right\|_n \tag{4}$$

$\|x, y\|_n$ Denotes the norm x and y. If $n > 0$,

$$\begin{aligned}
\left\| \overline{f}_{11}, \overline{f}_{00} \right\| &= \sqrt[n]{(f_i(1) - f_i(0))^n + (f_j(1) - f_j(0))^n} \\
&= \sqrt[n]{(f_{10} - f_{00})^n + (f_{01} - f_{00})^n}
\end{aligned} \tag{5}$$

$$\begin{aligned}
\left\| \overline{f}_{10}, \overline{f}_{01} \right\| &= \sqrt[n]{(f_i(1) - f_i(0))^n + (f_j(0) - f_j(1))^n} \\
&= \sqrt[n]{(f_{11} - f_{01})^n + (f_{10} - f_{11})^n}
\end{aligned} \tag{6}$$

If $n = 0$, we have

$$|f_{10} - f_{00}| + |f_{01} - f_{00}| = |f_{11} - f_{01}| + |f_{10} - f_{11}| \tag{7}$$

Assume that $Q^n(x)$ denotes the condition for different n. Note that both two condition are necessary conditions to induce linearity, nonlinearity can be easily obtain by negate $P(x)$ and $Q^n(x)$:

$$\neg(P(x) \wedge Q^0(x) \wedge Q^1(x) \cdots Q^n(x)) \tag{8}$$

The above logic expression shows nonlinearity, "$\neg$" denotes logic "not" and "$\wedge$" denotes logic "or". We can change n to form a stronger condition. Since there may exist linearity inside a gene block in some context, it is not enough to check nonlinearity in just one string. Therefore, all the coupled genes on a string must be checked in a population properly sized. We proposed strategy that dynamically check the nonlinearity as the generation pass down. The following procedure for each pair of loci in each string is conducted to find nonlinearity.

- If $\neg P(x)$, the s_i and s_j are surely members of a possible gene component
- If P(x), may not construct a gene component or a building block is exist but linearity exists in the current context of a particular string. Check $Q^0(x) \cdots Q^n(x)$, if one of condition is satisfied assign $L[i] = j$, else turn to another generation.

To store tightly linked loci to form a larger gene component, a vector L is used to organize the group of loci. The notation $L[i]$ denotes the parents of variable i. Under the assumption that the property of nonlinearity is transmittable, gene components are easy to be constructed.

3.3   Evolution Mechanism: Reward and Punishment

In each step the the evolution, the best and worst, individuals are selected to compete. this competition result in the higher opportunity to reproduce of winner and the extinction of loser. this is different most GAs and EDAs , which almost ignores the information implicated by individuals with lower fitness. Therefore, we employ a reward and punishment scheme to generate the survival rate.

Suppose the winder is $gBEST$ and the looser is $gWORST$, and the genetic competitions are already calculated. the survival rate $M = (P_1, P_2, \cdots, P_m)$ is generate as follows. For each genetic component G_i, supposed that $\Pi = (\pi_1, \pi_2, \cdots, \pi_l)$ denotes the permutation of loci classified as Gi. for each genetic component on $gBEST$. $p_{\pi_1} = p_{\pi_1} + \varepsilon$ and $p_{\pi_i, \pi_{i-1}} = p_{\pi_i, \pi_{i-1}} + \varepsilon$, whereas for $gWORST$, the addition operation is replaced by subtraction.

4   Experimental Results and Analysis

Four well-known benchmark problems, include Four Peaks problem, Satisfactory problem, Weight One-Max problem, and deceptive problem [5,14,13], are used to evaluate the performance of SGEGC, comparing the results with that of MIMIC, BMDA, and COMIT. the problems sizes of each benchmark problems vary from 10 to 200 with step 10. For MIMIC , COMIT , and BMDA , 200 samples per generation is employed with a fixed truncation selection ratio(5%). For SGEGC, the incremental learning factor α=0.1 and the value of ε in Reward and Punishment Scheme sets to default value. All parameters are held constant through all runs. For each problem and problem size, 20 successful independent runs are performed. Each run is terminated either when the global optimum is found or when the best fitness is unchanged for 2000 evaluations.

The Fig.2 shows the convergent reliability of MIMIC, BMDA , COMIT and SGEGC under different numbers of problem size through computing the deviation of fitness between the optimal solutions and converged result. From Fig.2, we can see that SGEGC perform better than MIMIC, BMDA and COMIT are not. Actually, SGEGC successfully find the all the optimal solution of three problems except for For Peaks problem. This may due the fact that the all the variables of Four Peaks Problem are completely nonlinear, which means inefficacy of exchanging genetic components. However, MIMIC, BMDA, and COMIT are not satisfied for all tested four benchmark problems. For example, the difference between the converged value of the Deceptive problem and the global optimal value of Deceptive problem of other three methods is linearly increased withe the number of variable. It is clearly depicted from the Fig.2 that the stability of SGEGC because the averagely higher quality of its solutions than that of the others.

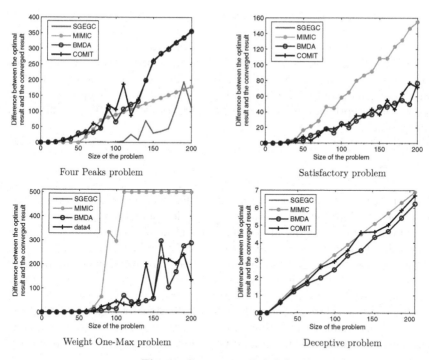

Fig. 2. Convergent Reliability

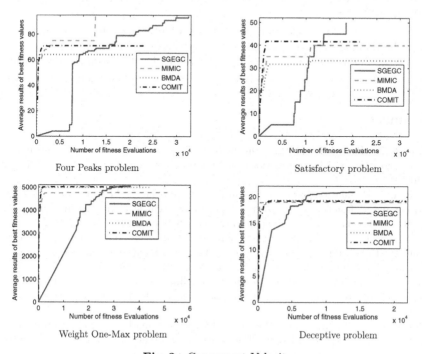

Fig. 3. Convergent Velocity

Moreover, we verify the convergence process of MIMIC, BMDA , COMIT and SGEGC; and the results are shown in Fig.3. Although an extra evaluations are need to perform the nonlinearity detecting procure, the least times of evaluation are $2n \times (n-1)$, SGEGC successfully balance the convergence and population diversity. From the Fig.3 , we can see that the convergence speed of SGEGC is slower than BMDA and COMIT in early stage, but SGEGC can avoid getting trapped in local optima;and the convergence process of SGEGC is both steady and persistent.

5   Conclusion

In this paper, we have proposed an improved Estimation of Distribution Algorithm named SGEGC which is based on genetic component to solve discrete optimization problem. In the algorithm, a novel nonlinear detecting approach is proposed, which check the nonlinearity of the a problem. At the same time, we use exchange detected genetic component as a relative block to construct three individuals, from which the two ones that have the highest or lower fitness are chosen. Then based on the selfish gene theory, we assume that the evolve process is relied on relative gene rather than individual or organism. While the traditional EDAs require much time in the statistic learning progress owning to the complexity of relationships among variables, we focus only on the survival rate of each gene, only a vector M is needed to represent the population. Experimental results illustrate that SGEGC significantly superior than the BMDA , COMIT and MIMIC.

However, it is also noted that the number of fitness evaluates is increased because the nonlinearity checking progress is actually based on the evaluation of the function. the further study will concentrate on the extension of nonlinearity checking progress that can effectively represent the relationship among variables.

References

1. Ahn, C.W., Ramakrishna, R.S.: On the scalability of real-coded bayesian optimization algorithm. IEEE Transactions on Evolutionary Computation 12(3), 307–322 (2008)
2. Baluja, S.: Population-based incremental learning: A method for integrating genetic search based function optimization and competitive learning. Technical Report CMU-CS-94-163, Carnegie Mellon University Pittsburgh, PA, USA (1994)
3. Baluja, S., Davies, S.: Using optimal dependency-trees for combinational optimization. In: ICML 1997: Proceedings of the Fourteenth International Conference on Machine Learning, San Francisco, CA, USA, pp. 30–38 (1997)
4. Baluja, S., Davies, S.: Fast probabilistic modeling for combinatorial optimization. In: Proc. of 15th National Conf. on Artificial Intelligence(AAAI), pp. 469–476 (1998)
5. Bonet, J., Isbell, C.L., Viola, P.: Mimic: Finding optima by estimating probability densities. In: Advances in Neural Information Processing Systems, vol. 9, pp. 424–430. MIT Press, Cambridge (1997)

6. Corno, F., Reorda, M.S., Squillero, G.: A new evolutionary algorithm inspired by the selfish gene theory. In: ICEC 1998: IEEE International Conference on Evolutionary Computation, pp. 575–580 (1998)
7. Corno, F., Reorda, M., Squillero, G.: The selfish gene algorithm: a new evolutionary optimization strategy. In: SAC 1998: 13th Annual ACM Symposium on Applied Computing, pp. 349–355 (1998)
8. Corno, F., Reorda, M., Squillero, G.: Exploiting the selfish gene algorithm for evolving cellular automata. In: Proceedings of the IEEE-INNS-ENNS International Joint Conference on Neural Networks, 2000. IJCNN 2000, vol. 6, pp. 577–581 (2000)
9. Harik, G.R., Lobo, F.G., Goldberg, D.E.: The compact genetic algorithm. IEEE Transactions on Evolutionary Computation 3(4), 287–297 (1999)
10. Muhlenbein, H., Paass, G.: From recombination of genes to the estimation of distributions i. binary parameters. In: PPSN IV: Proceedings of the 4th International Conference on Parallel Problem Solving from Nature, London, UK, pp. 178–187 (1996)
11. Larranaga, P., Lozano, J.A.: Estimation of Distribution Algorithms: A New Tool for Evolutionary Computation. Kluwer Academic Publishers, Boston (2002)
12. Muhlenbein, H., Mahnig, T.: The factorized distribution algorithm for additively decomposedfunctions. In: Proceedings of the 1999 Congress on Evolutionary Computation,1999.CEC 1999, vol. 1 (1999)
13. Pelikan, M., Goldberg, D.E., Cant-Paz, E.: Boa: The bayesian optimization algorithm. In: Proceedings of the Genetic and Evolutionary Computation Conference(GECCO-1999), pp. 525–532. Morgan Kaufmann, San Francisco (1999)
14. Pelikan, M., Muhlenbein, H.: The bivariate marginal distribution algorithm. In: Advances in Soft Computing:Engineering Design and Manufacturing, pp. 521–535. Springer, London (1999)
15. Dawkins, R.: The Selfish Gene - new edition. Oxford University Press, Oxford (1989)
16. Harik, G.R., Lobo, F.G., Sastry, K.: Linkage learning via probabilistic modeling in the extended compact genetic algorithm(ecga). Scalable Optimization via Probabilistic Modeling, 39–61 (2006)
17. Zhou, S.D., Sun, Z.Q.: A survey on estimation of distribution algorithms. Acta Automatica Sinica 33(2), 113–124 (2007)
18. Yang, S.Y., Ho, S.L., Ni, G.Z., Machado, J.M., Wong, K.F.: A new implementation of population based incremental learning method for optimizations in electromagnetics. IEEE Transactions on Magnetics 43(4), 1601–1604 (2007)
19. Yang, S.X., Yao, X.: Population-based incremental learning with associative memory for dynamic environments. IEEE Transactions on Evolutionary Computation 12(5), 542–561 (2008)

Appendix

The first benchmark problem is Four Peaks:

Given an N-dimensional input vector X ,the four peaks evaluation function is defined as:

$$f\left(X, T\right) = \max\left[tail\left(0, X\right), head\left(1, X\right)\right] + R\left(X, T\right)$$

where

$$tail\left(b, X\right) = number\ of\ trailing\ b's\ in\ X$$

$$head\,(b, \boldsymbol{X}) = number\ of\ trailing\ b's\ in\ \boldsymbol{X}$$

$$R\,(\boldsymbol{X}, T) = \begin{cases} N & if\ tail\,(0, \boldsymbol{X}) > T\ and\ head\,(1, \boldsymbol{X}) > T \\ 0 \end{cases}$$

In all trails, T was set to be 10% of N, the size of the problem.

The second benchmark problem is Satisfaction Problem:

$$\max\left(\sum_{i}^{n} f(x_{5i-1}, x_{5i-2}, x_{5i-3}, x_{5i-4}, x_{5i})\right) \qquad x \in \{0, 1\}$$

where $f(x_{5i-1}, x_{5i-2}, x_{5i-3}, x_{5i-4}, x_{5i})$ equals to 5 if and only if all variables equal to 1.Otherwise it equals to 0.

The third benchmark problem is Weighed One-Max:

$$\max\left(\sum_{i=1}^{n} i \cdot x_i\right) \qquad x_i \in \{0, 1\}$$

The fourth benchmark problem is 3-deceptive problem:

$$\max \sum_{i=0}^{\frac{n}{3}} f(x_{3i-1}, x_{3i-2}, x_{3i-3})$$

where

$$u = x_{3i-1} + x_{3i-2} + x_{3i-3}$$

and

$$f_{3-deceptive}(u) = \begin{cases} 0.9 & if\ u = 0 \\ 0.8 & if\ u = 1 \\ 0 & if\ u = 2 \\ 1 & otherwise \end{cases}$$

Where u is the number of bit '1' in the input string.

A Novel RM-Based Algorithm for Reversible Circuits[*]

Dong Wang[1,2], Hanwu Chen[1], Bo An[1], and Zhongming Yang[1]

[1] School of Computer Science and Engineering, Southeast University, 210096, China
[2] Computer Center, Henan University, 415002, China
122062815@qq.com

Abstract. This paper presents a heuristic fast-matching algorithm for quantum reversible logic circuits synthesis. The algorithm uses the quantum gate formula as the heuristic rules to perform forward-matching. This can avoid blind matching and decrease the matching complexity. Simple, smaller overhead and better to simplify circuits, the algorithm can perform well in the multi-quantum reversible logic circuits synthesis.

Keywords: quantum reversible circuits; Reed-Muller expansion; CNOT gate; Toffoli gate.

1 Introduction

According to physics laws, irreversible operation in computing plays the important role in energy consumption on chips, thus converting an irreversible operation to a reversible one is the key of reducing the energy loss. Bennett has proved that the energy consumption can be cut by using reversible logic gates to construct reversible circuits (the lowest energy consumption can be reached in theory [1]). Each quantum logic gate is corresponding to a unitary operator, which means the quantum logic gate is reversible, so the circuits constructed by cascading quantum logic gates is reversible too. In theory, quantum circuits can be used to establish more powerful quantum computer with lower energy consumption, higher integration and higher speed. Hence, the research on quantum reversible circuits becomes a rapidly growing field.

Different from the classical irreversible circuit, the 1-1 mapping between inputs and outputs is required in reversible circuits, so there is no any fan-in, fan-out and feedback in it. Therefore, the synthesis of reversible circuits is more complex than the irreversible one. At present, no general efficient algorithm exists, some are usually chosen such as truth table approach by Maslov [2,3], exhaustive search approach by Shende [4] and group theory methodology by Song [5]. Either mature technology or sophisticated mathematical theory and formal deduction is adopted in these algorithms with good solution, however all of them are so complicated.

---

[*] This work was supported by The National Natural Science Foundation of China under Grant 60572071 and 60873101, Jiangsu Natural Science Foundation under Grant BK2007104 and BK2008209.

Z. Cai et al. (Eds.): ISICA 2009, LNCS 5821, pp. 63–69, 2009.

A fast synthesis algorithm is proposed in this paper, which is based on RM expansion, using CNT gate library, adopting forward-matching by using the quantum gate formula as heuristic rules. Since RM expansion has been of the simplest and only one gate is chosen to substitute in the process of pattern matching, without deadlock and backtracking, the algorithm is simple, fast, lower time and space complexity, and easy to implement.

2 Preliminaries

Definition 1. Let B= {0, 1}, a Boolean logic function f with n inputs and n outputs variables is $f(x_1,\cdots,x_n)=(y_1,\cdots y_n)$, $f:B_n \to B_n$. A Boolean logic function is reversible if and only if it is a one-to-one, onto function (bijection).

A logic gate is reversible if and only if it realizes a reversible function. A reversible circuit is a cascade of all the reversible gates.

Definition 2. The expansion of the Boolean function $f(x_1,\cdots,x_n)=(y_1,\cdots,y_n)$ can be represented as follows:

$$f(x_n,\cdots,x_1)=\oplus_{i=0}^{2^n-1}(d_i p_i)$$

This expansion is called Polarity Reed-Mull expansion (RM). That is, any Boolean function can be represented as the XOR of the variables products. $p_i = \prod_{k=1}^{n}(x_k)^{i_k}$, i_k represents the kth binary bit of i, $i=(i_n i_{n-1}\cdots i_k \cdots i_1)_2$. i_k determines whether x_k appears. $d_i \in \{0,1\}$ determines whether p_i appears. When n is fixed, the only variable is d_i in RM expansion. So calculating the value of d_i is the nature of generating RM expansion. 3 variables RM is:

$$f(x_1,x_2,x_3) = d_0 \oplus d_1 x_1 \oplus d_2 x_2 \oplus d_3 x_2 x_1 \oplus d_4 x_3 \oplus d_5 x_3 x_1 \oplus d_6 x_3 x_2 \oplus d_7 x_3 x_2 x_1$$

Algorithm 1. The algorithm of Generating RM expansion $GRM(i,j)$

Input: i is input of the reversible function, j represents the jth RM expansion

Output: the jth RM expansion

```
if i = 0 then return y_{0,j}

else   return GRM(i-1, j) ⊕ (⊕_{h=0}^{i}(e(h|i,i) y_{h,j})) p_i

endif
```

Generating the jth RM expansion should call $GRM(2^n-1,j)$. '|' is 'OR' operation, function $e(i,j)=\begin{cases}0, i\neq j\\1, i=j\end{cases}$ is that: if all 1-bits in the binary bits of h are included in 1-bits of i, then $e(h|i,i)=1$, else $e(h|i,i)=0$. $y_{h,j}$ represents the value of the jth bit of the hth output in the truth table. $\oplus_{h=0}^{i}\left(e(h\,|\,i,i)\,y_{h,j}\right)$ means that select all $y_{h,j}$, $0 \le h \le i$ and $e(h\,|\,i,i)=1$, the value of d_i is their XOR.

Definition 3. Reversible quantum gates: NOT, CNOT, and standard Toffoli are defined as follows:

1*1 NOT: $x_0 = 1 \oplus x$

2*2 CNOT: $x_0 = x$, $y_0 = y \oplus x$

3*3 Standard Toffoli: $x_0 = x$, $y_0 = y$,
$$z_0 = z \oplus xy$$

NOT   CNOT   Standard Toffoli

Fig. 1. Quantum Logic Gates

3 Synthesis Algorithm

A quantum gate represents a unitary operation, and the result of the unitary operation can be expressed by the quantum gate formulas. That is, the cascade of the quantum gates is the unitary operation's continuous actions. Each RM expansion at the output end is the result that the corresponding inputs are continuously transformed by the quantum gates composed quantum reversible circuit [6]. Since the quantum circuit is reversible, the synthesis approach that uses converse transform based on RM to get the circuit is feasible [7]. In the transform process, if one quantum gate formula is successfully matched, then the corresponding gate is identified, so the circuit is derived from the cascade of these gates.

Now, with which RM we begin to match is the key problem to improve the algorithm efficiency because the different orders can conduce to different circuits that can complete same function. We always hope to get the circuit with the lower cost.

Definition 4. The length of the RM expansion is the amount of the symbolic ' $\oplus$ '.

Synthesis of the reversible circuit is in essence dynamic programming problem. From the view of dynamic programming, the optimal sub-process should be kept in the process of exploring optimal solution. For this goal, every time we should begin with the shortest RM to match quantum gate, one gate one time, all of the RM length doesn't become longer besides that at least one RM becomes shorter. This substitution order is the fastest order to make the RM identical. Furthermore, simplifying circuit is easier because the controlled-ends of the quantum gates will be arranged together as much as possible with the above substituting order.

Algorithm 2. synthesis of the reversible circuits
Input: the reversible specification;
Output: the cascade of the quantum gates completing the reversible function;
The array *gate*: store the quantum gates;
The array *identity*: store the identical signal of the ith RM, identity(i)=1, the ith RM is identical, otherwise identity(i)=0, the ith RM is not identical, every item of identity is initialized 0;

```
call GRM(2ⁿ-1,j) to generate n RM;

sort the RM in terms of their length's ascending order;

i=the number of the shortest RM;

nofidentityRM = 0;   //* the variable nofidentityRM *//
          //*records the amount of the identical RM*//

while (NofIdentityRM != n)   //* NofIdentityRM = n *//
          //* is on behalf that all RM is identical *//

{

    if (j gate is found in the iᵗʰ RM with forward-
          matching and the length of the RM is shorter
          after substituting the j gate )

    {

        gate(x)=j;

        x=x+1;

        for (k=1; k<=n; k++)

            {

                if (identity(k)!=1)

                    {

                        substitute variable related j of the
                        kᵗʰ RM for j gate formula and simplify the
                        kᵗʰ RM;

                        if (the kᵗʰ RM becomes identical )

                            {

                                identity(k)=1;

                                NofIdentityRM= NofIdentityRM+1;

                            }

                    }

            }

        sort the rest non-identical RM in terms of their
              length's ascending order;

        i=the number of the shortest RM;

    }

    else i=(i+1) mod n ;

}

return gate;
```

Example1: Consider a reversible specification

$f(x, y, z) = (7,1,4,3,0,6,2,5)$ defined as table 1.

Step 1: According to the table 1, call $GRM(2^3 - 1, j)$ to generate 3 RM, sort the RM in terms of their length's ascending order;

$$x_0 = 1 \oplus x \oplus z \tag{1}$$

$$y_0 = y \oplus 1 \oplus x \oplus z \tag{2}$$

$$z_0 = y \oplus xy \oplus yz \oplus 1 \oplus x \tag{3}$$

Table 1. Truth-table of reversible function

x	y	z	x_0	y_0	z_0
0	0	0	1	1	1
0	0	1	0	0	1
0	1	0	1	0	0
0	1	1	0	1	1
1	0	0	0	0	0
1	0	1	1	1	0
1	1	0	0	1	0
1	1	1	1	0	1

Step 2: matching substitution process.

① The matching substation begin with equation (1) because of its shortest length. $x' = x \oplus z$ is found by forward-matching, the first CNOT gate is identified, then x is substituted for $x \oplus z$ in the equations (1) (2) (3) and these equations are simplified.

$$x_0 = 1 \oplus (x \oplus z) \oplus z = 1 \oplus x \oplus z \oplus z = 1 \oplus x \tag{1.1}$$

$$y_0 = y \oplus 1 \oplus (x \oplus z) \oplus z = y \oplus 1 \oplus x \oplus z \oplus z = y \oplus 1 \oplus x \tag{2.1}$$

$$z_0 = y \oplus (x \oplus z)y \oplus yz \oplus 1 \oplus (x \oplus z) = y \oplus xy \oplus yz \oplus yz \oplus 1 \oplus x \oplus z$$
$$= y \oplus xy \oplus 1 \oplus x \oplus z \tag{3.1}$$

② Now, equation(1.1) is shortest, therefore it is searched. $x' = 1 \oplus x$ is found by forward-matching, the second NOT gate is identified. x is substituted for $1 \oplus x$ in the equations (1.1) (2.1) (3.1) and these equations are simplified.

$$x_0 = 1 \oplus 1 \oplus x = x \tag{1.2}$$

$$y_0 = y \oplus 1 \oplus 1 \oplus x = y \oplus x \tag{2.2}$$

$$z_0 = y \oplus (1 \oplus x)y \oplus 1 \oplus 1 \oplus x \oplus z = y \oplus y \oplus xy \oplus 1 \oplus 1 \oplus x \oplus z$$
$$= xy \oplus x \oplus z \tag{3.2}$$

③ This time, equation (1.2) have became identical, so equation (2.2) is the shortest. The same approach as above is used to find substitution $y' = y \oplus x$, the third CNOT gate is identified, after the substitution and simplification□the equations is:

$$y_0 = y \oplus x \oplus x = y \tag{2.3}$$

$$z_0 = x(y \oplus x) \oplus x \oplus z = xy \oplus x \oplus x \oplus z = xy \oplus z = z \oplus xy \tag{3.3}$$

④ Adopting the above approach, formula $z' = z \oplus xy$ is found, the fourth CNOT gate is identified and equation(3.3) becomes as follows:

$$z_0 = z \oplus xy \oplus xy = z \tag{3.4}$$

So far, all RM is identical, the forward-matching substitution process have completed. The circuit is formed by cascading all the quantum gates identified above. It is shown in Fig 2.

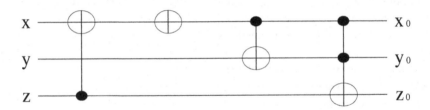

Fig. 2. quantum reversible circuit

4 Performance Analysis

At present, all the synthesis methods based on the Reed-Muller expansion use the exhaustive search methods, the deadlock and the backtracking cannot be avoided, so the time and space complexity are higher and the algorithm is inefficient. Our algorithm avoid blind matching, decrease the matching complexity and the amount of the substitution, so the deadlock and the backtracking are avoided and the efficiency is higher. Since the algorithm of generating RM has been very mature, the RM generated by this algorithm has been the simplest form, substitution always begins with the shortest RM, from the view of the dynamic programming, this is the easiest method to get the optimal circuit. During the process of the matching substitution, one gate one time, every step can make the whole length of the RM shorter and no redundant gates are identify, so the generated circuit always is optimal or near-optimal. Furthermore, during the synthesis process, the algorithm was designed subtly to make the controlled-ends of the gates together as much as possible, which can reduce the movement of the gates during the simplification of the circuit.

The synthesis for more than 3 bits reversible circuit is still a very difficult problem. Synthesis of 4-qubit circuit as example, because the memory is consumed too quickly, in [8], only the first eighth layer optimal circuits are synthesized with the shortest length by using the CNT library. If using the bidirectional cascade, without any more memory consumption, the optimal circuits with 16 layers are constructed and it is the best synthesis results so far. Our algorithm is not restricted by the amount of the quantum and need not save all the optimal circuits, so it can save memory efficiently and build any multi-quantum circuits with less cost.

The algorithm's idea is simpler than group theory methodology. Compared with exhaustive search and trial method, the time and space complexity is cut a lot.

5 Conclusions

In this paper, a heuristic fast matching algorithm is proposed for synthesis of quantum reversible logic circuits. It is RM-based and can always generate optimal or near-optimal quantum reversible circuits efficiently. The algorithm uses the quantum gate formulas as the heuristic rules and forward-matching technology to avoid blind searching, deadlock, backtracking. The other important advantage of this algorithm is that it makes preparation for simplifying the circuits.

Our further research includes ①further optimizing the algorithm. ②finding the better optimization rules of the circuits. ③finding the better representation method in the computer[9](such as Quantum Decision Diagram, QDD[10]) in order to use computer to analyze, optimize and test the circuits.

References

1. Bennett, C.: Logical reversibility of computation. I. B. M. J. Res. Dev. 17, 525–532 (1973)
2. Maslov, D., Dueck, G.W., Miller, D.M.: Toffoli network synthesis with templates. In: IEEE Trans CADICS, vol. 24(6), pp. 807–817 (2005)
3. Miller, D.M., Maslov, D., Dueck, G.W.: A transformation based algorithm for reversible logic synthesis. In: IEEE DAC, vol. 40, pp. 318–323 (2003)
4. Shende, V.V., Prasad, A.K., Markov, I.l.: Synthesis of reversible logic circuits. In: IEEE Trans CADICS, vol. 22(6), pp. 710–722 (2003)
5. Yang, G., Song, X., Perkowski, M.A., et al.: Four-level realization of 3-qubit reversible function. In: IET Comput. Digit. Tech, vol. 1(4), pp. 382–388 (2007)
6. Kerntopf, P.: A new heuristic algorithm for reversible logic synthesis. In: IEEE DAC, vol. 41, pp. 834–837 (2004)
7. Shende, V.V., Prasad, A.K., Markov, I.L., Hayes, J.P.: Reversible logic circuits synthesis. In: IEEE ACM, pp. 353–360 (2002)
8. Li, Z.Q., Chen, H.W., et al.: Fast algorithms for 4-qubit reversible logic circuits synthesis. Acta Electronic Sinica 36(11), 2081–2089 (2008)
9. Saeedi, M., Sedighi, M., Zamani, M.S.: A novel synthesis algorithm for reversible circuits. In: IEEE DAC, pp. 65–68 (2007)
10. Abdollahi, A., Pedram, M.: Analysis and synthesis of quantum circuits by using quantum decision diagrams, pp. 317–322. DAT, Europe (2006)

A Novel Transformation-Based Algorithm for Reversible Logic Synthesis[*]

Sishuang Wan, Hanwu Chen, and Rujin Cao

School of Computer Science and Engineering, Southeast University
Nanjing, Jiangsu, 210096, China
{hw_chen,wansishuang}@seu.edu.cn

Abstract. Reversible logic studies have promising potential on energy lossless circuit design, quantum computation, nanotechnology, etc. This paper proposes an analogic selection sorting algorithm essentially based on the transformation-based algorithm. It uses an unweighted, undirected graph for the representation of all transformable paths. During the synthesis process, a sequence of transformations are performed to enable all the output patterns to appear in the right place. The whole process can be implemented by a sequence of Toffoli gates. In addition, a simplification algorithm is put forward to further optimize the generated circuit. The experimental results show that this algorithm, compared with other exact methods, can achieve optimal or nearly optimal solutions with less computation time. Furthermore, it is more easily understood and implemented.

Keywords: Quantum computing; Reversible logic synthesis; Toffoli gate; Selection sorting.

1 Introduction

Quantum computers can be equivalent to the quantum Turing machine, and the theory has been proved that the quantum Turing machine can be equivalent to quantum logic circuits [1]. Thus the quantum computers can be cascaded with the combinations of quantum logic gates. Reversible logic synthesis results from the study on the reversible computer and now has applications in quantum computing, low-power CMOS, nanotechnology and optical computing. Synthesis of reversible networks is an emerging research topic.

At present, the reversible quantum logic circuit synthesis methods mainly used the Toffoli gate. The method can be divided into two broad categories. One kind of the method which is similar to the exhaustive search method such as the Boolean satisfiability (SAT) method [2], quantified Boolean formula (QBF) [3], dynamic programming [4] and symbolic reachability [5] can provide optimal solutions. However, they many suffer from long computation time because of their extensive exploration

---

[*] This work was supported by The National Natural Science Foundation of China under Grant 60572071 and 60873101, Natural Science Foundation under Grant BK2007104 and BK2008209.

processes. Plus, the search space intends to grow exponentially as the circuit size increases, which likely imposes limits on their practical usage. The other is the Heuristic search method, such as spectral technique [6], shared binary decision diagrams for complexity measurement [7], template-based transformation [8] and positive polarity Read-Muller (PPRM) expansions [9]. This kind of methods that add the heuristic rules on the exhaustive method can narrow the scope of the search and short the running time, but the cost of circuit synthesis is not the smallest, and also the synthesis algorithm does not guarantee of convergence.

In this paper, we present a novel transformation-based synthesis heuristic. It uses an unweighted, undirected graph for the representation of all transformable paths which is called PGraph. During the synthesis process, we first find the minimum output pattern, and then do a transformation to make it appeared in the first position and repeat the steps for remainder of the output patterns until all of them are already sorted. Since every transformation can be realized by one or several Toffoli gates, the whole process can be regarded as the circuit at the output in a reverse order. In addition, In order to reduce the cost of circuit, we proposed a simplification algorithm to further optimize the generated circuit.

The rest of this paper is organized as follows. Section 2 introduces the background materials of reversible logic. Section 3 presents the definitions and theorems as preliminaries for our synthesis method. Section 4 describes our design methodology and gives an illustration in detail. The optimization is discussed in Section 5. Section 6 demonstrates the experimental results. Finally Section 7 concludes.

2 Background

This paper assumes that the reader is familiar with the concepts of the reversible function and *TOFn* gates.

Definition 1: The hamming distance between two strings of equal length is the number of positions for which the corresponding symbols are different.
Specially, the hamming distance between a reversible function's any pair of the input pattern and the output pattern is called the output pattern's hamming distance.

Definition 2: The complexity of a reversible function f is the sum of all the output pattern's the hamming distance. For example, the reversible function f as shown in Fig.2 has a complexity of $C(f) = 3+1+2+1+3+1+2+1 = 14$.

3 Preliminaries

In this section, we present the definitions and the theorems for our synthesis heuristic.

Definition 3: For an n-bit reversible function f, if two output patterns A and B with only one bit difference, we can interchange them and get a new reversible function f. The interchange operation is called **SWAP[A,B]**. A **SWAP** can be realized by adding a single Toffoli gate at the output of the function.

Example 1: Let us consider the function $f=\{0,1,2,7,4,6,3,5\}$ given in Fig.2. The output patterns [000] and [001] only differ on the third bit, so a **SWAP**[000,111] can be done and a new function $f'=\{1,0,2,7,4,6,3,5\}$ is generated, whose truth table is shown in Fig.1(a). The corresponding Toffoli gate $TOF3(\overline{x_3},\overline{x_2},x_1)$ is shown in Fig.1(b).

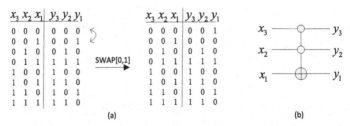

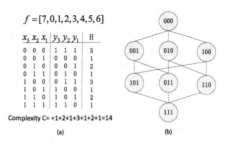

Fig. 1. (a) The truth table of f and f', (b) The Toffoli gate realization of **SWAP**[0, 1]

Theorem 1: A **SWAP** changes the hamming distance of the output pattern by one.

Proof: A **SWAP** only flips one bit of the output pattern, so the change of the hamming distance is 1.

Definition 4: A Path-Selection graph of an n-bit reversible function is an unweighted, undirected graph, denoted by $G=(V,E)$ where the vertex set $V=\{0,1,...,2^n-1\}$ represents the 2^n input or output truth values, and the edge set $E=\{e_{ij}|\exists \textbf{SWAP}[i,j].\ i,j\in V\}$ represents there exists a **SWAP** between the vertex i and j. The path means i can be achieved by applying a consecution of **SWAP**s from j. The path length is the number of the edges on the path. The Path-Selection graph is called PGraph for short.

Example 2: The PGraph of *3*-bit reversible function is shown in Fig. 2(b). The edge between the vertex $(0)_2=000$ and $(1)_2=001$ represents there is a **SWAP**[000, 111] between them. If we need to interchange the output patterns 0 and 7, we can first find a path from 0 to 7 in the PGraph: eg.000->001->101->111. Then we can use **SWAP**[000,001], **SWAP**[001,101], **SWAP**[101,111] to interchange them and the path length is 3.

Fig. 2. $f = [7,0,1,2,3,4,5,6]$ (a) The truth table (b) PGraph

Theorem 2: If the hamming distance between the output pattern A and the output pattern B is k, there exists a path with the length k from A to B, i.e. the interchange of the output patterns A and B needs k **SWAP**s at least.

Proof: Obviously, the PGraph is connected, so there is a path from the vertex A to the vertex B. According to the Theorem 1, a **SWAP** can change the Hamming distance 1. And the Hamming distance between A and B is k, so it needs k steps at least to interchange them, i.e. the path length from the vertex A to the vertex B is k at least. According to the Theorem 2, it is easy to get the following lemma.

Lemma 1: For a *3*-bit reversible function, suppose we need to interchange two output patterns A and B, the Hamming distance between them meets the condition $1 \leq H(A,B) \leq 3$, and

1. When $H(A,B)=1$, A and B exists a direct edge, i.e. the path length from A to B is 1. So we can interchange them immediately by the **SWAP[A,B]**.
2. When $H(A,B)=2$, the path length from A to B is 2 at least, i.e. there is a vertex C on the path and we can do the **SWAP[A,C]** and **SWAP[C,B]** to interchange them.
3. When $H(A,B)=3$, the path length from A to B is 3 at least, i.e. there are two vertexes C and D on the path and we can do the **SWAP[A,C]**, **SWAP[C,D]**, **SWAP(D,B)** to interchange them.

Proof: 1. When $H(A,B)=1$, according to the Lemma 1, there is a direct edge from A to B, so the number of the path from A to B with the length 1 is only one.
2. When $H(A,B)=2$, A and B differ on two bits. We can assume $A=[a,b,c], B=[a,\bar{b},\bar{c}]$ without loss of generality. The interchange of the vertexes A and B only can be realized through the vertex $C=[a,\bar{b},c]$ or $C=[a,b,\bar{c}]$, i.e. we can do **SWAP[A,C]**, **SWAP[C,B]** to interchange them. So the number of the path with the length 2 is two at most.
3. When $H(A,B)=3$, A and B differ on three bits. We can assume $A=[a,b,c], B=[\bar{a},\bar{b},\bar{c}]$ without loss of generality. If we first change the bit a, and get $C=[\bar{a},b,c]$, and next we can change b, and get $D=[\bar{a},\bar{b},c]$. Finally, we change the bit c and get B. Similarly, we can first change b or c. So the most number of the path from A to B is 3! =6.

From the proof of Lemma 2, we can get the following corollary.

Corollary 1: Suppose we need to interchange two output patterns A and B, if $H(A,B)=k$, the number of the path from A to B with the length k is 2*k at most.

Theorem 3: A **SWAP** changes the function complexity by 2, 0 or -2.

Proof: Suppose a **SWAP** interchanges two output patterns A and B, we use H_A, H_B to denote the Hamming distance of the A and B. We can assume $A=[x_1,x_2,...,x_{n-1},x_n]$, $B=[x_1,x_2,...,x_{n-1},\bar{x_n}]$ the last bit is different without loss of generality. After the **SWAP**, $A=[x_1,x_2,...,x_{n-1},\bar{x_n}]$, $B=[x_1,x_2,...,x_{n-1},x_n]$. Obviously, H_A, H_B =1 or -1. Since H_A and H_B is independent, the changed value of the complexity are independent. If H_A and H_B both are 1, the complexity increases 2; if both are -1, the complexity decreases 2; otherwise, the complexity is not changed.

Proof: According to the Theorem 2, it needs to do k **SWAP**s from f to f'. According to the Theorem 3, a **SWAP** decreases the complexity of the function f at most. As a result, the complexity decreases 2*k at most.

According to the Lemma 3, it is easy to get the following lemma.

Corollary 2: For a *3*-bit reversible function, suppose we need to interchange two output patterns A and B, the Hamming distance between them meets the condition:
$1 \leq H(A,B) \leq 3$, and

1. When $H(A,B)=1$, the complexity decreases 2 at most after the interchange.
2. When $H(A,B)=2$, the complexity decreases 4 at most after the interchange.
3. When $H(A,B)=3$, the complexity decreases 6 at most after the interchange.

4 Methodology

We present our reversible logic synthesis methodology in this section. Given a reversible function *f*, we want to do a sequence of **SWAP**s to transform *f* to an identity function. Since each **SWAP** corresponds to a Toffoli gate, the transformation process can be regarded as a realization of *f* by cascading primitive Toffoli gates at the output in a reverse order. The algorithm similar to the selection sorting:

   1. Find the minimum output pattern in all the output patterns.

   2. Swap it with the output pattern in the first position (here swap means a sequence of **SWAP**s through the path in the PGraph).

   3. Repeat the steps above for remainder of the output patterns (starting at the second position).

The algorithm ends when all the output patterns are already sorted. The algorithm is made up of the path selection and the circuit generation. We will next describe the key components in detail and give an example to illustrate the algorithm.

A. The Path Selection

Suppose we need to interchange two output patterns A and B, and the Hamming distance between them is *k*. From the PGraph we can see that:

   1) There may be a number of different length routes from A to B. But according to the Theorem 2, we only need to find the path which length is *k*.

   2) Even if the path length is *k*, it may be not unique. According the Theorem 3, we can first find a path which decreases the complexity of the function by $2*k$.

   3) If not exists, according to the Corollary 1, we can traversal all the $2k$ routes and find the path which can decrease the complexity most.

   4) Since the traversed output patterns are already in order, we can remove them from the PGraph.

According to the above, we can get a suitable path L from the PGraph.

B. The Gate Generation

After a sequence of **SWAP**s by the path L, if the remaining function is the identity function, the process terminates and the Toffoli network synthesis result is generated by converting the sequence of applied **SWAP**s to cascaded TOF*n* gates. In the final synthesis result, Toffoli gates are placed in the reverse order of the applied **SWAP**s.

C. Methodology Convergence

Theorem 4: The Path-Selection is connected after removing the vertex in the increasing order.

Proof: Suppose we are going to delete the vertex $V(V \neq 2^n\text{-}1)$. A 0 exists in the vertex V such that we can assume $V = (x_0, x_1, \ldots, 0, \ldots, x_n)$ without loss of generality. Since the vertex is deleted in the increasing order, a vertex $V' > V$ exists where the 1 appears in the 0 position of the vertex V, i.e. $V' = (x_0, x_1, \ldots, 1, \ldots, x_n)$. Obviously, there exists an edge between V and V' and so the PGraph is connected all the same.

Lemma 4: The proposed synthesis methodology always converges to a feasible solution.

Proof: From the proof of the Theorem 4, a path always exists such that the reversible function can do a sequence of SWAPs to become an identity function (when the first $2^n\text{-}1$ outputs are in order, the final output is already in place). We can conclude that our methodology can always transform a given function to an identity function.

D. Example

Next we give an example to illustrate our algorithm in detail.

Example 4: Let us consider the function $f = [7,0,1,2,3,4,5,6]$, whose truth table and PGraph are shown in Fig. 2(a) and (b).

Step 1: Similar to the Selection Sorting, we first find the minimum output pattern 000 which is not in the right place($y[000]=111\neq000$), so we need to do the interchange: $[111,000]$ where the hamming distance between 000 and 111 is $H(000,111) =3$, the complexity $C(f) =14$.

$f_1 = [0,1,5,2,3,4,7,6]$

x_3 x_2 x_1	y_3 y_2 y_1	H
0 0 0	0 0 0	0
0 0 1	0 0 1	0
0 1 0	1 0 1	3
0 1 1	0 1 0	1
1 0 0	0 1 1	3
1 0 1	1 0 0	1
1 1 0	1 1 1	1
1 1 1	1 1 0	1

Complexity C=0+0+3+1+3+1+1+1=10

(a)

$f_1' = [0,4,1,2,3,5,7,6]$

x_3 x_2 x_1	y_3 y_2 y_1	H
0 0 0	0 0 0	0
0 0 1	1 0 0	2
0 1 0	0 0 1	2
0 1 1	0 1 0	1
1 0 0	0 1 1	3
1 0 1	1 0 1	0
1 1 0	1 1 1	1
1 1 1	1 1 0	1

Complexity C=0+2+2+1+3+0+1+1=10

(b)

$f_1'' = [0,1,3,2,7,4,5,6]$

x_3 x_2 x_1	y_3 y_2 y_1	H
0 0 0	0 0 0	0
0 0 1	0 0 1	0
0 1 0	0 1 1	1
0 1 1	0 1 0	1
1 0 0	1 1 1	2
1 0 1	1 0 0	1
1 1 0	1 0 1	2
1 1 1	1 1 0	1

Complexity C=0+0+1+1+2+1+2+1=8

(c)

Fig. 3. The truth table after the interchange of the output patterns 000 and 111

Next, we find the path to interchange the output patterns 000 and 111 from the PGraph. We first find a path 1) 111-101-001-000. The truth table of the f after the interchange on the path is shown in Fig. 3(a). Since the complexity decreases $\triangle C = 14$-10=4, according to the Corollary 2, a better path maybe exist. Then we find another path 2)111-101-100-000. Same to the 1), the f after the interchange is shown in Fig. 3(b) and $\triangle C = 14$-10=4. We continue traversing and find another path 3) 111-011-001-000. It's shown in Fig. 3(c) after the interchange and$\triangle C = 14$-8=6. According to the Corollary 2, the path is the best. So we stop traversing and do the interchange by the path and get a new function $f_1=[0,1,3,2,7,4,5,6]$.

At last, we remove the vertex 000 from the PGraph because the output pattern 000 is in the right place.

Step2: As shown in Fig. 3(c) y[001]=001. i.e. 001 is already in the right place. We only need to remove 001 from the PGraph. The function is still f_1=[0,1,3,2,7,4,5,6].

f_2=[0,1,2,3,7,4,5,6]						
x_3	x_2	x_1	y_3	y_2	y_1	H
0	0	0	0	0	0	0
0	0	1	0	0	1	0
0	1	0	0	1	0	0
0	1	1	0	1	1	0
1	0	0	1	1	1	2
1	0	1	1	0	0	1
1	1	0	1	0	1	2
1	1	1	1	1	0	1

Complextiy C=2+1+2+1=6

(a)

f_3=[0,1,2,3,4,5,7,6]						
x_3	x_2	x_1	y_3	y_2	y_1	H
0	0	0	0	0	0	0
0	0	1	0	0	1	0
0	1	0	0	1	0	0
0	1	1	0	1	1	0
1	0	0	1	0	0	0
1	0	1	1	0	1	0
1	1	0	1	1	1	1
1	1	1	1	1	0	1

Complexity C=1+1=2

(b)

f_4=[0,1,2,3,4,5,6,7]						
x_3	x_2	x_1	y_3	y_2	y_1	H
0	0	0	0	0	0	0
0	0	1	0	0	1	0
0	1	0	0	1	0	0
0	1	1	0	1	1	0
1	0	0	1	0	0	0
1	0	1	1	0	1	0
1	1	0	1	1	0	0
1	1	1	1	1	1	0

Complexity C=0

(c)

Fig. 4. The truth table,(a) step 3 and step 4, (b) step 5 and step 6, (c)step 7 and step 8

Step3: Next, we consider the output pattern 010 where y[010]=011≠010, so we need to do the interchange: [011,010]. Since $H(010,011)$ =1, $C(f)$ =8, according to the Corollary 2, we can interchange [010,011] immediately i.e. **SWAP**[010,011] and get the function f_2=[0,1,2,3,7,4,5,6] which is shown in Fig.4(a) and then remove the vertex 010 from the PGraph.

Step 4: y[011]=011.We only need to remove the vertex 011 from the PGraph.

Step 5: y[100]=111≠100, H=2.We can find a best path 111-101-100 which can decreases the complexity△C= 14-10=4 and get f_3=[0,1,2,3,4,5,7,6] shown in Fig.4(b).

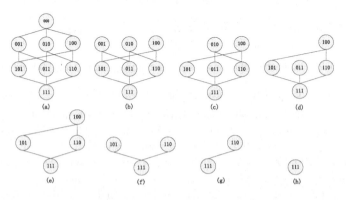

Fig. 5. The change process of the PGraph: (a) to (h) corresponding the step1 to step 8, remove the vertex 000,001,010,011,100,101,110,111

Step 6: y[101]=011.We only need to remove the vertex 011 from the PGraph.

Step 7: y[110]=111 ≠ 110,H=1.We can find a direct path 111-110 and get f_4=[0,1,2,3,4,5,6,7] shown in Fig.9.

Step 8: When the first 7 outputs are in order, the final output is already in place.

According to above steps we get the sequence of **SWAP**s: **SWAP**[111,011], **SWAP**[011,001], **SWAP**[001,000], **SWAP**[010,011], **SWAP**[111,101], **SWAP**[101,100],**SWAP**[110,111].

The corresponding Toffoli gates are $TOF3(x_2,x_1,x_3)$, $TOF3(\overline{x_3},x_1,x_2)$, $TOF3(\overline{x_3},\overline{x_2},x_1)$, $TOF3(\overline{x_3},x_2,x_1),TOF3(x_3,x_1,x_2),TOF3(x_3,\overline{x_2},x_1),TOF3(x_3,x_2,x_1)$.

The final synthesis result is that the Toffoli gates are placed in the reverse order of the sequence which is shown in Fig.6.

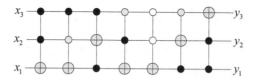

Fig. 6. The Toffoli network implementation of the f=[7,0,1,2,3,4,5,6]

5 Simplification

Since the generated circuits by the above algorithm can be simplified, we developed a simplification algorithm to further reduce the number of the gates.

Theorem 5: If two Toffoli gates A=$TOFk(x_1,x_2...x_{k-1},x_k)$ and B=$TOFl(y_1,y_2...y_{l-1},y_l)$

satisfy: $x_k \notin \{y_1, y_2...y_{l-1}\}$ Or $\exists i \in [1, k-1], j \in [1,l-1]$ meets $x_i = \overline{y_j}$,we can see that the gate

A has no influence to the gate B.

Property 1: If the Toffoli gate A and B don't react upon each other, we can interchange the position of them.

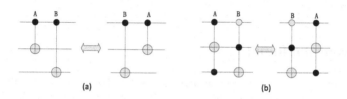

Fig. 7. In (a), A's control bit is not in front of the B's target bit and the B's control bit is also not in front of the A's target bit, In (b), since A and B are mutually exclusive

Theorem 6: If two adjacent Toffoli gates only difference on one control bit, the bit can be removed and the two gates can be merged with the left bit.

Proof: Supposed the two adjacent Toffoli gates are A and B whose first n-1 inputs are the control bits and the nth input is the target bit. It is assumed that A and B only have the difference on the n-1 pattern. Let $A= TOFn(x_1,x_2,...,x_{n-1},x_n)$ and $B=TOFn(x_1,x_2,...,\overline{x_{n-1}},x_n)$. After the influence of A and B :

$$x_n'' = \overline{x_1 x_2...x_{n-1}} \oplus (x_1 x_2...x_{n-1} \oplus x_n) = x_1 x_2...x_{n-2}(\overline{x_{n-1}} \oplus x_n) \oplus x_n = x_1 x_2...x_{n-2} \oplus x_n$$

And the control line is not changed. So A and B can be merged with the left bit. Some merge examples is shown in Fig.8.

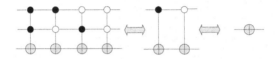

Fig. 8. An example of the Toffoli gates merging

Theorem 7: If two adjacent Toffoli gates are the same, the two gates can be removed. According to the Theorem 6 and Theorem 7, let us do the simplification on the circuit in the Example 4. The process is shown inFig.9.

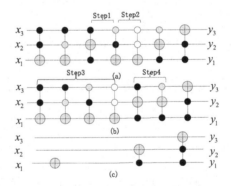

Fig. 9. An example of the simplification process. The original circuit is shown in (a) where Step1 and Step2 mean the interchange operation. The Step3 and Step4 mean the merge operation.

6   Experimental Results

In this section, we present our experimental results. The proposed synthesis algorithm is implemented in C++ and the experiments are performed on an Intel Core™2 CPU 2.13GHz PC with 2GB memory running windows XP SP2. We first synthesized all reversible functions of three variables which number is 8! = 403020. The whole process takes 0.410s after the simplification. Table 1 compares our results

Table 1. Results for all the three-bit reversible functions

Gate count	Circuit count		
	Optimal	POT	Ours After Simplification
14			
13			2
12		25	21
11		258	158
10		1265	699
9		3788	2241
8	577	7820	4981
7	10253	10630	8095
6	17049	9126	9731
5	8921	4996	8112
4	2780	1833	4471
3	625	476	1499
2	102	90	282
1	12	12	27
0	1	1	1
Avg.	5.87	6.83	6.14

which uses a library of *NOT*, *CNOT* and *TOF*3 gate with the optimal results generated by [4] (Column Optimal) which uses a library of *NOT*, *CNOT* and *TOF3* gates and the POT method results generated by [10] which uses a library of *TOF*3 gates and is the best heuristics until now. It can be observed that our average circuit size after the simplification is 6.14, which is closer to the optimal average of 5.87 than the POT method.

Next, we compared our method with other heuristics, specifically, the PPRM expansion method [9] (column *PPRM*), non-search method [12] (column *Non-search*) and the POT method [10] (column *POT*). The benchmark circuits are discussed in [11]. Table 2 illustrates the synthesis results. Our method can yield less number of gates than the non-search method and similar to the POT method on average. Although the results yield more number of gates than the PPRM expansion method, our method only takes 0.01ms on average to synthesize a 3-bit reversible function, which is several orders of magnitude better than 0.2ms by the POT method and 0.5s by the PPRM expansion method (An Intel Xeon 3GHZ workstation with 2G memory which is better than our PC) [10]. Thus it can be seen that our algorithm, compared with other exact methods, can achieve optimal or very close to optimal solutions with less computation time which efficiency is dozens of or hundreds of times compared with other heuristics.

Table 2. Synthesis comparisons with other heuristics

Function	Toffoli gate count				Our Synthesized Circuits (x_4=d,x_3=c, x_2=b, x_1=a)
	PPRM	Non-search	POT	Ours	
[1,0,3,2,5,7,4,6]	4	6	4	4	TOF3(c,b,a) TOF3(c,a,b) TOF3(c,b´,a) TOF3(c´,a)
[7,0,1,2,3,4,5,6]	3	3	3	3	TOF1(a)TOF2(c,b)TOF(c,b,a)
[0,1,2,3,4,6,5,7]	3	3	3	3	TOF3(c,b,a)TOF3(c,a,b)TOF3(c,b,a)
[0,1,2,4,3,5,6,7]	5	7	5	5	TOF3(c,b´,a)TOF3(c,a,b)TOF3(b,a,c) TOF(c,a,b) TOF(b´,c,a)
[0,1,2,3,4,5,6,8,7,9, 10,11,12,13,14,15]	7	15	7	7	TOF4(d,c´,b´,a)TOF4(d,c´,a,b) TOF4(d,b,a,c)TOF4(b,c,a,d) TOF4(d,b,a,c)TOF4(d,c´,a,b) TOF4(d,c´,b´,a)
[1,2,3,4,5,6,7,0]	3	3	3	5	TOF3(b,a,c)TOF2(c,a)TOF2(c,b) TOF2(a,b)TOF3(c´,a)
[1,2,3,4,5,6,7,8,9,10 ,11,12,13,14,15,0]	4	4	4	4	TOF4(d´,c´,b´,a)TOF3(d,c,a) TOF2(d´,c)TOF1(d)
[0,7,6,9,4,11,10,13, 8,15,14,1,12,3,2,5]	4	3	6	3	TOF2(d,a)TOF2(c,b)TOF2(d,c)
[3,6,2,5,7,1,0,4]	7	8	8	6	TOF3(c,b,a)TOF2(a,c)TOF3(c´,b,a) TOF3(c,a,b)TOF2(a´,b)TOF2(b,a)
[1,2,7,5,6,3,0,4]	6	8	7	8	TOF3(c,b,a)TOF3(c,a,b)TOF3(b,a,c) TOF2(c,b)TOF3(c´,b,a)TOF3(b,a,c) TOF3(c´,a,b)TOF2(c´,a)
[4,3,0,2,7,5,6,1]	7	8	5	7	TOF3(c,a´,b)TOF3(b´,a´,c)TOF3(c,b,a)TOF3(b,a´,c)TOF2(c,b)TOF2(a,b) TOF(b´,c´,a)
[7,5,2,4,6,1,0,3]	7	6	6	6	TOF3(c,b,a)TOF3(b,a,c)TOF2(b,c) TOF2(a´,b)TOF3(c´,b,a) TOF2(a,c)
Avg.	5.00	6.17	5.08	5.08	

7 Conclusions

We propose an analogic selection sorting algorithm essentially based on the transformation-based algorithm. During the synthesis process, we do a sequence of transformation to make all the output patterns appeared in the right place. The whole process can be implemented by a sequence of Toffoli gates. In addition, we proposed a simplification algorithm to further optimize the generated circuit. The experimental results show that our algorithm, compared with other exact methods, can achieve optimal or very close to optimal solutions with less computation time. Furthermore, our algorithm is more easily understood and implemented.

References

1. Deutsch, D.: Quantum theory, the Church-Turing principle and the universal quantum computer. J. Proc. Royal Soc. London 400, 97–117 (1985)
2. Wille, R., Große, D.: Fast exact Toffoli network synthesis of reversible logic. In: Proc. Int. Conf. Computer-Aided Design, pp. 60–64 (2007)

3. Wille, R., Le, H.M., Dueck, G.W., Große, D.: Quantified synthesis of reversible logic. In: Proc. Design Automation & Test Europe Conf., pp.1015–1020 (2008)
4. Shende, V.V., Prasad, A.K., Markov, I.L., Hayes, J.P.: Synthesis of reversible logic circuits. In: Proc. Int. Conf. Computer-Aided Design, pp. 353–360 (2002)
5. Hung, W.N.N., Song, X., Yang, G., Yang, J., Perkowski, M.: Quantum logic synthesis by symbolic reachability analysis. In: Proc. Design Automation Conf., pp. 838–841 (2004)
6. Miller, D.M., Dueck, G.W.: Spectral techniques for reversible logic synthesis. In: Proc. 6th Int. Symp. Representations Methodology of Future Computing Technologies, pp. 56–62. Trier (2003)
7. Kerntopf, P.: A new heuristic algorithm for reversible logic synthesis. In: Proc. Design Automation Conf., San Diego, pp. 834–837 (2004)
8. Maslov, D., Dueck, G.W., Miller, D.M.: Toffoli network synthesis with templates. J. IEEE Trans. Computer-Aided Design of Integrated Circuits & Systems. 6, 807–817 (2005)
9. Gupta, P., Agrawal, A., Jha, N.K.: An algorithm for synthesis of reversible logic circuits. J. IEEE Trans. Computer-Aided Design of Integrated Circuits & Systems 11, 2317–2530 (2006)
10. Zheng, Y., Huang, C.: A novel Toffoli network synthesis algorithm for reversible logic. In: Design Automation Conference, 2009. ASP-DAC 2009, Asia and South Pacific, pp. 739–744 (2009)
11. Saeedi, M., Saheb Zamani, M., Sedighi, M.: On the Behavior of Substitution-Based Reversible Circuit Synthesis Algorithms. In: Investigation and Improvement, ISVLSI, pp. 428–436 (2007)
12. Saeedi, M., Sedighi, M., Zamani, M.S.: A novel synthesis algorithm for reversible circuits. In: Proc. Int. Conf. Computer-Aided Design, pp. 65–68 (2007)

Estimation of Distribution Algorithms for the Machine-Part Cell Formation

Qingbin Zhang[1], Bo Liu[2], Lihong Bi[1], Zhuangwei Wang[3], and Boyuan Ma[1]

[1] Shijiazhuang Institute of Railway Technology, Shijiazhuang 050041, China
[2] Hebei Academy of Sciences, Shijiazhuang 050081, China
[3] Information Center of Hebei Education Department, Shijiazhuang 050000, China
zqbin2002@sina.com

Abstract. The machine-part cell formation is a NP- complete combinational optimization in cellular manufacturing system. Previous researches have revealed that although the genetic algorithm (GA) can get high quality solutions, special selection strategy, crossover and mutation operators as well as the parameters must be defined previously to solve the problem efficiently and flexibly. The Estimation of Distribution Algorithms (EDAs) has recently been recognized as a new computing paradigm in evolutionary computation which can overcome some drawbacks of the traditional GA mentioned above. In this paper, two kinds of the EDAs, UMDA and EBNA$_{BIC}$, are applied to solve the machine-part cell formation problem. Simulation results on six well known problems show that the UMDA and EBNA$_{BIC}$ can attain satisfied solutions more simply and efficiently.

Keywords: machine-part cell formation, UMDA, EBNA$_{BIC}$, grouping efficacy.

1 Introduction

Cellular manufacturing has been recognized as a desirable compromise between flow line production and job shop production. With properly grouped machines and parts based on group technology, a cellular manufacturing system can take advantages of the efficiency of a flow line system and the flexibility offered by a job shop system [1]. One fundamental problem in cellular manufacturing system is to identify the part families and machine groups and consequently to form manufacturing cells, which is named as the machine-part cell formation or manufacturing cell design.

The machine-part cell formation is a NP-complete combinational optimization problem, so it is appropriate to adopt heuristic based approaches to obtain good solutions. Among those approaches, genetic algorithms (GAs) have been widely used to solve the machine-part cell formation problem. Joines, Culbreth and King developed an integer programming model and used GA to solve the machine-part cell formation problem [2]. Cheng et al. formulated the problem as a traveling salesman problem and solved the model using GA [3]. Onwubolu and Muting developed a GA taking into account cell-load variation [4]. Brown and Sumichrast proposed a grouping genetic algorithm (GGA) for the machine-part cell formation problem [5]. Eduardo Vila Gonçalves Filho and Alexandre José Tiberti also proposed an approach using GGA based

Z. Cai et al. (Eds.): ISICA 2009, LNCS 5821, pp. 82–91, 2009.

on group encoding instead of simple machine encoding [6]. Adnan Tariq, Iftikhar Hussain and Abdul Ghafoor developed an approach that combines a local search heuristic with GA [7]. All these researchers have concluded that GA can get high quality solutions to the problems in the literature.

However, the past research has also shown that the performance of GA for the machine-part cell formation depends heavily on encoding methods and determination of selection, crossover and mutation operators as well as choice of related parameters, thus needs prior knowledge about the problem at hand, otherwise extensive experiments have to been done to choose an effective configuration of the operators and the parameters for a GA.

Estimation of distribution algorithms (EDAs) [8-10] has recently been recognized as a new computing paradigm in evolutionary computation which can overcome some drawbacks exhibited by traditional genetic algorithms mentioned above. So there has been a considerable growth of interest in the use of EDAs to deal with optimization problems. In this paper, we adopt EDAs for the machine-part cell formation. Two kinds of EDAs, UMDA and EBNA$_{BIC}$, are applied to solve a set of well known machine-part cell formation problems in the literature. Experimental results compared with that of the GA are reported.

The remainder of this paper is organized as follows: The machine-part cell formation problem is described in section 2. The principle of the UMDA and EBNA$_{BIC}$ are analyzed in section 3. The performance on six well known problems in the literature is shown in section 4. Finally, conclusion is made in section 5.

2   The Machine-Part Cell Formation Problem

2.1   Problem Definition

The machine-part cell formation problem includes the identification of the parts that have similar processing requirements and the identification of the machines that can process each family of parts. For cells to operate efficiently, all of the machines within a cell should be fully utilized and the amount of the traveling between cells should be kept to a minimum [5].

At the conceptual level, the machine-cell formation problem can be represented by a binary machine-part incidence matrix. Consider an m machine and n part cell formation problem with k cells, machine-part incidence matrix is a zero-one matrix of order $m \times n$ in which a element a_{ij} has a value of 1 if part j needs processing on machine i, and a value 0 otherwise. At the same time, the model must fulfill the follow constraints [2]:

$$x_{il} = \begin{cases} 1, & \text{if machine } i \text{ is assigned to cell } j \\ 0, \text{otherwise} \end{cases} \tag{1}$$

$$y_{jl} = \begin{cases} 1, & \text{if part } j \text{ is assigned to part family } l \\ 0, \text{ otherwise} \end{cases} \tag{2}$$

$$\sum_{l=1}^{k} x_{il} = 1, i = 1, 2, ..., m \qquad (3)$$

$$\sum_{l=1}^{k} y_{jl} = 1, j = 1, 2, ..., n \qquad (4)$$

In order to determine the utilization of machines and the inter-cell moment of parts, previous research has mainly focused on the block diagonalization of the given machine-part incidence matrix. When columns and rows are arranged in the order corresponding to the groups identified by a machine-part cell formation problem solution, the incidence matrix can be evaluated to determine the performance of the solutions. The best solutions are those that contain a minimal number of voids (zeros in the diagonal blocks) and a minimal number of exceptional elements (ones outside the diagonal blocks).

2.2 Measure of the Performance

The most widely used performance measures on the machine-part cell formation problem are probably the grouping efficiency and the grouping efficacy because they are simple to implement and generate block diagonal matrices.

The grouping efficiency was first proposed by Chandrasekharan and Rajagopalan [11]. It incorporates both machine utilization and inter-cell movement and is defined as the weighted sum of η_1 and η_2 using the formula:

$$\eta = q\eta_1 + (1-q)\eta_2 \qquad (5)$$

where η_1 is the ratio of the number of ones in the diagonal blocks to the total number of elements in the diagonal blocks of the final matrix, η_2 is the ratio of the number of zeros in the off-diagonal blocks to the total number of elements in the off-diagonal blocks of the final matrix, and q is the weight factor.

The drawback of the grouping efficiency lies in its low discriminating capability and choosing the weight factor often involves subjective judgment in reality.

The grouping efficacy was suggested by Kumar and Chandrasekharan [12]. It can be defined as:

$$\Gamma = \frac{1 - {e_0}/{e}}{1 + {e_v}/{e}} = \frac{e - e_0}{e + e_v} \qquad (6)$$

where e is the number of ones in the incidence matrix, e_0 is the number of the exceptional elements, and e_v is the voids in the diagonal blocks.

The grouping efficacy does not require a weight factor, so it can effectively avoid the possible bias introduced by a subjectively specified weight factor. At same time, it has a high capability to differentiate between well-structured and ill-structured matrices, so we choose the grouping efficacy as the measure of performance.

Given the definition of the grouping efficacy and the assignment variables above, Γ can be defined in detail as follows:

$$\Gamma = \frac{\sum_{l=1}^{kmax}\sum_{j=1}^{n}\sum_{i=1}^{m} y_{jl}x_{il}a_{ij}}{\sum_{j=1}^{n}\sum_{i=1}^{m}a_{ij} + \sum_{l=1}^{kmax}[(\sum_{j=1}^{n} y_{jl})(\sum_{i=1}^{m} x_{il})] - \sum_{l=1}^{kmax}\sum_{j=1}^{n}\sum_{i=1}^{m} y_{jl}x_{il}a_{ij}} \qquad (7)$$

3 Estimation of Distribution Algorithms

Unlike other evolutionary algorithms, EDAs do not use crossover or mutation. Instead, they explicitly extract global statistical information from the selected solutions and subsequently build a probabilistic model of promising solutions, based on the extracted information. New solutions are sampled from the probabilistic model thus built. Because EDAs can get competitive and robust results on many complicated optimization problems which conventional GA can only get poor performance, they have been applied to a variety of practical problems from different domains such as engineering optimization, biomedical informatics and machine learning, etc [8,13,14].

According to the complexity of probabilistic models they use, EDAs can be classified into three classes [8]: (1) no interactions among variables. Algorithms in this class include the PBIL, cGA and UMDA. (2) pairwise interactions among variables. These algorithms include the MIMIC, COMIT and BMDA. (3) models with multivariate interactions. These algorithms mainly include EBNA, ECGA and BOA. Although the algorithms use models that can cover multivariate interactions require increased computational time, they work well on problems which have complex interactions among variables.

The UMDA was proposed by Mühlenbein and Paaß [9]. UMDA uses the simplest model to estimate the joint probability distribution of the selected individuals at each generation. This joint probability distribution is factorized as a product of independent univariate marginal distributions:

$$p_t(x) = \prod_{i=1}^{n} p_t(x_i) = \prod_{i=1}^{n} p(x_i | D_{t-1}^{se}) \qquad (8)$$

Usually each univariate marginal distribution is estimated from marginal frequencies as follows:

$$p(x_i | D_{t-1}^{se}) = \frac{\sum_{j=1}^{N} \delta_j(X_i = x_i | D_{t-1}^{se})}{N} \qquad (9)$$

where

$$\delta_j(X_i = x_i | D_{t-1}^{se}) = \begin{cases} 1, & \text{if in the } j^{th} \text{ case of } D_{t-1}^{se}, X_i = x_i \\ 0, & \text{otherwise} \end{cases} \qquad (10)$$

A pseudo-code for the UMDA algorithm can be seen in Figure 1.

UMDA

$D_0 \leftarrow$ Generate M individuals to form the initial population

Repeat for $t=1,2,\ldots$ until the stopping criterion is met

$D_{t-1}^{se} \leftarrow$ Select $N<M$ individuals from D_{t-1} according to the selection method

Estimate the joint probability distribution:

$$p_t(x) = p(x \mid D_{t-1}^{se}) = \prod_{i=1}^{n} p_i(x_i) = \prod_{i=1}^{n} \frac{\sum_{j=1}^{N} \delta_j (X_i = x_i \mid D_{t-1}^{se})}{N}$$

$D_t \leftarrow$ Sample M individuals to form the new population from $p_t(\text{x})$

Fig. 1. Pseudo-code for the UMDA

The EBNA was introduced by Etxeberria and Larrañaga [15]. In EBNA, the joint probability distribution is encoded by a Bayesian network that is learnt from the database containing the selected individuals at each generation.

Bayesian networks is a pair $(S;\theta)$ representing a graphical factorization of a probability distribution [16]. The structure S is a directed acyclic graph which reflects the set of conditional (in) dependencies among the variables. The factorization of the probability distribution is codified by S:

$$p(x) = \prod_{i=1}^{n} p(x_i \mid pa_i) \tag{11}$$

where pa_x is the parent set of X_H (variables from which there exists an arc to X_i in the graph S). On the other hand, θ is a set of parameters for the local probability distributions associated with each variable. If the variable X_i has r_i possible values, $x_i^1,\ldots,x_i^{r_i}$ ⇔ the local distribution $p(x_i \mid pa_i^j,\theta_i)$ is an unrestricted discrete distribution:

$$p(x_i^k \mid pa_i^j,\theta_i) \equiv \theta_{ijk} \tag{12}$$

where $pa_i^1,\ldots,pa_i^{q_i}$ denote the values of pa_i and the term q_i denotes the number of possible different instances of the parent variables of X_i. In other words, the parameter θ_{ijk} represents the conditional probability of variable X_i being in its kth value, knowing that the set of its parent variables is in its jth value. Therefore, the local parameters are given by $\theta_i = (((\theta_{ijk})_{k=1}^{r_i})_{j=1}^{q_i})$.

Learning the probabilistic model at each generation in EBNA means learning a Bayesian network from the selected promising individuals. Once the structure has been learnt, the conditional probability distributions required to completely specify the model are estimated from the database.

There are two kinds of strategies to learn the structure of a Bayesian network: by detecting conditional (in)dependencies or with a method called "score+ search". Several criteria for guiding the search for good model structures based on BIC or K2+pen score as well as on detecting conditional (in)dependencies between variables-PC algorithm-have been implemented, giving the different instantiations of EBNA: $EBNA_{BIC}$, $EBNA_{K2+pen}$, $EBNA_{PC}$ [8,15].

In EBNA, the simulation of the Bayesian network is done using the Probabilistic Logic Sampling (PLS) method [17]. Figure 2 represents a pseudo-code of the EBNA algorithm.

EBNA

$BN_0 \leftarrow (S_0, \theta_0)$ where S_0 is an arc less DAG, and θ_0 is uniform distribution:

$$p_0(x) = \prod_{i=1}^{n} p(x_i) = \prod_{i=1}^{n} \frac{1}{r_i}$$

$D_0 \leftarrow$ sample M individuals to form the initial population

Repeat for $t=1,2,...$ until the stopping criterion is met

$D_{t-1}^{se} \leftarrow$ Select $N<M$ individuals from D_{t-1}

$S_t^* \leftarrow$ find the best structure according to the criterion:

penalized maximum likelihood+search$\rightarrow EBNA_{BIC}$

penalized Bayesian score+search$\rightarrow EBNA_{K2+pen}$

conditional (in)dependencies tests$\rightarrow EBNA_{PC}$

$\theta^t \leftarrow$ calculate θ_{ijk}^t using D_{t-1}^{se} as the data set

$BN_t \leftarrow (S_t^*, \theta^t)$

$D_t \leftarrow$ sample M individuals from BN_t using PLS method

Fig. 2. Pseudo-code for the EBNA

4 Experiments and Results

4.1 Individual Representation

Joines developed a representation in which each variable or individual comes from an alphabet consisting of the integers between the variable's upper and lower bounds for the machine-part cell formation [2]. So for a machine-part cell formation problem with an m machines and n parts, an integer alphabet $1,...,k_{max}$ is employed, where k_{max} represents an upper bound on the number of the cells. For an individual, the first m

variables represent the machines while the last n variables are associated with the parts. Therefore, each individual can be represented as a vector of $m + n$ integer variables:

$$individual \rightarrow (\underbrace{x_1, x_2, ..., x_m}_{machines}, \underbrace{y_1, y_2, ..., y_n}_{parts}) \tag{13}$$

4.2 Selection Methods

Selection methods determine which the set of individuals will be used to build the probabilistic model in EDAs. Although any selection method in the evolutionary algorithms can be used in the EDAs, truncation selection has been the most popular used method for it has been shown that truncation selection can get more accurate linkage learning information about the optimization problem at hand [18], so in this paper, we use the truncation selection in which the best $\tau\%$ individuals in the population are selected to be the promising individuals.

4.3 Learning Methods

Another key feature when dealing with an EDA is the way that probabilistic model is learned. According to the complexity of the probabilistic model, there are two alternatives: induce both the model structure and its associated parameters, or induce just the set of parameters for an a priori given model. The first class includes two subtasks: structure learning and parameter learning, whereas the second class only needs parameter learning.

In UMDA, there are no interactions among variables in each individual, so the algorithm uses a simple fixed model which only the parameters representation joint probability distribution are needed to be identified.

In EBNA, however, the joint probability distribution is encoded by a Bayesian network, so the learning in EBNA includes structure learning which to identify the topology of the Bayesian network and parameter learning which to identify the conditional probabilities for a given network topology. In this paper, we consider EBNA$_{BIC}$ which use penalized maximum likelihood+search method to learn the structure of the Bayesian network for its popularity. In EBNA$_{BIC}$, given a database D and a Bayesian network whose structure is denoted by S, a value which evaluates how well the Bayesian network represents the probability distribution of the database D is:

$$BIC(S, D) = \sum_{i=1}^{n} \sum_{j=1}^{q_i} \sum_{k=1}^{r_i} N_{ijk} \log \frac{N_{ijk}}{N_{ij}} - \frac{\log N}{2} \sum_{i=1}^{n} (r_i - 1) q_i \tag{14}$$

where n is the number of variables of the Bayesian network, r_i is the number of different values that variable X_i can take, q_i is the number of different values that the parent variables of X_i can take, N_{ij} is the number of individuals in D in which the parent variables of X_i take their j^{th} value and N_{ijk} is the number of individuals in D in which variable X_i takes its kth value and parent variables take their j^{th} value.

4.4 Experimental Results

To demonstrate the performance of the EDAs on the machine-part cell formation problem, we use UMDA and EBNA$_{BIC}$ for six well known problems collected from the literature, the grouping efficacy obtained by the UMDA and EBNA$_{BIC}$ are compared with that of the GA. Experimental results are presented in Table1 and Table 2. GA1 represents the experimental results from Joines[2].GA2 represents the experimental results from Cheng et al.[3] and GA3 represents the experimental results from Onwubolu and Mutingi[4]. In our experiments, initial population are generated randomly with uniform distribution, the elitist is copied to next generation and 50% of the top individuals in the population are selected to construct the probabilistic model. The k is set equal to the best known number of cells determined by other algorithms. All the results of the UMDA and EBNA$_{BIC}$ are averaged by 20 run.

From the Table 1 we can see that for all the experimental problems, both the UMDA with simple no interaction model and the EBNA$_{BIC}$ with Bayesian network model can get same grouping efficacy as that of the GA1, which performs the best among three GAs. For Chandrasekharan&Rajagopalan problem and Stanfel problem, the UMDA and EBNA$_{BIC}$ can even get higher grouping efficacy than that of the GA2 and GA3.

In the Table 2, P represents the population size; G means the average generations needed to run before convergence; F represents the number of function evaluations of the algorithms. It can be concluded that for the Chandrasekharan &Rajagopalan problem and the Burbidge problem, the function evaluations of the UMDA and EBNA$_{BIC}$ are less than that of the GA1, for other problems, the UMDA and EBNA$_{BIC}$ have a little higher function evaluations. The reason is that the EDAs need more individuals to get effective probabilistic model in each generation.

Table 1. Group efficacy of the UMDA, EBNA$_{BIC}$ and GA

problem	Matrix size	k	e	GA			UMDA	EBNA$_{BIC}$
				GA1	GA2	GA3		
Boctor	7×11	3	20	--	0.7037	0.7037	0.7037	0.7037
Simple Chan&Miller	10×15	3	46	0.9200	0.9200	--	0.9200	0.9200
Chandrasekharan& Rajagopalan	8×20	3	61	0.8525	0.8524	0.8525	0.8525	0.8525
Stanfel	14×24	5	61	0.7051	0.6744	0.6348	0.7051	0.7051
Srinivasan	16×30	4	116	0.6783	--	--	0.6783	0.6783
Burbidge	20×35	4	136	0.7571	--	--	0.7571	0.7571

Table 2. Function evaluations required of the UMDA, EBNA$_{BIC}$ and GA

problem	GA1			UMDA			EBNA$_{BIC}$		
	P	G	F	P	G	F	P	G	F
Boctor	--	--	--	500	17	8500	500	14.4	7200
Simple Chan&Miller	80	97	7760	500	18.9	9450	500	18.3	9150
Chandrasekharan &Rajagopalan	80	119.9	9592	400	18.7	7480	400	17.6	7040
Stanfel	80	895	71600	2000	38.4	76800	2500	33.8	84500
Srinivasan	80	432	34560	1500	34.5	51750	1500	32	48000
Burbidge	80	680.4	54432	1000	34.3	34300	1500	32	48000

5 Conclusion

In this paper, two kinds of the EDAs, UMDA which uses the simplest probabilistic model and the EBNA$_{BIC}$, which uses the Bayesian network encode the variables, are applied to solve the machine-part cell formation problem. Experimental results on six well cited problems show that both the simple UMDA and the complicated EBNA$_{BIC}$ can get the same grouping efficacy as that of the GA proposed by Joines with approximated function evaluations. For some problems, the UMDA and EBNA$_{BIC}$ can get higher grouping efficacy than that of GA approaches proposed by Cheng and Onwubolu et al. At same time, the EDAs, especially the UMDA, can solve the problem more simply and efficiently with less operators and parameters.

Acknowledgments. This work was supported by Nature Science Foundation of Hebei Province (F2008001166) and Mentoring Programs of Scientific and Technological Research & Development in Hebei Province (072135133).

References

1. Saeed, Z., Ming, L.: A new genetic algorithm for the machine/part grouping problem involving processing times and lot sizes. Computers & Industrial Engineering 45, 713–731 (2003)
2. Joines, J.A., Culbreth, C.T., King, R.E.: Manufacturing cell design: an integer programming model employing genetic algorithms. IIE Transactions 28, 69–85 (1996)
3. Cheng, C.H., Gupta, Y.P., Lee, W.H., Wong, K.F.: A TSP-based heuristic for forming machine groups and part families. International Journal of Production Research 36, 1325–1337 (1998)

4. Onwubolu, G.C., Mutingi, M.: A genetic algorithm approach to cellular manufacturing systems. Computers & Industrial Engineering 39, 125–144 (2001)
5. Brown, E.C., Sumichrast, R.T.: CF-GGA: a grouping genetic algorithm for the cell formation problem. International Journal of Production Research 39, 3651–3670 (2001)
6. Vila Goncalves Filho, E., JoséTiberti, A.: A group genetic algorithm for the machine cell formation problem. International Journal of Production Economics 102, 1–21 (2006)
7. Tariq, A., Hussain, I., Ghafoor, A.: A hybrid genetic algorithm for machine-part grouping. Computers & Industrial Engineering 56, 347–356 (2008)
8. Larrañaga, P., Lozano, J.A.: Estimation of Distribution Algorithms: A New Tool for Evolutionary Computation. Kluwer Academic Publishers, Dordrecht (2002)
9. Mühlenbein, H., Paaß, G.: From Recombination of Genes to the Estimation of Distributions I. Binary Parameters. In: Ebeling, W., Rechenberg, I., Voigt, H.-M., Schwefel, H.-P. (eds.) PPSN 1996. LNCS, vol. 1141, pp. 178–187. Springer, Heidelberg (1996)
10. Pelikan, M., Goldberg, D.E., Lobo, F.: A Survey of Optimization by Building and Using Probabilistic Models. Computational Optimization and Applications 21, 5–20 (2002)
11. Chandrasekharan, M.P., Rajagopalan, R.: An ideal seed non-hierarchical clustering algorithm for group technology. International Journal of Production Research 11, 835–850 (1986)
12. Kumar, C.S., Chandrasekharan, M.P.: Grouping efficacy: a quantities criterion for goodness of block diagonal forms of binary matrices in group technology. International Journal of Production Research 28, 223–243 (1990)
13. Armañanzas, R., Inza, I., Santana, R., et al.: A review of estimation of distribution algorithms in bioinformatics. BioData Mining 1, 1–6 (2008)
14. Pelikan, M., Sastry, K., Cantú-Paz, E.: Scalable optimization via probabilistic modeling: From algorithms to applications. Springer, Heidelberg (2006)
15. Etxeberria, R., Larrañaga, P.: Global optimization using Bayesian networks. In: Rodriguez, A.A.O., Ortiz, M.R.S., Hermida, R.S. (eds.) Second Symposium on Artificial Intelligence (CIMAF 1999) Habana, Cuba. Institute of Cybernetics, Mathematics, and Physics and Ministry of Science, Technology and Environment. pp. 332–339 (1999)
16. Jensen., F.V. (ed.): Introduction to Bayesian Networks. Springer, Secaucus (1996)
17. Henrion, M.: Propagation of uncertainty by probabilistic logic sampling in Bayes' networks. Uncertainty in Artificial Intelligence 2, 149–164 (1988)
18. Lima, C.F., Pelikan, M., Goldberg, D.E., et al.: Influence of selection and replacement strategies on linkage learning in BOA. In: IEEE Congress on Evolutionary Computation CEC 2007, Singapore, pp. 1083–1090 (2007)

Global Exponential Stability of Delayed Neural Networks with Non-lipschitz Neuron Activations and Impulses

Chaojin Fu and Ailong Wu

Department of Mathematics, Hubei Normal University,
Huangshi 435002, China
chaojinfu@126.com, alequ@126.com

Abstract. This paper investigates global convergence for a novel class of delayed neural networks with non-Lipschitz neuron activations and impulses based on the topological degree theory and Lyapunov functional method. Some suffcient conditions are derived to ensure the existence, and global exponential stability of the equilibrium point of neural networks. Finally, a numerical example is given to demonstrate the effectiveness of the obtained result.

Keywords: Neural networks, Global exponential stability, Impulses.

1 Introduction

In the design of neural networks, the model of neural networks is descried by the system of nonlinear ordinary differential equations or the system of nonlinear functional differential equations. In generality, these nonlinear systems possibly show complex dynamic behaviors, such as, periodic oscillatory, bifurcation, chaos, etc. However, in practical applications, especially for solving linear and quadratic programming problems in real time, it requires that networks have good convergent property, such as global asymptotic stability and global exponential stability. Under these good convergent property, the validity can be guaranteed during numeral solving. Due to these, stability analysis for neural networks with or without time delays has received a great of attention (see [1 − 8]). Recently, impulsive neural networks have been extensively studied in both theory and applications (see [5 − 8]). However, in the existing literatures, almost all results on the stability of neural networks are obtained under Lipschitz neuron activations [1 − 7]. When neuron activation functions do not satisfy Lipschitz conditions, people want to know whether the neural networks is stable. In practical engineering applications, people also need to present new neural networks. Therefore, developing a new class of neural networks without Lipschitz neuron activation functions and giving the conditions of the stability of new neural networks are very interesting and valuable.

In this paper, we investigate a general class of delayed neural networks with impulses where the neuron activations are non-Lipschitz functions. To the best

Z. Cai et al. (Eds.): ISICA 2009, LNCS 5821, pp. 92–100, 2009.

of authors' knowledge, this is the first time to study the existence and global exponential stability of equilibrium point for the neural networks developed by us.

For convenience, we give the following notations:

If A is a given $n \times n$ matrix, A' denotes the transpose of A. A^{-1} denotes the inverse of A. For a real symmetric matrix A, $A > 0 (A \geq 0)$ means that A is positive definite (positive semidefinite). Similarly $A < 0 (A \leq 0)$ means that A is negative definite (negative semidefinite). E represents an identity matrix with appropriate dimension. Given the column vectors $x = (x_1, \cdots, x_n)' \in R^n$, the vector norm is the Euclidean, i.e., $\|x\| = (\sum_{i=1}^{n} x_i^2)^{\frac{1}{2}}$.

The rest of this paper is organized as follows. Preliminaries and model description are given in Section 2. In Section 3, we give main results and their proof. An example is given in Section 4 to show the improvement of this paper.

2   Model Description and Preliminaries

In this paper, we consider the following delayed neural networks with impulses:

$$\begin{cases} \dot{x}(t) &= -Dx(t) + Af(x(t)) + A^\tau g(x(t - \tau)) + I, \quad t \neq t_k, \\ \triangle x(t_k) &= J_k(x(t_k)), \quad k = 1, 2, \cdots, \end{cases} \quad (1)$$

where $x(t) = (x_1(t), \cdots, x_n(t))'$ is the vector of neuron states at time t; $D = diag(d_1, \cdots, d_n)$ is an $n \times n$ constant diagonal matrix, where $d_i > 0, i = 1, \cdots, n$, are the neural self-inhibitions; $A = (a_{ij})_{n \times n}$ is an $n \times n$ interconnection matrix; $A^\tau = (a_{ij}^\tau)_{n \times n}$ is an $n \times n$ delayed interconnection matrix; $f(x) = (f_1(x_1), \cdots, f_n(x_n))'$, $g(x) = (g_1(x_1), \cdots, g_n(x_n))'$. Continuous functions f_i and g_i, represent the neuron input-output activation, and f_i are monotonic increasing with $f_i(0) = 0, i = 1, \cdots, n$; $I = (I_1, \cdots, I_n)'$ is a constant vector denoting inputs of neural networks; τ is the delayed parameter; $J_k(x) : R^n \rightarrow R^n$ is a continuous mapping; $\triangle x(t_k) = x(t_k^+) - x(t_k^-), k = 1, 2, \cdots$, are the impulses at moments t_k, and $0 < t_1 < t_2 < \cdots$ is a strictly increasing sequence such that $\lim_{k \to \infty} t_k = +\infty$.

The system (1) is supplemented with the initial values of the type $x(t) = \phi(t), -\tau \leq t \leq 0$ in which $\phi(t) \in C([-\tau, 0]; R^n)$ is a continuous function. $C([-\tau, 0]; R^n)$ is a Banach space of continuous mapping which maps $[-\tau, 0]$ into R^n with a topology of uniform convergence.

Definition 1. A function $x : [-\tau, +\infty] \rightarrow R^n$ is said to be a solution of system (1) with initial conditions $x(t) = \phi(t), t \in [-\tau, 0]$, if the following conditions are satisfied:

(1) $x(t)$ is piecewise continuous with first kind discontinuity at points $t_k, k = 1, 2, \cdots$. Moreover, $x(t)$ is right continuous at each discontinuity points;

(2) $x(t)$ satisfies system (1) for $t \geq 0$, and $x(s) = \phi(s)$ for $s \in [-\tau, 0]$.

Definition 2. An equilibrium point of system (1) is a constant vector $x^* \in R^n$ which satisfies the equation

$$-Dx^* + Af(x^*) + A^\tau g(x^*) + I = 0 \tag{2}$$

and the impulsive jumps $J_k(\cdot)$ are assumed to satisfy $J_k(x^*) = 0$, $k = 1, 2, \cdots$.

Definition 3. The equilibrium point x^* of system (1) is said to be globally exponentially stable, if there exist constants $\beta > 0, T > 0$ and $M_\phi > 0$, such that for any $\phi(t) \in C([-\tau, 0]; R^n), t \geq T, \|x(t, \phi) - x^*\| \leq M_\phi e^{-\beta t}$.

Throughout this paper, we make the following assumptions about activation functions f_i, $i = 1, \cdots, n$,

(H_1) For any $\rho_0 \in R$, then $\lim\limits_{|\rho| \to \infty} \int_{\rho_0}^{\rho} [f_i(\theta) - f_i(\rho_0)] \mathrm{d}\theta = +\infty, i = 1, \cdots, n$;

(H_2) There exist constants $\alpha > 0, q_0 > 0$ and $r_0 > 0$, such that

$$|f_i(x_i)| \geq q_0 |x_i|^\alpha, \forall |x_i| \leq r_0; \quad |f_i(x_i)| \geq q_0 |r_0|^\alpha, \forall |x_i| \geq r_0, i = 1, \cdots, n.$$

It is easy to check that $f_i(\theta) = \arctan\theta$, $f_i(\theta) = \theta^3$, $f_i(\theta) = \theta^3 + \theta$ all satisfy (H_1) and (H_2).

Lemma 1. Let $\varepsilon > 0$, for any $x, y \in R^n$ and matrix A, then $x'Ay \leq \dfrac{1}{2\varepsilon} x'AA'x + \dfrac{\varepsilon}{2} y'y$.

3   Main Results

Theorem 1. Assume that (H_1) and (H_2) hold, for any $x, y \in R^n$, $\|g(x) - g(y)\| \leq \ell \|f(x) - f(y)\|$, $\ell > 0$ is a constant. If there exist a $P = diag(p_1, \cdots, p_n) > 0$ and a constant $\varepsilon > 0$ such that

$$PA + A'P + \frac{1}{\varepsilon}(PA^\tau)(PA^\tau)' + \varepsilon\ell^2 E < 0 \tag{3}$$

then Eq.(2) has a unique solution.

Proof. In order to complete the proof, we divide the proof into two steps.

Step 1. Set $U(x) = Dx - Af(x) - A^\tau g(x) - I$. $x^* \in R^n$ is a solution of Eq.(2) if and only if $U(x^*) = 0$. Rewrite $U(x)$ as follows

$$U(x) = Dx - A\tilde{f}(x) - A^\tau \tilde{g}(x) + U(0),$$

where $\tilde{f}(x) = f(x) - f(0)$, $\tilde{g}(x) = g(x) - g(0)$, and $\tilde{f}(0) = \tilde{g}(0) = 0$. It is easy to see that $\tilde{f}_i$ also satisfy (H_1) and (H_2), $x_i \tilde{f}_i(x_i) \geq 0$, $i = 1, \cdots, n$. Let $\Omega_\Re = \{x \in R^n : \|x\| < \Re\}, \Re > 0$ and

$$H(\lambda, x) = Dx - \lambda\left\{A\tilde{f}(x) + A^\tau \tilde{g}(x)\right\} + \lambda U(0), x \in \overline{\Omega}_\Re, \lambda \in [0, 1],$$

where $\overline{\Omega}_\Re = \{x \in R^n : \|x\| \leq \Re\}$. By Lemma 1 and the assumptions of Theorem 1, we can get

$$
\begin{aligned}
(\tilde{f}(x))'PH(\lambda, x) &= (\tilde{f}(x))'P(Dx + \lambda U(0)) - \lambda\{(\tilde{f}(x))'PA\tilde{f}(x) \\
&\quad + (\tilde{f}(x))'PA^\tau \tilde{g}(x)\} \\
&\geq (\tilde{f}(x))'P(Dx + \lambda U(0)) - \lambda\{(\tilde{f}(x))'\frac{PA + A'P}{2}\tilde{f}(x) \\
&\quad + \frac{1}{2\varepsilon}(\tilde{f}(x))'(PA^\tau)(PA^\tau)'\tilde{f}(x) + \frac{\varepsilon}{2}(\tilde{g}(x))'\tilde{g}(x)\} \\
&\geq (\tilde{f}(x))'P(Dx + \lambda U(0)) - \frac{1}{2}\lambda(\tilde{f}(x))'\{PA + A'P \\
&\quad + \frac{1}{\varepsilon}(PA^\tau)(PA^\tau)' + \varepsilon\ell^2 E\}\tilde{f}(x) \\
&\geq (\tilde{f}(x))'P(Dx + \lambda U(0)) \\
&\geq \sum_{i=1}^n \left[p_i d_i \left| \tilde{f}_i(x_i) \right| |x_i| - \left| \tilde{f}_i(x_i) \right| |(PU(0))_i| \right] \\
&\geq \sum_{i=1}^n p_i d_i \left| \tilde{f}_i(x_i) \right| \left[|x_i| - \frac{|(PU(0))_i|}{p_i d_i} \right]
\end{aligned}
$$

By (H_2), there exist constants $\alpha > 0$, $q_0 > 0$ and $r_0 > 0$, such that

$$\left| \tilde{f}_i(x_i) \right| \geq q_0 |r_0|^\alpha, \forall |x_i| \geq r_0, i = 1, \cdots, n. \tag{4}$$

Let $a = \max\limits_{1 \leq i \leq n} \dfrac{|(PU(0))_i|}{p_i d_i}$, $\mathcal{N}_k = \{n_1, \cdots, n_k\} \subset \{1, \cdots, n\}, \forall k < n$. Define

$$\Omega_{\mathcal{N}_k} = \left\{x : |x_i| \leq a, i \in \mathcal{N}_k, x \in R^k\right\}, \tilde{f}_{\mathcal{N}_k}(x) = \sum_{i \in \mathcal{N}_k} p_i d_i \left| \tilde{f}_i(x_i) \right| \left[|x_i| - a \right].$$

It is obvious that $\Omega_{\mathcal{N}_k}$ is a compact subset of R^k, and $\tilde{g}_{\mathcal{N}_k}$ is continuous on $\Omega_{\mathcal{N}_k}$. Hence, $\tilde{g}_{\mathcal{N}_k}$ can reach its minimum $\min\limits_{x \in \Omega_{\mathcal{N}_k}} \tilde{g}_{\mathcal{N}_k}(x)$ on $\Omega_{\mathcal{N}_k}$.

Let $l = q_0 |r_0|^\alpha \max\limits_{1 \leq i \leq n} \{p_i d_i\}$, $\mathcal{M}_{\mathcal{N}_k} = \min\limits_{x \in \Omega_{\mathcal{N}_k}} \tilde{f}_{\mathcal{N}_k}(x)$, and $\mathcal{M} = \min\{\mathcal{M}_{\mathcal{N}_k} : \mathcal{N}_k \subset i = 1, \cdots, n\}$. Set $\Re > \max\{\sqrt{n}(a - \frac{\mathcal{M}}{l}), \sqrt{n}r_0)\}$ and $x \in \partial\Omega_\Re$, then there exist two index sets $\mathcal{N}$ and $\overline{\mathcal{N}}$ such that

$$|x_i| \leq a, i \in \mathcal{N} \text{ and } |x_i| > a, i \in \overline{\mathcal{N}},$$

where $\mathcal{N} \cup \overline{\mathcal{N}} = \{1, \cdots, n\}$. Furthermore, we can find an index i_0 in $\overline{\mathcal{N}}$ such that

$$|x_{i_0}| \geq \frac{\Re}{\sqrt{n}} \geq \max\{a, r_0\} \tag{5}$$

By (4) and (5), for any $x \in \partial\Omega_\Re$, and $\lambda \in [0, 1]$, we can get

$$(\tilde{f}(x))'PH(\lambda, x) \geq \sum_{i \in \mathscr{N}} p_i d_i \left|\tilde{f}_i(x_i)\right| [|x_i| - a] + \sum_{i \in \mathscr{N}} p_i d_i \left|\tilde{f}_i(x_i)\right| [|x_i| - a]$$

$$\geq p_{i_0} d_{i_0} q_0 |r_0|^\alpha [|x_{i_0}| - a] + \mathscr{M}$$

$$\geq p_{i_0} d_{i_0} q_0 |r_0|^\alpha [|x_{i_0}| - a + \frac{\mathscr{M}}{l}]$$

$$\geq p_{i_0} d_{i_0} q_0 |r_0|^\alpha [\frac{\Re}{\sqrt{n}} - a + \frac{\mathscr{M}}{l}] > 0$$

So we can obtain that for $x \in \partial\Omega_\Re$ and $\lambda \in [0, 1], H(\lambda, x) \neq 0$. Then

$$deg(H(0, x), \Omega_\Re, 0) = deg(H(1, x), \Omega_\Re, 0),$$

i.e., $deg(U(x), \Omega_\Re, 0) = deg(Dx, \Omega_\Re, 0) \neq 0$. So $U(x) = 0$ has at least a solution in $\Omega_\Re$, i.e., Eq.(2) has at least a solution.

Step 2. Assume that x_1^* and x_2^* are two different solutions of Eq.(2), then

$$D(x_1^* - x_2^*) = A(f(x_1^*) - f(x_2^*)) + A^\tau(g(x_1^*) - g(x_2^*)).$$

Then we get

$$0 < (f(x_1^*) - f(x_2^*))PD(x_1^* - x_2^*)$$
$$= (f(x_1^*) - f(x_2^*))PA(f(x_1^*) - f(x_2^*)) + (f(x_1^*) - f(x_2^*))PA^\tau(g(x_1^*) - g(x_2^*))$$
$$\leq (f(x_1^*) - f(x_2^*))\frac{1}{2}[PA + A'P + \frac{1}{\varepsilon}(PA^\tau)(PA^\tau)' + \varepsilon \ell^2 E](f(x_1^*) - f(x_2^*)) < 0$$

This is a contradiction. Hence, $x_1^* = x_2^*$. This completes the proof of Theorem 1.

Theorem 2. Under assumptions of Theorem 1, further if the following conditions are satisfied

$$J_k(x(t_k)) = -\gamma_k(x(t_k) - x^*), k = 1, 2, \cdots,$$

where x^* is the solution of Eq.(2), $\gamma_k = diag(\gamma_{1k}, \cdots, \gamma_{nk}), 0 < \gamma_{ik} < 1, i = 1, \cdots, n, k = 1, 2, \cdots$, then system (1) has a unique equilibrium point which is globally exponentially stable.

By Definition 2 and Theorem 1, under the conditions of Theorem 2, it is obvious that the constant vector $x^* \in R^n$ is the unique equilibrium point of system (1). In the following, we will prove that the unique equilibrium point x^* of system (1) is globally exponentially stable.

Proof. In order to complete the proof, we divide the proof into three steps.

Step 1. Consider the following system:

$$\begin{cases} \dot{x}(t) = -Dx(t) + Af(x(t)) + A^\tau g(x(t - \tau)) + I, & t \in [0, t_1], \\ x(t) = \phi(t), & t \in [-\tau, 0]. \end{cases} \tag{6}$$

By (H_1) and (H_2), g_i is a continuous function, $i = 1, \cdots, n$, $\tilde{U}(x(t)) = -Dx(t) + Af(x(t)) + A^\tau g(x(t - \tau)) + I$ is continuous and local bounded. It is easy to obtain the existence of a solution of system (6) on $[0, t^*(\phi))$, where $t^*(\phi) \in (0, t_1)$ or $t^*(\phi) = t_1$, and $[0, t^*(\phi))$ is the maximal right-side existence interval of the solution of system (6). We denote this solution by $x(t, \phi)$, $x(t, \phi) = (x_1(t, \phi_1), \cdots, x_n(t, \phi_n))'$.

Make a transformation $y(t) = x(t) - x^*$, system (6) is transformed into

$$\dot{y}(t) = -Dy(t) + A\hat{f}(y(t)) + A^\tau \hat{g}(y(t - \tau)), \quad t \in [0, t_1] \tag{7}$$

where $y(t) = (y_1(t), \cdots, y_n(t))'$, $\hat{f}(y) = (\hat{f}_1(y_1), \cdots, \hat{f}_n(y_n))'$, $\hat{g}(y) = (\hat{g}_1(y_1), \cdots, \hat{g}_n(y_n))'$, and $\hat{f}_i(y_i) = f_i(y_i + x_i^*) - f_i(x_i^*)$, $\hat{g}_i(y_i) = g_i(y_i + x_i^*) - g_i(x_i^*)$, $i = 1, \cdots, n$. Hence, $y(t, \phi) = x(t, \phi) - x^*$ is a solution of system (7) with initial values $y(t) = \tilde{\phi}(t), t \in [-\tau, 0]$ on $[0, t^*(\phi))$, where $\tilde{\phi}(t) = \phi(t) - x^*$. By (3), we can choose a constant $\gamma > 0$ satisfying

$$PA + A'P + \frac{1}{\varepsilon}(PA^\tau)(PA^\tau)' + e^{\gamma\tau}\varepsilon\ell^2 E < 0 \tag{8}$$

and $\gamma < \min\{d_i : i = 1, \cdots, n\}$.

Consider the following Lyapunov functional

$$V(t) \equiv V(t, y(t)) = 2e^{\gamma t}\sum_{i=1}^{n} p_i \int_0^{y_i(t)} \hat{f}_i(\theta)d\theta + \varepsilon \int_{t-\tau}^{t} (\hat{g}(y(\theta)))'\hat{g}(y(\theta))e^{\gamma(\theta+\tau)}d\theta \tag{9}$$

where $p_i, i = 1, \cdots, n$, are diagonal entries of P. Calculating the derivative of $V(t)$ along the solution $y(t, \tilde{\phi})$ of system (7) on $[0, t^*(\phi))$, then we can get

$$\dot{V}(t) = 2\gamma e^{\gamma t}\sum_{i=1}^{n} p_i \int_0^{y_i(t,\tilde{\phi})} \hat{f}_i(\theta)d\theta + 2e^{\gamma t}(\hat{f}(y(t, \tilde{\phi})))'P[-Dy(t, \tilde{\phi}) + A\hat{f}(y(t, \tilde{\phi}))$$
$$+ A^\tau \hat{g}(y(t - \tau, \tilde{\phi}))] + \varepsilon e^{\gamma t}[(\hat{g}(y(t, \tilde{\phi})))'\hat{g}(y(t, \tilde{\phi}))e^{\gamma\tau}$$
$$- (\hat{g}(y(t - \tau, \tilde{\phi})))'\hat{g}(y(t - \tau, \tilde{\phi}))]$$
$$\leq 2e^{\gamma t}(\hat{f}(y(t, \tilde{\phi})))'(\gamma P - PD)y(t, \tilde{\phi}) + 2e^{\gamma t}[(\hat{f}(y(t, \tilde{\phi})))'PA\hat{f}(y(t, \tilde{\phi}))$$
$$+ \frac{1}{2\varepsilon}(\hat{f}(y(t, \tilde{\phi})))'(PA^\tau)(PA^\tau)'\hat{f}(y(t, \tilde{\phi})) + \frac{\varepsilon}{2}(\hat{g}(y(t-\tau, \tilde{\phi})))'\hat{g}(y(t-\tau, \tilde{\phi}))]$$
$$+ \varepsilon e^{\gamma t}[(\hat{g}(y(t, \tilde{\phi})))'\hat{g}(y(t, \tilde{\phi}))e^{\gamma\tau} - (\hat{g}(y(t - \tau, \tilde{\phi})))'\hat{g}(y(t - \tau, \tilde{\phi}))]$$
$$\leq 2e^{\gamma t}(\hat{f}(y(t, \tilde{\phi})))'(\gamma P - PD)y(t, \tilde{\phi}) + e^{\gamma t}(\hat{f}(y(t, \tilde{\phi})))'[PA + A'P$$
$$+ \frac{1}{\varepsilon}(PA^\tau)(PA^\tau)' + \varepsilon e^{\gamma\tau}\ell^2 E]\hat{f}(y(t, \tilde{\phi}))$$
$$\leq 0$$

This implies $V(t) \leq V(0), t \in [0, t^*(\phi))$. By (9), we can get

$$2\sum_{i=1}^{n} p_i \int_0^{y_i(t,\tilde{\phi})} \hat{f}_i(\theta)d\theta \leq V(0)e^{-\gamma t} \leq V(0) \tag{10}$$

According to (10) and (H_1), it is easy to derive that $y_i(t, \tilde{\phi}), i = 1, \cdots, n$, are bounded on $[0, t^*(\phi))$. By virtue of the continuous theorem of differential equations, we can conclude that system (7) has a solution on $[0, t_1]$, i.e., system (6) has a solution on $[0, t_1]$. We denote this solution of system (6) by $x^0(t)$.

Step 2. Consider the following system:

$$\begin{cases} \dot{x}(t) = -Dx(t) + Af(x(t)) + A^\tau g(x(t - \tau)) + I, & t \in [t_1, t_2], \\ x(t_1) = x^0(t_1) + J_1(x^0(t_1)). \end{cases} \tag{11}$$

Arguing as in step 1, system (11) has a solution $x^1(t)$ on $[t_1, t_2]$. As inductive step, we can derive that the following system:

$$\begin{cases} \dot{x}(t) = -Dx(t) + Af(x(t)) + A^\tau g(x(t - \tau)) + I, & t \in [t_m, t_{m+1}], \\ x(t_m) = x^{m-1}(t_m) + J_m(x^{m-1}(t_m)), \end{cases}$$

also has a solution $x^m(t)$ on $[t_m, t_{m+1}], m = 2, 3, \cdots$.
Define

$$x(t, \phi) = \begin{cases} x^0(t), t \in [0, t_1], \\ x^1(t), t \in (t_1, t_2], \\ \cdots, \\ x^m(t), t \in (t_m, t_{m+1}], \\ \cdots \end{cases}$$

then $x(t, \phi)$ is the solution of system (1) with initial values $x(s) = \phi(s)$. This completes the proof of the existence of solutions of system (1).

Step 3. Assume that $x(t)$ is a solution of system (1), and x^* is the unique equilibrium point of system (1). Make a transformation $y(t) = x(t) - x^*$, then system (1) is transformed into the following system:

$$\begin{cases} \dot{y}(t) = -Dy(t) + A\hat{f}(y(t)) + A^\tau \hat{g}(y(t - \tau)), & t \neq t_k, \\ \triangle y(t_k) = J_k(y(t_k)) = -\gamma_k y(t_k), & k = 1, 2, \cdots. \end{cases} \tag{12}$$

Consider Lyapunov functional $V(t)$, the $V(t)$ is the same as (9). Calculating the derivative of $V(t)$ along the solution $y(t)$ of system (12) for any $t, t \neq t_k, k = 1, 2, \cdots$. Arguing as in step 1, we have $\dot{V}(t) \leq 0, t \neq t_k, k = 1, 2, \cdots$. Also,

$$V(t_k + 0) = 2e^{\gamma(t_k + 0)} \sum_{i=1}^n p_i \int_0^{y_i(t_k + 0)} \hat{f}_i(\theta) d\theta$$

$$+ \varepsilon \int_{(t_k + 0) - \tau}^{(t_k + 0)} (\hat{g}(y(\theta)))' \hat{g}(y(\theta)) e^{\gamma(\theta + \tau)} d\theta$$

$$= V(t_k) + 2e^{\gamma t_k} \sum_{i=1}^n p_i \int_{y_i(t_k)}^{(1 - \gamma_{ik}) y_i(t_k)} \hat{f}_i(\theta) d\theta$$

$$\leq V(t_k), \quad k = 1, 2, \cdots.$$

It follows that $V(t) \leq V(0)$ for $t > 0$, i.e.,

$$2 \sum_{i=1}^n p_i \int_0^{y_i(t, \tilde{\phi})} \hat{f}_i(\theta) d\theta \leq V(0) e^{-\gamma t} \leq V(0) \tag{13}$$

By (H_1), from (13) we can get $\lim\limits_{t \to +\infty} y_i(t, \tilde{\phi}) = 0, i = 1, \cdots, n$. Hence, there exists a constant $T > 0$, such that $y_i(t, \tilde{\phi}) \in [-r_0, r_0], i = 1, \cdots, n, \forall t > T$. Let $p = \min\{p_i, i = 1, \cdots, n\}$. By (H_2), we can get

$$\sum_{i=1}^{n} p_i \int_0^{y_i(t,\tilde{\phi})} \hat{f}_i(\theta) d\theta \geq \sum_{i=1}^{n} p_i \int_0^{|y_i(t,\tilde{\phi})|} q_0 |\theta|^\alpha d\theta$$

$$\geq \frac{pq_0}{\alpha+1} \left\{ \max_{1 \leq i \leq n} \left| y_i(t, \tilde{\phi}) \right| \right\}^{\alpha+1}, \quad t \geq T,$$

i.e.,

$$\max_{1 \leq i \leq n} \left| y_i(t, \tilde{\phi}) \right| \leq \left[\frac{\alpha+1}{2pq_0} V(0) \right]^{\frac{1}{\alpha+1}} e^{-\frac{\gamma}{\alpha+1}t}, \quad t \geq T,$$

$$\| x(t, \phi) - x^* \| \leq \sqrt{n} \left[\frac{\alpha+1}{2pq_0} V(0) \right]^{\frac{1}{\alpha+1}} e^{-\frac{\gamma}{\alpha+1}t}, \quad t \geq T.$$

This means the equilibrium point x^* of system (1) is globally exponentially stable. This proof is completed.

The system (1) includes as a special case neural network, which is obtained by choosing $f(x) = g(x)$ in (1), i.e.,

$$\begin{cases} \dot{x}(t) = -Dx(t) + Af(x(t)) + A^\tau f(x(t-\tau)) + I, & t \neq t_k, \\ \Delta x(t_k) = J_k(x(t_k)), & k = 1, 2, \cdots, \end{cases} \tag{14}$$

Corollary 1. Assume that (H_1) and (H_2) hold, if:
(1)There exist a $P = diag(p_1, \cdots, p_n) > 0$ and a constant $\varepsilon > 0$ such that $PA + A'P + \frac{1}{\varepsilon}(PA^\tau)(PA^\tau)' + \varepsilon E < 0$;
(2) $J_k(x(t_k)) = -\gamma_k(x(t_k) - x^*), k = 1, 2, \cdots$, where x^* is the equilibrium point of system (14), $\gamma_k = diag(\gamma_{1k}, \cdots, \gamma_{nk})$, $0 < \gamma_{ik} < 1, i = 1, \cdots, n, k = 1, 2, \cdots$. then system (14) is globally exponentially stable.

When $A^\tau = 0$, the system (1) changes into the following system:

$$\begin{cases} \dot{x}(t) = -Dx(t) + Af(x(t)) + I, & t \neq t_k, \\ \Delta x(t_k) = J_k(x(t_k)), & k = 1, 2, \cdots, \end{cases} \tag{15}$$

Corollary 2. Assume that (H_1) and (H_2) hold, if:
(1)There exists a $P = diag(p_1, \cdots, p_n) > 0$ such that $PA + A'P < 0$;
(2) $J_k(x(t_k)) = -\gamma_k(x(t_k) - x^*), k = 1, 2, \cdots$, where x^* is the equilibrium point of system (15), $\gamma_k = diag(\gamma_{1k}, \cdots, \gamma_{nk})$, $0 < \gamma_{ik} < 1, i = 1, \cdots, n, k = 1, 2, \cdots$. then system (15) is globally exponentially stable.

4 Illustrative Example

Consider the second-order neural network (1) descried by $f_1(\theta) = f_2(\theta) = \theta^3$, $g_1(\theta) = g_2(\theta) = \sin(\theta^3)$, $\tau = 1$, $D = diag(1, 1)$, $I = (0, 0)'$, $A = \begin{pmatrix} -2 & 5 \\ -1 & -2 \end{pmatrix}$,

$A^\tau = diag(1, 0.5)$, $\gamma_k = diag(0.2, 0.3)$, $t_k = kT$, T is any given positive number, $k = 1, 2, \cdots$.

Obviously, those results in [5-8] would fail when applying to this example. However, we can see that $\|g(x) - g(y)\| \leq \|f(x) - f(y)\|$, and $(0, 0)'$ is the unique equilibrium point. Choose $\varepsilon = 1$, $P = diag(1, 5)$, by Theorem 2, we see that the neural network in above example has a unique equilibrium point which is globally exponentially stable.

Acknowledgements. The work is supported by Key Science Foundation of Educational Department of Hubei Province under Grant D20082201 and Innovation Teams of Hubei Normal University.

References

1. Zhou, L., Hu, G.: Global Exponential Periodicity and Stability of Cellular Neural Networks with Variable and Distributed Delays. Applied Mathematics and Computation 195, 402–411 (2008)
2. Li, T., Fei, S.: Stability Analysis of Cohen-Grossberg Neural Networks with Time-Varying and Distributed Delays. Neurocomputing 71, 1069–1081 (2008)
3. Zhang, Q., Wei, X., Xu, J.: Delay-Dependent Exponential Stability Criteria for Non-Autonomous Cellular Neural Networks with Time-Varying Delays. Chaos, Solitons and Fractals 36, 985–990 (2008)
4. Zhao, W.: Dynamics of Cohen-Grossberg Neural Network with Variable Coefficients and Time-Varying Delays. Nonlinear Analysis: Real World Applications 9, 1024–1037 (2008)
5. Xiong, W., Zhou, Q., Xiao, B., Yu, Y.: Global Exponential Stability of Cellular Neural Networks with Mixed Delays and Impulses. Chaos, Solitons and Fractals 34, 896–902 (2007)
6. Huang, Z., Yang, Q., Luo, X.: Exponential Stability of Impulsive Neural Networks with Time-Varying Delays. Chaos, Solitons and Fractals 35, 770–780 (2008)
7. Long, S., Xu, D.: Delay-Dependent Stability Analysis for Impulsive Neural Networks with Time-Varying Delays. Neurocomputing 71, 1705–1713 (2008)
8. Wu, H., Xue, X.: Stability Analysis for Neural Networks with Inverse Lipschitzian Neuron Activations and Impulses. Applied Mathematical Modelling 32, 2347–2359 (2008)

Modeling and Verification of Zhang Neural Networks for Online Solution of Time-Varying Quadratic Minimization and Programming

Yunong Zhang[1,*], Xuezhong Li[2], and Zhan Li[1]

[1] School of Information Science and Technology
Tel.: +86-20-84113597; Fax: +86-20-84113597
[2] School of Software
Sun Yat-Sen University (SYSU), Guangzhou 510275, China
zhynong@mail.sysu.edu.cn, lixzh@mail2.sysu.edu.cn

Abstract. In this paper, by following Zhang *et al*'s neural-dynamic method proposed formally since March 2001, two recurrent neural networks are generalized to solve online the time-varying convex quadratic-minimization and quadratic-programming (QP) problems, of which the latter is subject to a time-varying linear-equality constraint as an example. In comparison with conventional gradient-based neural networks or gradient neural networks (GNN), the resultant Zhang neural networks (ZNN) can be unified as a superior approach for solving online the time-varying quadratic problems. For the purpose of time-varying quadratic-problems solving, this paper investigates comparatively both ZNN and GNN solvers, and then their unified modeling techniques. The modeling results substantiate well the efficacy of such ZNN models on solving online the time-varying convex QP problems.

Keywords: time-varying, quadratic program, gradient neural networks, recurrent neural networks (RNN), Zhang neural networks.

1 Introduction

The online solution of (equality-constrained) quadratic programs (including the quadratic-minimization problems solving as its special case) is widely encountered in various areas; e.g., optimal controller design [1], power-scheduling [2], robot-arm motion planning [3], and digital signal processing [4]. A well-accepted approach to solving linear-equality constrained quadratic-programs is the numerical algorithms/methods performed on digital computers (e.g., nowadays computers). However, the minimal arithmetic operations of a numerical QP algorithm are proportional to the cube of the related Hessian matrix's dimension, and consequently such a numerical algorithm may not be efficient enough [4].

In the past decades, many neural-dynamic models have been proposed, developed and implemented on specific architectures, e.g., analog RNN solvers

---

* Corresponding author.

Z. Cai et al. (Eds.): ISICA 2009, LNCS 5821, pp. 101–110, 2009.

[5,6,7]. The neural-dynamic approach is now regarded as a powerful alternative to real-time computation and optimization in view of its parallel-processing distributed nature, self-adaptation ability, and hardware-implementation convenience. A large number of neural-dynamic models aforementioned, however, belong to the well-known gradient (or termed, gradient-descent, negative-gradient) method, being feasible and efficient intrinsically for static (or termed, constant, time-invariant) problems solving (e.g., static quadratic-minimization and QP).

Different from conventional design methods of numerical algorithms and gradient neural networks [3,4,5,6,7], in this paper, Zhang neural networks (ZNN), together with their modeling techniques and results, are presented for online solution of time-varying convex quadratic-minimization and quadratic-programs subject to time-varying linear-equality constraints. Theoretical and modeling results both demonstrate the ZNN superiority on "moving"-problems solving.

2   Time-Varying Quadratic Minimization

Let us consider the time-varying quadratic-minimization (QM) problem below:

$$\text{minimize} \quad f(x) = x^T(t)P(t)x(t)/2 + q^T(t)x(t) \in R, \tag{1}$$

where the given Hessian matrix $P(t) \in R^{n \times n}$ is smoothly time-varying and positive-definite for any time instant $t \in [0, +\infty)$, and the given coefficient vector $q(t) \in R^n$ is smoothly time-varying as well. In QM (1), the unknown vector $x(t) \in R^n$ is to be solved all over the time interval $[0, +\infty)$ (or $[t_0, t_f]$ of interest), so as to make the value of $f(x)$ always smallest for any time instant $t \in [0, +\infty)$.

For solving such a time-varying quadratic-minimization problem, we can follow Zhang et al's method [8,9,10]. By utilizing the ZNN-design formula [10,11], the following implicit dynamic equation as of Zhang neural network can readily be used for minimizing online the time-varying quadratic function (1) [11]:

$$P(t)\dot{x}(t) = -\dot{P}(t)x(t) - \gamma \mathcal{F}\big(P(t)x(t) + q(t)\big) - \dot{q}(t), \tag{2}$$

where $x(t) \in R^n$, starting from any initial condition $x(0) \in R^n$, denotes the neural-state vector corresponding to the theoretical time-varying minimum solution $x^*(t) \in R^n$ of time-varying quadratic function (1). The block diagram of ZNN (2) can be seen from Fig. 1 (by ignoring the dotted-rectangle parts and deleting the tildes "~" above the symbols). In addition, from ZNN (2), design parameter $\gamma > 0$ should be set as large as the hardware permits or be selected appropriately for simulation and modeling purposes. Here, as usual, $\mathcal{F}(\cdot) : R^n \to R^n$ denotes an activation-function array used in constructing the neural networks, of which each scalar-valued activation-function $f(\cdot)$ should be odd and monotonically-increasing. The following two types of $f(\cdot)$ are investigated in this paper: 1) linear activation-function $f(e_i) = e_i$, and 2) power-sigmoid activation-function (with error-input $e_i := [Px + q]_i$) [3,8,9,10,11]

$$f(e_i) = \begin{cases} e_i^\rho, & \text{if } |e_i| \geqslant 1; \\ \dfrac{1+\exp(-\xi)}{1-\exp(-\xi)} \cdot \dfrac{1-\exp(-\xi e_i)}{1+\exp(-\xi e_i)}, & \text{otherwise.} \end{cases} \tag{3}$$

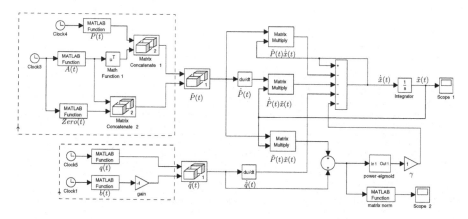

Fig. 1. A unified overall model of ZNN (2) and (11) for time-varying QP solving

Moreover, it is worth pointing out the following linear ZNN model, which is simplified from (2), also for time-varying quadratic-minimization purposes:

$$P(t)\dot{x}(t) = -\big(\dot{P}(t) + \gamma P(t)\big)x(t) - \big(\gamma q(t) + \dot{q}(t)\big). \tag{4}$$

For comparison with GNN models, we can present below the gradient-based solver applied to online minimization of time-varying quadratic function (1):

$$\dot{x}(t) = -\gamma P^T(t)\mathcal{F}\big(P(t)x(t) + q(t)\big), \tag{5}$$

of which the block diagram can be seen readily from Fig. 2 (by ignoring the dotted-rectangle parts and deleting the tildes "∼" above the symbols). In addition, computer-simulation results in [11] have shown and substantiated well the superiority of ZNN model (2) for online solution of time-varying quadratic minimization problem (1) [as compared to GNN model (5)].

3   Time-Varying Quadratic Program

Facing the efficacy of ZNN (2) on time-varying quadratic minimization, as a further investigation, we consider the following time-varying quadratic-program [subject to a time-varying linear-equality-constraint, $A(t)x(t) = b(t)$]:

$$\text{minimize} \quad x^T(t)P(t)x(t)/2 + q^T(t)x(t), \tag{6}$$
$$\text{subject to} \quad A(t)x(t) = b(t), \tag{7}$$

where time-varying decision-vector $x(t) \in R^n$ is unknown and to be solved at any time instant $t \in [0, +\infty)$. In addition to the coefficients' description in Section 2, the smoothly time-varying coefficient matrix $A(t) \in R^{m \times n}$ in equality constraint (7) is assumed to be of full row rank. Likewise, without loss of generality, the coefficient matrices and vectors, together with their time derivatives, are assumed to be known or at least can be estimated accurately.

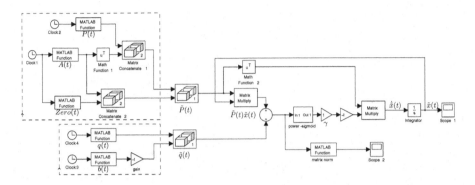

Fig. 2. A unified overall model of GNN (5) and (13) applied to time-varying QP solving

Based on the knowledge on static QP problems solving [12,13], we can similarly transform the time-varying QP problem (6)-(7) into the following time-varying linear matrix-vector equation {to be solved in real time $t \in [0, +\infty)$}:

$$\tilde{P}(t)\tilde{x}(t) = -\tilde{q}(t), \tag{8}$$

where the augmented coefficient matrix $\tilde{P}(t)$ and vector $\tilde{q}(t)$ are defined below:

$$\tilde{P}(t) := \begin{bmatrix} P(t) & A^T(t) \\ A(t) & \mathbf{0}_{m \times m} \end{bmatrix} \in R^{(n+m) \times (n+m)}, \quad \tilde{q}(t) := \begin{bmatrix} q(t) \\ -b(t) \end{bmatrix} \in R^{n+m},$$

in addition to defining the augmented vector $\tilde{x}(t) = [x^T(t), \lambda^T(t)]^T \in R^{n+m}$.

To monitor the solution process of time-varying quadratic program (7) via time-varying linear equation (8) [i.e., to solve for $\tilde{x}(t)$], we can firstly define the following vector-valued indefinite error-function {instead of conventional scalar-valued lower-bounded (or nonnegative) energy-functions usually employed in gradient-based or Hopfield-type neural-network approaches [3,5,6,7,10]}:

$$\tilde{e}(t) := \tilde{P}(t)\tilde{x}(t) + \tilde{q}(t) \in R^{n+m}, \tag{9}$$

of which each element can be positive, negative, or even not lower-bounded. Then, to make each element of the error vector $\tilde{e}(t) \in R^{n+m}$ convergent to zero, the following ZNN design formula can be adopted again [8,9,10,11,14]:

$$\frac{d\tilde{e}(t)}{dt} = -\gamma \mathcal{F}\big(\tilde{e}(t)\big). \tag{10}$$

Expanding the above ZNN design formula (10) leads to the following specific ZNN model depicted in an implicit dynamic equation, which solves online the augmented time-varying linear matrix-vector equation (8) as well as the time-varying equality-constrained quadratic-program (6)-(7):

$$\tilde{P}(t)\dot{\tilde{x}}(t) = -\dot{\tilde{P}}(t)\tilde{x}(t) - \gamma \mathcal{F}\left(\tilde{P}(t)\tilde{x}(t) + \tilde{q}(t)\right) - \dot{\tilde{q}}(t), \tag{11}$$

or written in a more complete form as below:

$$\begin{bmatrix} P(t) & A^T(t) \\ A(t) & 0 \end{bmatrix} \begin{bmatrix} \dot{x}(t) \\ \dot{\lambda}(t) \end{bmatrix} = - \begin{bmatrix} \dot{P}(t) & \dot{A}^T(t) \\ \dot{A}(t) & 0 \end{bmatrix} \begin{bmatrix} x(t) \\ \lambda(t) \end{bmatrix}$$

$$- \gamma \mathcal{F} \left(\begin{bmatrix} P(t)x(t) + A^T(t)\lambda(t) + q(t) \\ A(t)x(t) - b(t) \end{bmatrix} \right) - \begin{bmatrix} \dot{q}(t) \\ -\dot{b}(t) \end{bmatrix},$$

where state vector $\tilde{x}(t) \in R^{n+m}$, staring from an initial condition $\tilde{x}(0) \in R^{n+m}$, corresponds to the theoretical time-varying solution of augmented linear equation (8), of which the first n elements [i.e., $\tilde{x}_1(t), \tilde{x}_2(t), \cdots, \tilde{x}_n(t)$] constitute the neural-network solution/output corresponding to the optimal solution of time-varying quadratic program (6)-(7). The block diagram of ZNN model (11) is shown in Fig. 1, which is based on Simulink (see [14,15] and references therein). In addition, it is worth writing out the following linear ZNN model [simplified from ZNN (11)] for the online solution of time-varying quadratic program (6)-(7):

$$\tilde{P}(t)\dot{\tilde{x}}(t) = - \left(\dot{\tilde{P}}(t) + \gamma \tilde{P}(t) \right) \tilde{x}(t) - \left(\gamma \tilde{q}(t) + \dot{\tilde{q}}(t) \right), \tag{12}$$

or writing out in a more complete form as below:

$$\begin{bmatrix} P(t) & A^T(t) \\ A(t) & 0 \end{bmatrix} \begin{bmatrix} \dot{x}(t) \\ \dot{\lambda}(t) \end{bmatrix} = - \left(\begin{bmatrix} \dot{P}(t) + \gamma P(t) & \dot{A}^T(t) + \gamma A^T(t) \\ \dot{A}(t) + \gamma A(t) & 0 \end{bmatrix} \right) \begin{bmatrix} x(t) \\ \lambda(t) \end{bmatrix}$$

$$- \begin{bmatrix} \gamma q(t) + \dot{q}(t) \\ -\gamma b(t) - \dot{b}(t) \end{bmatrix}.$$

Moreover, we have the following theoretical results on global exponential and/or superior convergence of ZNN (11) and (12) [and, similarly, ZNN (2) and (4)] with proof omitted due to space limitation.

Theorem 1. Consider smoothly time-varying strictly-convex quadratic program (6)-(7). If a monotonically-increasing odd activation-function array $\mathcal{F}(\cdot)$ is used, then the state vector $\tilde{x}(t)$ of ZNN (11), starting from any initial state $\tilde{x}(0) \in R^{n+m}$, globally converges to the unique theoretical solution $\tilde{x}^*(t) := [x^{*T}(t), \lambda^{*T}(t)]^T$ of time-varying linear matrix-vector equation (8). In addition, the first n elements of theoretical solution $\tilde{x}^*(t)$ constitute the time-varying optimal solution $x^*(t)$ to the time-varying quadratic program (6)-(7) of interest.

Theorem 2. In addition to Theorem 1, if linear activation function $f(\tilde{e}_i) = \tilde{e}_i$ is used, then the state vector $\tilde{x}(t)$ of ZNN (11) [i.e., (12)] globally exponentially converges to the unique theoretical solution $\tilde{x}^*(t)$ of time-varying linear matrix-vector equation (8), with the first n elements of $\tilde{x}^*(t)$ constituting $x^*(t)$ as the time-varying optimal solution to time-varying quadratic program (6)-(7).

Theorem 3. In addition to Theorems 1 and 2, if the power-sigmoid activation function (3) is used with suitable design parameters $\xi \geqslant 2$ and $\rho \geqslant 3$ (being an integer), then the state vector $\tilde{x}(t)$ of ZNN model (11) globally and superiorly converges to theoretical solution $\tilde{x}^*(t)$, of which the $x^*(t)$ part is the optimal solution to time-varying quadratic program (6)-(7), as compared to the situation of using linear activation functions [i.e., ZNN (12)] presented in Theorem 2.

For comparison with GNN models, we can develop the following gradient-based neural network applied to solving online the time-varying problem (6)-(7):

$$\dot{\tilde{x}}(t) = -\gamma \tilde{P}^T(t)\mathcal{F}\left(\tilde{P}(t)\tilde{x}(t) + \tilde{q}(t)\right),\tag{13}$$

with its block-diagram in Fig. 2. In addition, the gradient-based neural network (13) can also be written in the following more-complete form:

$$\begin{bmatrix}\dot{x}(t)\\\dot{\lambda}(t)\end{bmatrix} = -\gamma\begin{bmatrix}P(t)\ A^T(t)\\A(t)\ \ 0\end{bmatrix}\mathcal{F}\left(\begin{bmatrix}P(t)x(t) + A^T(t)\lambda(t) + q(t)\\A(t)x(t) - b(t)\end{bmatrix}\right).$$

Furthermore, comparing ZNN model (11) and GNN model (13), we can draw the following remarks (also for the completeness of this research and paper).

1) ZNN model (11) is designed based on the elimination of every element of vector-valued indefinite error-function $\tilde{e}(t) = \tilde{P}(t)\tilde{x}(t) + \tilde{q}(t)$. In contrast, GNN model (13) is designed based on the elimination of scalar-valued norm-based nonnegative energy function $\|\tilde{P}\tilde{x} + \tilde{q}\|_2^2$. Generally speaking, the GNN design method can only be used for handling static problems with constant coefficients.

2) ZNN model (11) is depicted in an implicit dynamics, i.e., $\tilde{P}(t)\dot{\tilde{x}}(t) = \cdots$, which coincides well with the systems in nature and in engineering (e.g., the analogue electronic circuits and mechanical systems owing to Kirchhoff's and Newton's laws, respectively [8,10,14,15]). In contrast, GNN model (13) is depicted in an explicit dynamics, i.e., $\dot{\tilde{x}}(t) = \cdots$, which is usually associated with conventional gradient-based and/or Hopfield-type models. Comparing the implicit and explicit dynamics, we can see that ZNN model (11) appears to have higher capacities in representing dynamic systems, as it can even preserve physical parameters in the coefficient matrix on the left-hand side of the system equation, i.e., the so-called mass matrix $\tilde{P}(t)$ on the left-hand side of (11) [9,15].

3) ZNN model (11) can systematically and methodologically exploit the time-derivative information of coefficient matrices and vectors [namely, $\dot{P}(t)$, $\dot{A}(t)$, $\dot{q}(t)$ and $\dot{b}(t)$] during its real-time solving process (which may thus belong to the predictive approach) [8,9,10,11,14]. In contrast, GNN model (13) has not exploited such important time-derivative information [3,5,6,7], which may comparatively belong to the passively-tracking approach and is thus less effective on solving the time-varying quadratic-optimization problems.

4   Modeling Techniques and Illustrative Example

To simulate and/or model the above-presented ZNN and GNN solvers, the following MATLAB Simulink modeling techniques (see [14,15] and references therein) are investigated in this section to show the RNN-solution characteristics. A Simulink model is a representation of the design and/or implementation of a dynamic system satisfying a set of requirements. The modeling techniques are related to those basic function-blocks and their parameters' setting. By interconnecting the basic function-blocks with appropriate parameters, the diagrams of ZNN (11) and GNN (13) can be built up, as shown in Figs. 1 and 2, which are exploited to solve online the time-varying quadratic program (6)-(7).

With the overall ZNN and GNN models built up and depicted in Figs. 1 and 2, prior to running them, we may have to change some of the default simulation options by opening the "Configuration Parameters" dialog box and setting

- Solver: "ode45 (Dormand-Prince)";
- Absolute tolerance: "1e-6 (i.e., 10^{-6})";
- Relative tolerance: "1e-6 (i.e., 10^{-6})";
- Algebraic loop: "none".

Then, for illustration and comparison purposes, ZNN (11) and GNN (13), activated by the power-sigmoid activation function with design parameters $\rho = 3$ and $\xi = 4$, could both be modeled and employed to solve online such a time-varying quadratic-programming problem depicted in (6)-(7).

More specifically, let us consider the time-varying quadratic-program (6)-(7) with the following coefficient matrices and vectors (as an example):

$$P(t) = \begin{bmatrix} 0.5\sin t + 2 & \cos t \\ \cos t & 0.5\cos t + 2 \end{bmatrix}, \; q(t) = \begin{bmatrix} \sin 6t \\ \cos 6t \end{bmatrix},$$

$$A(t) = [\sin 4t, \cos 4t], \; b(t) = \cos 2t.$$

It follows from equation (8), ZNN (11) and GNN (13) that

$$\tilde{P}(t) = \begin{bmatrix} 0.5\sin t + 2 & \cos t & \sin 4t \\ \cos t & 0.5\cos t + 2 & \cos 4t \\ \sin 4t & \cos 4t & 0 \end{bmatrix},$$

$$\tilde{q}(t) = \begin{bmatrix} \sin 6t, \cos 6t, -\cos 2t \end{bmatrix}^T.$$

ZNN (11) is thus formulated in the following specific form [so will be GNN (13)]:

$$\begin{bmatrix} 0.5\sin t + 2 & \cos t & \sin 4t \\ \cos t & 0.5\cos t + 2 & \cos 4t \\ \sin 4t & \cos 4t & 0 \end{bmatrix} \begin{bmatrix} \dot{x}_1(t) \\ \dot{x}_2(t) \\ \dot{\lambda}(t) \end{bmatrix}$$

$$= - \begin{bmatrix} 0.5\cos t & -\sin t & 4\cos 4t \\ -\sin t & -0.5\sin t & -4\sin 4t \\ 4\cos 4t & -4\sin 4t & 0 \end{bmatrix} \begin{bmatrix} x_1(t) \\ x_2(t) \\ \lambda(t) \end{bmatrix} - \begin{bmatrix} 6\cos 6t \\ -6\sin 6t \\ 2\sin 2t \end{bmatrix}$$

$$- \mathcal{F}\left(\begin{bmatrix} 0.5\sin t + 2 & \cos t & \sin 4t \\ \cos t & 0.5\cos t + 2 & \cos 4t \\ \sin 4t & \cos 4t & 0 \end{bmatrix} \begin{bmatrix} x_1(t) \\ x_2(t) \\ \lambda(t) \end{bmatrix} + \begin{bmatrix} \sin 6t \\ \cos 6t \\ -\cos 2t \end{bmatrix} \right).$$

Then we could have the specific ZNN and GNN models built up and depicted in Figs. 1 and 2, respectively. After running them, we can obtain their online solutions as shown in Fig. 3(a) and (b): evidently, the ZNN and GNN solution-curves are quite different. In addition, as seen from Fig. 4(a), by using ZNN model (11) to solve the time-varying quadratic program (6)-(7), its residual error $\|\tilde{P}(t)\tilde{x}(t) + \tilde{q}(t)\|_2$ decreases to zero fast. For comparison, as seen from

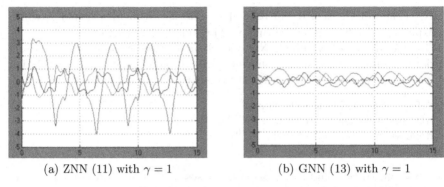

(a) ZNN (11) with $\gamma = 1$ (b) GNN (13) with $\gamma = 1$

Fig. 3. Output $\tilde{x}(t)$ of Scope 1 exploited in ZNN and GNN modeling

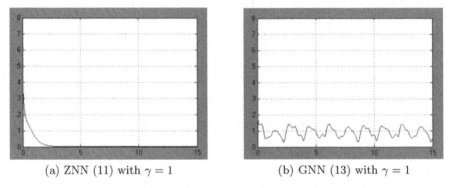

(a) ZNN (11) with $\gamma = 1$ (b) GNN (13) with $\gamma = 1$

Fig. 4. Output $\|\tilde{P}(t)\tilde{x}(t) + \tilde{q}(t)\|_2$ of Scope 2 exploited in ZNN and GNN modeling

Fig. 4(b), by using GNN model (13) to solve the time-varying quadratic program (6)-(7), under the same modeling conditions, its residual error $\|\tilde{P}(t)\tilde{x}(t) + \tilde{q}(t)\|_2$ is however much larger (than the ZNN one) and is also with very clear fluctuations. Furthermore, corresponding to the above RNN-solution process, we could also show the value of time-varying equality-constraint satisfaction [i.e., the value of $A(t)x(t) - b(t)$] for QP (6)-(7). The results are in Fig. 5, where the rapid convergence of $A(t)x(t) - b(t)$ to zero [or to say, the satisfaction of time-varying equality-constraint $A(t)x(t) = b(t)$] has been achieved well by ZNN model (11). In contrast, as seen especially from Fig. 5(b), by using GNN model (13) to solve the time-varying quadratic program (6)-(7), the time-varying equality-constraint $A(t)x(t) = b(t)$ can not be satisfied accurately in view of the observation that the steady-state scalar-value of $A(t)x(t) - b(t)$ is not zero but fluctuating around.

In summary, from the modeling and verification results, we can say that, about the online solution of time-varying QP problems, the resultant ZNN models could perform much better than gradient-based models. This may further imply that the ZNN method and models might be a powerful alternative to the relevant time-varying optimization problems solving.

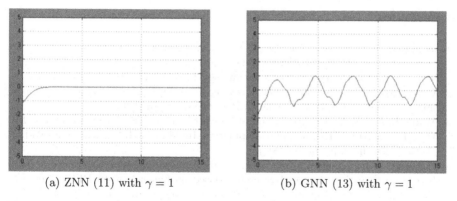

(a) ZNN (11) with $\gamma = 1$ (b) GNN (13) with $\gamma = 1$

Fig. 5. RNN-synthesized scalar-values of equality-constraint satisfaction $A(t)x(t) - b(t)$

5   Conclusions

By following Zhang *et al*'s design method, a kind of recurrent neural networks (i.e., Zhang neural networks) has been proposed, unified and modeled for solving online the time-varying convex quadratic-minimization and quadratic-program problems (of which the latter is subject to a time-varying linear matrix-vector equality-constraint). Instead of writing simulation-codes, we could build up the neural-network models readily and rapidly by employing, creating and connecting the modeling blocks. An illustrative example has demonstrated the feasibility and efficacy of Zhang *et al*'s neural-dynamic design-method and solvers for handling time-varying problems. Compared to conventional gradient-based solvers, superior performance can be achieved by the ZNN models for time-varying problems solving, especially using the power-sigmoid activation-function array.

Acknowledgments. This work is supported by the Program for New Century Excellent Talents in University (NCET-07-0887). Before joining SYSU in 2006, Yunong Zhang had been with National University of Ireland at Maynooth, University of Strathclyde, National University of Singapore, Chinese University of Hong Kong, South China University of Technology, and Huazhong University of Science and Technology, since 1992. Yunong had been supported by those research fellowships, assistantship and studentships, which had been related to this research explicitly or implicitly. His web-page is now available at http://www.ee.sysu.edu.cn/teacher/detail.asp?sn=129. In addition, Yunong would like to thank the student-coauthors for their important contribution (e.g., graphical modeling and illustrations) to this work by sharing the following thoughts: "An educational principle which I inherit and believe in is that the better the students are, the better the teacher is".

References

1. Johansen, T.A., Fossen, T.I., Berge, S.P.: Constrained Nonlinear Control Allocation with Singularity Avoidance Using Sequential Quadratic Programming. IEEE Transactions on Control Systems Technology 12, 211–216 (2004)
2. Grudinin, N.: Reactive Power Optimization Using Successive Quadratic Programming Method. IEEE Transactions on Power Systems 13, 1219–1225 (1998)
3. Wang, J., Zhang, Y.: Recurrent Neural Networks for Real-Time Computation of Inverse Kinematics of Redundant Manipulators. In: Machine Intelligence Quo Vadis? World Scientific, Singapore (2004)
4. Leithead, W.E., Zhang, Y.: $O(N^2)$-Operation Approximation of Covariance Matrix Inverse in Gaussian Process Regression Based on Quasi-Newton BFGS Method. Communications in Statistics – Simulation and Computation 36, 367–380 (2007)
5. Tank, D.W., Hopfield, J.J.: Simple "Neural" Optimization Networks: An A/D Converter, Signal Decision Circuit, and a Linear Programming Circuit. IEEE Transactions on Circuits and Systems 33, 533–541 (1986)
6. Costantini, G., Perfetti, R., Todisco, M.: Quasi-Lagrangian Neural Network for Convex Quadratic Optimization. IEEE Transactions on Neural Networks 19, 1804–1809 (2008)
7. Zhang, Y.: Revisit the Analog Computer and Gradient-Based Neural System for Matrix Inversion. In: Proceedings of IEEE International Symposium on Intelligent Control, pp. 1411–1416. IEEE Press, Limassol (2005)
8. Zhang, Y., Jiang, D., Wang, J.: A Recurrent Neural Network for Solving Sylvester Equation with Time-Varying Coefficients. IEEE Transactions on Neural Networks 13, 1053–1063 (2002)
9. Zhang, Y., Chen, K., Ma, W.: MATLAB Simulation and Comparison of Zhang Neural Network and Gradient Neural Network for Online Solution of Linear Time-Varying Equations. In: Proceedings of International Conference on Life System Modeling and Simulation, pp. 450–454. Watam Press, Shanghai (2007)
10. Zhang, Y., Ge, S.S.: Design and Analysis of a General Recurrent Neural Network Model for Time-Varying Matrix Inversion. IEEE Transactions on Neural Networks 16, 1477–1490 (2005)
11. Zhang, Y., Li, Z., Yi, C., Chen, K.: Zhang Neural Network versus Gradient Neural Network for Online Time-Varying Quadratic Function Minimization. In: Huang, D.-S., Wunsch II, D.C., Levine, D.S., Jo, K.-H. (eds.) ICIC 2008. LNCS (LNAI), vol. 5227, pp. 807–814. Springer, Heidelberg (2008)
12. Boyd, S., Vandenberghe, L.: Convex Optimization. Cambridge University Press, New York (2004)
13. Nocedal, J., Wright, S.J.: Numerical Optimization. Springer, Heidelberg (1999)
14. Zhang, Y., Chen, K., Li, X., Yi, C., Zhu, H.: Simulink Modeling and Comparison of Zhang Neural Networks and Gradient Neural Networks for Time-Varying Lyapunov Equation Solving. In: Proceedings of the Fourth International Conference on Natural Computation, Jinan, pp. 521–525 (2008)
15. The MathWorks Inc.: Using Simulink,
http://www.mathworks.com/access/helpdesk/help/toolbox/simulink

New Product Design Based Target Cost Control with BP Neural Network and Genetic Algorithm - A Case Study in Chinese Automobile Industry

Bo Ju, Lifeng Xi, and Xiaojun Zhou

State Key Laboratory of Mechanical System and Vibration, Shanghai Jiao Tong University,
Shanghai, China
samediee@hotmail.com, lfxi@sjtu.edu.cn, zzhou745@sjtu.edu.cn

Abstract. Implementing target cost control at the design stage can better reduce the cost. However, for automakers in the Chinese market, no adequate attention is paid to the target cost control during design stage for various reasons. Among these reasons, the lack of an effective cost control tool is a substantial one. In this study, a target cost control method is proposed and artificial intelligence is employed for new product cost reduction. At the early design stage, Back Propagation (BP) neural network is introduced to estimate and evaluate the target cost of different designs. Consequently, a cost saving design can be chosen. The target cost can be mainly achieved through procurement cost control. A procurement model is designed for balancing procurement cost reduction and supplier satisfaction. To search the optimal solution for this model, genetic algorithm is introduced. A case study of the proposed method in a Chinese automobile company is also discussed .

Keywords: target cost control, Chinese automobile industry, new product design, Back Propagation neural network, genetic algorithm, procurement cost, supplier satisfaction.

1 Introduction

As the second largest automobile producer in the world, the annual output of automobiles in China in 2008 is 9.35 million. While the importance of Chinese automobile market increases, especially at the time when the automakers worldwide are heavily beaten by the financial crisis, this market is also getting more and more competitive. To survive in such a market, the automakers must pay special attention to cost control and provide the customers with products of high performance cost ratio.

According to several research findings, among all the factors, design has the largest influence on cost and 70%-80% of the product cost is determined during the design stage [1]. However, little attention is paid to target cost control at the design stage in China. One reason is that the prevailing joint-ventures preferred introducing matured automobile models from their overseas headquarters, the new products design were not paid enough attention to in China in the past. Another reason is that the domestic automotive companies persisted in the traditional cost control method and concentrated on the manufacturing process. But the situation is changing after the Chinese government starts to encourage the independent innovation rather than introducing

Z. Cai et al. (Eds.): ISICA 2009, LNCS 5821, pp. 111–122, 2009.
© Springer-Verlag Berlin Heidelberg 2009

existing technology. However, at present, there is no effective tool to estimate the product target cost while designing in China.

Among all cost related factors, the procurement cost takes up 70-80% of the complete vehicle cost. Consequently, reducing the procurement cost becomes the first priority for automakers to realize the target cost. Procurement plans should be combined with the new product design and evaluated before the procurement activity starts. If the target cost can not be achieved, the purchaser should find the bottleneck in the supply chain and provide feedback to the designer. Then the designer should check the origin design to clarify the problem and find a solution. As a result, the target cost can be more easily achieved in the procurement process. However, the loss caused by such cost reduction will be finally shifted onto the suppliers and drop their satisfaction and loyalty. Excessively low satisfaction of the supplier may cause their refusal to supply products and damage the security of the supply chain. Especially, the small or medium Chinese domestic automobile companies which are in relatively weak position in the market should be alert to such situation. But at present there are few researches concerning the supplier satisfaction, particularly in China.

Therefore, this study presents a methodology used for the target cost control during the automobile design stage. The methodology further comprises two steps: the target cost estimation and target cost realization. A Back Propagation (BP) neural network based method is developed to estimate the target costs of varied designs at the early stage. To realize the target cost, reducing the procurement cost becomes the top priority since it takes the largest part in the total automobile product cost. But to ensure the security of supply chain, supplier satisfaction must be taken into consideration, especially for the medium or small domestic automakers in China. A mathematic model for balancing the procurement target cost reduction and supplier satisfaction is developed. Genetic algorithm is introduced to find the optimum solution for this model. A case study of the methodology in a Chinese automobile company is also given.

2 BP Neural Network Based Target Cost Estimation and Reduction Method

Target costing is the most widely used cost control method for product design [2]. According to Moden [3], the two objects of target costing system are: reducing the product cost during design while keeping the quality; motivating all the employees to participate the activities of target costing.

As a crucial technique to target cost control, cost estimation is studied by many researchers. Layer et al. [4] generally classifies the cost estimation approaches into two categories: qualitative approaches and quantitative approaches. Qualitative methods possess high flexibility and can accommodate varied situations, while quantitative cost estimation methods are suitable for further cost analysis where quantification is required. At present, quantitative cost estimation methods in literatures can be retrieved can be classified into four categories: detail based method, analogy based method, parametric based method and neural networks based method [5]. The effectiveness of neural networks based method for product cost estimation is demonstrated in the researches of Zhang and Fuh [6] and Seo, et al [7]. Zhang et al apply BP neural networks in cost estimation of packaging products. However, the package product is relatively simple so that many important details could be specified at the early design stage. Seo et al use BP neural networks to estimate costs of home appliances such as vacuum cleaner, washing machine and so on. The attributes they choose to train the neural networks include the mass, material proportion, lifetime, use mode, modularity, serviceability etc. Their research does not focus on one specified product and many attributes like material components proportion, are not available at the early design stage.

The process of the BP neural network based target cost estimation method is demonstrated in Figure 1.

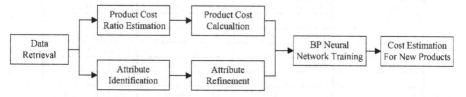

Fig. 1. Flow chart of BP Neural network based target cost estimation

2.1 Data Retrieval

The difficulty for automobile cost study exists in the inaccessibility to the cost data directly since they are confidential information. However, the cost can be estimated by analyzing the retail price which has a close relation with it.

The data concerning the automobile's parameters and retail prices are collected from a major Chinese automobile website–Cheshi (www.cheshi.com), which has the complete, comprehensive, daily updated database. Therefore, it becomes the main data source in this study.

2.2 Design Attributes Identification and Refinement

Before building the BP neural network based target cost estimation model, the cost-related design attributes should be identified and refined.

In this study, sedan, which takes the largest market share in passenger vehicle, is made the research focus. The whole system of sedan can be divided into three subsystems: automobile body subsystem, chassis subsystem and power subsystem. However, only with them, the very kind of sedan can not be clearly described and some extra information should be supplemented. Such information includes interior parts and exterior parts, safety appliance, the type of the automobile, its sales figure, the year when it came into market and so on. For instance there are 34 automotive manufacturers studied in this paper, of which 20 are joint ventures and 14 are domestic companies. According to the market share and the company size, they are classified into 5 grades.

Some attributes are quantitative and can be directly used to train the neural networks. Other qualitative attributes can also be quantified since their variations are limited. For instance, there are generally two types of materials used for automobile body and - sheet steel is encoded with 1 and aluminium alloy is encoded with 2.

Initially, 41 attributes are chosen. Through analyzing the data of 150 different sedans in market, 6 of the attributes are eliminated. For instance, ABS and AM/FM radio can be found in every sedan manufactured in China today, so the two attributes are taken off from the attributes list. Next, the remaining 35 attributes are tested of correlation coefficient to find those attributes which are replaceable. The replacement reduces the number of total attributes from 35 to 31.Table 1 shows the 31 attributes used for Back Propagation neural network training.

Table 1. Design attributes for neural network training

Body subsystem	Chassis subsystem	Power subsystem	Other attributes
Width	Transmission	Engine type	Front Airbags
Height	Front suspension	Amount of cylinders	Front side airbag
Wheelbase	Rear suspension	Amount of Valves	Front lamp
Clearance to ground	Front wheel brake	Rpm of Max Power	Air-conditioning
Fuel capacity	Rear wheel brake	Max Torque	Material of Seats
Automobile Type	Wheel style	Rpm of Max Torque	Sunroof
		Power output per liter	Manufacturer
		Emission standard	Manufacturers' status
		Compression ratio	Annual output
			Time-to-market

2.3 Product Cost Ratio Estimation and Product Cost Calculation

The target cost studied in this paper is restricted in the scope of product cost, which is defined as the cost needed to manufacture an automobile. Thus, marketing or sales cost is not taken into account. For this reason, gross profit margin can not be used and the concept of product cost ratio is introduced to correlate product cost with its retail price. The product cost ratio is defined in Equation (1).

$$\text{Retail price} = \text{Product cost}*(1+ \text{Product cost ratio}) \tag{1}$$

The product cost ratio is estimated through Delphi method developed by Rand Corporation. The Delphi method [8] is a kind of method that carried out among a panel of geographically dispersed experts. Although these experts are separated, they can communicate with each other anonymously through the "facilitator" who is in charge of sending out the questionnaires to the experts, collecting the answers and analyzing them, offering feedbacks to the experts to refine their work. There may be several rounds of "ask and answer" before a stable analysis could be conducted.

In this study, eight experts were chosen to form the panel for estimating the product cost ratio of automakers. In order to increase the estimation precision, in the second round, extra information besides the answers of first round was offered to aid their judgments. Such extra information, which included the profiles of the companies, their production capacities, market shares, government policies etc, was all gathered through public sources like company's annual report, newspaper and website.

After 5 rounds, the replies stabilized to the pre-set level and the product cost ratio is obtained. Next, the product is calculated backward for the retail prices with the Equation (1).

2.4 BP Neural Network Training and Cost Estimation

The BP neural networks based cost model is trained by the Neural Networks Toolbox of Matlab 7.1. Data from 112 kinds of sedans with 31 attributes are used to train the BP networks. To correspond with the dimension of the input data, the number of input layer neurons is endowed with 31. Obviously the output layer needs only one neuron to produce cost value. As one hidden layer networks have the similar performance with two hidden layers networks but need far fewer training time [6], so in this experiment, one hidden layer networks are adopted. However, the number of neurons in hidden layer is not decided yet. To solve this problem, 6 different architectures of networks are proposed for choosing. The scaled conjugate gradient algorithm (scg) and Levenberg-Marquardt algorithm (lm) are tested for this study. The data from the remaining 38 automobiles out of the total 150 are used to test the trained networks. The performances of the neural networks are evaluated by
  (a) Training time,
  (b) Mean square errors (mse) of the difference between actual automobile cost and the experiment results,
  (c) Percentage of absolute errors over 10%. (Absolute error is calculated by $|Target-Result|/Target*100\%$)

Though experiment, the BP neural networks which have 25 neurons in hidden layer and are trained with scg algorithm is chosen in this study. The simulation results shows that 19 out of 38(50.00%) estimations have absolute error less than 5%, 36 out of 38(94.74%) estimations have absolute error less than 10%. Given that detailed design parameters are missing at the early design stage, the performance of the neural networks based cost estimation method is satisfactory.

3   Mathematical Model for Balancing the Procurement Cost Reduction and Supplier Satisfaction

Since the procurement cost occupies the largest fraction of the total cost for a vehicle, reducing the procurement cost is the most efficient way to achieve the target cost for sedans. Table 2 has shown the impacts of procurement cost, direct labor cost, overhead cost, marketing cost and management cost on the profits. The cost structure for different items is from our survey in one Chinese domestic automobile company.

Table 2. Impacts of different cost items on profits

Cost items	Cost structure	Cost changes
Procurement cost	70	↓1%
Direct labor cost	7	↓10%
Overhead cost	6	↓11.7%
Marketing cost	8	↓8.8%
Management cost	4	↓17.5%
Profits	5	↑14%

Table 2 clearly shows that 1% drop in the procurement cost will increase the profits by 14%. To achieve the same result, the direct labor cost must be reduced by 10%, the overhead cost by 11.7%, the marketing cost by 8.8% and the management cost by 17.5%.

Since cost control implemented at the design stage is the most effective, the procurement plans, especially the procurement prices and volume plans can be made after the product is designed. The cost reduction of different procurement plans can be simulated to find the one which can achieve the target cost. If the cost of some parts can not agree with the target cost, the designer should redesign these parts or find the substitutes for them. Therefore, before the procurement process begins, the purchase cost can be controlled in advance.

In the Chinese automobile market, the larger joint-ventures have procurement advantage over the small or medium size Chinese domestic automakers. These Chinese manufacturers have relative small procurement quantity, which weakens their position in the procurement price negotiation with the suppliers. Since the acute competition in the automobile market, the suppliers hesitantly develop the long-term relationship with the Chinese domestic companies whose future prospects are still in question. If the procurement prices under their bottom line, the suppliers will not accept the offers from the Chinese domestic automakers and will stop providing parts to them. In that case, these Chinese companies have to search for new supplier to fill the vacancy of former supplier. Such finding process is costly and time consuming. What is worse, if they can not find proper supplier in time, the security of the supply chain is damaged which may cause unaffordable loss. Therefore, the Chinese domestic automobile producers should balance the supplier satisfaction and the procurement cost reduction in order to guarantee the safety of their supply chains.

However, at present, there are not many researches focusing on the supplier satisfaction. Among them, there are fewer papers referring the quantification of supplier satisfaction.

Supplier Relation Management (SRM) is an important issue in the Supply Chain Management (SCM). However, traditional Supplier Relation Management (SRM) seldom covers the supplier satisfaction management. Donath [9] makes the points that the supplier satisfaction can improve supply process and believes supplier satisfaction is the new frontier to be discovered in companies.

Wong's study [10] explores the role of suppliers in improving customer satisfaction and finds that companies can make use of their suppliers in achieving high customer satisfaction. Wong states that companies need to integrate supplier satisfaction with customer satisfaction.

In Susanna's study [11] supplier satisfaction is defined as implementing the supply chain smoothly, without any adverse consequences. Susanna develops a set of questionnaire to investigate the suppliers' satisfaction for a famous mobile phone manufacturer. However, Susanna does not propose a quantitative model for evaluate the supplier satisfaction.

In this study, a supplier satisfaction function is proposed. Based on this function, a mathematic model is developed to balance the procurement cost control and the suppliers' satisfaction.

Firstly, the factors which have influence on the supplier satisfaction are classified. The most important satisfaction related element is the profit. If one supplier gains fewer profits from providing products, its satisfaction will decrease certainly. The profits are affected by both prices and volume of purchase. However, since the effect of experience curve, the price reduction does not necessarily mean the decrease in the profits. In the late 1960s, Bruce Henderson of the Boston Consulting Group (BCG) began to employ the experience curve for cost analysis [12]. According to research of BCG in the 1970s, the experience curve effects ranged from 10 to 25 percent for different industries. In this study, the experience curve should be estimated for each supplier. To make allowance, the estimation for experience curve should be conservative in order to leave more profits for supplier. The percentage of price reduction should be compared with that of the cost reduction caused by the curve. It is assumed that the satisfaction is unchanged if the price reduction percentage is smaller than that of the experience curve drops down.

The size of supplier should be taken into consideration. Commonly, it is hard to please large or gigantic supplier since the purchaser's offer takes only fraction of its total sales. Therefore, the larger the supplier is, the smaller its satisfaction fluctuates. Facing this kind of supplier, the purchaser can hardly decide the price. On the contrary, for medium or small supplier, the changes in the prices and volume of purchase will dominate their satisfaction. Though the purchaser can have more influence on the pricing, it is not suitable to declare the procurement price unilaterally without giving consideration to the supplier.

The price of raw materials is also important factor. If the material price falls down, the suppliers can be more profitable. Thus, they can accept the price decreasing demand from the purchaser if such drop will not slash their profits.

The early involvement of supplier is also a factor for supplier satisfaction. Many researches have proved that the product design has influence on over 70% of the life cycle cost. If the supplier is involved in the new product development from the start, it is better for them to understand the technique demands and initiate product cost control project. The close cooperation can also boost the trust between the purchaser and the supplier.

The suppliers' forecasting on the prospect of the purchaser is also a factor for satisfaction. If the suppliers have the confidence in the purchaser's future success, they will cultivate the present supply in the long run. Consequently, they can more easily accept the price drop as an early investment for future business.

In this study, the supplier satisfaction function is the sum of the satisfaction functions of relevant factors.

The S_r (satisfaction function of profit) is defined by:

$$S_r(p,v)=f(p,v)*g(p,v) \tag{2}$$

where $f(p,v)$ is a function of parameters p (price) and v (volume of procurement). It represents the satisfaction changes caused by price.

$$f(p,v) = \begin{cases} 1, & \text{if } (p_0 - p)/p_0 < 1 - C_0(v_0 + v)^{-\alpha} \\ p/p_0, & \text{if } (p_0 - p)/p_0 \geq 1 - C_0(v_0 + v)^{-\alpha} \end{cases} \tag{3}$$

where p_0 is the previous procurement price, v_0 is the previous procurement volume, and C_0 is the cost of first unit of production, α is the elasticity of cost with regard to output.

$$g(p,v)=(v/v_0)*(p*v/O) \tag{4}$$

where O is the annual output of the supplier, and $(p*v/O)$ can calculate the percentage of the procurement in the whole output of the supplier. Therefore, it can reflect the effect of supplier's size factor.

The S_m (satisfaction function of raw material price) is defined by:

$$S_m(p)=\begin{cases} 1, & if\ (p_0-p)/\,p_0 < (m_0-m_1)/\,m_0 \\ p/\,p_0, 1, & if\ (p_0-p)/\,p_0 \geq (m_0-m_1)/\,m_0 \end{cases} \tag{5}$$

where m_0 is the previous material price and m_1 is the present material price.

The satisfaction function of the early involvement of supplier and the suppliers' confidence are relatively simple since they have no relation with the prices and volume of procurement. They can be acquired by questionnaire or survey of the supplier, or can be estimated by the purchasing personnel who have insights on the suppliers. These two functions can be binary, like:

$$S_i=\begin{cases} 1, & if\ with\ EIS \\ a, & if\ without\ EIS \end{cases} \tag{6}$$

$$S_c=\begin{cases} 1, & if\ with\ sufficient\ confidence \\ b, & if\ without\ sufficient\ confidence \end{cases} \tag{7}$$

where EIS is the early involvement of supplier, and $0<a,b<1$

In this study, the default choice is $p_0>p$, which means that the procurement price is decreasing. But in reality, such price can be increasing sometimes. However, if the prices go up, the suppliers are generally satisfied and it is not necessary to study their satisfaction.

Since the status of above factors is varied, different weights are assigned to the functions of the factors. The weights are decided by experience and the sum of them is one.

The supplier satisfaction is then defined as:

$$S(p,v)=w_r*S_r+w_m*S_m+w_i*S_i+w_c*S_c \tag{8}$$

After defining the supplier satisfaction function, a mathematical model can be developed to balancing the satisfaction descent and the procurement cost control.

The object is to minimize the average decrease in the supplier satisfaction for the whole supply chain while achieving the cost control goal. If there are n suppliers and j parts to be purchased in the supply chain, the model can be defined as:

$$Minimize\ S = (1/n)*\sum_{i=1}^{n}(S_i(p_i,v_i)-S_{i0}(p_{i0},v_{i0}))$$

Subject to

$$S_i(p_i,v_i) \geq T_i \tag{9}$$

$$\sum_{i=1}^{n} p_i*v_i = (1-r\%)*\sum_{i=1}^{n} p_{i0}*v_{i0} \tag{10}$$

$$V_k = \sum_{i \in Q_k} v_i, \ 1 \leq k \leq j \tag{11}$$

$$0 < p \leq p_{i0} \tag{12}$$

$$0 < v_i < V_k, \ i \in Q_k \tag{13}$$

where p_i is the procurement price for supplier i this time, and v_i is the procurement volume for supplier i this time, while p_{i0} and v_{i0} are the procurement price and volume for supplier i last time. T_i is the predetermined lower limit for satisfaction of supplier i. $r\%$ is the procurement cost reduction percentage. Since there are j parts to be purchased, V_k stands for the total procurement volume for part k. And Q_k is the set of all suppliers who provide the part k.

The supplier number in this study is determined based on the parts to be bought. For instance, if part A has two suppliers and part B has three suppliers, the number of suppliers should be the sum of two and three. However, in many cases, one supplier can provide more than one parts. But in this study, such supplier should be deemed as several suppliers. Such treatment is reasonable since the satisfaction of the supplier on varied parts is independent with each other. The supplier can stop providing one part due to the low satisfaction while it can continue providing another profitable part because of the high satisfaction.

This optimization problem is a non-linear one. In order to find out the optimal solution, the genetic algorithm is introduced. Unlike the BP neural network target cost estimation method which can train a generic neural network to carry out the cost estimation for different designs, the supplier satisfaction model is unique for each automobile company. Therefore, one specific genetic algorithm can only correspond to a concrete instance and no universal genetic algorithm can applied for all different supplier satisfaction models. Therefore, the genetic algorithm is detailed with a case study in the Chinese automobile company in following Section 4.

4 Target Cost Reduction in a Chinese Automobile Company with BP Neural Network and Genetic Algorithm Based Method

The BP neural network and genetic algorithm based method is employed in a medium sized Chinese domestic company H, which is a private automaker in China whose products are mainly economical sedans with relatively low prices. Aiming at the middle grade market, H was developing a new sedan and preparing to launch it in 2007. H planed to equip the new product with 1.8L engine rather than widely adopted 1.5L engine. During the development, the management wanted to estimate the target cost of the new sedan and accordingly position it in market. And the BP neural network model developed in this paper was used for this task.

Firstly, the product cost was estimated and the result was provided to H as reference. They reported that the estimation error was within 10% relative to their estimation with experience. Secondly, the product cost of the new sedan made by other competitors was estimated by changing the input data attributes concerning the manufacturers. This would help the management of H learn the competition status of this sedan in market and set the cost benchmark. Including 2 Sino-European joint ventures (E), 2 Sino-American joint ventures (A), 2 Sino-Japanese joint ventures (J), 2 Sino-Korean joint ventures (K), 2 Chinese state-owned companies (S), and 2 Chinese private companies (P), total 12 automotive companies in Chinese market were chosen for the test.

The simulation results of other companies were divided by the result of H. As shown in Table 3, H had cost advantages over all the joint ventures. However, emerged as a new comer in market, H's brand influence was far feebler than those joint ventures established by the world famous automobile giants. Unless providing a product of high performance but low price, H could barely make the customers turn to it given their preferences for famous brands. Compared with its Chinese counterparts, H's cost advantage weakened or even disappeared. H could set the competitors whose product costs were lower as benchmarks and endeavour to exceed them.

The neural networks based method could also help the designers compare various design concepts. Hence, product costs of different companies for the new sedan with 1.5L engine could be simulated. The simulation results shown in Table 3 revealed that that H might have cost advantage over all the other automakers with 1.5L engine. This might be attributed to the fact that sedans with 1.5L engine were in absolute majority in H. The experiment demonstrated that the new sedan should also install 1.5L engine. As a matter of fact, H finally decided to place both models into market.

Table 3. The product cost comparison of different companies with H

	H	E1	E2	A1	A2	J1	J2
1.8 L	1	1.0401	1.0709	1.0623	1.084	1.0531	1.0603
1.5 L	1	1.0351	1.0802	1.0774	1.0823	1.0783	1.0665
	H	K1	K2	S1	S2	P1	P2
1.8 L	1	1.0351	1.0856	0.985	1.0458	0.9983	1.0242
1.5 L	1	1.033	1.0739	1.014	1.0239	1.0033	1.0372

To reduce the procurement cost and achieve the target, the mathematic model was also employed by H to manage its supplier satisfaction. Compared with the joint-ventures, H's relatively small position in the market forced it to put emphasis on the supplier satisfaction in order to boost the security of supply chain.

The supplier satisfaction model was applied in the supply chain for chassis system. 20 suppliers which provided the interior parts were chosen and their satisfaction functions were founded.

The cost control target was to decrease the procurement cost by 2% and the purchasing price should be determined and the volume should be allocated for each supplier.

Several genetic algorithms were tested for this optimization problem. The running time and accuracy were considered. Finally, a genetic algorithm which had a population size of 200 was used for this model. The crossover probability P_c was 0.4 and the crossover pattern was single point; the mutation probability P_m was 0.2 and the

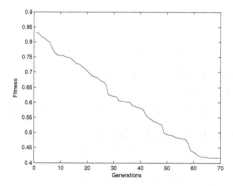

Fig. 2. The fitness of the genetic algorithm

mutation pattern was uniform. The best three individuals' information was recorded according to the Elitist model.

After 70 generations, the Minimum S was 0.0417, which meant that if the total procurement cost decreased the 2%, the average supplier satisfaction would drop 4.17%. Figure 2 shows the fitness value of the genetic algorithm. With the optimum solution, the satisfaction decrease of each supplier's could also be calculated. If some suppliers' satisfaction were on the brink of the lower limit, the automobile company should be alert to the potential risk of the supply chain caused by these suppliers.

5   Conclusion and Future Study

This research proposes a target cost control methodology which can be applied at the new product design stage for the small or medium sized Chinese domestic automakers. To set the target cost, this study presents a BP neural network based method which comprises data collecting, design attributes processing, product cost ratio estimation, BP neural network training and target cost estimation. To achieve such target, supplier satisfaction is studied and a mathematic model to balance the satisfaction decrease and procurement cost reduction is developed. The optimum solution can be obtained with the genetic algorithm. The case study on the method in a Chinese company is also given. In future research, the criteria for selecting design attributes for neural network training should be studied and more attributes combination should be tested. The multi-object mathematic model for supplier satisfaction should also be studied. For instance, future model should include the object to minimize the mean-squared error of the satisfaction decrease.

Acknowledgements

This research is supported by the Innovation Team of National Natural Science Foundation of China (NSFC) under the project 50821003. This research is also supported by the Program of Introducing Talents of Discipline to Universities under the project B06012.

References

1. Dowlatshahi, S.: Product design in a concurrent engineering environments an optimization approach. J. Prod. Res. 30, 1803–1818 (1992)
2. Cooper, R., Slagmulder, R.: Develop Profitable New Products with Target Costing. Sloan Manage. Rev. 40, 22–33 (1999)
3. Monden, Y.: Cost Reduction Systems: Target Costing and Kaizen Costing. Productivity Press, Oregon (1995)
4. Layer, A., Brinke, E.T., Houten, F., Kals, H., Haasis, S.: Recent and future trends in cost estimation. Int. J. Comp. Integ. M. 15, 499–510 (2002)
5. Ju, B., Xi, L.F.: A product cost estimation for the early design of sedans using neural networks. Int. J. Auto. Tech. Manage. 8, 331–349 (2008)
6. Zhang, Y.F., Fuh, J.Y.H.: A neural network approach for early cost estimation of packaging products, Comp. Ind. Engi. 34, 433–450 (1998)
7. Seo, K.K., Park, J.H., Jang, D.S., Wallace, D.: Prediction of the life cycle cost using statistical and artificial neural network methods in conceptual product design. Int. J. Comp. Integ. M. 15, 541–554 (2002)
8. Linstone, H.A., Turoff, M.: Delphi method: techniques and applications. Addison-Wesley, Massachusetts (1975)
9. Donath, R.: Have you hugged supplier today? Mark. News 11, 4 (1991)
10. Wong, A.: Integrating supplier satisfaction with customer satisfaction. Total Qual. Manag. 11, S427–S432 (2000)
11. Susana, M.: Supplier satisfaction: the concept and a measurement system. Thesis, University of Oulu (2003)
12. Hax, A.C., Majluf, N.S.: Competitive cost dynamics: the experience curve. Interfaces 12, 50–61 (1982)

Hard Real Time Task Oriented Power Saving Scheduling Algorithm Based on DVS

Daliang Zhang and Shudong Shi

College of Computer Science & Technology, Hubei Normal University, Hubei, China

Abstract. This paper first gives a general review of the present situation of the hard real time power saving scheduling algorithm and then demonstrates its currently related technology and several classic power saving scheduling algorithms. Moreover, it studies the power saving sheduling algorithm of hard real time periodical task based on DVS technology and sonducts a comparison simulation of three different scheduling algorithms.

Keywords: hard real time, power saving scheduling, task division.

1 Introduction

With the substantial growth of the semi-conductor chip's density and working frequency, the power consumption of the VLSI system is getting larger and larger, power consumption problem is increasingly prominent. Power consumption has been the crucial non-functional design constraint, so power optimization and power saving technology has been the research focus of system designers. In the real time (esp distributional real time) application field, power saving issue is quite complex, how to lower down the system's power consumption as far as possible on the premises that the real time demand can be met has become the focus of present research.

In the current power consumption oriented design field, the consideration of the power consumption attribution has been taken into each design layer. Research shows that: the higher the layer of research the bigger the potential of power saving will be. So, in recent years the research focus of this area has been transferred from the traditional low power consumption circuit to the system-level power optimization. Especially in the real time field, combined with existing methods of real-time scheduling hardware technology and emerging energy-saving mechanism provided by dynamic voltage scaling technology, focus on the overall system behavior, and excavation from its inherent energy-saving potential, has become the most effective strategy of real time power optimum design[1].

2 Real Time Scheduling and Dynamic Voltage Scaling

With the rapid development of the scale of integrated circuits, the power consumption problem becomes all the more prominent. High power consumption has been the obstacle that hinders the processor's design. Real time system's application makes the

Z. Cai et al. (Eds.): ISICA 2009, LNCS 5821, pp. 123–135, 2009.

optimization of system power consumption important factor that should be taken into consideration of real time system's design. How to optimize the system power consumption on the premises that real time system rigid time constraint demand can be met has been the present real time system' research focus.

Since the DVS technology was introduced into the real time system, power saving scheduling algorithm has developed by leaps and bounds, there are a large number of processors which has adopted DVS technology. For instance: Strong ARM and XScale processor of Intel company, Crusoe processor of Transmeta company, Power Now processor of AMD company and Motorola 6805 processor of Motorola company etc.

2.1 Real Time Scheduling Basic Concept

The basic issue of real time scheduling is to find an execution order of a task which can make the task set satisfy its time constraints when under execution, while real time power saving scheduling is to fulfill this process with least resource consumption. In the real time scheduling, task refers to the software entity that fulfills a certain function of the system. A certain execution of the task in its life period is called an operation of this task. Those task with real time requirement is called real time task. Time of arrival of each task of the mission is called the release time. The time a task fulfills its function is called its execution time. The time interval from the task release to completion is called responding time. The time the task was required to completed by is called the absolute time limit for the task. The interval between the absolute time limit and release time is the relative time limit of the task, the time limit for a task completion is called the time limit constraint. Tasks to meet their time frame is called the schedulability. The system that all the tasks can be scheduled is called schedulable system[2].

According to the difference of the law of the arrival time of the task operation, the task can be divided as periodical task, non-periodical task and accidental task. Non-periodical task's operation release time has no law. Accidental task is the subset of non-periodical task, the interval of its two adjacent operation release time is not fixed, but there is a lower limit, namely accidental task's operation achieved in accordance with a rate no higher than a value. Environmental changes may influence the cyclic nature of the periodical task. Therefore result in the gap between the actual release time of the periodical task and the expected value. The gap is called periodical task's release time vibration[3].

2.2 Dynamic Voltage Scaling(DVS)

System layer's energy-saving design in the real time system is still relatively new research field, in the 90s of the twentieth century, power saving design is mainly considered from the physical layer. Constantly improve the performance of the hardware is of course can reduce the power consumption, but the system's operation need to be realized through creating, scheduling and destruction of all kinds of task by the operating system. So as the most important system software operation system, the power consumption generated from it accounts for a significant percentage of the entire consumption of the system [4].

3 The Real Time Power Saving Scheduling Relative Technology

With the wide application of portable devices, Battery life of these devices become increasingly unable to meet the needs of the people, so there emerged a lot of effective energy-saving technology to reduce system power consumption, thus, extended the battery life.

3.1 Slack Time Recycle

To know slack time recycle technology, we must first understand the concept of slack time. The so called slack time refers to the left time of the task completed before the deadline. (the margin between the deadline and the actual execution time) , as is shown in the below figure. The slack time has 3 features, respectively they are: individuality, non-superposition, and non-linear.

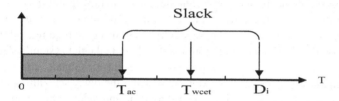

Fig. 1. Slack time schematic

Slack time is independent from the task being scheduled, although it can be defined as the characteristic parameter of the task, it doesn't belong to its basic parameter. There is no need to provide before the inception of power saving scheduling, in the scheduling process it will be taken over by the extended task running time caused by the lowered down voltage. After the scheduling, it will deplete in the ideal circumstances.

Slack time has no superposition feature, according to the definition of the task slack time, the total sum of each task slack time is larger than or equals to the whole scheduling slack time. When and only when two successive running tasks' deadline coincides with the beginning time the two equal.

Due to the non linear relationship between the slack time's extent and the drop extent of the power consumption, if the same length of slack time for different tasks, the voltage range ready for dropping is the same, But the savings in power consumption vary due to the difference of the battery working current needed by different task.

If the processor's running speed can be appropriately reduced, and the slack time can be fully exploited, the real time system's power consumption can be lowered down comparatively effective. Presently many real time power saving scheduling algorithm are combined with slack recycling principal. During the slack time recycling how to reasonably and effectively allocate the slack time to task is the key.

3.2 Delay Scheduling

From previous introduction, we can see the processor mainly include static power consumption and dynamic power consumption, the dynamic power consumption accounts for relatively higher percentage in the total power consumption, so the usual power saving algorithm only analyses the dynamic part in the system. Presently dynamic voltage scaling's principal is at the cost of increase the execution time of the task to lower down the processor's voltage and frequency, so that lower down the system's power consumption, however, the increase of the task's execution time will inevitably result in the rise of system's static power consumption. With the development of electronic technology, the smaller the electronic device is the larger the currency leakage will be, and the static power consumption caused by the currency leakage will become bigger and bigger, thus, simply only consider the dynamic power consumption's power saving algorithm can not make the system get better power saving effect, thus, we must take the dynamic and static power consumption into consideration simultaneously when design the power saving algorithm.

By using the delay scheduling technology we can minimum the static power consumption, as the name implies, delay scheduling is to meet the requirement that all the tasks postpone the task execution before the deadline, make the system's slack cluster as much as possible, then make the processor enter the sleep state, consequently reduce the static power consumption. Merely by using the delay scheduling technology can not get optimum power saving effect, based on the delay scheduling, combined with dynamic slack time recycling technology can make the total sum of the dynamic and static power consumption minimum.

In the power saving algorithm, by recycling the slack time can lower down the processor speed, consequently reduce the processor's dynamic power consumption, but too much processor speed reducing can lead to the boost of the processor's static power consumption. If recycle the slack time to expand the task execution slack time interval can reduce the system static power consumption better. Below is an instance to analyse the circumstance that slack time recycling and the delay scheduling schedule the dynamic task. Let's assume a task series comprise the following two tasks:

$$\tau_1 = \{5,5,2\} \qquad \tau_2 = \{10,10,6\}$$

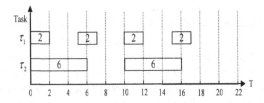

Fig. 2. Scheduling of task under the worst execution circumstance

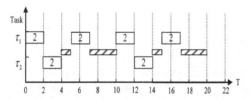

Fig. 3. Scheduling of task based on EDF(scheduling without delay)

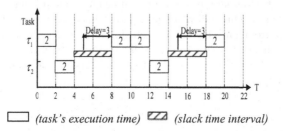

▭ *(task's execution time)* ▨ *(slack time interval)*

Fig. 4. Expand the task's slack time interval by using the delay scheduling

Fig 2 depicted the execution picture of the tasks arriving at the same time under the worst circumstance, judging from the feature of the tasks queue we can make out that the processor's utilization ratio is:

$$U = \sum_{i=1}^{m} C_i / T_i = 2/5 + 6/10 = 1 \tag{3-1}$$

From the processor's utilization ratio we can see, task execution slack time interval is 0, through static analysis can not reduce the static power consumption by using the delay scheduling; fig 3-3 depict the task's execution picture by using EDF scheduling, at 0 time task $\tau_{1,1}$ execute first because of the top priority among the ready tasks. $\tau_{1,1}$ finishes execution at the moment t=2 meanwhile task $\tau_{2,1}$ is ready for execution, task $\tau_{2,1}$ finishes the task in advance, less than the worst circumstance by 4 time units, therefore can spare 4 units slack time, the processor is idle at the moment t=4, $\tau_{1,2}$ arrives at the moment t=5, its deadline is t=10, in the period [10,20] tasks have similar scheduling circumstance. Fig 3-4 depicted the slack time scheduling circumstance generated by the high priority task dynamic delay recycling. On the premises that all the tasks meet the deadline requirement, recycle the usable slack time to postpone the task execution slack time interval. Judging from the fig we can see through dynamic slack time recycling combined with delay scheduling the switch of context can be reduced, while the task is idle for a long time we can make the system enter the sleep state, so this way can effectively reduce the system's total power consumption.

3.3 Feedback Control

To real time system, performance indicators relating to time is one of the important factors that must be considered for the system's scheduling method, for instance:

responding time, deadline missing ratio etc. In the real time system whether each task can be accomplished in the expected time, depends on whether they can be timely allocated the necessary system resource for the operation, such as processor, network bandwidth etc, this is what the real time scheduling mechanism is responsible for. So, when the system's internal environment (such as: task load) or external environment (such as: the number of web request) change, if we still want to guarantee the real time task's time constraint can be met, more often than not require the system's real time scheduling relating component can make appropriate adjustment to follow the environment, so that the system's resource allocation can still adapt to the circumstance after changing. This will naturally require the system to conduct constant detection to the environment change and scheduling result, and constantly adjust the scheduling component according to the feedback information. Because this process is endless, which is identical to a close-loop system, it is as well called based on feedback control strategy.

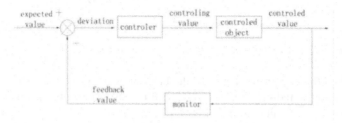

Fig. 5. Basic feedback control structure

Presently, the real time scheduling strategy based on feedback control has been paid attention to, it is self-adaptive scheduling method universally adopted mode currently. Feedback control origin from automatic control theory, its basic element include three parts: measurement, comparison and execution. The variant got by measurement, compared with the expected value will generate deviation, use this deviation execution action to correct and regulate the control system's response. This control method's crucial problem lies in; after make right measure and comparison, how to correct the system in better ways.

Fig 5 is the basic structure chart of feedback control method, the controlled object's output (the controlled variable) is sampling by sensors, comparing with expected value as feedback value, commonly by means of minus operation, and transfer to the controller as deviation, the latter generate controlling value according to certain algorithm, then pass by to the controlled object, bring forth the controlled object's regulation, henceforth makes its output change. When the feedback control method is applied to the real time scheduling field, the scheduling relating component then parallel to the controlled object in it, it determines the system's resource allocation and ultimately influence the system's real time performance indicators; such indicator then be sampling as the controlled object; the deviation generated by the comparison of the expected value and factual sampling value is transferred to the controller. The expected value and factual sampling value is of the same indicator. Then the latter conduct the calculation according to certain algorithm. Generate controlling value to regulate the scheduling device's parameter. Because the sampling and controlling action is ongoing according to certain cycle, real time system's scheduling component then will regulate itself periodically to constantly suit the environment's change.

4 DVS Power Saving Scheduling Algorithm Based On Feedback Control

4.1 System Model

Let's assume this system is a hard real time system which adopts EDF algorithm and can grab the task scheduling strategy, in this system task set $\Gamma = \{\tau_i \mid 1 \le i \le n\}$ is period task set, each task τ uses four-element group $(T_i, WCET_i, D_i, ACET_i)$ to represent, in it T_i is the task's period, D_i is the task's deadline, $WCET_i$ and $ACET_i$ are the worst execution time (WCET) and the average execution time (ACET) respectively, in which, $WCET_i \ge ACET_i$, and they are both the maximum speed based on the processor. Let's assume $Load_i = BCET_i / WCET_i$ represents the system's load (BCETi represents the task's best execution time), the smaller Load is the more time the task generates. Meanwhile, we introduce the factor α ($0 < \alpha \le 1$) to regulate the system processor's running speed instantly, if $\alpha = 1$ means the processor is running at the maximum speed. Let assume the task's $WCET_i$ and $ACET_i$ is known before execution, the real execution time AET can be determined when running.

Besides, we assume the task set meets the following conditions:

- any task do not have the part that can not be grabbed;

- all the tasks are irrelevant, they are independent one another, there is on constraint by the order.

- Processor's running speed can be constantly modified by regulating the factor α in the range of $[S_{\min}, S_{\max}]$, $S_{\min}$ represents the minimum speed that the processor can guarantee the system run properly, $S_{\max}$ represents the maximum speed of the processor, and $0 \le S_{\min} \le S_{\max} \le 1$.

- Neglect the system's overheads, such as interrupt process, overheads of task grabbing and switch.

We define the system's utilization as.

$$U = \sum_{i=1}^{n} C_i / T_i . \tag{4-1}$$

4.2 Power Model

Compared with dynamic static power consumption is negligible, moreover the technology to lower down the static power consumption is rather complex, therefore, most power saving scheduling algorithm only consider the dynamic power consumption. The power saving algorithm in this paper only takes the dynamic power consumption into consideration, below is the detailed analysis of dynamic power consumption P_d :

$$P_d = C_{eff} \cdot V_{dd}^2 \cdot S. \tag{4-2}$$

C_{eff} represents effective switch capacitor, V_{dd} is power supply voltage, S is the clock the frequency of processor, which is equivalent to the processor's running speed. Besides processor's speed and voltage is approximate linear relationship.

$$S = k \cdot \frac{(V_{dd} - V_t)^2}{V_{dd}}. \tag{4-3}$$

k is constant,   is threshold voltage. From (4-2) and (4-3) we can get:

$$P_d \approx C_{eff} \cdot \frac{S^3}{k^2}. \tag{4-4}$$

For the task's execution time is the result of CN divided by S, CN is the period number of task execution S is the processor's speed, the energy consumed by the task is :

$$E = P_d \cdot \frac{CN}{S} \approx CN \cdot C_{eff} \cdot \frac{S^2}{k^2}. \tag{4-5}$$

After regulating the processor by the regulating factor α the speed is:

$$S = \alpha S_{max}. \tag{4-6}$$

From (4-5) and (4-6) It is not difficult to infer:

$$E \propto \alpha^2 \cdot CN. \tag{4-7}$$

4.3 Algorithm Example

Let's assume a hard real time periodical task set Γ shown as TABLE I, all the tasks arrive at the same time, and the tasks' execution period equals to their deadline, each task uses four-element group $(D_i, WCET_i, ACET_i, AET_i)$ to represent. Fig 1 shows the tasks set's scheduling sequence based on EDF-NON algorithm(with EDF scheduling but without dynamic voltage regulation), fig4-2 shows the scheduling process based on the EDF-DVS algorithm of this task set, finally focus on this task set, fig4-3 shows how MSF-DVS algorithm realizes the scheduling process.

  Under the EDF-DVS scheduling algorithm, task set is scheduling in accordance to the strategy that the minimum deadline first. When t=0ms, task τ_1 release begin to execute, to guarantee the hard time restriction we must assume that the task execution is under the worst circumstance, then the task τ_1's frequency regulation factor $\alpha_1 = 1$, task τ_1's remain slack time is: $slack = WCET_1 - AET_1 = 3 - 1 = 2$ when t=1ms, task τ_1 accomplishes and task τ_2 begins to execute, use DVS technology to recycle the former task's slack time, then task τ_2's frequency regulating factor $\alpha_2 = WCET_2 / (WCET_2 + slack) = 4 / (4 + 2) = 2/3$, see fig 7(a) when t=4ms, task τ_2 finishes, and task τ_3 begins to execute, for the same reason can get the regulating factor $\alpha_3 = 5/6$, as is shown of fig 7(b); when t=5.2ms, task τ_3 accomplishes, task τ_4 begins to execute, for the same reason can get the regulating factor $\alpha_4 = 30/49$, as is shown of fig 7(c), the entire task set accomplishes when t=6.8ms.

Table 1. Example of task set

Task's name	D_i	$WCET_i$	$ACET_i$	AET_i
τ_1	10	3	1	1
τ_2	12	4	2	2
τ_3	15	5	2	1
τ_4	20	6	2	1

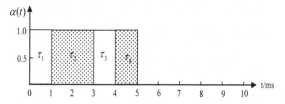

Fig. 6. The task set's scheduling based on EDF-NON algorithm

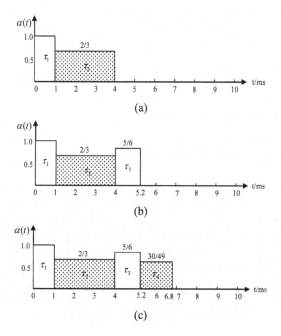

(a)

(b)

(c)

Fig. 7. Task set's scheduling under EDF-DVS algorithm

Under MSF-DVS scheduling algorithm, task set is scheduling in accordance with MSF strategy, according to $WCET_i$ and $ACET_i$ calculate each task's possible slack time, and sort the task set according to MSF, therefore, the execution order of the task set is τ_4, τ_3, τ_1, τ_2, regarding to the slack time's recycling method, it is the same with EDF-DVS algorithm, so we can derive the task set's scheduling under MSF-DVS algorithm (as is shown in fig 8).

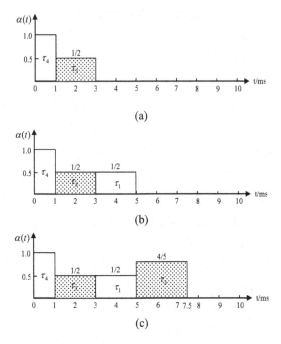

Fig. 8. Task set's scheduling under MSF-DVS algorithm

4.4 Simulation Experiment and Analysis

In order verify MSF-DVS algorithm's superiority, we conducted the simulation by adopting Intel Pentium4 CPU+2.40GHZ processor, 512MB RAM platform and Visual C++ 6.0.

We choosed 100 tasks generated randomly, and assumed that each task's period and deadline is the same, system's utilization rate is between 10%~90%, the worst execution time of the task (WCETi) conforms to the average distribution U(10,100) and the unit is ms, the best execution time (BCETi)is Load*WCETi the Load in it represents the system's working load, it is between 0.1~0.9, the average execution time is $(WCET_i + BCET_i)/2$, the actual execution time conforms to the Gauss normal distribution, $\mu = (WCET_i + BCET_i)/2$ and the variance is $\sigma = (WCET_i - BCET_i)/6$. With the change of U and Load, we can calculate the algorithm EDF-NON、EDF-DVS and MSF-DVS's power consumption under the same task set.

a) system's work load's influence on power consumption
In order to facilitate calculation and analyse the system's power consumption, according to the equation (4-4) we can set the proportional coefficient 1; power consumption unit milliwatt (mw), when the system's utilization U is fixed, with the system's work load (Load) constantly getting larger the three algorithms' power consumption is getting larger and larger. Below is the tableII about the three algorithms' power consumption when the system's utilization is 60%. Fig 9 is the histogram power consumption contrast.

Table 2. The three algorithms power consumption when the system's utilization is 60%

Work load	Power consumption （mw）			Power saving percentage （%）	
	EDF-Non	EDF-DVS	MSF-DVS	EDF-DVS	MSF-DVS
0.1	30.1007	20.7584	18.6006	31.04%	38.21%
0.2	32.5629	24.2282	21.7027	25.60%	33.35%
0.3	34.1918	26.1276	24.1105	23.59%	29.48%
0.4	35.9192	28.1074	26.3914	21.75%	26.53%
0.5	43.7583	34.5964	34.1345	20.94%	21.99%
0.6	46.5035	38.2106	37.3846	17.83%	19.61%
0.7	50.5621	43.7119	43.1566	13.55%	14.65%
0.8	53.3012	48.2729	48.2805	9.43%	9.42%
0.9	60.4026	56.2412	56.2287	6.89%	6.91%

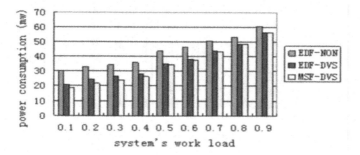

Fig. 9. Power consumption contrast histogram when the system's utilization is 60%

From Table 2 and Fig 9 we can see: under the same task set, when the system's utilization is 60%, MSF-DVS algorithm and EDF-DVS can effectively lower down the system's power consumption, when the system's load is relatively small(less than 0.5), compared with EDF-DVS algorithm, MSF-DVS algorithm can recycle the system's slack time better, it has better power saving effect; when the system's load is relatively big(more than 0.5), the two algorithms have similar power saving effect.

The reason is mainly due to that : when the system's work load is relatively small, there is more slack time in it, through MSF algorithm to sort the order of the task, then the merit of short task first and long task first can be manifested, that is to make the task generate more slack time, in doing so the following task can have more execution time and smaller speed regulating factor, consequently can lower down the system's power consumption. When the system's load is relatively big, the slack time in the system is relatively small, the task's slack time generated by the two algorithms is similar, so there is little difference in the last system's power saving effect.

b) system utilization's influence on the power consumption

When the system's load (Load) is fixed, with the system utilization U constantly getting larger power consumption's variation is not conspicuous under the three algorithms. The below Table 3 is the power consumption circumstance of the three algorithms when the system's working load is 0.5, fig 10 is the power consuming contrast histogram.

Table 3. The power consumption of the three algorithms when the work load is 0.5

utilization	Power consumption（mw）			Power saving percentage（%）	
	EDF-NON	EDF-DVS	MSF-DVS	EDF-DVS	MSF-DVS
10%	41.142	32.6071	31.45	20.75%	23.56%
20%	39.3026	31.2368	29.9863	20.52%	23.71%
30%	42.4985	33.8977	32.6037	20.24%	23.28%
40%	43.3154	35.1036	33.8331	18.96%	21.89%
50%	42.8389	34.5086	33.0701	19.45%	22.80%
60%	43.7583	34.5964	34.1345	20.94%	21.99%
70%	41.252	33.4323	32.9017	18.96%	20.24%
80%	40.6728	32.6957	31.8473	19.61%	21.70%
90%	43.2489	34.7455	33.9829	19.66%	21.42%

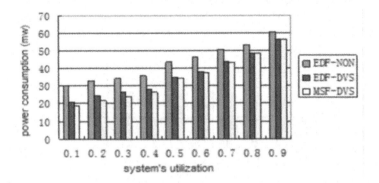

Fig. 10. the power consumption contrast histogram when the system's work load is 50%

Through Table 3 and Fig 5 we can easily make out: under the same task set, when the system's work load is 0.5, MSF-DVS and EDF-DVS both can get lower power consumption compared with EDF-NON algorithm, with the utilization's constant getting larger, the total trend is that the power saving effect is getting worse. Meanwhile, the MSF-DVS algorithm is superior to the EDF-DVS algorithm, can get more power saving, and has better power saving effect. The reason is due to that the MSF-DVS grasped the point of power saving, utilize the system's slack time to the maximum extent.

5   Concluding Remarks

This paper came up with a new power saving scheduling algorithm MSF-DVS, static algorithm is used for off-line calculate the static slack time possibly generated by each task, and sort the order of the task based on the maximum slack time first strategy. Dynamic algorithm get the task's actual execution time by using the feedback control, then based on the task's actual running circumstance and generated dynamic slack time to regulate the speed of the following task. Meanwhile, we illustrated the MSF-DVS algorithm's superiority, and made comparison to the EDF-NON algorithm and the EDF-DVS algorithm, through the comparison of the simulation of the three algorithms, the result manifests that: when the system's work load is less than 0.5(the system's utilization is 60%),MSF-DVS algorithm can reduce the system's power consumption better compared with EDF-DVS, when the system's work load is 0.5(the system's utilization is between 10%~90%), the MSF-DVS algorithm is always superior to the EDF-DVS algorithm, and has the better power saving result.

Reference

1. Pollack, F.: New Micro architecture Challenges in the Coming Generations of CMOS Process Technologies. In: Keynote Talk. 32nd International Symposium on Micro architecture, MICRO-32 (November 1999)
2. Haiye, X., Wei, L., Chenhui, Y., Yun, W.: Low Power System Design. pp.1001–9081 (2004);03-0158-03. pp.158–159 (2002)
3. Weiser, M., Welch, B., Demers, A., Shenker, S.: Scheduling for reduced CPU energy. In: Proc. USENIX Symposium on Operating Systems Design and Implementation, pp. 13–23 (1994)
4. Pillai, P., Shin, K.G.: Real-Time Dynamic Voltage Scaling for Low-Power Embedded Operating Systems. In: Proc. of 18th ACM Symposium on Operating Systems Principles, pp. 89–102 (October 2001)

A Globally Convergent Smoothing Method for Symmetric Conic Linear Programming

Xiaoni Chi[*] and Ping Li

College of Mathematics and Information Science, Huanggang Normal University,
Huangzhou 438000, Hubei, China
chixiaoni@126.com

Abstract. Based on the Chen-Harker-Kanzow-Smale smoothing function, a smoothing Newton method is developed for solving the symmetric conic linear programming. Without any restrictions for its starting point, this algorithm solves only one linear system of equations at each iteration and proves to be globally convergent in absence of uniform nonsingularity. Numerical results indicate that it is promising in future applications.

Keywords: symmetric conic linear programming, smoothing method, Chen-Harker-Kanzow-Smale smoothing function, global convergence.

1 Introduction

The symmetric conic linear programming (SCLP) is to minimize or maximize a linear function over the intersection of an affine space with a symmetric cone. Consider the SCLP problem and its dual problem [7] in the following standard form:

$$(P) \quad \min\{<c,x>: Ax=b, x\in K\}, \tag{1}$$

$$(D) \quad \max\{<b,y>: A^T y+s=c, s\in K\}. \tag{2}$$

Here J is a real n-dimensional Euclidean space with inner product $<\cdot,\cdot>$, $K \subset J$ is a symmetric cone, and $c\in J$, $b\in R^m$ are the data.

The sets of strictly feasible solutions of (1) and (2) are

$$F^0(P) = \{x: Ax=b, x\in \text{int } K\},$$

$$F^0(D) = \{(y,s): A^T y+s=c, s\in \text{int } K\},$$

respectively. Throughout this paper, we assume that $F^0(P)\times F^0(D) \neq \varnothing$. Thus, it follows from the strong dual theory [7] that both (1) and (2) have optimal solutions and their optimal values coincide.

The SCLP has wide applications and covers linear programming [10], second-order cone programming (SOCP) [1] and semidefinite programming as special cases.

As a new kind of algorithms for solving mathematical programming problems, smoothing Newton methods perform well [2,3,7,8] due to their encouraging

---

[*] Corresponding author.

Z. Cai et al. (Eds.): ISICA 2009, LNCS 5821, pp. 136–143, 2009.
© Springer-Verlag Berlin Heidelberg 2009

convergent properties and numerical results. However, there is little work on smoothing methods for the SCLP. Moreover, some algorithm [3] depends on the uniform nonsingularity condition. without uniform nonsingularity, some algorithms [2,7] need to solve two linear systems of equations and to perform two or three line searches at each iteration.

To overcome these deficiencies, we propose a globally convergent smoothing Newton method for solving the SCLP in this paper.

The rest of this paper is organized as follows. Section 2 presents our novel algorithm. To illustrate the effectiveness and superiority of the algorithm, the convergence analysis and numerical results are given in Section 3 and Section 4, respectively. Section 5 concludes this paper.

2 Smoothing Method

In this section, we give a brief introduction to Euclidean Jordan algebras [4]. Based on the Jordan algebras, we present a globally convergent smoothing method for the SCLP and show the well-definedness of our algorithm.

$(J, \circ)$ is called a Jordan algebra if a bilinear mapping $J \times J \to J$ denoted by " $\circ$ "is defined for any $x, y \in J$ such that

$$x \circ y = y \circ x \text{ and } L_x L_{x^2} = L_{x^2} L_x,$$

where $x^2 = x \circ x$, and L_x is a linear transformation of J defined by $L_x y = x \circ y.$

A Jordan algebra is called Euclidean if an associate inner product " $< \cdot, \cdot >$ " is defined, i.e., $< x \circ y, z >=< x, y \circ z >$ holds for any $x, y, z \in J$. A Jordan algebra has an identity, if there exists a unique element $e \in J$ such that $x \circ e = e \circ x = x$ holds for all $x \in J$. Throughout this paper, we assume that J is a Euclidean Jordan algebra with an identity element e.

The set of squares of some Euclidean Jordan algebra $K := \left\{ x^2 \mid x \in J \right\}$ is called a symmetric cone. Let $x^2 := x \circ x$. For any $x \in K$, $\sqrt{x}$ denotes the unique vector such that $(\sqrt{x})^2 = \sqrt{x} \circ \sqrt{x} = x.$

It is well known that the SCLP problems (1) and (2) are equivalent to [7] the optimality conditions

$$\begin{cases} Ax = b, & x \in K, \\ A^T y + s = c, & s \in K, \\ x \circ s = 0. \end{cases} \tag{3}$$

The algorithm to be discussed here reformulates the optimality conditions (3) as a nonlinear system of equations. By applying Newton's method to the system of equations, one can find a solution of the SCLP problems (1) and (2). For this purpose, let $\phi_\mu : J \times J \to J$ denote the Chen-Harker-Kanzow-Smale (CHKS) smoothing function [6]

$$\phi_\mu (x,s) = x + s - \sqrt{(x-s)^2 + 4\mu^2 e},$$

where $\mu \in R$ is the smoothing parameter. It is not difficult to verify

$$\phi_0 (x,s) = 0 \Leftrightarrow x \circ s = 0, x \in K, s \in K. \tag{4}$$

Let $z = (x, y, s) \in J \times R^m \times J$ and define

$$\Phi_\mu(z) = \begin{pmatrix} Ax - b \\ A^T y + s - c \\ \phi_\mu (x,s) \end{pmatrix}, \tag{5}$$

with the parameter $\mu \in R$. By (3) and (4), $z^* := (x^*, y^*, s^*)$ is the optimal solution of (1) and (2) if and only if z^* is a root of the system of equations $\Phi_0(z) = 0$. Since the function $\Phi_0(z)$ is nonsmooth, it is difficult for us to solve the system of equations $\Phi_0(z) = 0$ directly. Thus, we can apply Newton's method to the smooth system of equations $\Phi_\mu(z) = 0$ and make $\|\Phi_\mu(z)\|$ decrease gradually by reducing μ to zero.

Algorithm 2.1

Step 0. Choose $\sigma, \delta, \gamma \in (0,1)$ and $\mu_0 \in (0, \infty)$. Let $(x_0, y_0, s_0) \in J \times R^m \times J$ be an arbitrary point and $z_0 := (x_0, y_0, s_0)$. Choose $\beta > 0$ such that $\|\Phi_{\mu_0}(z)\| \leq \beta \mu_0$. Set $k := 0$.

Step 1. If $\Phi_0(z_k) = 0$, stop.

Step 2. Compute the search direction $\Delta z_k = (\Delta x_k, \ \Delta y_k, \Delta s_k) \in J \times R^m \times J$ by solving the linear system of equations

$$D\Phi_{\mu_k}(z_k)\Delta z = -\Phi_{\mu_k}(z_k). \tag{6}$$

Step 3. Let $\lambda_k = \max\{\delta^l \mid l = 0,1,2,\ldots\}$ such that

$$\|\Phi_{\mu_k}(z_k + \lambda_k \Delta z_k)\| \leq (1 - \sigma \lambda_k)\|\Phi_{\mu_k}(z_k)\|, \tag{7}$$

and set $z_{k+1} := z_k + \lambda_k \Delta z_k$.

Step 4. Compute $\tau_k = \max\{\gamma^l \mid l = 0,1,2,\ldots\}$ such that

$$\left\| \Phi_{(1-\tau_k)\mu_k}(z_{k+1}) \right\| \le \beta(1-\tau_k)\mu_k, \tag{8}$$

and set $\mu_{k+1} := (1-\tau_k)\mu_k$. Set $k := k+1$ and go to Step 1.

To design and analyze Algorithm 2.1, we need the following properties of the function $\Phi_\mu(z)$.

Lemma 2.1. Let $\Phi_\mu : J \times R^m \times J \to R^m \times J \times J$ be defined as in (5). Then for any $\mu > 0$, the following results hold.

(i) The function Φ_μ is continuously differentiable everywhere in $J \times R^m \times J$ with its Jacobian

$$D\Phi_\mu(z)(u,w,v) = \begin{pmatrix} Au \\ A^T w + v \\ D\phi_\mu(x,s)(u,v) \end{pmatrix},$$

where

$$D\phi_\mu(x,s)(u,v) = u + v - L_c^{-1}[(x-y) \circ (u-v)],$$

$$c := \sqrt{(x-s)^2 + 4\mu^2 e}.$$

(ii) If A has full row rank, $D\Phi_\mu(z)$ is nonsingular for any $z \in J \times R^m \times J$.

Proof. By using Theorem 4.2 in [6] and following the proof of Theorem 5.1 in [5], it is not difficult to show the conclusions hold.

Theorem 2.2. If A has full row rank, Algorithm 2.1 is well-defined.

Proof. Since $\mu_k > 0$ by the algorithm and A has full row rank, it follows from Lemma 2.1 (ii) that $D\Phi_{\mu_k}(z_k)$ is nonsingular. This demonstrates the well-definedness of Step 2. By Lemma 2.1 (i) and induction on k, it is not difficult to show that Step 3 is well-defined.

3 Global Convergence

To analyze the global convergence of Algorithm 2.1, we need the following lemma, which may be shown by a simple induction argument.

Lemma 3.1. Suppose that A has full row rank. Then

(i) $Ax_k - b \to 0$ as $k \to \infty$;

(ii) $A^T y_k + s_k - c \to 0$ as $k \to \infty$;

(iii) $\mu_k = (1 - \tau_{k-1}) \cdots (1 - \tau_0) \mu_0 \geq 0$ for any $k > 0$;

(iv) $\left\| \Phi_{\mu_k}(z_k) \right\| \leq \beta \mu_k$ for any $k \geq 0$.

Theorem 3.2. Suppose that A has full row rank and that the iteration sequence $\{(z_k, \mu_k)\}$ generated by Algorithm 2.1 has at least one accumulation point. Then $\{\mu_k\}$ converges to 0, and hence any accumulation point of $\{z_k\}$ is a solution of $\Phi_0(z) = 0$.

Proof. First we show that $\{\mu_k\}$ converges to 0. Since $\{\mu_k\}$ is monotonically decreasing and bounded from below by zero by Lemma 3.1 (iii), it converges to a number $\mu^* \geq 0$. If $\mu^* = 0$, we obtain the desired result. On the contrary, we assume $\mu^* > 0$. Using the fact $\mu_k \to \mu^* > 0$ and Lemma 3.1 (iii), we obtain for all sufficiently large k that

$$\lim_{k \to \infty} \tau_k = 0. \tag{9}$$

Let z^* be an accumulation point of the sequence $\{z_k\}$. By taking a subsequence if necessary, we assume

$$\lim_{k \to \infty} (z_k, \mu_k) = (z^*, \mu^*).$$

Since $\lambda_k \geq 0$ for any $k \geq 0$, we consider the following two cases separately.

Case (i). If $\liminf_{k \to \infty} \lambda_k = 0$, we have $\lim_{k \to \infty} \lambda_k = 0$ by taking a subsequence if necessary. Since Φ is continuously differentiable in both z and μ for any $\mu > 0$ by Lemma 2.1, we obtain

$$\lim_{k \to \infty} \Phi_{\mu_k}(z_k) = \Phi_{\mu^*}(z^*), \quad \lim_{k \to \infty} D\Phi_{\mu_k}(z_k) = D\Phi_{\mu^*}(z^*).$$

On the one hand, it follows from Step 4 in Algorithm 2.1 that τ_k / γ does not satisfy relation (8), i.e.,

$$\| \Phi_{(1 - \tau_k / \gamma)\mu_k}(z_{k+1}) \| > \beta(1 - \tau_k / \gamma)\mu_k.$$

Taking the limit $k \to \infty$ in the last relation and using (9), we have

$$\| \Phi_{\mu^*}(z^*) \| \geq \beta \mu^* > 0. \tag{10}$$

On the other hand, the Armijo condition (7) is not satisfied for $\bar{\lambda}_k := \lambda_k / \delta$ from Step 3 in Algorithm 2.1, i.e.,

$$\frac{\| \Phi_{\mu_k}(z_k + \bar{\lambda}_k \Delta z_k) \| - \| \Phi_{\mu_k}(z_k) \|}{\bar{\lambda}_k} > -\sigma \| \Phi_{\mu_k}(z_k) \|.$$

Taking the limit $k \to \infty$ in the above relation and using $\bar{\lambda}_k \to 0$, we obtain

$$\Phi_{\mu^*}(z^*)^T D\Phi_{\mu^*}(z^*) \Delta z^* \geq -\sigma \| \Phi_{\mu^*}(z^*) \|^2. \tag{11}$$

By (6), we have

$$D\Phi_{\mu^*}(z^*) \Delta z^* = -\Phi_{\mu^*}(z^*).$$

Using (11), the last relation and the fact $\sigma \in (0,1)$, we have

$$\Phi_{\mu^*}(z^*) = 0,$$

which is a contradiction to (10).

Case (ii). If $\liminf_{k \to \infty} \lambda_k > 0$, there exists a constant $\lambda > 0$ such that $\lambda_k \geq \lambda$ for all sufficiently large k. It follows from Corollary 4.1 in [6] that

$$\| \Phi_\mu(z) - \Phi_{\mu'}(z) \| \leq 2 \, |\mu - \mu'| \tag{12}$$

holds for any $\mu, \mu' > 0$ and any $z \in J \times R^m \times J$. By (7) and Lemma 3.1 (iv), we have

$$\| \Phi_{\mu_k}(z_{k+1}) \| \leq (1 - \sigma\lambda) \| \Phi_{\mu_k}(z_k) \| \leq \beta(1 - \sigma\lambda)\mu_k. \tag{13}$$

It follows from (12), (13) and Step 4 in Algorithm 2.1 that

$$\begin{aligned} &\beta(1 - \tau_k/\gamma)\mu_k \\ &\leq \| \Phi_{(1-\tau_k/\gamma)\mu_k}(z_{k+1}) \| \\ &\leq \| \Phi_{\mu_k}(z_{k+1}) \| + \| \Phi_{(1-\tau_k/\gamma)\mu_k}(z_{k+1}) - \Phi_{\mu_k}(z_{k+1}) \| \\ &\leq \beta(1 - \sigma\lambda)\mu_k + 2\tau_k\mu_k/\gamma. \end{aligned}$$

This implies $\tau_k \geq \beta\sigma\lambda\gamma/(\beta + 2)$ holds for all sufficiently large k, which is a contradiction to (9).

Combining Case (i) and Case (ii) yields that $\{\mu_k\}$ converges to 0.

Next we show that z^* is a solution of $\Phi_0(z) = 0$. By Lemma 3.1 (iv), we have

$$\| \Phi_{\mu_k}(z_k)\| \le \beta\mu_k. \tag{14}$$

Similar to Lemma 2.1, it is not difficult to show that Φ is a continuous function in both z and μ. Then taking the limit $k \to \infty$ in (14) yields

$$\| \Phi_0(z^*)\| = \| \Phi_{\mu^*}(z^*)\| \le \beta\mu^* = 0.$$

4 Numerical Results

To see the behavior of Algorithm 2.1, we implemented the smoothing method for solving the SCLP in MATLAB 7.0.1. As the interior point algorithm for the SCLP, the SDPT3 solver [9] was used for comparison purpose. All the experiments were performed on Windows XP system running on a Intel (R) Pentium(R) 4 CPU 3.00 GHz with 512 MB memory.

The test problems are randomly generated second-order cone programming (SOCP) problems with size $n = 2m = 100$. Choose $x_0 = s_0 = 1.0e$, $y_0 = 0 \in R^m$ as initial points. The parameters used in Algorithm 2.1 were $\sigma = 0.2$, $\delta = 0.9, \gamma = 0.9$ and

$$\mu_0 = \min\{1, \| \Phi_0(z_0)\|\}, \quad \beta = \| \Phi_{\mu_0}(z_0)\|/\mu_0.$$

We used $\| \Phi_0(z)\| \le 10^{-6}$ as our stopping criterion. The numerical results in Table 1 indicate that Algorithm 2.1 is comparable to SDPT3 and hence is promising.

Table 1. Comparison of Algorithm 2.1 and SDPT3 on SOCPs

Algorithm 2.1		SDPT3	
Iter	Cpu(s)	Iter	Cpu(s)
6	0.09	9	0.20
5	0.07	8	0.10
6	0.08	8	0.10
4	0.06	7	0.10
5	0.07	8	0.10
5	0.07	8	0.20

5 Numerical Results

Based on the CHKS smoothing function, we propose a smoothing Newton method for solving the SCLP. Our algorithm is shown to possess the following good properties: (i) if A has full row rank, the algorithm is well-defined and globally convergent; (ii) without any restrictions regarding its starting points, the algorithm solves only one linear system of equations at each iteration; (iii) in absence of uniform nonsingularity, any accumulation point of the iteration sequence generated by our algorithm is a solution of the SCLP.

Acknowledgments. This research was supported by the Excellent Youth Project of Hubei Provincial Department of Education (No. Q20092701), and the Doctorial Foundation of Huanggang Normal University (No. 08CD158), China.

References

1. Alizadeh, F., Goldfarb, D.: Second-order cone programming. Mathematical Programming 95(1), 3–51 (2003)
2. Burke, J., Xu, S.: A non-interior predictor-corrector path following algorithm for the monotone linear complementarity problem. Math. Program. 87(1), 113–130 (2000)
3. Chen, B., Xiu, N.: A global linear and local quadratic non-interior continuation method for nonlinear complementarity problems based on Chen-Mangasarian smoothing functions. SIAM J. Optim. 9(3), 605–623 (1999)
4. Faraut, J., Korányi, A.: Analysis on Symmetric Cones. Oxford University Press, Oxford (1994)
5. Huang, Z.H., Ni, T.: Smoothing algorithms for complementarity problems over symmetric cones. Comput. Optim. Appl. doi:10.1007/s10589-008-9180-y
6. Liu, Y., Zhang, L., Liu, M.: Extension of smoothing functions to symmetric cone complementarity problems. Applied Mathematics–A Journal of Chinese Universities 22(2), 245–252 (2007)
7. Liu, Y., Zhang, L., Wang, Y.: Analysis of a smoothing method for symmetric conic linear programming. J. Appl. Math. Comput. 22(1-2), 133–148 (2006)
8. Qi, L., Sun, D., Zhou, G.: A new look at smoothing Newton methods for nonlinear complementarity problems and box constrained variational inequalities. Math. Program. 87(1), 1–35 (2000)
9. Toh, K.C., Tütüncü, R.H., Todd, M.J.: SDPT3 Version 3.02 –a MATLAB software for semidefinite-quadratic-linear programming (2002), http://www.math.nus.edu.sg/~mattohkc/sdpt3.html
10. Yong, L.: Primal-dual Interior Point Algorithm for Linear Programming. In: Proceedings of First International Conference of Modelling and Simulation, vol. II, pp. 432–436. World Academic Press, UK (2008)

A New Optimizaiton Algorithm for Function Optimization

Xuesong Yan[1], Qinghua Wu[2], and Hanmin Liu[3]

[1] School of Computer Science, Chin University of Geoscience, Hubei, Wuhan, 430074, China
Yanxs1999@yahoo.com.cn
[2] Faculty of Computer Science and Engineering, WuHan Institute of Technology, Hubei, Wuhan, 430074, China
wuqinghua@sina.com
[3] Wuhan Institute of Shipbuilding Technology, Hubei, Wuhan, 430050, China

Abstract. Particle Swarm Optimization (PSO) algorithm was developed under the inspiration of behavior laws of bird flocks, fish schools and human communities. In order to get rid of the disadvantages of standard Particle Swarm Optimization algorithm like being trapped easily into a local optimum, this paper improves the standard PSO and proposes a new algorithm to solve these problems. The new algorithm keeps not only the fast convergence speed characteristic of PSO, but effectively improves the capability of global searching as well. Compared with standard PSO on the Benchmarks function, the new algorithm produces more efficient results.

1 Introduction

Particle Swarm Optimization (PSO) algorithm [1] was an intelligent technology first presented in 1995 by Eberhart and Kennedy, and it was developed under the inspiration of behavior laws of bird flocks, fish schools and human communities. If we compare PSO with Genetic Algorithms (GAs), we may find that they are all maneuvered on the basis of population operated. But PSO doesn't rely on genetic operators like selection operators, crossover operators and mutation operators to operate individual, it optimizes the population through information exchange among individuals. PSO achieves its optimum solution by starting from a group of random solution and then searching repeatedly. Once PSO was presented, it invited widespread concerns among scholars in the optimization fields and shortly afterwards it had become a studying focus within only several years. A number of scientific achievements had emerged in these fields [2] [3] [4]. PSO was proved to be a sort of high efficient optimization algorithm by numerous research and experiments [5]. This paper improves the disadvantages of standard PSO's being easily trapped into a local optimum and presents a new algorithm which proves to be more simply conducted and with more efficient global searching capability.

2 Standards PSO

PSO was presented under the inspiration of bird flock immigration during the course of finding food and then be used in the optimization problems. In PSO, each optimization

Z. Cai et al. (Eds.): ISICA 2009, LNCS 5821, pp. 144–150, 2009.

problem solution is taken as a bird in the searching space and it is called "particle". Every particle has a fitness value which is determined by target functions and it has also a velocity which determines its destination and distance. All particles search in the solution space for their best positions and the positions of the best particles in the swarm. PSO is initially a group of random particles (random solutions), and then the optimum solutions are found by repeated searching. In the course of every iteration, a particle will follow two bests to renew itself: the best position found for a particle called pbest; the best position found for the whole swarm called gbest. All particles will determine following steps through the best experiences of individuals themselves and their companions.

For particle id, its velocity and its position renewal formula are as follows:

$$V_{id}^{'} = \omega V_{id} + \eta_1 rand()(P_{idb} - X_{id}) + \eta_2 rand()(P_{gdb} - X_{id}) \tag{1}$$

$$X_{id}^{'} = X_{id} + V_{id}^{'} \tag{2}$$

In here: ω is called inertia weight, it is a proportion factor that is concerned with former velocity, $0 < \omega < 1$, η_1 and η_2 are constants and are called accelerating factors, normally $\eta_1 = \eta_2 = 2$; $rand()$ are random numbers, X_{id} represents the position of particle id ; V_{id} represents the velocity of particle id ; P_{id} , P_{gd} represent separatively the best position particle id has found and the position of the best particles in the whole swarm.

In formula(1), the first part represents the former velocity of the particle, it enables the particle to possess expanding tendency in the searching space and thus makes the algorithm be more capable in global searching; the second part is called cognition part, it represents the process of absorbing individual experience knowledge on the part of the particle; the third part is called social part, it represents the process of learning from the experiences of other particles on the part of certain particle, and it also shows the information sharing and social cooperation among particles.

The flow of PSO can briefly describe as following: First, to initialize a group of particles, e.g. to give randomly each particle an initial position X_i and an initial velocity V_i, and then to calculate its fitness value f. In every iteration, evaluated a particle's fitness value by analyzing the velocity and positions of renewed particles in formula (1) and (2). When a particle finds a better position than previously, it will mark this coordinate into vector P_1, the vector difference between P_1 and the present position of the particle will randomly be added to next velocity vector, so that the following renewed particles will search around this point, it's also called in formula (1) cognition component. The weight difference of the present position of the particle swarm and the best position of the swarm P_{gd} will also be added to velocity vector for adjusting the next population velocity. This is also called in formula (1) social component. These two adjustments will enable particles to search around two bests.

The most obvious advantage of PSO is that the convergence speed of the swarm is very high, scholars like Clerc [6] has presented proof on its convergence. Here a fatal weakness may result from this characteristic. With constant increase of iterations, the velocity of particles will gradually diminish and reach zero in the end. At this time, the whole swarm will be converged at one point in the solution space, if gbest particles haven't found gbest, the whole swarm will be trapped into a local optimum; and the capacity of swarm jump out of a local optimum is rather weak. The probability of the occurrence is especially high so far for multi-peaks functions, we have test the algorithm for the multi-peaks functions to verify these. In order to get through this disadvantage, in this paper we presents a new algorithm based on PSO.

3   A New Algorithm Based on PSO

In the standard PSO algorithm, the convergence speed of particles is fast, but the adjustments of cognition component and social component make particles search around P_{gd} and P_{id}. According to velocity and position renewal formula, once the best individual in the swarm is trapped into a local optimum, the information sharing mechanism in PSO will attract other particles to approach this local optimum gradually, and in the end the whole swarm will be converged at this position. But according to velocity and position renewal formula (1), once the whole swarm is trapped into a local optimum, its cognition component and social component will become zero in the end; still, because $0 < \omega < 1$ and with the number of iteration increase, the velocity of particles will become zero in the end, thus the whole swarm is hard to jump out of the local optimum and has no way to achieve the global optimum. In order to avoid being trapped into a local optimum, the new PSO adopts a new information sharing mechanism. We all know that when a particle is searching in the solution space, it doesn't know the exact position of the optimum solution. But we can not only record the best positions an individual particle and the whole swarm have experienced, we can also record the worst positions an individual particle and the whole swarm have experienced, thus we may make individual particles move in the direction of evading the worst positions an individual particle and the whole flock have experienced, this will surely enlarge the global searching space of particles and enable them to avoid being trapped into a local optimum too early, in the same time, it will improve the possibility of finding gbest in the searching space. In the new strategy, the particle velocity and position renewal formula are as follows:

$$V_{id}^{'} = \omega V_{id} + \eta_1 rand()(X_{id} - P_{idw}) + \eta_2 rand()(X_{id} - P_{gdw}) \tag{3}$$

$$X_{id}^{'} = X_{id} + V_{id}^{'} \tag{4}$$

In here: P_{idw}, P_{gdw} represent the worst position particle id has found and the worst positions of the whole swarm has found.

In standard PSO algorithm, the next flying direction of each particle is nearly definite, it can fly to the best individual and the best individuals for the whole swarm. From the above conclusion we may easily to know it will be the danger for being trapped into a local optimum. In order to decrease the possibility of being trapped into the local optimum, the new PSO introduces genetic selection strategy: To set particle number in the swarm as m, father population and son population add up to $2m$. To select randomly q pairs from m; as to each individual particle i, if the fitness value of i is smaller than its opponents, i will win out and then add one to its mark, and finally select those particles which have the maximum mark value into the next generation. The experiments conducted show that this strategy greatly reduces the possibility of being trapped into a local optimum when solving certain functions. The flow of the new PSO is as follows:

Step 1: to initialize randomly the velocity and position of particles;

Step 2: to evaluate the fitness value of each particle;

Step 3: as to each particle, if its fitness value is smaller than the best fitness value P_{idb}, renew the best position P_{idb} of particle id ; or else if its fitness value is bigger than the worst fitness value P_{idw}, renew P_{idw} ;

Step 4: as to each particle, if its fitness value is smaller than the best whole swarm fitness value P_{gdb}, renew the best fitness value P_{gdb} of particle id ; or else if bigger than the worst whole swarm fitness value P_{gdw}, renew P_{gdw} ;

Step 5: as to each particle,

1) To produce new particle t by applying formula (1) (2),

2) To produce new particle t' by applying formula (3) (4),

3) To make a comparison between t and t' and then select the better one into the next generation;

Step 6: to produce next generation particles according to the above genetic selection strategy;

Step 7: if all the above steps satisfy suspension needs, suspend it; or turn to Step 3.

4 Experiment and Results

In order to verify the validity of the new algorithm, we using eight benchmarks function to verify the effectiveness of improvement. Specific details of the test function see table 1. In the table 1, n behalf of the dimension number of the function, S behalf of the range of variables, f min behalf of the minimization of the function.

In order to compare the standard PSO and the new algorithm performance of these two algorithms, the two algorithms of the same experimental parameters set. Each function in table 1 is run 50 times with the two algorithms, their experimental results such as table 2.

Table 1. Test Function

Test Function	n	S	f_{min}
$f_1(x) = \sum_{i=1}^{n} x_i^2$	30	(-100,100)	0
$f_2(x) = 6 \cdot \sum_{i=1}^{5} \lfloor x_i \rfloor$	30	(-5.12, 5.12)	0
$f_3(x) = \sum_{i=1}^{n} i \cdot x_i^4 + U(0,1)$	30	(-1.28,1.28)	0
$f_4(x) = \dfrac{(\sin^2 \sqrt{x_2 + y_2}) + 0.5}{(1.0 + 0.001(x_2 + y_2))_2} + 0.5$	2	(-100.0,100.0)	0
$f_5(x) = \dfrac{1}{4000} \sum_{i=1}^{n} (x_i - 100)_2 - \prod_{i=1}^{n} \cos(\dfrac{x_i - 100}{\sqrt{i}}) + 1$	30	(-300.0,300.0)	0
$f_6(x) = -20 \cdot \exp(-0.2 \sqrt{\dfrac{1}{n} \sum_{i=1}^{n} x_i^2}) - \exp(\dfrac{1}{n} \cdot \sum_{i=1}^{n} \cos(2\pi \cdot x_i)) + 20 + e$	30	(-32.0,32.0)	0
$f_7(x) = \sum_{i=1}^{n} 100((x_{i+1} - x_i^2)_2 + (x_i - 1)_2)$	30	(-2.048,2.048)	0
$f_8(x) = \sum_{i=1}^{n} - x_i \sin(\sqrt{|x_i|})$	30	(-500,500)	-12569.5

By analyzing the experimental results we know, in solving function f_1, f_5 and f_8, use PSO algorithm is easily into local optimum, but uses the new algorithm, functions convergence soon, and finds a better solution, the average fitness and the best fitness was both superior to PSO algorithm. For the function f_2, the new algorithm and PSO all can find the global optimum, these two algorithms for this test function is very effective. For function f_6, two algorithms can find the best solutions are the same (see table 2), but the new algorithm's convergence speed faster than the PSO, and the new algorithm to get the best value of the average is better than PSO algorithm.

In sum, we can see that in solving function f_1, f_5, f_6 and f_8, the new algorithm more efficient than PSO algorithm, in solving other functions, the performance almost same of the two algorithms. In short, this new algorithm has the following values: better global search capability and faster convergence, so the information sharing mechanism is effective.

Table 2. New algorithm and PSO experiments

Function	Algorithm	Best Value	Worst Value	Average Value	Standard deviation
$f_1(x)$	PSO	1495.71	7032.89	4224.775	201.038
	New	4.13731 E-26	1.0882E-24	4.46015E-26	2.28015E-26
$f_2(x)$	PSO	0	0	0	0
	New	0	0	0	0
$f_3(x)$	PSO	0.00177 094	0.00833963	0.004630085	0.000210055
	New	0.00193 565	0.0103595	0.004941903	0.000259903
$f_4(x)$	PSO	0	0.00971591	0.005246591	0.000684817
	New	1.41681 E-07	0.00971591	0.003697618	0.000509981
$f_5(x)$	PSO	72.5069	123.954	101.410452	1.52289
	New	2.18559 E-12	8.63194E-25	0.010377	0.00177512
$f_6(x)$	PSO	-3.19744E-14	4.4229	1.306447538	0.148418
	New	-3.19744E-14	1.50229	0.27769	0.0749509
$f_7(x)$	PSO	1.84889E-28	8.63194E-25	4.59643E-26	1.83991E-26
	New	2.55147E-28	1.20401E-23	3.46992E-25	2.41678E-25
$f_8(x)$	PSO	-5038.62	-3233.13	-4005.02	54.0123
	New	-9535.19	-8203.56	-8741.27	45.1661

5 Conclusion

This paper introduce a new algorithm based on the standard PSO algorithm, for the standard PSO algorithm the new algorithm has done two improvements: 1. By introducing a new information sharing mechanism, make particles moved on the contrary direction of the worst individual positions and the worst whole swarm positions, thus enlarge global searching space and reduce the possibility of particles to be trapped into a local optimum; 2. By introducing genetic selection strategy, decreased the possibility of being trapped into a local optimum. Compared with the standard PSO algorithm, the new algorithm enlarges the searching space and the complexity is not high. By analyzing the testing results of eight Benchmarks optimization, we reach the conclusion: in the optimization precision and the optimization speed, the new algorithm is efficiency than the standard PSO algorithm and the new algorithm is more efficient than PSO in coping with function optimization problems.

Acknowledgement

This paper is supported by Astronautics Research Foundation of China (NO. C5220060318). The author will thank for Prof. Lishan Kang and Dr. Changhe Li.

References

[1] Kennedy, J., Eberhart, R.C.: Particle Swarm Optimization. In: IEEE International Conference on Neural Networks, pp. 1942–1948 (1995)

[2] Clare, M., Kennedy, J.: The Particle Swarm - Explosion, Stability, and Convergence in a Multidimensional Complex Space. IEEE Trans. on Evolutionary Computation 6(1), 58–73 (2002)

[3] Coello, C.A., Lechuga, M.S.: Mopso: A proposal for multiple objective particle swarm optimization. In: IEEE Proceedings World Congress on Computational Intelligence, pp. 1051–1056 (2002)

[4] Kennedy, J.: The particle swarm: social adaptation of knowledge. In: Proc. IEEE int. Conf. on evolutionary computation, pp. 3003–3008 (1997)

[5] Oscan, E., Mohan, C.K.: Analysis of A Simple Particle Swarm Optimization System. In: Intelligence Engineering Systems Through Artificial Neural Networks, pp. 253–258 (1998)

[6] Clerc, M., Kennedy, J.: The Particle Swarm: Explosion, Stability and Convergence in a Multi-Dimensional Complex Space. IEEE Trans. on Evolutionary Computation 6, 58–73 (2002)

[7] van den Bergh, F.: An Analysis of Particle Swarm Optimizers. PhD thesis, Department of Computer Science, University of Pretoria, South Africa (2002)

[8] Parsopoulos, K.E., Vrahatis, M.N.: Particle Swarm Optimization Method in Multiobjective Problems. In: Proceedings of the 2002 Congress on Evolutionary Computation, Piscataway, NJ, pp. 46–53 (2000)

[9] Clerc, M.: Discrete Particle Swarm Optimization Illustrated by the Traveling Salesman Problem (2000), http://www.mauriceclerc.net

[10] Clerc, M., Kennedy, J.: The Particle Swarm: Explosion, Stability and Convergence in a Multi-Dimensional Complex Space. IEEE Trans. on Evolutionary Computation 6, 58–73 (2002)

[11] Eberhart, R.C., Shi, Y.: Comparing inertia weights and constriction factors in particle swarm optimization. In: Proceedings of the 2000 Congress on evolutionary computation, vol. 1, pp. 84–88 (2000)

A Point Symmetry-Based Automatic Clustering Approach Using Differential Evolution

Wenyin Gong[1], Zhihua Cai[1], Charles X. Ling[2], and Bo Huang[1]

[1] School of Computer Science,
China University of Geosciences, Wuhan 430074, P.R. China
cug11100304@yahoo.com.cn, zhcai@cug.edu.cn
[2] Department of Computer Science,
The University of Western Ontario, London, Canada
cling@csd.uwo.ca

Abstract. Clustering is a core problem in data mining and machine learning though it is widely applied in many fields. Recently, it is very popular to use the evolutionary algorithm to solve the problem. This paper proposes an automatic clustering differential evolution (DE) technique for the problem. This approach can be characterized by (i) proposing a modified point symmetry-based cluster validity index (CVI) as a measure of the validity of the corresponding partitioning, (ii) using the Kd-tree based nearest neighbor search to reduce the complexity of finding the closest symmetric point, and (iii) employing a new representation to represent an individual. Experiments conducted on 6 artificial data sets of diverse complexities indicate that this approach is suitable for both the symmetrical intra-clusters and the symmetrical inter-clusters. In addition, it is able to find the optimal number of clusters of the data. Furthermore, based on the comparison with the original point symmetry-based CVI, this proposed point symmetry-based CVI shows better performance in terms of the F-measure and the number of clusters found.

1 Introduction

Clustering is the unsupervised classification of objects (patterns) into different groups, or more precisely, the partitioning of a data set into subsets (clusters), so that the data in the same clusters is similar and the data in different clusters is dissimilar according to some defined distance measure. Data clustering is a common technique for statistical data analysis, which is used in many fields, including machine learning, data mining, pattern recognition, image analysis, and bioinformatics [1], [2].

Clustering techniques may broadly be divided into two categories: hierarchical and partitional clustering [3], [4]. Hierarchical clustering algorithms generate a cluster tree by using heuristic splitting or merging techniques. Algorithms that use splitting to generate the cluster tree are called divisive. On the other hand, the more popular algorithms that use merging to generate the cluster tree are called agglomerative [2]. There are two main advantages of the hierarchical clustering algorithms: i) the number of clusters need not to be specified a priori, and ii) they are independent of the initial conditions [2]. However, the main drawbacks of these algorithms are: i) they are static; that is, data

Z. Cai et al. (Eds.): ISICA 2009, LNCS 5821, pp. 151–162, 2009.
© Springer-Verlag Berlin Heidelberg 2009

points assigned to a cluster can not move to another cluster; ii) they may fail to separate overlapping clusters due to a lack of information about the global shape or size of the clusters; and iii) they are computationally expensive. On the other hand, partitional clustering algorithms try to decompose the data set directly into a set of disjoint clusters. They try to optimize certain criteria. The advantages of the hierarchical algorithms are the disadvantages of the partitional algorithms, and vice versa. Two extensive surveys of the clustering algorithms can be found in [1] and [2].

Since a priori knowledge is generally not available, it is difficult to estimate the exact number of clusters from the given data set. Recently, many automatic clustering algorithms based on evolutionary algorithms (EAs) have been introduced [5], [6], [7], [8], etc. Based on some clustering validity index (CVI) [9], these techniques are more efficient than the traditional method.

Differential evolution (DE) [10] algorithm is a novel evolutionary algorithm for faster optimization, which mutation operator is based on the distribution of solutions in the population. Among DE's advantages are its simple structure, ease of use, speed and robustness. Based on the successful applications of DE [11], [12] in many fields, some researchers adopted it to solve the clustering problems [13], [14], [7]. Experimental results have shown that the DE-based clustering algorithms can provide higher performance than GA-based clustering algorithms. However, the work of using DE for clustering problems is still preliminary. In addition, most of the previous work need to give the number of clusters in advance.

In this paper, in order to automatically determine the optimal number of clusters in the data set, we propose an automatic clustering DE technique based on the point symmetry-based CVI. Our approach is referred as ACDEPS. It is characterized by (i) proposing a modified point symmetry-based cluster validity index (CVI) as a measure of the validity of the corresponding partitioning, (ii) using the Kd-tree based nearest neighbor search to reduce the complexity of finding the closest symmetric point, and (iii) employing a new representation to represent an individual.

The remainder of this paper is organized as follows. In Section 2, we briefly introduce the clustering problem definition and the DE algorithm. Our proposed approach is presented in detail in Section 3. In Section 4, we verify our approach through 6 artificial data sets of diverse complexities. The last section, Section 5, is devoted to conclusions and future work.

2 Preliminary

2.1 Problem Definition

Generally, a clustering problem can be formally defined as follows [2]: Given a data set $X = \{x_1, x_2, \cdots, x_n\}$, where n is the number of patterns in X, x_i is a pattern in a d-dimensional feature space, then the clustering of X is the partitioning of X into k clusters $\{C_1, C_2, \cdots, C_k\}$ satisfying the following conditions:

- Each pattern should be assigned to a cluster, i.e. $\cup_{i=1}^{k} C_i = X$.
- Each cluster has at least one pattern assigned to it, i.e. $C_i \neq \phi$, for $i = 1, 2, \cdots, k$.
- Each pattern is assigned to one and only one cluster (in case of hard clustering only), i.e. $C_i \cap C_j = \phi$, for $i = 1, 2, \cdots, k$, $j = 1, 2, \cdots, k$, and $i \neq j$.

2.2   Differential Evolution

The DE algorithm [10] is a simple EA that creates new candidate solutions by combining the parent individual and several other individuals of the same population. A candidate replaces the parent only if it has better fitness. This is a rather greedy selection scheme that often outperforms traditional EAs. In addition, DE is a simple yet powerful population-based, direct search algorithm with the generation-and-test feature for globally optimizing functions using real-valued parameters. Among DE's advantages are its simple structure, ease of use, speed and robustness. Due to these advantages, it has many real-world applications, such as data mining [15], [7], pattern recognition, digital filter design, neural network training, etc. [11], [12].

The DE algorithm in pseudo-code is shown in Algorithm 1. d is the number of decision variables, NP is the size of the parent population P, F is the mutation scaling factor, CR is the probability of crossover operator, U^i is the offspring, rndint$(1, d)$ is a uniformly distributed random integer number between 1 and d, and rnd$_j[0, 1)$ is a uniformly distributed random real number in $[0, 1)$. Many schemes of creation of a candidate are possible. We use the DE/rand/1/bin scheme (see lines 6 - 13 of Algorithm 1) described in Algorithm 1 (more details on DE/rand/1/bin and other DE schemes can be found in [16] and [11]).

Algorithm 1. DE algorithm with DE/rand/1/bin

1: Generate the initial population
2: Evaluate the fitness for each individual
3: **while** The halting criterion is not satisfied **do**
4:      **for** $i = 1$ to NP **do**
5:          Select uniform randomly $r_1 \neq r_2 \neq r_3 \neq i$
6:          j_{rand} = rndint$(1, d)$
7:          **for** $j = 1$ to d **do**
8:              **if** rnd$_j[0, 1) > CR$ or $j == j_{rand}$ **then**
9:                  $U_j^i = X_j^{r_1} + F \times (X_j^{r_2} - X_j^{r_3})$
10:             **else**
11:                 $U_j^i = X_j^i$
12:             **end if**
13:         **end for**
14:         Evaluate the offspring U^i
15:         **if** U^i is better than P^i **then**
16:             $P^i = U^i$
17:         **end if**
18:     **end for**
19: **end while**

From Algorithm 1, we can see that there are only three control parameters in this algorithm. These are NP, F and CR. As for the terminal conditions, one can either fix the maximum number of fitness function evaluations (NFFEs) Max_NFFEs or the precision of a desired solution VTR (value to reach).

2.3 Point Symmetry-Based Distance Measures

In natural senses, symmetry is one of the basic feature of shapes and objects, and hence, it is reasonable to assume some kinds of symmetry exist in the structures of clusters. Based on this idea, some symmetry-based distance measures are proposed in literature recently [17], [18], [19]. Since in this work we only employ the point symmetry-based distance measure proposed in [19], we will briefly discuss this measure in the following.

Recently, Bandyopadhyay and Saha proposed a genetic clustering technique based on a new point symmetry-based distance measure [19]. In addition, they adopted the Kd-tree based nearest neighbor search method to reduce the complexity of finding the most symmetrical point. The proposed point symmetry-based distance measure is defined by

$$d_{ps}(x_i, c_t) = \frac{d_1 + d_2}{2} \times d_e(x_i, c_t) \tag{1}$$

where $d_e(x_i, c_t)$ is the Euclidean distance between the pattern x_i and the cluster centroid c_t, d_1 and d_2 are the first and the second unique nearest neighbors of the symmetrical point (i.e. $2 \times c_t - x_i$) of x_i with respect to a particular center c_t, respectively. To reduce the complexity of finding d_1 and d_2, an ANN search using the Kd-tree method is used. After applying the genetic clustering technique based on point symmetry distance measure (GAPS) to different types of data sets, they concluded that the GAPS method is able to detect any type of clusters as long as they possess the characteristic of symmetry.

In [19], the authors pointed out that the complexity of assigning the points to the different clusters is $O(kn^2)$ when adopting the point symmetry-based distance measure. In order to reduce the complexity, the Kd-tree based nearest neighbor search technique, which reduces the complexity from $O(kn^2)$ to $O(kn \log{(n)})$, is adopted. ANN is a library written in C++ [20], which supports data structures and algorithms for both exact and approximate nearest neighbor searching in arbitrarily high dimensions.

2.4 Point Symmetry-Based CVI

For automatic clustering techniques, there are two fundamental questions that need to be addressed: i) how many clusters are actually present in the data, and ii) how real or good is the clustering itself [9]. To measure the goodness of the clustering result, the cluster validity index (CVI) is used to evaluate the results of a clustering algorithm on a quantitative basis. In [8], they proposed a point symmetry-based CVI and defined as:

$$Sym(k) = \left(\frac{1}{k} \times \frac{1}{\xi_k} \times D_k \right) \tag{2}$$

Where,

$$\xi_k = \sum_{i=1}^{k} E_i \tag{3}$$

such that

$$E_i = \sum_{j=1}^{n_i} d_{ps}^*(x_j^i, c_i) \tag{4}$$

and

$$D_k = max_{i,j=1}^{k} \| c_i - c_j \| \tag{5}$$

k is the number of clusters. D_k is the maximum Euclidean distance between two cluster centers among all pairs of centers. $d_{ps}^*(x_j^i, c_i)$ is computed by Equation 1 with some constraint. Here, the first $knear$ nearest neighbors of $2 \times c_i - x_j$ will be searched among only those points with are in cluster i. The objective is to maximize this index in order to obtain the actual number of clusters. More details about this index can be found in [8].

3 Our Approach: ACDEPS

As above-mentioned, DE is a simple and versatile global optimizer. The DE-based clustering algorithms can provide higher performance than GA-based clustering algorithms [13]. Motivated by this idea, in this work, we propose an automatic clustering DE approach for the clustering problems. Our approach is referred as ACDEPS, i.e., Automatic Clustering DE based on Point Symmetry-based measure. It is explained in detail in the following subsections.

3.1 Individual Representation

In our approach, the individual representation proposed in [7] is used. For n data points, each d dimensional, and for a maximum number of clusters $k_{max} = \sqrt{n}$ [6], an individual is a vector of real numbers of dimension $k_{max} + k_{max} \times d$. It is defined as:

$$X_i = \left(T_{i,1}, T_{i,2}, \cdots, T_{i,k_{max}}, c_{i,1}, c_{i,2}, \cdots, c_{i,k_{max}} \right)^T \tag{6}$$

Where the first k_{max} entries are positive floating-point numbers in $[0, 1]$, each of which controls whether the corresponding cluster is to be used or not. Only if $T_{i,j} > 0.5$, then the j-th cluster center in the i-th individual is active. The rest entries are the d-dimensional cluster centers.

3.2 Modified Point Symmetry-Based CVI

From Equation 2 we can see that Sym-index is a composition of three factors, $1/k$, $1/\xi_k$, and D_k. The first factor increases as k decreases. The second and the third factors decrease as k decreases. Since the Sym-index needs to be maximized for optimal clustering, only the first factor prefers to decrease k. While the other two factors prefer to increase k. Thus, in the beginning of the evolutionary process, the individuals prefer to find more clusters. In order to make the algorithm find the optimal cluster centers faster and then obtain the optimal partitioning, in this work, we propose a modified point symmetry-base CVI, where the k is penalized dynamically. It is described as follows.

$$Sym'(k) = \left(\frac{1}{k'} \times \frac{1}{\xi_k} \times D_k \right) \qquad (7)$$

Here, $1/\xi_k$ and D_k are defined by Equations 3 and 5, respectively. k' is defined as:

$$k' = k^{2^t} \qquad (8)$$

and

$$t = 1.0 - \alpha \times \frac{gen}{G_{max}} \qquad (9)$$

where gen is the current generation number. G_{max} is the maximum generations. $\alpha \geq 1$ is a constant; it controls the dynamic penalty of k. When $\alpha = 1$, it means that k is penalized in the entire evolution, except for the last generation. When $\alpha = 2$, it indicates that k is penalized if $gen < 0.5 \times G_{max}$; while when $gen \geq 0.5 \times G_{max}$, k is not penalized, i.e. $k' = k$. Based on the penalized dynamic Sym'-index, the algorithm is able to avoid finding too more clusters in the beginning of the evolutionary process.

3.3 Avoiding Erroneous Individuals

In our approach, calculation of the Sym'-index needs to find the first and the second symmetrical points. In this work, the Kd-tree based nearest neighbor search method is employed to find the two points, and hence, there are at least two data points for each cluster. For an individual if any cluster has fewer than two dada points in it, the individual is reinitialized to k randomly selected points from the data set. After the special individual is reinitialized, all data points are reassigned to this individual.

Furthermore, when a new offspring is created according to DE/rand/1/bin strategy as shown in Algorithm 1, if some $T_{i,j}$ in the offspring is greater than 1 or less than 0, it is forcefully fixed to 1 or 0, respectively. If the number of $T_{i,j} \geq 0.5$ is less than 2, we randomly select two $T_{i,j}$ and reinitialize them to a random value in $[0.5, 1.0]$. Thus, the minimum number of clusters is 2.

4 Experimental Results and Analysis

To evaluate the performance of our approach, we test the ACDEPS approach for both Sym'-index and Sym-index, then the two methods are referred to as ACDEPS1 and ACDEPS2, respectively. Moreover, we compare the two ACDEPS methods with GCUK proposed in [5][1]. To make a fair comparison, in GCUK, the Sym'-index and Sym-index are also used; they are referred to as GCUK1 and GCUK2, respectively.

4.1 Experimental Setup

In our proposed approach, there are four parameters to be specified: i) the population size NP, ii) the crossover probability CR, iii) the maximum number of generations

---

[1] Since we can not obtain the VGAPS method [8] code, we don't make a comparison with VGAPS.

G_{max}, and iv) the dynamic control factor α. In the original DE, the scaling factor F requires to be specified in advance. However, in this work, the dither technique is used to avoid tuning this parameter, where F is uniformly distributed random number generated from $[0.0, 1.0]$. The reason is that the dither technique can improve the performance of DE [11], [12]. Moreover, it can avoid tuning this parameter for the user. For all experiments, we use the following parameters unless a change is mentioned. For GCUK, the parameter settings are used as mentioned in [5].

- Population size: $NP = 100$;
- Crossover probability: $CR = 0.3$;
- DE scheme: DE/rand/1/bin;
- Dynamic control factor: $\alpha = 2.0$;
- Maximum generations: $G_{max} = 30$.

In our experiments, each data set is optimized over 10 independent runs. We also use the same set of initial random populations to evaluate different algorithms. All the algorithms are implemented in standard C++ and the experiments are done on a P-IV (Core 2) 2.1 GHz laptop with 1.0 GB RAM under WIN-XP platform.

4.2 Data Sets

In order to validate the performance of ACDEPS, we have carried out different experiments using a test suite, which consists of 6 artificial data sets of diverse complexities chosen from literature. They are artificial data sets and are briefly described as follows.

- **data1**: This data set has been used in [8]. It consists of two crossed ellipsoid shells, where each ellipsoid shell contains 200 data points.
- **data2**: This data set, used in [17], [19], [8], is a combination of ring-shaped, compact and linear clusters. It contains 350 data points.
- **data3**: This data set, used in [19], contains 400 data points and three clusters, which consists of a ring-shaped cluster, a rectangular cluster and a linear cluster.
- **data4**: This data set, used in [19], [8], is in 3-d space, and has 4 hyper-spherical disjoint clusters. The total number of points is 400.
- **data5**: This data set has 6 different clusters in 2-d space. It contains 300 data points used in [19] and [8].
- **data6**: This data set, used in [8], contains 850 data points distributed on five clusters.

4.3 Performance Criteria

To compare the performance of the four algorithms, three performance criteria are selected to evaluate the performance of the algorithms. These criteria are described as follows.

- **F-measure**: F-measure [21] is associated to the information retrieval field, recall and precision are measures that give us some idea of how well a clustering algorithm is identifying the classes present in the data set. In the context of classification, recall is define as $r(i, j) = n_{ij}/n_i$ where n_{ij} is the number if items of class

Table 1. Comparison of the F-measure value for the four algorithms after 3, 000 NFFEs. Where "Mean" indicates the mean f-measure values found in the last generation; "Std Dev" stands for the standard deviation. The best results are highlighted in **Bold** face.

Dataset	ACDEPS1			GCUK1			ACDEPS2			GCUK2		
	Mean	Std Dev	SR	Mean	Std Dev	SR	Mean	Std Dev	SR	Mean	Std Dev	SR
data1	**0.982**	0.015	**1.0**	0.084	0.266	0.1	0.492	0.519	0.5	0.000	0.000	0.0
data2	**0.942**	0.021	**1.0**	0.645	0.453	0.7	0.762	0.402	0.8	0.278	0.448	0.3
data3	0.999	0.001	**1.0**	**1.000**	0.000	**1.0**	0.300	0.482	0.3	0.100	0.316	0.1
data4	**1.000**	0.000	**1.0**	0.300	0.483	0.3	**1.000**	0.000	**1.0**	0.899	0.316	0.9
data5	**1.000**	0.000	**1.0**	0.800	0.242	0.0	**1.000**	0.000	**1.0**	0.900	0.316	0.9
data6	0.365	0.472	0.4	**0.699**	0.482	**0.7**	0.197	0.415	0.2	0.690	0.477	0.6

Table 2. Comparison of the number of clusters found by the four algorithms after 3, 000 NFFEs. Where "Mean" indicates the mean number of clusters found in the last generation; "Std Dev" stands for the standard deviation. The best results are highlighted in **Bold** face.

Dataset	ACDEPS1			GCUK1			ACDEPS2			GCUK2		
	Mean	Std Dev	SR	Mean	Std Dev	SR	Mean	Std Dev	SR	Mean	Std Dev	SR
data1	**2.000**	0.000	**1.0**	4.200	2.201	0.1	3.100	1.663	0.5	7.200	1.229	0.0
data2	**3.000**	0.000	**1.0**	2.700	0.483	0.7	3.200	0.422	0.8	5.600	1.897	0.3
data3	**3.000**	0.000	**1.0**	**3.000**	0.000	**1.0**	4.400	0.966	0.3	4.800	0.632	0.1
data4	**4.000**	0.000	**1.0**	2.600	0.966	0.3	**4.000**	0.000	**1.0**	4.100	0.316	0.9
data5	**6.000**	0.000	**1.0**	5.800	0.323	0.0	**6.000**	0.000	**1.0**	6.100	0.316	0.9
data6	5.800	0.789	0.4	**5.200**	0.422	**0.7**	7.000	1.333	0.2	4.100	1.449	0.6

i in cluster j and n_i is the number of elements of class i. Precision is defined as $p(i, j) = n_{ij}/n_j$ where n_j is the number of elements in cluster j. For a class i and cluster j the F-measure is define by

$$F(i, j) = \frac{2p(i, j)r(i, j)}{p(i, j) + r(i, j)} \qquad (10)$$

The overall F-measure for the classification generated by the clustering algorithm is give by

$$F = \sum_{i=1}^{k} \left(\frac{n_i}{n} \max_j F(i, j) \right) \qquad (11)$$

where n is the size of the data set. F is limited to the interval $[0, 1]$ with a value of 1 with a perfect clustering.

– **Number of clusters**: The number of clusters found of each algorithm in the final generations. The average value and the standard deviation are calculated over 10 runs.
– **Successful rate (SR)**: If the algorithm can find the actual number of clusters of a given data set in one run, it means that the algorithm obtains a successful run. The SR value is the ratio of the successful runs over the total runs.

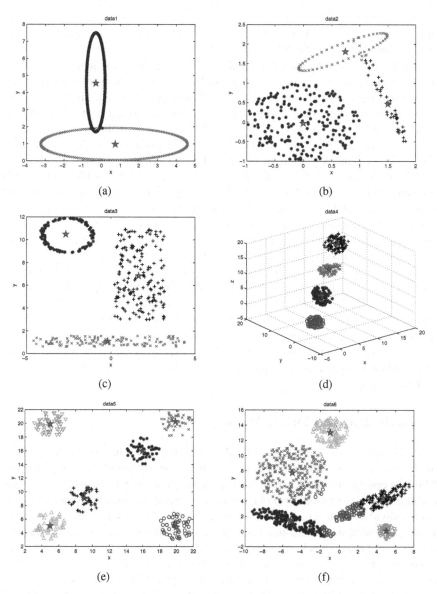

Fig. 1. Clustered results of ACDEPS1 for all data sets. (a) data1. (b) data2. (c) data3. (d) data4. (e) data5. (f) data6. The ⋆ indicates the cluster center.

4.4 Experimental Results

In this section, we compare the performance of the four algorithms. The parameters used for ACDEPS1, ACDEPS2, GCUK1, and GCUK2 are described above. All data sets are conducted for 10 independent runs. The experimental results for the four algorithms are shown in Table 1 and Table 2, respectively. And some representative clustering results are illustrated in Fig. 1.

From Table 1, it can be seen that ACDEPS1 can find the actual number of clusters for five out of six data sets over all 10 runs. And the average F-measure values for these five data sets (data1 - data5) are very close to 1.0. It indicates that ACDEPS1 can obtain the near-optimal partitioning of these data sets. When compared with ACDEPS2, we can see that ACDEPS1 is superior to ACDEPS2 in terms of both the F-measure and the success rate. This phenomenon means that our proposed Sym'-index is better than the original Sym-index when used in the ACDEPS method. Compared the results of ACDEPS with those of GCUK (ACDEPS1 vs GCUK1, and ACDEPS2 vs GCUK2), the results show that ACDEPS is better than GCUK on the majority of the data sets. Except for data6, GCUK performs better than ACDEPS.

From Table 2 we can see that for five data sets (data1 - data5) ACDEPS1 can automatically determine the optimal number of clusters over all 10 runs. It can also obtain the best results compared with ACDEPS2, GCUK1, and GCUK2.

In addition, from Fig. 1 it is apparent to see that for data1 to data5, ACDEPS1 can obtain both the optimal number of clusters and their corresponding optimal partitioning. However, for data6, ACDEPS1 is failed to cluster this data set.

In summary, for the majority of the data sets used in this work, our proposed ACDEPS1 approach is able to automatically determine the optimal number clusters, also it can obtain the optimal partitioning as long as the data sets possess the characteristic of symmetry. And the proposed Sym'-index can make the ACDEPS method more robust than the original Sym-index.

5   Conclusions and Future Work

The DE algorithm is a simple yet powerful evolutionary algorithm for global optimization. In this paper, we adopt the DE algorithm for the automatic clustering problem. To find the optimal number of clusters, we propose a modified Sym'-index, which can avoid finding too more number of clusters in the beginning of the evolutionary process. A new individual representation is employed to make DE suitable for the automatic clustering. In addition, the Kd-tree based nearest neighbor search is used to reduce the complexity of finding the closest symmetric point.

In order to test the performance of our approach, 6 artificial data sets are chosen from literature. Experimental results indicate that our proposed ACDEPS1 approach is able to automatically determine the optimal number clusters, also it can obtain the optimal partitioning as long as the data sets possess the characteristic of symmetry. Furthermore, based on the comparison with the original Sym-index, our proposed Sym'-index shows better performance in terms of the F-measure and the number of clusters found.

In our proposed Sym'-index, an additional parameter α is used to control the dynamic penalty of k. It may be problem-dependent. Our future work will conduct further experiments, both for the artificial data sets and the real world data sets, to test the influence of this parameter.

Acknowledgments

The first author would like to thank Dr. S. Saha for providing the data sets and her suggestions on this work. This work was supported by the Fund for Outstanding Doctoral Dissertation of CUG, China Scholarship Council under Grant No. 2008641008, and the National High Technology Research and Development Program of China under Grand No. 2009AA12Z117.

References

1. Jain, A.K., Murty, M.N., Flynn, P.J.: Data clustering: a review. ACM Comput. Surv. 31(3), 264–323 (1999)
2. Omran, M.G.H., Engelbrecht, A.P., Salman, A.: An overview of clustering methods. Intell. Data Anal. 11(6), 583–605 (2007)
3. Frigui, H., Krishnapuram, R.: A robust competitive clustering algorithm with applications in computer vision. IEEE Trans. Pattern Anal. Mach. Intell. 21(5), 450–465 (1999)
4. Leung, Y., Zhang, J.S., Xu, Z.B.: Clustering by scale-space filtering. IEEE Trans. Pattern Anal. Mach. Intell. 22(12), 1396–1410 (2000)
5. Bandyopadhyay, S., Maulik, U.: Genetic clustering for automatic evolution of clusters and application to image classification. Pattern Recognition 35(6), 1197–1208 (2002)
6. Sheng, W., Swift, S., Zhang, L., Liu, X.: A weighted sum validity function for clustering with a hybrid niching genetic algorithm. IEEE Transactions on Systems, Man, and Cybernetics, Part B 35(6), 1156–1167 (2005)
7. Das, S., Abraham, A., Konar, A.: Automatic clustering using an improved differential evolution algorithm. IEEE Transaction on Systems Man and Cybernetics: Part A 38(1), 218–237 (2008)
8. Bandyopadhyay, S., Saha, S.: A point symmetry-based clustering technique for automatic evolution of clusters. IEEE Trans. on Knowl. and Data Eng. 20(11), 1441–1457 (2008)
9. Pakhira, M.K., Bandyopadhyay, S., Maulik, U.: Validity index for crisp and fuzzy clusters. Pattern Recognition 37(3), 487–501 (2004)
10. Storn, R., Price, K.: Differential evolution - a simple and efficient heuristic for global optimization over continuous spaces. Journal of Global Optimization 11(4), 341–359 (1997)
11. Price, K., Storn, R., Lampinen, J.: Differential Evolution: A Practical Approach to Global Optimization. Springer, Berlin (2005)
12. Chakraborty, U.: Advances in Differential Evolution. Springer, Berlin (2008)
13. Paterlini, S., Krink, T.: High performance clustering with differential evolution. In: Proceedings of 2004 Congress on Evolutionary Computation, pp. 2004–2011. IEEE Press, Los Alamitos (2004)
14. Paterlini, S., Krink, T.: Differential evolution and particle swarm optimisation in partitional clustering. Comput. Stat. Data Anal. 50, 1220–1247 (2006)
15. Alatas, B., Akin, E., Karci, A.: Modenar: Multi-objective differential evolution algorithm for mining numeric association rules. Applied Soft Computing 8(1), 646–656 (2008)
16. Storn, R., Price, K.: Home page of differential evolution (2008),
http://www.icsi.berkeley.edu/~storn/code.html

17. Su, M.C., Chou, C.H.: A modified version of the k-means algorithm with a distance based on cluster symmetry. IEEE Trans. Pattern Anal. Mach. Intell. 23(6), 674–680 (2001)
18. Chung, K.L., Lin, J.S.: Faster and more robust point symmetry-based k-means algorithm. Pattern Recogn. 40(2), 410–422 (2007)
19. Bandyopadhyay, S., Saha, S.: Gaps: A clustering method using a new point symmetry-based distance measure. Pattern Recogn. 40(12), 3430–3451 (2007)
20. Mount, D., Arya, S.: Ann: A library for approximate nearest neighbor searching (2008), http://www.cs.umd.edu/~mount/ann
21. van Rijsbergen, C.: Information Retrieval, 2nd edn. Butterworths, London (1979)

Balanced Learning for Ensembles with Small Neural Networks

Yong Liu

The University of Aizu
Aizu-Wakamatsu, Fukushima 965-8580, Japan
yliu@u-aizu.ac.jp

Abstract. By introducing an adaptive error function, a balanced ensemble learning had been developed from negative correlation learning. In this paper, balanced ensemble learning had been used to train a set of small neural networks with one hidden node only. The experimental results suggest that balanced ensemble learning is able to create a strong ensemble by combining a set of weak learners. Different to bagging and boosting where learners are trained on randomly re-sampled data from the original set of patterns, learners could be trained on all available data in balanced ensemble learning. It is interesting to be discovered that learners by balanced ensemble learning could be just be slightly better than random guessing even if they had been trained on the whole data set. Another difference among these ensemble learning methods is that learners are trained simultaneously in balanced ensemble learning when learners are trained independently in bagging, and sequentially in boosting.

1 Introduction

By introducing an adaptive error function, a balanced ensemble learning had been developed from negative correlation learning [1]. The idea of balanced ensemble learning is to introduce adaptive learning error functions for different individual neural networks in an ensemble, in which different individuals could have different formats of error functions in the learning process, and these error functions could be changed as well. It is different from previous work in ensemble learning where error functions are often set to the same or the fixed ones in the whole learning process. Generally speaking, on learning data where the ensemble has learned well, the error functions in balanced ensemble learning would be changed to allow the ensemble to have a little larger values in error so that the ensemble could shift its attention of learning away from these well-learned data. On other learning data where the ensemble has not yet learned, enlarged error signals are given to each individual so that the ensemble could focus on these not-yet-learned data. Through shifting away from well-learned data and focusing on not-yet-learned data, a good balanced learning could be achieved in the ensemble.

Different to bagging [2] and boosting [3] where learners are trained on randomly re-sampled data from the original set of patterns, learners could be trained

Z. Cai et al. (Eds.): ISICA 2009, LNCS 5821, pp. 163–170, 2009.
© Springer-Verlag Berlin Heidelberg 2009

on all available patters in balanced ensemble learning. It is interesting to be discovered that learners could be still weak even if they had been trained on the whole data set. Another difference among these ensemble learning methods is that learners are trained simultaneously when learners are trained independently in bagging, and sequentially in boosting. Besides bagging and boosting, many other ensemble learning approaches have been developed from a variety of backgrounds [4,5,6,7,8].

For a two-class classification problem, the target values for two classes are often defined as 1 and 0. However, it is unnecessary to fix the target values to 1 or 0. One target value could be any value larger than 0.5 while the other target value could be an value smaller than 0.5. The adaptive error function is defined by shifting the target values away from 1 or 0, and moving the target values to 0.5. This paper investigated how learners change their behaviors at ensemble level and individual level with the changes of shifting parameters. Such shifting parameters also play a similar role of scaling target values. Generally speaking, when the target values move closer to 0.5, learners by balanced ensemble learning become weaker

The rest of this paper is organized as follows: Section 2 describes ideas of balanced ensemble learning. Section 3 display the learning behaviors of balanced ensemble learning on both ensemble level and individual level. Finally, Section 4 concludes with a summary of the paper.

2   Balanced Ensemble Learning

A balanced ensemble learning was developed by changing error functions in negative correlation learning (NCL). In NCL, the output y of a neural network ensemble is formed by a simple averaging of outputs F_i of a set of neural networks. Given the training data set $D = \{(\mathbf{x}(1), y(1)), \cdots, (\mathbf{x}(N), y(N))\}$, all the individual networks in the ensemble are trained on the same training data set D

$$F(n) = \frac{1}{M} \Sigma_{i=1}^{M} F_i(n) \tag{1}$$

where $F_i(n)$ is the output of individual network i on the nth training pattern $\mathbf{x}(n)$, $F(n)$ is the output of the neural network ensemble on the nth training pattern, and M is the number of individual networks in the neural network ensemble.

The idea of NCL [8] is to introduce a correlation penalty term into the error function of each individual network so that all the individual networks can be trained simultaneously and interactively. The error function E_i for individual i on the training data set D in negative correlation learning is defined by

$$E_i = \frac{1}{N} \Sigma_{n=1}^{N} E_i(n) = \frac{1}{N} \Sigma_{n=1}^{N} \left[\frac{1}{2}(F_i(n) - y(n))^2 - \lambda \frac{1}{2}(F_i(n) - F(n))^2 \right] \tag{2}$$

where N is the number of training patterns, $E_i(n)$ is the value of the error function of network i at presentation of the nth training pattern, and $y(n)$ is the desired output of the nth training pattern. The first term in the right side of Eq.(2) is the mean-squared error of individual network i. The second term is a correlation penalty function. The purpose of minimizing is to negatively correlate each individual's error with errors for the rest of the ensemble. The parameter λ is used to adjust the strength of the penalty.

The partial derivative of E_i with respect to the output of individual i on the nth training pattern is

$$\frac{\partial E_i(n)}{\partial F_i(n)} = F_i(n) - y(n) - \lambda(F_i(n) - F(n))$$
$$= (1 - \lambda)(F_i(n) - y(n)) + \lambda(F(n) - y(n)) \tag{3}$$

In the case of $0 < \lambda < 1$, both $F(n)$ and $F_i(n)$ are trained to go closer to the target output $y(n)$ by NCL. $\lambda = 0$ and $\lambda = 1$ are the two special cases. At $\lambda = 0$, there is no correlation penalty function, and each individual network is just trained independently based on

$$\frac{\partial E_i(n)}{\partial F_i(n)} = F_i(n) - y(n) \tag{4}$$

At $\lambda = 1$, the derivative of error function is given by

$$\frac{\partial E_i(n)}{\partial F_i(n)} = F(n) - y(n) \tag{5}$$

where the error signal is decided by $F(n) - y(n)$, i.e. the difference between $F(n)$ and $y(n)$. For the classification problems, it is unnecessary to have the smallest difference between $F(n)$ and $y(n)$. For an example of a two-class problem, the target value y on a data point can be set up to 1.0 or 0.0 depend on which class the data point belongs to. As long as F is larger than 0.5 at $y = 1.0$ or smaller than 0.5 at $y = 1.0$, the data point will be correctly classified.

In balanced ensemble learning, the error function for each individual on each data point is defined based on whether the ensemble has learned the data point or not. If the ensemble had learned to classify the data point correctly, a shifting parameter β with values of $0 \leq \beta \leq 0.5$ could be introduced into the derivative of error function in Eq.(refrelation) for each individual

$$\frac{\partial E_i(n)}{\partial F_i(n)} = F(n) - |y(n) - \beta| \tag{6}$$

Otherwise, an enforcing parameter α with values $\alpha \geq 1$ would be added to the the derivative of error function for each individual

$$\frac{\partial E_i(n)}{\partial F_i(n)} = \alpha(F(n) - y(n)) \tag{7}$$

By shifting and enforcing the derivative of error function, the ensemble would not need to learn every data too well to prevent from learning hard data points too slowly.

3   Experimental Results

3.1   Experimental Setup

Two real-world problems, i.e. the Australian credit card assessment problem and the heart disease problem, were tested. The two data sets were obtained from the UCI machine learning benchmark repository. It is available by anonymous ftp at ics.uci.edu (128.195.1.1) in directory /pub/machine-learning-databases.

The Australian credit card assessment data set is to assess applications for credit cards based on a number of attributes. There are 690 cases in total. The output has two classes. The 14 attributes include 6 numeric values and 8 discrete ones, the latter having from 2 to 14 possible values.

The purpose of the heart disease data set is to predict the presence or absence of heart disease given the results of various medical tests carried out on a patient. This database contains 13 attributes, which have been extracted from a larger set of 75. The database originally contained 303 examples but 6 of these contained missing class values and so were discarded leaving 297. 27 of these were retained in case of dispute, leaving a final total of 270. There are two classes: presence and absence (of heart disease).

10-fold cross-validation were used in both the Australian credit card data set and the heart disease data set. 5 runs of 10-fold cross-validation had been conducted to calculate the average results. In another word, 50 runs for each of data sets had been executed in estimating average results.

The ensemble architecture used in the experiments has 50 networks. Each individual network is a feedforward network with one hidden layer and one hidden node only. The number of training epochs was set to 2000.

3.2   Results of Balanced Ensemble Learning

Balanced ensemble learning had been examined under different values of shifting parameter β from 0 to 0.4, in which NCL is the special case of balanced ensemble learning with $\beta = 0$. In the results of balanced ensemble learning discussed in this section, enforing parameter α was set to 1.

Table 1 presented the average results of error rates of the learned ensembles consisting of 50 small neural networks by balanced ensemble learning after 2000 training epochs over 5 runs of 10-fold cross-validation on the Australian credit card data set and the heart disease data set. The average results of error rates

Table 1. Average of error rates of the learned ensembles by balanced ensemble learning from 50 runs on the Australian credit card data set and the heart disease data set

	0		0.1		0.2		0.3		0.4	
	Train	Test	Train	Test	Train	Test	Train	Test	Train	Test
Card	0.081	0.135	0.067	0.139	0.053	0.138	0.027	0.141	0.015	0.140
Heart	0.062	0.105	0.044	0.079	0.024	0.068	0.011	0.055	0.004	0.041

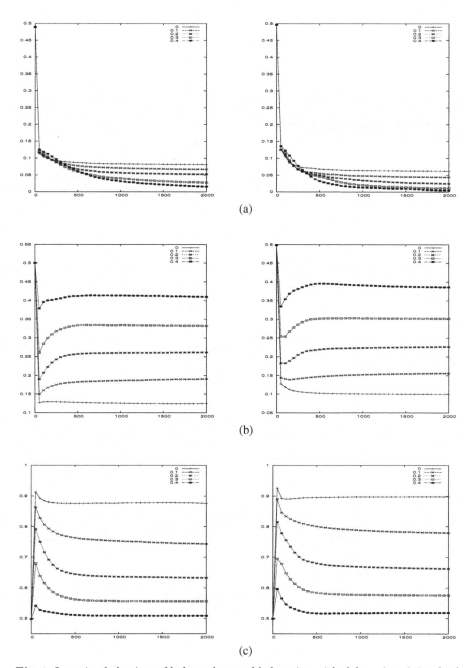

Fig. 1. Learning behaviors of balanced ensemble learning with β from 0 to 0.4 at both ensemble and individual levels on the training set of the Australian credit card data set (left) and the heart disease data set (right). (a) Average error rate of learned ensemble; (b) Average error rate of individual networks; (c) Average overlapping rates of output between every two individual networks in the ensemble.

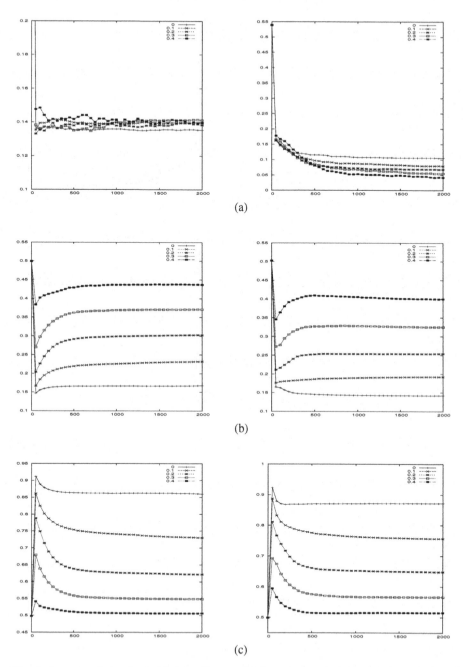

Fig. 2. Learning behaviors of balanced ensemble learning with β from 0 to 0.4 at both ensemble and individual levels on the testing set of the Australian credit card data set (left) and the heart disease data set (right). (a) Average error rate of learned ensemble; (b) Average error rate of individual networks; (c) Average overlapping rates of output between every two individual networks in the ensemble.

of the learned ensembles with different shifting parameters through the learning process are also shown in in Figures 1 and 2.

With larger shifting parameters β, balanced ensemble learning could learn much better on training set. For example, with increasing β from 0 to 0.4, the error rate was reduced from 8.1% to 1.5% on the training set for the Australian credit card data set, and from 6.2% to 0.4% on the training set for the heart disease data set. Not only had balanced ensemble learning dramatically reduced the error rates on the training set, but also maintained comparable or better generalization on the testing sets of two data sets. That is, balanced ensemble learning is capable of improving performance of the learned ensemble on both the training set and the testing set.

By observing the learning process in Figures 1 and 2, balanced ensemble learning with larger shifting parameters was faster on the training set for both data sets. On the testing set, balanced ensemble learning performed a little worse with increased shifting parameters on the Australian credit card data while it kepts its better performance on the heart disease data.

3.3 Weak Learners by Balanced Ensemble Learning

After knowing the performance of the learned ensemble, it would be interesting to examine each individual neural network in the ensemble. Two values were measured among the individual networks, including the average error rates of individual networks and the average overlapping rates of output between every two individual networks. The first value represents the average performance of individuals, while the second value shows how similar those individuals are. The overlapping rate with value 1 means that every two learners have the same classification on the measured data points, while the overlapping rate with value 0 implies that every two learners give the different classification on the measured data points.

The changes of the average error rates of individual networks and the average overlapping rates on both the training set and the testing set through the learning process are shown in Figures 1 and 2. When the shifting parameter increased from 0 to 0.4, the error rates of individuals jumped to nearly 50% while the overlapping rates dropped to 50%. It suggests that the individuals could be just slightly better than the random guessing in balanced ensemble learning. When the individual learners became so weak, they were also almost independent.

4   Conclusions

Although negative correlation learning was developed to create negatively correlated learners for regression tasks, such negatively correlated learners had not been able to generated by negative correlation learning on classification problems. Actually, for classification problems, the individual networks in the learned ensemble by negative correlation learning are likely positive. By shifting target values, balanced ensemble learning is able to create a set of neural networks that are nearly independent.

By shifting target values only, balanced ensemble learning could generate weak learners without re-sampling. Because of re-sampling at the same probability from the training data in bagging, learners generated by bagging could likely be so positive that their combined ensemble might not perform well on training data. Therefore, bagging might lead to underfitting. Boosting could guarantee to reach nearly perfect performance on training data. However, usually only a few learners had been created in boosting for the practical problems. These few learners by boosting are often much better than random guessing, and therefore not so weak. In contrast, weak learners by balanced ensemble learning could be just slightly better than random guess while their combined ensemble could be rather strong.

References

1. Liu, Y.: A balanced ensemble learning with adaptive error functions. In: Kang, L., Cai, Z., Yan, X., Liu, Y. (eds.) ISICA 2008. LNCS, vol. 5370, pp. 1–8. Springer, Heidelberg (2008)
2. Breiman, L.: Bagging predictors. Machine Learning 24, 123–140 (1996)
3. Schapire, R.E.: The strength of weak learnability. Machine Learning 5, 197–227 (1990)
4. Hansen, L.K., Salamon, P.: Neural network ensembles. IEEE Trans. on Pattern Analysis and Machine Intelligence 12(10), 993–1001 (1990)
5. Sarkar, D.: Randomness in generalization ability: a source to improve it. IEEE Trans. on Neural Networks 7(3), 676–685 (1996)
6. Jacobs, R.A., Jordan, M.I., Nowlan, S.J., Hinton, G.E.: Adaptive mixtures of local experts. Neural Computation 3, 79–87 (1991)
7. Jacobs, R.A., Jordan, M.I., Barto, A.G.: Task decomposition through competition in a modular connectionist architecture: the what and where vision task. Cognitive Science 15, 219–250 (1991)
8. Liu, Y., Yao, X.: Simultaneous training of negatively correlated neural networks in an ensemble. IEEE Trans. on Systems, Man, and Cybernetics, Part B: Cybernetics 29(6), 716–725 (1999)

Estimating Geostatistics Variogram Parameters Based on Hybrid Orthogonal Differential Evolution Algorithm

Dongmei Zhang, Xiaosheng Gong, and Lei Peng

School of Computer Science, China University of Geosciences, Wuhan,
430074, China
jjielee@163.com

Abstract. Variogram is a basic tool of geostatistics, used to describe the randomicity and structural property of regionalized variable. While estimating variogram parameters is the basic issue of spatial statistics analysis. Estimate of the parameters is always made by using the theoretical variogram model to fit experimental variogram model. However, it is difficult to obtain the optimization results because the theoretical variogram is not successively derivable if traditional numerical algorithm is used. Differential evolution algorithm is a new evolution algorithm which adopts real number encoding format and has a fast convergence. In this paper, it is the first time to use differential evolution algorithm to estimate variogram parameters. Orthogonal experiments are conducted to ensure the diversity of initial species. The results illustrate that the approach of DE can work out the problem with fast convergence, strong optimization and excellent stability.

Keywords: geostatistics; variogram; parameters estimation; orthogonal differential evolution algorithm.

1 Introduction

Geostatistics is a branch of geology that deals with the analysis of mining processes through mathematical models. It is currently applied in disciplines such as petroleum geology, hydrogeology, meteorology and other fields of agriculture (esp. in precision farming). Geostatistics study on the spatial distribution which is random and possesses the structural phenomenon by regionalized variable theory and variogram. Variogram is a basic tool of geostatistics, which is used to describe the randomicity and structural property of regionalized variable. It is the basic question of spatial statistical analysis to determine the parameters of variogram, which is a prerequisite for the realization of Kriging interpolation.

In practice, it is difficult to carry out structural analysis by using the experimental variogram directly because the value of variogram changes dramaticly when the distance or direction of space changes. However, it is very difficult to fit parameter because the theoretical variogram is non-continuous derivative. According to the experimental variogram curve characteristics, traditional research methods usually give full consideration to the basis of geological factors and select an appropriate theoretical variogram

Z. Cai et al. (Eds.): ISICA 2009, LNCS 5821, pp. 171–179, 2009.

to determine the parameters by hand-fitting. But this method is the lack of a unified objective criteria. Wang Renduo proposed weighted polynomial regression method to fit the parameters of theoretical variogram model. But it required determine weights by manual methods and fit nested model successively[1]. Jiao Xiguo and Liu Chao made use of the non-negative solutions theory of linear equations to fit parameters of theoretical variogram model[2]. It is difficult to obtain ideal optimization results by using of traditional numerical algorithm for complex function optimization problems. In recent years, Huang Shifeng and Jin Juliang adopted the accelerated genetic algorithm to implement parameter estimation of variogram, which have achieved good results. But the genetic algorithm easy to premature convergence and slow convergence in the complex optimize issues and the efficiency is weakened especially when the optimize parameters are interrelated significantly[3].

Differential evolution algorithm (referred to as DE) is a rapid evolutionary algorithm based on the difference between groups, which was proposed by Rainer Storn and Kenneth Price in 1995[4]. The algorithm uses real-coded and guides the search of new individual by using of the differential information of individual. DE algorithm can avoid local optimization by the unique mutation operation. Compared with the basic genetic algorithm, DE algorithm has the characteristics of simple structure, easy implementation, robustness and so on. In this paper we use orthogonal experiment to ensure the diversity of initial species[7]. It is the first time to use differential evolution algorithm estimate variogram parameters. The experimental results illustrates that the approach of DE can carry out the problem with fast convergence strong optimization and excellent stability.

2   Theoretical Variogram and Experimental Variogram

2.1   Variogram

Definition 1. Variogram is semivariance of the difference between $Z(x)$ and $Z(x+h)$ which represent the value of regionalization variable $Z(x)$ at x and $x+h$ (h means spatial distance) respectively, which recorded as follow.

$$\gamma(x,h) = \frac{1}{2} E[Z(x) - Z(x+h)]^2 - \frac{1}{2}\{E[Z(x)] - E[Z(x+h)]\}^2 \qquad (1)$$

Definition 2. Smooth second-order assumption is that the mathematical expectation in the study area $Z(x)$ is a constant or covariance function and is smooth.

$$E[Z(x+h)] = E[Z(x)], \forall h \qquad (2)$$

Under second-order stationary assumption, formula (3) is rewritten as follow if the variance function has nothing to do with the location x.

$$\gamma^*(h) = \frac{1}{2N(h)} \sum_{i=1}^{N(h)} [z(x_i + h) - z(x_i)]^2 \qquad (3)$$

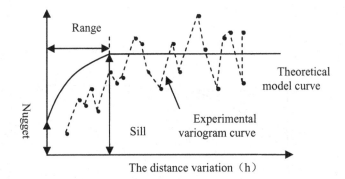

Fig. 1. Variogram curve

Where h represents step length, $N(h)$ represents the number of sample pairs with distance being h. Range, sill and nugget of the semivariance function will be determined by fitting experimental variogram functions with theoretical ones.

Generally we use the variogram curves, the tendency of the value of variation function $\gamma(x)$ and the distance variation h, express variogram curve in Fig.1.

It is difficult to carry out structural analysis by using the experimental variogram directly because the value of variogram changes dramaticly when the distance or direction of space changes. So we find the fitting model of experimental variogram and get the main spatial structure of regionalization variable by fitting the parameters of theoretical variogram.

2.2 Theoretical Variogram

Common theoretical variogram model has sill model, such as spherical model, exponential model and gaussian model; linear model, such as the pure nugget effect model; no sill model, such as power function model, non-linear units value-based model, the parabolic model; hole effect model and so on. Spherical model is one of the most widely used model of geostatistics and is often selected to fit experimental variogram model for the samples which have an obvious spatial autocorrelation. Spherical model, also known as Matheron model, generally expressed as follow:

$$r(h) = \begin{cases} 0 & h = 0 \\ C_0 + C[\frac{3}{2}\left(\frac{h}{a}\right) - \frac{1}{2}(\frac{h}{a})^3] & 0 < h < a \\ C_0 + C & h \geq a \end{cases} \tag{4}$$

Where C_0 represents gold nugget constant and expresses the change of stochastic part, the smaller the value, the stronger the spatial correlation; C represents arch rise and expresses the change of the structural parameters; $C_0 + C$ represents sill and expresses the greatest magnitude of changes; a represents range and expresses the range of spatial correlation.

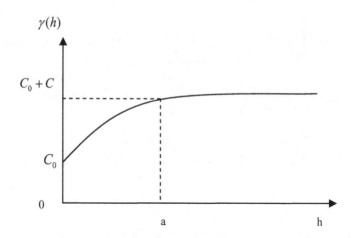

Fig. 2. Spherical model

The value of the model parameters C_0, C, a can be get through theoretical variogram model fit the experimental variogram. In the practical application, the variogram is often fitted by a number of nested theoretical models with different scales and spatial orientation.

3   Orthogonal Experimental Design

3.1   Orthogonal Design of Initialization Species

The uniformity of the distribution of the initial groups ensure the initial groups diversity and patterns rich, which makes the algorithm converge in the global scope in more rapid rate. In accordance with the orthogonal form, orthogonal experimental design selects some representative points for trials. In this paper, orthogonal experimental method is used to generate initial population.

3.2   Orthogonal Design of Control Table

The orthogonal design allow each individual species of vector has 50% probability cross-operation, the traditional differential algorithm adopts randomized crossover operation, which makes the new algorithm more reasonable and easy to control than the traditional differential algorithm. The algorithm design for orthogonal is $L_8(2^3)$ which is shown in table 1.

3.3   The Crossover Operation by Orthogonal Control

L_{ij} express the column j of the No.i experiments, when $L_{ij} = 1$ the crossover operation for No. j parameters is implemented and when $L_{ij} = 2$ the crossover operation for No. j parameters is not implemented. For example the No.3 Vector $L_3(1,2,2)$ is selected as as a guide vector variation ,which represents only the first parameter will implement cross

Table 1. $L_8(2^3)$ orthogonal table

Row Test Number	1	2	3
1	1	1	1
2	1	1	1
3	1	2	2
4	1	2	2
5	2	1	2
6	2	1	2
7	2	2	1
8	2	2	1

over operation. This will not only ensure each parameter has the same cross-operation probability (50%) but also ensure the process variation of species are diversity.

4   Orthogonal Differential Evolution Algorithm Design

Differential evolution algorithm is a new evolution algorithm which is based on the difference between groups and adopted real number encoding format. Each vector of the groups represents a set of solutions of the problem. The most prominent feature is the mutation strategy by use of the recombinant of the difference between the vector to get new individual. Different DE algorithms adopt different mutation strategy.

4.1   The Formation of the Initial Species

The solution of the optimization problem will be composed of D-dimensional solution vectors and each vector of the solution is the basic individual of the evolution. According to the literature [8] select orthogonal table $L_M(Q^F)=[b_{ij}]_{M\times F}$ and produce M individuals by the experiments.

$$\begin{cases} \left(f_1(b_{1,1}), f_2(b_{1,2}), \cdots, f_F(b_{1,F})\right) \\ \left(f_1(b_{2,1}), f_2(b_{2,2}), \cdots, f_F(b_{2,F})\right) \\ \cdots\cdots\cdots\cdots\cdots \\ \left(f_1(b_{M,1}), f_2(b_{M,2}), \cdots, f_F(b_{M,F})\right) \end{cases} \qquad (5)$$

4.2   Mutation Operation

In the mutation operation of the DE algorithm the new individual is formed by scaling the difference between any two individual vector of target species and superimposed to the third vector of species. Suppose $X_{i,G}(\ i=1,2\ldots,N)$

$$V_{i,G+1} = X_{i_1,G} + F*(X_{i_2,G} - X_{i3,G}) \qquad (6)$$

This is the basic pattern of variation, $X_{i1,G}$, $X_{i2,G}$, $X_{i3,G}$ groups are randomly selected from three separate individuals, F for the scaling factor, the general value range [0, 1]. This is the basic pattern of variation, $X_{i1,G}$, $X_{i2,G}$, $X_{i3,G}$ three separate individuals are randomly selected from groups, where F is the scaling factor, [0, 1] is the general value range. In this paper DE/best/1/exp strategy is used as the mutation strategy.

4.3 Crossover Operation

Crossover operation has two types of model such as index cross and binomial cross, that the aim is increasing the diversity of the groups and jumping out of the local optimum. In this paper the binomial crossover is used and the new individual is recorded as follow:

$$U_{i,G+1} = (u_{1i,G+1}, u_{2i,G+1}, \cdots, u_{Di,G+1}) \tag{7}$$

$$u_{ji,G+1} = \begin{cases} v_{ji,G+1} & if \quad L_{ij} = 1 \quad or \quad j = rn_i; \\ v_{ji,G} & if \quad L_{ij} = 2 \quad and \quad j \neq rn_i; \end{cases} \tag{8}$$

Where j represents $1,2,\ldots,D$.

4.4 Select Operator

In order to ensure the better individuals access to the next generation elite reservation strategy is be taken.

$$x_{i,G+1} = \begin{cases} u_{i,G} & if(f(u_{i,G}) \leq f(x_{i,G})) \\ x_{i,G} & if(f(u_{i,G}) > f(x_{i,G})) \end{cases} \tag{9}$$

5 Simulation

Based on orthogonal differential evolution algorithm and the theoretical variogram, we adopt spherical model to fit the experimental variogram on the vertical direction of a molybdenum ore grade.

5.1 Algorithm Parameter Settings

In the present study, the following parameters were used:
(1) Set Generation with 500 because population size N directly affects convergence rate of the algorithm and the general settings is 5-10 times of the vector dimension ;
(2) Set F with 0.3 because the greater the variability factor F, the stronger the algorithm's global search ability ;
(3) Set Crossover probability with 0.5 and orthogonal table set to $L_8(2^5)$;

5.2 The Experimental Results and Analysis

According to the literature [3] we use two nested spherical model to fit the experimental variogram on the vertical direction of a molybdenum ore grade.

Table 2. The results comparison table of fitting variogram

Distance h	The values of variogram $r(h)$	The fitting value of literature [2]	The fitting value of GA	The fitting value of DE
0.8	2.4	2.6	2.78	2.71
1.5	5.0	4.38	4.72	4.72
2.3	6.4	5.68	6.07	6.19
3.1	7.1	6.86	7.12	7.19
3.8	7.8	7.80	7.96	8.00
4.6	8.6	8.76	8.81	8.81
5.3	9.6	9.47	9.42	9.41
6.1	10.1	10.11	9.96	9.94
6.8	10.2	10.5	10.27	10.26
7.6	10.7	10.73	10.41	10.43
8.3	10.2	10.74	10.41	10.43
9.1	10.4	10.74	10.41	10.43

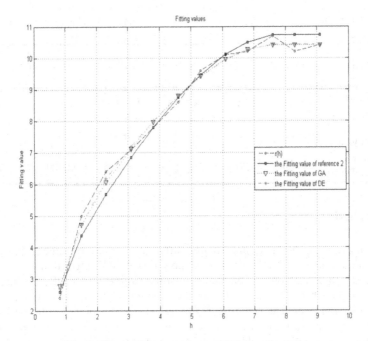

Fig. 3. The results comparison of fitting variogram

$$r(h) = \begin{cases} 0 & h = 0 \\ C_0 + C_1\left(\frac{3h}{2a_1} - \frac{h^3}{2a_1^3}\right) + C_2\left(\frac{3h}{2a_2} - \frac{h^3}{2a_2^3}\right) & 0 < h \leqslant a_1 \\ C_0 + C_1 + C_2\left(\frac{3h}{2a_2} - \frac{h^3}{2a_2^3}\right) & a_1 < h \leqslant a_2 \\ C_0 + C_1 + C_2 & h > a_2 \end{cases} \quad (10)$$

Where C_0 represents sill, C_1 and C_2 represents the firth and the second arch rise respectively; a_1, a_2 represents range respectively; Firstly, design the orthogonal table; Then, computer model parameters by differential evolution algorithm. Fitting results are shown as follows in table 2.

Table 2 lists the variogram results of three fitting algorithm. Table 3 lists all parameters of the theoretical variogram model(formular 10) and the estimated value of parameters corresponding to the smallest residual sum of squares in accordance with the literature [2]. Compared with the results of the smallest residual sum of squares, the fitting results of DE algorithm is better than the literature [2] and the GA algorithm results. The results show DE algorithm not only can derive the optimal feasible solution, but also has good stability and convergence, which can converge to the same solution every time.

Table 3. The results of variogram parameter estimation comparison table of fitting variogram

Parameter	C_0	C_1	C_2	a_1	a_2	The smallest residual sum of squares
The fitting value of literature [2]	0.000	1.9490	8.7955	1.7031	7.9058	1.55
The fitting value of GA	0.0769	2.6206	7.7132	1.9849	7.6639	0.59
The fitting value of DE	0.000000	3.000000	7.437569	2.182456	7.900000	0.509597

6   Conclusion

In this paper, it is the first time to use differential evolution algorithm estimate variogram parameters. Simulation results show that the DE algorithm is superior to genetic algorithms and other weighted polynomial regression method, which illustrates the approach of DE can carry out the problem with fast convergence, strong optimization and excellent stability. However, similar to other evolutionary algorithms, differential evolution algorithm in solving the global optimal solution will also appear slower convergence problem at the late evolution. In the future work we intend to use the differences of the best and the worst individual such as adaptive control methods to impove the algorithm.

Acknowledgments. This paper was supported by the Research Foundation for Outstanding Young Teachers, China University of Geosciences (Wuhan) (CUGQNL0328) and the open issues of Geological and mineral resources of State Key Laboratory.

References

1. Renduo, W., Guangdao, H.: Linear geostatistics[M], pp. 68–75. Geological Publishing House, Beijing (1988)
2. Xiguo, J., Chao, L.: Estimation of variation parameter. Computing techniques for geophysical and geochemical exploration 16(2), 157–161 (1996)
3. Shifeng, H., Jinjun, D., Jidiang, J., Yiuning, W.: A new method for estimating variogram parameters in geostatistics. Geology and prospecting 35(1), 41–43 (1999)
4. Storn, R., Price, K.: Differential evolution-a simple and efficient adaptive scheme for global optimization over continuous space. Technical report, International Computer Science Institute, Berkley (1995)
5. Vesterstrom, J., Thomsen, R.: A Comparative Study of Differential Evolution, Particle Swarm Optimization, and Evolutionary Algorithms on Numerical Benchmark Problems. In: Proceedings of Congress on Evolutionary Computation(CEC 2004), Poland (2004)
6. Krink, T., Filipic, B., Fogel, G.B.: Noisy optimization problems-a particular challenge for differential evolution. In: Proceedings of Congress on Evolutionary Computation (CEC2004), Poland (April 2004)
7. Zhong-yang, J., Zi-xing, C., Yong, W.: Hybrid Orthogonal Genetic Algorithm for Global Optimization[J]. Computer Application 35(4), 204–206 (2009)
8. Jingfeng, Y., Bo-ping, Z., Wen-ying, G., Shuimu, T.: Application study on a novel differential evolution algorithm. Computer Application 28(03), 719–722 (2008)

Memetic Strategies for Global Trajectory Optimisation

Massimiliano Vasile and Edmondo Minisci

Department of Aerospace Engineering,
University of Glasgow, G12 8QQ, Glasgow, UK
{m.vasile,e.minisci}@aero.gla.ac.uk
http://www.aero.gla.ac.uk/Research/SpaceArt/

Abstract. Some types of space trajectory design problems present highly multimodal, globally non-convex objective functions with a large number of local minima, often nested. This paper proposes some memetic strategies to improve the performance of the basic heuristic of differential evolution when applied to the solution of global trajectory optimisation. In particular, it is often more useful to find families of good solutions rather than a single, globally optimal one. A rigorous testing procedure is introduced to measure the performance of a global optimisation algorithm. The memetic strategies are tested on a standard set of difficult trajectory optimisation problems. Key words: global trajectory optimisation, differential evolution, memetic algorithms.

Keywords: global trajectory optimisation, differential evolution, memetic algorithms.

1   Introduction

In the last decade many authors have used global optimization techniques to find optimal solutions to space trajectory design problems. Many different methods have been proposed and tested on a variety of cases. From pure Genetic Algorithms [1,2,3] to Evolutionary Algorithms (such as Differential Evolution) [4] to hybrid methods [5], to memetic algorithms [6], the general intent is to improve over the pure grid or enumerative search. The need for global optimisation tools is motivated by the high multimodality of most of space trajectory optimisation problems. The traditional approach was to rely on the experience of the mission analyst but the use of global optimisation methods was proven to provide significant improvements in the quality of the solutions with a reduced workload [12]. However, efficiently finding good solutions to a generic space trajectory optimisation method is still an open problem. Moreover the reliability (the ability of a method to consistently return good local optima or the global optimum) of some global methods can be considered questionable. In this paper, we present some strategies to improve Differential Evolution, which, among all evolutionary algorithms, has displayed reasonably good performance in many test cases [4].

A rigorous testing procedure is proposed to evaluate the performance of global optimisation methods. In particular, we are not interested in ability of a method

Z. Cai et al. (Eds.): ISICA 2009, LNCS 5821, pp. 180–190, 2009.

to identify the global optimum (or alternatively the best known solution) but in the ability of a method to repeatedly find solutions belonging to a level set defined by the values of the objective function below a given threshold. In fact, this latter characteristic is more useful in practical applications.

2   Problem Description

We consider a benchmark made of three different test-cases, with increasing complexity: a direct bi-impulsive transfer from the Earth to an asteroid, a multi-gravity assist transfer from the Earth to a comet, a multi-gravity assist transfer to Mercury. In all of these cases the objective is to minimize the total variation of the velocity of the spacecraft due to all propelled maneuvers, or total Δv. However, in this paper, we propose a level-set approach to the problem in which the aim is to find all solutions with a value of the objective function within a given range.

2.1   Problem Formulation

Rather looking for the global optimum we are here interested in all the solutions with a value of the objective function within a given range. This is practically more useful than finding the absolute global minimum because, during the design of a space mission, the main interest is to find multiple alternative mission options with similar cost function. Therefore, the general problem is to find a set X, contained in a given domain D, of solutions $\mathbf{x}$ such that the property $\Pi(\mathbf{x})$ is true for all $\mathbf{x} \in X \subseteq D$,

$$X = \{\mathbf{x} \in D \mid \Pi(\mathbf{x})\} , \qquad (1)$$

where the domain D is a hyper-rectangle defined by the upper and lower bounds on the components of the vector $\mathbf{x}$, $D = \left\{x_i \mid x_i \in [b_i^l \ b_i^u] \subseteq \Re, \ i = 1, ..., n_d\right\}$, with n_d the dimension of the problem. In our case:

$$\Pi(\mathbf{x}) = f_L \leq f(\mathbf{x}) \leq f_U . \qquad (2)$$

2.2   Test Cases

A complete description of the trajectory model for all the test cases in this paper can be found in [12]. Furthermore, in order to make the comparison with other methods easy and to avoid ambiguities due to the specific implementation of the trajectory model, we use the code that can be downloaded from the ESA/ACT web site[1].

---

[1] *http://www.esa.int/gsp/ACT/inf/op/globopt/edvdvdedjds.htm*

Earth-Apophis Transfer. A simple, but already significant, test case is to find the best launch date t_0 and time of flight T_1 to transfer a spacecraft from the Earth to the asteroid Apophis. The objective function for this problem is the sum of the departure velocity change Δv_0 and the arrival velocity change Δv_f, $f(\mathbf{x}) = \Delta v_0 + \Delta v_f$, with the solution vector $\mathbf{x} = [t_0, T_1]^T$. The search space D is a box defining the limits of the two components of the solution vector. In particular, the launch date from the Earth was taken in the interval [3653   10958]MJD2000 (i.e. number of elapsed days since January 1st 2000), while the time of flight was taken in the interval [50 900] days. The known best solution in D has objective value f_{best}=4.3745658 km/s.

Earth to Comet Transfer. The second test case is a multi gravity assist trajectory from the Earth to the comet 67P/Churyumov-Gerasimenko following the gravity assist sequence that was planned for the spacecraft Rosetta: Earth-Earth-Mars-Earth-Earth-Comet. The solution vector has 22 components. The best known solution (also on the ESA website) has objective value $f_{best} = 1.343$ km/s.

Earth to Saturn Transfer. The third test case is a multi gravity assist trajectory from the Earth to Saturn following the sequence Earth-Venus-Venus-Earth-Jupiter-Saturn (EVVEJS) corresponding to the space mission Cassini-Huygens. The solution vector has 22 components and the best known solution has objective value f_{best}=8.384 km/s.

3   Solution Strategy

If we consider that a candidate solution vector in D is associated to an agent a, then the heuristics governing the motion of the agents in D can be written as:

$$\mathbf{x}_{i,k+1} = \mathbf{x}_{i,k} + S(\mathbf{x}_{i,k} + \mathbf{u}_{i,k})\mathbf{u}_{i,k} \ . \tag{3}$$

The control $\mathbf{u}_{i,k}$ defines the next point that will be sampled for each one of the existing points in the solution space. In addition to Eq. (3), a general evolutionary algorithm has heuristics responsible for selecting the new candidate points generated with $\mathbf{u}_{i,k}$. The selection operator can be expressed through the function $S(\mathbf{x}_{i,k} + \mathbf{u}_{i,k+1})$ which can be either 1 if the candidate point is accepted or 0 if it is not accepted. For example, Differential Evolution [7], in its basic form, has the $\mathbf{u}_{i,k}$ defined by:

$$\mathbf{u}_{i,k+1} = \mathbf{e}[(\mathbf{x}_{i_3,k} - \mathbf{x}_{i,k}) + F(\mathbf{x}_{i_2,k} - \mathbf{x}_{i_1,k})] \ , \tag{4}$$

where i_1 and i_2 are integer numbers randomly chosen in the interval $[1 \ n_{pop}] \subset \mathbb{N}$ of indexes of the population, and is $\mathbf{e} = \mathbf{r} < C_R$. The vector $\mathbf{r}$ is made of random numbers taken from a random uniform distribution $r(j) \in U[0 \ 1]$ with $j = 1, ..., n_d$ and C_R is a constant. The index i_3 can be chosen at random or can be the index of the best solution vector $\mathbf{x}_{best}$. We assume here that the indices i_1, i_2 and i_3 can take any value, thus including the cases: $i_1 = i_2 = i_3$, $i_1 = i_2 \neq i_3$, $i_1 \neq i_2 = i_3$ and $i_1 = i_3 \neq i_2$. Here we also propose a particular choice of the indexes corresponding to a strategy called *better-worse* in the following: the population is ranked and $\mathbf{x}_{i_3,k}$ and $\mathbf{x}_{i,k}$ are selected so that $f(\mathbf{x}_{i_3,k}) > f(\mathbf{x}_{i,k})$.

It can be proven [11] that, when a population P_k, of agents a whose dynamics is given by (3), at each iteration k lies in the neighborhood of a local minimum satisfying some regularity assumption (e.g., the Hessian at the local minimum is positive definite, implying strict convexity in the neighborhood), the map (3) will converge to a fixed point. For general functions, we can not always guarantee that the population will converge to a fixed point, but we can show [11] that the maximum difference between the objective function values in the population converges to 0, i.e. the points in the population tend to belong to the same level set. In both cases the population contracts within a limited region of D. The contraction of map (3) suggests that after a certain iteration k the population can have exhausted its exploration capability. Therefore, when the maximum distance $\rho_A = \max(\|\mathbf{x}_i - \mathbf{x}_j\|)$ among the elements in the population collapses below a value $tol_{conv}\rho_{A,max}$, where $\rho_{A,max}$ is the maximum ρ_A recorded during the convergence of the map (3), the process can be terminated and restarted. In order to guarantee convergence to a local minimum every time the process is terminated, a local search is started from the best solution $\mathbf{x}_{best}$ in P and the corresponding local minimum $\mathbf{x}_l$ is saved in an archive A_g (in this implementation we used the Matlab® function *fmincon* as local optimiser) together with the population.

3.1 Local Search Strategy

If the search space is characterized by a single or multi-funnel structure [9], it is worthwhile to proceed the exploration of D in a neighborhood of an existing minimum. We can then associate to an agent a the position of a local minimum, a bubble $D_l \subseteq D$ with radius ρ_l, and local search process guided by dynamics (4). In other words we can restart a subpopulation P_{sub} in the bubble D_l. If the search process in the bubble terminates successfully we can move the agent to the new local minimum. This process is conceptually equivalent to the search strategy of MBH (Monotonic Basin Hopping) [13]. Every time a new search in a bubble is terminated and a local search with *fmincon* is performed, the local minimum and the population are stored in A_g.

3.2 Clustering, Sampling and Restart Strategy

If multiple funnels or multiple isolated minima exist, the local search strategy might not be effective to identify all the funnels, even if multiple local searches are run in parallel. Therefore, after a number of local searches iun, the solutions in the archive are grouped into n_c clusters [8] with baricenter $\mathbf{x}_{c,j}$ for $j = 1, ..., n_c$, and a new population is generated. Each agent $\mathbf{x}_i$ of the new population is generated so that:

$$\|\mathbf{x}_i - \mathbf{x}_{c,j}\| > \delta_c .\tag{5}$$

Algorithm 1. Inflationary Differential Evolution Algorithm (IDEA)

1: Set values for n_{pop}, C_R, F and tol_{conv}, set $n_{feval} = 0$ and $k = 1$
2: Initialize $\mathbf{x}_{i,k}$ and $\mathbf{v}_{i,k}$ for all $i \in [1, ..., n_{pop}]$
3: Create the vector of random values $\mathbf{r} \in U[0\ 1]$ and the mask $\mathbf{e} = \mathbf{r} < C_R$
4: **for all** $i \in [1, ..., n_{pop}]$ **do**
5:     Apply dynamics (3), $n_{feval} = n_{feval} + 1$
6: **end for**
7: $k = k + 1$
8: Compute $\rho_A = \max(\|\mathbf{x}_{i,k} - \mathbf{x}_{j,k}\|)$ for $\forall \mathbf{x}_{i,k}, \mathbf{x}_{j,k} \in P_{sub} \subseteq P_k$
9: **if** $\rho_A < tol_{conv}\rho_{A,max}$ **then**
10:     Run a local optimizer a_l from $\mathbf{x}_{best}$ and let $\mathbf{x}_l$ be the local minimum found by a_l
11:     **if** $f(\mathbf{x}_l) < f(\mathbf{x}_{best})$ **then**
12:         $f_{best} \leftarrow f(\mathbf{x}_l)$
13:     **end if**
14:     **if** $f(\mathbf{x}_{best}) < f_{min}$ **then**
15:         $f_{min} \leftarrow f(\mathbf{x}_{best})$
16:         $iun = 0$
17:     **else**
18:         $iun = iun + 1$
19:     **end if**
20:     **if** $iun \leq iun_{max}$ **then**
21:         Define a bubble D_l such that $\mathbf{x}_{i,k} \in D_l$ for $\forall \mathbf{x}_{i,k} \in P_{sub}$ and $P_{sub} \subseteq P_k$
22:         $A_g = A_g + \{\mathbf{x}_{best}\}$ where $\mathbf{x}_{best} = \arg\min_i f(\mathbf{x}_{i,k})$
23:         Initialize $\mathbf{x}_{i,k}$ and $\mathbf{v}_{i,k}$ for all $\in [1, ..., n_{pop}]$, in the bubble $D_l \subseteq D$
24:     **else**
25:         Define clusters in A_g and their baricenters $\mathbf{x}_{c,j}$, with $j = 1, ..., n_c$.
26:         Re-generate P in D such that $\forall i, j, \|\mathbf{x}_{i,k} - \mathbf{x}_{c,j}\| > \delta_c \sqrt{n_d}$
27:     **end if**
28: **end if**
29: **Termination** Unless $n_{feval} \geq n_{fevalmax}$, *goto* Step 3

The re-generation of the population is performed by over-sampling the solution space with Latin Hypercube: if the population has size n_{pop}, $2n_{pop}$ samples are generated. The subset of n_{pop} samples fulfilling condition (5) become the new population. The overall process leads to algorithm 1.

4   Testing Procedure

In this section we describe a rigorous testing procedure that can be used to assess the performance of a global optimization algorithm. A detailed description of the testing procedure can be found in [11] and it is here summarized in Algorithm 2 for a generic solution algorithm A and a generic problem p. The index of performance j_s is the number of successes of the algorithm A. In the following we use the f_{best} values reported above in place of f_{global} and we consider $\delta_f(\bar{\mathbf{x}})$ because we are interested in condition (2). A key point is setting properly the

---

Algorithm 2. Testing Procedure

1: Set to N the max number of function evaluations for A
2: Apply A to p for n times and set $j_s = 0$
3: **for all** $i \in [1, ..., n]$ **do**
4: $\quad \phi(N, i) = \min f(A(N), p, i)$
5: $\quad \bar{\mathbf{x}} = arg\ \phi(N, i)$
6: $\quad$ Compute $\delta_f(\bar{\mathbf{x}}) = | f_{global} - f(\bar{\mathbf{x}}) |$;
7: $\quad\quad$ **if** $(\delta_f(\bar{\mathbf{x}}) < tol_f)$ **then** $j_s = j_s + 1$
8: $\quad\quad$ **end if**
9: **end for**

---

value of n to have a reliable estimate of the success probability of an algorithm, or success rate $p_s = j_s/n$. The success rate, p_s, will be used for the comparative assessment of the algorithm performance instead of the commonly used best value, mean and variance because: the success rate gives an immediate and unique indication of the algorithm effectiveness, and, second, it can be always represented with a binomial probability density function (pdf), independently of the number of function evaluations, the problem and the type of optimization algorithm. Furthermore it should be noted that reporting the best value the mean and the variance as indexes of performance is generally misleading. In fact, there is a nonzero probability of finding the global minimum (best value) for any given stochastic algorithm regardless of its quality and the distribution of the solutions found by an algorithm is not gaussian. On the other hand, since the success is binomial (assumes values that are either 0 or 1) we can set a priori the value of n to get the required confidence on the value of p_s. A commonly adopted starting point for sizing the sample of a binomial distribution is to assume a normal approximation for the sample proportion p_s of successes (i.e. $p_s \sim N\{\theta_p, \theta_p(1-\theta_p)/n\}$, where θ_p is the unknown true proportion of successes) and the requirement that $Pr[|p_s - \theta_p| \leq d_{err}|\theta_p]$ is at least equal to $1 - \alpha_p$ [10]. This leads to the expression $n \geq \theta_p(1-\theta_p)\chi^2_{(1),\alpha_p}/d^2_{err}$ that can be approximated conservatively with

$$n \geq 0.25\chi^2_{(1),\alpha_p}/d^2_{err}, \tag{6}$$

valid for $\theta_p = 0.5$. For most of the tests we required an error ≤ 0.05 ($d_{err} = 0.05$) with a 95% of confidence ($\alpha_p = 0.05$), which, according to Eq.(6), yields $n = 176$. This is extended to 200 in order to have a higher confidence in the result. For the Earth-Apophis case instead we required an error of 0.02 which corresponds to $n = 1000$.

4.1   Test Results

Three algorithms were tested: Differential Evolution, Monotonic Basin Hopping and Algorithm 1, called IDEA. For the Earth-Apophis case we tested DE with a wide variety of settings: population size from 5 to 20 individuals, $F \in [0.7\ 1.1]$, $C_R \in [0.6\ 1]$ and all available strategies. MBH run a local search from a random point within a subdomain D_l enclosing a neighborhood of a local minimum. The local minimum is updated every time the local search leads to an improvement. The size of D_l is a critical parameter and we used two values 0.1 and 0.3. For all the other cases we considered two different settings for the DE, resulting from combining two sets of populations, $[5\,d, 10\,d]$, where d is the dimensionality of the problem, with single values of step-size and crossover probability $F = 0.75$ and $C_R = 0.8$ respectively, on the basis of repeated tests on this benchmark of problems. The index i_3 corresponds to the best individual in all test cases except for the Earth-Apophis case where we used a random individual. In the following the two settings will be denominated with DE5,DE10. For MBH, we considered a neighborhood of radius 0.1. We also tested a variant that restarts globally the algorithm by sampling a random point in D after 30 unsuccessful trials (MBH-GR). The search space for each one of the trajectory models was normalized so that D is a unit hypercube with each component of the solution vector belonging to the interval $[0\ 1]$. Furthermore, all solution algorithms were run for a progressively increasing number of function evaluations N. We can therefore introduce the efficiency of convergence as $\eta_c = p_s/N$. For the Earth-Apophis case, IDEA was run with a population of 5 agents, strategy *better-worse*, with no local strategy, $F = 0.9$, $C_R = 0.9$, $\delta_c = 0.1$, $tol_{conv} = 0.1$. For the Earth-comet case, IDEA was run with a population of 50 agents, i_3 of the best individual, with no local strategy, $F = 0.8$, $C_R = 0.8$, $\delta_c = 0.3$, $tol_{conv} = 0.2$. For the other cases IDEA was run with a population of 25 agents, i_3 of the best individual, with local strategy, $F = 0.9$, $C_R = 0.9$, $\rho_l = 0.4$, $\delta_c = 0.4$, $tol_{conv} = 0.2$. Note that a C_R and an F in the range $[0.75\ 0.9]$ led to no significant change in the results. The tolerance tol_f was set 0.01 for the Earth-Apophis case, 0.057 for the Earth-comet case and, 0.12 for the Earth-Saturn case. These values are arbitrary and a different choice would lead to a different performance for the same algorithm but would not change the relative performance among different algorithms.

Fig. 1 represents the success rate for the Earth-Apophis case together with the efficiency η_c for IDEA. Only the best performing settings of DE are reported, i.e. $F = 0.9$, $C_R = 0.9$, index i_3 chosen randomly, DE7, or corresponding to the best individual, DE6, and the best performing settings of MBH, i.e. with D_l of size 0.3. The figure shows that DE performs badly for a low number of function evaluations, mainly because of a lack of local convergence. As the number of function evaluations increases above 1000, on the other hand, DE6 and DE7 with 10 individuals display no improvement. The main reason is that the population contracts rapidly and loses any exploration capability. DE7 with a population of 20 individuals, instead, has a nice progression reaching about 87% of success at 2000 function evaluations. The low performance for a lower n is again due to a lack of local convergence. The performance of MBH is almost linearly increasing with the number of function evaluations, this is a trend that was registered also in the other tests. IDEA performs better than all the other algorithms for a low n and is marginally better than DE7 for $n = 2000$. Note that as p_s approaches 1, all the algorithms are expected to be comparable. For the same reason the value of η_c is expected to decrease as the success rate approaches 1. On the other hand

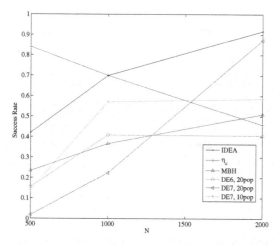

Fig. 1. Success rate for the Earth-Apophis case

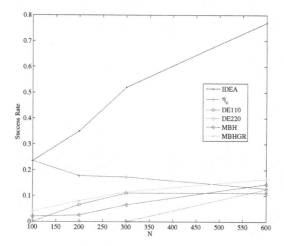

Fig. 2. Success rate for the Earth-comet case

the peak efficiency of IDEA is at 500 function evaluations and rapidly decreases as the success rate reaches 0.92 very fast.

Fig. 2 shows the performance of the tested algorithms on the Earth-comet case. IDEA outperforms the other algorithms already for the lowest number of function evaluations. DE110 exhausts its exploration capability quite soon and displays no improvement for $n > 300000$ while DE220 has zero performance up to $n = 300000$ but then seems to improve over DE110. However, for $n > 600000$ DE220 did not show further improvements. MBH shows again a linear improvement with the restart version of the algorithm performing slightly better. The better performance of IDEA is due to the restart mechanism that avoid the stagnation, displayed by DE, and to dynamics (3) that avoids the costly use

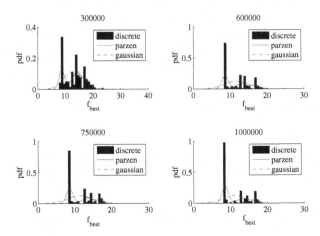

Fig. 3. Distribution of the solutions for Earth-Saturn trajectory problem

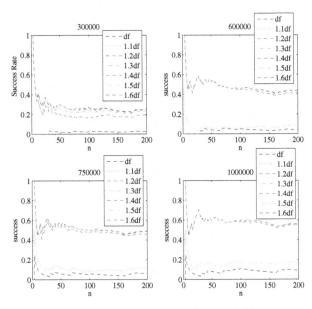

Fig. 4. Number of successes for the solutions of the Earth-Saturn trajectory problem

of the gradient as in MBH, until a promising region is identified. The Earth-comet problem, in fact, seems to be characterised by a multi-funnel structure with the best known solution at the bottom of a narrow funnel next to a larger one. Dynamics (3) explores the funnels faster than MBH but requires frequent restarts to avoid stagnation. Even in this case we registered a decrease of the efficiency, though less rapid than in the Earth-Apophis case.

Fig. 3 shows the distribution of the best local minima f_{best} found by IDEA in the Earth-Saturn case in every run. It can be noted that the distribution is not Gaussian. On the same graph we reported the Gaussian pdf corresponding to the value of the mean and variance of the f_{best}. The Gaussian pdf hardly predict the behaviour of the algorithm, a better pdf would be the Parzen one although it does not provide a single performance index. Fig. 4 shows the success rate for a variable number of runs and different numbers of function evaluations. As predicted by the theory developed for the testing procedure, at 200 runs we have a stable and reliable value for the success rate. Note that for $n < 50$ the value of the success rate could be extremely unreliable. The performance of IDEA in this case is not particularly good despite the higher tol_f and the local search strategy. Note that the local search strategy was effective in this case because the other algorithms tend to get stuck at a local minima with objective value above 8.7, apparently belonging to the same funnel of the best known solution. The local strategy in IDEA brings all the values to 8.52 or below. This can be seen in Fig. 4 from the success rate for a $\delta_f < 1.2 tol_f$ (curve labeled 1.2df in the figure).

5   Conclusions

In this paper we presented few simple strategies to modify the basic DE heuristic and improve its performance when applied to the solution of some global trajectory optimisation problems. Some of the proposed strategies appear to be very effective, like the restart strategies together with the use of the archive, the clustering and the sampling strategy. The *better-worse* dynamics performed better than the standard DE on the Earth-Apophis case but still needs to be tested on the other cases. The local strategies appear to be necessary when the local convergence within a funnel is problematic while the proposed restart strategy is essential when multiple funnels are present. The paper introduced also a testing procedure and two performance indexes: the success ratio and the efficiency. It was demonstrated that the distribution of the best solutions found by an algorithm is not gaussian, therefore the use of mean and variance is not a good indicator of the performance because cannot be used to predict the future behaviour of the algorithm. Furthermore, the use of the success rate, which gives a rigorous way of selecting the number of runs, is consistent with the level-set formulation of the problem that we proposed in this paper.

References

1. Gage, P.J., Braun, R.D., Kroo, I.M.: Interplanetary trajectory optimization using a genetic algorithm. Journal of the Astronautical Sciences 43(1), 59–75 (1995)
2. Rauwolf, G., Coverstone-Carroll, V.: Near-optimal low-thrust orbit transfers generated by a genetic algorithm. Journal of Spacecraft and Rockets 33(6), 859–862 (1996)
3. Kim, Y.H., Spencer, D.B.: Optimal Spacecraft Rendezvous Using Genetic Algorithms. Journal of Spacecraft and Rockets 39(6), 859–865 (2002)

4. Olds, A.D., Kluever, C.A., Cupples, M.L.: Interplanetary Mission Design Using Differential Evolution. Journal of Spacecraft and Rockets 44(5), 1060–1070 (2007)
5. Vasile, M., Locatelli, M.: A hybrid multiagent approach for global trajectory optimization. Journal of Global Optimization (2008), doi:10.1007/s10898-008-9329-3
6. Pisarevsky, D., Gurfil, P.: A Memetic Algorithm for Optimizing High-Inclination Multiple Gravity-Assist Orbits. In: IEEE CEC 2009, Trondheim, Norway, May 18-21 (2009)
7. Price, K.V., Storn, R.M., Lampinen, J.A.: Differential Evolution. In: A Practical Approach to Global Optimization. Natural Computing Series. Springer, Heidelberg (2005)
8. Funkunaga, K., Hosteler, L.D.: The Estimation of the Gradient of a Density Function, with Applications in Pattern Recognition. IEEE Transactions on Information Theory 21(1), 32–40 (1975)
9. Locatelli, M.: On the multilevel structure of global optimization problems. Computational Optimization and Applications 30, 5–22 (2005)
10. Adcock, C.J.: Sample size determination: a review. The Statistician 46(2), 261–283 (1997)
11. Vasile, M., Minisci, E., Locatelli, M.: On Testing Global Optimization Algorithms for Space Trajectory Design. In: AIAA/AAS Astrodynamic Specialists Conference, Honolulu, Hawaii, USA (2008)
12. Vasile, M., De Pascale, P.: Preliminary Design of Multiple Gravity-Assist Trajectories. Journal of Spacecraft and Rockets 43(4) (2006)
13. Wales, D.J., Doye, J.P.K.: Global optimization by basin-hopping and the lowest energy structures of Lennard-Jones clusters containing up to 110 atoms. J. Phys. Chem. A 101, 5111–5116 (1997)

Effects of Similarity-Based Selection on WBMOIA: A Weight-Based Multiobjective Immune Algorithm

Jiaquan Gao, Zhimin Fang, and Lei Fang

Zhijiang College, Zhejiang University of Technology, Hangzhou 310024, China
gaojiaquan@gmail.com

Abstract. With a comparison to the random selection approach used in the weight-based multiobjective immune algorithm (WBMOIA), this paper proposes a new selection approach based on the truncation algorithm with similar individuals (TASI). Then the effect of the proposed selection approach is examined on the performance of WBMOIA. On one hand, the performance is compared between WBMOIA with the random selection approach and WBMOIA with the proposed selection approach. On the other hand, simulation results on a number of problems are presented to investigate if there exists any value of the reduction rate where WBMOIA performs well. Experiment results show that the performance of WBMOIA can be improved by the proposed selection approach and a better reduction rate can be obtained for each test problem.

Keywords: Multiobjective optimization, Immune algorithm, Similar individuals, Evolutionary algorithm.

1 Introduction

During the last decade, based on principles of the immune system, a new computational intelligence approach, called immune algorithm (IA), has been developed. When compared to artificial neural networks, evolutionary algorithms (EAs), fuzzy systems, although immune algorithm is still in its infancy, it has been successfully applied to many fields such as clustering, classification, pattern recognition, computer defense, optimization, and others[1,2]. In 1999, Yoo and Hajela firstly proposed an approach which uses IA for solving MOOPs [3]. In their approach, Yoo and Hajela made use of a utility function and weighting mechanism to convert a multi-criteria problem into a single-objective problem. IA was used for modifying the fitness values of a genetic algorithm (GA). Although Yoo and Hajela's algorithm cannot be considered a true multiobjective immune algorithm (MOIA), it is a pioneer in using IA ideas for MOOPs. Next, Coello Coello and Cruz Cortés in 2002 developed a MOIA directly based on the emulation of the immune system [4]. The algorithm, called the multiobjective immune system algorithm (MISA), can be considered the really first attempt to solve MOOPs directly with IA. The performance of MISA has been improved in

Z. Cai et al. (Eds.): ISICA 2009, LNCS 5821, pp. 191–200, 2009.
© Springer-Verlag Berlin Heidelberg 2009

further work of the same authors in 2005 [5]. In 2006, based on opt-aiNET, the artificial immune system algorithm for multi-modal optimization proposed by Castro and Timmis [6]. Freschi and Repetto presented a vector immune system (VIS) [7]. In the Freschi and Repetto study, VIS follows the elementary structure of the opt-aiNET optimization algorithm, and the differences between opt-aiNET and VIS are very few. Besides them, many approaches using the metaphor of the immune system for MOOPs have been presented in recent years [8,9,10].

In the literature [11,12], like VIS, a novel multiobjective immune algorithm based on opt-aiNET was presented. The proposed algorithm follows the elementary structure of opt-aiNET. Compared to the other MOIA based on opt-aiNET, the proposed algorithm, called the weight-based multiojective immune algorithm (WBMOIA), has the following distinct features: (1) A randomly weighted sum of multiple objectives is used as a fitness function. (2) The individuals of the population are chosen from the memory, which is a set of elite solutions, and a local search procedure is utilized to facilitate the exploitation of the search space. (3) A new diversity approach, named truncation algorithm with similar individuals (TASI), is presented. For WBMOIA, two diversity approaches, TASI and the clonal suppression algorithm which is similar to that used in opt-aiNET, are utilized together to eliminate similar cells in memory, and TASI is used as the main diversity approach in order to obtain a better distribution of Pareto-optimal solutions.

Recently, it is observed that the performance of WBMOIA is related to the approach of the selection of the new population. For WBMOIA, a random selection approach is presented to guide the selection of the new population. The approach is as follows: assume that a set R_t is composed of dominated ones among offspring and memory cells in the t-th generation, N_{pop} cells are randomly selected from the memory Q_{t+1} to create the population P_{t+1} when $|Q_{t+1}| >= N_{\text{pop}}$. If $|Q_{t+1}| < N_{\text{pop}}$, the cells of Q_{t+1} are copied to P_{t+1} and then randomly select $(N_{\text{pop}} - |Q_{t+1}|)$ cells from R_t and add them to P_{t+1}. However, it can be seen that the random selection approach cannot ensure diversity along the current non-dominated front. In many problems, when this happens, the search slows down. Therefore, in this study we present a new selection approach based on TASI in order to preserve diversity of the created population P_{t+1}. Then we examine the effect of the proposed selection approach.

The remainder of this paper is organized as follows. In the second section, the weight-based multiobjective immune algorithm (WBMOIA) is described. In the third section, we present the new selection approach based on TASI. Numerical experiments for examining the effect of the proposed selection approach are presented in the fourth section. The fifth section contains our conclusions.

2   WBMOIA

Here we list the weight-based multiobjective immune algorithm (WBMOIA) suggested in the literature [11,12]. The framework of WBMOIA is shown in Fig.1. Assuming that the population is a set of cells, and each of them represents a

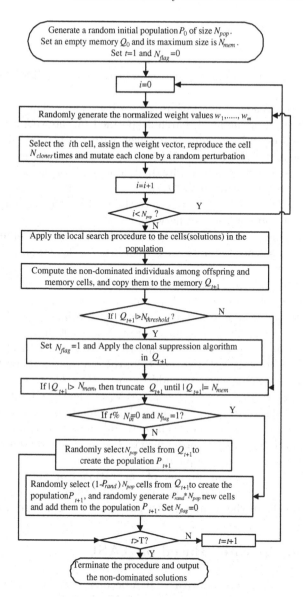

Fig. 1. The framework of WBMOIA

solution to the optimization problem, we list the main procedures of WBMOIA as follows.

(1) A random initial population P_0 of size N_{pop} is created. Set the memory $Q_0 = \emptyset$ and its maximum size $= N_{mem}$. Set a counter $t = 1$, and set a flag $N_{flag} = 0$ (one of the conditions to decide that the algorithm will go to (9) or (10)).

(2) For each cell in the population, do
   (a) Randomly specify the weight values $w_1, w_2, \ldots, w_m$, where $w_1 + w_2 + \cdots + w_m = 1$, and $w_i \in [0,1], i = 1, 2, \ldots, m$.
   (b) Reproduce the cell N_{clones} times and mutate each clone by a random perturbation [12].

(3) Apply the local search algorithm [12] to each clone. For each clone, the search direction of the local search is specified by the weight values in the fitness function and the clone is replaced with the fittest cell obtained by the local search if this fittest cell is not worse than the clone.

(4) Compute the non-dominated individuals among offspring and memory cells, and copy them to the memory Q_{t+1}.

(5) If the size of Q_{t+1} exceeds $N_{\text{threshold}}$ (a threshold of the memory size), then set $N_{\text{flag}} = 1$ and continue. Otherwise, go to (7).

(6) Apply the clonal suppression algorithm [12] in Q_{t+1} to eliminate those memory clones whose affinity with each other is less than a pre-specified threshold.

(7) If $|Q_{t+1}| > N_{\text{mem}}$, then perform TASI (see Section 3).

(8) If t can be exactly divided by N_{in} (number of inner loops) and $N_{\text{flag}} = 1$, then set $N_{\text{flag}} = 0$ and go to (10). Otherwise, continue.

(9) If $|Q_{t+1}| \geqslant N_{\text{pop}}$, then randomly select N_{pop} cells from Q_{t+1} to create the population P_{t+1}. Otherwise, copy the cells of Q_{t+1} to P_{t+1} and then randomly select $N_{\text{pop}} - |Q_{t+1}|$ cells from the dominated individuals among offspring and memory cells and add them to P_{t+1}. Go to (11).

(10) If the size of Q_{t+1} exceeds $(1 - p_{\text{rand}})N_{\text{pop}}$, then randomly select $(1 - p_{\text{rand}})N_{\text{pop}}$ cells from Q_{t+1} to create the population P_{t+1}, and then randomly generate $p_{\text{rand}}N_{\text{pop}}$ new cells and add them to the population P_{t+1}. Otherwise, the cells in Q_{t+1} are copied to P_{t+1} and new randomly generated cells to fill the remaining population.

(11) If $t > T$ (the maximum number of generations) or another termination condition is satisfied, then terminate the algorithm and output the non-dominated cells in the memory. Otherwise, $t = t + 1$ and return to (2).

3   Selection Operator Based on TASI

A selection operator is important to a MOEA because it is responsible for guiding the selection process at the various stages of the algorithm toward a uniformly spread-out Pareto-optimal front. For WBMOIA mentioned above, a random selection approach (RSA) is presented to guide the selection of the new population. It can be observed that RSA cannot ensure diversity along the current non-dominated front. In many problems, when this happens, the search slows down. Therefore, here we present a new selection operator based on TASI in order to preserve diversity of the created population P_{t+1}.

Before suggesting the new selection approach, we list the definition of similar individuals and the procedures of TASI [12] in order to let the reader easily understand our proposed selection approach.

Definition 1. (*Similar individuals*): *For a given multiobjective optimization problem and the solution set P, the solutions P_1 ($P_1 \in P$) and P_2 ($P_2 \in P$) are referred to as similar individuals, if their Euclidean distance in the objective space is the shortest in set P.*

Given the above definition of similar individuals, the truncation algorithm, TASI, is listed as follows.

(1) Calculate the Euclidean distance (in objective space) between any two solutions i and j in the memory Q_{t+1}.
(2) Select two similar individuals i and j from Q_{t+1} and remove one of them from Q_{t+1}. The solution i is chosen for removal if the following condition is true.

$$\exists\, 0 < k < |Q_{t+1}|, \text{ such that } d_i^k < d_j^k, \text{ and } \forall\, 0 < l < k, d_i^l = d_j^l,$$

where d_i^k denotes the distance of i to its k-th nearest neighbor in Q_{t+1}. Otherwise, the solution j is chosen for removal.
(3) If $|Q_{t+1}| > N_{\text{mem}}$, then return to (2). Otherwise, terminate the procedure.

Based on TASI mentioned above, the detailed procedures of our proposed selection approach are listed as follows.

(1) If $|Q_{t+1}| \geqslant N_{\text{pop}}$, copy cells of Q_{t+1} to a set ϕ_{t+1}, and use TASI to reduce the size of ϕ_{t+1} to N_{pop}, and then let the new population $P_{t+1} = \phi_{t+1}$. Terminate the procedure.
(2) If $|Q_{t+1}| < N_{\text{pop}}$, then copy cells of Q_{t+1} to P_{t+1}. Next, the set R_t is sorted for non-domination. Let us say that the number of non-dominated fronts in R_t is K. The maximum number of cells allowed in the i-th front ($i = 1, 2, \ldots, K$) in the new population P_{t+1} of size N_{pop} is calculated according to the following equation.

$$N_i = (N_{\text{pop}} - |Q_{t+1}|)\frac{1 - r}{1 - r^K}r^{i-1}, \tag{1}$$

where $0 < r < 1$.
(3) Assume that N_i^t is the number of cells of the i-th front in R_t. If $N_1^t > N_1$ (that is, there are more cells than allowed), we copy cells of the first front in R_t to a set ϕ_{t+1}, and use TASI to truncate ϕ_{t+1} until its size is equal to N_1, and then add cells in ϕ_{t+1} to P_{t+1}. On the other hand, if $N_1^t \leqslant N_1$ (that is, there are less or equal number of cells in R_t than allowed), we choose all N_1^t cells and count the number of remaining slots $\delta_1 = N_1 - N_1^t$. The maximum allowed number of cells in the second front is now increased to $N_2 + \delta_1$. Thereafter, the actual number of solutions N_2^t present in the second front is counted and is compared with N_2 as above. This procedure is continued until $N_{\text{pop}} - |Q_{t+1}|$ cells are selected.

In this procedure, when the number of non-dominated cells in Q_{t+1} is less or equal than N_{pop}, we attempt to maintain a predefined distribution of number of cells in each front except for the current best non-dominated front. Specifically, we use a geometric distribution for this purpose:

$$N_i = rN_{i-1}, \tag{2}$$

where N_i is the maximum number of allowed cells in the i-th front and r is the reduction rate.

4   Experiments

In this section, we will investigate the effect of our proposed selection approach (NSA). All experiments are conducted on an IBM computer, which is equipped with a Pentium IV 2.8G processor and 1GB of internal memory. The operating system is Windows XP and the programming language is C++. The compiler is Borland C++ 6.0.

4.1   Comparison Experiment

We compare WBMOIA with WBMOIA-II for examining which is better between RSA and NSA. The algorithm, called WBMOIA-II, is the same as WBMOIA except that RSA is replaced by NSA. For effectively investigating the effect of NSA, we do not use the local search algorithm for WBMOIA and WBMOIA-II.

In this comparison experiment, the specification of parameters for two algorithms is listed as follows. For WBMOIA, the results indicated below are obtained using the following parameters: population size $N_{\text{pop}} = 100$, size of external memory $N_{\text{mem}} = 200$, number of clones for each cell $N_{\text{clones}} = 5$, number of inner iterations $N_{\text{in}} = 5$, threshold of external memory size $N_{\text{threshold}} = 400$, percentage of random cells at each outer iteration $p_{\text{rand}} = 20\%$, and $\beta = 0.85$. For WBMOIA-II, the same parameters as WBMOIA are used except that the reduction rate $r = 0.65$.

Test Problem 1: ZDT6

The first test problem was proposed by Zitzler et al. [13].

$$\min \begin{cases} f_1(\mathbf{x}) &= 1 - \exp(-4x_1)\sin^6(6\pi x_1), \\ f_2(\mathbf{x}) &= g(\mathbf{x})[1 - (f_1(\mathbf{x})/g(\mathbf{x}))^2], \\ g(\mathbf{x}) &= 1 + 9[(\sum_{i=2}^{10} x_i)/9]^{0.25}, \end{cases} \tag{3}$$

where $x_i \in [0,1], i = 1,2,\ldots,10$. The Pareto-optimal region corresponds to $x_1^* \in [0,1]$ and $x_i^* = 0$ for $i = 2,3,\ldots,10$. For ZDT6, the adverse density of solutions across the Pareto-optimal front, coupled with the nonconvex nature of the front, may cause difficulties for many multiobjective optimization algorithms to converge to the true Pareto-optimal front.

In this case, the number of fitness function evaluations for all two algorithms has been set to 36,000. We show the comparison of results between the

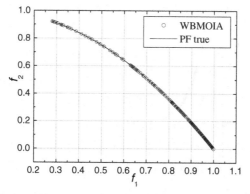

Fig. 2. Pareto-optimal front obtained using WBMOIA for ZDT6

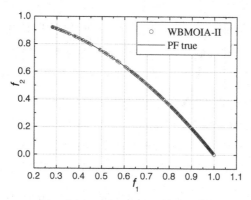

Fig. 3. Pareto-optimal front obtained using WBMOIA-II for ZDT6

true Pareto front of ZDT6 and the Pareto front obtained by WBMOIA and WBMOIA-II in Fig.2 and Fig.3, respectively.

From Fig.2 and Fig.3, it can be observed that WBMOIA and WBMOIA-II both are able to approximate the true Pareto front but WBMOIA-II shows better spread of solutions than WBMOIA.

Test Problem 2: DEB

The second test problem was presented by Deb in 1999 [13].

$$
\min \begin{cases} f_1(\mathbf{x}) & = x_1, \\ f_2(\mathbf{x}) & = \frac{g(\mathbf{x})}{x_1}, \\ g(\mathbf{x}) & = 2 - \exp\left[-\left(\frac{x_2-0.2}{0.004}\right)^2\right] \\ & \quad -0.8\exp\left[-\left(\frac{x_2-0.6}{0.4}\right)^2\right], \end{cases} \tag{4}
$$

where $x_i \in [0.1, 1], i = 1, 2$. In the range allowed for x_2, the function $g(\mathbf{x})$ has $x_2 = 0.2$ as a global minimum and $x_2 = 0.6$ as a local one. It can be proved that this behavior of $g(\mathbf{x})$ results in a multi-modal and multiobjective problem.

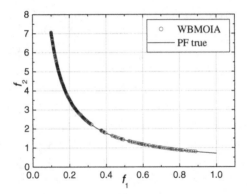

Fig. 4. Pareto-optimal front obtained using WBMOIA for DEB

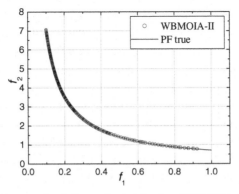

Fig. 5. Pareto-optimal front obtained using WBMOIA-II for DEB

Moreover most of the search space leads to the local Pareto front whereas only a few solutions lead toward the global one.

For DEB, two algorithms will stop when the number of fitness function evaluations exceeds 12,000. The comparison of results between the true Pareto front of DEB and the Pareto front produced by two algorithms is respectively shown in Fig.4 and Fig.5.

From Fig.4 and Fig.5, it can be found that WBMOIA-II shows better performance and has better spread of solutions than WBMOIA.

4.2   Experimental Analysis

The selection operator in Section 3 will help maintain diversity in the solutions across many non-dominated fronts. In solving MOOPs, this additional feature may be helpful in progressing towards the true Pareto-optimal front. However, it is intuitive that the parameter r is important. If r is small, it is obviously observed that the extent of exploration is large from Eq.1, and vice versa. In general, the optimal value of r will depend on the problem and it will be difficult to determine it theoretically. Next, we present simulation results on a number of

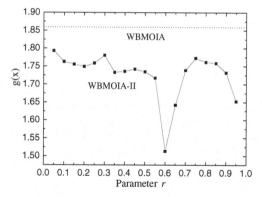

Fig. 6. Convergence observed for WBMOIA and WBMOIA-II

problems to investigate if there exists any value of r where WBMOIA-II performs well.

A Test Problem

The test problem is defined as follows:

$$\min \begin{cases} f_1(\mathbf{x}) & = x_1, \\ f_2(\mathbf{x}) & = g(\mathbf{x})(1 - \sqrt{x_1/g(\mathbf{x})}). \\ g(\mathbf{x}) & = 1 + (\sum_{i=2}^{10} |x_i|)^{0.25} \end{cases} \quad (5)$$

where $x_1 \in [0,1]$, $x_i \in [-5,5]$, $i = 2, 3, \ldots, 10$. For WBMOIA and WBMOIA-II, the same parameters as in the above experiment are used except that they are run until 20,000 fitness function evaluations are completed. In all simulations, 20 independent runs from different initial populations are taken.

One advantage of the above test problem is that the function $g(\mathbf{x})$ indicates the convergence of the obtained front near the true Pareto-optimal front. For an ideal convergence, the value of $g(\mathbf{x})$ should be one. A simulation with a smaller $g(\mathbf{x})$ is better. Here, we set the parameter r to 0.05, 0.1, 0.15, 0.2, 0.25, 0.3, 0.35, 0.4, 0.45, 0.5, 0.55, 0.6, 0.65, 0.7, 0.75, 0.8, 0.85, 0.9, and 0.95, in that order. For each r, we randomly run WBMOIA 20 times, and calculate the average value (denoted by g_i^r, $i = 1, 2, \ldots, 20$) of the value of $g(\mathbf{x})$ in the memory for each run, and then obtain the average value $g^r = \frac{1}{20} \sum_{i=1}^{20} g_i^r$. The change curve of g^r with respect to r is plotted in Fig.6.

From Fig.6, it is clear that all runs for WBMOIA-II have converged better than runs with WBMOIA. The average $g(\mathbf{x})$ value is closer to one than that in WBMOIA. Among the different r values, r=0.6 performed the best.

5   Conclusion

In this study, we suggest a new selection approach based on WBMOIA, and examine its effect. Numerical experiments show that WBMOIA with the new selection approach performs WBMOIA with the random selection approach, and a good reduction rate can be obtained for each test problem.

References

1. de Castro, L.N., Timmis, J.: Artifical Immune System: A New Computational Intelligence Approach. Springer, Heidelberg (2002)
2. Hart, E., Timmis, J.: Application Areas of AIS: The Past, the Present and the Future. Appl. Soft. Comput. 3, 191–201 (2008)
3. Yoo, J., Hajela, P.: Immune Network Simulations in Multicriterion Design. Struct. Opt. 18, 85–94 (1999)
4. Coello Coello, C.A., Cruz Cortés, N.: An Approach to Solve Multiobjective Optimization Problems Based on an Artificial Immune System. In: Timmis, J., Bentley, P.J. (eds.) First International Conference on Artificial Immune Systems (ICARIS 2002), pp. 212–221. University of Kent, Canterbury (2002)
5. Coello Coello, C.A., Cruz Cortés, N.: Solving Multiobjective Optimization Problems Using an Artificial Immune System. Genet. Prog. Evol. Mach. 6, 163–190 (2005)
6. de Castro, L.N., Timmis, J.: An Artificial Immune Network for Multimodal Function Optimization. In: Proc. 2002 Congress on Evolutionary Computation, CEC 2002, Honolulu, vol. 1, pp. 699–704. IEEE Press, Los Alamitos (2002)
7. Freschi, F., Repetto, M.: VIS: An Artificial Immune Network for Multi-Objective Optimization. Eng. Optimiz. 38(18), 975–996 (2006)
8. Luh, G.C., Chueh, C.H., Liu, W.W.: Multi-Objective Optimal Design of Truss Structure with Immune Algorithm. Comput. Struct. 82, 829–844 (2004)
9. Wang, X.L., Mahfouf, M.: ACSAMO: an Adaptive Multiobjective Optimization Algorithm Using the Clonal Selection Principle. In: Proc. 2nd European Symposium on Nature-inspired Smart Information Systems, Puerto de la Cruz, Tenerife, Spain (2006)
10. Zhang, Z.H.: Multiobjective Optimization Immune Algorithm in Dynamic Environments and Its Application to Greenhouse Control. Appl. Soft. Comput. 8, 959–971 (2008)
11. Gao, J., Fang, L.: A Novel Artificial Immune System for Multiobjective Optimization Problems. In: Yu, W., He, H., Zhang, N. (eds.) 6th International Symposium on Neural Networks. LNCS, vol. 5553, pp. 88–97. Springer, Heidelberg (2009)
12. Gao, J., Wang, J.: WBMOAIS: A Novel Artificial Immune System for Multiobjective Optimization. Computers and Operations Research (2009), doi:10.1016/j.cor, 03.009
13. Deb, K.: Multi-Objective Optimization Using Evolutionary Algorithms. John Wiley & Sons, Ltd., New York (2001)

A Novel Evolutionary Algorithm Based on Multi-parent Crossover and Space Transformation Search

Jing Wang[1,2], Zhijian Wu[1], Hui Wang[1], and Lishan Kang[1]

[1] State Key Lab of Software Engineering, Wuhan University, Wuhan 430072, China
[2] Software College, Jiangxi University of Finance and Economics, Nanchang 330013, China
wj.jxufe@gmail.com

Abstract. This paper presents a novel hybrid evolutionary algorithm for function optimization. In this algorithm, the space transformation search (STS) is embedded into a novel genetic algorithm (GA) which employs a novel crossover operator based on a nonconvex linear combination of multiple parents and elite-preservation strategy (EGT). STS transforms the search space to increase more opportunities for finding the global optimum and accelerate convergence speed. Experimental studies on 15 benchmark functions show that the STS-EGT not only has good ability to help EGT jump out of local optimum but also obtains faster convergence than the STS-GT which has no elitepreservation strategy.

Keywords: space transformation search, multi-parent crossover, elite-preservation strategy, evolutionary algorithm.

1 Introduction

Evolutionary algorithm is a parallel problem solver which uses ideas and gets inspirations from natural evolutionary processes. It consists of genetic algorithm, evolutionary strategy, evolutionary programming, and genetic programming [1]. Due to its intrinsic parallelism and some intelligent properties such as self-organizing, adaption and self-learning, evolutionary computation has been applied effectively to solve complicated problems, while these problems are almost impossible to be solved by traditional optimization algorithms.

Research in the field of evolutionary algorithm, genetic algorithm operator is one of the key issues to improve the algorithm performance. Evolutionary strategy and evolutionary programming researchers stressed the importance of mutation operators, and their research also confirmed that the mutation operators were very effective [2]. D.Fogle stated: crossover operators , in the general sense, are not better than the mutation operators [3]. On the other hand, genetic algorithm researchers are convinced that the crossover operators are more efficient operators, and they have done a lot of work to analyze the performance of the crossover operator's impact [4-5]. Schaffer and Eshelman compare the mutation operator with crossover operator, and

Z. Cai et al. (Eds.): ISICA 2009, LNCS 5821, pp. 201–210, 2009.
© Springer-Verlag Berlin Heidelberg 2009

come to the conclusion: the only variation is not always sufficient [6]. Over the years, it is not clear that whether it is necessary to make a distinction between the mutation and crossover, but designing a more general operator will be a promising approach.

Every optimization algorithm has its own advantages and disadvantages, while the hybrid optimization algorithms that are produced by combining these algorithms with each other can own some advantages of these algorithms simultaneously [7]. In this paper, we propose a hybrid approach through combining a novel evolutionary algorithm which has multi-parent crossover operators with space transformation search technique. The paper is organized as follows. The related works is introduced in section 2. STS used in the multi-parent evolutionary algorithm is explained in section 3. Experimental results and analysis are presented in section 4. Finally, summaries and future work are concluded in section 5.

2 Related Works

The general aim of optimization algorithms is to find a solution that represents a local maximum or minimum in a suitably defined solution domain, which means to find the best solution to a considered problem among all the possible ones. In this paper, an hybrid evolutionary algorithm based on space transformation search technique and multi-parent crossover technique is proposed. This part briefly describes the two techniques.

2.1 Space Transformation Search(STS)

In our previous work, we presented a new evolutionary technique to transform solutions in current search space to a new search space, we called it space transformation search (STS) [8]. By simultaneously evaluating the solutions in current search space and transformed space, it can improve the chance to find solutions more closely to the global optimum than current solutions.

The STS technique is described briefly as follows.

Let $X = (X_1, X_2, ..., X_n,)$ be a solution in an n-dimensional space, then $X = (X_1^*, X_2^*, ..., X_n^*)$ is the corresponding solution of X in the transformed search space. The new dynamic STS model is defined by equation (1).

$$X_{ij}^* = k[a_j(t) + b_j(t)] - X_{ij} \tag{1}$$

where X_{ij} is the jth vector of the ith solution in the population, X_{ij}^* is the transformed solution of X_{ij}, k can be set as a random number within [0,1]. $a_j(t)$ and $b_j(t)$ are the minimum and maximum values of the jth dimension in current search space respectively, and $t=1,2,...$, indicates the generations, $i=1,2,...$, indicates the size of the population, $j=1,2,...$, indicates the dimensions.

Assume $f(X)$ is a fitness function which is used to evaluate the solution's fitness. If $f(X^*)$ is better than $f(X)$, then update X with X^*; Otherwise keep the current solution X. Hence, the current solution and its transformed solution are evaluated simultaneously, and the better one will be choiced.

When the STS is conducted, new solutions in transformed population (TP) are calculated according to the STS model (see equation (1)). The specific steps are as follows.

(1) Calculate the fitness of solutions in current population P.
(2) Calculate the new solutions in transformed population TP by equation (1).
(3) Select the PopSize fittest individuals from P□TP as the new current population.

2.2 Multi-parent Crossover

Multi-parent crossover operators, where more than two parents are involved in generating offspring, are a more flexible version, generalizing the traditional two-parent crossover of nature. They have attracted increasing attention in the field of evolutionary computation (EC) as well as evolutionary strategies (ES), and Guo presents a simple, highly efficient operation of the evolutionary algorithm (we called GT algorithm)[9]. Based on this algorithm, a elite-preservation strategy has been proposed in this paper and we called it EGT algorithm.

The EGT is described briefly as follows.

(1) Select M individuals $x_1,x_2,...,x_z,x_{z+1},...,x_M$ from the population, $x_1,x_2,...,x_z$ are z best individuals and $x_{z+1},...,x_M$ are the random individuals;
(2) M random real numbers a_i, $i = 1,2,...,M$, are generated, subject to

$$\sum_{i=1}^{M} a_i = 1, -0.5 \le a_i \le 1.5 \tag{2}$$

(3) The offspring vector x is generated as follows:

$$V = \{x \mid x \in S, x = \sum_{i=1}^{M} a_i x_i\} \tag{3}$$

In EGT, by adopting the elite-preservation strategy, good information in the solution space will be utilized fully and make the algorithm converges quickly. For the selection of elites, that z is larger doesn't mean the better. When z is large, undoubtedly, the solving information can be used fully, but the larger z is, the smaller diversity of the subspace V is, in which the solution lingers over the certain local region in the search space, especially, for the multimodal. The selection of z relates to the size of M. The larger M is, the larger z can be.

3   STS Used in the Novel Algorithm(STS-EGT)

The evolutionary operation, an important role in EAs, determines the search ability and efficiency of the algorithms. However, when the searching easily stagnates, the population will easily fall into local optima. Under these circumstances, the current search space hardly contains the global optimum. So it is difficult for the current population to achieve better solutions. In this process, STS is embedded in EGT and improves the performance of the algorithm. STS transforms current search space into a new search space, which provides more opportunities for the algorithm to find the global optimum and accelerates convergence speed.

The main steps of STS-EGT are given as follows.

Algorithm. STS-EGT

Begin
 Initialize the population P(t), P(t)={$x_1(t)$, $x_2(t)$,…,$x_n(t)$}, $x_i(t) \in S$;
 Evaluate the population P(t);
 Calculate evaluation times;
 Sort (P(t));
 while ($x_1(t)$.fitness > accuracy && NE ≤ MAXNE)
  if(rand(0,1)<p_s)
   Execute STS operation and form TP(t) by equation (1)
   Evaluate the population TP(t);
   Calculate evaluation times;
   Add TP(t) to P(t);
   Sort (P(t), 2*PopSize);
  else
   Execute EGT/GT operation;
   Evaluate the population P(t);
   Calculate evaluation times;
   Sort (P(t), PopSize);
  end if
 end while
 Output x_{best} and $f(x_{best})$;
End

In STS-EGT, the allowed maximum numbers of evaluation (MAXNE) is set to 200,000. If the best fitness reaches to the fixed accuracy described in table 1, the current population is considered to obtain the global optimum, and then the algorithm is terminated. The value of k is related to the characteristics of given problems. Different values of k will result in different search spaces which may cover the global optimum(s). It is also very important to set the value of p_s which determines the implementation probability of the STS. In this paper, k and ps in STS-EGT are empirical studies. We will focus on the investigations of k, ps in future work.

4 Experiments and Analysis

4.1 Parameter Settings and Measures

There are 15 well-known benchmark functions including 6 unimodal functions, 5 multimodal functions and 4 multimodal functions with low dimensionalities and only a few local minima [10]. The description of the benchmark functions are listed in the Appendix. All the experiments are conducted 30 times with different random seeds, and the average results throughout the optimization runs are recorded. All the functions used in this paper are to be minimized.

The settings for the STS-EGT algorithms are:
- stopping criterion: 200,000 function evaluations
- population size:50
- dimension size: f_1-f_{11} is 30, f_{12} is 4, f_{13}-f_{15} is 2
- the probability p_s: 0.20
- the elite size of z in the EGT: 3
- the value of M in the EGT: 8
- the value of k in the STS: rand $(0,1)$

Table 1. Fixed accuracy level for each function and dimensions

Function	Accuracy	Function	Accuracy	Function	Accuracy
f_1	1.00E-15	f_2	1.00E-15	f_3	1.00E-15
f_4	1.00E-15	f_5	1.00E-15	f_6	1.00E-15
f_7	1.00E-15	f_8	1.00E-15	f_9	1.00E-15
f_{10}	1.00E-15	f_{11}	1.00E-15	f_{12}	0.0003075
f_{13}	-1.0316284	f_{14}	0.398	f_{15}	3

4.2 Results

The results of comparison among GT, STS-GT, STS-EGT are given by table 2, table3 and table4, where "ANE" is the average number of evaluations, "Mean" indicates the mean best function values found in the last generation and "Std Dev" stands for the standard deviation. "Best" and "Worst" are the best and worst fitness value throughout 30 runs respectively. "SR" indicates the number of runs reached the fixed accuracy in the percentage of total number of runs (successful running rate). The larger SR means that the algorithm is more reliable.

The results from f_1-f_6 are about unimodal functions. For STS-EGT□all functions have found the optimal solution with 100 percent success rate except f_5 which has got the optimal solution with 93 percent success rate. For STS-GT, all functions have achieved the optimal solution except f_5. Compared STS-EGT with the convergence rate of STS-GT, STS-EGT is significantly faster than that of STS-GT. GT is always trapped in local optimum while STS-GT and STS-EGT almost find the optimal solution every time, which indicates that STS helps both STS-GT and STS-EGT to jump out of the local optimum, and eventually find the optimal solution.

Multimodal functions, having many local minima, are often regarded as being difficult to optimize. f_7-f_{11} are multimodal functions with many local minima. For STS-EGT, all functions have found the optimal solution with 100 percent success rate except f_{10} which has got the optimal solution with 97 percent success rate. However, for STS-GT, f_7, f_8 and f_9 have got the optimal solution while both f_{10} and f_{11} haven't, and GT is trapped in local optimum every time. By comparing the results of this part with table 4, the fact that STS-EGT has more advantages in response to multimodal functions with many local minima is indicated.

To evaluate more fully, additional multimodal benchmark functions were also included in our experiments, i.e., f_{12}-f_{15} where the number of local minima for each function and the dimension of the function are small. For STS-EGT, f_{12} has got the optimal solution with 60 percent success rate, f_{13} hasn't found the optimal solution, and both f_{14} and f_{15} have achieved the optimal solution with 100 percent success rate. For STS-GT, f_{12} and f_{13} haven't found the optimal solution, f_{14} has discovered the optimal solution with 53 percent success rate, and f_{15} has achieved the optimal solution with 100 percent success rate. For STS-GT, all functions have achieved the optimal solution with 100 percent success rate except f_{12} which has got the optimal solution with 50 percent success rate. For f_{12}-f_{15}, the convergence rate of GT is significantly faster than that of STS-EGT and STS-GT. In general, the overall performance of GT is superior to that of STS-EGT and STS-GT, which confirm No-Free-Lunch theorem [11].

Table 2. Unimodal functions, Comparsion among GT, STS-GT, STS-EGT on f_1-f_6

Function	Model	ANE	Mean Best	Best	Worst	Std Dev	SR
f_1	GT	200000	1.59E+03	3.67E+02	4.71E+03	1.18E+06	0%
	STS-GT	52126	5.47E-16	1.10E-16	9.73E-16	5.45E-32	100%
	STS-EGT	31514	5.49E-16	9.34E-17	9.54E-16	8.17E-32	100%
f_2	GT	200000	1.17E+01	5.60E+00	2.20E+01	2.56E+01	0%
	STS-GT	86192	7.21E-16	2.61E-16	9.87E-16	3.31E-32	100%
	STS-EGT	55364	6.90E-16	2.85E-16	9.89E-16	3.48E-03	100%
f_3	GT	200000	2.34E+03	4.56E+02	1.14E+04	5.26E+06	0%
	STS-GT	44411	4.81E-16	2.44E-17	9.79E-16	8.47E-32	100%
	STS-EGT	27902	5.52E-16	7.48E-17	9.99E-16	7.79E-32	100%
f_4	GT	200000	9.76E+00	3.16E+00	1.95E+01	1.65E+01	0%
	STS-GT	87923	6.92E-16	1.04E-16	9.86E-16	6.05E-32	100%
	STS-EGT	56873	6.87E-16	2.02E-16	9.95E-16	3.89E-32	100%
f_5	GT	200000	1.43E+02	4.90E+01	3.60E+02	5.75E+03	0%
	STS-GT	200000	4.65E-06	7.73E-08	2.92E-03	2.84E-07	0%
	STS-EGT	173010	6.37E-16	6.46E-17	5.23E-15	7.79E-31	93%
f_6	GT	200000	1.19E+03	2.64E+02	3.30E+03	5.52E+05	0%
	STS-GT	9995	0.00E+00	0.00E+00	0.00E+00	0.00E+00	100%
	STS-EGT	7016	0.00E+00	0.00E+00	0.00E+00	0.00E+00	100%

Table 3. Multimodal functions with many minimal, Comparsion among GT, STS-GT, STS-EGT on f_7–f_{11}

Function	Model	ANE	Mean Best	Best	Worst	Std Dev	SR
f_7	GT	200000	1.04E+02	8.40E+01	1.37E+02	2.01E+02	0%
	STS-GT	37789	0.00E+00	0.00E+00	0.00E+00	0.00E+00	100%
	STS-EGT	25553	0.00E+00	0.00E+00	0.00E+00	0.00E+00	100%
f_8	GT	200000	5.89E+00	5.82E-14	2.00E+01	5.61E+01	0%
	STS-GT	78833	-9.96E-15	-2.71E-14	-2.22E-15	5.00E-29	100%
	STS-EGT	51088	-1.23E-14	-3.77E-14	-2.22E-15	8.90E-29	100%
f_9	GT	200000	1.77E+01	3.53E+00	6.39E+01	1.56E+02	0%
	STS-GT	39244	3.89E-16	0.00E+00	9.99E-16	1.12E-31	100%
	STS-EGT	27481	3.77E-16	0.00E+00	9.99E-16	1.07E-31	100%
f_{10}	GT	200000	2.88E+01	1.29E+00	1.30E+04	5.58E+06	0%
	STS-GT	200000	6.12E-07	2.07E-10	1.41E-04	6.57E-10	0%
	STS-EGT	162937	7.25E-16	3.60E-16	1.27E-15	4.83E-32	97%
f_{11}	GT	200000	7.25E+03	1.10E+01	4.43E+05	6.76E+09	0%
	STS-GT	200062	1.54E-07	7.58E-10	3.16E-06	3.81E-13	0%
	STS-EGT	166176	6.11E-16	1.30E-16	8.86E-16	3.06E-32	100%

Table 4. Multimodal functions with low dimensionalities and only a few local minimal, Comparsion among GT, STS-GT, STS-EGT on f_{12}–f_{15}

Function	Model	ANE	Mean Best	Best	Worst	Std Dev	SR
f_{12}	GT	101844	3.28E-03	3.07E-04	2.04E-02	5.45E-05	50%
	STS-GT	200000	9.32E-04	3.08E-04	2.16E-03	1.73611e	0%
	STS-EGT	136898	6.42E-04	3.07E-04	2.04E-02	1.32E-05	60%
f_{13}	GT	4182	-9.97E-01	-1.03E+00	-1.03E+00	1.18E-03	100%
	STS-GT	200000	-9.93E-01	-1.03E+00	-9.51E-01	1.26E-03	0%
	STS-EGT	200000	-9.92E-01	-1.03E+00	-1.00E+00	1.18E-03	0%
f_{14}	GT	2891	3.85E-01	3.98E-01	3.98E-01	1.76E-04	100%
	STS-GT	154795	3.85E-01	3.98E-01	4.00E-01	1.78E-04	53%
	STS-EGT	49742	3.85E-01	3.98E-01	4.02E-01	1.80E-04	97%
f_{15}	GT	2063	3.00E+00	3.00E+00	3.00E+00	1.00E-02	100%
	STS-GT	97162	3.00E+00	3.00E+00	3.00E+00	1.00E-02	100%
	STS-EGT	50334	3.00E+00	3.00E+00	3.00E+00	1.00E-02	100%

4.3 Analysis of Experiment Results

From experiment results on the fifteen benchmark functions, we can get the following conclusions:

1) GT/EGT is a highly efficient algorithm, especially for the functions with low-dimensionalities and a few local minima, it perform superiorly. But for the functions with high-dimensionalities and many minima, it act interiorly.
2) Through transforming the search space, STS-EGT□which contains space transformation technique, can get the algorithm out from local optimum, and ultimately achieve the optimal solution. Particularly, for the functions with high-dimensionalities and many minima, the effects would be more obvious.
3) For the functions with low-dimensionalities and a few local minima, both STS-EGT and EGT can find the optimal solution nearly. But the convergence rate of EGT is faster than that of STS-EGT apparently, the reason for the result is that STS transforms the search space and cause the search scope of STS-EGT increased. However, for the functions with high-dimensionalities and many minima, EGT-STS is distinctly better than EGT no matter in terms of the quality of solution or the convergence rate.

5 Conclusions

In this paper, a novel hybrid EAs named STS-EGT is proposed based on merging multi-parent crossover and space transformation technique. The main idea is to embed space transformation search (STS) into a novel genetic algorithm GA) which employs a novel crossover operator based on the non-convex linear combination of multiple parents and elite strategy (EGT). With a certain probability, STS transforms the search space to provide more opportunities for finding the global optimum and accelerate convergence speed. Experimental results show that the GT or EGT deals with the functions which have only a few local minima well but show low efficiency in optimization of functions which are high-dimensionalities, multimodal and have many local minima. When the GT or EGT employs the space transformation technique, the performance can be prompted significantly.

In future research works, we shall focus on how to apply this novel hybrid algorithm to solve more practical problems.

References

1. Pan, Z.J., Kang, L.S., Chen, Y.P.: Evolutionary Computation. Tsinghua University Press (1998) (in Chnese)
2. Baeck, T., Hoffme, F., Schwefel, H.P.: A survey of evolution strategies. In: Proceedings of the Fourth International Conference on Genetic Algorithms and Their Application. Morgan Kaufmann, CA (1991)
3. Fogel, D.B., Atmar, J.W.: Comparing Genetic Operators with Gaussian Mutations in Simulated Evolutionary Processes Using Linear Systems. Biol. Cybern. 63, 111–114 (1990)

4. Spears, W.M., De Jong, K.A.: On the Virtues of Parameterized Uniform Crossover. In: Proceedings of the Fourth International Conference on Genetic Algorithms and Their Application. Morgan Kaufmann, CA (1991)
5. Vose, M.D., Liepms, G.E.: Schema Disruption. In: Proceedings of the Fourth International Conference on Genetic Algorithms and Their Application. Morgan Kaufmann, CA (1991)
6. Schaffer, J.D., Eshelman, L.J.: On crossover as an evolutionarily viable strategy. In: Proceedings of the Fourth International Conference on Genetic Algorithms and Their Application. Morgan Kaufmann, CA (1991)
7. Shi, X.H., Lu, Y.H.: Hybrid Evolutionary Algorithms Based on PSO and GA. In: proceeding of IEEE int. Congress on Evolutionary Computation, vol. 4, pp. 2393–2399 (2003)
8. Wang, H., Wu, Z.J., Liu, Y., Wang, J.: Space Transformation Search: A New Evolutionary Technique. In: Proceedings of World Summit on Genetic and Evolutionary Computation, Shanghai, china (in press, 2009)
9. Guo, T.: Evolutionary Algorithm and Optimization. PHD Dissertation. Wuhan University (1999)
10. Yao, X., Liu, Y., Lin, G.L.: Evolutionary programming made faster. IEEE Trans. Evol. Comput. 3, 82–102 (1999)
11. Wolpert, D.H., Macready, W.G.: No free lunch theorems for optimization. IEEE Trans. Evol. 1, 67–82 (1997)

Appendix

The 15 benchmark functions we employed are given below. All the functions used in this paper are to be minimized.

f_1: *Sphere Model*

$$f_1 = \sum_{i=1}^{30} x_i^2, -100 \le x_i \le 100$$

$$\min(f_1) = f_1(0,...,0) = 0$$

f_2: *Schwefel's Problem 2.22*

$$f_2 = \sum_{i=1}^{30} |x_i| + \prod_{i=1}^{30} x_i, -10 \le x_i \le 10$$

$$\min(f_2) = f_2(0,...,0) = 0$$

f_3: *Schwefel's Problem 1.2*

$$f_3 = \sum_{i=1}^{30} \left(\sum_{j=1}^{i} x_j \right)^2, -100 \le x_i \le 100$$

$$\min(f_3) = f_3(0,...,0) = 0$$

f_4: *Schwefel's Problem 2.21*

$$f_4(x) = \max_i \{ |x_i|, 1 \le i \le 30 \}, -100 \le x_i \le 100$$

$$\min(f_4) = f_4(0,...,0) = 0$$

f_5: *Generalized Rosenbrock's Function*

$$f_5(x) = \sum_{i=1}^{29} [100(x_{i+1} - x_i^2)^2 + (x_i - 1)^2], -30 \le x_i \le 30$$

$$\min(f_5) = f_5(1,...,1) = 0$$

f_6: *Step Function*

$$f_6(x) = \sum_{i=1}^{30} (x_i + 0.5)^2, -100 \le x_i \le 100$$

$$\min(f_6) = f_6(0,...,0) = 0$$

f_7: *Generalized Rastrigin's Function*

$$f_7 = \sum_{i=1}^{30} [x_i^2 - 10\cos(2\pi x_i) + 10], -5.12 \le x_i \le 5.12$$

$$\min(f_7) = f_7(0,...,0) = 0$$

f_8: *Ackley's Function*

$$f_8(x) = -20\exp(-0.2\sqrt{\frac{1}{30}\sum_{i=1}^{30} x_i^2}) - \exp(\frac{1}{30}\sum_{i=1}^{30}\cos 2\pi x_i) + 20 + e$$

$$-32 \le x_i \le 32, \min(f_8) = f_8(0,...,0) = 0$$

f_9: *Generalized Griewank Function*

$$f_9(x) = \frac{1}{4000}\sum_{i=1}^{30} x_i^2 - \prod_{i=1}^{30}\cos(\frac{x_i}{\sqrt{i}}) + 1$$

$$, -600 \le x_i \le 600$$

$$\min(f_{11}) = f_{11}(0,...,0) = 0$$

f_{10}: *Generalized Penalized Functions I*

$$f_{10} = \frac{\pi}{30}\{10\sin^2(\pi y_1) + \sum_{i=1}^{29}(y_i - 1)^2[1 + 10\sin^2(\pi y_{i+1})] + (y_n - 1)^2$$

$$+ \sum_{i=1}^{30} u(x_i, 10, 100, 4)\}$$

$$y_i = 1 + \frac{1}{4}(x_i + 1), u(x_i, a, k, m) = \begin{cases} k(x_i - a)^2, x_i > a \\ 0, -a \le x_i \le a \\ k(-x_i - a)^2, x_i < a \end{cases}$$

$$-50 \le x_i \le 50, \min(f_{10}) = f_{10}(1,...,1) = 0$$

f_{11}: *Generalized Penalized Functions II*

$$f_{10} = \frac{\pi}{30} \{\sin^2(\pi 3 x_i) + \sum_{i=1}^{29} (x_i - 1)^2 [1 + \sin^2(3\pi x_{i+1})] + (x_n - 1)^2$$

$$[1 + \sin^2(2\pi x_{30})]\} + \sum_{i=1}^{30} u(x_i, 5, 100, 4)$$

$$u(x_i, a, k, m) = \begin{cases} k(x_i - a)^2, x_i > a \\ o, -a \le x_i \le a \\ k(-x_i - a)^2, x_i < a \end{cases}$$

$$-50 \le x_i \le 50, \min(f_{10}) = f_{10}(1,...,1) = 0$$

f_{13}: *Six-Hump Camel-Back Function*

$$f_{13} = 4x_1^2 - 2.1x_1^4 + \frac{1}{3}x_1^6 + x_1 x_2 - 4x_2^2 + 4x_2^4$$

$$-5 \le x_i \le 5, x_{min} = (0.08983, -0.7126), (-0.08983, 0.7126)$$

$$\min(f_{13}) = -1.0316285$$

f_{12}: *Kowalik's Function*

$$f_{12}(x) = \sum_{i=1}^{11} \left[a_i - \frac{x_1(b_i^2 + b_i x_2)}{b_i^2 + b_i x_3 + x_4} \right]^2$$

$$a_i = \{0.1957, 0.1947, 0.1735, 0.1600, 0.0844, 0.0627, 0.0456$$
$$, 0.0342, 0.0323, 0.0235, 0.0246\}$$

$$b_i = \{0.25, 0.5, 1, 2, 4, 6, 8, 10, 12, 14, 16\}$$

$$-5 \le x_i \le 5, \min f_{12}(x) \approx f_{15}(0.1928, 0.1908, 0.1231, 0.1358)$$

$$\approx 0.0003075$$

f_{14}: *Branin Function*

$$f_{14}(x) = (x_2 - \frac{5.1}{4\pi^2}x_1^2 + \frac{5}{\pi}x_1 - 6)^2 + 10(1 - \frac{1}{8\pi})\cos x_1 + 10$$

$$-5 \le x_1 \le 10, 0 \le x_2 \le 15$$

$$x_{min} = (-3.1421, 2.275), (3.142, 2.275), (9.425, 2.425), \min(f_{14})$$
$$= 0.398$$

f_{15}: *Goldstein-Price Function*

$$f_{15}(x) = [1 + (x_1 + x_2 + 1)^2 (19 - 14x_1 + 3x_1^2 - 14x_2 + 6x_1 x_2 + 3x_2^2)] \times [30 + (2x_1 - 3x_2)^2 \times (18 - 32x_1 + 12x_1^2 + 48x_2 - 36x_1 x_2 + 27x_2^2)]$$

$$-2 \le x_i \le 2, \min(f_{15}) = f_{15}(0, -1) = 3$$

An Evolutionary Algorithm and Kalman Filter Hybrid Approach for Integrated Navigation

Zhiqiang Du, Zhihua Cai, Leichen Chen, and Huihui Deng

School of Computer, China University of Geosciences, Wuhan, Hubei, 430074, China
wolfdzq@gmail.com, zhcai@cug.edu.cn

Abstract. Kalman filter perform optimally when the noise statistics for the measurement and process are completely known in integrated navigation system. However, the noise statistics could change with the actual working environment and so the initial priori value would represent the actual state of noise incorrectly. To solve this problem, this paper presents an adaptive Kalman Filter based on evolutionary algorithm. The hybrid method improves the real-time noise statistics by the procedure of global search. Field test data are processed to evaluate the performance of the proposed method. The results of experiment show the proposed method is capable of improving the output precision and adaptive capacity of filtering, and thus is valuable in application.

Keywords: Kalman filter, Evolutionary Algorithm, Integrated Navigation.

1 Introduction

Evolutionary algorithm is a heuristic search algorithm based on the populations, which search optimal result in the solution space by individuals in groups and has been widely used in function optimization, combinatorial optimization and the solving of other optimization problems at recent years.

The traditional Kalman filter works well when the mathematical models were accurate and the statistical properties of system noise were well be known. However, the models are often uncertainty and the statistical properties of interference signals are not fully known. In recent years, the idea of robust controlling, such as fuzzy logic method [1,2] and genetic algorithm [3], was introduced into the filtering, which achieved fairly good effect. However, there are some drawbacks that fuzzy adaptive reasoning requires a lot of empirical data, which may be inaccurate because of the changes in the environment and the parameters, such as the cycle of optimization, the number of models and so on, need repeated test and research in order to get good results for genetic algorithm.

In this paper we build an adaptive Kalman filter model based on the evolutionary algorithm, and apply it to the integrated navigation system, so make it a new method for solving the problem that the statistical properties of the system noise change with the time and environment.

Z. Cai et al. (Eds.): ISICA 2009, LNCS 5821, pp. 211–216, 2009.
© Springer-Verlag Berlin Heidelberg 2009

2 INS/GPS Integrated Techniques

GPS and INS are usually integrated with a KF to overcome drawbacks associated with each system, and provide a robust navigation solution. Since GPS has a consistent, long-term accuracy, it is used to correct INS measurements and thus to prevent the long-term growth of their errors. On the other hand, the accurate short-term measurement provided by INS is used to solve problems related to GPS such as cycle slips and clock biases. KF is the optimal filter for modeled processes, and the core of most GPS/SINS integrated systems implemented to date [5]. It can optimally estimate the position, velocity and attitude of a moving vehicle using precise GPS measurements to update the filter states. KF is computationally efficient, which is especially useful for real-time applications. With correct dynamic models and stochastic models of GPS and INS errors, KF can produce very accurate geo-referencing solutions provided that there is a continuous access to GPS signals.

Traditionally, this integration is accomplished by means of Kalman filter as shown in Fig.1, in which the INS outputs are compared with the outputs of the global positioning system (GPS). The errors in between are subjected to Kalman filtering, which enhances the performance of the navigation system by removing the effect of residual random errors during the surveying process [6].

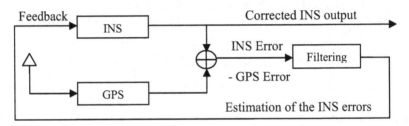

Fig. 1. INS/GPS integration navigation system using Kalman Filter

There are several considerable drawbacks of KF. The necessity of accurate stochastic modeling may not be possible in the case of low cost and tactical grade sensors. It is demanding to accurately determine the parameters of the system and measurement covariance matrices for each new sensor.

3 Differential Evolution

Differential evolution [10] (DE) in fact is a steady-state evolutionary algorithm which adopt a multi-parent restructuring operator to generate the new individuals. The selection operator of DE is simple and easy to implement. The procedure of DE is summarized as follows:

Step1: Randomly initialize the population for DE, where each individual contain d variables.
Step2: Evaluate the objective values of all individuals, and determine X_{best} which has the best objective value.

Step3: Perform mutation operation for each individual in order to obtain each individual's mutant counterpart.

Step4: Perform crossover operation between each individual and its corresponding mutant counterpart in order to obtain each individual's trial individual.

Step5: evaluate the objective values of the trial individuals.

Step6: Perform selection operation between each individual and its corresponding trial counterpart so as to generate the new individual for the next generation.

Step7: Determine the best individual of the current new population with the best objective value. If the objective value is better than the objective value of X_{best}, then update X_{best} and its objective value with the value and objective value of the current best individual.

Step8: If a stopping criterion is met, then output X_{best} and its objective value; otherwise go back to Step 3.

4 Evolutionary Kalman Filter (EvoKF)

Using the evolutionary algorithm shown above, we can design an adapted Kalman filter based on the evolutionary algorithm, which can optimize the observed noise matrix and the process noise matrix each time to make the filter's estimated error covariance matrix smallest. The block diagram of proposed KF and DE hybrid method is presented in Fig.2.

- Individual representation

In this paper DE adopts the real-coded genomes with corresponding genetic operators performed. The values of process noise matrix and measurement noise matrix were coded to generate an individual.

- Fitness function

The fitness of an individual of the population is the criterion for DE to optimize all the parameters encoded into an individual. Because the criteria for the performance of integrated navigation system is RMSE or the max error, so we defined the fitness function as follows:

$$X.f = \sqrt{\left(\hat{L}-L_{GPS}\right)^2+\left(\hat{\lambda}-\lambda_{GPS}\right)^2+\left(\hat{\upsilon}_E-\upsilon_E^{GPS}\right)^2+\left(\hat{\upsilon}_N-\upsilon_N^{GPS}\right)^2}$$

where L represent longitude, λ represent latitude, υ_E represent east velocity, υ_N represent north velocity.

- The stopping criteria

In this paper the stopping criterion is set according to one criterion. While the specified maximum number of generations is reached, the evolution process is terminated. The process of EvoKF is similar to the normal evolutionary algorithm as follows:

Step1: First, using Differential Evolution or other evolutionary algorithm search the best individual in the solution space before filtering. The best individual after reaching the max generation could be the covariance matrix of the process noise and the measurement noise used by the classical Kalman filter.

Step2: Using the classical Kalman filter with good covariance matrix obtained above to get the estimated value about position and velocity.

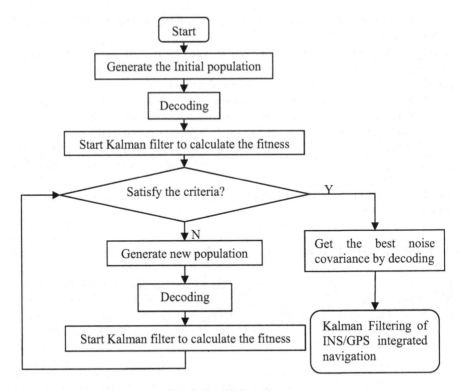

Fig. 2. EvoKF flow chart

5 Experiments

To test the performance of EvoKF, we not only use DE but also use Guo's Algorithm[11] as the evolutionary algorithm used in the EvoKF. The max generation numbers of two evolution algorithm are both 100, the size of population is 10. In the Guo's Algorithm, the parent number is 3. In DE, we set the mutation probability 0.9 and the strategy is DE/rand/1/exp. The experiment data was collected in Beijing, China by an INS/GPS Integrated Navigation system. The minimum number of available satellites was 7, and the frequency of INS was 0.01(s), the frequency of GPS was 1(s).

From the fitness function, we know the element with bigger estimated error would make bigger effective on the fitness value than the element with smaller estimated error, so we designed three kinds of weights for position estimated error to balance the effective made by position estimated error and velocity estimated error. They are represented by *weight-a*, *weight-b*, *weight-c* showed below. *weight-a* is obtained by the exponential difference of estimated error between position and velocity; *weight-b* is obtained by the exponential difference of relative estimated error between position and velocity; *weight-c* is an experience value based on the above two.

Table 1. Three kinds of weight

Weight	Longitude	Latitude
weight-a	e^8	e^8
weight-b	e^10	e^8
weight-c	e^9	e^9

The compared results are presented below.

Table 2. RMSE of each method in position and velocity with weight-a

Method	Longitude	Latitude	East velocity	North velocity
Kalman	4.8942e-005	2.8176e-005	0.30061	0.296
EvoKF(GT)	**4.2484e-005**	**2.4514e-005**	**0.28442**	**0.28277**
EvoKF(DE)	**4.1399e-005**	**2.4065e-005**	**0.28139**	**0.28027**

Table 3. RMSE of each method in position and velocity with weight-b

Method	Longitude	Latitude	East velocity	North velocity
Kalman	4.8942e-005	2.8176e-005	0.30061	0.296
EvoKF(GT)	**2.2853e-005**	**2.5713e-005**	**0.28499**	**0.28767**
EvoKF(DE)	**2.1936e-005**	**2.4073e-005**	**0.28409**	**0.28486**

Table 4. RMSE of each method in position and velocity with weight-c

Method	Longitude	Latitude	East velocity	North velocity
Kalman	4.8942e-5	2.8176e-5	0.30061	0.296
EvoKF(GT)	**2.7315e-5**	**1.5355e-5**	**0.27971**	**0.27974**
EvoKF(DE)	**2.4119e-5**	**1.4277e-5**	**0.27662**	**0.27475**

Table 5. Max-error of each method in position and velocity with weight-a

Method	Longitude	Latitude	East velocity	North velocity
Kalman	0.00013441	0.00011977	2.0268	3.022
EvoKF(GT)	**0.00013668**	**0.00011864**	**1.9117**	**2.894**
EvoKF(DE)	0.00013901	**0.00011604**	**1.8879**	**2.8832**

Table 6. Max-error of each method in position and velocity with weight-b

Method	Longitude	Latitude	East velocity	North velocity
Kalman	0.00013441	0.00011977	2.0268	3.022
EvoKF(GT)	**8.834e-005**	**0.00011641**	**1.9112**	**2.8727**
EvoKF(DE)	**9.845e-005**	**0.00010969**	**1.9392**	**2.8152**

Table 7. Max-error of each method in position and velocity with weight-c

Method	Longitude	Latitude	East velocity	North velocity
Kalman	0.00013441	0.00011977	2.0268	3.022
EvoKF(GT)	**0.00010768**	**0.00010058**	**1.8586**	**2.8569**
EvoKF(DE)	**0.00010045**	**0.0001044**	**1.8217**	**2.7555**

6 Conclusion

In this paper, we proposed a new adaptive Kalman filter algorithm and solved the problem that filtering will be divergence with the changing of noises statistical properties. The experiment result proved the hybrid method works optimally compared with the classical Kalman Filter. The EvoKF estimate the state of noises, and overcome difficulty that the sensitive to the initial values of statistical properties of the noises.

References

1. Jing, B., Jian-ye, L., Xin, Y.: Study of Fuzzy Adaptive Kalman Filtering Technique. Information and Control. J. 31, 193–197 (2002) (in Chinese)
2. Tian-lai, X., Wen-hu, Y., Ping-yuan, C.: Research on GPS/INS Integrated navigation System Based on Fuzzy Adaptive Kalman Filtering. Journal of Astronautics. J. 26, 571–575 (2005)
3. Zi-liang, W., Jian-cheng, F., Wei, Q.: Multi-model Kalman filter algorithm based on GA. Journal of Beijing University of Aeronautics and Astronautics. J. 30, 748–752 (2004)
4. Bäck, T., Schwefel, H.-P.: An overview of evolutionary algorithms for parameter optimization. Evolutionary Computation. J. 1, 1–23 (1993)
5. Farrell, J., Barth, M.: The Global Positioning System and Inertial Navigation, p. 333. McGraw-Hill, New York (1999)
6. Titterton, D.H., Weston, J.L.: Strapdown inertial naviagation technology. Peter Peregrinus Ltd., London (1997)
7. Kalman, R.E.: A New Approach to Linear Filtering and Prediction Problems. Journal of Basic Engineering, J. 82, 35–45 (1960)
8. Noureldin, A., Irvine-Halliday, D., Mintchev, M.P.: Accuracy limitations of FOG-based continuous measurement-while-drilling surveying instruments for horizontal wells. IEEE Transactions on Instrumentation and Measurement, J 51(6), 1177–1191 (2002)
9. Nassar, S., Noureldin, A., El-Sheimy, N.: Improving positioning accuracy during kinematic DGPS outage periods SINS/DGPS integration and SINS data de-noising. Survey Review Journal. J. 37, 426–438 (2004)
10. Storn, R., Price, K.: Differential evolution, A simple and efficient heuristic for global optimization over continuous spaces. Journal of Global Optimization. J. 11, 341–359 (1997)
11. Tao, G., Li-shan, K., Yan, L.: A New Algorithm for Solving Function Optimization Problems with Inequality Constrains. Wuhan University Journal (Natural Science Edition). J. 45, 771–775 (1999) (in Chinese)
12. Chan, Z.S.H., Ngan, H.W., Rad, A.B.: A practical mutation operator and its application to the Kalman filter. In: Proceedings of International Conference on Power System Technology, pp. 491–495 (2000)
13. Shin, E.-H., El-Sheimy, N.: Accuracy Improvement of Low Cost INS/GPS for Land Applications. In: Proceedings of the 14th ION Meeting, San Diego, USA (2002)

Clonal and Cauchy-mutation Evolutionary Algorithm for Global Numerical Optimization

Jing Guan[1] and Ming Yang[2]

[1] Institute for Pattern Recognition and Artificial Intelligence, Huazhong University of Science and Technology, Wuhan, 430074, China
g_jing0414@yahoo.com.cn
[2] School of Computer Science, China University of Geosciences, Wuhan, 430074, China
yangming0702@gmail.com

Abstract. Many real-life problems can be formulated as numerical optimization of certain objective functions. However, for an objective function possesses numerous local optima, many evolutionary algorithms (EAs) would be trapped in local solutions. To improve the search efficiency, this paper presents a clone and Cauchy-mutation evolutionary algorithm (CCEA), which employs dynamic clone and Cauchy mutation methods, for numerical optimization. For a suit of 23 benchmark test functions, CCEA is able to locate the near-optimal solutions for almost 23 test functions with relatively small variance. Especially, for f_{14}-f_{23}, CCEA can get better solutions than other algorithms.

Keywords: numerical optimization, evolutionary algorithm, clone, Cauchy.

1 Introduction

As optimization problems exist widely in all domains of scientific research and engineering application, research on optimization methods is of great theoretical significance and practical value. Most function optimization problems, such as the optimization of fuzzy system structure and parameters or the optimization of control system, are all multi-peaks function optimization problems , this kind of problems is to search the best point, which is the minimum point commonly from all the search space. For those problems to get the maximum point, they can make minus and are changed to search the minimum point. The minimum function optimization problem can be described as follows:

$$\min f(x), x \in D \tag{1}$$

where f is an N-dimension function, D is a limited space and $D \subseteq R^N$.

A number of evolutionary algorithms have been used to solve these function optimization problems [1-9]. This success is due to EAs essentially are search algorithms based on the concepts of natural selection and survival of the fittest. They guide the evolution of a set of randomly selected individuals through a number of generations in

Z. Cai et al. (Eds.): ISICA 2009, LNCS 5821, pp. 217–227, 2009.

approaching the global optimum solution. Besides that, the fact that these algorithms do not require previous considerations regarding the problem to be optimized and offers a high degree of parallelism is also true.

Fast evolutionary strategy (FES), applying Cauchy mutation in the evolution strategies to generate each new generation, can find near-optima very fast [4]. Especially, evolutionary programming (EP) has been applied with success to many function optimization problems in recent years [3,5,6], such as classical evolutionary programming (CEP) [5] and fast evolutionary programming (FEP) [6]. For CEP, there are some versions with different mutation operators, namely, (a) Gaussian mutation operator (CEP/GMO), designed for fast convergence on convex function optimization; (b) Cauchy mutation operator (CEP/CMO), aimed for effective escape from the local optima; (c) mean mutation operator (CEP/MMO), which is a linear combination of Gaussian mutation and Cauchy mutation. FEP essentially employs a CMO but incorporates the GMO in an effective way, and it performs much better than CEP for multimodal functions with many local minima while being comparable to CEP in performance for unimodal and multimodal functions with only a few local minima. Evolutionary optimization (EO) [7] uses a mutation operator and a selection scheme to evolve a population. Stochastic genetic algorithm (StGA), employing a novel stochastic coding strategy so that the search space is dynamically divided into regions using a stochastic method and explored region-by-region, and in each region, a number of children are produced through random sampling, and the best child is chosen to represent the region, can get very good results for many function optimization problems [8]. Quantum-inspired evolutionary algorithm, inspired by the multiple universes principle of quantum computing, can also solve some function optimization problems effectively [9]. Some other algorithms such as particle swarm optimization (PSO) [7,10-12] and differential evolution (DE) [13-15] are proposed to solve function optimization problems. PSO is a new evolutionary computing scheme, which explores the insect swarm behavior, and seems to be effective for optimizing a wide range of functions. DE is a practical approach to global function optimization that is easy to understand, simple to implement, reliable, and fast. Basically, DE adds the weighted difference between two population vectors to a third vector and is completely self-organizing.

In this paper, a clone and Cauchy-mutation evolutionary algorithm (CCEA) for function optimization is proposed, using dynamic clone, the number of which is direct proportion to "affinity" between individuals, and Cauchy mutation methods.

2   Clone and Cauchy-mutation Evolutionary Algorithm (CCEA)

Suppose that $A(k) = \{A_1(k+1), A_2(k+1), ..., A_n(k+1)\}$ is the population at the k generation and n is the size of population.

The individual $A(k)$ is coded by real number:

$$A_i(k) = (x_{i1}, x_{i2}, ..., x_{im}), i = 1, 2, ..., n \tag{2}$$

where m is the dimension of function and $x_{ij} \in [a_j, b_j]$; a_j, b_j is the boundary of x_j.

CCEA clones an individual according to "affinity" between individuals, operates Cauchy mutation on the population and then generation the offspring population. The course of CCEA is as follow:

$$A(k) \xrightarrow{T_c} Y(k) \xrightarrow{T_g} A(k) \cup Y'(k) \xrightarrow{T_s} A(k+1) \tag{3}$$

where T_c is the dynamic clone operation, T_g is the genetic operation and T_s is the selection operation to generate offspring population, $Y(k)$ is the clone of $A(k)$ got by T_c, $Y'(k)$ is the clone population after T_g. The three operations are described as Fig. 1.

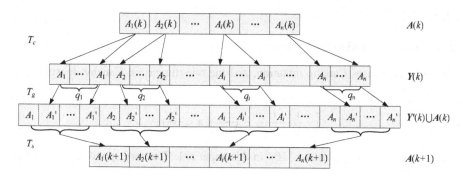

Fig. 1. The three operations of CCEA: T_c, T_g and T_s

2.1 Clone Operation T_c

For an individual, the number of clone got by T_c is determined by the density of its nearby individuals, which is called "affinity". If the density is large, the clone number is small; if the density is small, the number is large. And the number changes with the distribution of population. With this clone operation, domains with smaller density can get larger possibility of genetic operations. So CCEA can search the whole space most possibly and get the global optimal solution.

Suppose that $Y(k)$ is the clone population after T_c. $Y(k)$ is:

$$Y(k) = T_c(A(k)) = \begin{bmatrix} Y_1(k) & Y_2(k) & \cdots & Y_n(k) \end{bmatrix}^T \tag{4}$$

where $Y_i(k) = T_c(A_i(k)) = I_i \times A_i(k) = \begin{bmatrix} A_i(k) & A_i(k) & \cdots & A_i(k) \end{bmatrix}_{1 \times q_i}$, $i = 1, 2, ..., n$, I_i is the q_i-dimension row vector in which each element is 1 and the value of q_i is:

$$q_i = \lceil low + (up - low) \times \Theta_i \rceil \tag{5}$$

where *low* and *up* is respectively the minimum and maximum value of clone size, Θ_i is the affinity between A_i and other individuals and $\Theta_i \in [0,1]$:

$$\Theta_i = \frac{d_i - d_{min}}{d_{max} - d_{min}} \tag{6}$$

where d_i is the Euclidian distance between A_i and other individuals A_j:

$$d_i = \min\|A_i - A_j\|, j = 1, 2, ..., n, i \neq j$$
$$d_{min} = \min\{d_i\}, i = 1, 2, ..., n \tag{7}$$
$$d_{max} = \max\{d_i\}, i = 1, 2, ..., n$$

From Equation (5) and (6), it can be seen that q_i changes with Θ_i which indicates how dense the population's distribution is near the individual A_i. The more dense distribution, the less Θ_i is, vice versa.

2.2 Cauchy Mutation Operation T_g

This algorithm uses Cauchy mutation, and the one-dimension Cauchy density function is defined by:

$$f(x) = \frac{1}{\pi} \frac{t}{t^2 + x^2}, \quad (-\infty < x < +\infty) \tag{8}$$

where $t>0$ is a scale parameter [16], in this paper $t=1$. The corresponding distribution function is:

$$F(x) = \frac{1}{2} + \frac{1}{\pi} \arctan\left(\frac{x}{t}\right) \tag{9}$$

There are some papers use the Gaussian mutation as their mutation operator, in paper [6], experiments proved that Cauchy density function is similar to Gaussian density function and less than it in vertical direction. The Cauchy distribution changes as slowly as it approaches the horizontal axis, as a result, the variance of the Cauchy distribution is infinite. Fig. 2 shows the difference between Cauchy and Gaussian density functions by plotting them in the same scale.

According to the similarity between Cauchy and Gaussian distribution, especially Cauchy distribution has two sides probability characteristics, the Cauchy distribution can generate a random number far away from origin easily, whose distribution range is wider than that generated from Gaussian mutation, it means Cauchy mutation can jump out of the local optimum quickly.

$\forall A_i(k) \in Y_i(k), A_i(k) = (x_{i1}, x_{i2}, ..., x_{im})$, after the Cauchy mutation operation T_g, the clone individuals of $A_i(k)$ is $Y'(k) = T_g(A_i(k)) = [A'_i(k) \; A'_i(k) \; \cdots \; A'_i(k)]_{1 \times q_i}$,

where $A'_i(k) = (x'_{i1}, x'_{i2}, ..., x'_{im})$. The following is the description of T_g.

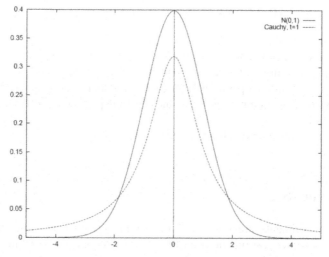

Fig. 2. Comparison between Cauchy and Gaussian density functions

for $(1 \leq j \leq m)$
{
    if $(random(0,1) < P_m)$
    {
        if $(random(0,1) < 0.5)$
            $x'_{ij} = x_{ij} + \delta_{ij}, 1 \leq j \leq m$;
        else
            $x'_{ij} = x_{ij} - \delta_{ij}, 1 \leq j \leq m$;
        if $(x'_{ij} < a_j)$ $x'_{ij} = a_j$;
        else if $(x'_{ij} > b_j)$ $x'_{ij} = b_j$;
    }
}

where $P_m = m^{-(n+1)/(n+t_i)}$, $P_m \in \left[\dfrac{1}{m}, \sqrt{\dfrac{1}{m}} \right]$, t is the ranking of $A_i(k+1)$ in the sort sequence

according to fitness; δ_{ij} is a Cauchy variable and $\delta_{ij} \in \left[0, r * b_j \right]$.

Relative to the individual of better fitness, the ones of worse fitness can get greater probability. This can guarantee the whole population is good.

2.3 Selection Operation T_s

After Cauchy mutation operation, the offspring population is: $\forall i = 1, 2, ..., n$

$$A_i(k+1) = \begin{cases} B_i(k) & \text{if } B_i(k) \text{ is better than } A_i(k) \\ A_i(k) & \text{else} \end{cases} \tag{10}$$

where $B_i(k) = best \left\{ Y'_i(k) \right\} = best \left\{ A'_i(k) \mid i = 1, 2, ..., q_i \right\}$.

2.4 The Framework of CCEA

1. Suppose that k is the number of evolution, $k=0$;
2. Initialize the population $A(k)$ randomly, the size of population is n;
3. Clone operation T_c for each individual in $A(k)$, generate $Y(k)$;
4. Cauchy mutation operation T_g for each individual in $Y(k)$, generate $Y'(k)$;
5. Selection Operation T_s, generate the offspring population $A(k+1)$;
6. $k:=k+1$;
7. If not termination condition, go to step 4;
8. Stop.

3 Experiments

Numerical experiments are conducted to test the effectiveness and efficiency of CCEA. Twenty-three test functions in [6] of three categories are used in experiments, covering a broader range than in some other relevant studies for the purpose to demonstrate the robustness and reliability of the present algorithm.

Table 1 lists the 23 test functions and their key properties. These functions can be divided into three categories of different complexities. f_1-f_7 are unimodal functions, which are relatively easy to optimize, but the difficulty increases as the problem dimension goes high. f_8-f_{13}, representing the most difficult class of problems for many optimization algorithms, are multimodal functions with many local optima, and the number of local minima increases exponentially with the problem dimension [17,18]. f_{14}-f_{23} are likewise multimodal functions, but they only contain a few local optima [18]. The major difference between f_8-f_{13} and f_{14}-f_{23} is that functions f_{14}-f_{23} appear to be simpler than f_8-f_{13} due to their low dimensionalities and a smaller number of local minima. As examples of the three categories, Fig. 3 shows the surface landscapes of f_3, f_8 and f_{23} when the dimension is set to 2. It is interesting to note that some functions possess rather unique features. For instance, f_6 is a discontinuous step function having a single optimum; f_7 is a noisy function involving a uniformly distributed random variable within [0, 1).

Generally speaking, for unimodal functions the convergence rates are of main interest as optimizing such functions to a satisfactory accuracy is not a major issue. For multimodal functions, however, the quality of the final results is more crucial since it reflects the algorithm's ability in escaping from local deceptive optima and locating the desired near-global solution.

In this paper, CCEA is compared with FEP and StGA, where results of FEP and StGA are from [6] and [8]. The parameters of algorithm are set as Table 2. For each test function, 50 runs with different seeds from the random number generator are performed to observe the consistency of the outcome. The results of this comparison are shown in Table 3 and Table 4 with respect to the mean best values found and the standard deviations for each function.

Table 1. The 23 benchmark functions used in experiment, where N is the dimension of function, f_{min} is the minimum value of function, and D is the search space ($x \in D$), the sign "≈" in column f_{min} means the value is approximate

Functions	N	S	f_{min}
f_1	30	$[-100, 100]^N$	0
f_2	30	$[-10, 10]^N$	0
f_3	30	$[-100, 100]^N$	0
f_4	30	$[-100, 100]^N$	0
f_5	30	$[-30, 30]^N$	0
f_6	30	$[-100, 100]^N$	0
f_7	30	$[-1.28, 1.28]^N$	0
f_8	30	$[-500, 500]^N$	-12569.5
f_9	30	$[-5.12, 5.12]^N$	0
f_{10}	30	$[-32, 32]^N$	0
f_{11}	30	$[-600, 600]^N$	0
f_{12}	30	$[-50, 50]^N$	0
f_{13}	30	$[-50, 50]^N$	0
f_{14}	2	$[-65.536, 65.536]^N$	≈1
f_{15}	4	$[-5, 5]^N$	≈0.0003075
f_{16}	2	$[-5, 5]^N$	-1.0316285
f_{17}	2	$[-5, 10] \times [0, 15]$	0.398
f_{18}	2	$[-2, 2]^N$	3
f_{19}	3	$[0, 1]^N$	-3.86
f_{20}	6	$[0, 1]^N$	-3.32
f_{21}	4	$[0, 10]^N$	≈-10.1422
f_{22}	4	$[0, 10]^N$	≈-10.3909
f_{23}	4	$[0, 10]^N$	≈-10.5300

From Table 3, it can be seen that CCEA can get the near-global solution except f_8 and f_9. In the experiment, we found because there are so many local optima, the steps between optima are large, and the probability of generating large Cauchy variables is very small, CCEA can not jump out of local optima and get the global solution. From Table 3 and Table 4, for from f_1 to f_{13}, we can see CCEA have the same performance to FEP and StGA, except f_8 and f_9. For from f_{14} to f_{23}, CCEA performs better than FEP and StGA.

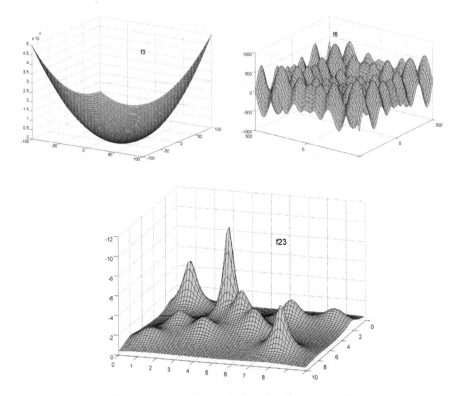

Fig. 3. Graphs of f_3, f_8 and f_{23} with a dimension of 2

Table 2. Algorithm's parameters setting

n	low	up	r_1	t
50	10	20	0.1	1

Table 3. Comparison between CCEA and FEP. All results have been averaged over 50 runs, where "Mean Best"indicates the mean best function values found in the last generation, and "Std Dev" stand for the standard deviation.

TF	Number of generation		Mean Best		Std Dev	
	CCEA	FEP	CCEA	FEP	CCEA	FEP
f_1	10000	1500	5.27×10^{-5}	5.7×10^{-4}	8.99×10^{-6}	1.3×10^{-4}
f_2	50000	2000	2.89×10^{-3}	8.1×10^{-3}	2.49×10^{-4}	7.7×10^{-4}
f_3	50000	5000	4.40×10^{-2}	1.6×10^{-2}	9.46×10^{-3}	1.4×10^{-2}

Table 3. (*Continued*)

TF	Number of generation		Mean Best		Std Dev	
	CCEA	FEP	CCEA	FEP	CCEA	FEP
f_4	50000	5000	$6.29{\times}10^{-3}$	0.3	$3.86{\times}10^{-4}$	0.5
f_5	50000	20000	0.2	5.06	0.24	5.87
f_6	500	1500	0	0	0	0
f_7	10000	3000	$1.29{\times}10^{-3}$	$7.6{\times}10^{-3}$	$1.63{\times}10^{-3}$	$2.6{\times}10^{-3}$
f_8	10000	9000	-8315.98	-12554.5	383.29	52.6
f_9	10000	5000	161.681	$4.6{\times}10^{-2}$	19.92	$1.2{\times}10^{-2}$
f_{10}	50000	1500	$8.82{\times}10^{-4}$	$1.8{\times}10^{-2}$	$1.19{\times}10^{-4}$	$2.1{\times}10^{-3}$
f_{11}	10000	2000	$3.89{\times}10^{-6}$	$1.6{\times}10^{-2}$	$1.58{\times}10^{-6}$	$2.2{\times}10^{-2}$
f_{12}	10000	1500	$4.38{\times}10^{-7}$	$9.2{\times}10^{-6}$	$1.36{\times}10^{-7}$	$3.6{\times}10^{-6}$
f_{13}	10000	1500	$5.69{\times}10^{-6}$	$1.6{\times}10^{-4}$	$1.04{\times}10^{-6}$	$7.3{\times}10^{-5}$
f_{14}	500	100	0.998004	1.22	0	0.56
f_{15}	50000	4000	$3.11{\times}10^{-4}$	$5.0{\times}10^{-4}$	$3.14{\times}10^{-6}$	$3.2{\times}10^{-4}$
f_{16}	100	100	-1.03163	-1.03	$1.49{\times}10^{-6}$	$4.9{\times}10^{-7}$
f_{17}	100	100	0.397889	0.398	$1.45{\times}10^{-6}$	$1.5{\times}10^{-7}$
f_{18}	500	100	3	3.02	$2.01{\times}10^{-6}$	0.11
f_{19}	100	200	-3.86278	-3.86	$1.22{\times}10^{-6}$	$1.4{\times}10^{-5}$
f_{20}	100	100	-3.32188	-3.27	$4.63{\times}10^{-5}$	$5.9{\times}10^{-2}$
f_{21}	1000	100	-10.1532	-5.52	$2.19{\times}10^{-5}$	1.59
f_{22}	1000	100	-10.4029	-5.52	$1.79{\times}10^{-5}$	2.12
f_{23}	1000	100	-10.5364	-6.57	$4.10{\times}10^{-5}$	3.14

4 Conclusions

This paper introduced a clone and Cauchy-mutation evolutionary algorithm (CCEA), which employs dynamic clone and Cauchy mutation methods, for numerical optimization. With clone operation, domains with smaller density can get larger possibility of genetic operations. So CCEA can search the whole space most possibly, jump out of the local optima, and get the global optimal solution. For a suit of 23 benchmark test functions, CCEA is able to locate the near-optimal solutions for almost 23 test functions with relatively small variance, indicating that the algorithm is both effective and statistically stable.

The future work is to improve the mutation random variables, and to jump out of local optima and locate the global optima with larger possibility.

Table 4. Comparison between CCEA and StGA. All results have been averaged over 50 runs, where "Mean Best"indicates the mean best function values found in the last generation, and "Std Dev" stand for the standard deviation.

TF	Number of generation		Mean Best		Std Dev	
	CCEA	StGA	CCEA	StGA	CCEA	StGA
f_1	10000	30000	5.27×10^{-5}	2.45×10^{-15}	8.99×10^{-6}	5.25×10^{-16}
f_2	50000	17600	2.89×10^{-3}	2.03×10^{-7}	2.49×10^{-4}	2.95×10^{-8}
f_3	50000	23000	4.40×10^{-2}	9.98×10^{-29}	9.46×10^{-3}	6.9×10^{-29}
f_4	50000	32000	6.29×10^{-3}	2.01×10^{-8}	3.86×10^{-4}	3.42×10^{-9}
f_5	50000	45000	0.2	0.04435	0.24	0
f_6	500	1500	0	0	0	0
f_7	10000	25500	1.29×10^{-3}	8.4×10^{-4}	1.63×10^{-3}	1.0×10^{-3}
f_8	10000	1500	-8315.98	-12569.5	383.29	0
f_9	10000	28500	161.681	4.42×10^{-13}	19.92	1.14×10^{-13}
f_{10}	50000	10000	8.82×10^{-4}	3.52×10^{-8}	1.19×10^{-4}	3.51×10^{-8}
f_{11}	10000	52500	3.89×10^{-6}	2.44×10^{-17}	1.58×10^{-6}	4.54×10^{-17}
f_{12}	10000	8000	4.38×10^{-7}	8.03×10^{-7}	1.36×10^{-7}	1.96×10^{-14}
f_{13}	10000	16000	5.69×10^{-6}	1.13×10^{-5}	1.04×10^{-6}	4.62×10^{-13}
f_{14}	500	800	0.998004	1	0	0
f_{15}	50000	30000	3.11×10^{-4}	3.1798×10^{-4}	3.14×10^{-6}	4.7262×10^{-6}
f_{16}	100	4000	-1.03163	-1.03034	1.49×10^{-6}	1.0×10^{-3}
f_{17}	100	5000	0.397889	0.3986	1.45×10^{-6}	6.0×10^{-4}
f_{18}	500	/	3	/	2.01×10^{-6}	/
f_{19}	100	/	-3.86278	/	1.22×10^{-6}	/
f_{20}	100	/	-3.32188	/	4.63×10^{-5}	/
f_{21}	1000	10000	-10.1532	-9.828	2.19×10^{-5}	0.287
f_{22}	1000	4800	-10.4029	-10.40	1.79×10^{-5}	0
f_{23}	1000	8500	-10.5364	-10.450	4.10×10^{-5}	0.037

References

1. Bäck, T., Fogel, D.B., Michalewicz, Z. (eds.): Handbook of Evolutionary Computation. Institute to Physics Publishing (1997)
2. Michalewicz, Z.: Genetic algorithms + data structures = evolution programs, 2nd edn. Springer, New York (1994)
3. Gehlhaar, D.K., Fogel, D.B.: Tuning evolutionary programming for conformationally flexible molecular docking. In: Fogel, L.J., Angeline, P.J., Bäck, T. (eds.) Evolutionary Programming V: Proc. Of the Fifth Annual Conference on Evolutionary Programming, pp. 419–429. MIT Press, Cambridge (1996)

4. Yao, X., Liu, Y., Lin, G.M.: Fast evolutionary strategy. In: Angeline, P.J., Reynods, R., McDonnell, J., Eberhart, R. (eds.) Proc. Evolutionary Programming VI, pp. 151–161 (1997)
5. Chellapilla, K.: Combining mutation operators in evolutionary programming. IEEE Trans. Evol. Comput. 2, 91–98 (1998)
6. Yao, X., Liu, Y., Lin, G.M.: Evolutionary programming made faster. IEEE Trans. on Evolutionary Computation 3, 82–102 (1999)
7. Angeline, P.J.: Evolutionary optimization versus particle swarm optimization: Philosophy and performance differences. In: Porto, V.W., Saravanan, N., Waagen, D., Eiben, A.E. (eds.) Proc. Evolutionary Programming VII, pp. 601–610 (1998)
8. Tu, Z., Lu, Y.: A robust stochastic genetic algorithm (stga) for global numerical optimization. IEEE Trans. on Evolutionary Computation 8(5), 456–470 (2004)
9. André, V., da Curz, A., Vellasco, M.M.B.R.: Quantum-Inspired Evolutionary Algorithm for Numerical Optimization. In: 2006 IEEE Congress on Evolutionary Computation, pp. 9181–9187 (2006)
10. Clerc, M., Kennedy, J.: The particle swarm-explosion, stability, and convergence in a multidimensional complex space. IEEE Trans. on Evolutionary Computation 6(1), 58–73 (2002)
11. Parsopoulos, K.E., Vrahatis, M.N.: Recent approaches to global optimization problems through particle swarm optimization. Natural Computing, 235–306 (2002)
12. Andrews, P.S.: An Investigation into Mutation Operators for Particle Swarm Optimization. In: 2006 IEEE Congress on Evolutionary Computation, pp. 3789–3796 (2006)
13. Storn, R., Price, K.V.: Differential evolution-A simple and Efficient Heuristic for Global Optimization over Continuous Spaces. Journal of Global Optimization 11, 341–359 (1997)
14. Lampinen, J., Zelinka, I.: Mixed Variable Non-linear Optimization by Differential Evolution. In: Proceedings of Nostradamus 1999 2nd International Prediction Conference, pp. 45–55 (1999)
15. Price, K., Storm, R., Lampinen, J.: Differential Evolution-A Practical Approach to Global Optimization. Springer, Heidelberg (2005)
16. Feller, W.: An Introduction to Probability Theory and Its Applications, 2nd edn., vol. 2, p. 51. John Wiley & Sons, Inc., Chichester (1971)
17. Törn, A., Žilinskas, A.: Global Optimization. LNCS, vol. 350. Springer, Heidelberg (1989)
18. Schwefel, H.P.: Evolution and Optimum Seeking. Wiley, New York (1995)

Construction of Hoare Triples
under Generalized Model with Semantically
Valid Genetic Operations

Pei He[1,2], Lishan Kang[2,3], and Daochang Huang[1]

[1] School of Computer and Communication Engineering, Changsha University
of Science and Technology, Chnagsha 410114, P. R. China
bk_he@126.com
[2] State Key Laboratory of Software Engineering, Wuhan University
Wuhan 430072, P. R. China
kang_whu@yahoo.com
[3] School of Computer, China University of Geosciences
Wuhan 430074, P. R. China
40588154@qq.com

Abstract. This paper is a technical supplement of our original research in the combination of genetic programming (GP), Hoare logic, model checking, and finite state automaton for Hoare triple constructions. Although there is no problem in achieving this goal by first constructing the generalized models for some given Hoare triples, the desired Hoare triples from the application of general GP approaches to them still produce ineffective results and hence needs further improvement. In this paper, we solve it through the use of some semantically valid genetic operations. Precisely, we check logic relationships among Hoare triples and generalized models for their consistence.

Keywords: Genetic programming, Hoare logic, model checking, finite state automaton.

1 Introduction

Genetic programming (GP) ([1], [2]) is one of the most important means to automatically generate programs solving given problems. It can be dated back to John R. Koza's pioneering work in 1992, when he borrowed essential idea from genetic algorithm (GA) ([2], [3]) to construct computer programs by random techniques. Although GP is developed currently into a big family ([4], [5], [6], [7]) of GEP (Gene Expression Programming), STGP (Strongly Typed Genetic Programming), ADF-GP (Automatic Defined Function Genetic Programming), LGP(Linear Genetic Programming) etc, it almost deals with fitness evaluation based only on testing ([8], [9]).

Formal GPs are promising program generation methods worthy of in-depth research. The major advantage they provide lies in their reliability. For example, if one can automatically create Hoare triples ([10], [11], [12], [13]) in some way, he can also say with certainty that the programs of the concern are correct with respect to their

Z. Cai et al. (Eds.): ISICA 2009, LNCS 5821, pp. 228–237, 2009.
© Springer-Verlag Berlin Heidelberg 2009

requirements. As a result, this makes Formal GPs visibly different from their traditional competitors.

In view of this, paper [9] has initiated a formal study in the combination of genetic programming, Hoare logic, model checking, and finite state automaton, etc. Although it is successful in doing that like constructing Hoare triples under certain generalized models, the heuristic algorithm used there is inefficient, therefore deserving of further improvement. In the present paper, we will solve it through the use of some semantically valid genetic operations. Precisely, we check logic relationships among Hoare triples and generalized models for their consistency.

2 Elements of the Theory

Software reliability ([14]) is an important issue of common concern among researchers all over the world. One of the most common solutions to it is Hoare logic ([10], [11], [12], [13]). This paper focuses on Hoare triple constructions. Before discussing it, we first introduce some concepts as well as our formal result.([9]).

2.1 Concepts and Result

Definition 1 (Hoare triple).   Let P, Q be two first-order logic formulas, and f a program segment. A formula, denoted $\{P\}\,f\,\{Q\}$, is a Hoare triple, if it can be interpreted as that if P holds before execution of f, and that the running of f can terminate under P, then Q will hold.

Definition 2 (Generalized Hoare triple).   Let P, Q be sets of first-order logic formulas, and f a program segment. A formula, denoted $P\,\{f\}_G\,Q$, is a generalized Hoare triple or formula, if for each q in Q, there is some p in P such that $\{p\}\,f\,\{q\}$ forms a Hoare triple. In this case, $\{p\}\,f\,\{q\}$ is also called an instance of $P\,\{f\}_G\,Q$.

Definition 3 (Generalized representation).   Given a set H of Hoare triples and a set R of generalized Hoare triples, R is a generalized representation of H, if for each h in H, there is some r in R such that h is an instance of r and none r in R shares the same program segment with the other elements in R.

Definition 4 (Generalized model).   Given a set H of Hoare formulas and one of its generalized representations R, A directed graph G=<V, E> is a generalized model with respect to R, if :

1) Each v in V is either the generalized pre-condition or the generalized post-condition of some generalized Hoare triple in R.
2) Each e in E is either labeled with an epsilon (ε) symbol, standing for an empty statement, or a string, standing for a program segment of some Hoare formula in H.
3) $v1$, $v2$ in V is linked from $v1$ to $v2$ by a ε arrow, iff there are some formulas p_1, p_2 in $v1$, $v2$ such that $|-p_1 \rightarrow p_2$ holds.
4) $v1$, $v2$ in V is linked from $v1$ to $v2$ by an arrow of label name f, a program segment of some generalized Hoare triple in R, iff $v1\,\{f\}_G\,v2$ in R.

Definition 5 (Passage). Given a directed graph $G = <V, E>$, a path $V_1 f_1 V_2 f_2 \ldots f_{n-1} V_n$ in G is called a passage, if it defines a maximum expansion function $m(V_i)$ for some nonempty subset P $(\subseteq V_1)$ as follows. Where V_i stands for vertex of G. The string α $(= f_1 f_2 \ldots f_{n-1})$ concatenated from edge labels along the passage is called a generalized body; $m(V_i)$ the maximum expansion of $f_1 f_2 \ldots f_{i-1}$ on P.

1) $m(V_1) = P \neq \varnothing$;

2) $m(V_i) = \begin{cases} \{x \in V_i \mid \exists p \in m(V_{i-1})(p \rightarrow x)\} \neq \varnothing & V_{i-1} \text{ and } V_i \text{ are linked by } \varepsilon \\ \{x \in V_i \mid \exists p \in m(V_{i-1})(\{p\}f\{x\} \in H)\} \neq \varnothing & V_{i-1} \text{ and } V_i \text{ are linked by } f \end{cases}$

for $2 \leq i \leq n$

Theorem 1. Given a set H of Hoare triples as well as its generalized representation R, and Let $GM(H)$ be the corresponding generalized model. If α is a passage in $GM(H)$ with respect to a nonempty subset P of some vertex V of $GM(H)$, then $\{\wedge P\} \alpha \{\wedge Q\}$ for each nonempty set Q of α's maximum expansion over P is a Hoare formula. Where $\wedge X$ for a set X of logic formulas stands for a conjunction of all elements of X.

The proof can easily be completed by using the composition rule of Hoare logic ([11], [12]).

So, if an efficient algorithm is available for figuring out the appropriate passage meeting some requirements, we can create desired programs automatically.

2.2 Hoare Triple Generation

As we know, whether for two given vertices and an integer k there will exist a simple path of edge number over k in a directed graph is a NP-Complete problem ([15]). So, in light of the above result, we can construct Hoare triples meeting some requirements in evolutionary approaches. Paper ([9]) conducts a research in this topic, presenting a novel method called Hoare logic based genetic programming (HGP). Since HGP is a kind of genetic programming, we will focus on its differences from classical ones, describing it based on a given set H of Hoare triples as well as its generalized representation R, and its generalized model $GM(H)$.

Representation   A program is represented as a string of program segments , thus different from tree depended GPs in representation.

Fitness function The fitness function used by HGP is :

$$f(Gpre, S, Gpos) = \begin{cases} n(m(S, Gpre) \cap Gpos) & otherwise \\ -\lfloor b(S) \div l(S) * 100 \rfloor & breaking\ point \end{cases} \tag{1}$$

Where symbol conventions are:
S: a string of program segments;
Gpre: an assumed precondition;
Gpos: the target post-condition.
$n(Set)$: the number of the elements of the set Set ;

m(*S, Gpre*): the maximum expansion of program *S* over *Gpre*. It is calculated against definition 5 as follows.

$$m(S, Grep) = \begin{cases} Grep & S \text{ is an empty string} \\ \{v \in V_2 \mid \exists u \in V_1(\land Grep \to u \land \{u\}f\{v\} \in H)\} & S \text{ is } f, V_1\{f\}_G V_2 \text{ in } R \\ m(S_2, m(S_1, Grep)) & S \text{ is } S_1; S_2 \end{cases}$$

l(*S*): the length of the sequence of program components *S*. For example, let $S = f_1 f_2 f_3$, *l*(*S*) will be 3;

b(*S*): the number of the breaking points in a sequence *S*. For example, if there is no edge in a generalized model *GM*(*H*) linking two program components, there must exist a breaking point preventing *S* from being a path.

So to evaluate whether a randomly generated program is the best solution to a given problem, we can calculate the similarity between it and the desired requirement based on the intersection principle, i.e. the fitness function. Fig. 1 gives a schematic overview of genetic programming ([16]). In principle, our method is the same.

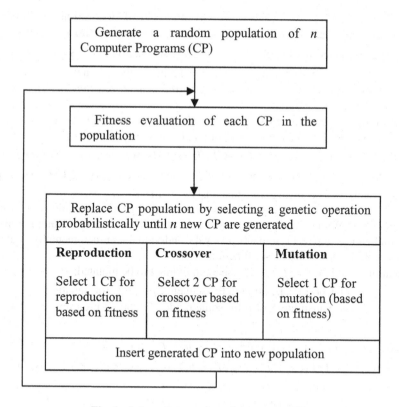

Fig. 1. Schematic overview of the present GP

3 Semantic Improvement on Genetic Operations

Obviously, execution of the above algorithm can generate approximate program to solving a giving problem, but many strings of program segments which conflict with the generalized model may also be created, therefore hindering its efficiency greatly. To overcome this shortcoming, we can improve the algorithm of fig. 1 by focusing on all semantically valid programs. This shares some ideas with reference [17]. In paper [17], Daniel Manrique, et. al. are painstaking with all possibly valid crossover positions, proposing a sophisticatedly new crossover operator for grammar based genetic programming systems based on such 3 factors as main derivation, crossover node and derivation length. Our method is as follows.

Definition 6 (Successor function). Given a set H of Hoare triples as well as its generalized representation $R = \{P_i\{f_i\}_G Q_i \mid 1 \le i \le n\}$, and let $GM(H)$ be the corresponding generalized model, $S = \{f_i \mid 1 \le i \le n\}$. A function $Succ: S \to 2^S$ is a successor function, if for each f in S, $Succ(f) = \{g$ in S | there is an empty edge in $GM(H)$ linking the generalized post-condition of f to the generalized pre-condition of g $\}$. Particularly, $Succ(\varepsilon) = S$.

Definition 7 (Predecessor function). Given a set H of Hoare triples as well as its generalized representation $R = \{P_i\{f_i\}_G Q_i \mid 1 \le i \le n\}$, and let $GM(H)$ be the corresponding generalized model, $S = \{f_i \mid 1 \le i \le n\}$. A function $Pred: S \to 2^S$ is a predecessor function, if for each f in S, $Pred(f) = \{g$ in S | there is a ε arrow in $GM(H)$ linking the generalized post-condition of g to the generalized pre-condition of f $\}$. Particularly, $Pred(\varepsilon) = S$.

Definition 8 (Embedment). Given H, R, $GM(H)$ and S as above, we call $Succ(f) \cap Pred(g)$ the embedment of f and g in S, denoted $Embedment(f, g)$.

Definition 9 (Crossover-set). Given H, R, $GM(H)$ and S as above, we call a subset of S a crossover-set of two strings $\alpha, \beta \in S^*$, denoted $C(\alpha, \beta)$, if $C(\alpha, \beta)$ are program segments of S occurring simultaneously in both strings.

Now, we can algorithmically realize semantic-based genetic operations in terms of definitions 6 to 9. For example, the mutation and crossover operators are as follows. For initialization step, each semantically valid individual can incrementally be generated through the use of successor function.

Mutation: 1) Let $P = f_1 f_2 \cdots f_m$ be an individual to be mutated;
2) Choose a position in the sequence p, say i, for mutation;
3) Substitute f_i of p for some randomly chosen program, say f, in $Embedment(f_{i-1}, f_{i+1})$.

Note that f_{i-1} for $i = 1$ stands for ε, and so does f_{i+1} for $i = m$.

Crossover: 1) Let $P_1 = f_1 f_2 \cdots f_m$, $P_2 = h_1 h_2 \cdots h_n$ with $C(P_1, P_2) \ne \varnothing$ be two individuals for the crossover;
2) Locate positions, say i and j, in P_1, P_2 for some randomly chosen program in $C(P_1, P_2)$ for crossover operation;

3) Conduct crossover on P_1, P_2 through substituting $h_{j+1} \cdots h_n$ of P_1 for $f_{i+1} \cdots f_m$, and $f_{i+1} \cdots f_m$ of P_2 for $h_{j+1} \cdots h_n$ to get semantically valid novel individuals for further use.

Certainly, combining these techniques with the algorithm of fig. 1 can give birth to an effective approach to reliable program generation. For this improved *HGP*, the fitness function is:

$$f(Gpre, S, Gpos) = n(m(S, Gpre) \cap Gpos) \tag{2}$$

4 Experiment and Analysis

In order for demonstrating why the improved *HGP* is correct and why it is more efficient than *HGP* in [9], we have conducted a comparative study between them in the following experiment. For the detail theoretical analysis, one can refer to what was discussed above or those of [9].

Problem. Given a set H (table 1) of Hoare triples, and one of its generalized representation $R = \{\{P_1, P_2, P_3\} \{ f_1 \}_G \{P_2, P_3, P_4\}, \{P_2, P_4, P_6\} \{ f_2 \}_G \{P_1, P_5, P_6\}, \{P_3, P_4, P_2\} \{ f_3 \}_G \{P_2, P_4, P_6\}, \{P_1, P_5, P_6\} \{ f_4 \}_G \{P_1, P_5, P_7\}\}$, generating a correct program such that its pre- and post-conditions are $(P_1 \wedge P_5 \wedge P_7)$ and $(P_1 \wedge P_5 \wedge P_7 \wedge (u=0 \vee r<z))$ respectively ([9]).

Table 1. Set of Hoare triple. Each row stands for a Hoare formula.

	Pre-condition	Program segment	Post-condition	
P1	$y + uz = xz$	f_1	$y + (u-1)z = xz$	P4
P2	$u > 0$	f_1	$u > 0$	P2
P3	$x = r + qz \wedge r \geq z \wedge z > 0$	f_1	$x = r + qz \wedge r \geq z \wedge z > 0$	P3
P4	$y + (u-1)z = xz$	f_2	$y + uz = xz$	P1
P2	$u > 0$	f_2	$u \geq 0$	P5
P6	$x = r + (q+1)z \wedge r \geq 0 \wedge z > 0$	f_2	$x = r + (q+1)z \wedge r \geq 0 \wedge z > 0$	P6
P3	$x = r + qz \wedge r \geq z \wedge z > 0$	f_3	$x = r + (q+1)z \wedge r \geq 0 \wedge z > 0$	P6
P4	$y + (u-1)z = xz$	f_3	$y + (u-1)z = xz$	P4
P2	$u > 0$	f_3	$u > 0$	P2
P6	$x = r + (q+1)z \wedge r \geq 0 \wedge z > 0$	f_4	$x = r + qz \wedge r \geq 0 \wedge z > 0$	P7
P1	$y + uz = xz$	f_4	$y + uz = xz$	P1
P5	$u \geq 0$	f_4	$u \geq 0$	P5

Theoretical analysis. By Hoare logic, if there exists a program X which together with $(P_1 \wedge P_5 \wedge P_7) \wedge (u \neq 0 \wedge r \geq z)$ and $(P_1 \wedge P_5 \wedge P_7)$ forms a Hoare triple $\{ (P_1 \wedge P_5 \wedge P_7) \wedge (u \neq 0 \wedge r \geq z) \} X \{P_1 \wedge P_5 \wedge P_7\}$, then:

$\{P_1 \wedge P_5 \wedge P_7\}$ while ($u \neq 0 \wedge r \geq z$) do X $\{P_1 \wedge P_5 \wedge P_7 \wedge (u=0 \vee r < z)\}$.

So the desired program is: *while ($u \neq 0 \wedge r \geq z$) do X*. Now we solve to find the value for *X*. The major steps includes the following:

Step 1: Constructing the generalized model *GM(H)* of fig. 2 for *H* based on *R*;

Step 2: By theorem 1, searching for a desired passage *X* in *GM(H)*.

Clearly, there is a passage in *GM(H)* giving a proof of $\{P_1 \wedge P_2 \wedge P_3\}$ $f_1 f_3 f_2 f_4$ $\{P_1 \wedge P_5 \wedge P_7\}$ being a Hoare triple. Furthermore by logic knowledge and Hoare logic, we have $1 - ((P_1 \wedge P_5 \wedge P_7) \wedge (u \neq 0 \wedge r \geq z)) \rightarrow (P_1 \wedge P_2 \wedge P_3)$, therefore deducing the Hoare triple $\{ (P_1 \wedge P_5 \wedge P_7) \wedge (u \neq 0 \wedge r \geq z) \} f_1 f_3 f_2 f_4 \{P_1 \wedge P_5 \wedge P_7\}$, i.e. $\{P_1 \wedge P_5 \wedge P_7\}$ *while ($u \neq 0 \wedge r \geq z$) do begin $f_1 f_3 f_2 f_4$ end* $\{P_1 \wedge P_5 \wedge P_7 \wedge (u=0 \vee r < z)\}$.

Experimental analysis. The simulation is as follows.

Step 1: Calculating both the *successor* and *predecessor* functions for any program segment, and *embedment, crossover-set* for each pair of program segments involved in *H* based on *GM(H)* ;

Step 2: For each randomly generated programs, using $\{x$ in GC1 $|$ $(P_1 \wedge P_5 \wedge P_7 \wedge u \neq 0 \wedge r \geq z) \rightarrow x\} = \{P_1, P_2, P_3\}$ and tPost = $\{P_1, P_5, P_7\}$ as the generalized pre-condition *Gpre* and the target requirement *Gpos* to invoke the fitness function.

Step 3: Let the population size be 8, pressing the "*Run*" button, we obtain screenshots of both novel and previous methods in fig. 3 and fig. 4.

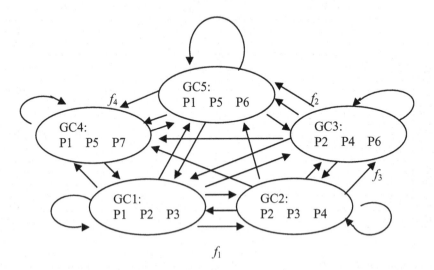

Fig. 2. The generalized model *GM(H)* of the experiment. Where each node GC_i represents a generalized condition; edges without labels are ε arrows.

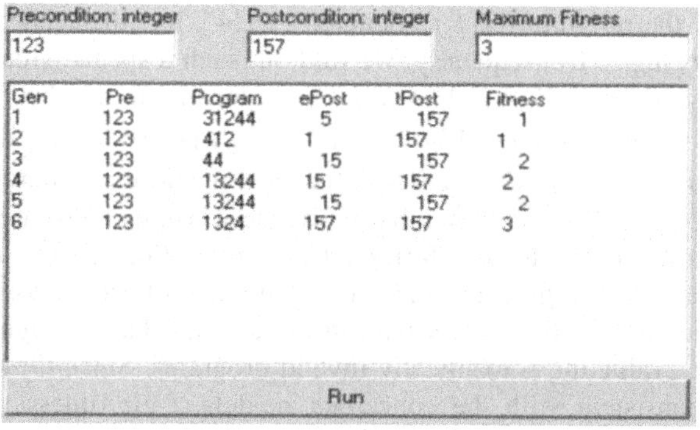

Fig. 3. Screenshot of result

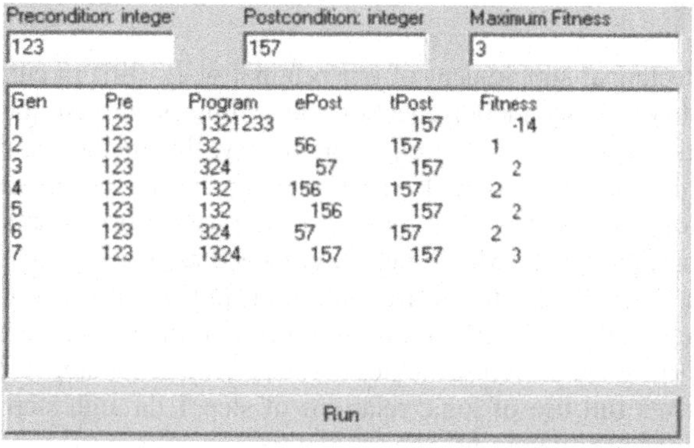

Fig. 4. Screenshot of result

Annotations to fig. 3 and fig. 4. In these figures, the datum under the name Gen are generation numbers. The Data under the names Pre, ePost and tPost represent sets of properties of some program. For instance, for "123" under the name Pre, it is $\{P_1, P_2, P_3\}$; for "157" under either the name ePost or the name tPost, it stands for $\{P_1, P_5, P_7\}$. The data under the name Program indicate sequences of program segments. For example, the data "1324" in the two figures means the program $f_1 f_3 f_2 f_4$. Finally, the numbers under the name Fitness express fitness values, which were calculated in fig. 3 based on formula (2):

$$f(Gpre, S, Gpos) = n(m(S, Gpre) \cap Gpos)$$

and in fig. 4 on formula (1):

$$f(Gpre, S, Gpos) = \begin{cases} n(m(S, Gpre) \cap Gpos) & otherwise \\ -\lfloor b(S) \div l(S) * 100 \rfloor & breaking\ point \end{cases}$$

So fitness values for either generations 3 through 5 in fig. 3 or through 6 in fig. 4 are 2. Because for each generation in these cases, the data under the names ePost and tPost share two digits with each other. For example, "156" in generation 5 of fig. 4 shares the two digits "1" and "5" with 157. So does the same reason for both the fitness values of the program $f_1 f_3 f_2 f_4$, denoted "1324", in either generation 6 or 7 in the two figures being 3. Consequently, we find out such a special Hoare formula $\{P_1 \land P_2 \land P_3\} f_1 f_3 f_2 f_4 \{P_1 \land P_5 \land P_7\}$ in $GM(H)$. According to the theoretical analysis, we have $\{ (P_1 \land P_5 \land P_7) \land (u \neq 0 \land r \geq z) \} f_1 f_3 f_2 f_4 \{P_1 \land P_5 \land P_7\}$. Thus what we want is: *while ($u \neq 0 \land r \geq z$) do begin $f_1 f_3 f_2 f_4$ end*, the desired program.

Of course, we should point out that basically, these two methods are the same; but, solving with formula (2) instead of formula (1) as fitness function is a far more efficient way to deal with large scale generalized models of Hoare formulas. As was shown in generation 1 of fig. 4, we may, in these cases, have a high probability of wasting time for evaluating semantically invalid programs. Since these programs are semantically inconsistent with the concerned models, their fitness values must be negatives.

5 Conclusion

This paper is a technical supplement of our original work ([9]) in combining genetic programming, Hoare logic, model checking, and finite state automaton for reliable program generations. As was discussed in the theory, this method is divided into the following steps: 1) Managing to get Hoare triples, i.e. basic facts about program components, by various approaches. 2) Grouping Hoare triples based on such concept as generalized representation. 3) Modeling search space as generalized models of verified components. 4) Searching for desired programs in the concerned models by some heuristic approach like genetic algorithm. So given that the first three steps have been completed (see [9]), good search strategies are very critical for step 4. To this end, the present work makes full use of logic relations of step 1 through step 3 to create semantically valid genetic operations.

What follows are our future works: novel modeling techniques, efficient search approaches, implementations, and extensions of existing work to grammar based genetic programming, etc.

Acknowledgments. This work was supported by the State Key Laboratory of Software Engineering (SKLSE), P. R. China under Grant No. SKLSE 20080701.

References

1. Koza, J.R.: Genetic Programming: On the Programming of Computers by Means of Natural Selection. The MIT Press, Cambridge (1992)
2. Holland, J.: Adaptation in Natural and Artificial Systems. The University of Michigan Press, Michigan (1975)
3. Mitchell, M.: An Introduction to Genetic Algorithms. MIT Press, Cambridge (1976)
4. Oltean, M., Grosan, C.: A Comparison of Several Linear Genetic Programming Techniques. Complex Systems 14(4), 1–29 (2004)
5. Abraham, A., Nedjah, N., de Mourelle, L.M.: Evolutionary Computation: from Genetic Algorithms to Genetic Programming. In: Nedjah, N., et al. (eds.) Studies in Computational Intelligence. Springer, Heidelberg (2006)

6. Montana, D.J.: Strongly Typed Genetic Programming. Evolutionary Computation 3(2), 199–230 (1995)
7. Koza, J.R.: Genetic Programming II: Automatic Discovery of Reusable Programs. MIT Press, Cambridge (1994)
8. Johnson, C.G.: Genetic Programming with Fitness Based on Model Checking. In: Ebner, M., O'Neill, M., Ekárt, A., Vanneschi, L., Esparcia-Alcázar, A.I. (eds.) EuroGP 2007. LNCS, vol. 4445, pp. 114–124. Springer, Heidelberg (2007)
9. He, P., Kang, L.S., Fu, M.: Formality Based Genetic Programming. In: Proc. of IEEE Congress on Evolutionary Computation, pp. 4081–4088. IEEE Press, Los Alamitos (2008)
10. Hoare, C.A.R.: An Axiomatic Basis for Computer Programming. CACM 12(10), 576–583 (1969)
11. Winskel, G.: The Formal Semantics of Programming Language: A Introduction. MIT Press, MA (1993)
12. Huth, M., Ryan, M.: Logic in Computer Science: Modelling and Reasoning about System. Cambridge University Press, England (2004)
13. Manna, Z.: Mathematical Theory of Computations. McGraw-Hill, New York (1974)
14. Chen, H.W., Wang, J., Dong, W.: High Confidence Software Engineering Technologies. Acta Electronica Sinica 31(12A), 1933–1938 (2003) (in Chinese)
15. Garey, M., Johnson, D.S.: Computers and Intractability - A Guide to the Theory of NP-completeness. Freeman, San Francisco (1979)
16. Sette, S., Boullart, L.: Genetic Programming: Principles and Applications. Engineering Applications of Artificial Intelligence 14(6), 727–736 (2001)
17. Manrique, D., Márquez, F., Ríos, J., Rodríguez-Patón, A.: Grammar Based Crossover Operator in Genetic Programming. In: Mira, J., Álvarez, J.R. (eds.) IWINAC 2005. LNCS, vol. 3562, pp. 252–261. Springer, Heidelberg (2005)

Evaluation of Cobalt-Rich Crust Resources Based on Fractal Characteristics of Seamount Terrain

Hongbo Mei[1,2], Guangdao Hu[1,2], Linli Zhou[2], and Huiqin Zeng[2]

[1] State Key Laboratory of Geological Processes and Mineral Resources, China University of Geosciences, Wuhan 430074, China
hbmei@cug.edu.cn
[2] The Faculty of Earth Resources, China University of Geosciences, Wuhan 430074, China

Abstract. In order to ensure the target selection of the cobalt-rich crust exploration and thus to benefit the mining area application in the future, it is necessary to conduct the method research for the resources calculation and the exploration area circling. In this paper, we employ the fractal parameters of the seamount terrain isoline to explore the relationship, that exists in the distribution and enrichment of the seamount cobalt-rich crusts and the seamount distribution fractal parameters, to provide quantitative basis for judgment of the blocks to be estimated. Finally, we carry out an empirical research with the terrain and station sampling data of a certain seamount in the Central Pacific and establish the scheme of circle mines by selecting the suitable threshold value of fractal box dimension. Then we use Ordinary Kriging method to complete the resources evaluation of cobalt-rich crust.

Keywords: Cobalt-rich crust, Fractal box dimension, Ordinary Kriging, Resources evaluation.

1 Introduction

Ocean cobalt-rich crusts is a polymetallic ore, which grows in 500-3000m water depth in the sea surface slope. It is rich in metal and rare earth elements of high economic value, such as Co, Au, Ni, Ti, Mn, Pt,etc.. The mass fraction of Co and Pt, which are rare in land, is up to 2.5% and 2×10^6 particularly[1]. As potential mineral resources, ocean cobalt-rich crusts attracts people's general concern.

Some countries led by America had carried out a number of attempts on cobalt-rich crust resources evaluation. Early in the 1980s, America used the geological block method to calculate resources quantity of some seamounts in the Pacific. Russia and France had used the methods of adjacent area and Kriging to respectively resources assessment in their own survey area. In our country, resources quantity evaluation of cobalt-rich crust is in early stage. We use methods of arithmetic average and geometric mean to do preliminary resources estimation in general survey. Wu Guanghai had used the methods of the nearest domain and geological block in preliminary resources quantity evaluation of a certain seamount in the eastern Pacific, and confirmed the seamount has long-term reserves[2].

Z. Cai et al. (Eds.): ISICA 2009, LNCS 5821, pp. 238–247, 2009.

The goal, that our country carries out resources evaluation in the cobalt-rich curst investigation area, is to circle the mine area that we intend to apply for the International Seabed Bureau and make the resources quantity as far as possible and as well as possible. And gradually establish an effective evaluation system of ocean mineral resources.

Increasing information indicates that mineral resources distribution belongs to the fractal distribution[3], which is the basis of the fractal research of ocean seamount cobalt crust resources evaluation.

2 Methodology

Crust resources evaluation generally includes two aspects: circling mine scheme and resources evaluation.

Delineation of the blocks to be estimated is the most important factor to impact the reliability of crust resources quantity. As the grid of crust resources investigation is dilute, area of the blocks to be estimated based on the grid is relatively large. Although misjudgment of a few blocks to be estimated, resources increase or decrease caused by is very significant. So it is very necessary to explore a way, which can quantitatively judge the block to be estimated, to improve the reliability of delineation of the block to be estimated. This paper uses fractal parameters of the seamount terrain isoline to explore the relationship, that exists in the distribution and enrichment of the seamount cobalt-rich crust and the seamount distribution fractal parameters, to find out methods which can quantificationally estimate crust distribution and enrichment and provide quantitative basis for judgment of block to be estimated.

Cobalt-rich crust is basically regarded as a two-dimensional distribution of the seabed sediment deposits. The resources quantity estimation is easy to test and has high reliability. Existing methods of cobalt-rich crust resources evaluation include the methods of arithmetic average, the weighted average, geological block, and Kriging. Kriging, suitable for the area of higher investigation degree, is used to calculate estimated value of the variable related to resources calculating. Kriging reflects the randomicity and constitutive property of the geological variable, not only can get estimation value of different blocks, but also can give estimation error. This paper intends to use ordinary Kriging to evaluate ocean crust resources.

2.1 Methods of Ore Delineation

2.1.1 Calculating Fractal Eigenvalue with the Fractal Box Dimension Method

This paper intends to use the fractal box dimension(hereafter short for FBD) method to calculate fractal. Basic principle of this method is: cover the fractal sets with the E-scale box and count the number N of boxes. And then paint E-scale and boxes N(E) points in the logarithmic coordinates or paint $\ln(E)$ and $\ln(N)$ in the general coordinates. Finally we use linear regression method to confirm slope of the straight line of the interval-scaled points and get fractal dimension D. We calculate the FBD on a collection of two-dimensional plane as follows: increase Tn gradually and calculate the corresponding value of Nn (A) to get data pairs of $(-\ln Tn , \ln Nn(A))$ and then use minimum mean square deviation to derive the slope, that is the FBD we want, of lnNn (A) relative lnTn[4].

2.1.2 Delineation of the Blocks to be Estimated

We calculate the delineation of block to be estimated, by using seamount terrain fractal parameters[5], as follows:

(1) DEM(digital elevation model) data griding of the seamount terrain

According to the grid of seamount station sampling, we can rarefy DEM data with grid. The grid size rarefied by DEM data is consistent with the size and location of the block to be estimated, which used by crust resources calculation.

(2) Use the box method to calculate the FBD value of the grid (block to be estimated).

Use the box method to calculate the FBD value of the grid rarefied. Traverse the entire seamount areas and get the box dimensions of all of the grids.

(3) Determine the threshold value of FBD.

Extract the FBD of stations sampling location and get statistical data of the FBD distribution character of sampling location. List to compare with the crust abundance of sampling locations and the relevance of FBD. Select threshold value of FBD, which is critical value to basically distinguish whether it has crust distribution, to provide quantitative basis for delineation of the blocks to be estimated.

(4) Determine the blocks to be estimated.

Use the threshold value of FBD to filter the seamount grids. Grids, that satisfy the given conditions (greater than a certain threshold or in a threshold range), are the blocks to be estimated to form block lithology file. Blocks determined in the file are the blocks to be estimated and then use methods to calculate resource quantity.

2.2 Evaluation of Resources Quantity

Kriging, which is the core of geological statistics, is a method to get optimal, linear and unbiased interpolation estimation. Kriging uses variogram as the basic tool and gives full consideration to the geometric characteristics of the sample information, such as the shape, size and the spatial distribution location with the blocks to be estimated. It also considers about the spatial structure of variables.

2.2.1 Variogram Calculation

Variogram is the basic and specific tool of geological, which can describe both the space structural and the stochastic changes of the regionalized variables. Common definition of variogram is: variogram is the mathematical expectation of increment square of the regionalized variable, that is, the variance of increment of the regionalized variable.

The establishment of variogram is the key of Kriging valuation. Kriging valuation will be carried through only after the establishment of effective variogram and fitting.

Variogram means a half of the variance of the increments of regionalized variable value $Z(x)$ and $Z(x+h)$ at two points, x and x+h, which divided by vector h. That is:

$$\gamma(\chi, h) = \frac{1}{2} Var[Z(\chi_i) - Z(\chi_i + h)] \tag{1}$$

2.2.2 Fit to First-Order Spherical Model

We need to select an appropriate model of variogram theory to fit after calculating the variogram, and then can study structural analysis of the regionalized variable.

Calculation equation of spherical model which has the abutment (also known as Matheron model) is as follows:

$$\gamma(r) = \begin{cases} C_0 + C\left(\dfrac{3r}{2a} - \dfrac{r^3}{2a^3}\right) & 0 \le r \le a \\ C_0 + C, r > a \end{cases} \tag{2}$$

Where γ is the variation, r is the step (or distance), a is the range, C_0 is the nugget, C is the arch height , $(C + C_0)$ is the sill.

2.2.3 Combined Spherical Model

For two directions of a variogram model fitting, assume the model parameters are: Va, Vc, Vc_0 and Wa, Wc, Wc_0. The model parameters after combining are: a_1, C_1, C_0, a_2, C_2. Then combined model parameters are calculated as follows: $C_0 = 0.5(Vc_0 + Wc_0)$, $Uv = (Vc + Vc_0) - C_0$, $Uw = (Wc + Wc_0) - C_0$.

If $Uv < Uw$, then $a_1 = Va$, $a_2 = Wa$, $C_1 = Uv$, $C_2 = Uw - Uv$.

If $Uv \ge Uw$, then $a_1 = Wa$, $a_2 = Va$, $C_1 = Uw$, $C_2 = Uv - Uw$.

The calculation equation is:

$$\gamma(r) = \begin{cases} C_0 + C_1\left(\dfrac{3r}{2a_1} - \dfrac{r^3}{2a_1{}^3}\right) + C_2\left(\dfrac{3r}{2a_2} - \dfrac{r^3}{2a_2{}^3}\right) & 0 \le r \le a_1 \\ C_0 + C_1 + C_2\left(\dfrac{3r}{2a_2} - \dfrac{r^3}{2a_2{}^3}\right), & a_1 < r \le a_2 \\ C_0 + C_1 + C_2, r > a_2 \end{cases} \tag{3}$$

Where $(C_0 + C_1 + C_2)$ is the sill.

2.2.4 Kriging Evaluation

We get Kriging evaluation of variable mean through giving a certain weight coefficient to each sample and then get weighted average. That is:

$$Z_v{}^* = \sum_{i=1}^{n} \lambda_i Z_i \tag{4}$$

Where λ_i is Kriging weights coefficient, that is, the impact of the sample when we evaluate $Z_v{}^*$, Z_i (i = 1,2 ... ... n) is the information of known sample.

The main process of Kriging is solving Kriging equations set to obtain the Kriging weights coefficient, that is, to solve the following two questions: First, list and solve Kriging equations to get the Kriging weights coefficient λ_i; Second, get the estimation variance of Kriging. By the premise of meet the second-order stationary hypothesis, ordinary Kriging equations (Eq.5) and ordinary Kriging variance (Eq.6) can be expressed by the two variogram equations formulas as follows.

$$\begin{cases} \sum_{j=1}^{n} \lambda_i \overline{\gamma}(x_i, x_j) + \mu = \overline{\gamma}(x_i, V), i = 1,2,\dots n \\ \sum_{i=1}^{n} \lambda_i = 1 \end{cases} \tag{5}$$

$$\delta_k^2 = \sum_{i=1}^{n} \lambda_i \overline{\gamma}(x_i, V) - \overline{\gamma}(V, V) + \mu \tag{6}$$

Where $\overline{\gamma}$ is the variogram, μ is the Lagrange coefficient, V is the blocks to be estimated.

3   Experiment and Result

Take the terrain and sampling station data of a certain seamount in the Central Pacific as an example to carry out case studies.

3.1   Results of Delineation of the Block to be Estimated

3.1.1   Basic Conditions of the Seamount Terrain Data and Sampling Station Data
The seamount terrain DEM is shown in Fig. 4. The abundance values of sampling points are shown in Table 1.

3.1.2   Seamount Terrain Gridding
According to the sampling grid, the seamount terrain is divided into the grid of 100×50, that is, equally divided into 100 parts in latitude direction with 0.016079 degree as the grid spacing, and 50 parts in longitude direction with 0.015960 degree as the grid spacing.

3.1.3   Calculating the FBD Values of Grids
After the division of grids, give the grid divided above the number with X(m,n), in which m is the number of rows and n is the number of columns. So corresponding to each X(m, n) , there is the FBD value D(m, n).

Calculate the FBD value of each grid by using the FBD method described above.The statistical results demonstrate that almost all the FBD values of grids fall between 0 ~ 0.325 as shown in Fig. 1 For the 44 sampling points of the seamount, count the grids which the sampling points fall into and get the FBD values of corresponding grids as shown in Table1 and Fig.2.

Table 1. Statistical of the relations between seamount samples abundance and FBD Value

Sample Number	Abundance (Kg/m^2)	FBD Value	Sample Number	Abundance (Kg/m^2)	FBD Value
1	36.8	0.0077	23	170.6	0.3191
2	45	0.2624	24	57.28	0.0742
3	55.5	0.0235	25	173.47	0.0936
4	107.25	0.1287	26	197.61	0.0196
5	42	0.1084	27	44.18	0.0069
6	43.8	0.3048	28	142.82	0.0481
7	149.84	0.2025	29	94.6	0.2768
8	132.1	0.0465	30	80.84	0.1736
9	140.1	0.3237	31	80.74	0.1579
10	120.8	0.1376	32	226.18	0.2256
11	38.73	0.0035	33	74.36	0.1280
12	62.62	0.2810	34	47.6	0.0510
13	120.2	0.1829	35	175.61	0.2129
14	26.2	0.2347	36	95.13	0.0081
15	127	0.0057	37	67.11	0.0624
16	139.1	0.0347	38	78.5	0.0362
17	14.56	0.0375	39	63.5	0.0362
18	86.2	0.1921	40	85.8	0.0335
19	201	0.3512	41	129.4	0.1772
20	160.6	0.0617	42	56.98	0.2820
21	14.55	0.1475	43	50.16	0.2340
22	149.35	0.1572	44	144.02	0.3190

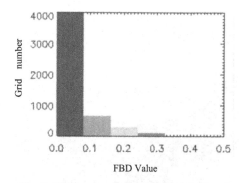

Fig. 1. Histogram of seamount terrain fractal

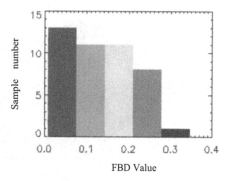

Fig. 2. Histogram of the sample grid fractal

From Table 1 and Fig.2 ,we can clearly see that the sampling points grids with the FBD values less than 0.10 are accounted for more than 70%. We draw the conclusion that for this seamount the vast area where the FBD value of the grids is less than 0.10 basically can not produce crust. There is not clear relationship between the abundance and fractal value of the samples of the area where the FBD value is greater than 0.10. So we take the FBD value '0.1' for the threshold value. The grids with the FBD values less than 0.10 will not be considered in the crust resources calculation. But only the grids, the FBD value of which is greater than 0.10, can be calculated resources quantity.

3.1.4 Lithology and Projection Diagram of the Blocks to be Estimated

Lithology diagram of the blocks to be estimated is shown in Fig. 3 when the threshold value of the seamount FBD is equal to 0.10. The mark '+' is the location of the blocks to be estimated.

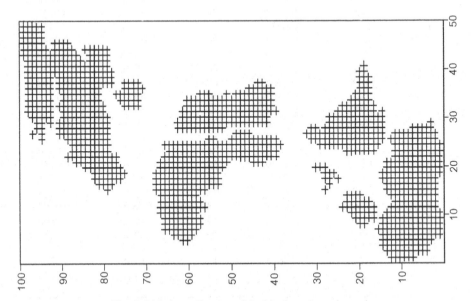

Fig. 3. Lithology diagram of the blocks to be estimated

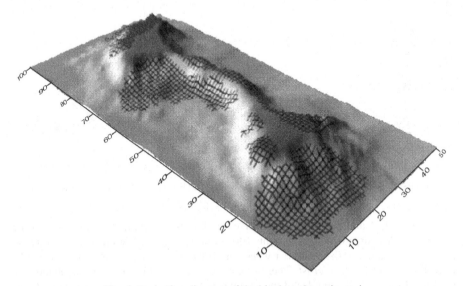

Fig. 4. Projection diagram of the blocks to be estimated

As shown in Fig. 4(the coordinates represent grid numbers), we can further make projection diagram of the blocks to be estimated to judge whether the scope of the delineation of the blocks to be estimated is reasonable. Delineation of the blocks to be estimated can be tested through projection diagram of itself.

As shown in Fig. 3 and Fig. 4, the distribution of blocks to be estimated is in the seamount slopes, and relatively much less in the seamount flat ceiling, which is basically consistent with the research conclusions that plate crust is mostly more grown in slopes[6].

3.2 Results of the Resources Evaluation

3.2.1 Results of Variogram Calculation

There are 44 sampling data of crust abundance of the seamount in total. We carried out variogram calculation in the directions of 0°, 45°, 90°and 135°and the results are shown in Fig. 5(the unit of pace length is degree in latitude or longitude direction).

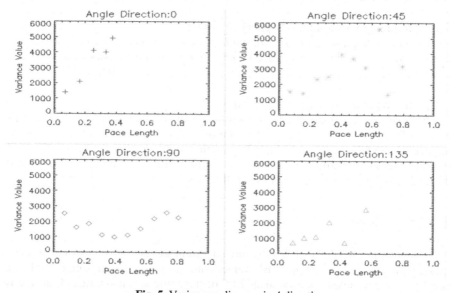

Fig. 5. Variogram diagram in 4 directions

3.2.2 Results of Fitting to First-Order Spherical Model

According to Fig. 5, the directions of 45°and 135°are confirmed to be the main change directions of the seamount crust abundance. On the basis of this, spherical model is used to the theoretical variogram fitting. Fig. 6 is the fitted curve in the 45° direction and the model parameters are: a=0.577566, c=3299.33, c_0=477.679; Fig. 7 is the fitted curve in the 135°direction and the model parameters are: a=0.560935, c=814.933, c_0=602.444. We can see that the variability of the abundance of the seamount crust, in every direction of the space, is quite different. Variation range in the directions of 45°and 135°are 0.577566 and 0.560935, which means that in this two directions space affect distance of the samples is not large but the difference of space variation amplitude is relatively large which is accompany with the structural

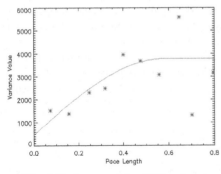

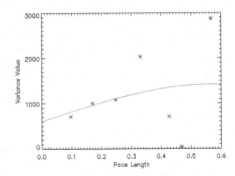

Fig. 6. Variogram of the 45°direction

Fig. 7. Variogram of the 135°direction

characteristics of zonal anisotropy. Both the variation amplitude of crust abundance and the terrain change are the greatest in the 45°direction.

3.2.3 Results of the Combined Spherical Model

Combine the fitting model of the variogram in the directions of 45°and 135°in accordance with Eq. 3 to get new combined model. The correlative model parameters are: $a_1 = 0.560935$, $a_2 = 0.577566$, $c_1 = 877.315$, $c_2 = 2359.63$, $c_0 = 540.061$.

3.2.4 Results of the Resources Calculation

On the basis of Eq. (5) and Eq.(6), we get the results of the resources calculation by using ordinary Kriging valuation. The minimum and maximum evaluation value is respectively 35.9061 Kg/m^2 and 134.567 Kg/m^2, the average evaluation value is 74.1411 Kg/m^2, the valuation variance is 559.12, the overall valuation variance is 308.236, and the total resources evaluation is 0.18891 billion tons.

4   Conclusions

According to the FBD calculation of seamount terrain and the statistics of sample data, we find that the area , where the FBD value of the seamount terrain isoline is relative small (<0.1), accounted for more than 70% of the entire seamount area. That means the research seamount is relative flat and the trend of terrain change is relative small, which is consistent with the three-dimensional topographic map drew in Fig. 4. Most sample data of the sampling points fall in the area, where the FBD value is relative large (> 0.1), and almost no sample points fall in the area with the relative small FBD value. As the FBD value reflects the characteristics of the regional terrain changes, regional terrain changes a lot in the area with the relative large FBD value and is relative flat in the area with the relative small FBD value. It can be considered that crusts generally grow in the area where local terrain is relative steep and almost do not grow in the area where local terrain slope is relative flat. So we can get the conclusion that the FBD of the seamount terrain isoline can be used to judge the crust status of spatial distribution. And we have the theories and methods basis to circle the seamount blocks to be estimated through the threshold value.

In addition, because of limitations of the sampling data amount and the complexity of cobalt-rich crusts itself, the fitted model of variogram is not very satisfactory and need further research after the abundance of sample data.

Reference

1. Witshire, J., Wen, X.Y., Yao, D.: Ferromanganese crusts near Johnston Island: geochemistry, stratigraphy and economic potential. Marine Georesourcess and Geotechnology (17), 257–270 (1999)
2. Wu, G.H.: Combined application of the methods of the nearest domain and geological block to resources evaluation of cobalt-rich crust of a seamount in the Pacific. Marine Geology & Quaternary Geology 20(4), 87–92 (2000)
3. Lian, C.Y., Su, X.S.: Fractal estimation for resources extent of gold in jiaodong exploration field. Journal of Changchun University of Science and Technology 30(1), 24–27 (2000)
4. Liang, D.F., Li, Y.B., Jiang, C.B.: Research on the Box Counting Algorithm in Fractal Dimension Measurement. Journal of Image and Graphics 7(3), 246–250 (2002)
5. Hu, G.D., Zhou, L.L., Mei, H.B.: Delineation and evaluation on estimated blocks in the calculation scheme of cobalt crust resourcess. In: 12th Conference of Int. Association for Mathematical Geology, Beijing, China, pp. 603–606 (2007)
6. Chu, F.Y., Sun, G.S., Li, X.M.: The growth habit and controlling factors of the cobalt-rich crusts in seamount of the central pacific. Journal of Jiling University (Earth Science Edition) 35(3), 320–325 (2005)

Hybridizing Evolutionary Negative Selection Algorithm and Local Search for Large-Scale Satisfiability Problems

Peng Guo[1,2], Wenjian Luo[1,2], Zhifang Li[1,2], Houjun Liang[1,2], and Xufa Wang[1,2]

[1] Nature Inspired Computation and Applications Laboratory (NICAL), School of Computer Science and Technology, University of Science and Technology of China, Hefei 230027, China
[2] Anhui Key Laboratory of Software in Computing and Communication, University of Science and Technology of China, Hefei 230027, China
gplc123@mail.ustc.edu.cn, wjluo@ustc.edu.cn,
zhifangl@mail.ustc.edu.cn, ahlhj@mail.ustc.edu.cn,
xfwang@ustc.edu.cn

Abstract. This paper introduces a hybrid algorithm called as the HENSA-SAT for the large-scale Satisfiability (SAT) problems. The HENSA-SAT is the hybrid of Evolutionary Negative Selection Algorithm (ENSA), the Flip Heuristic, the *BackForwardFlipHeuristic* procedure and the *VerticalClimbing* procedure. The Negative Selection (NS) is called twice for different purposes. One is used to make the search start in as many different areas as possible. The other is used to restrict the times of calling the *BackForwardFlipHeuristic* for local search. The Flip Heuristic, the *BackForwardFlipHeuristic* procedure and the *Vertical-Climbing* procedure are used to enhance the local search. Experiment results show that the proposed algorithm is competitive with the GASAT that is the state-of-the-art algorithm for the large-scale SAT problems.

Keywords: SAT, Evolutionary Negative Selection Algorithm, Flip Heuristic.

1 Introduction

The Satisfiability problem (SAT) was firstly proved to be an NP-complete problem by Cook [1] in 1971. The SAT problem could be defined as follows. Given a conjunctive formula F, determine whether there exists an assignment of boolean variables to make F become true. A formula F is defined as the conjunction of clauses, while a clause is defined as the disjunction of several literals. A literal is a boolean variable or the negation of the boolean variable. If the number of literals contained in each clause is the same value of k, the problem could be called k-SAT. An assignment of the variables which makes F become true is a solution.

Some algorithms [2-9] have been proposed to solve the SAT problems. These algorithms could be classified into 2 categories, which are the complete algorithms [2-4] and the incomplete algorithms [5-9]. The complete algorithms check the whole search space, and ensure they can find a solution unless there is no solution, while the time complexity is exponential in the worst case. The incomplete algorithms check part of the whole search space. When the incomplete algorithms do not find a solution for a SAT problem, they can not determine whether there exists a solution or not.

Z. Cai et al. (Eds.): ISICA 2009, LNCS 5821, pp. 248–257, 2009.
© Springer-Verlag Berlin Heidelberg 2009

The Evolutionary Negative Selection Algorithms (ENSAs) are proposed by drawing the mechanisms of evolution and negative selection in biological immune system. ENSAs have been developed to solve the logic circuits design [10], function optimization [11], etc. Some works [11, 12] have demonstrated that the Negative Selection (NS) can help the EAs (Evolutionary Algorithms) to escape from the local optima.

In this paper, a hybrid algorithm called as the HENSA-SAT for the large-scale SAT problems is proposed. The HENSA-SAT is designed by combining the Evolutionary Negative Selection Algorithm (ENSA), the Flip Heuristic [13], the *BackForwardFlipHeuristic* procedure and the *VerticalClimbing* procedure. The Flip Heuristic proposed in the FlipGA [13] has a good ability of local search. The introduction of the NS could help the HENSA-SAT to escape from the local optima. The NS is called twice in the HENSA-SAT for different uses. One is used to make the search start in different area as much as possible. The other is used to restrict the times of local search. Experimental results show that the proposed algorithm is effective for the large-scale SAT problems.

The rest of the paper is organized as follows. Section 2 introduces the related work about Evolutionary Algorithms (EAs) for the SAT problems. The ENSAs are also briefly stated in this section. The HENSA-SAT for the SAT problems is detailed in Section 3. Experimental results and analyses are given in Section 4. Section 5 gives the conclusions of this paper.

2 Related Work

The Evolutionary Algorithms (EAs) have been developed to solve the SAT problems. Early work demonstrated that EAs have poor performance for the SAT problems. De Jong and Spears [14] pointed out that GAs may not outperform the highly tuned and problem-specific algorithms. Fleurent and Ferland [15] also pointed out that pure GAs have poor performance when compared to traditional local search algorithms.

Recent work demonstrates that the EAs could solve the SAT problems efficiently by combining some heuristic techniques. Typical works are given as follows. The Stepwise Adaption of Weights Evolutionary Algorithm (SAWEA) [16] uses the clause weights to guide the search direction. The refining function is introduced in the Refining function Evolutionary Algorithm (RFEA) [17, 18] to discriminate those assignments which have the same fitness but are different. The FlipGA [13] takes the Flip Heuristic as one of the main operators. The Adaptive evolutionary algorithm for the SAtisfiability Problem (ASAP) [19] maintains a tabu-like table and resorts to the adaptive Flip Heuristic and the adaptive mutation rate. In the GASAT [20], the tabu search procedure is used as a local search procedure to improve the performance. An overview of the SAWEA, the RFEA, the FlipGA and the ASAP is depicted in [21].

The ENSAs are developed for anomaly detection and optimization problem. For anomaly detection, two kinds of ENSAs for anomaly detection are designed in [22]. For the optimization problem, a new Path Planning Algorithm based on an ENSA for mobile robots is proposed in [23]. In [24], the gene library evolution is composed with the negative selection to solve the Travelling Salesman Problem (TSP). An ENSA called the ENSA-HSP is designed for solving Hardware/Software Partitioning Problem in [12].

Also, there are some works about theoretical analysis of ENSAs. Both the convergence and the ability of escaping from the local optimum of the ENSA-HSP are analyzed in [12]. In [25], the convergence of ENSAs with two different mutation operators for anomaly detection is analyzed.

3 The Proposed HENSA-SAT

The proposed HENSA-SAT is detailed in this section. In this paper, the bit string is taken as the individual structure. Each bit in the individual corresponds to a boolean variable. When a variable is true, the corresponding bit is set to 1, otherwise it is set to 0. The number of satisfied clauses is used as the fitness of the individual. If all clauses are satisfied, a solution is found. The individual *CBEST* is used to record the best individual found during the whole search process.

The HENSA-SAT is described in Fig. 1.

1.	Initialization
2.	Fitness evaluation
3.	**while** the stop conditions are not satisfied **do**
4.	**for** each individual in the parent population
5.	*VerticalClimbing*
6.	Flip Heuristic
7.	**if** (the number of individuals in the self set that match with the individual generated by Flip Heuristic $< T$) **then**
8.	*BackForwardFlipHeurisitc*
9.	Put the individuals generated by *BackForwardFlipHeuristic* to the offspring
10.	**else**
11.	Put the individuals generated by Flip Heuristic to the offspring
12.	Negative Selection
13.	Updating the self set
14.	Updating the Parent population
15.	**return** the best individual *CBEST*

Fig. 1. The description of the HENSA-SAT

In step 1 of Fig. 1, the *Popsize* individuals are randomly generated as the initial parent population. Each individual in the initial parent population is generated by randomly setting each bit to 0 or 1 with probability of 0.5.

In step 3 of Fig. 1, when a solution is found, or the maximum number of flips is reached, or the limited running time is reached, the algorithm terminates.

The *VerticalClimbing* procedure in step 5 of Fig. 1 is depicted in Fig. 2. The symbol m in step 5 of Fig. 2 denotes the number of clauses contained in the SAT instance. Each variable in unsatisfied clauses is evaluated and its gain is computed. The concept of the gain is from the FlipGA [13]. The gain of a variable is equal to the increment of satisfied clauses supposing it is flipped [13]. For convenience, the gain of a variable x in an individual *child* is denoted as *child.gain(x)*. The variables which have the maximum gain are firstly stored in a *pool*, and then checked again one by one before being flipped. For Fig. 2, it can be observed that a local optimum can be reached by the *VerticalClimbing* procedure with fewer number of flips.

| Input: an individual *child* |
| Output: an individual *child* |
| ***VerticalClimbing*** |

1.	*fittmp* ← 0
2.	**do**{
3.	*fittmp* ← *child.fitness*
4.	*pool* ← ϕ
5.	*max* ← - *m*
6.	**for** each variable *x* in unsatisfied clauses of *child*
7.	**if** (*child.gain(x)* > *max*) //Each variable is computed only once
8.	*max* ← *child.gain(x)*; clear the *pool*; put *x* to the *pool*
9.	**else if** (*child.gain(x)* is equal to *max*)
10.	put *x* to the *pool*
11.	**for** each variable *x* in the *pool*
12.	*gaintmp* ← *child.gain(x)* //the gain of *x* is recalculated
13.	**if** (*gaintmp* is equal to *max*)
14.	*child.fitness* ← *child.fitness* + *max*
15.	flip the variable *x* in *child*
16.	}**while**(*child.fitness* > *fittmp*)
17.	**return** *child*

Fig. 2. The procedure of *VerticalClimbing*

The Flip Heuristic in step 6 of Fig. 1 is from [13]. For convenience, it is briefly introduced as follows. Firstly, a random permutation of the variables is generated. Secondly, each variable is checked according to the permutation and its gain is computed. If the gain of a variable is greater than or equal to 0, the variable is flipped. After all the variables are checked, one round check is completed. If the accumulation of the gain (only the gain that is greater than or equal to 0 is accumulated) in one round is more than 0, the next round check begins according to the above permutation. Otherwise, the process of Flip Heuristic [13] ends and a new individual is generated.

If the number of individuals in the self set that match with the individual generated by the Flip Heuristic is lower than *T*, the *BackForwardFlipHeuristic* procedure is called, and the individuals generated by the *BackForwardFlipHeuristic* procedure are added into the offspring. Otherwise, the individuals generated by the Flip Heuristic are directly added to the offspring. Here, the matching threshold is $0.65 \times \mu_g$, where μ_g is the matching threshold of the self individual. It is noted that each individual in the offspring has its own coverage radius (denoted by *R*). The coverage radius (i.e. *R*) of the individuals generated by the *BackForwardFlipHeuristic* is the Hamming distance between the individual after back strategy (Step 5~19 in Fig. 3) and the individual after the forward strategy (Step 20 in Fig. 3). The coverage radius of the individuals generated by the Flip Heuristic is the Hamming distance between the individual after the *VerticalClimbing* and the individual after the Flip Heuristic.

In step 12 of Fig. 1, the NS would filter individuals in the offspring whose minimum Hamming distance to individuals in the self set is lower than a given threshold μ_g . Each individual in the self set has its own matching threshold μ_g . It is noted that the value of μ_g is set when the individual is added into the self set.

Input: an individual *child, NumChosen, Eb, Ec*	
Output: a set of individual *childtmpset*	
BackForwardFlipHeuristic	

1.	*childtmpset* ← ϕ
2.	**for** *i* ← 1 to *Eb*
3.	*childtmp* ← *child*
4.	**for** *j* ← 1 to *Ec*
5.	*max* ← - *m*
6.	*choice* ← ϕ
7.	**for** each variable *x* in *childtmp*
8.	**if** (*childtmp.gain(x)* > *max* && *childtmp.gain(x)* < 0)
9.	*max* ← *childtmp.gain(x)*; clear the *choice*; put *x* to *choice*
10.	**else if** (*childtmp.gain(x)* = *max*)
11.	put *x* to *choice*
12.	*numchoose* ← 0
13.	**while** (*numchoose* < *NumChosen* && *choice.size()* > 0)
14.	randomly choose a variable *x* in *choice* and flip it
15.	*numchoose* ← *numchoose* + 1
16.	delete *x* from *choice*
17.	**while** (*numchoose* < *NumChosen*)
18.	randomly choose a variable *x* in *childtmp* to flip
19.	*numchoose* ← *numchoose* + 1
20.	*childtmp* ← *Flip Heuristic*(*childtmp*)
21.	*childtmpset* ← *childtmpset* ∪ *childtmp*
22.	**return** *childtmpset*

Fig. 3. The procedure of *BackForwardFlipHeuristic*

In step 13 of Fig. 1, the self set is updated. The individuals left in the offspring after the NS are added to the self set. These self individuals have different matching thresholds μ_g . Exactly, the values of μ_g is equal to the coverage radius of the corresponding individual in the offspring. That is to say, $\mu_g = R$. It is noted that the self set is initially set to be empty.

In step 14 of Fig. 1, the parent population is updated. If the number of individuals left in the offspring after the NS is greater than or equal to *Popsize*, the best *Popsize* individuals in the offspring are selected and added to the new parent population. Otherwise, new individuals are generated and added to the new parent population. The generation procedure of new individuals is detailed as follows. An individual *child* is randomly chosen from the individuals filtered by the NS. For convenience, the individual in the self set which has minimum Hamming distance to *child* is denoted as *childref*, and the Hamming distance between *child* and *childref* is denoted as *H(child, childref)*. Some bits of *child* are flipped, which are randomly chosen from the bits that the corresponding value of both *child* and *childref* is identical. The number of bits chosen to be flipped is *rnd* -*H(child, childref)*, where *rnd* is a random number chosen between $\mu_g +1$ and $0.5 \times (n+\mu_g)+1$. The individual after the above operation is added to the new parent population. The process repeats until the size of the parent population is equal to *Popsize*.

4 Experiments

The test instances and parameter settings are briefly described in section 4.1. The experimental results and analyses are given in section 4.2.

4.1 Test Instances and Parameter Settings

Nine instances are used to test the HENSA-SAT. All these instances are from the SAT2002 or the SAT2003 competitions[1]. The average number of unsatisfied clauses by the GASAT [20] on these instances are more than 50. The first two instances listed in Table 1 are handmade benchmarks. The following three instances in Table 1 are structured benchmarks. They are transformed into the 3-SAT format, and the transformation is conducted according to the method in [20]. The sixth instance is a random benchmark, and the last three instances are industrial benchmarks.

The parameter settings are given as follows. The population size *Popsize* is set to 4. The parameters *Eb* and *Ec* in the *BackForwardFlipHeuristic* procedure are set to 2 and 15, respectively. The parameter *NumChosen* in the *BackForwardFlipHeuristic* is usually set to $0.02{\times}n$, where n denotes the number of variables contained in the test instance.

The value of parameter T for each instance is obtained by the preprocessing experiments. Firstly, the parameter T is set to $+\infty$, and the *BackForwardFlipHeuristic* procedure is always called in the HENSA-SAT. Secondly, the number of individuals in self set that match with the best individual found by the HENSA-SAT (i.e. *CBEST*) is counted, and this number is denoted by δ. Generally, the value of T should be greater than δ. Here, the sixth instance in Table 1 is taken as an example.

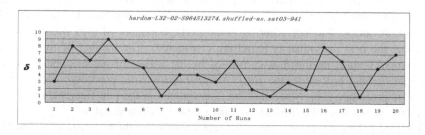

Fig. 4. The number of individuals in the self set that match with *CBEST* in 20 runs

Fig. 4 gives the values of δ in 20 independent runs. From Fig. 4, the values of δ are usually less than 10. So the parameter T for the sixth instance is set to 10. The values of T for other instances are set in the same way like the sixth instance.

Furthermore, Fig. 5 gives the number of individuals in the self set that match with the individuals generated by the Flip Heuristic in one run. For convenience, this number is also denoted by δ. From Fig. 5, it can be observed that some values of δ is

[1] http://www.satlib.org/

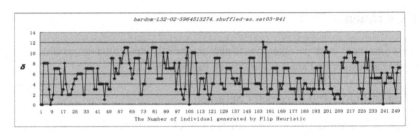

Fig. 5. The number of individuals in the self set that match with the individuals generated by the Flip Heuristic in one run

more than or equal to 10. If the T is set to 10, the *BackForwardFlipHeuristic* procedure is called less than 10 times. Therefore, the times of local search with the *BackForwardFlipHeuristic* procedure could be restricted.

4.2 Experimental Results and Analyse

The experimental results are listed in Table 1. Each test instance is conducted 20 runs independently. The maximum number of flips is set to 101×10^5, and the running time is limited to 1 hour. The termination condition is the same as that in [20]. However, the machine configurations are different. The results of the FlipGA and the GASAT are from [20]. They are tested on a cluster with Linux and Alinka (with 2 CPU Pentium IV 2.2 GHZ with 1 GB RAM) used sequentially. The results for the HENSA-SAT are also shown in Table 1. They are tested on a 2-core 1.6 GHZ Pentium IV PC with 1.5 GB RAM.

Three comparison criteria are used to evaluate the performance of different algorithms. The first two criteria are the average number of unsatisfied clauses and its standard deviation. Another criterion is the average number of flips used (only the runs that the best individual is found are considered). The number of flips for the HENSA-SAT sums up the flips consumed by the update of parent population, the *VerticalClimbing* procedure, the *BackForwardFlipHeuristic* procedure and the Flip Heuristic procedure [13]. Noted that the flips counted in the Flip Heuristic procedure [13] only include the valid flips whose gain are more than or equal to 0.

The first column in Table 1 gives the serial number of the test instances. The following three columns in Table 1 give the basic property of the test instances. Column 2 gives the name of the test instance. Column 3 and column 4 give the number of variables and that of clauses contained in the test instances, respectively. The following three columns give the results of the FlipGA on the test instances. Column 5 (f.c. avg) and column 6 (f.c. s.d.) give the average number of unsatisfied clauses and its standard deviation, respectively. Column 7 gives the average number of flips used when the best individual is found. Columns 8 to 10 give the results of the GASAT and the following three columns give the results of the HENSA-SAT, respectively. The last column gives the values of the parameter T in HENSA-SAT for each test instance. The symbol "N/A" means that the corresponding result is not given in [20].

Table 1. Comparative results of the FlipGA, the GASAT and the HENSA-SAT

No	Benchmarks			FlipGA			GASAT			HENSA-SAT			T
	instances	n	M	f.c. avg	f.c. s.d.	fl. ×10³	f.c. avg.	f.c. s.d.	fl. ×10³	f.c. avg.	f.c. s.d.	fl. ×10³	
1.	bqwh.33.381.shuffled-as.sat03-1642	1555	9534	N/A	N/A	N/A	50.05	7.32	985	**12.20**	2.04	2082	6
2.	pyhala-braun-unsat-35-4 03.shuffled-as.sat03-1543	7383	24320	N/A	N/A	N/A	80.15	53.88	2008	**56.40**	4.12	9126	7
3.	difp_19_0_arr_rcr.3SAT	5157	10560	87.60	7.23	20340	84.25	6.13	657	**38.50**	5.73	8160	60
4.	difp_19_99_arr_rcr.3SAT	5157	10560	87.95	9.75	20172	81.40	7.14	639	**38.00**	5.71	8666	70
5.	color-18-4.3SAT	97200	191808	2064.35	363.65	2818	**248.50**	0.50	27	250.00	0.45	2446	4
6.	hardnm-L32-02-S964513 274.shuffled-as.sat03-941	1024	4096	N/A	N/A	N/A	53.85	1.28	1078	**15.70**	2.03	2309	10
7.	k2fix_gr_2pinvar_w9. shuffled-as.sat03-436	5028	307674	N/A	N/A	N/A	174.55	10.50	553	**174.00**	7.31	985	2
8.	cnt10.shuffled-as. sat03-418	20470	68561	N/A	N/A	N/A	163.65	22.39	966	**47.10**	5.50	5222	2
9.	dp11u10.shuffled-as.sat03-422	9197	25271	N/A	N/A	N/A	**79.67**	9.52	873	86.30	6.48	8351	14

Experimental results in Table 1 demonstrate that the performance of the HENSA-SAT is very competitive with the FlipGA and the GASAT on the test instances. For the average number of unsatisfied clauses, the HENSA-SAT has lower values than the GASAT on most test instances except the fifth test instance and the ninth test instance.

The standard deviation of the unsatisfied clauses of the HENSA-SAT is also much lower than that of the GASAT on most test instances except for the sixth test instance. It can be concluded that the proposed algorithm has good stability for the large-scale SAT problems.

Additionally, the number of flips used in the HENSA-SAT is much higher than that of the GASAT on all the test instances. This is mainly because the flips consumed by the Flip Heuristic [13] and the *BackForwardFlipHeuristic* procedure are relatively large.

5   Conclusions

The HENSA-SAT algorithm is proposed in this paper for the large-scale SAT problems. The proposed algorithm is a hybrid of the Evolutionary Negative Selection Algorithm, the Flip Heuristic [13], the *BackForwardFlipHeuristic* procedure and the *VerticalClimbing* procedure. This efficient algorithm for the SAT problems has a good ability of local search, and can exploit different areas in the whole search space. Exactly, in the HENSA-SAT, the Flip Heuristic [13], the *BackForwardFlipHeuristic* procedure and the *VerticalClimbing* procedure make it have a good local search ability, while the Negative Selection could help it to escape from local optima. The NS in the HENSA-SAT is used for two purposes. One is used to make the search start in different area as much as possible. The other is used to restrict the times of local search. Experimental results show that the HENSA-SAT is very competitive with the FlipGA and the GASAT.

Future work will focus on the experimental test on more benchmarks, and analyze the effect of different parameter settings.

Acknowledgments. This work is partly supported by the National Natural Science Foundation of China (NO. 60774075).

References

1. Cook, S.A.: The Complexity of Theorem-proving Procedure. In: Proceedings of the 3rd Annual ACM Symposium on Theory of Computing, New York, pp. 151–158 (1971)
2. Gent, I.P., Toby, W.: The Search for Satisfaction. Department of Computer Science. University of Strathclyde (1999)
3. Davis, M., Putnam, H.: A Computing Procedure for Quantification Theory. Journal of the ACM 7, 201–215 (1960)
4. Martin, D., George, L., Donald, L.: A Machine Program for Theorem-proving. Communication of ACM 5(7), 394–397 (1962)
5. Papadimitriou, C.H.: On Selecting a Satisfying Truth Assignment. In: The 32nd Annual Symposium of Foundations of Computer Science, pp. 163–169 (1991)
6. Selman, B., Levesque, H., Mitchell, D.: A New Method for Solving Hard Satisfiability Problems. In: Proceedings of the 10th National Conference on Artificial Intelligence, San Jose, CA, pp. 440–446 (1992)
7. Selman, B., Kautz, H.A., Cohen, B.: Noise Strategies for Improving Local Search. In: Proceedings of the 12th National Conference on Artificial Intelligence, Seattle, WA, pp. 337–343 (1994)
8. McAllester, D., Selman, B., Kautz, H.: Evidence for Invariants in Local Search. In: Proceedings of the 14th National Conference on Artificial Intelligence, pp. 321–327 (1997)
9. Hirsch, E.A., Kojevnikov, A.: UnitWalk: A New SAT Solver that Uses Local Search Guided by Unit Clause Elimination. Annals of Mathematics and Artificial Intelligence 43(1-4), 91–111 (2001)
10. Zhang, Y., Luo, W., Wang, X.: A Logic Circuits Designing Algorithm Based on Immune Principles. Computer Engineering and Applications 42(11), 38–40 (2006) (in Chinese)
11. Luo, W., Zhang, Y., Wang, X., Wang, X.: Experimental Analyses of Evolutionary Negative Selection Algorithm for Function Optimization. Journal of Harbin Engineering University 27(B07), 158–163 (2006)
12. Zhang, Y., Luo, W., Zhang, Z., Li, B., Wang, X.: A Hardware/Software Partitioning Algorithm Based on Artificial Immune Principles. Applied Soft Computing 8(1), 383–391 (2008)
13. Marchiori, E., Rossi, C.: A Flipping Genetic Algorithm for Hard 3-SAT Problems. In: Proceedings of the Genetic and Evolutionary Computation Conference, pp. 393–400. Morgan Kaufmann, San Francisco (1999)
14. Jong, K.A.D., Spears, W.M.: Using Genetic Algorithms to Solve NP-complete Problems. In: Proceedings of the 3rd International Conference on Genetic Algorithms, Mason University, United States, pp. 124–132. Morgan Kaufmann Publishers Inc., San Francisco (1989)
15. Fleurent, C., Ferland, J.: Object-oriented Implementation of Heuristic Search Methods for Graph Coloring, Maximum Clique, and Satisfiability. In: Trick, M., Johnson, D.S. (eds.) DIMACS Series in Discrete Mathematics and Theoretical Computer Science, vol. 26, pp. 619–652 (1996)
16. Thomas, B., Eiben, A.E., Marco, E.V.: A Superior Evolutionary Algorithm for 3-SAT. In: Proceedings of the 7th International Conference on Evolutionary Programming VII. Springer, Heidelberg (1998)\

17. Gottlieb, J., Voss, N.: Improving the Performance of Evolutionary Algorithms for the Satisfiability Problem by Refining Functions. In: Eiben, A.E., Bäck, T., Schoenauer, M., Schwefel, H.-P. (eds.) PPSN 1998. LNCS, vol. 1498, pp. 755–764. Springer, Heidelberg (1998)
18. Gottlieb, J., Voss, N.: Adaptive Fitness Functions for the Satisfiability Problem. In: Proceedings of the 6th International Conference on Parallel Problem Solving from Nature. Springer, Heidelberg (2000)
19. Rossi, C., Marchiori, E., Kok, J.N.: An Adaptive Evolutionary Algorithm for the Satisfiability Problem. In: Proceedings of the 2000, ACM symposium on Applied computing, Como, Italy, vol. 1, pp. 463–469. ACM, New York (2000)
20. Lardeux, F., Saubion, F., Hao, J.-K.: GASAT: A Genetic Local Search Algorithm for the Satisfiability Problem. Evolutionary Computation 14(2), 223–253 (2006)
21. Gottlieb, J., Marchiori, E., Rossi, C.: Evolutionary Algorithms for the Satisfiability Problem. Evolutionary Computation 10(1), 35–50 (2002)
22. Luo, W., Wang, J., Wang, X.: Evolutionary Negative Selection Algorithms for Anomaly Detection. In: Proceedings of the 8th Joint Conference on Information Sciences (ICIS 2005), Salt Lake City, Utah, vol. 1-3, pp. 440–445 (2005)
23. Zhang, Z., Luo, W., Wang, X.: Research of Mobile Robots Path Planning Algorithm Based on Immune Evolutionary Negative Selection Mechanism. Journal of Electronics and Information Technology 29(8), 1987–1991 (2007)
24. Cao, X., Zhang, S., Wang, X.: Immune Optimization System based on Immune Recognition. In: Proceedings of the 8th International Conference on Neural Information Processing, Shanghai, China, vol. 2, pp. 535–541 (2001)
25. Luo, W., Guo, P., Wang, X.: On Convergence of Evolutionary Negative Selection Algorithms for Anomaly Detection. In: Proceedings of the 2008 IEEE Congress on Evolutionary Computation, Hongkong, pp. 2938–2944 (2008)

Novel Associative Memory Retrieving Strategies for Evolutionary Algorithms in Dynamic Environments

Yong Cao[1,2] and Wenjian Luo[1,2]

[1] Nature Inspired Computation and Applications Laboratory, School of Computer Science and Technology, University of Science and Technology of China, Hefei, 230027, Anhui, China
[2] Anhui Key Laboratory of Software in Computing and Communication, University of Science and Technology of China, Hefei 230027, China
caoyll@mail.ustc.edu.cn, wjluo@ustc.edu.cn

Abstract. Recently, Evolutionary Algorithms (EAs) with associative memory schemes have been developed to solve Dynamic Optimization Problems (DOPs). Current associative memory schemes always retrieve both the best memory individual and the corresponding environmental information. However, the memory individual with the best fitness could not be the most appropriate one for new environments. In this paper, two novel associative memory retrieving strategies are proposed to obtain the most appropriate memory environmental information. In these strategies, two best individuals are first selected from the two best memory individuals and the current best individual. Then, their corresponding environmental information is evaluated according to either the survivability or the diversity, one of which is retrieved. In experiments, the proposed two strategies were embedded into the state-of-the-art algorithm, i.e. the MPBIL, and tested on three dynamic functions in cyclic environments. Experiment results demonstrate that the proposed retrieving strategies enhance the search ability in cyclic environments.

Keywords: dynamic optimization problems, evolutionary algorithms, memory, associative memory, memory retrieving strategy.

1 Introduction

Evolutionary Algorithms (EAs) have been used to solve Dynamic Optimization Problems (DOPs) and demonstrate powerful search ability [1-3]. So far, some improved EAs have been developed for DOPs. Cobb [4] developed a Genetic Algorithm to promote the population diversity with hypermutation operator when the environment changed. To maintain the population diversity throughout the run, in [1, 5], EAs with different immigrant schemes have been developed. Meanwhile, the memory schemes [6, 7] and the multi-population strategies [8-10] have also been introduced into EAs for DOPs.

Among these approaches, the memory schemes have proved to be very effective, especially in cyclic dynamic environments. Generally, there are two memory schemes, i.e. the implicit memory [11, 12] and the explicit memory [6, 7, 13-16]. Furthermore, the explicit memory schemes include the direct memory [6, 17] and the

Z. Cai et al. (Eds.): ISICA 2009, LNCS 5821, pp. 258–268, 2009.
© Springer-Verlag Berlin Heidelberg 2009

associative memory [13, 16]. Especially, the memory-enhanced PBIL (MPBIL) proposed by Yang and Yao [16] is the state-of-the-art evolutionary algorithm for DOPs, which introduces the associative memory scheme into the population-based incremental learning algorithms (PBIL) [18].

Different from traditional memory schemes, the associative memory scheme can retrieve both the best memory individual and the corresponding environmental information [16]. However, current associative memory schemes retrieve the memory individual and the corresponding environmental information only in terms of the fitness, which could not retrieve the most appropriate one for the current environment.

In this paper, two novel associative memory retrieving strategies are proposed. In these two strategies, firstly, two best individuals are selected from the two best memory individuals and the current best individual. Secondly, the associated environmental information of these two best individuals is evaluated according to either their survivability or their diversity, and one of them is retrieved to enhance the search ability in the current environment. Three dynamic test problems in [16] are adopted in the experiments. Experimental results demonstrate that associative memory-enhanced EAs with the proposed novel retrieving strategies have better performance than the state-of-the-art algorithm, i.e. the MPBIL in [16].

The rest of this paper is organized as follows. In Section 2, the existing memory retrieving strategies are reviewed. The disadvantage of the current retrieving strategy is discussed, and two novel associative memory retrieving strategies are described in Section 3. Section 4 demonstrates the experimental results. Some discussions are given in Section 5, and Section 6 summaries the whole paper briefly.

2 Related Work

Both the direct memory scheme and the associative memory scheme are explicit memory schemes. As for explicit memory schemes, when retrieving the memory, the memory individuals often compete with the individuals of the current population to survive in the next generation population [6, 16].

The direct memory scheme only memorizes good solutions, while the associative memory scheme stores both good solutions and the associated environmental information. Because the environmental information is also stored together with the memorized individuals, the associative memory scheme can reuse the environmental information with different ways.

The Case-based Initialization of Genetic Algorithm by Ramsey and Grefenstette [13] reactivated the memory controller solution whose associated environmental information was most similar to the current environment. The MPBIL by Yang and Yao [16] retrieved the memory individual with the best fitness, and reused the corresponding enviromental information to generate new candidate solutions.

To our best knowledge, the work in [13] and [16] has covered the existent ways about the associative memory retrieving strategies. In [13], because the dynamic environment is detectable and comparable, it retrieves the memory individual according to the similarities between old environments and new environments. While in [16], the dynamics of DOPs are difficult to be detected and compared, it retrieves the environmental information in terms of the fitness of the corresponding memory individuals.

The associative memory retrieving strategies proposed in this paper are incorporated into the MPBIL [16] by replacing its retrieving strategy. Here the MPBIL is introduced briefly. The MPBIL [16] first stores the best sample as well as the associated probability vector in the memory set, and then reuses them when the environment changes. When the memory set is updated, the current best sample and the working probability vector are stored in the memory set. If the memory set is full, the memory sample closest to the current best sample in terms of the Hamming distance is picked out. If its fitness is worse than the current best sample, the memory sample and its associated probability vector will be replaced by the current best sample and the corresponding working probability vector, respectively. Otherwise, the memory remains the same as before.

3   The Proposed Associative Memory Retrieving Strategies

In the MPBIL[16], the retrieving strategy always retrieves the memory point with the best fitness value. However, the fitness value cannot reflect its adaptability in new environments.

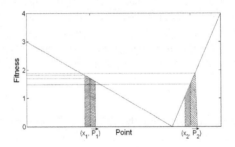

Fig. 1. The point ($x_2, \vec{P}_2$) is more suitable for the current environment although the fitness of its associated candidate solution x_2 is worse than that of x_1.

Fig. 1 demonstrates an example. In Fig. 1, a point consists of a sample (candidate solution) and its associated probability vector (environmental information). In terms of the fitness, the point ($x_1, \vec{P}_1$) is better than the point ($x_2, \vec{P}_2$) in the current environment. The point ($x_1, \vec{P}_1$) will be retrieved in the MPBIL because its associated sample x_1 has a higher fitness. However, retrieving the point ($x_2, \vec{P}_2$) could obtain a better result. As shown in Fig. 1, the samples generated by ($x_2, \vec{P}_2$) distribute in a relatively favorable terrain, and these samples may contain a better solution.

In order to retrieve such points, e.g. ($x_2, \vec{P}_2$), two novel associative memory retrieving strategies are described as follows.

3.1 The Survivability-Based Retrieving Strategy

Algorithm 1. The survivability-based retrieving strategy

1: In iteration t, let x_C denote the current best sample, $\overrightarrow{P_C}$ denote the working probability vector, and the corresponding point $P_C = (x_C, \overrightarrow{P_C})$.

2: **IF** *environmental change is detected in iteration t* **THEN**

3: Pick out two best points P_M' and P_M'' from the memory set according to their fitness values. Let $P_M' = (x_M', \overrightarrow{P_M'})$, and $P_M'' = (x_M'', \overrightarrow{P_M''})$.

4: Pick out two best points P_1 and P_2 from $\{ P_C$, P_M', $P_M'' \}$ according to their fitness values. Let $P_1 = (x_1, \overrightarrow{P_1})$, $P_2 = (x_2, \overrightarrow{P_2})$.

5: Mutate $\overrightarrow{P_1}$ and $\overrightarrow{P_2}$, and use them to generate half samples of the sample set $S(t)$, respectively.

6: **IF** *the best sample generated by* $\overrightarrow{P_1}$ **THEN**

7: Retrieve $\overrightarrow{P_1}$ as the new working probability vector.

8: **ELSE**

9: Retrieve $\overrightarrow{P_2}$ as the new working probability vector.

10: Let $t = t+1$.

As for associative memory schemes, the memory point with higher environmental adaptability should be retrieved when a new environment comes. In order to compare the environmental adaptabilities of two points, a straightforward approach is to compare their survivability. That is to say, the better point could generate fitter samples for new environments. Inspired by such an idea, the *survivability-based retrieving strategy* is given in Algorithm 1.

As shown in Algorithm 1, when an environmental change is detected in iteration t, firstly, two best points are picked out from the memory set and the current best point in terms of the fitness. Secondly, their associated probability vectors are mutated and used to generate half samples of the sample set $S(t)$, respectively. The probability vector which generates the best sample will be retrieved as the new working probability vector, and used to generate samples for later generations.

For fair, because a sample set is generated and evaluated in this retrieving operation, the evolutionary generation is increased by one. Therefore, the total number of fitness evaluations is not increased.

Additionally, the *survivability-based retrieving strategy* is different from the multi-population strategies [8-10] in essence. This is because the samples generated by the two candidate probability vectors do not participate in the process of evolution in this step. They are just used to decide which probability vector should be retrieved.

3.2 The Diversity-Based Retrieving Strategy

The diversity is the necessity for EAs to track the moving optima in dynamic environments. So the diversity can be used as the auxiliary information to decide which point should be retrieved.

In [16, 19], the population diversity is represented by the allele distribution of the population, while its computation cost is relatively large. In this paper, only the diversity of the probability vector is needed to be evaluated. Therefore, a simple approach to calculate the diversity of the probability vector is given as follows.

When a bit of a probability vector is closer to the central value (i.e. 0.5), the corresponding bit of the generated sample will be more stochastic. Therefore, the diversity of the probability vector $\vec{P} = (p_1, ..., p_l)$ (l is the binary-encoding length) can be calculated as Eq. (1).

$$Div(\vec{P}) = \frac{1}{l}\sum_{i=1}^{l}(P_i - 0.5)^2 \tag{1}$$

The retrieving strategy based on the diversity of the probability vector is denoted as the *diversity-based retrieving strategy* in Algorithm 2.

Algorithm 2. The diversity-based retrieving strategy

1:   In iteration t, let x_C denote the current best sample, $\vec{P_C}$ denote the working probability vector, and the corresponding point $P_C = (x_C, \vec{P_C})$.

2:   **IF** *environmental change is detected* **THEN**

3:   Pick out two best points P_M' and P_M'' from the memory set according to their fitness values. Let $P_M' = (x_M', \vec{P_M'})$, and $P_M'' = (x_M'', \vec{P_M''})$.

4:   Pick out two best points P_1 and P_2 from { P_C, P_M', P_M'' } according to their fitness values. Let $P_1 = (x_1, \vec{P_1})$ and $P_2 = (x_2, \vec{P_2})$.

5:   **IF** $|f(x_1) - f(x_2)| < \varepsilon$ **THEN**

6:   Calculate the diversity of $\vec{P_1}$ and $\vec{P_2}$ by Eq. (1).

7:   **IF** $Div(\vec{P_1}) > Div(\vec{P_2})$ **THEN**

8:   Retrieve $\vec{P_2}$ as the new working probability vector.

9:   **ELSE**

10:   Retrieve $\vec{P_1}$ as the new working probability vector.

11:   **ELSE**

12:   Retrieve $\vec{P_1}$ as the new working probability vector.

As shown in Algorithm 2, when an environmental change is detected, firstly, two best points are picked out from the memory set and the current best point. Secondly, for safety, if and only if the two candidate points have close fitness values, i.e. $|f(x_1) - f(x_2)| < \varepsilon$, the probability vector with higher diversity will be retrieved. Otherwise, the probability vector with a fitter associated sample will be retrieved. This is because the fitness value is also an important factor to reflect the environmental adaptability of a point. In this paper, the parameter ε is set to 3.0.

4 Experiments

4.1 Experimental Settings

In this paper, to test the performance of the proposed two novel associative memory retrieving strategies, they are embedded into the MPBIL [16] by replacing its retrieving strategy.

For convenience, the MPBIL with the *survivability-based retrieving strategy* is denoted as the sbrMPBIL, and the MPBIL with the *diversity-based retrieving strategy* is denoted as the dbrMPBIL. The sbrMPBIL and dbrMPBIL are given in Algorithm 3.

Algorithm 3. The MPBILs

1: **Initialization.** Set $t := 0$, the memory set $M(t) := \phi$, the working probability vector
     $\vec{P}(t) := (0.5,...,0.5)$. Use $\vec{P}(t)$ to generate the first generation sample set $S(t)$ and
     calculate the fitness value of samples in $S(t)$.
2: **REPEAT**
3:      **Updating.** If it is time to update the memory, memorize the current best sample as well
         as the corresponding probability vector according to the updating strategy in [16].
4:      **Retrieving.**
         IF *environmental change is detected* **THEN**
             for sbrMPBIL: Do retrieval with the *survivability-based retrieving strategy*.
                 Go to step 6.
             for dbrMPBIL: Do retrieval with the *diversity-based retrieving strategy*.
5:      **Evolution.**
         Learn $\vec{P}(t)$ towards the best sample if no environmental change is detected.
         Mutate $\vec{P}(t)$, and use it to generate a new sample set $S(t)$.
         Calculate the fitness value of samples in $S(t)$ and $M(t)$.
6: **UNTIL** the termination condition is satisfied.

Three dynamic test problems from [16], denoted by DDUF1, DDUF2 and DDUF3, respectively, are adopted to compare the performance of the MPBIL, sbrMPBIL and dbrMPBIL. The settings of dynamic environments are the same as [16]. Because the memory scheme is a preferred approach in cyclic environments, the sbrMPBIL, dbrMPBIL and MPBIL are tested and compared in cyclic environments.

The common parameters of all algorithms including the sbrMPBIL, dbrMPBIL and MPBIL are the same as [16], and are given as follows. The total population size n is set to 100, including the memory size of $m = 0.1n$. The learning rate $\alpha = 0.25$, and the mutation shift $\delta_m = 0.05$. The bit flip mutation happens in every generation with a probability of $p_m = 0.02$.

Each experiment runs 50 times independently. In each experiment, the MPBIL [16], sbrMPBIL and dbrMPBIL use the identical random seed. The total evolutionary generation is 5000 for each run.

The performance of the algorithms is compared according to Eq. (2) [16].

$$\overline{F}_{BOT} = \frac{1}{T}\sum_{t=1}^{T}(\frac{1}{R}\sum_{r=1}^{R}f_{BOT}^{tr}) \qquad (2)$$

Where T denotes the total number of generations in a run, R denotes the total run times in each experiment, and f_{BOT}^{tr} is the best fitness value of the tth generation in the rth run.

4.2 Experimental Results

The experimental results are given in Table 1 and Table 2.

The t-test results are given in Table 1. The t-test adopted in this paper is the same as that in [16] (i.e. one-tailed, 98 freedom degrees and 0.05 significance level). In Table 1, for each comparison of "Algorithm 1 – Algorithm 2", "$s+$" means that

Table 1. The t-test results of comparisons between sbrMPBIL, dbrMPBIL and MPBIL

t-test Result	DDUF1				DDUF2				DDUF3			
$\tau=10$, $\rho \Rightarrow$	0.1	0.2	0.5	1.0	0.1	0.2	0.5	1.0	0.1	0.2	0.5	1.0
sbrMPBIL – MPBIL	$s+$	$s+$	$+$	$s+$	$s+$	$s+$	$s+$	$s+$	$s+$	$+$	$+$	$+$
dbrMPBIL – MPBIL	$+$	$s+$	$s+$	$-$	$s+$	$s+$	$s+$	$s+$	$s+$	$s+$	$+$	$s-$
$\tau=25$, $\rho \Rightarrow$	0.1	0.2	0.5	1.0	0.1	0.2	0.5	1.0	0.1	0.2	0.5	1.0
sbrMPBIL – MPBIL	$s+$	$s+$	$s+$	$-$	$s+$	$s+$	$s+$	$s+$	$s+$	$+$	$s+$	$s+$
dbrMPBIL – MPBIL	$+$	$s+$	$s+$	$s-$	$+$	$s+$	$s+$	$s+$	$s+$	$+$	$+$	$s-$

Table 2. Experimental results of $\overline{F}_{BOT}$

DDUFs	τ	ρ	MPBIL	sbrMPBIL	dbrMPBIL
DDUF1	10	0.1	90.92 (0.2551)	**91.45 (0.2207)**	90.96 (0.2873)
		0.2	90.68 (1.2893)	**91.31 (0.9881)**	91.26 (0.9095)
		0.5	98.26 (0.0960)	**98.41 (1.9609)**	98.36 (0.0607)
		1.0	98.99 (0.0351)	**99.37 (0.0192)**	98.92 (0.0583)
	25	0.1	91.20 (0.1572)	**91.54 (0.1619)**	91.31 (0.1255)
		0.2	91.17 (0.5280)	91.75 (0.5502)	**91.87 (0.6506)**
		0.5	96.33 (16.928)	**98.45 (2.0755)**	98.29 (4.1838)
		1.0	**99.57 (0.0065)**	99.56 (0.0028)	99.47 (0.0379)
DDUF2	10	0.1	78.66 (2.2070)	**80.03 (2.4506)**	79.26 (1.6800)
		0.2	77.70 (7.5016)	**80.61 (5.5936)**	79.95 (5.2982)
		0.5	86.88 (11.370)	**91.38 (6.6576)**	88.92 (7.2275)
		1.0	83.59 (88.623)	**93.85 (9.7141)**	87.99 (33.372)
	25	0.1	79.57 (1.2447)	**80.34 (1.5342)**	79.85 (1.8260)
		0.2	79.45 (1.5393)	**81.33 (2.8599)**	81.14 (2.0075)
		0.5	88.54 (37.194)	**92.45 (13.048)**	92.35 (9.3258)
		1.0	93.24 (20.207)	**96.08 (4.5275)**	95.42 (6.0340)
DDUF3	10	0.1	78.78 (1.0817)	79.49 (1.1228)	**79.58 (1.4333)**
		0.2	84.38 (1.6736)	84.43 (3.0280)	**84.86 (0.5014)**
		0.5	86.55 (0.0803)	**86.63 (0.0964)**	86.55 (0.1007)
		1.0	87.31 (0.0045)	**87.33 (0.0224)**	87.22 (0.0273)
	25	0.1	79.10 (0.8408)	**79.73 (0.5585)**	79.63 (0.6279)
		0.2	84.12 (2.9486)	84.13 (3.6053)	**84.26 (3.7795)**
		0.5	86.72 (0.0931)	**86.89 (0.0504)**	86.79 (0.0861)
		1.0	87.33 (0.0035)	**87.36 (0.0121)**	87.25 (0.0214)

"Algorithm 1" is significantly better than "Algorithm 2". And "+" means that "Algorithm 1" is better than "Algorithm 2", but not significantly better. For "−" and "s−", they mean "Algorithm 2" is better and significantly better than "Algorithm 1", respectively.

The values of $\overline{F}_{BOT}$ of the MPBIL, sbrMPBIL and dbrMPBIL are given in Table 2. The numbers in the parentheses are the variance.

From Table 1 and Table 2, the results demonstrate that both sbrMPBIL and dbrMPBIL perform significantly better than the MPBIL in most cases on three dynamic test problems.

From the experimental results in Table 2, it can be observed that the sbrMPBIL is the best algorithm among them. For the sbrMPBIL, before retrieving, the two candidate points generate half samples of the sample set, respectively. This can help to test which point has better environmental adaptability for new environments.

Table 3. Experimental results of the mean times of retrieving the second best points

DDUFs	τ	ρ	sbrMPBIL	dbrMPBIL
DDUF1	10	0.1	102.06 (121.241)	208.48 (107.561)
		0.2	135.58 (272.412)	101.90 (394.214)
		0.5	4.26 (197.502)	0.64 (0.64330)
		1.0	1.28 (0.20571)	27.94 (5527.65)
	25	0.1	32.32 (22.3445)	81.52 (37.8873)
		0.2	43.94 (28.0576)	51.96 (47.9167)
		0.5	2.18 (16.5996)	1.60 (5.75510)
		1.0	0.78 (7.84857)	22.16 (1642.79)
DDUF2	10	0.1	99.34 (141.821)	125.78 (120.012)
		0.2	126.38 (471.261)	38.58 (133.065)
		0.5	2.14 (1.18408)	1.04 (1.99837)
		1.0	1.3 (0.54082)	7.66 (1215.17)
	25	0.1	31.18 (24.9669)	66.26 (53.6249)
		0.2	41.48 (30.3363)	33.90 (36.4592)
		0.5	2.82 (42.3547)	1.38 (5.79143)
		1.0	0.32 (0.38531)	4.84 (223.729)
DDUF3	10	0.1	139.24 (432.553)	48.52 (178.255)
		0.2	22.2 (877.020)	6.44 (16.6188)
		0.5	3.92 (3.38122)	12.22 (980.338)
		1.0	17.72 (2467.72)	129.96 (21812.5)
	25	0.1	38.82 (55.1710)	31.94 (28.4657)
		0.2	9.44 (89.8024)	6.28 (30.5731)
		0.5	6.84 (411.566)	11.48 (392.540)
		1.0	11.26 (775.829)	36.70 (2953.32)

The most important characteristic of the proposed two memory retrieving strategies is that the second best individual could be retrieved, while traditional memory retrieving strategies always retrieve the best individual. In Table 3, as for the sbrMPBIL and the dbrMPBIL, the mean times of retrieving the second best points are given. The numbers in the parentheses are the variance. From Table 3, it can be seen that the proposed retrieving strategies indeed retrieve the second best point at a certain extent.

However, retrieving the second best point may produce negative effects. For example, on DDUF1, the dbrMPBIL is beaten by the MPBIL when $\rho = 1.0$, and the sbrMPBIL is a little worse than MPBIL when $\tau = 25$ and $\rho = 1.0$.

Additionally, on DDUF3, the dbrMPBIL is also beaten by the MPBIL when $\rho = 1.0$. In this case, compared with the sbrMPBIL, the dbrMPBIL retrieves too many second best points. Therefore, for the dbrMPBIL, a better balance between the diversity and the fitness should be studied in the future, i.e. adaptively adjusting the value of parameter ε in the *diversity-based retrieving strategy*.

5 Discussions

The memory scheme is an effective technique for DOPs, especially in cyclic dynamic environments. The explicit memory scheme is one kind of memory schemes, and its retrieving strategy is very important because the retrieved memory individuals could impact its performance.

In this paper, two novel effective memory retrieving strategies, the *survivability-based retrieving strategy* and the *diversity-based retrieving strategy* , are developed for the associative memory scheme in MPBIL [16] to retrieve the most appropriate memory environmental information. Experimental results demonstrate both the *survivability-based retrieving strategy* and the *diversity-based retrieving strategy* have better performance.

Because of the page limit, experiments are only tested in cyclic environments. The experiments in cyclic with noise environments and random environments will be tested in the future. Additionally, the performance of the proposed retrieving strategies on the dynamic real-valued multimodal problems needed to be tested.

These two retrieving strategies could also be useful in other situations. Yang [19] proposed the AMGA (i.e. Genetic Algorithms with an associative memory scheme) for DOPs. The two retrieving strategies proposed in this paper could be extended to replace the memory retrieving strategy of the AMGA. This will be done in the future.

6 Conclusion

For EAs with memory schemes, how to retrieve the memory correctly is significantly important to improve their environmental adaptability. Furthermore, for many dynamic problems, the fitness value of an individual is not the unique measure that reflects its environmental adaptability. Therefore, some other factors, such as the survivability and the diversity, should be considered when retrieving the memory.

In this paper, two novel associative memory retrieving strategies are developed to retrieve the most appropriate memory environmental information. Several experiments are done on three dynamic test problems. According to the experimental results, the proposed associative memory retrieving strategies have a competitive performance. Especially, the *survivability-based retrieving strategy* is the best one.

Acknowledgments. This work is partly supported by the 2006-2007 Excellent Young and Middle-aged Academic Leader Development Program of Anhui Province Research Experiment Bases.

References

1. Grefenstette, J.J.: Genetic Algorithms for Changing Environments. In: Proceedings of Parallel Problem Solving From Nature, Amsterdam, Netherlands, pp. 137–144 (1992)
2. Mori, N., Kita, H.: Genetic Algorithms for Adaptation to Dynamic Environments - a Survey. In: Proceedings of the 2000 IEEE International Conference on Industrial Electronics, Control and Instrumentation, Nagoya, Japan, vol. 4, pp. 2947–2952 (2000)
3. Jin, Y., Branke, J.: Evolutionary Optimization in Uncertain Environments - a Survey. IEEE Transactions on Evolutionary Computation 9(3), 303–317 (2005)
4. Cobb, H.G.: An Investigation into the Use of Hypermutation as an Adaptive Operator in Genetic Algorithms Having Continuous. Time-Dependent Nonstationary Environments, NRL-MR-6760, United States (1990)
5. Tinós, R., Yang, S.: A Self-Organizing Random Immigrants Genetic Algorithm for Dynamic Optimization Problems. Genetic Programming and Evolvable Machines 8(3), 255–286 (2007)
6. Branke, J.: Memory Enhanced Evolutionary Algorithms for Changing Optimization Problems. In: Proceedings of the IEEE Congress on Evolutionary Computation (CEC 1999), Washington, DC, USA, pp. 1875–1882 (1999)
7. Yang, S.: Explicit Memory Schemes for Evolutionary Algorithms in Dynamic Environments: Evolutionary Computation in Dynamic and Uncertain Environments, vol. 51, pp. 3–28. Springer, Heidelberg (2007)
8. Oppacher, F., Wineberg, M.: Reconstructing the Shifting Balance Theory in a GA: Taking Sewall Wright Seriously. In: Proceedings of the 2000 IEEE Congress on Evolutionary Computation (CEC 2000), vol. 1, pp. 219–226 (2000)
9. Ursem, R.K.: Multinational GAs: Multimodal Optimization Techniques in Dynamic Environments. In: Proceedings of the 2000 Genetic and Evolutionary Computation Conference (GECCO 2000), Riviera Hotel, Las Vegas, USA, vol. 1, pp. 19–26 (2000)
10. Branke, J., Kaussler, T., Smidt, C., Schmeck, H.: A Multi-Population Approach to Dynamic Optimization Problems. In: Proceedings of the 4th International Conference on Adaptive Computing in Design and Manufacture (ACDM 2000), Plymouth, England, pp. 299–307 (2000)
11. Goldberg, D.E., Smith, R.E.: Nonstationary Function Optimization Using Genetic Algorithms with Dominance and Diploidy. In: Proceedings of the 2nd International Conference on Genetic Algorithms, USA, pp. 59–68 (1987)
12. Yang, S., Yao, X.: Experimental Study on Population-Based Incremental Learning Algorithms for Dynamic Optimization Problems. Soft Computing 9(11), 815–834 (2005)
13. Ramsey, C.L., Grefenstette, J.J.: Case-Based Initialization of Genetic Algorithms. Australian Electronics Engineering 27(2), 84–91 (1994)
14. Yang, S.: Memory-Based Immigrants for Genetic Algorithms in Dynamic Environments. In: Proceedings of the 2005 Genetic and Evolutionary Computation Conference (GECCO 2005), Washington, DC, US, vol. 2, pp. 1115–1122 (2005)
15. Yang, S.: Population-Based Incremental Learning with Memory Scheme for Changing Environments. In: Proceedings of the 2005 Genetic and Evolutionary Computation Conference (GECCO 2005), Washington, DC, US, pp. 711–718 (2005)

16. Yang, S., Yao, X.: Population-Based Incremental Learning with Associative Memory for Dynamic Environments. IEEE Transactions on Evolutionary Computation 12(5), 542–561 (2008)
17. Louis, S.J., Xu, Z.J.: Genetic Algorithms for Open Shop Scheduling and Re-Scheduling. In: Proceedings of the 11th International Conference on Computers and Their Applications (ISCA), pp. 99–102 (1996)
18. Baluja, S.: Population-Based Incremental Learning: A Method for Integrating Genetic Search Based Function Optimization and Competitive Learning. CMU-CS-94-163, United States (1994)
19. Yang, S.: Associative Memory Scheme for Genetic Algorithms in Dynamic Environments. In: Proceedings of EvoWorkshops 2006: Applications of Evolutionary Computing, Heidelberg, Germany, pp. 788–799 (2006)

An Algorithm of Mining Class Association Rules

Man Zhao[1,2], Xiu Cheng[2], and Qianzhou He[3]

[1] State Key Laboratory of Software Engineering, Wuhan University, Wuhan 430072, China
[2] School of Computer, China University of Geosciences, Wuhan 430074, China
[3] School of Forgein Languages, China University of Geosciences, Wuhan 430074, China

Abstract. The relevance of traditional classification methods, such as CBA and CMAR, bring the problems of frequent scanning the database, resulting in excessive candidate sets, as well as the complex construction of FP-tree that causes excessive consumption. This paper studies the classification rules based on association rules - MCAR (Mining Class Association Rules). The database only needs scanning once, and the cross-support operation is used for the calculation as the format of databases is vertical layout for easily computing the support of the frequent items. Not only the minimum support and minimum confidence is used to prune the candidate set, but also the concept of class-frequent items is taken into account to delete the rules that may hinder the effective improvement of the algorithm performance.

Keywords: class-frequent items; class association rules; data mining; associative classification.

1 Introduction

Frequent patterns and their corresponding association or correlation rules characterize interesting relationships between attribute condition and class labels. And thus have been recently used for effective classification. The general idea is that we can search for strong associations between frequent patterns (conjunctions of attribute-value pairs) and class labels, because association rules explore highly confident associations among multiple attributes. This approach may overcome some constraints introduced by decision-tree induction, which considers only one attribute at a time. In many studies, associative classification has been found to be more accurate than some traditional classification methods, such as C4.5[7].

Methods of associative classification differ primarily in the approach used for frequent item-sets mining and in how the derived rules are analyzed and used for classification. We now look at some of the various methods for associative classification, such as CBA[5] and CMAR[5]. CBA uses an iterative approach to frequent item-sets mining, similar to that described for Apriority[6], where multiple passes are made over the data and the derived frequent item-sets are used to generate and test longer item-sets. In general, the number of passes made is equal to the length of the longest rule found. CMAR (Classification based on Multiple Association Rules) differs from CBA in its strategy for frequent item-sets mining and its construction of the classifier. CMAR adopts a variant of the FP-growth algorithm to find the complete set of rules

Z. Cai et al. (Eds.): ISICA 2009, LNCS 5821, pp. 269–275, 2009.

satisfying the minimum confidence and minimum support thresholds and it. This requires two scans of D and employs another tree structure to store data. However, these two approaches may also suffer some weakness as show below. CBA needs to scan the data several times, and there are too much frequent items, and the structure of FP-tree is so complex.

How can we solve the above three problems? In this paper, we develop a new technique MCAR, for efficient classification and make the following contributions.

First, instead of scanning database several times, MCAR just construct the rule set at once. Second, to prune the redundant items that cannot product effective rules, we developed a criterion of redundant class-frequent items to prune weak rules before they are actually generated. Third, to improve the complex structure such as FP-tree, MCAR transform the horizontally formatted data to the vertical format by scanning the data once and counting support by intersecting the C-Tidset.

2   Definitions

Consider a relational data set D with n attribute domains. A record of D is a set of attribute-value pairs, denoted by T. A pattern is a subset of a record. We say a pattern is a k-pattern if it contains k attribute-value pairs. All the records in D are categorized by a set of classes C.

An implication is denoted by P→c, where P is called the antecedent, and c is called the consequence . The support of pattern P is defined to be the ratio of the number of records containing P to the number of all the records in D, denoted by **supp(P)**[6]. The support of the implication P→c is defined to be the ratio of the number of records containing both P and c to the number of all the records in D , denoted by **supp(P→c)** [6]. The confidence of the implication P→c is defined to be the ratio of supp(P→c) to supp(P) , represented by **conf(P→c)**[6] .

Theorem 1[3]. Given two rules R_1 and R_2, R_1 is said **having higher rank** than R_2, denoted as $R_1 > R_2$, if and only if (1) $conf(R_1) > conf(R_2)$; (2) $conf(R_1) = conf(R_2)$ but $sup(R_1) > sup(R_2)$; or (3) $conf(R_1) = conf(R_2)$, $sup(R_1) = sup(R_2)$, but R_1 has fewer attribute values in its left hand side than R_2 does. In addition, a rule R_1:P→c is said a general rule w.r.t. rule R2: P'→c', if and only if P is a subset of P'.

Theorem 2. If the class-confidence of a superset items less than or equal the class-confidence of some already found class-frequent items, the superset is said a **redundant class-frequent items.**

We have to know that the confidence of class-frequent items is the confidence for every class in the class-frequent items. More details are in 3.1.3.

3   Mining Algorithm

3.1   Basic Idea of the Proposed Algorithm

In order to decrease the times of scan the database and the number of frequent items, as well as improve the complex structure, we present a new algorithm, which is

MCAR (Mining Classification associate Rules). For expressing the algorithm clearly, we will develop data format, how to count the support, and pruning the class-frequent items in this part.

3.1.1 Mining Frequent Item-Sets with Class in Vertical Data Format

Theorem 3.C-Tidset. Data can be presented in item-CTID format (that is, {item: Class-Tidset}), where item is an item name, class is a finite set of class labels, and TID-set is the set of transaction identifiers containing the item.

For instants, the transactions 1,2,3,4,5 contain item a, the class label of 1,2,3,4,5 are ABABC, so the C-Tidset of a, which denoted by C-Tidset(a) is{ A: 13, B: 24, C: 5}.

3.1.2 Counting Support

1. Counting (scanning the data set). We transform the horizontally formatted data to the vertical format by scanning the data set with its class label at once. For every transaction, if it includes the item, recording the item's TID on its corresponding class label.

2. Intersecting the C-Tidset. Given two items X and Y, their C-Tidset are CT(X) and CT(Y),support can be computed by |CT(X)| and |CT(Y)|,or the support count of an item-sets is simply the length of the C-Tidset of the item-sets; Suppose the new class-frequent items $Z=X \cup Y$, in this way, support(Z)= |CT(X)∩CT(Y)|,or the length of intersecting X and Y.

For example, ce=c $\cup$ e={1,2,4,5}∩{2,4,5}={2,4,5},so supp (ce) =3.

3.1.3 Class-Frequent Item-Sets Pruning

For the size of Graphics, we had not denoted the class label except 1- item-sets. The class-frequent items in Fig.1 were pruning just by minimum support, which denoted by a slant. And we prune the redundant class-frequent items in Fig.2 by theorem 2,

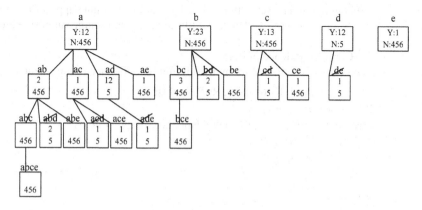

Fig. 1. Pruning just by minimum support, which denoted by a slant, without works by Theorem 2

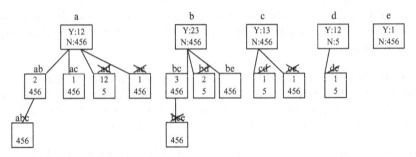

Fig. 2. Pruning by minimum support, which denoted by a slant, and at the same time, it is also works by Theorem 2,which denoted by a fork

denoted by a fork. First, we have to know that the confidence of class-frequent items is the confidence for every class in the class-frequent items. We use the following example to show it. The confidence of ae divide into two parts, they are Y25% (1) and N 75% (2). We prune (1) by the restriction of minimum confidence, and then for (2),we find out all its sub-items {a: Y 40%, a: N 60%,e: Y 25%,e: N 75%}.Since conf(e: N)=conf(ae: N), delete (2). At this moment, there is nothing in ae. In this way, it cannot product effective rules, so delete cf.. And we delete af, ap, bf, cm, cp, and fm in the same way. In this way, we can decrease the redundant class-frequent items in L_3 and L_4.

3.2   Algorithm Description

In this section, we develop a new associative-classification method, called MCAR, which performs Classification based on Association Rules.

   Algorithm: Mining Class Association Rules

   Input: database D with class attribute C, the minimum support and the minimum confidence.

   Output: class association rule set R.

          Scanning the data set with its class label at once, count support of items
          If supp>minsupp, add it to L_1 //Pruning by minimum support require-
ment
          Count confidence of items
          If conf>minconf // Pruning by minimum confidence requirement

             Form R_1 from L_1, R=R_1,L=L∪L_1
          Loop: Generate(L_{k-1})
          Pruning(L_k) //Remove the redundant class-frequent items
             Form R_k from L_k

             R=R∪R_k
          If L_k≠φ, GO Loop
       Return rule set R

In the following, we present and explain two unique functions in the proposed algorithm.

Function: Generate(L_{k-1})
Input: Lk-1 and minimum support
Output: class-frequent items that satisfy the minimum support requirement
        For all $X_i \in L_{k-1}$ do
        For all $X_j \in L_{k-1}, j < i$ do

        Potential class-frequent items $M_k = X_i \cup X_j$
            C-Tidset (M_k)= C-Tidset $(X_i) \cap$ C-Tidset(X_j)
// C-Tidset (M_k) is the Intersection of the TID based on class

                If supp(M_k)>minsupp// Pruning by minimum support requirement
                Add M_k to L_k
        Return L_k

Function: Prune(L_k)
Input: minimum confidence
Output: class-frequent items which satisfied the minimum confidence requirement
        For all l_i in L_k
        If conf (l_i) $\geq$ minconf do// Pruning by minimum confidence requirement
    Find out all the subsets l_{i-1} of l_i
                If conf (l_i) $\leq$ conf (l_{i-1})
                Delete l_i //Pruning by Theorem 2
        Return L_k

4 An Illustrative Example

We provide an example to show how the MCAR algorithm works in this section. In the following data set, Y and N are classes. We assume the minimum support is 0.5, and the minimum confidence is 0.5. Fig.2 shows the whole process of the MCAR algorithm. Since there are two classes Y and N, we just divide the box into two lines in order to separate the TID by different classes. The first line shows the transactions with class Y, and the second line show the transactions with class N. The class-frequent items which drawn by a slant for it is not satisfied the minimum support requirement, and which is drew by a fork since it works by Theorem 2.

Table 1. The transaction data set D in the illustrative example

TID	List of item_IDs	Class
1	a, c, d, e	Y
2	a, b, d	Y
3	b, c, f	Y
4	a, b ,c, e, f	N
5	a, b, c, d, e	N
6	a, b, c, e	N

Let us look at the following example:
1) For every transaction scanning the data set by their class label once. And, recording the frequency and the class label of the attribute in the database, counting the

support of items, using the minimum support of 0.5 to remove the items which are not satisfied the minimum support requirement, such as f, since its support is 0.33. In this way, we get the first class-frequent items $L_1=\{a, b, c, d, e\}$. Counting the confidence of them, selecting the rules with conf≥0.5 from L_1, we get the rule set $R_1=\{$ a→N 60%, b→N 60%, c→N 60%,d→Y 67%,e→N 75%$\}$.Finally, let R= R_1.There is one we have to notice is that L is empty at the beginning.

2) We descript how to generate L_2 in this section. We just combine the candidates in L_1 to product M_2, in the next stage, counting the support of items after intersecting the C-Tidset in L_1.After that, pruning the redundant items based on class by the minimum support 0.5, $L_2=\{ab, ac, ad, ae, bc, be, ce\}$. Computing the confidence based on class, in the next, we use the function Prune(L_k) to prune it. After pruning, $L_2=\{ab, ac, bc, be\}$ and form the rule set $R_2=\{$ ab→N 75%, ac→N 75%, bc→N 75%, be→N 100%$\}$,finally, let R=R∪R_2.

3) Repeat the above steps, $M_3=\{abc, bce\}$. Since conf(bce)=conf (be), we prune bce. In this way, $L_3=\{abc\}$.We get $R_3=\{$ abc→N 100%$\}$

4) Since $L_3=\{abc\}$, the number of item-sets in $L_3=1$,the algorithm stop working. Last, we get the rule set R= { a→N 60%, b→N 60%, c→N 60%,d→Y 67%, e→N 75%, ab→N 75%, ac→N 75%, bc→N 75%, be→N 100%, abc→N 100%},the total of 10 rules.

5   Conclusions

In the paper, we studied the problem of efficiently mining class association rules. And we proposed a new algorithm, which called MCAR (Mining Class Association Rules). We achieve 3 developments in this paper. First, it can decrease the times of scanning data set dramatically. Second, we improve the complex storage structure, such as FP-tree. Third, we expressed the data in item-CTID format, and counting support by intersecting the C-Tidset. In this way, we need not to scan the data several times; however we can get the rules set at once. Last, we developed a criterion of redundant class-frequent items to prune weak rules before they are actually generated, and presented an efficient algorithm to mine the class association rule set. We illustrated the proposed algorithm by an example and the results show that the our algorithm avoids much redundant computation required in mining the complete class association rule set, and hence improves efficiency of the mining process dramatically. Our example results show that the class association rule set which generated by MCAR has a much smaller size and has a more simple structure in comparison with other reported associative classification methods.

References

1. Liu, B., Hsu, W., Ma, Y.: Integrating classification and association rule mining. In: Proc. of the Int. Conf. on Knowledge Discovery and Data Mining (KDD 1998), New York, pp. 80–86 (1998-2008)
2. Wang, X.-z., Zhac, D.l.: Associative classification based on interestingness of rules. Computer Engineering and Applications 43(25), 168–171 (2007)

3. Li, W., Han, J., Pei, J.: CMAR: accurate and efficient classification based on multiple class-association rules. In: Proc. of 2001 IEEE Int. Conf. on Data Mining (ICDM 2001), San Jose, CA, pp. 369–376 (2001-2011)
4. Li, J.: On Optimal Rule Discovery. IEEE Transactions on knowledge and data engineering 18(4) (April 2006)
5. Han, J., Kamber, M.: Data Mining: Concepts and Techniques, pp. 181–184
6. Han, J., Kamber, M.: Data Mining: Concepts and Techniques, pp. 229–235
7. Han, J., Kamber, M.: Data Mining:Concepts and Techniques, p. 292
8. Zaki, M.J.: Mining Non-Redundant Association Rules. Data Mining and Knowledge Discovery 9, 223–248 (2004)

An Empirical Study on Several Classification Algorithms and Their Improvements

Jia Wu[1], Zhechao Gao[1], and Chenxi Hu[2]

[1] Faculty of Computer Science, China University of Geosciences,
Wuhan 430074, P.R. China
wujiawb@126.com
[2] State Key Laboratory of Information Engineering in Surveying,
Mapping and Remote Sensing, Wuhan University,
Wuhan 430079, P.R. China

Abstract. Classification algorithms as an important technology in data mining and machine learning have been widely studied and applied. Many methods can be used to build classifiers, such as the decision tree, Bayesian method, instance-based learning, artificial neural network and support vector machine. This paper focuses on the classification methods based on decision tree learning, Bayesian learning, and instance-based learning. In each kind of classification methods, many improvements have been presented to scale up the classification accuracy of the basic algorithm. The paper also studies and compares the classification performance on classification accuracy empirically, using the whole 36 UCI data sets obtained from various sources selected by Weka. The experiment results re-demonstrate the efficiency of all these improved algorithms.

Keywords: Classification, Decision tree learning, Bayesian learning, Instance-based learning, Empirical study, Classification accuracy.

1 Introduction

Classification plays an important role in data mining and machine learning. The purpose of classification algorithm is to construct a classifier, and then analyzes the characteristics of the unknown data to get an accurate model. The performance of the classifier is measured by its classification accuracy.

There are many ways to build classification algorithms, including decision tree method, Bayesian method, instance-based learning method, artificial neural network method [1], evolution algorithm [2], support vector machine [3], and so on. In the last few years, a lot of improved algorithms have been presented in these fields.

In this paper, we designed three sets of experiments, which can be expressed as decision tree methods (ID3, C4.5 [4], NBTree [5], Random Forest [6]), Bayesian methods (NB, HNB [7], AODE [8], Bayes Net [9]), and instance-based learning methods (KNN, KNNDW [10], LWNB [11], KStar [12]). In each experiment, we evaluate the performance of the improved algorithms compared with the traditional algorithms

Z. Cai et al. (Eds.): ISICA 2009, LNCS 5821, pp. 276–286, 2009.

using 10-fold cross validation. Finally, we conduct the information of two-tailed t-test with a 95% confidence level between each pair of algorithms.

The rest of paper is organized as follows. In Section 2, we give a formal description of the algorithms that we choose. Experimental process and results are presented in Section 3. Finally, we draw a conclusion of this paper.

2 Several Classification Algorithms and Their Improvements

2.1 Decision Tree Learning Algorithms

Decision tree is a tree-structure similar to the flow chart, which is one of the most basic inductive reasoning algorithms, and a discrete value function approximation methods. It searches from root node to leaf node to determine the class of instance. Each node represents the selected attribute, and splits according to the attribute values, where leaf nodes are the type of the instance. Each path from root node to leaf node corresponds to a classification rule. Each rule is the conjunction of the attribute. Then the tree can be represented in a disjunction expression.

The process of classification is recursively testing the node value from root to leaf, according to the attribute value of the testing instance.

- **Traditional algorithm (ID3)**
  ID3 is the basic algorithm in decision tree learning, the key point of ID3 is using information gain as an attribute selection standard to split at each step of building a tree. The attribute property which has the highest information gain is selected.
- **Improved algorithms (C4.5, NBTree, Random Forest)**
  C4.5 algorithm inherited the advantages of ID3 algorithm which uses information gain to split. The difference is that C4.5 trims the tree to avoid the "over-fitting". NBTree is the combination of decision tree and naive Bayes algorithm, which uses NB to split. Random Forest algorithm is a kind of decision tree combination classification method. It consists of a lot of regression trees, using the random selection to split which leads to a better noise tolerance.

In this paper, we use C4.5, NBTree, and Random Forest to compare with ID3.

2.2 Bayesian Learning Algorithms

Bayesian classification is a statistical classification method, which uses the methods of probability and statistics to classify. Its core is the Bayes theorem. The algorithm can be used for large-scale databases, which indicates the high accuracy and speed advantages.

- **Traditional algorithm (NB)**
  In the comparison with decision tree and neural network, a simple Bayesian classifier which is called Naive Bayes (NB) has a similar performance. In NB, we assume that the value of an attribute in a given category is independent to the other attribute value. In theory, when the assumption is establishment, the error rate of Bayesian is the smallest.

- **Improved algorithms (HNB, AODE, Bayes Net)**

    However, because of the inaccuracy of the assumption and the lack of available probability data, NB does not perform well in practice. Then there have been a lot of methods to reduce the independence assumption, such as HNB, AODE and Bayes Net. Hidden Naive Bayes (HNB) can be considered as a kind of restricted Bayesian network. A hidden parent is created for each attribute in HNB. It used the average of weighted one-dependence estimators to create hidden parents. HNB can be easily learned without structure learning because it inherits the structural simplicity of NB. Averaged One-Dependence Estimator (AODE) weakens the attribute independence assumption by averaging all models from a restricted class of one-dependence classifiers. It can achieve highly accurate classification. Bayes Net joints the conditional probability distribution, allowing defining the independence of the variables between subsets. And it also provides a graphical model of a causal relationship. Some other algorithms can be found in [13].

In this paper, we use HNB, AODE, and Bayes Net to compare with NB.

2.3 Instance-Based Learning Algorithms

Instance-based learning method, also known as "lazy-learning" method, simply puts the training sets stored until a test instance is given. It uses previously stored training sets to determine the class of the test sets.

Instance-based learning method includes nearest neighbor and locally weighted regression method. They all assume that the instance can be expressed as the point of European space, and can be used to approximate or discrete the objective function.

- **Traditional algorithm (KNN)**

    K-Nearest Neighbor (KNN) is the most basic algorithm of nearest neighbor method, which is based on the analog study. Each tuple of attribute corresponds to one point of the n-dimensional space. When given an unknown tuple, it searches the model space, to find k training tuples which are closest to the unknown. The k training tuples are known as the "nearest neighbor" of the unknown ones. We can use the Euclidean distance to find neighbors. KNN algorithm is on the nature of each attribute given equal weight. Its accuracy may be reduced when there is noise or unrelated data.

- **Improved algorithms(KNNDW, LWNB, KStar)**

    However, if we give the attribute different weights according to their distance, the nearer ones may get larger weight. The accuracy of the classification will be improved. This is called k-nearest neighbor algorithm on distance-weighted (KNNDW). Locally weighted naive Bayes (LWNB) method uses specific WeightedInstancesHandler (weight processor) to allocate the weight of attribute. KStar is an instance-based classifier, which is the class of a test instance is based upon the class of those training instances similar to it, which is determined by some similarity function. Some other algorithms can be found in [14].

In this paper, we use KNNDW, LWNB, and KStar to compare with the KNN.

3 Experiment

In this section, we designed three groups of experiments such as: decision tree (ID3, C4.5, NBTree, Random Forest), Bayesian (NB, HNB, AODE, Bayes Net), instance-based learning methods (KNN, KNNDW, LWNB, KStar). And we run our experiments under the framework of Weka [15] to validate the effectiveness of the novel algorithms.

3.1 Experimental Data

We run our experiments on 36 standard UCI data sets [16] which download from the main website of Weka. Detailed description of the data is shown in Table 1. Among them, the data preprocessing includes the following three steps [17]:

Table 1. Detailed information of experimental data

Dataset	Instances	Attributes	Classes	Missing	Numeric
anneal	898	39	6	Y	Y
anneal.ORIG	898	39	6	Y	Y
audiology	226	70	24	Y	N
autos	205	26	7	Y	Y
balance-scale	625	5	3	N	Y
breast-cancer	286	10	2	Y	N
breast-w	699	10	2	Y	N
colic	368	23	2	Y	Y
colic.ORIG	368	28	2	Y	Y
credit-a	690	16	2	Y	Y
credit-g	1000	21	2	N	Y
diabetes	768	9	2	N	Y
Glass	214	10	7	N	Y
heart-c	303	14	5	Y	Y
heart-h	294	14	5	Y	Y
heart-statlog	270	14	2	N	Y
hepatitis	155	20	2	Y	Y
hypothyroid	3772	30	4	Y	Y
ionosphere	351	35	2	N	Y
iris	150	5	3	N	Y
kr-vs-kp	3196	37	2	N	N
labor	57	17	2	Y	Y
letter	20000	17	26	N	Y
lymph	148	19	4	N	Y

Table 1. (*Continued*)

Dataset	Instances	Attributes	Classes	Missing	Numeric
mushroom	8124	23	2	Y	N
primary-tumor	339	18	21	Y	N
segment	2310	20	7	N	Y
sick	3772	30	2	Y	Y
sonar	208	61	2	N	Y
soybean	683	36	19	Y	N
splice	3190	62	3	N	N
vehicle	846	19	4	N	Y
vote	435	17	2	Y	N
vowel	990	14	11	N	Y
waveform-5000	5000	41	3	N	Y
zoo	101	18	7	N	Y

1. Replacing for the missing attribute values. In this paper, we use the unsupervised attribute filter *ReplaceMissingValues* in Weka to replace all the missing attribute value.
2. Discretizing for the numeric attribute values. In this paper, we used the unsupervised filter *Discretize* in Weka to handle all numeric attribute values in each data set.
3. Removing the useless attributes. In this paper, we used the unsupervised filter named *Remove* in Weka to remove these useless attributes. There are only three such attributes in the above-mentioned 36 data sets. They can be described as "Hospital Number" attribute in data set "colic.ORIG", "instance name" attribute in the data set "splice", as well as the "animal" attribute in data sets "zoo".

3.2 Experimental Methods

In this experiment, k value for k-nearest neighbor is set to Medium 5, and in LWNB it is set to 50. We use 10 runs of 10-fold cross validation to obtain the classification accuracy of each algorithm on each data set by Weka. And finally, we compare related algorithms via the information of two-tailed t-test with a 95% confidence level.

3.3 Experimental Results

Here, we assess the performance of three types improved algorithms (Decision tree methods, Bayesian methods, Instance-based learning methods) using the classification accuracy as the criterion. The higher the classification accuracy is, the better the corresponding classification effect is.

Table 2, Table 3, and Table 4 show the detailed results of the experiments about Decision tree methods, Bayesian methods, and Instance-based learning methods. If the data in the table is marked with "v", it means that the classification performance of this algorithm compared with the first algorithm in the table has significantly improved; if marked with "*", then has significantly lower.

The average value of the algorithm on 36 data sets in each table means the average classification accuracy. Then, to explain the w/t/l value of the t-test at the bottom of each table, we use Table 3 as an example. The w/t/l value of AODE is 14/21/1, it means that compared with NB, AODE wins 14, ties 21, and loses 1 on 36 standard data sets.

We also compared the Margin Num of the algorithms on 36 standard data sets. The Margin Num equals w value minus l value in w/t/l value at the bottom of tables. Now, let's summarize the highlights briefly as follows:

- Experiment 1: Decision tree methods (ID3, C4.5, NBTree, Random Forest)
  The experimental result is shown in Table 2. The classification accuracy of C4.5, NBTree, and Random Forest has markedly improved than ID3 (75.46). The ranking of these improved algorithms is NBTree (84.47), Random Forest (83.61), and C4.5 (82.64) from high to low according to classification accuracy. On the other hand, descending order according to the Margin Num is the Random Forest (26), NBTree (22), and C4.5 (22) on 36 standard data sets.

- Experiment 2: Bayesian methods (NB, HNB, AODE, Bayes Net)
  The experimental result is shown in Table 3. The classification accuracy of HNB, AODE, and Bayes Net has markedly improved than NB (82.34). The ranking of these improved algorithms is HNB (85.18), AODE (85.07), and Bayes Net (82.56) from high to low according to classification accuracy. On the other hand, descending order according to the Margin Num is the HNB (16), AODE (13), and Bayes Net (5) on 36 standard data sets.

- Experiment 3: Instance-based learning method (KNN, KNNDW, LWNB, KStar)
  The experimental result is shown in Table 4. The classification accuracy of KNNDW, LWNB, and KStar has markedly improved than KNN (82.09). The ranking of these improved algorithms is LWNB (85.65), KStar (83.69), and KNNDW (83.25) from high to low according to classification accuracy. On the other hand, descending order according to the Margin Num is LWNB (18), KNNDW (10), and KStar (8) on 36 standard data sets.

Table 2. Experimental results for C4.5, NBTree, Random Forest versus ID3: classification accuracy and standard deviation. The mean and w/t/l values are summarized at the bottom of the table.

Dataset	ID3	C4.5		NBTree		Random Forest	
anneal	99.62±0.66	98.65±0.97	*	98.40±1.53	*	98.82±1.11	
anneal.ORIG	89.63±2.93	90.36±2.51		91.27±3.03		91.28±2.98	
audiology	78.05±7.37	77.22±7.69		76.66±7.47		75.99±8.12	
autos	78.75±8.57	81.54±8.32		74.75±9.44		83.26±8.29	
balance-scale	37.74±4.92	64.14±4.16	v	91.44±1.30	v	76.61±4.01	v
breast-cancer	58.95±9.22	75.26±5.04	v	71.66±7.92	v	69.03±6.69	v
breast-w	90.12±3.11	94.01±3.28	v	97.23±1.76	v	95.91±2.42	v
colic	72.25±6.73	84.31±6.02	v	82.50±6.51	v	82.99±5.35	v
colic.ORIG	53.02±7.91	80.79±5.66	v	74.83±7.82	v	74.87±6.74	v
credit-a	73.84±5.32	85.06±4.12	v	84.86±3.92	v	83.72±4.06	v

Table 2. (*Contiued*)

Dataset	ID3	C4.5		NBTree		Random Forest	
credit-g	62.49±4.31	72.61±3.49	v	75.54±3.92	v	73.36±3.25	v
diabetes	60.31±4.85	73.89±4.7	v	75.28±4.84	v	72.59±4.77	v
glass	51.28±9.04	58.14±8.48		58.00±9.42		59.48±8.51	v
heart-c	62.42±9.04	79.14±6.44	v	81.10±7.24	v	77.45±7.22	v
heart-h	66.17±9.25	80.10±7.11	v	82.46±6.26	v	79.56±5.97	v
heart-statlog	62.07±9.12	79.78±7.71	v	82.26±6.50	v	78.33±7.92	v
hepatitis	71.01±9.72	81.12±8.42	v	82.90±9.79	v	81.70±8.04	v
hypothyroid	90.25±1.1	93.24±0.44	v	93.05±0.65	v	92.39±0.83	v
ionosphere	84.67±5.46	87.47±5.17		89.18±4.82	v	90.43±5.1	v
iris	90.80±7.26	96.00±4.64	v	95.27±6.16		94.87±5.35	v
kr-vs-kp	99.60±0.38	99.44±0.37		97.81±2.05	*	98.86±0.62	*
labor	73.40±16.26	84.97±14.24		95.60±8.39	v	88.37±12.24	v
letter	78.84±0.77	81.31±0.78	v	83.49±0.81	v	89.81±0.72	v
lymph	73.40±10.98	78.21±9.74		82.21±8.95	v	80.09±9.27	
mushroom	100.00±0	100.00±0		100.00±0.00		100.00±0	
primary-tumor	34.31±7.68	41.01±6.59	v	45.84±6.61	v	39.68±6.02	v
segment	92.11±1.77	93.42±1.67	v	92.64±1.61		95.59±1.39	v
sick	97.57±0.85	98.16±0.68	v	97.86±0.69		98.13±0.68	v
sonar	62.90±11.09	71.09±8.4	v	71.40±8.80	v	72.87±11.46	v
soybean	88.65±3.42	92.63±2.72	v	92.30±2.70	v	92.75±2.49	v
splice	89.75±1.65	94.17±1.28	v	95.42±1.14	v	90.09±1.78	
vehicle	61.28±4.25	70.74±3.62	v	68.91±4.58	v	70.70±4.05	v
vote	93.15±3.32	96.27±2.79	v	94.78±3.32		95.95±2.83	v
vowel	79.81±3.93	75.57±4.58	*	88.01±3.71	v	90.37±3.42	v
waveform-5000	61.31±2.18	72.64±1.81	v	81.62±1.76	v	77.52±1.93	v
zoo	97.12±4.96	92.61±7.33		94.55±6.54		96.52±4.77	
Average	75.46	82.64		84.47		83.61	
w/t/l	-	24/10/2		24/10/2		27/8/1	

Table 3. Experimental results for HNB, AODE, Bayes Net versus NB: classification accuracy and standard deviation. The mean and w/t/l values are summarized at the bottom of the table.

Dataset	NB	HNB		AODE		Bayes Net	
anneal	94.32±2.23	98.62±1.14	v	96.83±1.66	v	94.53±2.29	
anneal.ORIG	88.16±3.06	91.60±2.63	v	89.01±3.1		88.21±2.9	
audiology	71.40±6.37	73.15±6		71.66±6.42		75.99±6.48	v
autos	63.97±11.35	78.04±9.43	v	74.60±10.1	v	64.43±12.01	

Table 3. (*Continued*)

Dataset	NB	HNB		AODE		Bayes Net	
balance-scale	91.44±1.3	89.65±2.42	*	89.78±1.88	*	91.44±1.3	
breast-cancer	72.94±7.71	70.23±6.49		72.73±7.01		72.59±8.2	
breast-w	97.30±1.75	96.08±2.46		96.85±1.9		97.30±1.75	
colic	78.86±6.05	81.25±6.27		80.93±6.16		78.67±6.13	
colic.ORIG	74.21±7.09	75.50±6.57		75.38±6.41		73.97±6.49	
credit-a	84.74±3.83	84.84±4.43		85.86±3.72		84.62±3.85	
credit-g	75.93±3.87	76.86±3.64		76.45±3.88		75.89±3.89	
diabetes	75.68±4.85	75.83±4.86		76.57±4.53		75.57±4.82	
glass	57.69±10.07	59.33±8.83		61.73±9.69		58.48±10.88	
heart-c	83.44±6.27	81.43±7.35		82.84±7.03		83.41±6.19	
heart-h	83.64±5.85	80.72±6		84.09±6		83.40±5.98	
heart-statlog	83.78±5.41	81.74±5.94		83.63±5.32		83.81±5.39	
hepatitis	84.06±9.91	82.71±9.95		85.21±9.36		84.84±9.44	
hypothyroid	92.79±0.73	93.28±0.52	v	93.56±0.61	v	92.71±0.71	
ionosphere	90.86±4.33	93.02±3.98	v	91.74±4.28		90.86±4.26	
iris	94.33±6.79	93.93±6		94.00±5.88		94.33±6.45	
kr-vs-kp	87.79±1.91	92.35±1.32	v	91.03±1.66	v	87.81±1.9	
labor	96.70±7.27	90.87±13.15		94.57±9.72		96.50±7.82	
letter	70.09±0.93	86.13±0.69	v	85.54±0.68	v	70.34±0.92	v
lymph	85.97±8.88	82.93±8.96		85.46±9.32		85.50±8.87	
mushroom	95.52±0.78	99.96±0.06	v	99.95±0.07	v	96.22±0.75	v
primary-tumor	47.20±6.02	47.85±6.06		47.87±6.37		47.11±5.55	
segment	89.03±1.66	94.72±1.42	v	92.92±1.4	v	89.47±1.63	v
sick	96.78±0.91	97.78±0.73	v	97.52±0.72	v	96.83±0.91	
sonar	76.35±9.94	80.89±8.68		79.91±9.6		76.05±9.78	
soybean	92.20±3.23	94.67±2.25	v	93.31±2.85	v	93.06±2.98	v
splice	95.42±1.14	96.13±0.99	v	96.12±1	v	95.52±1.12	
vehicle	61.03±3.48	73.63±3.86	v	71.65±3.59	v	61.02±3.46	
vote	90.21±3.95	94.36±3.2	v	94.52±3.19	v	90.30±3.89	
vowel	66.09±4.78	92.99±2.49	v	89.64±3.06	v	66.80±4.87	
waveform-5000	79.97±1.46	83.58±1.61	v	84.24±1.6	v	79.98±1.44	
zoo	94.37±6.79	99.90±1	v	94.66±6.38		94.57±6.5	
Average	82.34	85.18		85.07		82.56	
w/t/l	-	17/18/1		14/21/1		5/31/0	

Table 4. Experimental results for KNNDW, LWNB, KStar versus KNN: classification accuracy and standard deviation. The mean and w/t/l values are summarized at the bottom of the table.

Dataset	KNN	KNNDW		LWNB		KStar	
anneal	97.12±1.54	97.78±1.43	v	98.85±0.90	v	98.73±1.01	v
anneal.ORIG	87.44±2.56	89.48±2.61	v	92.64±2.24	v	90.91±2.38	v
audiology	61.51±8.06	68.47±7.71	v	78.20±6.36	v	77.36±7.97	v
autos	66.46±9.92	73.89±9.63	v	78.52±9.59	v	79.90±8.31	v
balance-scale	84.54±3.16	84.54±3.16		85.92±2.87	v	87.71±2.21	v
breast-cancer	74.10±4.63	73.97±5.47		72.57±6.91		74.00±6.77	
breast-w	94.82±2.5	94.92±2.5		96.87±2.09	v	96.12±2.35	v
colic	80.46±6.1	81.68±6.15		79.70±6.43		77.64±5.73	
colic.ORIG	70.90±4.54	72.70±4.8	v	75.84±6.07	v	74.59±5.98	
credit-a	85.32±4.13	85.00±4.38		86.00±3.89		82.87±4.38	*
credit-g	71.99±2.5	72.60±2.8		73.36±3.14		71.53±3.53	
diabetes	70.31±3.68	70.58±3.94		72.97±4.23		70.39±3.9	
glass	58.71±9.19	59.33±8.7		65.19±8.70	v	61.22±8.92	
heart-c	79.93±7.99	80.59±7.9		80.10±7.98		80.17±7.83	
heart-h	82.39±5.79	82.46±5.92		82.69±5.71		82.97±5.62	
heart-statlog	81.04±5.96	81.15±6.16		81.04±5.50		82.22±6.27	
hepatitis	84.33±7.69	83.88±7.46		85.98±7.13		80.14±8.59	
hypothyroid	93.14±0.6	92.50±0.75	*	93.37±0.62		93.37±0.56	
ionosphere	89.72±4.69	89.77±4.68		92.42±4.07	v	90.97±4.35	
iris	93.00±6.24	94.13±5.86		95.40±5.58		92.93±6.62	
kr-vs-kp	96.16±1.02	96.44±1	v	97.79±0.80	v	96.91±0.92	v
labor	89.37±12.21	91.30±12.01		94.20±10.41		92.07±11.09	
letter	87.99±0.58	89.16±0.52	v	92.88±0.45	v	90.46±0.48	v
lymph	81.63±9.33	81.95±9.4		84.12±8.63		83.18±8.94	
mushroom	100.00±0.05	100.00±0		100.00±0.00		100.00±0	
primary-tumor	41.33±5.88	42.12±6.02		45.66±5.90		40.83±6.42	
segment	90.84±1.7	93.26±1.55	v	95.28±1.40	v	94.21±1.53	v
sick	97.44±0.66	97.76±0.69	v	98.14±0.66	v	97.69±0.68	
sonar	81.59±8.47	81.81±8.75		82.47±7.36		80.45±8.63	
soybean	90.73±3.02	90.75±3.06		93.72±2.62	v	92.25±2.72	
splice	79.86±1.86	82.14±1.7	v	94.25±1.35	v	78.84±1.96	
vehicle	70.13±3.91	70.67±3.9		71.63±3.65		69.75±4.54	
vote	93.84±3.41	93.40±3.46		95.95±2.74	v	92.80±3.63	
vowel	80.35±3.76	87.15±3.34	v	94.97±2.17	v	93.75±2.5	v

Table 4. (*Continued*)

Dataset	KNN	KNNDW	LWNB		KStar	
waveform-5000	74.02±1.71	74.08±1.67	78.38±1.67	v	67.75±1.71	*
zoo	92.57±6.52	95.53±5.17	96.25±5.57		96.23±5.44	
Average	82.09	83.25	85.65		83.69	
w/t/l	-	11/24/1	18/18/0		10/24/2	

4 Conclusion

In this paper, we firstly look back some improved algorithms of Decision tree methods, Bayesian methods, Instance based learning methods. Then, three groups of experiments are designed to compare the related improved algorithms with the basic algorithms on classification accuracy. The experimental results re-appeared the efficiency of all these improved algorithms. We believe that our work provide general knowledge for researchers to study all kinds of classification algorithms.

Acknowledgment

We very thank Mr. Liangxiao Jiang for his kindly guidance and help.

References

1. Fu, L.: A neural network model for learning domain rules based on its activation function characteristics. IEEE Transactions on Neural Networks 9, 787–795 (1998)
2. Hajela, P., Lee, E., Cho, H.: Genetic algorithms in topologic design of grillage structure. Computer-Aided Civil and Infrastructure Engineering 13, 13–22 (1998)
3. Mitchell, T.M.: Instance-Based Learning. In: Machine Learning, ch. 8. McGraw-Hill, New York (1997)
4. Quinlan, J.R.: C4.5: Programs for Machine Learning. Morgan Kaufmann, San Mateo (1993)
5. Kohavi, R.: Scaling up the accuracy of Naïve-Bayes classifiers: A decision tree hybrid. In: Proceedings of the Second International Conference on Knowledge Discovery and Data Mining, pp. 202–207. AAAI Press, Menlo Park (1996)
6. Breiman, L.: Random forests. Machine Learning 45, 5–32 (2001)
7. Zhang, H., Jiang, L., Su, J.: Hidden Naive Bayes. In: Proceedings of the 20th National Conference on Artificial Intelligence, AAAI 2005, pp. 919–924. AAAI Press, Menlo Park (2005)
8. Webb, B.J., Wang, Z.: Not So NaiveBayes: Aggregating One-Dependence Estimators. Machine Learning 58, 5–24 (2005)
9. Friedman, N., Geiger, D., Goldszmidt, M.: Bayesian network classifier. Machine Learning 29, 131–163 (1997)
10. Dudani, S.A.: The distance weighted k-nearest-neighbor rule. IEEE Transactions on Systems, Man, and Cybernetics 6, 325–327 (1976)

11. Frank, E., Hall, M., Pfahringer, B.: Locally Weighted Naive Bayes. In: Proceedings of the Conference on Uncertainty in Artificial Intelligence, pp. 249–256. Morgan Kaufmann, San Francisco (2003)

12. Cleary, J.G., Trigg, L.E.: K*: an instance-based learner using an entropic distance measure. In: Machine Learning: Proceedings of the 12th International, pp. 108–114 (1995)

13. Jiang, L., Wang, D., Cai, Z., Yan, X.: Survey of Improving Naive Bayes for Classification. In: Alhajj, R., Gao, H., Li, X., Li, J., Zaïane, O.R. (eds.) ADMA 2007. LNCS, vol. 4632, pp. 134–145. Springer, Heidelberg (2007)

14. Jiang, L., Cai, Z., Wang, D., Jiang, S.: Survey of Improving K-Nearest-Neighbor for Classification. In: Proceedings of the 4th International Conference on Fuzzy Systems and Knowledge Discovery, FSKD 2007, pp. 679–683. IEEE Computer Society Press, Haikou Hainan China (2007)

15. Witten, I.H., Frank, E.: Data Mining: Practical machine learning tools and techniques, 2nd edn. Morgan Kaufmann, San Francisco (2005)

16. Merz, C., Murphy, P., Aha, D.: UCI repository of machine learning databases. In: Department of ICS, University of California, Irvine (1997),
    http://prdownloads.sourceforge.net/weka/datasets-UCI.jar

17. Jiang, L., Li, C., Wu, J., Zhu, J.: A combined classification algorithm based on C4.5 and NB. In: Kang, L., Cai, Z., Yan, X., Liu, Y. (eds.) ISICA 2008. LNCS, vol. 5370, pp. 350–359. Springer, Heidelberg (2008)

Classification of Imbalanced Data Sets by Using the Hybrid Re-sampling Algorithm Based on Isomap

Qiong Gu[1,2], Zhihua Cai[2], and Li Zhu[2]

[1] Faculty of Mathematics & Computer Science, Xiangfan University, Xiangfan, Hubei, 441053, China
[2] School of Computer, China University of Geosciences, Wuhan, Hubei, 430074, China
gujone@163.com, zhcai@cug.edu.cn ,cugzhuli@163.com

Abstract. The majority of machine learning algorithms previously designed usually assume that their training sets are well-balanced, but data in the real-world is usually imbalanced. The class imbalance problem is pervasive and ubiquitous, causing trouble to a large segment of the data mining community. As the conventional machine learning algorithms have bad performance when they learn from imbalanced data sets, it is necessary to find solutions to machine learning on imbalanced data sets. This paper presents a novel Isomap-based hybrid re-sampling approach to improve the conventional SMOTE algorithm by incorporating the Isometric feature mapping algorithm (Isomap). Experiment results demonstrate that this hybrid re-sampling algorithm attains a performance superior to that of the re-sampling. It is clear that the Isomap method is an effective means to reduce the dimension of the re-sampling. This provides a new possible solution for dealing with the IDS classification.

Keywords: Isomap, Smote, NCR, re-sampling, Imbalanced data set.

1 Introduction

The majority of machine learning algorithms previously designed usually assume that their training sets are well-balanced, and implicitly assume that all misclassification errors cost equally. But data in real-world is usually imbalanced. The class imbalance problem is pervasive and ubiquitous, causing trouble to a large segment of the data mining community. Most of the existing state-of-the-art classification approaches are well developed by assuming the underlying training set is evenly distributed. However, they are faced with a severe bias problem when the training set is a highly imbalanced distribution. The resulting decision boundary is severely biased to the minority class,Thus, machine learning on imbalanced data sets becomes an urgent problem.

Imbalanced data classification often arises in many practical applications in the context of medical pattern recognition and data mining. For this purpose, many classification algorithms have been investigated intensively, such as the under-sampling technique over the majority class, the over-sampling technique over the minority class.

Z. Cai et al. (Eds.): ISICA 2009, LNCS 5821, pp. 287–296, 2009.

The synthetic minority over-sampling technique (SMOTE) [1]is an important approach by over-sampling the positive class or the minority class. However, it is limited to a strict assumption that the local space between any two positive instances is positive or belongs to the minority class, which may not always be true in the case when the training data is not linearly separable. However, mapping the training data into a more linearly separable space, where the SMOTE algorithm can be conducted, can circumvent this limitation. Once the positive class is over-sampled synthetically in the linearly separable space, the newly generated data should be transformed back into the original input space. The transformation mapping from input data space into the linearly separable space should be feasibly invertible in practice. For this purpose, the Isometric feature mapping (Isomap)[2] algorithm lends us a tool in design of an invertible mapping from the original input space to the linearly separable space. In this work, we present a novel hybrid re-sampling technique based on Isomap. The training data is first mapped into a lower-dimensional space by Isomap, where the input data is more separable, and thus can be over-sampled by SMOTE. The over-sampled samples were then under-sampled through NCR method yielding balanced low-dimensional data sets. The underlying re-sampling algorithm is implemented by incorporating the Isomap technique into the hybrid SMOTE and NCR algorithm. Experimental results demonstrate that the Isomap-based hybrid re-sampling algorithm attains a performance superior to that of the re-sampling. It is clear that the Isomap method is an effective mean of reducing the dimension of the re-sampling, which provides a new possible solution for dealing with the IDS classification.

The structure of this presentation is organized as follows: In section 2, we review the Isomap algorithm.Section 3 provides a brief overview of the resampling techniques considered in this work: random under-sampling, random over-sampling, SMOTE, NCR, et al. The Isomap-based hybrid re-sampling algorithm is presented in section 4, In Section 5,the existing evaluation measures of class imbalance problem are systematically analyzed and the performance comparison result of the Isomap-based hybrid re-sampling algorithm is analyzed and compared.Finally, the conclusion is drawn in Section 6.

2   Isometric Feature Mapping

Scientists working with large volumes of high-dimensional data, such as global climate patterns, or human gene distributions, regularly confront the problem of dimensionality reduction: finding meaningful low-dimensional structures hidden in their high-dimensional observations. Isomap[2] is an approach to solving dimensionality reduction problems that uses easily measured local metric information to learn the underlying global geometry of a data set. Unlike classical techniques such as principal component analysis (PCA) and multidimensional scaling (MDS), Isomap is capable of discovering the nonlinear degrees of freedom that underlie complex natural observations, such as human handwriting or images of a face under different viewing conditions. In contrast to previous algorithms for nonlinear dimensionality reduction, ours efficiently computes a globally optimal solution, and, for an important class of data manifolds, is guaranteed to converge asymptotically to the true structure. The Isomap algorithm consists of estimating geodesic distances using shortest-path distances and then finding an embedding of these distances in Euclidean space using MDS.

The complete isometric feature mapping, or Isomap, algorithm has three steps. The first step determines which points are neighbors on the manifold M, based on the distances $d_X(i, j)$ between pairs of points i, j in the input space X. Two simple methods are to connect each point to all points within some fixed radius ε, or to all of its K nearest neighbors. These neighborhood relations are represented as a weighted graph G over the data points, with edges of weight $d_X(i, j)$ between neighboring points. In its second step, Isomap estimates the geodesic distances $d_M(i, j)$ between all pairs of points on the manifold M by computing their shortest path distances $d_G(i, j)$ in the graph G. The final step applies classical MDS to the matrix of graph distances $D_G = \{d_G(i, j)\}$, constructing an embedding of the data in a d-dimensional Euclidean space Y that best preserves the manifold's estimated intrinsic geometry. The coordinate vectors y_i for points in Y are chosen to minimize the cost function

$$E = \left\| \tau(D_G) - \tau(D_Y) \right\|_{L^2} \tag{1}$$

where D_Y denotes the matrix of Euclidean distances $\{d_Y(i, j) = \left\| y_i - y_j \right\|\}$ and $\left\| A \right\|_{L^2}$ the L^2 matrix norm $\sqrt{\Sigma_{i,j} A_{ij}^2}$.

The τ operator converts distances to inner products, which uniquely characterize the geometry of the data in a form that supports efficient optimization. The global minimum of Eq. 1 is achieved by setting the coordinates y_i to the top d eigenvectors of the matrix $\tau(D_G)$.

3 Re-sampling

At the data level, the objective is to re-balance the class distribution by re-sampling the data space. These solutions include many different forms of re-sampling such as random over-sampling, random under-sampling, improved sampling techniques and combinations of the above techniques.

3.1 Basic Sampling Methods

One of the most direct ways for dealing with class imbalance is to alter the class distributions toward a more balanced distribution. There are two basic methods for balancing class distributions:

Random over-sampling is a non-heuristic method replicate examples of the minority class in order to achieve a more balanced distribution.

Random under-sampling is also a non-heuristic method aim to balance the data set by eliminating examples of the majority class.

Both under-sampling and over-sampling, have known drawbacks. Under-sampling can throw away potentially useful data, and random over-sampling can increase the likelihood of occurring over-fitting, since most of over-sampling methods make exact copies of the minority class examples.

The remainder balancing methods use heuristics in order to overcome the limitations of the non-heuristic methods.

3.2 Synthetic Minority Over-Sampling Technique (SMOTE)

SMOTE[3] is an over-sampling method. Its main idea is to form new minority class examples by interpolating between several minority class examples that lie together. Thus, the over-fitting problem is avoided and this causes the decision boundaries for the minority class to spread further into the majority class space.

If the amount of over-sampling needed is 200%, only two neighbors from the k nearest neighbor are chosen and one sample is generated in the direction of each. Synthetic samples are generated in the following way: Take the difference between the feature vector (sample) under consideration and its nearest neighbor. Multiply this difference by a random number between 0 and 1, and add it to the feature vector under consideration. This causes the selection of a random point along the line segment between two specific features. This approach effectively forces the decision region of the minority class to become more general.

3.3 Neighborhood Cleaning Rule (NCR)

Neighborhood Cleaning Rule (NCR) [4] uses the Wilson's Edited Nearest Neighbor Rule (ENN)[5] to remove majority class examples. ENN removes any example whose class label differs from the class of at least two of its three nearest neighbors. NCR modifies the ENN in order to increase the data cleaning. For a two-class problem the algorithm can be described in the following way: For each example E_i in the training set, its three nearest neighbors are found. If E_i belongs to the majority class and the classification given by its three nearest neighbors contradicts the original class of E_i, then E_i is removed. If E_i belongs to the minority class and its three nearest neighbors misclassify E_i, then the nearest neighbors that belong to the majority class are removed.

This algorithm is specific to K-nearest neighbor (KNN) classification method. This is often appropriate and can provide high generalization accuracy for real - world application, but the storage and computational requirements can be restrictive when the size of the training set is large. Results depend upon the order in which the data comes. This algorithm can be modified so that it will use the full data set and so as to remain unaffected by the order in which the data is coming. This algorithm removes noisy instances, as well as close border points which in turn smoothes decision boundary slightly. This helps avoiding over-fitting.

4 Isomap-Hybrid Re-sampling

SMOTE (Synthetic Minority Over-sampling Technique) is an approach by over-sampling the positive class or the minority class. However, it is limited to a strict assumption that the local space between any two minority class instances is minority class instances or belongs to the minority class, which may not be always true in the case when the training data is not linearly separable. Applicants note that mapping the training data into a more linearly separable space, where the SMOTE algorithm can be conducted, can circumvent this limitation. However, if the positive class is over-sampled synthetically in the linearly separable space, the newly generated data should be transformed back into the original input space. The transformation mapping from input data space into the linearly separable space should be feasibly invertible in practice. For this purpose, we presents a novel Isomap-based hybrid re-sampling approach to improving the conventional SMOTE algorithm by incorporating the Isomap algorithm.

The Isomap is employed for mapping from the original input space to the linearly separable space. Generally, the training data is first mapped into a lower-dimensional space by Isomap, where data is more separable. Then the SMOTE is applied to generate a desirable number of synthetic data points for the positive class. The over-sampled samples were then under-sampled through NCR method yielding balanced low-dimensional data sets. The implementation of this scheme is demonstrated in Table 1.The new re-sampled samples are created as follows:

Table 1. Isomap-hybrid re-sampling algorithm

Function Isomap-hybrid re-sampling(X,C+,C-,d,l,k) Return S
Input:
X: the original training set $X = \{x_1, x_2, ..., x_n \in R^N\}$
C-: majority class or negative class
C+: minority class or positive class
d: the dimension of original training set X
l: the reduced dimension by Isomap
k: a threshold for choosing a negative neighbor in Isomap
Output:
S:the reduced dimension hybrid re-sampled training set
Algorithm:
1、initialize parameter
2、Compute and find x_i's k nearest neighbors
3、Construct neighborhood graph
4、Compute shortest paths using Floyd method
5、Construct d-dimensional embedding using MDS method
6 、 generates new positive vectors by using SMOTE algorithm over embedding set Y
7 、 under-sampled the over-sampled samples through NCR method

5　Experiment

5.1　Data Set

We experimented with breast cancer data set, and it is summarized as follows. This data set is highly imbalanced and has been studied before by various researchers with different methods. We try to compare our proposed Isomap-based hybrid re-sampling method with hybrid re-sampling method. Here is the description of the data.

The breast cancer data set was first studied by Matjaz Zwitter & Milan Soklic[6] with their method, the multi-purpose incremental learning system AQ15.This data set includes 201 instances of no-recurrence-events class and 85 instances of recurrence-events class. The instances are described by 9 attributes, some of which are linear and some are nominal.

5.2 Performance Measurement

In learning extremely imbalanced data, the overall classification accuracy is often not an appropriate measure of performance. A trivial classifier that predicts every case as the majority class can still achieve very high accuracy. We use metrics such as true negative rate, true positive rate, G-mean, precision, recall, and F-measure to evaluate the performance of learning algorithms on imbalanced data. These metrics have been widely used for comparison. All the metrics are functions of the confusion matrix as shown in Table 2. The rows of the matrix are actual classes, and the columns are the predicted classes.

Table 2. Confusion matrix

	Predicted Positive Class	Predicted Negative Class
Actually Positive Class	True Positives (TP)	False Negatives (FN)
Actually Negative Class	False Positive (FP)	True Negatives (TN)

Based on Table 2, the performance metrics are defined as:

- $$\text{Accuracy} = \frac{TP + TN}{TP + TN + FP + FN}$$
- $$\text{True Positive Rate}(Acc^{+}) = \frac{TP}{TP + FN} = \text{Recall}^{+} = Sensitivity$$
- $$\text{True Negative Rate}(Acc^{-}) = \frac{TN}{TN + FP} = \text{Recall}^{-} = Specificity$$
- $$\text{False Positive Rate}(FPR) = \frac{FP}{TN + FP}$$
- $$\text{False Negative Rate}(FNR) = \frac{FN}{TP + FN}$$
- $$\text{Positive Predictive Value} = \frac{TP}{TP + FP} = Precision$$
- $$\text{Negative Predictive Value} = \frac{TN}{TN + FN}$$
- $$\text{G-mean} = \sqrt{Acc^{+} \cdot Acc^{-}}$$
- $$\text{F-measure} = \frac{2 \times Precision \times Recall}{Precision + Recall} \times 100\%$$

Traditionally, accuracy is the most commonly used measure for these purposes. However, for classification with the class imbalance problem, accuracy is no longer a proper measure since the rare class has very little impact on accuracy as compared to the prevalent class[7]. For example, in a problem where a rare class is represented by only 1% of the training data, a simple strategy can be to predict the prevalent class label for every example. It can achieve a high accuracy of 99%. However, this measurement is meaningless to some applications where the learning concern is the identification of the rare cases. For any classifier, there is always a trade off between true positive rate and true negative rate; and the same applies for recall and precision. In the case of learning extremely imbalanced data, quite often the rare class is of great interest. In many applications such as drug discovery and disease diagnosis, it is desirable to have a classifier that gives high prediction accuracy over the minority class (Acc+), while maintaining reasonable accuracy for the majority class (Acc−). The Geometric Mean(G-mean)[8] is used to assess the performance of their methods. Precision, recall and F-measure are commonly used in the information retrieval area as performance measures. We also use the area under a ROC curve to compare the performance of the Isomap-based hybrid re-sampling method. The ROC curve is a graphical representation of the trade off between the false negative and false positive rates for every possible cut off. The area under a ROC curve (AUC) provides a single measure of a classifier's performance for evaluating which model is better on average. There is a clear similarity between AUC and well-known Wilcoxon statistics. AUC can also be applied to evaluate the imbalanced data sets[9]. We will adopt all these measurements to compare our methods. Ten-fold cross-validations were carried out to obtain all the performance metrics.

5.3 Experiment and Experimental Results

The classifiers were considered since they are commonly-used in the machine learning community and in research on class imbalance. In order to validate the designing Isomap-hybrid re-sampling scheme, the imbalanced data set about breast cancer was examined. Data dimension reduction method was implemented in Matlab platform. Our re-sampling algorithms and classifier were built using WEKA, and don't changes to any default parameter values when experimentation showed a general improvement in the classifier performance across the datasets based on preliminary analysis.

Firstly, the original breast cancer input data dimension reduction were realized through Isomap method in MATLAB, and the low dimensional data sets were classified using J48 decision tree algorithm in weak platform.J48 uses the default WEKA parameter settings. Secondly, the SMOTE can be applied to generate a desirable number of synthetic data points for the positive class, the over-sampled samples were then under-sampled through NCR method. Then, we classified the balanced low dimensional data sets. Ten-fold cross-validations were carried out to obtain all the performance metrics.

The classification results are reported respectively in Table 3 and Table 4,Table 3 compare the classification performance of different dimension using Isomap method, and Table 4 compare the classification performance of different dimension using Isomap-hybrid re-sampling method.

The election of the Number of Nearest Neighbors, that is k, play a key role in data sets dimension reduction procedure using Isomap method, if the k value is too small, the graph will not be connected, and if the k value is too large, the Isomap algorithm will approximations to MDS algorithm, so the selection of k can directly affect classification performance, So the optimal k value is defined as "6 " by experiment.

Table 3. Performance coparison with Isomap method

Breast cancer	original data sets	9 dim.	8 dim.	7 dim.	6 dim.	5 dim.
AUC	0.955	0.967	0.967	0.974	0.967	0.973
F-measure+	0.958	0.971	0.971	0.972	0.971	0.972
F-measure-	0.921	0.947	0.947	0.949	0.947	0.949
TP_{rate}(Recall+)	0.956	0.965	0.965	0.965	0.961	0.959
TN_{rate}(Recall-)	0.925	0.959	0.959	0.963	0.967	0.975
G-mean	0.940	0.962	0.962	0.964	0.964	0.967
Accuracy	0.946	0.963	0.963	0.964	0.963	0.964

Table 4. Performance comparison with Isomap-based hybrid re-sampling method

Breast cancer	original data	9 dim.	8 dim.	7 dim.	6 dim.	5 dim.
AUC	0.955	0.991	0.988	0.988	0.992	0.986
F-measure+	0.958	0.994	0.989	0.990	0.987	0.991
F-measure-	0.921	0.995	0.990	0.991	0.989	0.992
TP_{rate}(Recall+)	0.956	0.993	0.989	0.995	0.991	0.991
TN_{rate}(Recall-)	0.925	0.996	0.990	0.985	0.985	0.992
G-mean	0.940	0.994	0.989	0.990	0.988	0.991
Accuracy	0.946	0.995	0.989	0.990	0.988	0.991

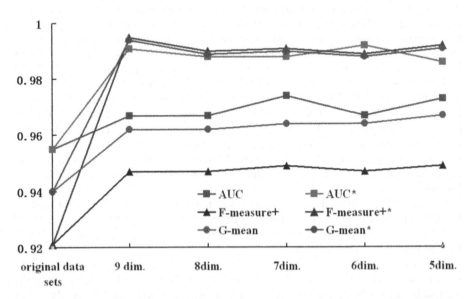

Fig. 1. Classification results with isomap method and Isomap-hybrid re-sampling method

Many practical classification problems are imbalanced,we pay special attention to the classification performance of positive class , for the sake of comparison,We combined classification results with Isomap method and Isomap-hybrid re-sampling method in fig.1 based on three measures(F-measure+, AUC and G-mean), the experimental results with Isomap method marked as F-measure+ , AUC , G-mean, and the experimental results with Isomap-hybrid re-sampling method marked as F-measure+*, AUC*, G-mean*.

From figure 1 we can see that,through the imbalanced input data sets dimension reduced processing ,By such a procedure, where the input data is more separable, and thus can be over-sampled by SMOTE. The over-sampled samples were then under-sampled through NCR method yielding balanced low-dimensional data sets. the evaluation measures were sequentially promoted and the classification performance is considerably improved, especially the F-measure of minority class. In fact, Not only is the classification performance of minority class improved significantly, but the overall classification performance is enhanced in a certain extent.

6 Conclusions

In this paper, we present a re-sampling technique, Isomap-based hybrid re-sampling, in classification of imbalanced data. The underlying re-sampling algorithm is implemented by incorporating the Isomap technique into the hybrid SMOTE and NCR algorithm. Experimental results demonstrate that the Isomap-based hybrid re-sampling algorithm attains a performance superior to that of the re-sampling. It is clear that the Isomap method is an effective mean of reducing the dimension of the re-sampling, which provides a new possible solution for dealing with the IDS classification.

References

1. Chawla, N.V., Bowyer, K.W., Hall, L.O., Kegelmeyer, W.P.: SMOTE: Synthetic Minority Over-sampling Technique. Journal of Artificial Intelligence Research 16, 321–357 (2002)
2. Tenenbaum, J.B., Silva, V., Langford, J.C.: A Global Geometric Framework for Nonlinear Dimensionality Reduction. Science 290, 2319–2323 (2000)
3. Chawla, N.V., Bowyer, K.W., Hall, L.O., Kegelmeyer, W.P.: SMOTE: Synthetic Minority Over-sampling Technique. Journal of Artificial Intelligence Research 16, 321–357 (2002)
4. Laurikkala, J.: Improving Identification of Difficult Small Classes by Balancing Class Distribution. In: Quaglini, S., Barahona, P., Andreassen, S. (eds.) AIME 2001. LNCS (LNAI), vol. 2101, pp. 63–66. Springer, Heidelberg (2001)
5. Wilson, L.D.: Asymptotic Properties of Nearest Neighbor Rules Using Edited Data. IEEE Transactions on Systems, Man and Cybernetics 2, 408–421 (1972)
6. Michalski, R.S., Mozetic, I., Hong, J., Lavrac, N.: The multi-purpose incremental learning system AQ15 and its testing application to three medical domains. In: The Fifth National Conference on Artificial Intelligence, pp. 1041–1045 (1986)

7. Weiss, G.M.: Mining with rarity: a unifying framework. In: Newsletter of the ACM Special Interest Group on Knowledge Discovery and Data Mining, vol. 6, pp. 7–19 (2004)
8. Kubat, M., Holte, R., Matwin, S.: Learning when negative examples abound. LNCS, pp. 146–153. Springer, Heidelberg (1997)
9. Bradley, A.P.: The use of the area under the ROC curve in the evaluation of machine learning algorithms. Pattern Recognition 30, 1145–1159 (1997)

Detecting Network Anomalies Using
CUSUM and EM Clustering

Wei Lu[1,2] and Hengjian Tong[3]

[1] Faculty of Computer Science, University of New Brunswick,
Fredericton, NB E3B 5A3, Canada
[2] Department of Electrical and Computer Engineering, University of Victoria,
Victoria, BC V8W 3P6, Canada
[3] Department of Computing Science and Technology, School of Computer Science
China University of Geosciences, Wuhan, Hubei, 430074, P.R. China
wlu@ece.uvic.ca

Abstract. Intrusion detection has been extensively studied in the last two decades. However, most existing intrusion detection techniques detect limited
number of attack types and report a huge number of false alarms. The hybrid
approach has been proposed recently to improve the performance of intrusion
detection systems (IDSs). A big challenge for constructing such a multi-sensor
based IDS is how to make accurate inferences that minimize the number of
false alerts and maximize the detection accuracy, thus releasing the security operator from the burden of high volume of conflicting event reports. We address
this issue and propose a hybrid framework to achieve an optimal performance
for detecting network traffic anomalies. In particular, we apply SNORT as the
signature based intrusion detector and the other two anomaly detection methods, namely non-parametric CUmulative SUM (CUSUM) and EM based clustering, as the anomaly detector. The experimental evaluation with the 1999
DARPA intrusion detection evaluation dataset shows that our approach successfully detects a large portion of the attacks missed by SNORT while also reducing the false alarm rate.

Keywords: Intrusion detection, clustering.

1 Introduction

Intrusion detection has been extensively studied since the seminal work by Anderson
[1]. Traditionally, intrusion detection techniques are classified into two categories:
misuse (signature-based) detection and anomaly detection. Misuse detection is based
on the assumption that most attacks leave a set of signatures in the stream of network
packets or in audit trails, and thus attacks are detectable if these signatures can be
identified by analyzing the audit trails or network traffic behaviors. However, misuse
detection is strictly limited to the known attacks. Detecting new attacks is one of the
biggest challenges faced by misuse detection.

To address the weakness of misuse detection, the concept of anomaly detection
was formalized in the seminal report of Denning [2]. Denning assumed that security

Z. Cai et al. (Eds.): ISICA 2009, LNCS 5821, pp. 297–308, 2009.
© Springer-Verlag Berlin Heidelberg 2009

violations could be detected by inspecting abnormal system usage patterns from the audit data. As a result, most anomaly detection techniques attempt to establish normal activity profiles by computing various metrics, and an intrusion is detected when the actual system behavior deviates from the normal profiles.

According to Axelsson [3], the early network anomaly detection systems are self-learning, that is, they automatically form an opinion of what the subject's normal behavior is. Self learning techniques combine the early statistical model based anomaly detection approaches, the AI based approaches, the biological models based approaches, and thus they still applied for current anomaly detection schemes. According to whether they are based on supervised or unsupervised learning techniques, anomaly detection schemes can be classified into supervised and unsupervised. Supervised anomaly detection establishes the normal profiles of systems or networks through training based on labeled datasets. In contrast, unsupervised anomaly detection attempts to detect intrusions without using any prior knowledge of attacks or normal instances. Although learning techniques achieve good results on network anomaly detection so far, they still face some challenges, such as "can machine learning be secure?" [4], "would behavioral non-similarity in training and testing data totally fail leaning algorithms on anomaly detection?" [5], and "what are the limitations for detecting previously unknown attacks due to large number of false alarms?" [6].

In order to overcome these challenges and keep the advantages of misuse detection, some researchers have proposed the idea of hybrid detection. There are currently two ways to achieve this goal, one is sequence based and the other is parallel based. Sequence based hybrid IDSs apply anomaly detection (or misuse detection) first and misuse detection (or anomaly detection) second [7-15]. Combing the advantages of both misuse and anomaly detection, hybrid IDSs achieve a better performance. However, the sequence based approaches might not provide a full coverage for the attack types due to the filtering of malicious (normal) traffic and also the sequence process will prolong the detection and make a real-time detection impossible. In contrast, parallel based hybrid IDSs apply multiple detectors in parallel and make an intrusion decision based on multiple output sources, which provide a wide coverage for intrusions and has the potential to detect previously unknown attacks [16-20]. One of the biggest challenges for parallel based IDSs is how to make accurate inferences that minimize the number of false alarms and maximize the detection accuracy.

In order to address the aforementioned issues, we propose in this paper a hybrid framework, combining the well-known SNORT signature based IDS and the other two anomaly detectors, namely non-parametric CUmulative SUM (CUSUM) and EM based clustering, As illustrated in Figure 1, the general architecture of our detection scheme consists of three major components, namely SNORT, feature analysis and CUSUM-EM detector. During feature analysis, we define and generate fifteen features to characterize the network traffic behavior, in which we expect the more the number of features, the more accurate the entire network will be characterized. These proposed features are then input to the CUSUM-EM detector, in which CUSUM based detector and EM clustering based detector are fused according to a set of scoring coefficients. The final intrusion decision is given through a fuzzy attacking probability output by the inference model.

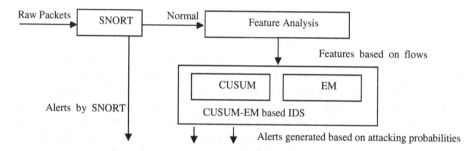

Fig. 1. General architecture of the detection framework

The rest of the paper is organized as follows. Section 2 introduces related work, in which we summarize some existing works on hybrid IDSs. Section 3 introduces the fifteen flow-based features and explains the reasons to select them. Section 4 overview the two existing anomaly detection approaches, namely CUSUM algorithm and the Expectation-Maximization (EM) based clustering algorithm. Section 5 presents the complete network anomalies analysis for the 1999 DARPA intrusion detection evaluation dataset by using our intrusion inference model. Section 6 makes some concluding remarks and discusses future work.

2 Related Work

Early research work on IDS suggest that intrusion detection capabilities can be improved through a hybrid approach consisting of both signature (misuse) detection as well as anomaly detection [8,9,10]. In such a hybrid system, the signature detection technique detects known attacks and the anomaly detection technique detects novel or unknown attacks. Typical recent research work for such a hybrid intrusion detection system are discussed in [7,11,12,13,14,15].

In [11], Tombini et al. applied an anomaly detection approach to create a list of suspicious items. Then a signature detection approach is employed to classify these suspicious items into three categories, namely false alarms, attacks, and unknown attacks. The approach is based on an assumption that a high detection rate can be achieved by the anomaly detection component because missed intrusions in the first step will not be found by the follow-up signature detection component.

Zhang et al. proposed a hybrid IDS combining both misuse detection and anomaly detection components, in which a random forest algorithm was applied firstly in the misuse detection module to detect known intrusions [12]. The outlier detection provided by the random forest algorithm is then utilized to detect unknown intrusions. Evaluations with a part of the KDDCUP'99 dataset showed that their misuse detection module generated a high detection rate with a low false positive rate and at the same time the anomaly detection component has the potential to find novel intrusions.

In [13], Peng et al. proposed a two-stage hybrid intrusion detection and visualization system that leverages the advantages of signature-based and anomaly detection methods. It was claimed that their hybrid system could identify both known and unknown attacks on system calls. However, evaluation results for their system were missed in the paper. The work is more like an introduction on how to apply a multiple stage intrusion detection mechanism for improving the detection capability of an IDS.

Similar with [12], Depren et al. proposed a novel hybrid IDS system consisting of an anomaly detection module, a misuse detection module and a decision support system [14]. The decision support system was used to combine the results of previous two detection modules. In the anomaly detection module, a Self-Organizing Map (SOM) structure was employed to model normal behavior and any deviation from the normal behavior would be classified as an attack. In the misuse detection module, a decision tree algorithm was used to classify various types of attacks. The final system was evaluated with the 1999 KDDCUP intrusion detection dataset and experimental results showed that the proposed hybrid approach gave better performance over individual approaches.

Based on the idea of combining the advantages of low false positive rate of signature based IDS and the ability of anomaly detection system (ADS) for detecting new or unknown attacks, Hwang et al. proposed and reported a new experimental hybrid intrusion detection system (HIDS) in [18]. The ADS was built in HIDS, in which anomalies were detected beyond the capabilities of well known signature based SNORT or Bro systems through mining anomalous traffic episodes from Internet connections. A weighted signature generation scheme was developed to combine ADS with SNORT through modeling signatures from detected anomalies. The HIDS scheme was evaluated with real Internet trace data mixed with 10 days of the 1999 DARPA intrusion detection data set. The obtained results showed that HIDS achieves a 60% detection rate, compared with 30% and 22% detection rate acquired by the SNORT and Bro systems, respectively.

Instead of combining signature detection techniques and anomaly detection techniques, some other hybrid systems fuse multiple anomaly detection systems according to some specific criteria considering that the detection capability for each anomaly detection technique is different. The main goal of such a hybrid system is to reduce the large number of false alerts generated by current anomaly detection approaches and at the same time keep an acceptable detection rate. Some examples of such research work are discussed in [16,17,18,19,20]. However, since such kinds of systems are just based on the idea of anomaly detection, they usually cannot outperform the other type of hybrid systems fusing misuse detection and anomaly detection.

3   Feature Analysis

The major goal of feature analysis is to select and extract robust network features that have the potential to discriminate anomalous behaviors from normal network activities. Since most current network intrusion detection systems use network flow data (e.g. netflow, sflow, ipfix) as their information sources, we focus on features in terms of flows.

The following five basic metrics are used to measure the entire network's behavior:

FlowCount: A flow consists of a group of packets going from a specific source to a specific destination over a time period. There are various flow definitions so far, such as netflow, sflow, ipfix, to name a few. Basically, one network flow should at least include source IP/port, destination IP/port, protocol, number of bytes and number of packets. Flows are often considered as sessions between users and services. Since attacking behaviors are usually different from normal user activities, they may be detected by observing flow characteristic.

PacketCount: The average number of packets in a flow over a time interval. Most attacks happen with an increased packet count. For example, Distributed Denial of Service (DDoS) attacks often generate a large number of packets in a short time in order to consume the available resources quickly.

ByteCount: The average number of bytes in a flow over a time interval. Through this metric, we can identify whether the network traffic consists of large size packets or not. Some previous Denial of Service (DoS) attacks use maximum packet size to consume the computation resources or to congest data paths, such as well known ping of death (pod) attack.

PacketSize: The average number of bytes per packet over a time interval.

FlowBehavior: The ratio between FlowCount and PacketSize. It measures the anomalousness of flow behavior. The higher the value of this ratio, the more anomalous the flows since most probing or surveillance attacks start a large number of connections with small packets in order to achieve the maximum probing performance.

Based on the above five metrics, we define a set of features to describe entire traffic behavior on networks. Let F denote the feature space of network flows, a 15-dimensional feature vector $f \in F$ can be represented as $\{f_1, f_2, ..., f_{15}\}$, where meaning of each feature is explained in Table 1.

Table 1. List of features

Features	Description
f_1	Number of TCP Flows per Minute
f_2	Number of UDP Flows per Minute
f_3	Number of ICMP Flows per Minute
f_4	Average Number of TCP Packets per Flow over 1 Minute
f_5	Average Number of UDP Packets per Flow over 1 Minute
f_6	Average Number of ICMP Packets per Flow over 1 Minute
f_7	Average Number of Bytes per TCP Flow over 1 Minute
f_8	Average Number of Bytes per UDP Flow over 1 Minute
f_9	Average Number of Bytes per ICMP Flow over 1 Minute
f_{10}	Average Number of Bytes per TCP Packet over 1 Minute
f_{11}	Average Number of Bytes per UDP Packet over 1 Minute
f_{12}	Average Number of Bytes per ICMP Packet over 1 Minute
f_{13}	Ratio of Number of flows to Bytes per Packet (TCP) over 1 Minute
f_{14}	Ratio of Number of flows to Bytes per Packet (UDP) over 1 Minute
f_{15}	Ratio of Number of flows to Bytes per Packet (ICMP) over 1 Minute

Empirical observations with the 1999 DARPA network traffic flow logs show that network traffic volumes can be characterized and discriminated through these features. For more information about the results of the empirical observation refer to [21].

4   Overview of Two Anomaly Detection Approaches

In this section, we briefly introduce the two network intrusion detection techniques, namely non-parametric Cumulative SUM (CUSUM) algorithm and

Expectation-Maximization (EM) based clustering algorithm. More information about CUSUM and EM clustering algorithm can be found in [22] and [23], respectively.

4.1 Non-parametric CUSUM Algorithm

The CUSUM algorithm is an approach to detect a change of the mean value of a stochastic process and it is based on the fact that if a change occurs, the probability distribution of the random sequence will also be changed. A basic assumption for the non-parametric CUSUM algorithm is that the mean value of the random sequence is negative during normal conditions, and becomes positive when a change occurs. Consequently, a transformation of $\{X_n\}$ into a new sequence $\{Z_n\}$ is necessary, which is given by $Z_n = X_n - \beta$, where β is a constant. The parameter β is set according to network normal conditions and it guarantees that the major part of values of the sequence Z_n is negative during normal conditions and becomes positive when a change occurs.

In practice, a recursive non-parametric CUSUM algorithm is used to detect anomalies online. The recursive version is presented in [22,24] and can be defined using a new sequence $\{Y_n\}$:

$$\begin{cases} Y_n = (Y_{n-1} + X_n - \beta)^+ \\ Y_0 = 0 \end{cases} \text{ where } x^+ = \begin{cases} x, & x > 0 \\ 0, & otherwise \end{cases}$$

where β is set in a fashion that the values of $X_n - \beta$ keep slightly negative during normal operations. As a result, increases in the metric are expected to be detected, once the values are bigger than β. A long time period of values larger than β will lead further increasing of the CUSUM function until a possible alarm level is reached.

A large value of Y_n is a strong indication of an attack. Based on this, we define an attacking probability p to measure the anomalous degree of initial sequence X_n:

$$p = \begin{cases} \dfrac{Y_n}{\alpha \times \beta}, & Y_n < \alpha \times \beta \\ 1.0, & otherwise \end{cases}$$

where p is the attacking probability for sequence X_n; α is an adjusting parameter, which is used to amplify the value of β and is set as such constant 1, 2,...; Y_n is the CUSUM value of sequence X_n.

4.2 EM Based Clustering Algorithm

EM algorithm is widely used to estimate the parameters of Gaussian Mixture Model (GMM). GMM is based on the assumption that the data to be clustered are drawn from one of several Gaussian distributions. It is suggested that Gaussian mixture distributions can approximate any distribution up to an arbitrary accuracy, as long as a sufficient number of components are used. Consequently, the entire data collection is seen as a mixture of several Gaussian distributions, and their corresponding probability density functions can be expressed as a weighted finite sum of Gaussian components with different parameters and mixing proportions. The conditional probability in EM describes the likelihood that data points approximate a specified Gaussian component. The greater the value of conditional probability for a data point belonging to a specified Gaussian component, the more accurate the approximation is. As a result, data points are assigned to the corresponding Gaussian components according to their conditional probabilities. However, in some cases, there exist some data points whose conditional probability of belonging to any component of a GMM is very low or close to zero. These data are naturally seen as the outliers or noisy data. All the outlier data will be deleted or considered as anomalies during anomaly detection, and their attacking probability is set to 1.0. Algorithm 1 illustrates a detailed EM based clustering algorithm in which C_m stands for the clustering results.

Algorithm 1. EM based clustering algorithm

Function EMCA (data) **returns**
 clusters C_m and posterior probability $p_r(i \mid x_n)$
  $C_m = \phi$, $1 \le m \le k$, k is the number of clusters
  Call EM (data);
  For $1 \le m \le k$, $1 \le n \le N$
   If ($p_{r-1}(m \mid x_n) = \max(p_{r-1}(m \mid x_n))$)
   Then assign x_n to C_m
  Return C_m, $m = 1, 2..., k$

In order to apply the EM based clustering technique for detecting network anomalies, we make two basic assumptions: (1) the input data points are composed of two clusters, namely anomalous cluster and normal cluster; (2) the size of the anomalous cluster is always smaller than the size of the normal cluster. Consequently, we can easily label the anomalous cluster according to the size of each cluster. The attack probability for each data point is equal to the conditional probability of the corresponding data point belonging to the anomalous cluster, which is defined as follows:

$$p = p_{r-1}(C_{anomalous} \mid x_n)$$

where x_n is the data point; $C_{anomalous}$ is the anomalous cluster; $p_{r-1}(C_{anomalous} \mid x_n)$ is the conditional probability of x_n belonging to anomalous cluster $C_{anomalous}$.

5 Performance Evaluation

We evaluate our hybrid IDS with the full 1999 DARPA intrusion detection dataset. In particular, we conduct a comprehensive analysis for network traffic provided by the dataset and identify the intrusions based on each specific day. Since most current existing network intrusion detection systems use network flow data (e.g. netflow, sflow, ipfix, etc.) as their information sources, we covert all the raw TCPDUMP packet data into flow based traffic data by using the public network traffic analysis tools (e.g. editcap [25], tshark [26]), similarly with the 1999 KDDCUP dataset [27] in which the 1998 DAPRA intrusion detection dataset [28] has been converted into connection based dataset. Although the 1998 and 1999 DARPA dataset was criticized in [29,30] due to the methodology for simulating actual network environment, they are the widely used and acceptable benchmark for the current intrusion detection research.

During the evaluation, the results are summarized and analyzed in three different categories, namely how many attack instances are detected by each feature and all features correlation, how many attack types are detected by each feature and all features correlation and how many attack instances are detected for each attack type. We do not use the traditional Receiver Operating Characteristic (ROC) curve to evaluate our approach and analyze the tradeoff between the false positive rates and detection rates because ROC curves are often misleading and incomplete [31].

Compared to most, if not all, other evaluations with the 1999 DARPA dataset, our evaluation covers all types of attacks and all days' network traffic and thus, we consider our evaluation as a comprehensive analysis for network traffic in the 1999 DARPA dataset. Next, we will analyze and discuss the intrusion detection results we obtain. More information about the 1999 DAPRA/MIT Lincoln intrusion detection dataset and the method for converting the TCPDUMP packet logs into network flow based logs can be found in [32] and [33], respectively.

The scoring coefficient is set up according to the detection rate (DR) and the false positive rate (FPR) for each detector over a long time history. The higher the DR, the better the performance of the detector; the lower the FPR, the better the detector performance. Therefore, the ratio of DR to FPR is used to measure the performance of each detector. We evaluate individually the two detectors with the 15 features and 9 days DARPA testing data on week 4 and week 5. The evaluation results are summarized and analyzed in three different categories described in above.

For the detector using EM based clustering technique, Table 2 illustrates the average value of DR, FPR and the ratio of DR to FPR for each feature over those 9 days. For the detector using CUSUM algorithm, Table 3 illustrates the average value of DR, FPR and the ratio of DR to FPR for each feature.

Based on the ratio of DR to FPR in Tables 2 and 3, we normalize them and use the normalized values as elements of the scoring coefficient matrix, which is given as follows:

$$\begin{bmatrix} 0.78 & 0.81 & 0.95 & 0.7 & 0.74 & 0.34 & 0.51 & 0.58 & 0.73 & 0.84 & 0.0 & 0.76 & 0.54 & 0.65 & 0.72 \\ 0.22 & 0.19 & 0.05 & 0.3 & 0.26 & 0.66 & 0.49 & 0.42 & 0.27 & 0.16 & 0.0 & 0.24 & 0.46 & 0.35 & 0.28 \end{bmatrix}$$

The coefficient matrix has 2 rows and 15 columns. Row 1 means the historical reputation weight for the detector using EM based clustering algorithm and row 2 stands for the historical reputation weight for CUSUM based detector. Columns 1 to 15 stand for the features F1 to F15.

During our evaluation, we have known that there are 15 features and 2 detectors included in the detection system, and we denote n and m the number of features and the number of detectors, respectively. We define S_1 as the detector using EM based clustering algorithm and S_2 as the CUSUM based detector. $C_{S_jF_i}$ stands for the scoring coefficient matrix, where i = 1,2,...,15 and j = 1,2. $p_{F_iS_j}$ is the attacking probability generated by feature F_i and detection agent S_j and p_{F_i} is the attacking probability of the hybrid detection system with a specific features F_i. Based on these, we have the attacking probability for the CUSUM-EM based IDS as follows:

$$p_{F_i} = \sum_{j=1}^{2} p_{F_iS_j} \times C_{S_jF_i} \qquad i = 1,2,...,15$$

Table 2. Performance of all 15 features over 9 days evaluation for EM detector

Features	Average DR (%)	Average FPR (%)	Ratio of Avg. DR to Avg. FPR
F1	39.83	81.84	0.487
F2	52.22	84.04	0.621
F3	32.25	84.14	0.383
F4	12.0	89.03	0.135
F5	51.8	85.74	0.604
F6	32.25	84.17	0.383
F7	3.2	82.92	0.0386
F8	49.26	84.19	0.585
F9	32.25	84.14	0.383
F10	6.81	86.71	0.0785
F11	0.0	0.0	0.0
F12	32.25	84.17	0.383
F13	8.57	94.59	0.0906
F14	52.41	83.59	0.627
F15	32.25	84.17	0.383

Table 3. Performance of all 15 features over 9 days evaluation for CUSUM detector

Features	Average DR (%)	Average FPR (%)	Ratio of Avg. DR to Avg. FPR
F1	11.04	80.43	0.137
F2	12.96	85.94	0.15
F3	1.6325	87.33	0.02
F4	4.9	84.44	0.058
F5	17.84	82.42	0.217
F6	7.23	95.5	0.757
F7	2.94	79.61	0.037
F8	33.57	78.18	0.429
F9	11.5	81.1	0.142
F10	1.4	94.87	0.015
F11	0.7	95.24	0.0074
F12	10.8	87.26	0.124
F13	6.015	77.18	0.078
F14	27.73	81.85	0.339
F15	12.87	86.12	0.15

We evaluated the detection system with one day's DARPA testing data (i.e. W4D1). There are 14 attack types on W4D1 and total 13 attack types are detected by our hybrid system. The DR in terms of attack types is 92.8%. The number of attack types detected by using the CUSUM technique only is 5, the number is 8 with the EM based clustering only and the number is 5 using the SNORT signature based IDS. More detailed detection results regarding the hybrid detection system see [20].

6 Conclusions and Future Work

We propose in this paper a new hybrid model for detecting network anomalies. In order to characterize the behavior of the network flows, we present a 15-dimensional feature vector and the empirical observation results with the 1999 DARPA intrusion detection dataset show that the proposed features have the potential to distinguish the anomalous activities from normal network behaviors. A complete traffic analysis for the 1999 DARPA intrusion detection dataset is conducted using the hybrid IDS with two well-known intrusion detection sensors. Based on the achieved evaluation results, we conclude that the proposed detection detect successfully the attacks missed by the signature based IDS, SNORT, and has the potential to find unknown intrusions through the attacking probability.

The future work mainly consists of the following three parts:

(1) We will include more detectors into our system in the near future. Currently we tested our model using only two existing detection techniques. We expect that the more the number of detection techniques involved with the system, the better the hybrid performance.

(2) We will develop more evaluation metrics to judge the fusion performance.

(3) Based on (1) and (2), we will improve the hybrid system through dynamic programming techniques. The final goal of this work is to answer such a theoretical question: how one plus one is bigger than two by exploring multi-detector techniques?

References

1. Anderson, J.P.: Computer Security Threat Monitoring and Surveillance. Technical Report, James P. Anderson Co., Fort Washington, Pennsylvania (1999)
2. Denning, D.E.: An Intrusion Detection Model. IEEE Transactions on Software Engineering 2, 222–232 (1987)
3. Axelsson, S.: The Base-Rate Fallacy and the Difficulty of Intrusion Detection. ACM Transactions on Information and System Security (TISSEC) 3(3), 186–201 (2000)
4. Barreno, M., Nelson, B., Sears, R., Joseph, A.D., Tygarcan, J.D.: Can Machine Learning be Secure? In: Proceedings of the 2006 ACM Symposium on Information, Computer and Communications Security, pp. 16–25 (2006)
5. Sabhnani, M., Serpen, G.: Analysis of a Computer Security Dataset: Why Machine Learning Algorithms Fail on KDD Dataset for Misuse Detection. Intelligent Data Analysis 8(4), 403–415 (2004)
6. Patcha, A., Park, J.M.: An Overview of Anomaly Detection Techniques: Existing Solutions and Latest Technologies Trends. Computer Networks: The International Journal of Computer and Telecommunications Networking 51(12), 3448–3470 (2007)
7. Barbarra, D., Couto, J., Jajodia, S., Popyack, L., Wu, N.: ADAM: Detecting Intrusions by Data Mining. In: Proceedings of the 2001 IEEE, Workshop on Information Assurance and Security, West Point, NY (June 2001)
8. Lunt, T.F., Tamaru, A., Gilham, F., Jagannathm, R., Jalali, C., Neumann, P.G., Javitz, H.S., Valdes, A., Garvey, T.D.: A Real-time Intrusion Detection Expert System (IDES). Technical Report, Computer Science Laboratory, SRI International, Menlo Park, USA (February 1992)
9. Anderson, D., Frivold, T., Tamaru, A., Valdes, A.: Next Generation Intrusion Detection Expert System (NIDES). Software Users Manual, Beta-Update release. Computer Science Laboratory, SRI International, Menlo Park, CA, USA, Technical Report SRI-CSL-95-0 (May 1994)
10. Porras, P., Neumann, P.: EMERALD: Event Monitoring Enabling Responses to Anomalous Live Disturbances. In: Proceedings of the 20th NIST-NCSC National Information Systems Security Conference, Baltimore, MD, USA, pp. 353–365 (1997)

11. Tombini, E., Debar, H., Mé, L., Ducassé, M.: A Serial Combination of Anomaly and Misuse IDSes Applied to HTTP traffic. In: Proceedings of the 20th Annual Computer Security Applications Conference, Tucson, AZ, USA (2004)
12. Zhang, J., Zulkernine, M.: A Hybrid Network Intrusion Detection Technique using Random Forests. In: Proceedings of the 1st International Conference on Availability, Reliability and Security, pp. 262–269. Vienna University of Technology (2006)
13. Peng, J., Feng, C., Rozenblit, J.W.: A Hybrid Intrusion Detection and Visualization System. In: Proceedings of the 13th Annual IEEE International Symposium and Workshop on Engineering of Computer Based Systems, pp. 505–506 (2006)
14. Depren, O., Topallar, M., Anarim, E., Ciliz, M.K.: An Intelligent Intrusion Detection System (IDS) for Anomaly and Misuse Detection in Computer Networks. Expert Systems with Applications 29(4), 713–722
15. Qin, M., Hwang, K., Cai, M., Chen, Y.: Hybrid Intrusion Detection with Weighted Signature Generation over Anomalous Internet Episodes. IEEE Transactions on Dependable and Secure Computing 4(1), 41–55
16. Xiang, C., Lim, S.M.: Design of Multiple-level Hybrid Classifier for Intrusion Detection System. In: Proceedings of the IEEE Workshop Machine Learning for Signal Processing, pp. 117–122 (2005)
17. Thames, J.L., Abler, R., Saad, A.: Hybrid Intelligent Systems for Network Security. In: Proceedings of the 44th ACM Annual Southeast Regional Conference, pp. 286–289
18. Peddabachigari, S., Abraham, A., Grosan, C., Thomas, J.: Modeling Intrusion Detection System using Hybrid Intelligent Systems. Special issue on Network and Information Security: A Computational Intelligence Approach. Journal of Network and Computer Applications 30(1), 114–132 (2007)
19. Shon, T., Moon, J.: A Hybrid Machine Learning Approach to Network Anomaly Detection. International Journal on Information Sciences 177(18), 3799–3821 (2007)
20. Sabhnani, M.R., Serpen, G.: Application of Machine Learning Algorithms to KDD Intrusion Detection Dataset within Misuse Detection Context. In: Proceedings of International Conference on Machine Learning: Models, Technologies, and Applications, pp. 209–215 (2003)
21. http://nsl.cs.unb.ca/wei/hybrid.htm
22. Wang, H.N., Zhang, D.L., Hin, K.G.: Detecting SYN flooding attacks. In: Proceedings of IEEE INFOCOM 2002 (June 2002)
23. Lu, W., Traore, I.: Unsupervised anomaly detection using an evolutionary extension of K-means algorithm. International Journal on Information and Computer Security 2(2), 107–139 (2008)
24. Peng, T., Leckie, C., Ramamohanarao, K.: Detecting distributed denial of service attacks using source IP address monitoring. Draft (November 2002)
25. http://www.ethereal.com/docs/man-pages/editcap.1.html
26. http://www.wireshark.org/docs/man-pages/tshark.html
27. http://kdd.ics.uci.edu/databases/kddcup99/
    kddcup99.html.kddcup
28. http://www.ll.mit.edu/IST/ideval/data/1998/
    1998_data_index.html
29. Mahoney, M.V., Chan, P.K.: An analysis of the 1999 DARPA/Lincoln Laboratory evaluation data for network anomaly detection. In: Proceedings of the 6th International Symposium on Recent Advances in Intrusion Detection, Pittsburgh, PA, USA, pp. 220–237 (2003)

30. McHugh, J.: Testing intrusion detection systems: a critique of the 1998 and 1999 DARPA intrusion detection system evaluations as performed by Lincoln Laboratory. ACM Transactions on Information and System Security 3(4), 262–294 (2000)

31. Gaffney, J.E., Ulvila, J.W.: Evaluation of intrusion detectors: a decision theory Approach. In: Proceeding of IEEE Symposium on Security and Privacy, pp. 50–61 (2001)

32. http://www.ll.mit.edu/IST/ideval/data/1999/1999_data_index.html

33. Lu, W., Ghorbani, A.A.: Network anomaly detection based on wavelet analysis. EURASIP Journal on Advances in Signal Processing (2008) (in press)

Multiobjective Optimization in Mineral Resources Exploitation: Models and Case Studies

Ting Huang and Jinhua Chen

China University of Geosciences, Wuhan 430074, China

Abstract. Economic models for mineral resources assessment are transferring from single objective to multiple objectives nowadays. However, common approaches to solve these multi-criteria problems are still staying in single-objective methods, by combining all objective functions into a single functional form, but such methods can only obtain one solution. In this paper, NSGA-II,a multiobjective optimization evolutionary algorithm, is adopted to optimize multiple objectives of mineral resource exploitation.Two case study prove that NSGA-II can offer multiple solutions and be irrelevant with starting point, moreover, results by NSGA-II are better than references.

1 Introduction

Traditional economic models for mineral resources assessment are of single objective - maximization of the profit. However, current assessment involves multi-objectives, such as population, resources, economy, environment. And these goals are conflictive, generally with constraint.

Common approaches to solve multi-objectives mineral resources assessment problem are transferring them into single objective problems by weighting these objectives, since the later is easy to be deal with by traditional methods, such as sequential quadratic programming (SQP), pattern search etc..

The earliest research about multi-criteria in mineral resource economic evaluation can be dated back in the early 1990s. Zhong Ziran, Pei Rongfu and Wu Liangshi proposed the optimization and economic evaluation models for regional mineral resources development planning system in 1990 ([24]). And Yang Changming and Chen Longgui considered regional mineral resources dominant level and its index system of evaluation ([3]) at the same year.

Subsequent research works on how to balance the weight of multiple objectives, in order to solve multi-attribute problems in mineral resource filed by single-objective solutions. Wei Yiming etc. developed an integrated intelligent decision system of mineral resource exploitation, using neural network ([22],[23]). Song Guangxing made some progress on multi-attribute decision-making in exploitation of mineral resources, on which a composed weight method was proposed ([11],[12]). Yan Junyin adopted analytic hierarchy process(AHP), a structured technique for dealing with complex decisions and the most popular method on

Z. Cai et al. (Eds.): ISICA 2009, LNCS 5821, pp. 309–317, 2009.

assigning weight, to establish the indexes system and evaluation model for evaluating the reasonable exhaustion of regional mineral resources([13]).

However, the above researches can only obtain one solution for multi-objective
problems. And one solution can't satisfy users who prefer to have more schemes
(choices).

Evolutionary algorithms(EA), the new popular approaches in multi-objective
optimization, are to provide a set of solutions, and therefore can meet the various needs of users. Successful cases in water resources management arouse our
interest to apply EA on mineral resource economic research([14,20,19,10]).

2 Multiobjective Optimization and Evolutionary Algorithms

2.1 Multiobjective Optimization and Solution Methods

Multi-objective optimization (or programming), also known as multi-criteria or
multi-attribute optimization, is the process of simultaneously optimizing two or
more conflicting objectives subject to certain constraints([16],[18],[2]).

In mathematical terms, the multiobjective problem can be written simply as:

$$Min/MaxZ = (Z_1, Z_2, .., Z_p)$$
$$Z_i = f_i(x)$$
$$Subject\ to:$$
$$h(x) = 0$$
$$g(x) < 0 \tag{1}$$
$$where$$
$$x - Decision variables$$
$$Z_i - The\ i_th Decision objectives$$
$$h(x), g(x) - Constraint conditions$$

Solution methods for the above problems are([2]):

1. Constructing a single aggregate objective function (AOF).
   The basic idea is to combine all of the objective functions into a single functional form, called the AOF. A well-known combination is the weighted linear
   sum of the objectives. Clearly, the solution obtained will depend on the values of the weights specified. Thus, it may be noticed that the weighted sum
   method is essentially subjective, in that a decision manager (DM) needs
   to supply the weights. Moreover, this approach cannot identify all non-
   dominated solutions([7]).
   Actually, most of the works listed in section 1 fall into this scope.
2. Normal Boundary Intersection (NBI) method.
   This approach is to find several Pareto optimal points, which collectively
   capture the trade-off among the various conflicting objectives. This is an
   improvement over continuation techniques for tracing the trade-off curve
   since continuation strategies cannot easily be extended to handle more than
   two objectives.([6])

3. Indirect Optimization on the basis of Self-Organization (IOSO). IOSO technology is based on the response surface methodology approach. At each IOSO iteration the internally constructed response surface model for the objective is being optimized within the current search region. This step is followed by a direct call to the actual mathematical model of the system for the candidate optimal point obtained from optimizing internal response surface model. During IOSO operation, the information about the system behavior is stored for the points in the neighborhood of the extremum, so that the response surface model becomes more accurate for this search area.([9])

4. Multiobjective Optimization Evolutionary Algorithms (MOEA). Evolutionary algorithms are very popular approaches in multiobjective optimization now. And genetic algorithms such as the Non-dominated Sorting Genetic Algorithm-II (NSGA-II) and Strength Pareto Evolutionary Approach 2 (SPEA-2) have become standard approaches. The former method is adopted in our research.([7])

5. Normal Constraint (NC) method. It can generate a set of evenly spaced solutions on a Pareto frontier for multiobjective optimization problems, using a new formulation of the NC method that incorporates a critical linear mapping of the design objectives and a Pareto filter which is useful in the application of the NC and other methods. ([15])

6. Pareto surface generation for convex multiobjective instances (PGEN). This algorithm presents a method for computing well distributed points on the (convex) Pareto optimal surface of a multiobjective programming problem, and is applied to intensity-modulated radiation therapy inverse planning problems, in three and four dimensions, investigating tradeoffs between tumor coverage and critical organ sparing. ([5])

2.2 NSGA & NSGA-II

The Non-dominated Sorting Genetic Algorithm (NSGA) proposed in Srinivas and Deb ([17]) is one of the first such evolutionary algorithms. Over the years, it have been criticized mainly for([8]):

1. Their $O(mN^3)$ computational complexity (where m is the number of objectives and N is the population size);
2. Their non-elitism approach;
3. The need to specify a sharing parameter δ_{share}.

To alleviates all of the above three difficulties, Deb, Pratap, Agarwal and Meyarivanwe propose a much improved version of NSGA ,a non-dominated sorting-based MOEA, called NSGA-II, which adopt a fast non-dominated sorting approach to decrease the computational complexity, a selection operator to create a mating pool and elitist approach to speed up the performance of the GA([8]).

Because of its efficiency and ability to obtain diverse solutions, it becomes one of the most popular GA method for multi-objective optimization problems.

3   Two Case Study

Two cases on mineral resources exploitation are chosen to be tested step-by-step by NSGA-II. We chose the GAToolbox ([1]) as the tool, which can be modify easily to adapt user's problems.

3.1   Study on Optimizing Service Year and Profit of Ore Bodies Exploitation in Gejiu Tin Mine

This case is from reference [4], which use a single-point iterative method, from one point to the next point, and finally to the best solution. However, a set of optimal solutions can be obtained by NSGA-II.

Models. A company, named Yunan Yuxi Co., planed to exploit two ore bodies, whose reserves are 1,782,940 and 7,523,200 tons. It wants to maximize both the profit and the time of mineral resource serve, with the constraint that production scales, by determining the ideal output of each body.

According to reference [4], the mathematical model can be written as:

$$Max(f_1(x_1), f_2(x_2))$$
$$f_1(x_1, x_2) = 13.346x_1 + 4.746x_2 \quad \%total\ profit$$
$$f_2(x_1, x_2) = -0.0056x_1 - 0.00133x_2 \quad \%total\ sevice\ year$$
$$subject\ to$$
$$5x_1 + 10x_2 \leqq 200 \tag{2}$$
$$x_1 \leqq 10 \quad \%x_1 : Output\ of\ Ore\ 1$$
$$x_2 \leqq 15 \quad \%x_2 : Output\ of\ Ore\ 2$$
$$x_1 \geqslant 0$$
$$x_1 \geqslant 0$$

However, this model is far from perfect. We make some improvements on it as following:

1. Delete the constraint: $5x_1 + 10x_2 \leqq 200$, which is redundant since the x_1 and x_2 domain are [0,10], [0,15] respectively,$5x_1 + 10x_2$ will be never larger than 200.
2. Narrow the x_1 and x_2 domain. Although it is right these two decision variables be declared to be larger than 0, based on mathematical analysis, they must bigger than 1 in real word. No ore production can be profitable if their output is less than $1t/year$.
3. Change the second objective function back to it original form as showed on equation 3.This change is the result of shrinking of x_1 and x_2 domain, so the two variables will never reach the zero, and will cause calculation overflow if they are assigned as the denominators.

We propose a simple and practical model(see Equation 3).

$$Max(f_1(x_1), f_2(x_2))$$
$$f_1(x_1, x_2) = 13.346x_1 + 4.746x_2$$
$$f_2(x_1, x_2) = 178.294/x_1 + 752.32/x_2$$
$$subject\ to$$
$$x_1 \leqq 10$$
$$x_2 \leqq 15 \tag{3}$$
$$x_1 \geqslant 1$$
$$x_1 \geqslant 1$$

Results. To illustrate the efficiency of NSGA-II, we chose the most general parameters(See Tab. 1).

Table 1. NSGA-II Parameters

Number of decision variables	2
Number of objectives	2
population size	100
Maximum generations	400
Replace proportion selection	0.9
Selection type	tournament, size 2
Crossover probability	0.9
Crossover types and parameters	SBX, 0.5, 10
Mutation probability	0.1
Mutation types and parameters	Polynomial, 20

We just ran once, and got the results, illustrated by Fig. 1, where "*" represents our results and "#" was calculated by reference [4].

Fig. 1 shows that almost all solutions were found, and most of them are close the Pareto front, while the result suggested by the reference [4] was not one of the best solutions, although it was very close to.

3.2 Study on Optimizing Multiple Objectives on Exploiting a Copper Ore Body

This case is from Ming Yang's PhD thesis ([21]), where a multi-objective development model of a mineral resource was proposed, based on considering the interactive relation of economies-resources-environment in the mining production.

Models. Since Ming Yang's model is designed for an improved Hooke and Jeeves search algorithm, we revise it for NSGA-II(see Equation 3.2).

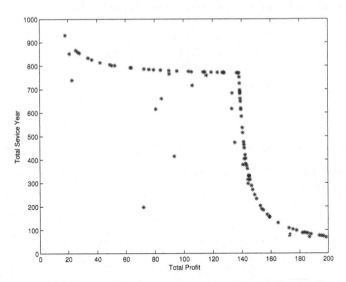

Fig. 1. NSGA-II Results of Total Profit and Total Service Year

$MaxGP(x_1, x_2)$ %*gross profit*
$MaxNPV(x_1, x_2)$ %*net present value*
$MaxROI(x_1, x_2)$ %*return on investment*
$MaxFIRR(x_1, x_2)$ %*Financial Internal Rate of Return*
$MaxMRUR(x_1, x_2)$ %*mineral resource utilization rate*
$MinPP(x_1, x_2)$ %*payback period*
subject to
$x_1 \leqq Q(x_2) * K / (T * (1 - \theta))$
$x_2 \leqq C_m$
$x_1 \leqslant A_{min}$
$x_1 \leqslant C_c$
where
   $GP(x_1, x_2), NPV(x_1, x_2), \ldots, PP(x_1, x_2)$ *their detail description*
      can be refereed to Ming Yang's PhD thesis ([21])
   $Q()$ *reserve calculate function*
   K *recovery ratio of mineral*
   T *time limit of mineral deposit serve*
   θ *ratio of waste rock*
   C_m *average grade*
   A_{min} *the minimum scale of operations*
   C_c *cutoff grade*

Results. We take the same parameters as 1 did, except that there 6 objectives this time.

Fig. 2 shows a 3-D scatter graph with NPV, FIRR and PP, the most interested objectives, since it is possible to put all 6 dimension result into one figure. Still,

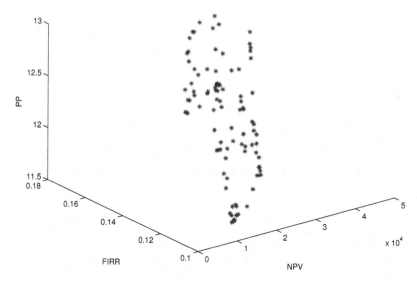

Fig. 2. NSGA-II Results of PV, FIRR and PP

"*" represents our results and "#" was calculated by reference . We can see that "#" is surrounded by "*"s, and suggest that solutions obtained by NSGA-II are so plenty[1].

3.3 Discussion

Two case study show that NSGA-II has obvious merits on multiple attributes optimization in economics assessment of mineral resource exploitation, comparing to traditional approaches.

1. Multiple solutions. NSGA-II offers plenty of solutions. In fact, each individual in the population is a solution.
2. Starting point independent. NSGA-II doesn't need the good initial points, actually, it just randomly generates the beginning points, unlike other iterative methods, who generally need a good start.

Besides an appropriate tool, extensive knowledge of the domain is also helpful to narrow the search, as we did in case1, proposing a simple and effective model.

4 Conclusions

For multi-objectives mineral resources assessment problem, NSGA-II is an efficient tool, whose features are to offer multiple solutions and to be irrelevant

---

[1] We can compare NSGA-II further with the method adopted by reference [21], on efficiency, success rate, and convergence etc., if Yang's program had less bugs and more clear description of the model parameters.

with starting point, while the transitional methods only give one solution and is sensitive to the initial point . Two case study prove the above merits of NSGA-II, moreover, NSGA-II gives better results than references.

References

1. Gatoolbox source code, `http://www.illigal.uiuc.edu/pub/src/GA/`
2. Multiobjective optimization,
   `http://en.wikipedia.org/wiki/Multiobjective_optimization#cite_note-0`
3. Changming, Y., Longgui, C.: Regional mineral resources dominant level and its index system of evaluation(in Chinese). Geological Science and Technology Information 9(4), 51–57 (1990)
4. Chunxue, L., Youbin, L., Yong, Z.: Application of multi-objective programming methods in setting the production and management parameters(in Chinese). Journal of Yunnan University of Finance and Economics 18(2), 91–94
5. Craft, D., Halabi, T., Shih, H., Bortfeld, T.: Approximating convex pareto surfaces in multiobjective radiotherapy planning. Medical Physics 33(9), 3399–3407 (2006)
6. Das, I., Dennis, J.E.: Normal-boundary intersection: A new method for generating the Pareto surface in nonlinear multicriteria optimization problems. SIAM Journal on Optimization 8(3), 631–657 (1998)
7. Deb, K.: Multi-Objective Optimization Using Evolutionary Algorithms. Wiley, Chichester (2001)
8. Deb, K., Pratap, A., Agarwal, S., Meyarivan, T.: A fast and elitist multiobjective genetic algorithm: NSGA-II. In: IEEE Evolutionary Computation, April 2002, vol. 6, pp. 182–197 (2002)
9. Egorov, I.: Indirect optimization method on the basis of self-organization. In: C.U. of Technology (ed.) Proceedings of International Conference on Optimization Techniques and Applications (ICOTA 1998), vol. 2 (1998)
10. Giustolisi, O., Doglioni, A., Savic, D.A., di Pierro, F.: An evolutionary multiobjective strategy for the effective management of groundwater resources. Water Resources Research 44(1) (January 3, 2008)
11. Guangxing, S.: Multi-attribute Decision-making in Exploitation Of Mineral Resources: Theory, Methods and Applications. PhD thesis, Kunming University of Science and Technology (2001)
12. Guangxing, S., Xin, Q., Huai, L.: An entropy technlogy-based evaluation method of the comprehensive exploitation and utilization of mineral resources (in Chinese). China Mining Magazine 9(3), 26–29 (2009)
13. Junyin, Y., Guojie, Z., Weidong, S.: On the sustainable development of regional allocation of mineral resources(in Chinese). Ecological Economy
14. Meixia, L., Xinmiao, W.: Water resources optimal allocation based on multi-objective genetic algorithm. In: Zhang, H., Zhao, R., Zhi, R. (eds.) Proceedings of The 2007 International Conference on Agriculture Engineering. International Conference on Agriculture Engineering, Baoding, Peoples R China, October 20-22, pp. 87–91. Orient Acad. Forum; Agr. Univ. Hebei; Blue Mt. Grp. Pty. Ltd.; Beijing Zhongjing Cent. Invest. Co. LTD (2007)
15. Messac, A., Ismail-Yahaya, A., Mattson, C.: The normalized normal constraint method for generating the Pareto frontier. Structural and Multidisciplinary Optimization 25(2), 86–98 (2003)

16. Sawaragi, Y., Nakayama, H., Tanino, T.: Theory of Multiobjective Optimization (Mathematics in Science and Engineering), p. 296. Academic Press, Orlando (1985)
17. Srinivas, N., Deb, K.: Multiobjective optimization using nondominated sorting in genetic algorithms. Evolutionary Computation 2(3), 221–248 (1995)
18. Steuer, R.E.: Multiple Criteria Optimization: Theory, Computation and Application, p. 546. John Wiley, New York (1986)
19. Tang, Y., Reed, P.M., Kollat, J.B.: Parallelization strategies for rapid and robust evolutionary multiobjective optimization in water resources applications. Advances in Water Resources 30(3), 335–353 (2007)
20. Yang, C.-C., Chang, L.-C., Yeh, C.-H., Chen, C.-S.: Multiobjective planning of surface water resources by multiobjective genetic algorithm with constrained differential dynamic programming. Journal of Water Resources Planning and Management-Asce 133(6), 499–508 (2007)
21. Yang, M.: Sustainable operation modes in mnining industry (in Chinese). PhD thesis, Central South University (2001)
22. Yiming, W., Guangxu, T.: Study on multi-objective decision-making system based on economic evaluation of mineral resources(in Chinese). Mining and Metallurgy 7(2), 1–6 (1998)
23. Yiming, W., Weixuan, X., Ying, F.: Multiple objective integrated methodology for global optimum decision making on resources exploitation(in Chinese). In: Systems Engineering-Theory and Practice
24. Ziran, Z., Rongfu, P., Liangshi, W.: Optimization and economic evaluation models for regional mineral resources development planning system(in Chinese). Geological Review 36(5), 436–443 (1990)

Robust and Efficient Eye Location and Its State Detection

Rui Sun and Zheng Ma

University of Electronic Science and Technology of China Zhongshan Institue, China
waltersun@foxmail.com, zma@zsc.edu.cn

Abstract. This paper proposes a robust and efficient eye state detection method based on an improved algorithm called LBP+SVM mode. LBP (local binary pattern) methodology is first used to select the two groups of candidates from a whole face image. Then corresponding SVMs (supporting vector machine) are employed to verify the real eye and its state. The LBP methodology makes it robust against rotation, illumination and occlusion to find the candidates, and the SVM helps to make the final verification correct.

Keywords: eye location, eye state, LBP, SVM.

1 Introduction

Eyes are the most important features of the human face, they can reflect the human physiological or psychological status. Eye state (open or closed) is very important in the driving fatigue detection, especially when it has been proven that the fatigue has a very high correlation with the PERCLOS [1]. Liu Zhaojie [2] also uses eye state to discuss the quality of the photos and makes the correction on those photos with closed eyes. Some methods to determine the eye state depend on establishing a classifier to distinguish two default types of states, which is strongly required to find the exact eyes location.

To determine the location of the eyes have a lot of ways. Obviously, projection [3,4] is a simple method, which is able to lock the eye region quickly by making use of the features of the eyes with lower gray value. But it is easily disrupted by the low quality of the photos, as well as the brows, mouth, and other regions of low gray scale. but the accuracy and the precision may not be available to the state classifier. We can also build up a classifier to distinguish between the eyes from the non-eyes, but first of all, we should choose a characteristic, which is associated with the eyes with a high degree, to select candidates of the location of the eyes, otherwise, the classifier would be very inefficient, especially in some real-time monitoring system.

Ying Zheng [5] adopts a robust and efficient algorithm to determine the location of the eyes. At first, the LBP of current picture is formed, then the Chi square distance of each points of the picture is calculated, through the projection method to obtain a group of candidates with higher eye-related degree, and finally a SVM is used as a grader, and it would choose the point which has the highest score as the eye position.

We improve this algorithm and call it LBP + SVM mode. first of all, we prepare two state (open and closed) LBP histogram templates, and calculate two Chi square

Z. Cai et al. (Eds.): ISICA 2009, LNCS 5821, pp. 318–326, 2009.
© Springer-Verlag Berlin Heidelberg 2009

distance value matrixes between current picture and the two templates separately, then select two groups of candidate points according to the matrixes, and finally make the judgment by putting the points with their pixel neighborhood through the corresponding SVMs to find the maximum score. The point with the maximum score is determined as the eye location and the eye state is determined according to which group the point is from. In this way, we can not only get eye state but also the eye location.(Fig. 1.)

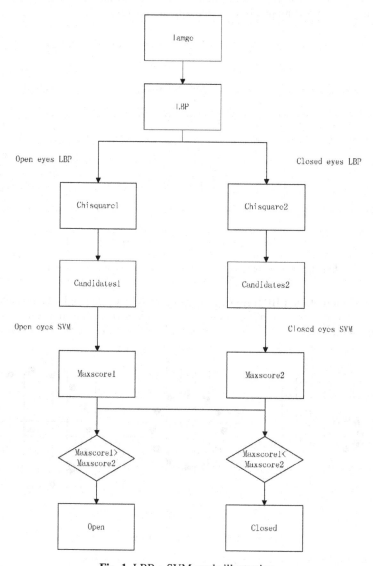

Fig. 1. LBP + SVM mode illustration

2 LBP + SVM Mode

2.1 LBP Methodology

The local binary pattern (LBP) operator was first introduced as a complementary measure for local image contrast [6]. The basic operator worked with the eight-neighbors of a pixel, using the value of the center pixel as a threshold. An LBP code for a neighborhood was produced by multiplying the thresholded values with weights given to the corresponding pixels, and summing up the result (Fig. 2.).

example

6	5	2
7	6	1
9	8	7

thresholded

1	0	0
1		0
1	1	1

weights

1	2	4
128		8
64	32	16

```
Pattern = 11110001
LBP = 128 + 64 + 32 + 16 + 0 + 0 + 0 + 1 = 241
```

Fig. 2. Calculating the original LBP code and a contrast measure

The derivation of the LBP follows that represented by Ojala [7]. It can be denoted as $LBP_{P,R}$ where P is the sampling points on the circle surrounding the center and R is the radius of the circle. Fig. 3. shows the examples of this kind of extended LBP.

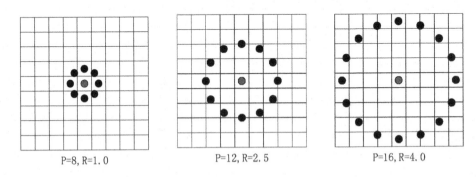

P=8, R=1. 0   P=12, R=2. 5   P=16, R=4. 0

Fig. 3. Circularly symmetric neighbor sets

To remove the effect of rotation, each LBP code must be rotated back to a reference position, effectively making all rotated versions of a binary code the same. This transformation can be defined as follows:

$$LBP_{P,R}^{ri} = \min\{ROR(LBP_{P,R},i) \mid i = 0,1,...,P-1\}$$

where the superscript ri stands for "rotation invariant". The function ROR(x,i) circularly shifts the P - bit binary number x i times to the right (| i |< P).

2.2 Candidates Selection

In this paper $LBP_{8,1}^{ri}$ operator is chosen, it has 36 unique rotation invariant binary patterns. As a result, we have a set of 36 LBP patterns denoted by {0,1,...,35}.

We first use two small training set of eye state images (40×20) and calculate each template of eye LBP histogram by averaging all the histograms extracted from the neighborhoods of the eye centre. When we start to analyze a new face image, we calculate LBP patterns for each pixel in the image, and then calculate the Chi square distance[8] between the LBP histogram of each pixel neighborhood (40×20) and the two templates. The Chi square is defined as follows:

$$\chi^2(S,M) = \sum_{i=1}^{B} \frac{(S_i - M_i)^2}{(S_i + M_i)}$$

where S and M denote (discrete) sample and model distributions, respectively. S_i and M_i correspond to the probability of bin i in the sample and model distributions. B is the number of bins in the distributions.

Now we can obtain two matrixes of the Chi square distance value according to the alternative eye state. We believe the value reflects the eye-related degree to the corresponding eye state and these points with local minimum value (valley) should contain the true eye position. Using projection method may miss some valley points sometimes when the valley points are close to the projection direction. So we first choose 2-D Gaussian filter to smooth the matrix value, then we select the points as the candidate obeying following rules:

1. The Chi square distance value of this point is in the part of the 20% smallest value points among the whole image.
2. It is the valley point, which has the smaller value than all the 8-connected neighbors.
3. If there are more than one pixels selected as candidates within 3 pixels, the mean position of them are used as an eye candidates.

After these works two groups of eye candidates are selected. (Fig. 4.)

2.3 SVM Verification

Two separated SVMs related to state are trained to verify real eyes. 37 acceptable points with their 40×20 neighbors pixels of each eye from training pictures are chosen as the positive samples for each state. (Fig. 5.) Each trained SVM has the form:

$$f(x) = \sum_{i=1}^{s} \alpha_i y_i K(x_i,x) + b$$

where $K(x_i, x)$ is a kernel function. The support vector x_i, the weight α_i and threshold b are obtained by training. When two groups of eye candidates are selected, they should be put through corresponding state SVM. The value of f(x) is considered as a

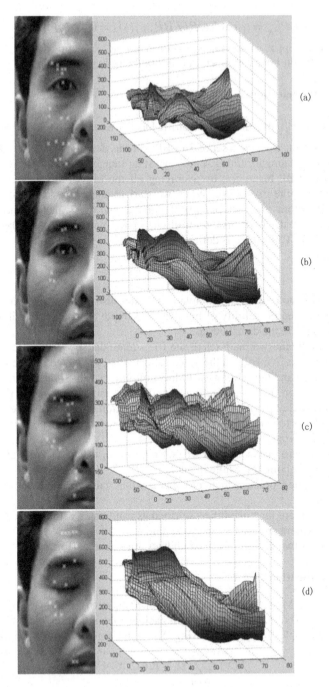

Fig. 4. Candidates of alternative eye state image and its Chi square distance value matrixes after Gaussian filter (a) (c) calculated with the open eye LBP histogram template (b) (d) calculated with the closed eye LBP histogram template

open   closed

Fig. 5. Acceptable location points

score, so the score of each candidate is calculated, and the max score from each group is obtained. If the max score from the open eye template group is greater than another max score from the closed eye group, the eye state is determined as open. Otherwise, eye state is determined as closed.

3 Experiments

The experiment is performed using images from CAS-PEAL database [9]. We collect 2969 frontal face images with open eyes including 1040 faces in normal status, 872 faces with accessory, 305 faces in different background and 752 faces with different expression and 376 normal face images with closed eyes. 200 eyes of 100 pictures of each state are selected randomly to form the template of LBP histogram and the acceptable location points neighborhood of these eyes are also used to be trained as the positive samples for the SVMs.

The LIBSVM [10] tool is selected to help to work out the parameters in the SVM function. The kernel is selected by default, while the cross-validation is used.

The result of the eye location with the right state recognition is shown in Table 1 and examples from different set of pictures are shown in Fig. 6. The failure represents the fault state detected. It is considered that if the eye location is determined more than 9 pixels away from the true eye position, the eye location with its neighborhood contains little information about the eye state, and the eye state detection result can be recognized as a failure. So, the final correct rate is fixed. It can be seen that the eye location is not very precise, but the deviation can be accepted in some cases.

Because the correctness of the closed state detection limits on the number of the samples from the database, one video including faces with alternate eye states is tested. The video is taken by the color digital camera and lasts for one minute, containing 25 frames per second. The result of the video test is shown in Table 2 and examples are shown in Fig. 7.

4 Conclusion

In this paper, we propose a new algorithm called LBP + SVM mode and use it to determine the eye state. The test result of the CAS-PEAL database is satisfying and the video test proves the possibility in practical use. It is also suggested the algorithm can be used to locate the eyes with the eye state unknown.

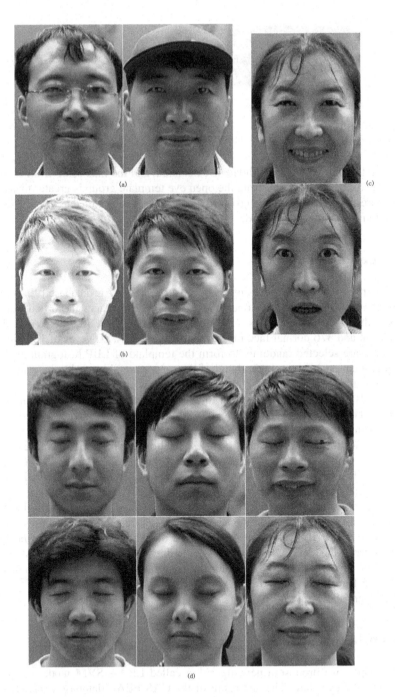

Fig. 6. Examples of faces from CAS-PEAL database (a) faces with accessory (b) faces in different background (c) faces with different expression (d) faces with closed eyes

Table 1. The result of the eye location with the right state recognition from CAS-PEAL database

Distance (pixels)	0~3	3~6	6~9	>9	Failure	Correct rate (fixed)
Open (5738 eyes)	1817	2636	1091	158	36	96.62%
Closed (552 eyes)	261	192	79	18	2	96.38%

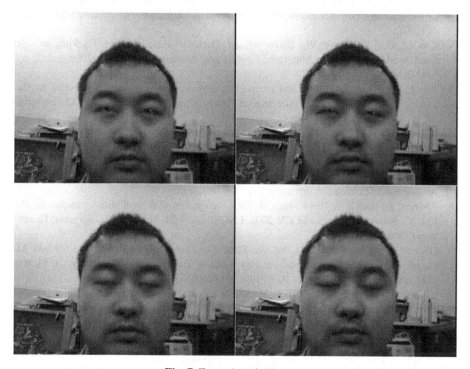

Fig. 7. Examples of video test

Table 2. The result of the video test

Eye state				Recognition rate
Open		Closed		
Frame	Recognized	Frame	Recognized	
1006	960	494	464	94.93%

Acknowledgments. The research in this paper use the CAS-PEAL-R1 face database collected under the sponsor of the Chinese National Hi-Tech Program and ISVISION Tech. Co. Ltd.

References

1. Dinges, D.F., Grace, R.: PERCLOS: a valid psychophysiological measure of alertness as assesed by psychomotor vigilance, Indianapolis. In: Federal Highway Administration, Office of Motor Carriers, Tech. Rep. MCRT-98-006 (1998)
2. Liu, Z., Ai, H.: Automatic Eye State Recognition and Closed-eye Photo Correction. In: 19th International Conference on Pattern Recognition (ICPR 2008), Tampa, Florida, USA, December 8-11 (2008)
3. Kith, V., El-Sharkawy, M., Bergeson-Dana, T., El-Ramly, S., Elnoubi, S.: A feature and appearance based method for eye detection on gray intensity face images. In: International Conference on Computer Engineering & Systems, ICCES 2008, November 25-27, pp. 41–47 (2008)
4. Gan, L., Cui, B., Wang, W.: Driver Fatigue Detection Based on Eye Tracking. In: The Sixth World Congress on Intelligent Control and Automation, WCICA 2006, vol. 2, pp. 5341–5344 (2006)
5. Zheng, Y., Wang, Z.: Robust and precise eye detection based on locally selective projection. In: 19th International Conference on Pattern Recognition, ICPR 2008, December 8-11, pp. 1–4 (2008)
6. Ojala, T., PietikaÈinen, M., Harwood, D.: A Comparative Study of Texture Measures with Classification Based on Feature Distributions. Pattern Recognition 29, 51–59 (1996)
7. Ojala, T., PietikaÈinen, M., MaÈenpaÈa, T.: Multiresolution gray-scale and rotation invariant texture classification with local binary patterns. IEEE Transactions on Pattern Analysis and Machine Intelligence 24(7), 971–987 (2002)
8. Ahonen, T., Hadid, A., Pietikainen, M.: Face recognition with local binary patterns. In: Pajdla, T., Matas, J(G.) (eds.) ECCV 2004. LNCS, vol. 3021, pp. 469–481. Springer, Heidelberg (2004)
9. Gao, W., Cao, B., Shan, S., Chen, X., Zhou, D., Zhang, X., Zhao, D.: The CAS-PEAL Large-Scale Chinese Face Database and Baseline Evaluations. IEEE Trans. on System Man, and Cybernetics (Part A) 38(1), 149–161 (2008)
10. Chang, C.-C., Lin, C.-J.: LIBSVM: a library for support vector machines (2009), http://www.csie.ntu.edu.tw/~cjlin/libsvm (updated, February 20)

A Neural Network Architecture for Perceptual Grouping, Attention Modulation and Boundary-Surface Interaction

Yong Chen[1] and Zhengzhi Wang[2]

[1] Institute of Automation, National University of Defense Technology,
Changsha, 410073, Hunan, China
literature_chen@nudt.edu.cn
[2] Institute of Automation, National University of Defense Technology,
Changsha, 410073, Hunan, China
wangzhengzhi@126.com

Abstract. A neural network architecture is introduced for context-sensitive binding processing in visual cortex areas such as perceptual grouping, attention and boundary-surface interaction. The present architecture, based on LAMINART and FAÇADE theory, shows how layered circuits in cortex areas enable feedforward, horizontal, and feedback interactions and intractions, together with balanced connections, to complete perceptual groupings with attention modulation. Thus, a pre-attentive/attentive interface for cortex has been established within the same circuits. Moreover, this architecture exhibits the invisible perceptual grouping and visible surface filling-in interaction with complementary computing property, introduced in FAÇADE theory. By implementing SOC filtering, preattentive perception can response well to contrast-sensitive stimuli. Also the simulations illustrates selective propagation of the attention along an object grouping as well as surface filling and the protection of them from competitive masking. At the same time it demonstrates the generation of attention modulation by boundary-surface interactions as well as translation of the attention across complementary visual processing streams.

Keywords: perceptual grouping; attention modulation; boundary-surface interaction; SOC filtering; complementary computing.

1 Introduction

Recent neurophysiological studies have shown that visual cortex, does more than passively process image features using the feedforward filters suggested by Hubel and Wiesel [1]. It also uses horizontal interactions to group features pre-attentively into object representations, and feedback interactions to selectively attend to these groupings, thus, implement context-sensitive bind process such as perceptual grouping and attention. LAMINART theory [2]-[5] proposed that all neocortical areas are organized into layered circuits. It embodies a new type of hybrid between feedforward and feedback computing, and digital and analog computing for processing distributed data. It realizes the perceptual grouping and top-down attention in the same circuit by providing the pre-attentive/attentive interface [2]-[5] which is proposed to exist between layer 6 and layer 4 where data-driven pre-attentive processing and task-directed

Z. Cai et al. (Eds.): ISICA 2009, LNCS 5821, pp. 327–336, 2009.
© Springer-Verlag Berlin Heidelberg 2009

top-down attentive processing are joined and solves the "binding problem" [2], whereby spatially distributed features are bound into representations of objects and events in the world.

1.1 Perceptual Grouping

Perceptual grouping, which is proposed to occur through the Retina-LGN Parvo-V1-V2-V4 processing stream, is the process whereby spatially distributed visual features become linked into object representations. There is evidence that it is a pre-attentive process that requires no top-down influences. In the process, the brain organizes image contrasts into emergent boundary structures that segregate objects and their backgrounds in response to texture, shading and depth cues in scenes and images, realizing a visual process called figure-ground separation [6]. Perceptual grouping is a basic step in solving the "binding problem". The past few years have seen an explosion of interest in the neurophysiological substrates of attention and perceptual grouping in visual cortex, at first in extrastriate areas but more recently also in striate cortex [8]. Anatomical studies have also revealed much of the intricate corticocortical and intra-cortical laminar circuitry of visual cortex which supports these processes [9].

1.2 Attention Modulation

In visual system, attention mechanisms are needed to allow the organism to select for further processing information that is currently task-relevant, whilst ignoring other information that also appears as part of the visual scene but that is not relevant. In another word, only a small amount of the information on the retina can be processed and one is aware of attended stimuli and largely filters out unwanted information at any given time. What is the type of representation on which selection is carried out is one of the currently controversial issues related to visual attention [10]. Given the importance of attention in generating conscious experience, it should be noted that at least three mechanistically-distinct types of attention have been distinguished by cortical modeling studies of visual perception and recognition [2], [10]: a) boundary attention, whereby spatial attention can propagate along an object boundary to select the entire object boundary to select the entire object for inspection; b) surface attention, whereby spatial attention can selectively fill in the surface shape of an object to form an "attention shroud"[9]; c) prototype attention whereby critical feature patterns of a learned object category can be selectively enhanced. Surface attention helps to intelligently search a scene with eye movements and to learn view-invariant object categories [11]. Prototype attention is the type of attention that is realized by ART [12] top-down category learning circuits. All three types of attention utilize one or another type of resonant feedback loops across what stream, which subserves visual object recognition through IT cortex, and Where streams, which subserves spatial localization through parietal cortex, with complementary computing property [13].

1.3 Boundary-Surface Interaction

Perceptual grouping generates the invisible boundaries which gate the visible filling-in of surface lightness and color via boundary-to-surface signals. In FAÇADE theory

[11], [14], surface-to-boundary feedback is to ensure perceptual consistency, even though boundaries and surfaces form according to complementary computations rules which are much like a lock fits its key, or two pieces of a puzzle fit together. Complementary principles in brain are similar to Heisenberg Uncertainty Principle of quantum mechanics which notes that precise measurement a particle's position forces uncertainty in measuring its momentum, and vice versa. With surface-boundary feedback, boundaries that are consistent to successful filling-in surfaces may be confirmed and strengthened, while others are inhibited. With such interaction, pre-attentive boundary and surface representations binds together into attentive object representations which generates categorical and prototypical representations for purposes of visual object recognition. Boundary attention gates filling-in process which transform visual information into spatial maps, and enable visual search [16] to be restricted to targets among distracters. The FAÇADE model predicts why and how contrast-sensitive surface-to-boundary feedback helps to define an object by ensuring that the correct object boundaries and surfaces are consistently bound together to form a pre-attentive object representation. Another, via boundary-surface interactions, surface attention, which primes the surface filling-in, can excite or modulate boundaries grouping.

2 Model Neural Network

We now present a neural network of visual cortex, which is based on LAMINART and FAÇADE theory, to show in computer simulations how contextual effects of attention, perceptual grouping and boundary-surface interactions can implemented. The model builds on and extends previous work presented by Grossberg.

The model is a network of point neurons whose single compartment membrane voltage $V(t)$ obeys [11], [15], [19]:

$$C_m \frac{dV(t)}{dt} = -\left[V(t) - E_{leak}\right] g_{leak}(t) - \left[V(t) - E_{excit}\right] g_{excit}(t) - \left[V(t) - E_{inhib}\right] g_{inhib}(t) \quad (1)$$

For similarity, equation can be rewritten as a membrane, or shunting equation:

$$\frac{d}{dt} v = -Dv + (U - v) g_{excit} - (v + L) g_{inhib} \quad (2)$$

Where A is a constant decay rate, U is a excitatory saturation potential, L is a hyper-polarization parameter, g_{excit} is the total excitatory input, and g_{inhib} is the total inhibitory input. At equilibrium,

$$V = f\left(\frac{(Ug_{excit} - Lg_{inhib})}{(D + g_{excit} + g_{inhib})}\right) \quad (3)$$

In (3), $f(x) = \max(x - \gamma, 0)$ represents the half-wave rectification operation, γ is the threshold.

2.1   Contrast Normalization Network, Retina/LGN

The model Retina has at each position both an ON-cell, u_{ij}^+ with a narrow on-center off-surround receptive field, and an OFF-cell, u_{ij}^- with a narrow off-center on-surround receptive field. The two channels implement complementary coding to respond both to light increments and light decrements. For ON channel:

$$g_{excit}^{ON} = \sum_{p,q} C_{pq} I_{p+i,q+j}; g_{inhibit}^{ON} = \sum_{p,q} S_{pq} I_{p+i,q+j}; g_{excit}^{OFF} = g_{inhibit}^{ON}; g_{inhibit}^{OFF} = g_{excit}^{ON} \quad (4)$$

The model Lateral Geniculate Nucleus (LGN) ON v^+ and OFF cells v^- receives input from Retina ON and OFF cells, as well as feedback from model cortical cells. Bottom-up retina input, is hypothesized to supraliminally activate LGN cells, while the role of top-down corticogeniculate feedback [15] helps to "focus attention" upon expected patterns of LGN activity, which appear to have the selective properties of an "automatic" attention process. For both channel

$$g_{excit} = \sum_{p,q} C_{pq} \left(1 + E_{p+i,q+j}\right) u_{p+i,q+j}^{\pm}; g_{inhib} = \sum_{p,q} S_{pq} \left(1 + M_{p+i,q+j}\right) u_{p+i,q+j}^{\pm} \quad (5)$$

In (5), E represents the excitatory input from cortical cells, while M represents inhibitory from LGN interneuron. For similarity:

$$E_{ij} = M_{ij} = \lambda f \left(\sum_k w_{ijk} \right) \quad (6)$$

In (6), λ represents the gain factor. The kernel used here is unoriented, symmetric, normalized Gaussian kernel

2.2   Static Oriented Contrast Filter (SOC Filter)

The SOC filtering is divided into two stages. The first stage is contrast-sensitive oriented filtering which models oriented simple cells that are bottom-up activated by LGN activities. The second stage is contrast-insensitive oriented filtering which models oriented, contrast-polarity insensitive and phase-insensitive complex cells.

In contrast-sensitive oriented filtering stage:

$$g_{excit} = \sum_{pq} \left(v_{i+p,j+q}^+ f\left(G_{pqk}\right) + v_{i+p,j+q}^- f\left(-G_{pqk}\right) \right) \quad (7)$$

$$g_{inhibit} = \sum_{pq} \left(v_{i+p,j+q}^+ f\left(-G_{pqk}\right) + v_{i+p,j+q}^- f\left(G_{pqk}\right) \right) \quad (8)$$

In (9) and (10), G_{pqk} represents the odd-symmetric Gabor kernels which provide optimum conjoint localization in both space and spatial frequency [20].

In contrast-insensitive oriented filtering, complex cell c_{ijk} is the sum of half-wave above-threshold rectified signals from pairs of like-oriented simple cells of opposite contrast-polarity:

$$c_{ijk} = y_{ijk} + y_{ij(k+K)} \qquad for \ \ 0 \le k \le K \qquad (9)$$

2.3 Spatial and Orientational Competition, Layer 6 and 4

The interactions between the two competitions establish pre-attentive/attentive interface. Top-down attentional feedback from higher cortical areas is predicted to be mediated by signals from layer 6, activates layer 6 in lower cortical areas, then modulate layer 4 cells via an layer-6-to-layer-4 on-center off-surround circuit, however, it cannot activate them because top-down attentional modulation is subliminal. Then modulatory effect is achieved by appropriately balancing the strength of excitatory and inhibitory signals within the on-center off-surround layer-6-to-layer-4 network.

In spatial competition, layer 6 cell x_{ijk} receive bottom-up input, as well as three types of folded-feedback [2]-[5]. The first type is intracortical feedback from above-threshold pyramidal cells z_{ijk} in layer 2/3. The second type is intercortical attentional feedback from upper visual areas. The third type is the surface contour feedback signals m_{ijk} .

$$g_{excit} = g_E + att^{upper} + J \qquad g_{inhib} = g_I \qquad (10)$$

$$\begin{cases} g_E = \sqrt{\left(c_{ijk} + z_{ijk} + m_{ijk}\right) \sum_{pq} G^E_{pqk} \left(c_{i+p,j+q,k} + z_{i+p,j+q,k} + m_{i+p,j+q,k}\right)} \\ g_I = \sqrt{\left(c_{ijk} + z_{ijk} + m_{ijk}\right) \sum_{pq} G^I_{pqk} \left(c_{i+p,j+q,k} + z_{i+p,j+q,k} + +m_{i+p,j+q,k}\right)} \end{cases} \quad (11)$$

In oriented competition, layer 4 cells y_{ijk} receive direct input from SOC outputs, as well as layer 6 cells. The competition acts at a smaller scale wherein in mutually orthogonal orientations inhibit each other the most, and embodies push-pull opponent processing mechanism [18].

$$g_E = \sum_r G^E_{kr} \bar{y}_{ijr}; g_I = \sum_r G^I_{kr} \bar{y}_{ijr}; \bar{y}_{ijk} = \sum_{pq} C'_{pqk} \left(x_{ijk} + c_{ijk}\right) \qquad (12)$$

In (10), att^{upper} is the boundary attention from higher cortex, J is a constant tonic activity [15]. In (12), C'_{pqk} is elongated ellipse Gaussian kernel, G^E_{kr} and G^I_{kr} generates orientation competition described above. The kernel used here are ON-center OFF-lateral ellipse kernels.

2.4 Bipole Grouping Layer 2/3

Long-range interactions among the pyramidal cells in layer 2/3 carry out perceptual grouping by forming and completing oriented boundaries in responses to inputs. These pooled boundaries realize boundary attention feedback to spatial competition, then folded-feedback to layer 2/3, as described above. These long-range connections also activate interneuron that inhibit each other and nearby pyramidal cells via short-range disynaptic inhibition, thus normalizing the total amount of inhibition emanating from the interneuron pool. The excitation and inhibition at targets cells get to a balance which helps to implement the bipole property: a) a cell can fire when it receive strong bottom-up excitatory input; b) when two collinearly aligned inducing stimuli are present, one on each flank of the cell, a boundary grouping can form even without direct bottom-up input. The bipole property has been reported in physiological recordings from cells in cortical areas V1 and V2 [2]-[5], [19].

$$g_{excit} = \gamma_1 f\left(y_{ijk}\right) + \gamma_2 \left(f\left(h_{ijk}^L\right) + f\left(h_{ijk}^R\right)\right); g_{inhib} = w_{ijk}^L + w_{ijk}^R \qquad (13)$$

The long-range horizontal excitatory inputs $h_{ijk}^{L/R}$ obey:

$$h_{ijk}^L = \sum_{pqr}\left(z_{i+p,j+q,r} - z_{i+p,j+q,R}\right) \bullet T\left(H_{pqrk}\right); h_{ijk}^R = \sum_{pqr}\left(z_{i+p,j+q,r} - z_{i+p,j+q,R}\right) \bullet T\left(-H_{pqrk}\right) (14)$$

In (14), $R = \left(r + K/2\right)\mathrm{mod}\left(K\right)$. This is to realize spatially impenetrability [17].

H_{pqrk} is the bipole kernel.

The interneuron activity $w_{ijk}^{L/R}$ is defined by:

$$w_{ijk}^{L/R} = \frac{f\left(h_{ijk}^{L/R}\right)}{1 + Qf\left(w_{ijk}^{R/L}\right)} \qquad (15)$$

In (13), γ_1 and γ_2 are the gain factor, In (15), Q is the interneuron cross-inhibitory weight.

2.5 Surface Filling-In Domain

Boundaries signals by the cells in layer 2/3 project to surface filling-in domains, where they gate the filling-in of surface feature signals arriving from the LGN. The boundary-gated spread of these surface features tends to generate uniform filled-in activity levels within each boundary compartment. The FIDOs in the present model are based on the diffusion network. FIDOs occurs separately via nearest-neighbor diffusion in ON and OFF filling-in domains. The final output is the difference of the ON and OFF FIDOs activities at each location, hence a double-opponent response.

Surface cells activities are defined:

$$\begin{cases} \dfrac{dY_{ij}^{+/-}}{dt} = -DY_{ij}^{+/-} + \sum_{p,q\in\Omega}(Y_{pq}^{+/-} - Y_{ij}^{+/-})\Psi_{pqij} + v_{ij}^{+/-} + att \\[2mm] Y_{ij} = Y_{ij}^+ - Y_{ij}^- \end{cases} \qquad (16)$$

In (16), att represents the surface attention. Ω, Ψ_{pqij} are defined in [11], [19].

2.6 Surface Contours

The activity of object surface is contrast-enhanced by on-center off-surround networks to generate contour output signals that feedback to layer 6 via SOC filtering process. The surface contour output signals $C^{+/-}$ are modeled like Retina process with different Gaussian kernel parameters. These two channels are filtered by SOC, and then generate the third type of boundary attention m_{ijk} described in spatial competition stage. The model equations in this stage are similar to Retina process and SOC filtering.

3 Simulation

3.1 Perceptual Grouping

This section illustrates that the perceptual grouping is competent to segment natural scenes. Within this model, cooperative boundary grouping and the boundary attentional modulation of these grouped boundaries results in relatively strong boundary activity. That is to say pre-attentive grouping is its own attention modulation.

3.2 Surface Filling-In

This section illustrates the boundary signals pool into surface process, and gate the outwardly filling-in of surface feature signals arriving from the LGN without the surface-boundary feedback. The boundary-gated spread of these surface features tends to generate uniform filled-in activity levels within each boundary compartment.

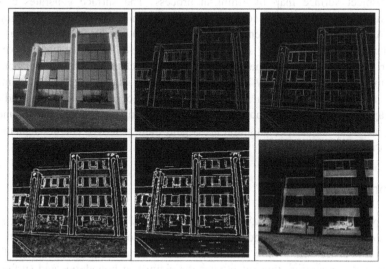

Fig. 1. Simulations on an example input image. Top-Left: Input image. Top-Middle: Output of LGN ON channel activities. Top-Right: Output of LGN OFF channel activities. Bottom-Left: Output of SOC filter. Bottom-Middle: Bipole cell outputs without surface attention. Bottom-Right: Output of Surface Filling-in without surface-boundary feedback.

3.3 Boundary-Surface Interaction

This section illustrates that the boundary-surface interactions while surface attention exists. See Fig. **2.**

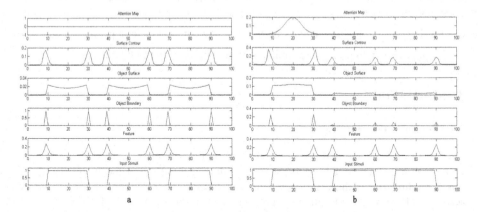

Fig. 2. Simulations on boundary-surface interaction. See text for detail.

In Fig. **2,** (a), (c) are consecutive instances in the dynamics of the model. (a) Initially, three inputs in the input stimuli map give rise to three sets of features and object boundaries in feature and object boundary map, by contrast enhancement. The features start diffusing and bounded inside the boundaries and re-create the surfaces in the object surface map by filling-in process. The surface generates contrast-sensitive contours in surface contour map by on-center off-surround shunting network. At this time, surface attention is not present. (c) The same map as in (a), but a Gaussian spot-light of surface attention exists around locations which are expected. Surface attention modulates the surface filling-in process, and then effect boundary grouping via surface-boundary interactions. Note that, the surface that is primed by surface attention is enhanced in the positive feedback loop between surface and attention map while the other is suppressed. Via surface-boundary interactions, boundaries which locate in the surface attention areas gain more activity. The other unattended boundaries are suppressed.

4 Conclusion

In this paper, a neural network, based on LAMINART and FAÇADE theory, is proposed to deal with boundary and surface perception. Boundary attention is critical for object form processing, while surface attention is critical in local surface feature learning and recognition, thus, elaborates the claim that boundaries and surfaces are the units of visual attention [4], [5]. Moreover, by simulation the boundary-surface interaction, the two of which are complementary processing in visual system, the model proposes that different kind of attention interaction with each other to complete a specific target, which is also a possible way by the brain to settle the uncertainty problem. However, this paper doesn't simulate how the boundary attention from higher cortex priming the perceptual grouping the boundary perception especially illusory boundary form. Present model does not clarify how the surface attention is mediated by the bottom-up stimuli and attention shifts between different targets to realize the visual search with eye opening and eye closing in Where stream. Present model neither take prototype attention into account which proved to be very important in visual recognition in What stream.

Acknowledgments. The authors would like to thank Professor Grossberg, S and his colleagues for their previous excellent work. This work was supported by the National Nature Science Foundation of China (60835005).

References

1. Hubel, D.H., Wiesel, T.N.: Functional architecture of macaque monkey visual cortex. Proceedings of the Royal Society of London (Series B) 198, 1–59 (1977)
2. Grossberg, S.: Consciousness CLEARS the mind. Technical Report CAS/CNS-TR-07-013. Neural Networks, 20, 1040–1053 (2007); special issue Consciousness and Brain
3. Grossberg, S.: Towards a unified theory of neocortex: Laminar cortical circuits for vision and cognition. Technical Report CAS/CNS-TR-2006-008. In: Cisek, P., Drew, T., Kalaska, J. (eds.): For Computational Neuroscience: From Neurons to Theory and Back Again, pp. 79–104. Elsevier, Amsterdam (2007)
4. Grossberg, S.: How does the cerebral cortex work? Development, learning, attention, and 3D vision by laminar circuits of visual cortex. Behavioral and Cognitive Neuroscience Reviews 2, 47–76 (2003)
5. Grossberg, S.: How does the cerebral cortex work? Learning, attention and grouping by the laminar circuits of visual cortex. Spatial Vision 12, 163–186 (1999)
6. Grossberg, S.: Figure-ground separation by visual cortex. In: Adelman, G., Smith, B.H. (eds.) Encyclopedia of neuroscience, 2nd edn. pp. 716–721. Elsevier Science Publishers, Amsterdam (1999)
7. Grossberg, S., Raizada, R.: Contrast-sensitive perceptual grouping and object-based attention in the laminar circuits of primary visual cortex. Vision Research 40, 1413–1432 (2000)
8. Callaway, E.M.: Local cicrcuits in primary visual cortex of the macaque monkey. Annual Review of Neuroscience 21, 47–74 (1998)
9. Soto, D., Blanco, M.J.: Spatial attention and object-based attention: a comparison within a single task. Vision Research 44, 69–81 (2004)
10. Grossberg, S.: Linking attention to learning, expectation, competition, and consciousness. In: Rees, L.I.G., Tsotsos, J. (eds.) Neurobiology of attention, pp. 652–662. Elsevier, San Diego (2005)
11. Fazl, A., Grossberg, S., Mingolla, E.: View-invariant object category learning, recognition, and search: How spatial and object attention are coordinated using surface-based attentional shrouds. Cognitive Psychology 58, 1–48 (2009)
12. Carpenter, G.A., Grossberg, S.: Adaptive resonance theory. In: Arbib, M.A. (ed.) The Handbook of Brain Theory and Neural Networks, 2nd edn. pp. 87–90. MIT Press, Cambridge (2003)

13. Grossberg, S.: The complementary brain: Unifying brain dynamics and modularity. Trends in Cognitive Sciences 4, 233–246 (2000)
14. Grossberg, S.: Filling-in the forms: Surface and boundary interactions in visual cortex. Technical Report CAS/CNS TR-2000-018, Boston University. In: Pessoa, L., DeWeerd, P. (eds.): Filling-in: From perceptual completion to skill learning, pp. 13–37. Oxford University Press, New York (2003)
15. Gove, A., Grossberg, S., Mingolla, E.: Brightness perception, illusory contours, and corticogeniculate feedback. Visual Neuroscience 12, 1027–1052 (1995)
16. Lanyon, L.J., Denham, S.L.: A model of active visual search with object-based attention guiding scan paths. Neural Networks 17, 873–897 (2004)
17. Grossberg, G., Williamson, J.R.: A neural model of how horizontal and interlaminar connections of visual cortex develop into adult circuits that carry out perceptual groupings and learning. Cerebral Cortex 11, 37–58 (2001)
18. Grossberg, S., Mingolla, E.: Neural dynamics of form perception: Boundary completion, illusory figures, and neon color spreading. Psychological Review 92, 173–211 (1985)
19. Bhatt, R., Carpenter, G., Grossberg, S.: Texture segregation by visual cortex: Perceptual grouping, attention, and learning. Vision Research 47, 3173–3211 (2007)
20. Kovesi, P.D.: MATLAB and Octave Functions for Computer Vision and Image Processing. School of Computer Science & Software Engineering, the University of Western Australia

Appendix: Convolution Kernel Used in This Model

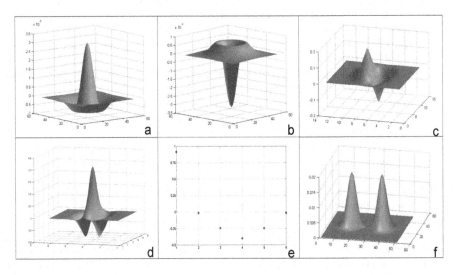

Fig. 3. Kernels used in each stage. (a): On-center Off-surround used in Contrast Normalization Network ON channel. (b): Off-center On-surround used in Contrast Normalization Network OFF channel. (c)Odd-symmetric Gabor kernel used in SOC filter. (d): On-center Lateral-surround kernels used in Spatial Competition. (e): orthogonal orientations inhibit efficiently in Orientation Competition. (f): bipole kernels in Bipole Grouping.

Adaptive Neighborhood Select Based on Local Linearity for Nonlinear Dimensionality Reduction

Yubin Zhan*, Jianping Yin, Xinwang Liu, and Guomin Zhang

Computer School, National University of Defense Technology, Changsha, China
zhanyubin_dm@yahoo.com.cn

Abstract. Neighborhood selection plays an important role in manifold learning algorithm. This paper proposes an Adaptive Neighborhood Select algorithm based on Local Linearity(ANSLL). Given manifold dimensionality d as a priori knowledge, ANSLL algorithm constructs neighborhood based on two principles: 1. data points in the same neighborhood should approximately lie on a d-dimensional linear subspace; 2. each neighborhood should be as large as possible. And in ASNLL algorithm PCA technique is exploited to measure the linearity of finite data points set. Moreover, we present an improved method of constructing neighborhood graph, which can improve the accuracy of geodesic distance estimate for isometric embedding. Experiments on both synthetic data sets and real data sets show that ANSLL algorithm can adaptively construct neighborhood according to local curvature of data manifold and then improve the performance of most manifold algorithms, such as ISOMAP and LLE.

Keywords: neighborhood, manifold learning, local linearity, geodesic distance.

1 Introduction

Manifold learning is an effective technology for nonlinear dimensionality reduction which is introduced to overcome the curse of dimensionality when dealing with high dimensional data. Due to the pervasiveness of high-dimensional data, it is widespread used in many applications such as pattern recognition, data analysis, and machine learning. The basic assumption of manifold learning that the high-dimensional data lie on or close to low-dimensional manifold is different from that of classical linear dimensional reduction technologies, such as PCA[1] and MDS[2]. And up to now, there are many manifold learning algorithms in the literature, such as ISOMAP[3] and LLE[5,4], which are the representative works in manifold learning. All of the existing manifold learning algorithms are in a unified framework which consists of three steps described in the following:

1. Computing neighborhood of each point in original space.

---

* Received: 2009-04-30, Accepted: 2009-06-15.

Z. Cai et al. (Eds.): ISICA 2009, LNCS 5821, pp. 337–348, 2009.

2. Constructing a special matrix based on the neighborhoods

3. Calculating spectral embedding using eigenvalue decomposition of that matrix.

Here in the first step the neighborhood parameter (k for k nearest neighbors or ε for ε-neighborhood) which should be manually specified beforehand plays an important role in constructing a faithful low-dimensional embedding. If the neighborhood parameter is too large, the local neighborhoods will include points in different patches of data manifold, and result in fatal errors in the final embedding. Too small neighborhood parameter, however, may divide the manifold into several disconnected sub-manifolds, which also are not the expected embeddings. So this paper concentrates on the problem of constructing neighborhoods automatically and presents a novel adaptive neighborhood select approach based on local linearity, then based on this approach we modify the method of constructing Neighborhood Graph(hereafter NG for short) used in ISOMAP algorithm, and the modified method can get more accurate geodesic distance estimate than that in ISOMAP algorithm.

The rest of the paper is organized as follows: the related work is introduced in section 2; then PCA is utilized to measure linearity of finite data points set in section 3; the algorithm ANSLL is proposed in section 4; modified method to construct NG for geodesic distance estimate is proposed in section 5; section 6 is the experiment results; a conclusion is made in section 7.

2   Related Work

There are two basic neighborhood selection algorithms: k nearest neighbors algorithm(k-NN) and ε-neighborhood. These two algorithms used in many manifold learning algorithms such as ISOMAP[3], LLE[5,4], Laplacian eigenmap[6], LTSA[7]. However, all those manifold learning algorithms are sensitive to neighborhood parameter which has to be specified manually beforehand[8]. What's more, these two algorithms can't guarantee a connected NG, which is essential requisition in most of manifold learning algorithms. Therefore, there are many researches concentrated on improving neighborhood select approach in the following ways:

1. Construct connected NG. Since most manifold learning algorithms can't work on disconnected NG, it is important for a neighborhood algorithm to guarantee a connected NG. However, the NG constructed by k-NN algorithm and ε-neighborhood cannot be guaranteed a connected one. Li Yang used k-edge-connected and k-connected spanning subgraph of complete Euclidean graph of all input data points to construct connected NG[7-10].

2. Select a fixed optimal neighborhood parameter automatically. The basic idea of this type of method is to exploit some heuristics to choose the optimal parameter. However, only some weak heuristics have been developed. For example the residual variance presented in ISOMAP algorithm is used to automatically determine the optimal neighborhood parameter in [13]. In fact

the residual variance, which is originally proposed to evaluate the quality of mapping between the input data and output data, is not reasonable to measure the quality of neighborhood parameter. Moreover, this method takes the fixed neighborhood size for all data points; obviously it is not suitable for manifold whose curvature varies sharply and the unevenly sampled manifolds, which are both the real cases in many real applications.

3. Delete the "short circuit" edge from the NG. The neighbors determined by the Euclidean distance always results in "short circuit" edges and some approaches try to delete all the "short circuit" edges from NG[15,16,14]. However, the true "short circuit" edges are always hard to distinguish. The approaches proposed in[15,16,14] regard edges that pass through low-density area as "short circuit" edges, sometimes this is not the real case.

Due to the drawbacks of existing neighborhood select approaches, this paper concentrates on constructing neighborhood for manifold learning. In ISOMAP algorithm, NG is only used to estimate the geodesic distance of all pairwise points, and the algorithm uses the Euclidean distances as the estimates of geodesic distance between a point and its neighbors. So it is obvious that if all data points in each neighborhood are in d-dimensional(assume d is the dimensionality of the data manifold) linear subspace, the ISOMAP will get more accurate geodesic distance estimate than estimation in other case, this will then further result in more faithful embedding. In another representative work LLE algorithm based on geometric intuition that data manifold is locally linear, it reconstructs every points by the linear combinations of neighbors. So in these two algorithms linearity can be the requisition for neighborhood. Moreover, many other manifold learning algorithms require that data points in each neighborhood are in or close to d-dimensional linear subspace. Meanwhile, in order to construct a connected NG, each neighborhood should contain points as more as possible. In summary, there are two requisitions for each neighborhood:

1. All data points in each neighborhood should be or approximate in a d-dimensional linear subspace.

2. The number of data points in each neighborhood should be as large as possible.

Based on the above two requisitions, this paper exploits PCA to evaluate the linearity of a finite data set and proposes an adaptive select approach and a modified method to construct NG. Paper[17] declares that they propose a method for neighborhood select, which constructs each neighborhood based on local geodesic distance estimate. However, comment on this method in paper [20] identifies the ineffectiveness of the algorithm, in addition, the response of the authors to this comment seems not so reasonable[21]. And in RML algorithm[18] the neighborhood selection algorithm obtains the neighborhood through deleting "invisible" edges and "unsafe" edges. Even though it can get good performance in RML algorithm, it is inclined to obtain small size neighborhood and not suitable for other manifold learning algorithms.

3   Using PCA to Measure Linearity of Finite Data Points Set

In this section, we first introduce the PCA and then exploit PCA to evaluate linearity of finite data points set.

PCA is a classical linear dimensionality reduction method and has widespread applications. Given a data matrix $X = [x_1, x_2, \cdots, x_n]$, where column vector $x_i \in R^D$ represents sample data. The goal the PCA is to project X into a d-dimensional $(d < D)$ linear subspace such that the projected data points are as close as possible to the original data points. This can be formalized as follows:

$$\min \sum_{i=1}^{n} \| x_i - V \cdot (V^T \cdot x_i) \|^2 \tag{1}$$

where V is a $D \times d$ matrix and $V^T V = I$. And the solution is given by the matrix consisted of eigenvectors corresponding to the first d largest eigenvalues of the covariance matrix XX^T (assume that the mean of sample data X is zero).

This is the traditional view of PCA. In fact we can understand PCA from another viewpoint. Suppose we want to evaluate how close data points in X to a d-dimensional linear subspace for a given dimensionality d(in manifold learning, the data manifold dimensionality d is always known as a priori). The formula (1) gives us a good heuristic. If the data set X is really in a d-dimensional linear subspace, then minimum of (1) is 0, and intuitively the less the minimum, the closer the data points set X to a d-dimensional linear subspace.

Denote the eigenvalues of the covariance matrix XX^T by $\lambda_i(0 < i \le D)$ where $\lambda_1 \ge \lambda_2 \ge \cdots \ge \lambda_D \ge 0$, and the corresponding eigenvectors are v_i. So the optimal solution of equation (1) is given by $V = [v_1, v_2, \cdots, v_d]$. Substituting the optimal solution into the equation (1), then it can be rewritten as follows:

$$\min \sum_{i=1}^{n} \|x_i - V \cdot (V^T x_i)\|^2 = \sum_{i=1}^{n} \|x_i\|^2 - \sum_{i=1}^{n} \|V^T x_i\|^2$$

$$= \sum_{i=1}^{n} \|x_i\|^2 - \sum_{j=1}^{d} \sum_{i=1}^{n} (v_j^T x_i)^2$$

$$= \operatorname{tr}(X^T X) - \sum_{j=1}^{d} \lambda_j = \sum_{j=1}^{D} \lambda_j - \sum_{j=1}^{d} \lambda_j$$

$$= \sum_{j=d+1}^{D} \lambda_j$$

Therefore the projection error $\sum_{j=d+1}^{D} \lambda_j$ can evaluate how close X to a d-dimensional linear subspace. However, this absolute projection error ignores the scatter of X and varies as different concrete problems. Therefore, it is necessary for us to normalize this absolute projection error by taking into account the scatter of X. Then the term $1 - \frac{\sum_{j=d+1}^{D} \lambda_j}{\sum_{j=1}^{D} \lambda_j} = \frac{\sum_{j=1}^{d} \lambda_j}{\sum_{j=1}^{D} \lambda_j}$ is adopted as the measurement to evaluate the linearity of X. Given a tolerable threshold η , if $\frac{\sum_{i=1}^{d} \lambda_i}{\sum_{i=1}^{D} \lambda_i} \geq \eta$ then data points in X can be seen in a d-dimensional linear subspace.

4 Adaptive Neighborhood Select Based on Local Linearity

As analysis in section 2, assume the dimensionality of the data manifold d is known as a priori knowledge, a good neighborhood select algorithm should follow two principles:

1. Data points in the neighborhood should be lie on or close to a d-dimension linear subspace.

2. The number of data points in the neighborhood should be as large as possible.

Then based on the PCA linearity measurement of finite data points set and the above two principles, we propose an adaptive neighborhood select algorithm. The basic idea is to expand each neighborhood while preserving its linearity. The detail is described in fig.1.

ANSLL algorithm

---

input: high-dimensional data set X, the manifold dimension d,
   the scope for candidate neighbors m, the tolerable threshold η.
output: the adaptive neighborhood of each point $\mathcal{N}(x_i)$.

Initialize: for each x_i, add its $d+1$ nearest neighbors to $\mathcal{N}(x_i)$
Expansion: for each $\mathcal{N}(x_i)$
1. $\forall x_{i_j} \in \mathcal{N}(x_i)$ that has not been processed
2. $\cdots$ for k-th neighbor $x_{i_j}^{(k)}(k = 1, 2, \cdots, m)$ of x_{i_j}
3. $\cdots\cdots$ if $x_{i_j}^{(k)} \notin \mathcal{N}(x_i)$
4. $\cdots\cdots\cdots$ compute eigenvalues $\lambda_l(0 < l \leq D)$ of covariance matrix of
    samples $\mathcal{N}(x_i) \cup x_{i_j}^{(k)}$
5. $\cdots\cdots\cdots$ if $\frac{\sum_{i=d}^{d} \lambda_i}{\sum_{i=1}^{D} \lambda_i} \geq \eta$, add $x_{i_j}^{(k)}$ into $\mathcal{N}(x_i)$,
6. $\cdots x_{i_j}$ has been processed.

Fig. 1. ANSLL algorithm

In order to construct neighborhood $\mathcal{N}(x_i)$, ANSLL algorithm firstly initialize it with $d+1$ nearest neighbors of x_i. Then algorithm expands it through iteratively checking the m nearest neighbors of each point in that neighborhood. For each candidate point $x_{i_j}^{(k)}$ that is not in $\mathcal{N}(x_i)$, ANSLL computes eigenvalues $\lambda_l(0 < l \leq D)$ of covariance matrix of samples points $\mathcal{N}(x_i) \cup x_{i_j}^{(k)}$ and ANSLL adds it to neighborhood $\mathcal{N}(x_i)$ if and only if $\mathcal{N}(x_i) \cup x_{i_j}^{(k)}$ is "in" a d-dimensional linear subspace according to the given tolerable threshold η. And this iterative procedure stops until no point can be added to $\mathcal{N}(x_i)$. In this iterative process, as a matter of factor, there is no need to recompute eigenvalues of covariance matrix of sample points $\mathcal{N}(x_i) \cup x_{i_j}^{(k)}$, which is time-consuming and costly, there are many Incremental updating techniques can be used, such as Incremental Principal Component Analysis(IPCA) and Incremental SVD techniques, which can quickly compute the eigenvalues and eigenvectors based on previous eigenvalues and eigenvectors when a new sample is arriving. In our implementation of ANSLL algorithm, LET-IPCA[19] is adopted.

5   Constructing Neighborhood Graph for Isometric Embedding

In ISOMAP algorithm the geodesic distance is estimated by the shortest path distance in the NG. And in this NG there is an edge between point x_i and x_j if and only if $x_j \in \mathcal{N}(x_i)$ or $x_i \in \mathcal{N}(x_j)$, the length w_{ij} of the edge (x_i, x_j) is the Euclidean distance $d_E(x_i, x_j)$ between x_i and x_j in the input space. Note that each neighborhood constructed by our ANSLL algorithm lies on or close to a d-dimensional linear subspace, for any two points in the same neighborhood, even though there is no edge between them(no point is in the neighborhood of the other), the direct Euclidean distance between them in input space is a more accurate geodesic distance estimate than others because of the linearity of the neighborhood. See an illustration example in fig. 2.

Therefore we improve the NG construction method used in ISOMAP as follows: connect any two points in the same neighborhood. Then the constructed NG is used to estimate the geodesic distance as the way in ISOMAP. As a matter of fact, if the entire input data set is in a d-dimensional linear subspace, then all the data points are in one neighborhood, then the nonlinear dimensionality reduction degenerates into linear method, such as ISOMAP, which degenerates into MDS[2].

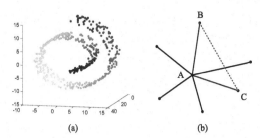

(a)   (b)

Fig. 2. An example to illustrate the superiority of the improved NG construction method. (a). 500 data points sampled from 2-dimensinal Swiss Roll manifold. (b). a representative neighborhood constructed by ANSLL when dealing with the 500 sampled data points in panel (a). All the points in panel b are in the neighborhood of point A. Suppose point B and C are not in the neighborhood of each other, and the shortest path between them is $B - A - C$. In original ISOMAP algorithm the estimate of the geometric distance between B and C is $d_E(B, A) + d_E(A, C)$, however, in the case that all points are in a plane, obviously $d_E(B, C)$ is a direct and still a more accurate estimate than $d_E(B, A) + d_E(A, C)$. Then we add a new edge connecting B and C in the NG.

6   Experiment Results

We conducted many experiments on both synthetic data set and real world data sets, all the experimental results show that our ANSLL can adaptively construct neighborhood and significantly improve the performance of most manifold learning algorithms such as ISOMAP and LLE. Moreover our algorithm is not sensitive to the parameters m as long as m is a comparatively large number, and the tolerable threshold η can be easily specified manually. In all the experiments showed below we set $m = 12$, $\eta = 0.95$ if they are not specified. And we call Isomap and LLE algorithm used our ANSLL algorithm ANSLL-Isomap and ANSLL-LLE respectively.

6.1   Z-Shape Curve Manifold

First, we do experiments on data set uniformly sampled from a Z-shape curve manifold. The fig. 3 shows the neighborhoods of two representative points constructed by two algorithms on the manifold. One point A is in the region where the manifold curvature is very large; the other point B is in the region where the curvature is very small.

Our ANSLL algorithm can adaptively construct the neighborhood according to the curvature of the manifold, this can be seen from the A's and B's neighborhood constructed by our ANSLL algorithm. The curvature of the manifold at point A is very large, therefore the number of points in A's neighborhood constructed by ANSLL is small whereas B's neighborhood contains much more points because of the small curvature of the manifold at B. Comparing the neighborhoods constructed by k-NN algorithm, we can see that k-NN has no such an ability.

Moreover, comparing the neighborhoods constructed under different sample size, A's neighborhoods constructed by ANSLL always cover the same region on the manifold in different sample size, the same is point B. However, region covered by neighborhood constructed by k-NN varies as the sample size. This phenomenon implies that our ANSLL constructs neighborhoods only according to the intrinsic structure of the manifold(curvatures in different region) and this construct process is little influenced by the sample size. We think this property is just what a superior neighborhood selection algorithm should have. However, the k-NN has no such a property either.

Then we apply LLE and ANSLL-LLE on 100 uniformly sampled data points, the unfolding results of these two algorithms and the real unfolding are shown on fig. 4. One can see that data points in the unfolding of LLE are no longer uniformly distributed, and the unfolding result of ANSLL-LLE algorithm is nearly the same as the real unfolding of the sampled data points, this demonstrates that our ANSLL algorithm can improve the performance of LLE significantly.

6.2   Swiss Roll Data Set

We run Isomap and ANSLL-isomap algorithms on 1000 data points randomly respectively sampled from Swiss Roll manifold and Swiss Roll with hole manifold.

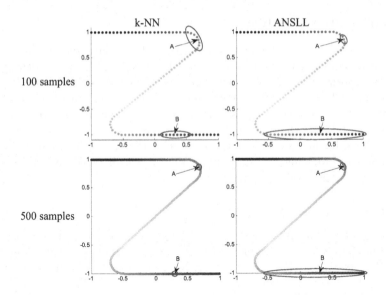

Fig. 3. The neighborhoods of A and B constructed by k-NN algorithm($k = 7$) and ANSLL algorithm. All the points in a red ellipse make up of a neighborhood respectively.

Fig. 4. The unfolding results of LLE and ANSLL-LLE and the real unfolding of 100 data points uniformly sampled from z-shape curve

The 2-D embeddings are shown in fig. 5. From the result we can see that ANSLL-isomap algorithm can produce more faithful embedding than Isomap algorithm. In particular, for swiss roll with hole manifold, Isomap amplifies the hole, while ANSLL-isomap can preserve the shape of the hole more faithfully.

We exploit the residual variance proposed in paper [3] and geodesic estimate error to quantitatively evaluate the performance of our method. Denote the true geodesic distance matrix by D_g and its estimate by $\hat{D}_g$, then the geodesic estimate error can be computed by the following formula:

$$error = \frac{\|D_g - \hat{D}_g\|_F}{n^2}$$

where $\|\cdot\|_F$ is the Frobenius-norm of matrix and n is the number of examples. In our experiment, the Swiss Roll data set is generated by the following matlab code:

```
t=3*pi/2*(1+2*rand(n,1));h=21*rand(n,1);
X=[t.*cos(t) h t.*sin(t)];
```

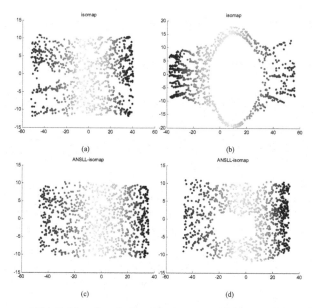

Fig. 5. Results of algorithm run on 1000 samples

So for any two points x_i and x_j, the true geodesic distance between them on data manifold can be calculated as follows:

$$d_g(x_i, x_j) =$$
$$\sqrt{(h_i - h_j)^2 + \frac{1}{4}\left(t_i\sqrt{t_i^2 + 1} + \ln\left|t_i + \sqrt{t_i^2 + 1}\right| - t_j\sqrt{t_j^2 + 1} - \ln\left|t_j + \sqrt{t_j^2 + 1}\right|\right)^2}$$

then we can easily obtain the true geodesic distance matrix D_g. Fig. 6 plots the residual variance and geodesic estimate error of Isomap and ANSLL-isomap under different parameters k and η when they obtain the 2-D embedding of 1000 data points randomly sampled from Swiss roll manifold. One can see that the residual variance and geodesic estimate error ANSLL-isomap are smaller than those of Isomap algorithm. So we can conclude that our ANSLL algorithm and the improved NG construction method can significantly improve the performance of Isomap algorithm.

6.3   Rendered Face Data Set

To further evaluate the performance of ANSLL algorithm on real world data set, we use Isomap algorithm and ANSLL-isomap to obtain 3-D embedding of Rendered face data set[1]. This data set consists of 698 face images with 64*64 pixels collected under different poses and light conditions. Each face image is represented as a 4096-dimensional vector. Denote the matrix that consists of

---

[1] http://isomap.stanford.edu

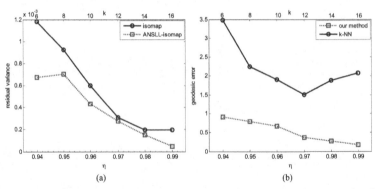

Fig. 6. Residual variance and geodesic estimate error of two algorithms under different parameters on 1000 data points randomly sampled from Swiss Roll manifold

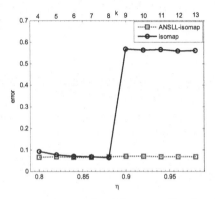

Fig. 7. Reconstruction error of two algorithms on Rendered face data set under different parameters

light parameters and poses parameters by P and $\hat{P} = P - (1/n)Pee^T$, then the reconstruction error of embedding algorithm can be defined as follows:

$$error = \min_{L \in R^{3\times3}} \|\hat{P} - LY\|_F$$

where Y is the embedding coordinates obtained by algorithm. Then we use the following relative reconstruction error to evaluate the performance:

$$error_r = \frac{error}{\|\hat{P}\|_F}$$

The less this relative reconstruction error is, the better the algorithm recovers the intrinsic parameters of this face data set. Fig. 7 plots the relative reconstruction error of the 3-D coordinates computed by isomap and ANSLL-isomap under different parameters k and η. One can clearly see that the relative reconstruct error of Isomap algorithm is sensitive to the parameter k, and ANSLL-isomap can get smaller relative reconstruction error, and the relative reconstruction error of ANSLL-isomap is not sensitive to the parameter η. This all demonstrates the superiority of our ANSLL algorithm and improved NG construction method.

7   Conclusion

This paper concentrates on the neighborhood select problem in manifold learning. Existing neighborhood select algorithms are not so satisfied. In this paper we propose an adaptive neighborhood select algorithm based on local linearity and improves the NG construction method originally used in ISOMAP algorithm. ANSLL algorithm adopts local linearity as the criterion of neighborhood. So it can adaptively construct the neighborhood of each point only according to data manifold curvature at that point. Meanwhile, the parameters can be specified easily because of their independence of the concrete input data set, such as the size of the input data. Experiments on both synthetic data set and real world data set demonstrate that our ANSLL algorithm can construct more reasonable neighborhoods than other algorithms, and the improved NG construction method can get more accurate geodesic distance estimate than the method originally used in ISOMAP. Moreover experiments also show that most manifold learning algorithms using our method can get more faithful low-dimensional embedding than that not use. There are, however, still some problems we have to solve in our ANSLL algorithm. ANSLL adopts the PCA to measure the linearity of finite data set, so sometimes over fitting can be happened. In the future, we will try to solve the over fitting problem.

Acknowledgments. This work is supported by the National Natural Science Foundation of China (NO.60603015).

References

1. Jolliffe, I.T.: Principal Component Analysis. Springer, Heidelberg (1989)
2. Cox, T., Cox, M.: Multidimensional Scaling. Chapman and Hall, Boca Raton (1994)
3. Tenenbaum, J.B., Silva, V.d., Langford, J.C.: A Global Geometric Framework for Nonlinear Dimensionality Reduction. Science 290, 2319–2323 (2000)
4. Saul, L.K., Roweis, S.T.: Think globally, fit locally: unsupervised learning of low dimensional manifolds. Journal of Machine Learning Research 4, 119–155 (2003)
5. Roweis, S.T., Saul, L.K.: Nonlinear Dimensionality Reduction by Locally Linear Embedding. Science 290, 2323–2326 (2000)
6. Belkin, M., Niyogi, P.: Laplacian eigenmaps for dimensionality reduction and data representation. Neural Comput. 15, 1373–1396 (2003)
7. Zhang, Z., Zha, H.: Principal Manifolds and Nonlinear Dimension Reduction via Local Tangent Space Alignment. SIAM J. Scientific Computing 26, 313–338 (2005)
8. Balasubramanian, M., Shwartz, E.L., Tenenbaum, J.B., Silva, V.d., Langford, J.C.: The Isomap Algorithm and Topological Stability. Science 295 (2002)
9. Yang, L.: Building k-edge-connected neighborhood graph for distance-based data projection. Pattern Recognit. Lett. 26, 2015–2021 (2005)

10. Yang, L.: Building k-connected neighborhood graphs for isometric data embedding. IEEE Transactions on Pattern Analysis and Machine Intelligence 28, 827–831 (2006)
11. Yang, L.: Building connected neighborhood graphs for isometric data embedding. In: Proceedings of the eleventh ACM SIGKDD international conference on Knowledge discovery in data mining. ACM, New York (2005)
12. Yang, L.: Building Connected Neighborhood Graphs for Locally Linear Embedding. In: ICPR 2006. 18th International Conference on Pattern Recognition,2006, vol. 4, pp. 194–197 (2006)
13. Samko, O., Marshall, A.D., Rosin, P.L.: Selection of the optimal parameter value for the Isomap algorithm. Pattern Recognit. Lett. 27, 968–979 (2006)
14. Xia, T., Li, J., Zhang, Y., Tang, S.: A More Topologically Stable Locally Linear Embedding Algorithm Based on R*-Tree. Advances in Knowledge Discovery and Data Mining, 803–812 (2008)
15. Shao, C., Huang, H., Zhao, L.: A More Topologically Stable ISOMAP Algorithm. Journal of Software 18, 869–877 (2007)
16. Shao, C., Huang, H., Wan, C.: Selection of the Suitable Neighborhood Size for the ISOMAP Algorithm. In: IJCNN 2007. International Joint Conference on Neural Networks, pp. 300–305 (2007)
17. Wen, G., Jiang, L., Wen, J.: Using locally estimated geodesic distance to optimize neighborhood graph for isometric data embedding. Pattern Recognit. 41, 2226–2236 (2008)
18. Lin, T., Zha, H.: Riemannian Manifold Learning. IEEE Trans. Pattern Anal. Mach. Intell. 30, 796–809 (2008)
19. Yan, S., Tang, X.: Largest-eigenvalue-theory for incremental principal component analysis. In: IEEE International Conference on Image Processing, 2005, vol. 1 (2005)
20. Zhong, C., Miao, D.: A comment on Using locally estimated geodesic distance to optimize neighborhood graph for isometric data embedding. Pattern Recognit. 42, 1012–1013 (2009)
21. Wen, G., Jiang, L., Wen, J.: Authors response to A comment on Using locally estimated geodesic distance to optimize neighborhood graph for isometric data embedding. Pattern Recognit. 42, 1014 (2009)

Anti-spam Filters Based on Support Vector Machines

Chengwang Xie[1], Lixin Ding[1], and Xin Du[1,2]

[1] State Key Lab of Software Engineering , Wuhan University, Wuhan 430072, China
[2] Department of Information and Engineering, Shijiazhuang University of Economics
Shijiazhuang 050031, China
chengwangxie@163.com

Abstract. Recently, spam has become an increasingly important problem. In this paper, a support vector machine (SVM) is used as the spam filter. Then a study is made of the effect of classification error rate when different subsets of corpora are used, and of the filter accuracy when SVM's with linear, polynomial, or RBF kernels is used. Also an investigation is made of the effect of the size of attribute sets. Based on the experimental results and analysis, it is concluded that SVM will be a very good alternative for building anti-spam classifiers, with consideration of a good combination of accuracy, consistency, and speed.

Keywords: anti-spam, support vector machines, classification, filter.

1 Introduction

The proliferation of unsolicited commercial e-mail(UCE), more commonly known as spam, over the last few years has been undermining constantly the usability of e-mail. The availability of bulk mailing software and lists of e-mail addresses harvested from Web pages, newsgroup archives, and service provider directories allows messages to be sent blindly to millions of recipients at essentially no cost. Spam messages are extremely annoying to most users, as they clutter their mail-boxes and prolong dial-up connections. They also waste the bandwidth and CPU time of ISPs, and often expose minors to unsuitable (e.g. pornographic) content.

Solutions to the proliferation of spam are either technical or regulatory [1]. Among the technical solutions, of more direct value are anti-spam filters, software tools that attempt to identify incoming spam messages automatically. The success of machine learning techniques in text categorization has led researchers to explore learning algorithms in anti-spam filtering. In this paper, we focused on the use of SVMs, which are currently placed among of the best-performing classifiers and have a unique ability to handle extremely large feature spaces (such as text), precisely the area where most of the traditional techniques fail due to the "curse of the dimensionality". Since SVMs have been shown to be very effective in the field of text categorization ([2],[8]), which we will utilize in this study.

In addition, due to a variety of practical reasons, the investigation of this paper considers only the text in the subjects and bodies of the messages, ignoring other headers, HTML markup, non-textual attributes, and attachments. Despite this limitation, we

Z. Cai et al. (Eds.): ISICA 2009, LNCS 5821, pp. 349–357, 2009.
© Springer-Verlag Berlin Heidelberg 2009

believe that the work of this paper is useful, in that it provides a detailed investigation of what can be achieved using only the text of the messages, thereby acting as a solid basis on which further improvements can be tried.

The remainder of this paper is organized as follows. In section 2, the feature extraction used in our work is presented, and in section 3 we simply describe SVM's learning mechanism. In section 4, we describe the corpora and experiments. The conclusions and future work are presented in section 5.

2 Feature Extraction

2.1 Feature Representation

A feature is a word. In the development below, w refers to a word, X is a feature vector that is composed of the various words from a dictionary formed by analyzing the documents. There is one feature vector per message. W refers to a weight vector usually obtained from some combination of the X 's. There are various alternatives and enhancements in constructing the X vectors. Some of them are considered as following [3]:

TF -Term Frequency: The i th component of the feature vector is the number of times that word w_i appears in that document. In our case, a word is a feature only if it occurs in three or more documents. (This prevents misspelled words and words used rarely from appearing in the dictionary).

$TF - IDF$ uses the above TF multiplied by the IDF (inverse document frequency). The document frequency ($DF(i)$) is the number of times that word w_i occurs in all the documents (excluding words that occur in less than three documents). The inverse document frequency (IDF) is defined as $IDF(w_i) = \log(\dfrac{|D|}{DF(w_i)})$,

where $|D|$ is the number of documents. Typically, the feature vector that consists of the $TF - IDF$ entries is normalized to unit length.

• Binary representation which indicates whether a particular word occurs in a particular document. A word is a candidate only if it occurs in three or more documents.

• Use of a stop list in addition to any of the above: Words like "of," "and," "the," etc., are used to form a stop list. Words on the stop list are not used in forming a feature vector. The rationale for this is that common words are not very useful in classification.

2.2 Feature Selection Method

A few of the mechanisms designed to find the optimum number of features (and the best features) are [3],[4] document frequency threshold, information gain, mutual information, term strength, and χ^2 . Yang and Pedersen [4] have found experimentally information gain to be one of the best attribute selection measures. Schneider [5] experimented with alternative versions of information gain attribute selection, intended to be more suitable to frequency-valued attributes. In this paper, the information gain $IG(X,C)$ of each remaining candidate attribute X with respect to the category-denoting random variable C was computed, using the Boolean values of the candidate attributes, as shown below; c_L and c_S denote the legitimate and spam categories, respectively. The m candidate attributes with the highest IG scores were then retained, with m depending on the experiment.

$$IG(X,C) = \sum_{x \in \{0,1\}, c \in \{c_L, c_S\}} P(X = x \wedge C = c) \cdot \log_2 \frac{P(X = x \wedge C = c)}{P(X = x) \cdot P(C = c)}$$

It can be shown that $IG(X,C)$ measures the average reduction in the entropy of C given the value of X [6]. Intuitive, it shows how much knowing X helps us guess correctly the value of C.

The main disadvantage of searching for the best features is that it requires additional time in the training algorithm. In the case of information gain, the features are ranked by the feature selection method from high to low, which is linear in the number of examples and linear in the number of features (giving quadratic complexity).

2.3 Performance Criteria

In information retrieval tasks, documents could be assigned multiple categories. For instance, a story about the high wages of basketball players could be categorized as belonging to both the term "financial" and the term "sports." When there are multiple categories, performance measures such as recall and precision [3],[4] are used. Since our problem is two-class classification task, recall and precision are not needed here.

In this paper, we use the following measures to indicate the filter's performance:

• Error Rate: Error rate is the typical performance measure for two-class classification schemes. However, two learning algorithms can have the same error rate, but the one which groups the errors near the decision border is the better one.

• False Alarm and Miss Rate: We define the false alarm and miss rates as

$$miss\ rate = \frac{nonspam\ samples\ misclassified}{total\ nonspam\ examples}$$

$$false\ alarm\ rate = \frac{spam\ samples\ misclassified}{total\ spam\ examples}.$$

The advantage of the false alarm and miss rate is that that they are a good indicator of whether the errors are close to the decision border or not. Given two classifiers with the same error rate, the one with lower false alarm and miss rates is the better one.

• Accuracy: We define the accuracy as that the filter can give the correct classification to all the examples classified.

$$Accuracy = \frac{spam\ found\ correct\ \text{and}\ nonspam\ found\ correct}{total\ examples\ classified}.$$

All of the experiments were performed using stratified ten-fold cross-validation [7]. That is, each message collection was divided into ten equally large parts, maintaining the original distribution of the two classes in each part. Each experiment was repeated ten times, reserving a different part for testing at each iteration, and using the remaining parts for training. The results were then averaged over the ten iterations, producing more reliable results, and allowing the entire corpus to be exploited for both training and testing. When we refer to the training corpus of cross-validation experiments, we mean the nine parts that were used for training at each iteration.

3   Support Vector Machines

Support vector machines were originally designed for binary classification, and they were discussed extensively in this issue ([3],[9],[10],[11]). The key concepts we want to use are the following: there are two classes, $y_i \in \{-1, 1\}$, and there are N labeled training examples: $(x_1, y_1), \cdots, (x_N, y_N), x \in R^d$ where d is the dimensionality of the vector.

If the two classes are linearly separable, then one can find an optimal weight vector w^* such that $\left\| w^* \right\|^2$ is minimum; and $w^* \bullet x_i - b \geq 1$ if $y_i = 1$, $w^* \bullet x_i - b \leq -1$ if $y_i = -1$, or equivalently $y_i(w^* \bullet x_i - b) \geq 1$. Training examples that satisfy the equality are termed support vectors. The support vectors define two hyperplanes, one that goes through the support vectors of one class and one goes through the support vectors of the other class. The distance between the two hyperplanes defines a margin and this margin is maximized when the norm of the weight vector $\left\| w^* \right\|$ is minimum. We may perform this minimization by maximizing the following function with respect to the variables α_j:

$$W(\alpha) = \sum_{i=1}^{N} \alpha_i - 0.5 \cdot \sum_{i=1}^{N} \sum_{j=1}^{N} \alpha_i \alpha_j (x_i \bullet x_j) y_i y_j$$

subject to the constraint: $\alpha_j \geq 0$ where it is assumed there are N training examples, x_i is one of the training vectors, and $\bullet$ represents the dot product. If $\alpha_j > 0$ then x_j is termed a support vector. For an unknown vector x_j classification then corresponds to finding $F(x_j) = sign\{w^* \bullet x_j - b\}$, where $w^* = \sum_{i=1}^{r} \alpha_i y_i x_i$, and the sum is over the r nonzero support vectors (whose α's are nonzero).

The advantage of the representation is that w^* can be calculated after training and classification amounts to computing the dot product of this optimum weight vector with the input vector.

For the nonseparable case, training errors are allowed and we now must minimize
$\left\| w^* \right\|^2 + C \sum_{i=1}^{N} \xi_i$, subject to the constraint $y_i(w^* \bullet x_i - b) \le (1 - \xi)$, $\xi \ge 0$. ξ is a
slack variable and allows training examples to exist in the region between the two
hyperplanes that go through the support points of the two classes. We can equiva-
lently minimize $W(\alpha)$ but the constraint is now $0 \le \alpha_i \le C$ instead of $\alpha_j \ge 0$.

Maximizing $W(\alpha)$ is quadratic programming techniques.

A range of kernel functions have been used in the literature, e.g., polynomial and
RBF kernels. The choice of kernel affects the model bias of the algorithm. For instance, the higher the degree n of a polynomial kernel, the higher the order of the dis-
criminant function that can be discovered in the original vector space. However, research in text classification has shown that simple linear SVMs usually perform as well
as non-linear ones [8]. In our paper, we will experiment with linear kernels, polynomial
kernels of various degrees and *RBF* kernels to compare the filters' performance.

4 Experiments

4.1 Benchmark Corpora for Anti-spam Filtering

In this paper, we used two publicly available data sets: PU1 and PU2. In order to
bypass privacy problem, each token was replaced by a unique number throughout the
corpus. The mapping between tokens and numbers is not released, making it extremely difficult to recover the original text.

The legitimate messages in PU1 are the English legitimate messages that Androutsopoulos [7] had received and saved over a period of 36 months, excluding self-
addressed messages; this led to 1182 messages. Legitimate messages with empty
bodies and regular correspondents, RC messages for brevity, were then removed. The
spam messages in PU1 are all the spam messages that Androutsopoulos had received
over a period of 22 months, excluding non-English messages and duplicates received
on the same day.

PU2 started from the legitimate and spam messages that Androutsopoulos' colleague
had received over a period of 22 months. The vast majority of his legitimate messages
were RC. Table 1 provides more information on the composition of the PU corpora.

Table 1. Composition and sizes of the PU collections. The third column shows the number of
legitimate messages from regular correspondents (RC), while the fourth column counts the
legitimate messages that were discarded for other reasons (e.g., empty bodies or duplicates); in
PU1 and PU2 both types of legitimate messages were discarded in one step. The last column
shows the legitimate-to-spam ratio in the retained messages.

collection name	legitimate initially	RC messages	other legit. discarded	legitimate retained	spam retained	total retained	L:S ratio
PU1	1182	564		618	481	1099	1.28
PU2	6207	5628		579	142	721	4.01

In all PU collections, attachments, HTML tags, and header fields other than the subject were removed, and the messages were then encoded as discussed above. Punctuation and other special symbols (e.g., "!", " $ ") were treated as tokens. Many of these symbols are among the best discriminating attributes in the PU corpora, because they are more common in spam messages than legitimate ones.

4.2 Corpus Experiments

We now move on to the presentation of our corpus experiments, which were performed using the PU1 and PU2 collections. All the experiments were performed using stratified 10-fold cross-validation.

All e-mail messages consist of a subject and body and the linear SVMs were tried on either the subject alone, the body alone, or the subject and body together. In addition, a stop list was either used or not used. We used all words in the messages as long as they occurred in at least three messages. The original feature entries are TF (term frequency) and could later be converted $TF - IDF$ or binary features. Thus there were six data sets constructed from the original 1099 messages (PU1), in the same way, six data sets were come from PU2 containing 721 messages:

- bodnostop – words from the body only without using a stop list.
- bodstop – words from the body only and the stop list was used.
- subbodnostop – words from the subject and body without using a stop list.
- subbodstop – words from the subject and body using a stop list.

Results are shown in Table 2 and Table 3. It can therefore be seen that the smallest error rates are given by using the subject and body without using a stop list (subbodnostop) and that SVM should be used with binary features. There are two reasons we believe that the training time for SVM's with binary features can be reduced. The first is that the vectors are binary and the second is that the feature vectors are sparse (typically only 4% of a vector is nonzero). This allows the dot product in the SVM optimization to be replaced with faster non-multiplicative routines.

It should be emphasized that the spam filter will never actually reject any messages classified as spam. The use of the false alarm and miss rates is a mechanism to compare performance.

The running times for training and testing have not been optimized for SVM's, however, since the SVM only has to execute one dot product, it would be expected to be fast.

Table 2. For PU1, false alarm rates corresponding to a 5% miss rate

	Linear SVM (TF features)	Linear SVM (binary features)	Linear SVM (TF-IDF features)
bodnostop	0.0982	0.0734	0.0908
bodstop	0.1202	0.1014	0.1302
subbodnostop	0.0182	0.0161	0.0176
subbodstop	0.0418	0.0402	0.0426
subnostop	0.5278	0.4304	0.5376
substop	0.7832	0.6525	0.6737

Table 3. For PU2, false alarm rates corresponding to a 5% miss rate

	Linear SVM (TF features)	Linear SVM (binary features)	Linear SVM (TF-IDF features)
bodnostop	0.1208	0.0978	0.1325
bodstop	0.3245	0.2578	0.3365
subbodnostop	0.0232	0.0202	0.0264
subbodstop	0.0525	0.0408	0.0448
subnostop	0.2343	0.2045	0.2796
substop	0.4575	0.4565	0.5054

The following experiments compare the performance of SVMs when using with linear, polynomial and RBF kernels. SVM training is carried out with the SVM[light] package, more information about SVM[light], readers can refer to [12]. The experiments also uses with all the features. Table 4 shows the results on PU1 and PU2. The accuracy is used as a performance measure.

Table 4. Various SVMs tested on PU1 and PU2, accuracy measure (%) was used

	SVM (linear)	SVM (poly) degree d=					SVM (RBF) $\gamma=$		
		1	2	3	4	5	0.6	0.8	1.0
PU1	93.4	93.5	92.6	94.1	92.9	93.1	92.1	93.4	92.9
PU2	94.1	93.7	94.2	93.2	94.5	93.9	94.0	93.6	94.1

We can see from Table 4 that simple linear SVMs usually perform as well as non-linear ones (e.g., polynomial and RBF kernels), moreover, the advantage of linear SVM's is that execution speed is very fast and there are no parameters to tune except the constant C. So, in our filter's architecture we use linear SVM, we can not only achieve comparable performance but also improve the time complexity of the filter.

The last experiments are to investigate the effect of the parameter: the size of the attribute set. Here, each attribute corresponded to one token. The best m attributes were retained based on information gain scores sorted, with m ranging from 40 to 3000 by 80. As shown in Figure 1, retaining large numbers of attributes does not always lead to significant improvements in accuracy, in most cases the accuracy curves are almost horizontal after the first few hundreds of attributes, which implies that one can often obtain very similar results with much fewer attributes, furthermore, [7] has shown that in almost all cases, there is a significant increase in both learning and classification time as more attributes are retained. Hence, in a real-life application one should be skeptical about using large attribute sets. In addition, the filters based on SVM's seemingly have similar accuracy in terms of accuracy between the PU1 and PU2, although the L:S ratio in PU1 is 1.28, and that in PU2 is 4.01. Since SVM's are not directly trying to minimize the error rate, but trying to separate the patterns in high dimensional space, the result is that SVM's are relatively insensitive to the relative numbers of each class.

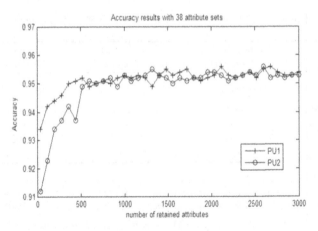

Fig. 1. 38 attribute sets were tested on PU1 and PU2 in terms of accuracy measure, using linear SVM filter

5   Conclusion and Future Work

In this paper, we investigate on the use of SVMs to construct effective anti-spam filters. Two publicly available corpora PU1 and PU2 were used. According to experiments, we come to the following conclusions:

1)   We can achieve the smallest error rates by using the subject and body without using a stop list (subbodnostop) and that SVM should be used with binary features.

2)   In a choice of between using a stop list and not using a stop list, it is preferable that a stop list not be used.

3)   Due to the simple linear SVMs perform as well as non-linear ones (e.g., polynomial and RBF kernels), we can use linear SVMs as filter's learning component.

4)   Attribute selection based on information gain leads to good performance with a few hundreds of attributes. Using much larger attribute sets may lead to further improvement in accuracy, but the improvements are usually small, and they are counter-balanced by increased computational cost.

For both data sets, SVM's had acceptable test performance in terms of accuracy and error rate, especially, its dot product optimization, we can reach that SVM's will be the perfect alternative as spam-filter's learning component.

The results of our experiments are promising, although we have not fully exploited the potential information in the email messages. Some papers in the literature suggest to consider other features than words in the messages, like the address of the sender, the number of capital letters, or some hand-crafted expressions like "win big money", to produce more accurate classifier ([13],[14],[15]). In fact, what we propose is to follow a complete Knowledge Discovery process, identifying good candidates for message features, and producing accurate classifiers in the context of a real usage scenario. The best users for building such an scenario are probably ISPs, because they are the most affected users by the problem of spam.

In the long run, mixtures of different filtering approaches, including collaborative filtering, are more likely to be successful, and machine learning has a central role to play in such mixed filters. Combining different learning algorithms also seems to be promising, as different classifiers often make different errors [16].

Acknowledgments. Our research is supported by Doctoral Fund of Ministry of Education of China (No.20070486081). At the same time, the work is also supported by Excellent Youth Foundation of Hubei Province of China (No.2005ABB017).

References

1. Faith Cranor, L., LaMacchia, B.H.: Spam. Commun. ACM 41(8), 74–83 (1998)
2. Dumais, S., Platt, J., Heckerman, D., Sahami, M.: Inductive learning algorithms and representations for text categorization. In: Proceedings of 7th International Conference on Information and Knowledge Management, pp. 229–237 (1998)
3. Drucker, H., Wu, D., Vapnik, V.N.: Support Vector Machines for Spam Categorization. IEEE transactions on neural networks 10(5) (September 1999)
4. Yang, Y., Pedersen, J.O.: A comparative study of feature selection in text categorization. In: Proc. 14th Int. Conf. Machine Learing (1997)
5. Schneider, K.–M.: A comparison of event models for Naive Bayes anti-spam e-mail filtering. In: Proceedings of the 10th Conference of the European Chapter of the Association for Computational Linguistics, Budapest, Hungary, pp. 307–314 (2003)
6. Manning, C., Schutze, H.: Foundations of statitical natural language processing. MIT Press, Cambridge (1999)
7. Androutsopoulos, I., Paliouras, G., Michelakis, E.: Learning to Filter Unsolicited Commercial E-Mail. NCSR "Demokritos" Technical Report, No. 2004/2 (March 2004)
8. Joachims, T.: Text Categorization with Support Vector Machines: Learning with many relevant features. In: Nédellec, C., Rouveirol, C. (eds.) ECML 1998. LNCS, vol. 1398, pp. 137–142. Springer, Heidelberg (1998)
9. Vapnik, V.: Estimation of Dependencies Based on Empirical Data. Springer, New York (1992)
10. Vapnik, V.: The Nature of Statistical Learning Theroy. Springer, New York (1995)
11. Drucker, H., Burges, C.J.C., Kauffman, L., Smola, A., Vapnik, V.: Support vector regression machines. In: Mczer, M.C., Joradn, J.I., petsche, T. (eds.) Neural Inform. Processing Syst., vol. 9, pp. 155–161. MIT Press, Cambridge (1997)
12. http://www-ai.informatik.uni-dortmund.de/thorsten/svm_light.html
13. Gomez Hidalgo, J.M., Ma na Lopez, M., Puertas Sanz, E.: Combining text and heuristics for cost-sensitive spam filtering. In: Proceedings of the Fourth Computational Natural Language Learning Workshop, CoNLL 2000. Association for Computational Linguistics (2000)
14. Sahami, M., Dumais, S., Heckerman, D., Horvitz, E.: A bayesian approach to filter junk e-mail. In: Learning for Text Categorization: Papers from the, Workshop, Madison, Wisconsin, AAAI Technical Report WS-98-05 (1998)
15. Maria, J., Hidalgo, G.: Evaluating Cost-Sensitive Unsolicited Bulk Email Categorization. In: International Conference Textual Data Statistical Analysis, Saint Malo, France, no. 6, pp. 323–334 (2002)
16. Sakkis, G., Androutsopoulos, I.: Stacking classifiers for anti-spam filtering of e-mail. In: Proceedings of the 6th conference on Empirical Methods in Natural Language Processing, pp. 44–50. Carnegie Mellon, Pittsburgh (2001a)

Multi-attribute Weight Allocation Based on Fuzzy Clustering Analysis and Rough Sets

Jing Wu[*], Xiaoyan Wu, and Zhongchang Gao

Missile Institute, Air Force Engineering University,
Sanyuan, Shaanxi, 713800, China
Ken1983414@126.com

Abstract. The reasonalbe and effective determination of the weight allocation is very critical to multi-attribute decision-making. This paper presents a novel multi-attribute weight allocation method based on the fuzzy clustering analysis and the information entropy theory in rough sets theory. It first studies the fuzzy clustering analysis method based on fuzzy transitive closure with the introduction of the information entropy theory in rough sets. Furthermore, it discusses the detailed steps of the proposed approach thoroughly . After the fuzzy clustering of the source data, the overall reasonable threshold is extracted based on F-statistics and the multi-attribute weight allocation is obtained using the information entropy theory. Finally, a case study is given to show the reasonability and validity of the proposed approach.

Keywords: fuzzy clustering; rough sets; information entropy; weight allocation.

1 Introduction

The precondition of multi-attribute decision-making is the multi-attribute weight allocation. How to avoid the effect of individual subjective judgment and favoritism on the weight allocation and confirm the multi-attribute weight allocation subjectively and reasonably is very important to multi-attribute decision-making.

Currently, there're many methods to solve the problem, such as AHP, Delphi, information entropy, rough sets (RS) theory, similar coefficient, fuzzy clustering analysis (FCA), etc. Although AHP method executes mathematical process to the expert's judgments, AHP and Delphi are still the same methods essentially, because they both depend on the expert's experience subjectively. The information entropy denotes the effectiveness of indicator's entropy, and the weight allocation by the method is more credible than the former. However, it lacks of the comparison among the indicators. The rough sets method doesn't need any prior information. However, it can only deal with the discrete decision table. And FCA method needs the prior information.

Aiming at the disadvantages of those methods above, based on the FCA and RS theory, a novel multi-attribute weight allocation method is proposed in this paper,

---

[*] Jing Wu is a Ph.D. student. He studies in 25#, Sanyuan, Shaanxi, China. His current research interests include M&S credibility evaluation and VV&A. His email address is <ken1983414@126.com>.

Z. Cai et al. (Eds.): ISICA 2009, LNCS 5821, pp. 358–365, 2009.
© Springer-Verlag Berlin Heidelberg 2009

which could reduce the effect of individual subjective judgment and favoritism on the weight allocation.

The remainder of this paper is organized as follows: Section 2 introduces the basic knowledge of related theory; Section 3 presents a weight allocation method based on FCA and RS; Section 4 gives a case study; and Section 5 gives the conclusions and the future work perspectives.

2 Basic Knowledge of Related Theory

2.1 Fuzzy Cluster Analysis

Cluster analysis or clustering is the assignment of objects into groups (called clusters) so that objects from the same cluster are more similar to each other than objects from different clusters. Often similarity is assessed according to a distance measure. Clustering is a common technique for statistical data analysis. Since Bellman et al. [1] and Ruspini [2] first initiated the research on clustering based on fuzzy sets, fuzzy clustering has been widely studied and applied in a variety of different areas, such as machine learning, data mining, pattern recognition, image analysis and bioinformatics.

Fuzzy clustering methods can be roughly divided into two categories. One involves distance-defined objective functions. The fuzzy c-means (FCM) algorithm and its variations are the well-known approaches in this category. However, the FCM-type methods need to have data presented in feature vectors so that the distance and prototypes can be calculated. The other category involves fuzzy relations. Since these fuzzy relation-based methods require only a relation matrix of the data set, they are simpler to use and are applied to many areas. In this paper, we mainly discuss the method based on transitive closure of fuzzy equivalent relation [3][4].

2.2 Data Normalization

Let $X = \{x_1, x_2, \cdots, x_n\}$ be a set of n objects to be classified and $x_j = (x_{j1}, x_{j2}, \cdots, x_{jm})$, where $x_{jk}(1 \leq k \leq m)$ is the kth feature of the ith object. Therefore, the features of an object set can be described by a $n \times m$ matrix $X = (x_{ij})_{n \times m}$. Then, the raw data should be normalized by the following formula:

$$x_{ij}' = x_{ij} / \max_{1 \leq k \leq m}(x_{kj}) \tag{1}$$

2.3 Construct Fuzzy Similar Matrix

Constructing fuzzy similar matrix to confirm the similarity r_{ij} between $x_i' = (x_{i1}', x_{i2}', \cdots, x_{im}')$ and $x_j' = (x_{j1}', x_{j2}', \cdots, x_{jm}')$. There are many methods to calculate r_{ij}, such as similar coefficient method, distance method, nearness degree method, subjective assessment method, etc. In this paper, we use the nearness degree method based on the following formula:

$$r_{ij} = \frac{\sum_{k=1}^{m} \min(x_{ik}^{'}, x_{jk}^{'})}{\sum_{k=1}^{m} \max(x_{ik}^{'}, x_{jk}^{'})} \tag{2}$$

Thus the fuzzy similar matrix R is built up as follows: $R = (r_{ij})_{n \times n}$.

2.4 Fuzzy Clustering

The paper adopts a clustering method based on the transitive closure of fuzzy equivalent relation. The transitive closure $t(R)$ is gained by means of the 'square method' that fuzzy similar matrix is squared gradually, just as the following formula:

$$R \rightarrow R^2 \rightarrow R^4 \rightarrow \cdots \rightarrow R^{2^i} \rightarrow \cdots$$
$$(R^2 = R \circ R = \bigvee_{k=1}^{n} (r_{ik} \wedge r_{kj})) \tag{3}$$

when $R^k = R^k \circ R^k$, it means that R^k is the transitive closure, and it is also the fuzzy equivalent matrix.

After establishing the fuzzy equivalent matrix, specific clustering process is to endow λ with different value from larger to smaller in turn. Then, get different clusters by calculating the λ-cut matrix.

2.5 Confirm Reasonable Threshold Interval

Obviously, there are different cluster as various λ according to the fuzzy clustering analysis. However, how to select a reasonable threshold is an intractable problem to be solved. Generally, we choose the value of λ according to expert's experience. F-statistics is an objective and feasible method to solve the problem. The method is described as follows.

$$\bar{x}_{ik} = \frac{1}{n_i} \sum_{j=1}^{n_i} x_{jk} \ , k = 1, 2, \cdots, m \tag{4}$$

Where n_i is the number of the ith cluster. $\bar{x}_{ik}$ is the mean value of kth feature of ith cluster.

$$\bar{x}_k = \frac{1}{n} \sum_{j=1}^{n} x_{jk} \ , k = 1, 2, \cdots, m \tag{5}$$

Where $\bar{x}_k$ is the mean value of kth feature of all clusters.

Then, the F-statistics can be denoted as follows:

$$F = \frac{\sum_{i=1}^{r} n_i \sum_{k=1}^{m} (\bar{x}_{ik} - \bar{x}_k)^2 / (r-1)}{\sum_{i=1}^{r} \sum_{j=1}^{n_i} \sum_{k=1}^{m} (x_{ik} - \bar{x}_{jk})^2 / (n-r)} \sim F(r-1, n-r) \tag{6}$$

Where r is the number of cluster corresponding to λ.

The nominator in (6) expresses the distance distances between clusters and the denominator expresses the inner-cluster distance. Therefore, the lager F is, the cluster is more reasonable [5]. Look up F_α in the upper critical values of the F distribution at α significance level. If $F > F_\alpha$, it means that the cluster is reasonable relatively and the reasonable threshold interval is also confirmed.

2.6 Rough Set Theory Based on Information Entropy

The uncertainty of knowledge could be measured by the information entropy. The roughness of knowledge and the information entropy have a close relationship. We give some basic definitions of rough set theory based on information entropy below [6].

Definition 1. Given a probability approximation space (U, R, P), the uncertainty of the system is denoted by its entropy $H(R^*)$, as the following formula:

$$H(R^*) = -\sum_{i=1}^{n} P(X_i) \log P(X_i) \tag{7}$$

Where $R^* = U / R = \{X_1, X_2, \cdots, X_n\}$

Definition 2. Suppose $S^* = \{Y_1, Y_2, \cdots, Y_m\}$ is another equivalent relationship. The conditional entropy or conditional uncertainty of knowledge S^* given knowledge R^* (also called the equivocation of S^* about R^*) is the average conditional entropy over R^*:

$$H(S^*|R^*) = -\sum_{i=1}^{n} P(X_i) \sum_{j=1}^{m} P(Y_j|X_i) \log P(Y_j|X_i) \tag{8}$$

Conditional entropy $H(S^*|R^*)$ is a reasonable measurement of the dependency of knowledge S^* relative to knowledge R^*.

Definition 3. Mutual information measures the amount of information that can be obtained about one random variable by observing another. It is important in communication where it can be used to maximize the amount of information shared between sent and received signals. The mutual information of R^* relative to S^* is given by:

$$I(R^*; S^*) = H(S^*) - H(S^*|R^*) = H(R^*) - H(R^*|S^*) \tag{9}$$

3 Weight Allocation Based on FCA and RS

In order to analysis the significance of each attribute in the sample, as to relational data model which involves both condition attributes and decision attributes, the weight allocation could be obtained based on the significance and dependence of the attributes in rough sets theory. When there are only condition attributes in the data model, the fuzzy clustering analysis method could be adopted to determine the weight allocation [7]. The detailed steps are as follows:

Step 1: Construct original data matrix $X = (x_{ij})_{n \times m}$ and perform fuzzy clustering based on the transitive closure of fuzzy equivalent relation. Confirm the reasonable threshold $\lambda_c \in [a_c, b_c]$ and its corresponding cluster when $F > F_\alpha$ based on F-statistics.

Step 2: After deleting condition attribute $c_i (i = 1, 2, \cdots, m)$, performing dynamic clustering of the data matrix and confirm the reasonable threshold interval $\lambda_{C-\{c_i\}} \in [a_{C-\{c_i\}}, b_{C-\{c_i\}}]$.

Step 3: In order to ensure the reasonability of each threshold interval, confirm the overall reasonable threshold interval $\lambda_k \in [\min(a_C, a_{C-\{c_i\}}), \max(b_C, b_{C-\{c_i\}})]$, $(1 \le k \le p)$.

Step 4: Confirm the information quantity $I(c_i)$ of each attribute. According to information entropy, after deleting a certain attribute, if obtaining more information from the original cluster, it means that the attribute provides more information, vice versa. Thus the information quantity $I_{\lambda_k}(c_i)$ at the threshold λ_k can be denoted as the following formula:

$$I_{\lambda_k}(c_i) = 1 / I_{\lambda_k}(C; C - \{c_i\}), (i = 1, 2, \cdots, m) \tag{10}$$

Synthesis all thresholds, the information quantity $I(c_i)$ is obtained as follows:

$$I(c_i) = \frac{1}{p} \sum_{k=1}^{p} I_{\lambda_k}(c_i) \tag{11}$$

Step 5: Confirm the weight allocation based on the information quantity of each attribute.

$$w_i = I(c_i) / \sum_{j=1}^{m} I(c_j) \tag{12}$$

4   Case Study

We applied the proposed method to the weigh allocation of a knowledge system (See Table 1). According to Step 1, performing fuzzy clustering analysis based on the transitive closure of fuzzy equivalent relation. The dynamic clustering of the datasets is depicted in Fig. 1.

Table 1. A knowledge system

No.	Condition attribute (C)			
	c_1	c_2	c_3	c_4
1	0.51	0.45	0.53	0.44
2	0.33	0.21	0.44	0.22
3	0.44	0.32	0.61	0.44
4	0.71	0.65	0.78	0.80
5	0.20	0.31	0.26	0.40
6	0.60	0.65	0.75	0.55
7	0.40	0.48	0.65	0.25
8	0.40	0.65	0.58	0.31
9	0.80	0.73	0.90	0.85
10	0.76	0.55	0.58	0.60

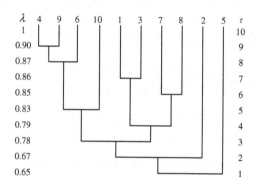

Fig. 1. Dynamic clustering results

Confirm the reasonable threshold interval based on F-statistics method. Calculating the F corresponding to each λ, and the results is shown in Table 2.

Table 2. Results based on F-statistics method

λ	0.90	0.87	0.86	0.85	0.83	0.79	0.78	0.67
r	9	8	7	6	5	4	3	2
F	10.55	4.04	6.03	8.04	7.63	8.54	2.75	2.24
$F_{0.1}(r-1,n-r)$	59.44	9.25	5.28	4.05	3.52	3.29	3.26	3.46
$F-F_{0.1}(r-1,n-r)$	-	-	0.75	3.99	4.11	5.25	-	-

It is insignificant that if all objects belong to one cluster or each object is a cluster. Therefore, we needn't calculate F when $\lambda = 1$ or $\lambda = 0.65$. Only when $\lambda_C \in [0.79, 0.86]$, $F > F_{0.1}$. Thus $\lambda_C \in [0.79, 0.86]$ is the reasonable threshold interval.

Similarly, according to Step 2, confirm the reasonable threshold interval after deleting conditional attribute $c_i (1 \leq i \leq 4)$. When deleting c_1, the reasonable threshold interval is $\lambda_{C-\{c_1\}} \in [0.84, 0.86]$; When deleting c_2, the reasonable threshold interval is $\lambda_{C-\{c_2\}} \in [0.82, 0.9]$; When deleting c_3, the reasonable threshold interval is $\lambda_{C-\{c_3\}} \in [0.78, 0.86]$; When deleting c_4, the reasonable threshold interval is $\lambda_{C-\{c_4\}} \in [0.82, 0.86]$.

According to Step 3, the overall reasonable threshold interval is obtained $\lambda_k \in [0.84, 0.86]$, $(1 \leq k \leq 3)$。

When $\lambda_1 = 0.84$, the original datasets including all attributes could be clustered to 6 clusters: {4, 6, 9}, {1, 3}, {7, 8}, {2}, {5}, {10}; After deleting attribute c_1, the datasets could be clustered to 6 clusters: {4, 6, 9, 10}, {1, 3}, {2}, {5}, {7}, {8}; After deleting attribute c_2, the datasets could be clustered to 7 clusters: {1, 3, 7, 8}, {4, 9}, {2}, {5}, {6}, {10}; After deleting attribute c_3, the datasets could be clustered to 6 clusters: {4, 6, 9, 10}, {1, 3}, {2}, {5}, {7}, {8}; After deleting attribute c_4, the datasets could be clustered to 5 clusters: {4, 6, 9, 10}, {1, 3, 7, 8}, {2}, {5}, {10}.

When $\lambda_1 = 0.84$, According to (7), the entropy of the knowledge system $H_{\lambda_1}(C) = 2.6464$. According to (8), the condition entropy $H_{\lambda_1}(C|C-\{c_i\})$ $(1 \leq i \leq 3)$ after deleting attribute c_i is (0.3245, 0.4, 0.3245, 0.7245). Thus, using (9), the mutual information $I_{\lambda_1}(C; C-\{c_i\})$ is (2.1219, 2.0464, 2.1219, 1.7219). According to (10), the information quantity $I_{\lambda_1}(c_i)$ is (0.4713, 0.4887, 0.4713, 0.5808).

Similarly, when $\lambda_2 = 0.85$, the information quantity of each attribute is (0.4088, 0.4887, 0.4452, 0.4606); when $\lambda_3 = 0.84$, the information quantity of each attribute is (0.4713, 0.4887, 0.4713, 0.5808).

According to (11), synthesizing all three thresholds, the information quantity of each attribute is (0.4505, 0.4887, 0.4626, 0.5407).

According to Step 5 and formula (12), the final weight allocation is obtained as follows: $w =$(0.2319, 0.2516, 0.2381, 0.2784).

As to the knowledge system in the case study, if adopting the method in [7][8], we should synthesis 16 thresholds to determine the final weight allocation. On one hand, this method involves more computation, on the other hand, only the overall reasonable threshold and its corresponding cluster is good for the computation of weight allocation. If adopting the method in [9], after extracting the optimal threshold and performing weight allocation based on the attribute significance in RS theory, we find that the final weight allocation of each attribute is 0. Therefore, the proposed method in this paper is more valid, which calculate the weight allocation within the overall reasonable threshold interval.

5 Conclusions

A valid and reasonable weight allocation is very critical to multi-attribute decision-making. Therefore, we need to find an objective solution to execute weight allocation by mining in the database. Based on FCA in fuzzy sets and the entropy theory in RS theory, a novel multi-attribute weight allocation method is proposed. Since the proposed method distills the inner information of the knowledge system and reduces the effect of individual subjective judgment and favoritism on the weight allocation, it is more objective and valid than other evaluation methods. The case study results demonstrate the reasonability and validity of the proposed approach.

The future work involves validating convergence property of this clustering and applying the method to other domains to validate the approach.

Acknowledgments. This paper is supported by the Nature Science Foundation of Shaanxi, China (NO. 2007F40).

References

1. Bellman, R., Kalaba, R.L., Zadeh, L.A.: Abstraction and pattern classification. Journal of Mathematical Analysis and Applications 2, 581–585 (1966)
2. Ruspini, E.H.: A new approach to clustering. Information and Control 15, 22–32 (1969)
3. Yang, M.S., Shih, H.M.: Cluster analysis based on fuzzy relations. Fuzzy Sets and Systems 120, 197–212 (2001)
4. Guh, Y.-Y., Yang, M.-S., Po, R.-W., Lee, E.S.: Establishing performance evaluation structures by fuzzyrelation-based cluster analysis. Computers and Mathematics with Applications 56, 572–582 (2008)
5. Zhang, L., Qi, J.: Evaluation Model for Grid Safe Production Based on Fuzzy Clustering and Rough Set. In: International Workshop on Modelling, Simulation and Optimization, pp. 196–199 (2008)
6. Chen, C.-B., Wang, L.-y.: Rough Set-Based Clustering with Refinement Using Shannon's Entropy Theory. Computers and Mathematics with Applications 52, 1563–1576 (2006)
7. Huang, D.-x.: Means of Weights Allocation with Multi-Factors Based on Impersonal Message Entropy. Systems Engineering Theory Methodology Applications 12(4), 321–325 (2003)
8. Huang, D., Wu, Z., Zong, Y.: An impersonal multi-attribute weight allocation method based on attribute importance. Systems Engineering Theory Methodology Applications 13(3), 203–208 (2004)
9. Liu, B., Li, H.: Method of factor weights allocation based on combination of fuzzy and rough set. Control and Decision 22(12), 1437–1441 (2007)

Spatio-temporal Model Based on Back Propagation Neural Network for Regional Data in GIS

Jing Zhu, Xiang Li, and Lin Du

Institute of Computer Science, China University of Geosciences, Wuhan, China
jingzhu723@163.com, lixiang@cug.edu.cn, dulin006@sohu.com

Abstract. This paper focuses on spatio-temporal non-linear intelligent prediction modeling for regional data, and discusses the application of Back-Propagation neural network (BPN) into analysis of regional data in geographic information system (GIS). With their characteristics of space-dependence and space volatility, the regional data determine the accuracy of the prediction model.With consideration of the sectional instability of the spatial pattern, the paper brings forward a modeling method based on regional neural network. First, the space units of researching regions are divided into different sub-regions by improved K-means algorithm based on spatial adjacency relationship, corresponding with sub-regions. Then, a modular BP network is built up, which is composed with main network, gate-network and sub-network. This network is thus named as regional spatio-temporal neural network (RSTN) model. Afterwards, the sub-networks are traiend respectively for every sub-region, and the output of sub-networks is input of main network with adjustment of gate-network The output of main network is predictive results. The spatio-temporal predictive capability of model is measured by average variance rate (AVR) and dynamic similar rate (DSR). At last, the RSTN model and the global BPN model are compared by the analysis of an example: prediction for influenza cases of 94 countries in France. The comparison declares that RSTN model has more powerful prediction capability.

Keywords: Spatio-temporal analysis, Regional data, Modular BP network, Regional spatio-temporal neural network model (RSTN model).

1 Introduction

Because of the imperative requirement in spatio-temporal functions of GIS like dynamic data update, management of history data, process simulation and trend prediction, temporal GIS aroused general interest over the last decade. Spatio-temporal model is the core and the main difficult issue in temporal GIS.

The purpose of building spatio-temporal model in GIS is to forecast system evolution trend through analyzing causal relationship of system variables come from actual observation data and make a best decision-making. Regression analysis model is a traditional method to solve it. But because the affect between various factors is very complex and the actual observation data is interfered by random factors inevitably,

Z. Cai et al. (Eds.): ISICA 2009, LNCS 5821, pp. 366–374, 2009.

causal relationship of system variables in GIS can't be determined accurately by this method [2]. Conventional regression analysis methods need approximate understanding of relationship between independent variable and dependent variable (linear and/or non-linear). So they will make wrong estimation to relationship of variables and lead to a predictive results with large error [4] [5].

Theory of artificial neural network (ANN) provides a new solution of this problem. Neural network have nice nonlinear characteristics, and it have more powerful capability of pattern recognition and non-linear mapping approximation with arbitrary precision because of its flexible and effective learning methods, complete distributed study structure and high degree parallel processing mechanism.

Prediction model based neural network widely used in weather forecast, groundwater exploration, environment monitor, ocean tides and many other areas of study. In this paper, research on the neural network model for regional GIS data in the temporal and spatial analysis. Some similar researches on the forecast modeling method based on neural network have been declared, such as the literature [6], [7], [8], [9] which involved in the study. They are almost all to establish global multi-layer feed-forward network based on test data set. However, spatial data in GIS have both global space-dependent property and local space volatility property. Simple global neural network model for temporal and spatial analysis of GIS may be unacceptable for the error from definition of boundary region.

With thinking of local instability of space pattern, first of all, this paper zone the space units of study area into many sub-regions by improved K-means clustering algorithm based on space adjacent relationship, in this process, make quantitative evaluation to different zoning programs by means of global and local Moran's I statistics. Then corresponding with the space partition pattern, construct a modular BP network, establish a multi-layer feed-network for each sub-region. For comparison, establish a global neural network for entire study area. At last, take the numbers of reported influenza cases in 94 countries of France from 1st week of 1990 to 53rd week of 1993 [14] as an example to do spatial and temporal analysis. Take the influenza cases of (t)th week in each sub-region as input, and take the case numbers of $(t+1)$th week as prediction data. Moran's I, Getis' G and Geary's C and other statistics are used to detect the two different scale (global and regional) spatial pattern of regional data [1].

2   Regional Data Spatio-temporal Model

Cressie divided spatial data into three major classes: point pattern data, geo-statistics data and lattice data. Lattice data is also called regional data, it refers to the data type that represent properties related fixed polygonal regions.

Spatio-temporal regional data has spatial and temporal attribute. First look at spatial aspect, just as Tobler's geography first theorem expound, spatial objects assume an interdependent space pattern, and this interdependence will become weakened with growth of distance between different objects. On the other hand, it's unrealistic to presume that space topology is fixed in researching region, especially in the situation that there are much more space units.

Look at temporal aspect, analyze by simple time series, to estimate properties of some one region at time t depend on properties of same region before time t. Some processes which have Markov properties at time like spatio-temporal modeling of infectious diseases even only consider the properties at time t-1. Otherwise, it will seriously affect the credibility and applicability of spatio-temporal model if ignore the other space-related regions' properties before time t.

2.1 Global and Regional Moran's I Statistics for Regional Data

From exploratory spatial data analysis point of view, spatial data that is composed of two parts: spatial smooth and spatial rough.

Spatial smooth reflect the global situation or the global characteristics of spatial data., Spatial rough reflect the local characteristics of spatial data.

Moran's I, Getis' G and Geary's C and other statistics are used to detect the two different scale (global and regional) spatial pattern of regional data [1].

2.2 Standards of Zoning

The purpose of zoning is dividing all space units into different sub-regions. The same attributes at different times can be regarded as different attributes.

Cliff thinks the optimal zoning programs should have three criteria: simplicity, contiguity and compactness. Based on regional neural network modeling needs, the paper adds another two additional criteria.

(1) Interdependence

Interdependence of the same sub-region's space units indicates that the space correlation among them.

(2) Instability

While each sub-district has a completely smooth is not possible, but the lower instability means that the better the forecast model. The stability of each sub-district can be measured by Std(I) [3].

2.3 K-Means Clustering Method Based on Space Adjacency Relations

In this paper, make use of K-means clustering method to partition the space units based on the space adjacency relationships [10].

3 Modular Artificial Neural Network

Conventional model of BP is relatively simple, just input, output and hidden layer three-tier architecture. Corresponding with the space partition pattern, this paper discusses a modular BP network. The idea of the model is to decompose complex task into several sub-tasks, through the various sub-tasks to achieve results throughout the mission. In the design of topological structure, there are several sub-networks and one gate-network be embedded in the main network. The main network has its own input, output and hidden layer. Sub-networks have their independent output and hidden layer.

Sub-networks and the main network share input layer. Gate-network control and comprehensive the output values from sub-network, integrate the results and then submit it to the main network to the hidden layer processing, final get system output. Sub-networks could be independent of the BP network. This structure will submit the mission about zoning high-dimensional spatial data to the various sub-networks. Sub-networks are highly targeted, easy to extract the details of information, so as to improve the geographical accuracy. Fig. 1 gives the structure of the modular network model.

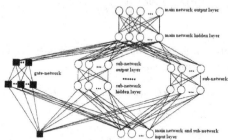

Fig. 1. Structure of the modular BP neural network model

In the training of modular networks model, the sub-networks and the gate-network is to be trained at the same time. For a given input vector, the gate-network will select one sub-network to deal with input data. Thus, the entire input space is divided into a number of sub-spaces, by the sub-networks to deal with space data. There is a number of modular network training at the same time, as the result, calculating intensity of modular BP model stronger than ordinary BP model.

In mathematical model, assume L is the number of processing units of gate-network output layer, $g=(g_1,g_2,...,g_L)$ is the activation vector of gate-network output layer, $S=(s_1,s_2,...,s_L)$ is pre-activation vector of gate network output layer, $y_K=(y_{k1},y_{k2},...,y_{kn})$ is the activation vector of the gate-network K output layer, $y=(y_1,y_2,...,y_n)$ is the output vector of main network. Output of the sub-network i was adjusted by gt which is output activation vector of the gate-network.

$$y = \sum_{t=1}^{L} gtyt \tag{1}$$

The training of modular network is complied by updating the weight value of each joint unit. Updating the weight values is complied by identify the maximum of target equation. The definition of target equation is:

$$J = \ln \sum_{t=1}^{L} gt\, e^{-0.5(d-yt)^T (d-yt)} \tag{2}$$

$d= (d1,d2,...,dn)$ is the desired output of the main network. h_K is used for the expression of the learning network equation, it is defined like formula (4):

$$h_K = \frac{g_K e^{-0.5(d-y_K)^T (d-y_K)}}{\sum\limits_{t=1}^{L} g_t e^{-0.5(d-yt)^T (d-yt)}} \tag{3}$$

The back propagation mode of error transmission is to be used for the main network to find the minimum error equation:

$$-\frac{\partial E}{\partial I} = -\frac{\partial E}{\partial y}\frac{\partial y}{\partial I} = (d - y)\frac{\partial y}{\partial I} \tag{4}$$

Training of modular network's back propagation transmission includes:
   (1) sub- network's error transmission:

$$\frac{\partial J}{\partial I_K} = -\frac{\partial J}{\partial y_K}\frac{\partial y_K}{\partial I_K} = h_K(d - y_K)\frac{\partial y_K}{\partial I_K} \tag{5}$$

$I_K = I_{k1}, I_{k2}, ..., I_{kn}$ is the pre-activation vector of Kth network's output layer:
   (2) gate-network processing units' error transmission:

g_K on behalf of a priori probability, and h_K on behalf of the posterior probability of the no. K sub-network's output vector. Formula (5), (6) show that each sub-network error was carried out processing by posterior probability weighted. Gate-network will be trained to match the priori and posterior probability of samples. Such a mechanism is to promote competition among sub-networks, because if a subset of the network

$$\frac{\partial J}{\partial S_K} = \sum_{t=1}^{L} \frac{\partial J}{\partial gt}\frac{\partial gt}{\partial S_K} = \sum_{t\neq K} (-\frac{ht}{gt}g_K gt) + \frac{h_K}{g_K}(g_K - g_K{}^2) = -g_K \sum_{t\neq K} ht - g_K h_K$$

$$= h_K - g_K \sum_{t=1}^{L} ht \tag{6}$$

$$= h_K - g_K$$

begins to control the importation of samples of a certain part of the deal, the doors of its network by the weighted influence.

4   Neural Network Modeling

After determining the final zoning districts, build neural network spatio-temporal model for every sub-region separately. In this paper, the model is named as the Regional Neural network Spatio-temporal model (RSTN model).

   The output of RSTN model is the predictive value X of each sub-region at time t and the input is the observations of relevant units before t time t. For the neural network mapping function as follows:

$$X_t = f(X_{t-1}, X_{t-2}, ..., X_{t-p}) . \tag{7}$$

p is the time step size of sliding window, used to determine the relevance of modeling the time lag. For example, there are T time observations vectors X_1, X_2, ..., X_T, each $X_i=[x_{t1}, x_{t2}, ..., x_{tN}]$ to express N observations of space units, when begin 1-step-ahead forecasting, the first input-output model's input is $X_1,X_2,...,X_p$, expected output is X_{p+1}, the second input-output model's input is X_2, $X_3,...,X_{p+1}$, expected output is X_{p+2}, so, the model $T-p,s$ input is $Xt-p$, $Xt-p+1,... ,X_{T-1}$, expected output is X_T.

At present, there are no suitable methods to determine the step P of sliding window. Some research literatures use spatial and temporal autocorrelation function and partial spatio-temporal autocorrelation function of a linear relationship to determine the time order of p. However, some scholars believe that this method is not appropriate to the lag of non-linear neural network. Practically use tests (try-and-error) approach.

Performance evaluation to the RSTN model is primarily through checking the test data set to measure the predictive power of new input (That is generalization ability), including two indicators: the average variance (ARV), which reflect the model predictive accuracy of the output, and dynamic similar rate (DSR), which reflects how close between the predict trend of model and the actual trend.

5 Application

Research data is France's 94 counties reported cases of influenza per week [14], from the 1st week of 1990 to the 53rd week of 1992, total 157 weeks. Fig. 2 (a) shows the 94 counties' numbers in the French figure.

Construct space statistics Q based on the average prevalence of influenza cases of every week, spatial distribution of is introduced in Fig. 2 (b). First-order space adjacency matrix W indicates the situation about directly adjacent sub-regions. Cases under the county average weekly of 94 counties to calculate the global Moran's I=1281, shows that the numbers of influenza cases in each county have spatial autocorrelation between each other, and shows a spatial pattern in which a high incidence area adjacent to a high incidence area, and a low incidence area adjacent to a low incidence area.

Take influenza cases per week as the county's property data, so every space unit has 157 attribute data. Partition 94 countries in France by K-means clustering algorithm with first-order adjacency matrix W as a constraint condition. As a result that the type number of clustering can not be determined in advance, take a K value one by one from 4-16, and cluster compute it respectively, After correlation testing to different partition programs, select several numbers of K with better space correlation: 8,9,10,12,14,16. Then calculate those six different partition programs' Std (I), finally select the most optimal number of K is 12.

The spatial distribution pattern of each sub-region with 12 districts is indicated in Fig. 2(c).From Fig. 2(b) and Fig. 2(c) contrast can be seen that the final program of the district also reflects the spatial distribution pattern of influenza cases.

To establish a RSTN model respectively for 12 sub-districts, each RSTN model forecast influenza cases of t week in every districts based on influenza cases of $t-1$, $t-2,...,t-p$ week in districts. As the transmission cycle of influenza is about 1 week, to the RSTN model whose time unit is week, input can only consider the cases of $t-1$ week, that is, $p=1$.

Therefore, the nodes of the RSTN model's output layer equal to the space unit number of corresponding sub-region, the nodes of RSTN model's input layer is sum of space unit number of local district and space unit number of boundary districts.

Fig. 2(d) for the No.1 promoter region and its adjacent border units, Table 1 for the nodes of each RSTN model's input layer and output layer.

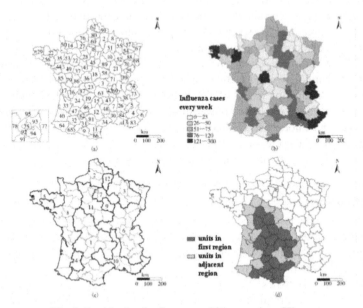

Fig. 2. Partitioning for flu cases of 94 countries of France

(a) IDs of 94 countries; (b) average weekly flu cases of 94 countries from 1st week of 1990 to 53th week of 1992; (c) the partition map of K=12 for 94 countries; (d) the first sub-region and it's adjacent areas

Table 1. The nodes of each RSTN model's input layer and output layer

Sub-region number	Nodes of input	Nodes of output
1	36	20
2	9	5
3	15	6
4	10	2
5	8	3
6	32	18
7	17	7
8	28	15
9	6	1
10	22	8
11	24	8
12	7	1

In order to compare the effect of RSTN model and ordinary BP model, establish a global BP model on the entire 94 study areas. The input of global BP is flu cases of t-1 week, expected output is influenza cases in t week, that is, the nodes number of both input layer and output layer are 94.

Put 156 number pairs (X_{t-1} , X_t) (X_{t-1} is observation vector of space unit at time $t-1$, X_t is observation vector of space unit at time t) into train dataset and test dataset according to 90%:10%. Training dataset includes 140 pair samples; testing dataset includes 16 pair samples.

Using BP algorithm to train and adjust model, then test model by test set, finally archive ARV, DSR of 94 countries of France from RSTN model and global BP model which indicated by Fig. 3 and Fig. 4 (Abscissa is the number of county code, according to Fig. 1(a)). It can be seen that the predictive capability of RSTN model is better than the global BP model.

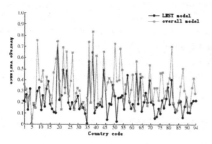

Fig. 3. Test dataset's ARV of RSTN and global model for 94 countries in France

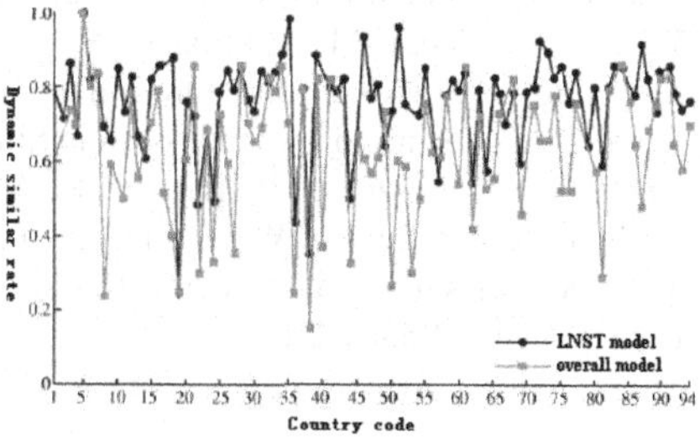

Fig. 4. Test dataset's DSR of RSTN and global model for 94 countries in France

6 Conclusion and Discussion

Modular BP model embed gate-network and sub-network into main network. Sub-networks decompose and process complex input data, and gate-networks adjust outputs of sub-networks. Complex task will be broken down into sub-tasks, and results are consolidated to obtain a higher accuracy output data.

It should be noted that it is necessary to refine further research on standards for the partitioning, corresponding spatio-temporal evaluation and testing methods. Its all are impact factors for the accuracy of the forecasts.

References

1. Matheron, G.: Principles of geostatistics. Econ Geo 58, 1246–1266 (1963)
2. Şen, Z.: Cumulative semivariogram model of regionalized variables. Int. J. Math. Geol. 21(8), 891–903 (1989)
3. Chang, H.-K., Lin, L.-C.: Multi-point tidal prediction using artificial neural network with tide-generating forces. Coastal Engineering 53, 857–864 (2006)

4. Fisher, M., Getis, A.: Recent Developments in Spatial Data Analysis. In: Spatial Statistics, Behavioral, Modeling and Neuro-computing, pp. 113–124. Springer, Berlin (1997)
5. Haining, R., Wise, S., Ma, J.: Designing and Implementing Software for Spatial Statistical Analysis in GIS Environment. Journal of Geographical Systems, 257–286 (2000)
6. Deo, M.C., Chaudhari, G.: Tide prediction using neural networks. Computer-Aided Civil and Infrastructure Engineering 13(2), 113–120 (1998)
7. Ruano, A.E., Crispim, E.M., Conceição, E.Z.E., Lúci, M.M.J.R.: Prediction of building's temperature using neural networks models. Energy and Buildings 38(6), 682–694 (2006)
8. Ruano, A.E., Crispim, E.M., Conceição, E.Z.E., Lúcio, M.M.J.R.: Temporal neural networks for downscaling climate variability and extremes. Neural Networks 19(2), 135–144 (2006)
9. Parkin, G., Birkinshaw, S.J., Younger, P.L., Rao, Z., Kirk, S.: A numerical modeling and neural network approach to estimate the impact of groundwater abstractions on river flows. Journal of Hydrology 339(1-2), 15–28 (2007)
10. Wieland, R., Mirschel, W.: Adaptive fuzzy modeling versus artificial neural networks. Environmental Modeling & Software 23(2), 215–224 (2008)
11. Wieland, R., Voss, M., Holtmann, X., Mirschel, W., Ajibefun, I.: Spatial Analysis and Modeling Tool (SAMT), structure and possibilities. Ecological Informatics 1, 67–76 (2006)
12. Korn, G.A.: Advanced Dynamic-system Simulation. Wiley, N.Y (2007)
13. Grzesiak, W., Blaszczyk, P., Lacroix, R.: Methods of prediction milk yield in dairy cows – predictive capabilities of Wood's lactation curve and artificial neural networks. Computers and Electronics in Agriculture 54, 101–114 (2006)
14. Data Source of France Flu,
    http://www.sph.umich.edu/geomed/data/France

Subject Integration and Applications of Neural Networks

Bowu Yan and Chao Gao

School of Computer Science and Technology, Huangshi Institue of Technology,
Hubei Huangshi 435003
hustybw@163.com

Abstract. The present paper introduces the development, valuable part and application of neural network. It also analyzes systematically the existing problems and the combination of neural network with wavelet analysis, fuzzy set, chaos, rough sets and other theories, together with its applications and the hot spots of the research on neural network. The analysis proves that the prospects of neural network will be primising with the combination method, and that subject integration will be the chief interest for the neural network research.

Keywords: Neural network. Rough set. Wavelet analysis. Chaos theory. Computational intelligence.

1 Introduction

Artificial neural networks(ANNs), fuzzy sets and evolutionary computing are regarded as the leading technologies of Computational Intelligence (CI). Recently, a great deal of attention has been paid to artificial neural networks and its related technologies. Neural networks were firstly brought forth by Warren McCulloch and Walter Pitts together in 1943[1]. They fabricate a simple artificial neural network neuron model, i.e., the M-P model. During the late 1940s, Donala O. Heb defined a kind of Hebbian rule [2]. During the late 1950s, Frank Rosenblatt put forth the perceptron network and ideal rule learning [3]. It was the enlightenment of neural networks research. During the 1960s, the perceptron and LMS algorithm arose. The research of neural networks turned to its first high tide. During the 1970s, adaptive resonance theory (ART) was brought forward by Grossberg. By that time, the *Perceptron* was published, the research of neural networks turned to its low tide. During the 1980s, Hopfield put forth Hopfield Networks Models. Back propagation(BP)-algorithm was put forth in 1974, but it did not go round until 1982. Now, the BP algorithm is used in all kind of networks. Chua and Yang put forth Cellular Neural Networks in 1988, and the research of neural networks turned to its new high tide. Since the beginning of the 1990s, the research of neural networks gained further development, at the meantime, it got integrated into fuzzy set, genetic algorithm, evolutionary algorithm, intelligent algorithm, etc.

Based on the comprehensive recognition of human brain's neural networks, artificial neural networks, as one kind of artificial neural network(ANN), were built. The functions of ANN are as follows: associative memory, nonlinear mapping, classification and identification, computational optimization and knowledge processing. Among the five

Z. Cai et al. (Eds.): ISICA 2009, LNCS 5821, pp. 375–381, 2009.

functions, the main functions are as follows: associative memory, nonlinear mapping. Associative memory refers to the function and process of neural networks that neural networks retrieve the complete original information by means of stored information beforehand, or by way of self-adaptive mechanism of learning. Nonlinear mapping refers to the function and process of neural networks that neural networks can fit nonlinear functions with arbitrary-precision by way of learning on system input-output original, and automatically grasping the latent mapping rules.

Architectures of artificial neural networks are shown in Fig.1. As shown in Fig.1, there are two kinds of architectures, one is feedforward ANN architecture, which allows signals to travel one way only; the other is recurrent ANN architecture, which has signals traveling in both directions by introducing loops in the networks.

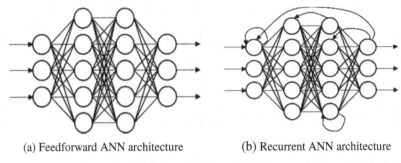

(a) Feedforward ANN architecture   (b) Recurrent ANN architecture

Fig. 1. Architectures of ANN

There are two kinds of learning models for neural networks, one is supervised learning, and the other is unsupervised learning. The main properties of neural networks are as follows: (1) the structural property of parallel processing, distributed storage and its fault tolerance; (2) ability characteristics of self-learning, self-organization and adaptability.

For their differentiated structures and information processing methods, neural networks have achieved remarkable success in many practical application fields, such as pattern recognition; image processing; nonlinear optimization; speech processing; natural language understanding; target identification target automatically; robot, expert system, etc.

2 Subject Integration

Main problems with ANNs are as follows: the learning sometimes is difficult and slow; the knowledge base is not transparent; the storage capability is limited. Now, the applied research hot spots of neural network are subjects' integration, on which the present paper focuses. As for subject integration, artificial neural networks have mainly integrated with wavelet analysis theory, fuzzy set, chaos theory, rough sets, genetic algorithm, expert system, gray system theory, etc.

2.1 Neural Networks and Wavelet Analysis Theory

In 1974, French engineer J. Morlet put forward the concept of wavelet transform. A wavelet basis is constructed by Y. Meyer in 1986. The paper *"Ten lectures on wavelets"*, which published by I. Daubechies in 1992, play an important role in promoting the popularization of wavelet analysis theory [4]. In 1994, *"Lifting Scheme"* was put forward by Wim Swelden in Bell Labs, which was regarded as the second wavelet analysis theory. The fundamental idea behind wavelets is to analyze the signal at different scales or resolutions, which are called multiresolution, Wavelets are a class of functions used to localize a given signal in both space and scaling domains [5].

The wavelet transform (WT) decomposes a signal $f(t)$ by performing inner products with a collection of analysis function ψ (a, b), which are scaled and translated version of the wavelet ψ. The wavelet coefficient $W(a,b)$ of the function $f(t)$ is defined as follows [5]:

$$W(a,b) =< f(t), \psi_{(a,b)}(t) >= \int_{-\infty}^{+\infty} f(t)\psi_{(a,b)}(t)dt . \qquad (1)$$

$$\psi_{(a,b)}(t) = a^{-\frac{1}{2}}\psi(\frac{t-b}{a}) . \qquad (2)$$

In recent years, wavelet transform (WT) techniques have been effectively used for multi-scale representation and analysis of signals. Wavelet analysis is becoming a common tool for analyzing localized variations of power within a time series. By decomposing a time series into time-frequency space, one is able to determine both the dominant modes of variability and how those modes vary in time.

Wavelet neural network is a new kind of hierarchical and multiresolution artificial neural network which based on wavelet analysis theory. It has recently attracted great interest, because of its advantages over radial basis function network as it is universal approximators but achieves faster convergence and is capable of dealing with the so-called "curse of dimensionality". Sheng-Tun Li presented a robust wavelet neural network based on the theory of robust regression for dealing with outliers in the framework of function approximation. In order to enhance the robustness of wavelet neural network, the training procedure of the initial wavelet neural network was performed by the least trimmed squares (LTS) in robust regression [6]. Yuehui Chen presented a local linear wavelet neural network. The difference of the network with the original wavelet neural network was that the connection weights between the hidden layer and output layer of the original wavelet neural network were replaced by a local linear model. A simple and fast training algorithm, particle swarm optimization (PSO), was also introduced for training the local linear wavelet neural network, and brought forth better feasibility and effectiveness[7].

Neural network, wavelet analysis theory and wavelet neural network have been used in many fields. For example, S.Cao presented a forecast method which was applied to forecast solar irradiance by combining recurrent BP network with wavelet transformation, and the method had been proved remarkable improvement through an example in the accuracy of the forecast for the day-by-day solar irradiance of a year compared with that without combining wavelet transformation[8]. B.-F. Chen showed that the addition of the wavelet analysis to ANN method could prominently improve the prediction quality[9]. Ghosh-dastidar Samanwoy proposed a novel wavelet-chaos-neural network methodology, which resulted in the highest classification accuracy, a high value of 96.7% [10].

2.2 Neural Networks and Fuzzy Sets

The name of Professor Lotfi A. Zadeh is one of the best known names in the modern mathematics. His seminal paper *"Fuzzy Sets"*, which was published in 1965 in *Information and Control*, has opened the fuzzy set theory, very dynamic area of the modern mathematical thinking. The fuzzy set theory enables us to structure and describe activities and observations which differ from each other only vaguely, to formulate them in models and to use these models for various purposes, such as problem-solving and decision-making. This is an ability we already have as human beings, but which is not present in classical mathematics and not as a consequence in any science-oriented methodology.

Now, Fuzzy set theory is applied into the fields of automatic control, decision analysis, pattern recognition and artificial intelligence. Fuzzy logic techniques often use verbal and linguistic information from experts, and neural network extracts information from system to be learned or controlled. Since neural networks and fussy system have different advantages in learning function and in explicit knowledge expression of fuzzy rules, respectively, they can complement each other. Fuzzy Neural Network is a product of integration of neural network with fuzzy system to obtain the benefits of both fuzzy systems and neural networks [11]. Since fuzzy neural networks are inherently neural networks, they are mostly used in pattern recognition applications.

In particular, neural fuzzy systems and genetic fuzzy systems hybridize the approximate inference method of fuzzy systems with the learning capabilities of neural networks and evolutionary algorithms [12]. A fuzzy neural network (FNN) controller which emulated the conventional IP controller was proposed for a vector controlled induction motor drive, a Sugeno type FNN was adopted for the proposed control system and the fuzzy neural network was so designed that the FNN controller behaved a robust nonlinear IP controller [13].

There are many different angles to neural networks and fuzzy logic. The fields are expanding rapidly with ever-new results and applications. This is especially useful for the more complicated neural network architectures like the Adaptive Resonance Theory of Stephen Grossberg (ART)[14]. Fuzzy ART incorporated computations from fuzzy set theory into ART networks [15].

2.3 Neural Networks and Chaos Theory

As we all know that studies in chaos and nonlinear science have been a hot research topic in the last two decades or so. Neural network is a highly complicated nonlinear dynamic system, and there exists the chaos phenomena, so Chaos Neural Network comes into being when neural network is combined with chaos. Chaos Neural Network is regarded as one of intelligent information systems which can be used to realize the computation of the practical world. At the present time, the study of Chaos Neural Network is still in its infancy. The research limited to the chaos properties of a neuron, to behavior analysis of a simple Chaos Neural Network. Many of the research focus on Aihara Chaos Neural Network model or Inoue Chaos Neural Network model. Chaos Neural Network which is formed by chaos neuron gains dynamic associative memory function. The artificial neural network model with chaos behavior is able to be used for image recognition or fault diagnosis, etc.

It was theoretically proved that one-dimensional transiently chaotic neural networks have chaotic structure in sense of Li-Yorke theorem with some given assumptions using that no division implies chaos. In particular, it is further derived sufficient conditions for the existence of chaos in sense of Li-Yorke theorem in chaotic neural networks, which lead to the fact that Aihara has demonstrated by numerical method [16].

The best indication that chaos can be practically utilized in artificial neural systems was the performance of one that had already been developed. The chaotic system, which was designed to optically recognize four different types of industrial parts and determine whether or not they appear to be defective, was compared to non-chaotic artificial neural system implementations of the same problem and was found to have significantly superior performance in positively identifying both acceptable and unacceptable parts [17]. Selective memorization, faster pattern recognition, and recognition of new patterns are the beneficial behaviors of integration of chaos and neural networks. Lipo Wang proposed a new model of cellular neural networks (CNNs) with transient chaos by adding negative self-feedbacks into CNNs after transforming the dynamic equation to discrete time via Euler's method. The new CNN model had richer and more flexible dynamics, and therefore may possessed better capabilities of solving various problems, compared to the conventional CNN with only stable dynamics [18].

2.4 Neural Networks and Rough Sets

Polish scholar Z Pawlak published the paper Rough Sets in 1982, which proclaimed the news of the birth of Rough Sets Theory. Rough Sets Theory is a theory which researches on the expression, learning and induction of deficient data or inexact knowledge, is to discover or uncover tacit knowledge or hidden laws by way of analyzing or approximatively classifying on data, deduction of the relation of data, based on the classification of observing and measuring data.

Rough Sets Theory can be used in the following application areas:

(1) express no definite or inaccurate knowledge; (2) acquire Knowledge through instances; (3) analyze nonconformity information; (4) infer from no definite or incomplete knowledge; (5) reduce data based on holding back valuable information; (6) close pattern classification; (7) recognize and evaluate reciprocal relationship among data.

Rough sets and neural network are chosen for the combined method study because they can discover patterns in ambiguous and imperfect data, and provide tools for data and pattern analysis. The common characteristic of rough sets and neural networks is that both approaches have the ability to learn decision models by examples. The rough neural networks used a combination of rough and conventional neurons[19]. F. Xue employed rough set approach and Elman neural network to construct five-category evaluation model commercial banks in China. The result shows that both the hybrid model of rough sets and Elman neural network is effective. The classification accuracies of hybrid model (83.19%) are higher than those of logistic model (77.31%). [20]. A rough neuron can be viewed as a pair of neurons. One neuron corresponds to the upper bound and the other corresponds to the lower bound. Upper neuron and lower neuron exchange information with each other during the calculation of their outputs. A rough set (RS) and fuzzy wavelet neural network (FWNN) were integrated, and the advantages and effectiveness of this method were verified by testing [21].

3 Conclusion

Neural networks are now a subject of interest to professionals in many fields, and also a tool for many areas of problem solving. We discover that neural networks are capable of solving complex problems with parallel computational architectures. Now, the researches of neural networks divide mainly into three aspects as follows: neural networks application research, neural networks implementation technique research, and neural networks' theory study. The orientation of this field development lies in several directions: applied research, theory study and implementation technique research, etc. Now, the hot spots of applied research are subjects' integration, on which the present paper focuses. The prospects of neural network will be bright by the way of subject integration.

References

1. McCulloch, W., Pitts, W.: A Logical Calculus of the Ideas Immanent in Nervous Activity. Bulletin of Mathematical Biophysics 1(5), 115–133 (1943)
2. Hebb, O.: The Oorganization Behaviour. Willey, New York (1949)
3. Rosenblatt, F.: The Perceptron: A Probabilistic Model for Information Storage and Organization in the Brain, Cornell Aeronautical Laboratory. Psychological Review 65(6), 386–408 (1958)
4. Daubechies, I.: Ten Lectures on Wavelets. SIAM, Philadelphia (1992)
5. Yang, M., Trifas, M., Bourbakis, C.C.: A Robust Information Hiding Methodology in Wavelet Domain. In: Proceeding of Signal and Image Processing, Honolulu, USA, pp. 200–245 (2007)
6. Li, S.-T., Chen, S.-C.: Function Approximation Using Robust Wavelet Neural Networks. In: Proceedings of the 14th IEEE International Conference on Tools with Artificial intelligence, pp. 483–488 (2002)
7. Chen, Y., Dong, J., Yang, B., Zhang, Y.: A Local Linear Wavelet Neural Network. In: Hangzhou, P.R. (ed.) Proceedings of the 5th world congress on intelligent control and automation, China, pp. 15–19 (2004)
8. Cao, S., Cao, J.: Forecast of solar irradiance using recurrent neural networks combined with wavelet analysis. Applied Thermal Engineering 25, 161–172 (2005)
9. Chen, B.-F., Wang, H.-D., Chu, C.-C.: Wavelet and artificial neural network analyses of tide forecasting and supplement of tides around Taiwan and South China Sea. Ocean Engineering 34, 2161–2175 (2007)

10. Samanwoy, G.-d., Hojjat, A., Nahid, D.: Mixed-band Wavelet-chaos- neural Network Methodology for Epilepsy and Epileptic Seizure Detection. In: IEEE transactions on biomedical engineering, vol. 54(9), pp. 1545–1551 (2007)
11. Zadeh, L.A.: Fuzzy sets. Information and Control 8(3), 338–353 (1965)
12. Kleinsteuber, S., Sepehri, N.: A polynomial network modeling approach to a class of large-scale hydraulic systems. Computers Elect. Eng. 22, 151–168 (1996)
13. Dandil, B.: Fuzzy neural network IP controller for robust position control of induction motor drive. Expert Systems with Applications 36, 4528–4534 (2009)
14. Grossberg, S.: Adaptive pattern classification and universal recoding: I. parallel development and coding of neural feature dectors. Biological Cybernetics 23, 121–134 (1976)
15. Carpenter, G.A., Grossberg, S., Rosen, D.B.: Fuzzy ART: fast stable learning and categorization of analog patterns by an adaptive resonance system. Neural Networks 4, 759–771 (1991)
16. jiong, R., weirui, Z., Rongsong, L.: Chaos in transiently chaotic neural networks. Applied Mathematics and Mechanics 24(8), 989–996 (2003)
17. Yao, Y., Freeman, W.J., Burke, B., Yang, Q.: Pattern recognition by a distributed neural network: an industrial application. Neural Networks 4, 103–121 (1991)
18. Wang, L., Liu, W., Shi, H., Zurada, J.M.: Cellular neural networks with transient chaos. In: IEEE transactions on circuits and systems-II:express briefs, vol. 54(5), pp. 440–444 (2007)
19. Hassanien, A.E., Ślezak, D.: Rough Neural Intelligent Approach for Image Classification: A Case of Patients with Suspected Breast Cancer. International Journal of Hybrid Intelligent System 3(4), 205–218 (2006)
20. Xue, F., Ke, K.-L.: Five-Category Evaluation of Commercial Bank's Loan by the Integration of Rough Sets and Neural Network. Systems Engineering -Theory & Practice 28(1), 40–45 (2008)
21. Dong, L., Xiao, D., Liang, Y., Liu, Y.: Rough set and fuzzy wavelet neural network integrated with least square weighted fusion algorithm based fault diagnosis research for power transformers. Electric power systems research 78, 129–136 (2008)

The Convergence Control to the ACO Metaheuristic Using Annotated Paraconsistent Logic

Luiz Eduardo da Silva[1], Helga Gonzaga Martins[2], Maurilio Pereira Coutinho[1],
Germano Lambert-Torres[2], and Luiz Eduardo Borges da Silva[2]

[1] Alfenas Federal University
[2] Itajuba Federal University
Av. BPS, 1303 – CEP 37500-903, Itajubá, Brasil
{luizedsilva,helgagonzaga,maurilio.coutinho,
germanoltorres}@gmail.com

Abstract. An approach to solve complex combinatorial optimizations problems is the Ant Colony Optimization Metaheuristic (ACO). There are several variations of this metaheuristic. One of them, the Max-Min Ant System, is an algorithm that presents excellent performance for some classes of combinatorial problems, such as Traveling Salesman Problem and the Quadratic Assignment Problem. This paper presents a method of convergence control of the Max-Min variation of Ant Colony Optimization Metaheuristic using paraconsistent logic. The proposed method can be adapted to any variation of the Ant Colony Optimization Metaheuristic.

Keywords: artificial intelligence, ant colony, hybrid system, paraconsistent logic.

1 Introduction

The Ant Colony Metaheuristic is a recent strategy that mimics the social behavior of ants looking for food. It has been showed effective for solving some classes of complex combinatorial problems. This strategy was first proposed by Dorigo in [2][3][4][5]. After this, several studies were developed to improve some algorithm aspects and provide a better convergence of the search method used by the ant colony. Some examples are the Elitist Ant System based on an elitist strategy [5-6], the rank based strategy (ASrank) [7], the MAX-MIN Ant System (MMAS) [8] and the Ant Colony System (ACS) [9].

In order to work with inconsistency, imprecision, and uncertain knowledge, which are not foreseen in the original implementation of this metaheuristic, this paper presents a new approach using a Non-Classical Logic called Paraconsistent Logic. This logic, described in [14], has the characteristic of non validation of the Law of Non-Contradiction. Evidently, if a contradiction may be accepted under the point of view of these logics, then the classical rule is invalid. Therefore the statement that any proposition is inferred from a contradiction is invalid. Paraconsistent Logic is based on analog methods to the ones used in standard logic. Nonetheless, it is more

Z. Cai et al. (Eds.): ISICA 2009, LNCS 5821, pp. 382–391, 2009.

appropriate for the treatment of inconsistencies, contradiction, and uncertain knowledge. Values may be attributed to the propositions so as to enable the paraconsistent logic application in practical computational problems.

The paper is organized as follows: metaheuristic Ant Colony Optimization (ACO) is presented in Section 2. In Section 3, the annotated paraconsistent logic is discussed. Section 4 describes the proposed hybrid algorithm which composes the characteristics of metaheuristic ACO and paraconsistent logic. It also shows the experimental results obtained with the application of this technique. The conclusions are presented in Section 5.

2 The Metaheuristic Ant Colony Optimization

The metaheuristic ACO is a swarm intelligence strategy which tries to imitate an ant colony behavior with the purpose of using it to solve combinatorial optimization problems. This type of problem is a NP-Complex, which is mathematical jargon for "hard". In this case the aim is to maximize or minimize a function defined over a finite domain. Although it is easy to determine a possible solution for this problem, to test all the possible solutions is computationally unfeasible.

In metaheuristic ACO, the ants build randomized solutions in a probabilistic form, based on the pheromone trail as well as on the heuristic problem specific information. The use of the pheromone trail to register the experience accumulated by the ants during the resolution of the problem makes the metaheuristic ACO different from the traditional heuristic methods.

2.1 Analogy with the Real Ants

The metaheuristic ACO was inspired in the experiences carried out by Goss et al [1], using an Argentine ant colony. To accomplish this experiment, the researchers built an environment with only two possible paths linking the nest and the food source, according to Fig. 1.

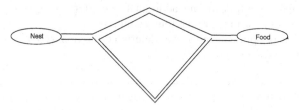

Fig. 1. Picture of the Argentine Ant Experiment

Each path has a different length. In order to get the food and return to the nest, the ant has to choose or the longer path or the shorter path. The experimental observation was that, after a transitory phase, most of the ants started using the shorter path. Also it was observed that the probability of the ants of selecting the shortest path increases when the difference of the path length increases. The choice for the shortest path may be explained in terms of a positive feedback loop and the different distances.

Therefore, the ants never need to interact directly. This indirect communication is based in the local changes in the environment.

When the Argentine ants travel from the nest to the food source, they deposit a chemical on the ground called "pheromone". When they arrive at an intersection point, they make a probabilistic decision based on the pheromone amount left on the paths. This behavior has an autocatalytic effect, because it increases the probability that this path will be chosen again in the future. In the beginning of the experiment, there is no pheromone on the path, and therefore, the ants travel from their nest to the food by choosing any path with the same probability. The ants that choose the shortest path get the food first. A new decision is made when they make the way back. The track that they used before will present a greater amount of pheromone. This means a higher probability of being chosen. During this iterative process, more pheromone is deposited on the shortest path than the longest path. This process makes the shortest path more and more attractive until all the ants start using it.

2.2 Overview of Metaheuristic ACO

The metaheuristic ACO may be summarized in the following way: the ants in the colony, in an asynchronous and competing way, construct solutions to the modeled problem through the path definition in graph G, which represents the problem. Each ant's choice is done through a probabilistic decision, by considering the pheromone trail and the heuristic information. During the construction process, or after the ant finalizes the path in the graph G, the (others) ants in the colony may assess the solution constructed, and thus deposit pheromone on the trail in order to favor the best solution found by the colony. In a simplified way, the metaheuristic ACO is represented through the pseudo-code in Fig. 2.

The iterations repeat until the end condition represented by the function *stopCondition*() is satisfied. The end condition may be the maximum time determined for the search or until some solution quality parameter is reached.

The metaheuristic ACO fundamental operations are: build the solution by the ant colony, update the statistics and structures utilized in the implementation of the metaheuristic, and the execution of any additional operation, such as the Local Search algorithm [7], in order to improve the found solution.

This operation is optional, but it can determine the quality and the metaheuristic convergence speed for a solution.

```
For(int t = 0; t < nTry; t++) {
    iter = 1;
    do {
        buildSolution(e);
        updatePheromone();
        updateStatistics();
        iter++;
    } while (!stopCondition());
}
```

Fig. 2. Pseudo-code of the Metaheuristic ACO

In the step *buildSolutions()*, each ant in the colony constructs a complete solution from a random component of the problem. According to the solutions found, additional operations may be executed in order to identify the good and bad solutions. The identification of the solutions computed in step *buildSolutions()* may be carried out in step *updateStatistic()*.

2.3 Implementation of the Metaheuristic ACO

Based on the experiment developed by Goss et al [1], Dorigo proposed an algorithm using ACO to solve The Traveling Salesman Problem (TSP) [8]. This problem is a good benchmark to test and compare the multiple variations constructed for this metaheuristic. An extended bibliography about the TSP topic can be found in [10].

The problem consists in determining a minimum route length to visit a group of cities. The traveler must visit all the cities only once. In order to use the ACO, firstly the problem must be modeled through a graph. The vertices represent the states of the problem and the edges determine the cost of the link between the vertices. Each ant traveling in the path spreads pheromone on its trail. The ant has a memory of the visited vertices in order to avoid the use of the same path more than once. When the ant is on vertex i, it chooses the next vertex j using the probability function according to Eq. 1.

$$p_{ij}^k(t) = \frac{[\tau_{ij}(t)]^\alpha [\eta_{ij}]^\beta}{\sum_{l \in J_i^k} [\tau_{il}(t)]^\alpha [\eta_{il}]^\beta} \tag{1}$$

Where $\tau_{ij}(t)$ determines the amount of pheromone between vertices i and j in iteration t. η_{ij} represents the heuristic function which is specific for each problem, α and β determine the relevance of the pheromone trail in relation to heuristic, and l represents the unvisited neighborhood of vertex i.

According to Eq. 2, the pheromone trail evaporates at a constant ρ, in order to avoid the convergence of all the ants to a sub-optimal trail.

$$\tau_{ij}(t+1) = (1 - \rho).\tau_{ij}(t) + \sum_{k=1}^{m} \Delta \tau_{ij}^k(t), \qquad \forall (i, j) \tag{2}$$

The whole process is repeated until all the ants find a path. The best path is chosen and a new iteration happens. The algorithm ends after n iterations, or until a time limit has been reached. After that, the best path found in all the iterations is chosen as the best solution. Several variations of this algorithm have been developed with the purpose of improving the performance and obtaining better results. For example, the *Elitist Ant System* based on an elitist strategy [5-6], the *rank based* algorithm (AS_{rank}) [7], the *MAX-MIN Ant System* (*MMAS*) [8] and the *Ant Colony System* (*ACS*) [9].

The Elitist-based strategy deposits an additional amount of pheromone to the best constructed solution. The AS_{rank} is a variation of the elitist algorithm, where only a rank of best solutions is allowed to update the pheromone trails, with a rate proportional to the quality of the solution. The *MAX-MIN Ant System* defines maximum and minimum values for the pheromone trail which limits the convergence of the results to local minimals. The *Ant Colony System* introduces the possibility of updating the local pheromone, differently from the other strategies which update at the end of the construction process.

3 Annotated Paraconsistent Logic

It is common the real world applications present characteristics like inconsistency, imprecision, and uncertain knowledge. Because the Classical Logic cannot deal with such characteristics, a new logic, called Paraconsistent Logic, was created in order to treat these characteristics [13, 14]. The results of several works and the possible applications about this logic were presented in [9 - 19].

In [15,16] the authors proposed an interpretation for the paraconsistent logic. The result is the Unit Square of Cartesian Plan (USCP) presented in the Fig. 3. In this interpretation a decision is made according to the degree of belief and disbelief about a fact. With this information, a taken decision could be *true* (D) or *false* (B), using the classical logic. And *paracomplete* (⊥), *inconsistent* (I) or *undefined* (U), using the paraconsistent logic.

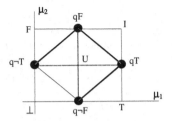

Fig. 3. Notable Points of USCP

For a given pair (μ_1, μ_2), representing respectively the *degree of belief and degree of disbelief*, it is estimated the Degree of Certainty (DC) and the Degree of Uncertainty (DU) as the equations Eq.3 and Eq 4 show:

$$DU = \mu_1 + \mu_2 - 1 \tag{3}$$

$$DC = \mu_1 - \mu_2 \tag{4}$$

If four extra notable points are considered, as suggested in [15, 16], then the representation divide the USCP in new regions. This fact represents different conclusions that can be taken depending on the degree of belief and degree of disbelief about a fact.

As suggested in [15, 16], four extra notable points are added: *almost-true, almost-false, almost-not-true and almost-not-false*. As illustrated in the Fig 3, new regions are added to the USCP. This work considers, specially, four regions: *totally inconsistent, totally paracomplete, totally true and totally false*.

Using the *degree of belief and disbelief*, these regions can be described in the following conditions:

If DC > 1/2 then output is totally true
If |DC| > 1/2 then output is totally false
If DU > 1/2 then output is totally inconsistent
If |DU| > 1/2 then output is totally paracomplete

In order to describe the problem in more realistic way, a third variable is added to this interpretation. It is called *Degree of Expertise (e)* [15, 16]. This variable is included in each diagnostic evaluation.

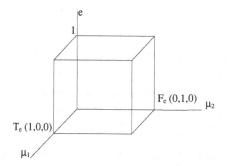

Fig. 4. The Analyzer Cube

The *degree of expertise* is represented by a perpendicular axis to the plane formed by the *degree of belief* and the *degree of disbelief* in the closed interval [0, 1]. In this case the 2-value Annotated Paraconsistent Logic (2vAPL) becomes the 3-value Annotated Paraconsistent Logic (3vAPL), as shown in the cube in the Fig.4.

Therefore the previous defined regions can be described by the following conditions:

> *If DC > e then output is totally true*
> *If |DC| >|- e| then output is totally false*
> *If DU > |1-e| then output is totally inconsistent*
> *If |DU| > |e-1| then output is totally paracomplete.*

4   The Proposed Algorithm

This section describes the proposed hybrid algorithm that performs a filtering method in the Colony Ant Algorithm, as showed in the Fig 5. During each iteration step, each ant uses the 3vAPL in order to decide which path to take. When the decision is assertive (D_x = totally true) this path is used by the ants. Otherwise, the probabilistic method based on Eq 1 is used. This mechanism can be used for any variation of the ACO metaheuristic.

In order to use the 3vAPL, each ant uses the path knowledge, which is represented by the product between the pheromone and the heuristic information. The value of the best option is used as a *belief degree* and the value of the second best option is used as *disbelief degree*. The *degree of expertise* varies according to the number of iterations. The variation purpose in the *degree of expertise* is to become the ants more assertive at the end of each iteration. Because each time the ants use more the paraconsistent logic than the original probabilistic method, they take, each time more, the same decisions and build similar solutions. The exceptions are the points where the difference between belief and disbelief does not allow a decision.

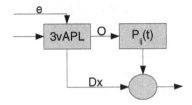

Fig. 5. Filtering the ACO Metaheuristic using 3vAPL

According to the 3vAPL and given the same *degree of belief* and *disbelief*, differ-ent *degrees of expertise* produce different diagnoses. The Fig. 6 shows the *degree of expertise* variation from 1 to 0. Each iteration the *degree of expertise* varies according to the Eq. 5.

The algorithm becomes the ants more assertive causing the increase of the ACO convergence. Each time the ants build closer solutions.

According to Fig. 6, if the *degree of expertise* is closer to 1, the diagnostic is al-most always different of D_x. When the *degree of expertise* varies towards zero the diagnostic changes. When the *degree of expertise* is equal zero, the ants choose D_x.

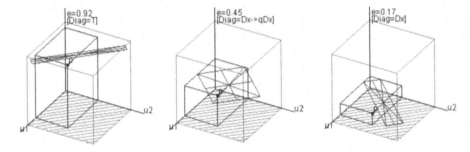

Fig. 6. The variation of the parameter in the cube 3vAPL and the different diagnoses to the same *degree of belief and disbelief*

In each iteration the degree of expertise varies according to the Eq. 5.

$$e_i = 1 - \left(\frac{i}{N}\right)^{\delta}, 0 \le i \le N \tag{5}$$

Where i represents the iteration, δ represents the convergence variation and N repre-sents the number of iterations. The convergence variation is showed in the Fig. 7. When $\delta = 1$, the variation of the expertise is linear and, therefore, the convergence is linear also. For $\delta > 1$, the convergence speed decreases and for $0 < \delta < 1$, the conver-gence speed increases.

The expertise variation goal is to increase the ant solution proximity. In a crescent manner the ants build solutions each time more similar. The difference is still the parts of the solution where it is not possible to use paraconsistent logic.

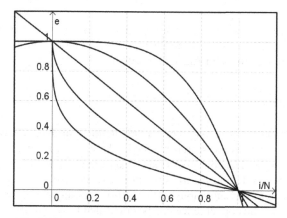

Fig. 7. Expertise variation determined by δ parameter

In order to demonstrate the convergence increasing of the colony, it is computed the distance between the solutions of each ant. The Eq. 6, proposed in [7], computes the distance between the two travels s and s'.

$$d(s,s') = n - |\{(i,j) : (i,j) \in s \wedge (i,j) \notin s'\}| \qquad (6)$$

Where n is the number of the cities visited in the tour. The average distance for all the ant colony is computed in order to verify the convergence of the colony for a solution. With the proposed hybrid algorithm it is possible to control the convergence of the colony. The Fig 8 compares the convergence of the colony using the Max-Min method and the Max-Min hybrid with paraconsistent logic.

In this experiment it is used the TSPLIB instance named eil76 with 76 ants, 5 trials, and 300 iterations [11]. It is observed that the colony has a better convergence when using paraconsistent logic at each iteration.

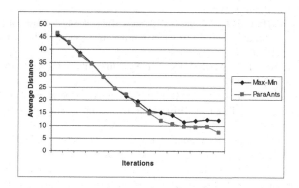

Fig. 8. Convergence of the Paraconsistent Method versus MAX-MIN ACO metaheuristic

The Fig. 8 shows the convergence of the ants during one iteration of the experiment. According to Eq. 6, the vertical axis denotes the average distance of the solution of the ants in the colony. The distance diminishes more sharply using the hybrid algorithm instead the Max-Min ACO metaheuristic.

5 Conclusions

An interesting strategy to solve complex computational problems is observed in how a colony of ants performs the search for food. The proposed approach uses the paraconsistent logic in the decision process and makes the colony able to deal with more realistic problems. As demonstrated in the previous sections, the proposed hybrid has better convergence of the ant colony at the end of each iteration. Another interesting characteristic is that the convergence can be controlled by the proposed method.

The proposal for future works is to implement new strategies for the variation process, such as, to increase or to decrease the convergence of the ant colony. It is also considered the proposal of a new evaluation criterion for belief and disbelief in order to enable more ant accurate decisions. The application of this methodology for engineering problems requires also further researches.

References

1. Goss, S., Aron, S., Deneubourg, J.L., Pasteels, J.M.: Self-organized Shortcuts in the Argentine Ant. Naturwissenschaften 76, 579–581 (1989)
2. Dorigo, M., Stützle, T.: The Ant Colony Optimization Metaheuristic: Algorithms, Applications, and Advances. In: Handbook of Metaheuristics (2002)
3. Dorigo, M., Birattari, M., Stützle, T.: Ant Colony Optimization– Artificial Ants as a Computational Intelligence Technique. In: IEEE Computational Intelligence Magazine (2006)
4. Dorigo, M., Maniezzo, V., Colorni, A.: Ant System: Optimization by a Colony of Cooperating Agents. In: IEEE Transactions on Systems, Man, and Cybernetics-Part B, vol. 26(1), pp. 29–41 (1996)
5. Dorigo, M.: Optimization, Learning and Natural Algorithms. Ph.D.Thesis, Politecnico di Milano, Italy, (in Italian) (1992)
6. Bullnheimer, B., Hartl, R.F., Strauss, C.: A New Rank Based Version of the Ant System: A Computational Study. Central European Journal for Operations Research and Economics 7(1), 25–38 (1999)
7. Stützle, T., Hoos, H.H.: MAX-MIN Ant System. Future Generation Computer Systems 16(8), 889–914 (2000)
8. Dorigo, M., Gambardella, L.M.: Ant Colony System: A Cooperative Learning Approach to the Traveling Salesman Problem. IEEE Transactions on Evolutionary Computation 1(1), 53–66 (1997)
9. Abe, J.M.: Fundamentals of Annotated Logic, Ph. D. thesis, FFLCH/USP, SP, Brazil (1992)
10. Da Costa, N. C. A., Hensche, L. J. and Subrahmanin, V. S.: Automatic Theorem Proving in Paraconsistent Logics: Theory and Implementation, Estudos Avançados, Coleção Documentos (3) USP, SP, Brazil (1990)
11. Subrahmanian, V.S.: On the Semantics of Quantitative Logic Programs. In: Proc. 4th IEEE Symposium on Logic Programming. Computer Society Press, Washington (1987)

12. Da Costa, N.C.A.: The Philosophic Importance of Paraconsistent Logic. Bol. Soc. Paranaense of Mathematic 11(2) (1990)
13. Da Costa, N.C.A.: On the Theory of Inconsistent Formal Systems. Notre Dame Journal of Formal Logic 11 (1974)
14. Da Costa, N.C.A., Subrahamanian, V.S., Vago, C.: The Paraconsistent Logic Pt, Zeitschrift fur Mathematische Logik und Grundlagen der Mathematik, vol. 37, pp. 139–148 (1991)
15. Martins, H.G.: The Four-Valued Annotated Paraconsistent Logic – 4vAPL Applied in a Case-Based Reasoning System for Restoration of Electrical Substations, Ph. D. Thesis, UNIFEI, Brazil (2003)
16. Martins, H.G., Lambert-Torres, G., Pontin, L.F.: Annotated Paraconsistent Logic, Ed. Communicar (2007) (in Portuguese)
17. Jünger, M., Reinelt, G., Rinaldi, G.: The Traveling Salesman Problem: a Bibliography. In: Dellamico, M., Maffioli, F., Martello, S. (eds.) Annotated Bibliography in Combinatorial Optimization, pp. 199–221. Willey (1997)
18. Reinelt, G.: TSPlib: A Traveling Salesman Problem Library. ORSA Journal on Computing 3, 376–384 (1991) (Accessed in 04/30/2009),
    http://www.iwr.uni-heidelberg.de/groups/comopt/software/
    TSPLIB95/

The Research of Artificial Neural Network on Negative Correlation Learning

Yi Ding[1,2], Xufu Peng[2], and Xian Fu[2]

[1] The Department of Computer Science and Technology,
Huazhong Science and Technology University, Wuhan Hubei 430072, China
[2] The College of Computer Science and Technology,
Hubei Normal University, Huangshi Hubei 435000, China
a_carrie@sina.com

Abstract. An Artificial Neural Network (ANN) is an information processing paradigm inspired by the biological nervous systems. It is composed of a large number of highly interconnected processing elements (neurones) working in unison to solve specific problems. The negative correlation learning encourages different individual network to study and trains different parts of the ensemble in order to make the whole ensemble study the whole training data better. This paper improves the method of negative correlation learning by using a BP algorithm with impulse in the error function. The method is an algorithm in batches with more powerful generalization and study speed because it combines primitive correlation learning with BP algorithm of impulse.

Keywords: Artificial Neural Networks, Neural Network Ensemble, Negative Correlation Learning.

1 Introduction

Neural network simu lations appear to be a recent development. However, this field was established before the advent of computers, and has survived at least one major setback and several eras.Many importand advances have been boosted by the use of inexpensive computer emu lations. Follo wing an initial period of enthusiasm, the field survived a period of frustration and disrepute. During this period when funding and professional support was minimal, important advances were made by relatively few reserchers. These pioneers were able to develop convincing technology which surpassed the limitations identified by Minsky and Papert. Minsky and Papert, published a book (in 1969) in which they summed up a general feeling of frustration (against neural networks) amo ng researchers, and was thus accepted by most without further analysis. Currently, the neural network field enjoys a resurgence of interest and a orresponding increase in funding.

2 Artificial Neural Networks

Artificial neural network (ANN) research is enlightened by biology to a certain extent, because the learning system of organism is made from an extremely complicated

Z. Cai et al. (Eds.): ISICA 2009, LNCS 5821, pp. 392–399, 2009.
© Springer-Verlag Berlin Heidelberg 2009

network of mutual joint neuron. And the artificial neural network is similar on the whole with it. It is formed by the intensively joint of a series of simple units. Every unit has certain amounts of real number values input. (It may be an output of other units) ,and produce single real number values output. (The output can become input of a lot of other units). At the beginning of the eighties, Scholars such as Rumelhart and Lecun[3] proposed the backpropagation algorithm of the multi-layer perceiving devices, which makes the research of the neural network become the focus of the study. From then on, the development of the neural network research is speedy.

2.1 Perceptron

By the end of the 50s ,the esthesia device that Rosenblatt had put forward is one of the main units forming the neural network. Esthesia device regards a real number value vector quantity as input, calculates the linear association of the input, then if the result is greater than a certain threshold value, exports 1, otherwise exports - 1. More precisely, if the input is x_1 to x_n ,the output calculating of the esthesia device is:

$$o(x_1, x_2, ... x_n) = \begin{cases} 1 & \text{if } w_0 + w_1 x_1 + ... + w_n x_n > 0 \\ -1 & \text{otherwise} \end{cases} \tag{1}$$

Every w_i is a real constant, or known as weight, which decides the contribution rate of output of every x_i . Among them, $-w_0$ is a threshold value, which is to make a sensor output, input and $w_1 x_1 + w_2 x_2 + w_3 x_3 ..... + w_n x_n$ must be weighted more than the threshold value.

To simplify the procedures, attached to a constant input $x_0 = 1$,the formula above can be written in the style:

$$o(\vec{x}) = \text{sgn}(\vec{w} . \vec{x}) \tag{2}$$

Among it:

$$\text{sgn}(y) = \begin{cases} 1 & \text{if } y > 0 \\ -1 & \text{otherwise} \end{cases} \tag{3}$$

Studying an esthesia device, which means selecting the value of the weigh .So what the esthesia device should consider is that the supposed candidate space is equal to the weigh vectorial gathering of all possible real number value .Formula (2)is called this unit to activate the function. In fact, it also can be the linear function, sigmoid function and so on, to activate the function.

2.2 Feed-Forward Neural Network

The neural network of feedforward is formed by several joint unit. A neuron of the feed-forward neural network accepts the input from the front ,and outputs to the behind, without feedback.It can be described by a direction figure without cy-cling.The nodes are divided into two groups in the picture, which are input nodes and calculation units. The input of every calculation unit is unconditional, but the output is only one. And the output can couple the inputs of other unconditional nodes. There are usually different layers in the feedforward network. The input of layer i is associative with $i-1$ only, considering the input node is the first layer. The nodes of input and output are called seen-layers for they can be linked up to the external world and influenced by the environment directly, and the other intermediate layers are called latent layers, as shown in Fig. 1. Feed-forward ANNs allow signals to travel one way only; from input to output. There is no feedback (loops) i.e. the output of any layer does not affect that same layer. Feed-forward ANNs tend to be straight forward networks that associate inputs with outputs. They are extensively used in pattern recognition. This type of organisation is also referred to as bottom-up or top-down.

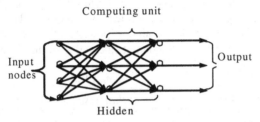

Fig. 1. Feedforward neural network sketch map

Kolmogorov proves that any continuous shining-upon function from input to output can be realized by a latent network of 3 layers when the activating function of a neuron is micro. The premise is that enough latent units, proper activating functions of nonlinearity and weighs values. Normally function to activate the neurons chooses Sigmoid function $f(x) = \dfrac{1}{1 + e^{-x}}$, because the sigmoid function is non-linear, monotone, an unlimited number of micro,approximately regarding as threshold function with great weigh and close to an linear function with small weigh.

The common neuron activation functions are also including hyperbolic function $f(x) = \tanh(x)$, and so on.

3 Negative Correlation Learning

1996, Solich and Krogh[4]provided the definition for the neural network ensemble, which was the neural network ensemble studied a same question with limited neural networks, The output of the ensemble under some input example is determined by all the output of the neural network forming the ensemble under the same input example.

In the respect of the individual network of producing ensemble, the process of two stage designing is adopted by most methods, that is, firstly the mission is to train individual networks independently and in turn, then make them form neural network ensemble . In this way, it not only loses the interaction between the individual networks, but also is without feedbacked between the stages of training and forming. So it could lead some individual networks having no contribution to the whole ensemble. In addition, the document points out, when the individual networks are   different greatly in the neural network ensemble, the effect of the ensemble is better. However, it's still a focus of research that how to get the individual networks with great difference and how to appraise difference degree between several networks at present. In this respect, the learning method of negative correlation provided by Liu and Yao in 1990 is a very potential method.

Negative correlation Learn ing (NCL) is a successful approach to designing neural network (NN) ensemble. Like many other learning methods, all the available data areused to train the ensemble during a single training session. However, in many real-world applications, the data are not available at one time. Therefore, it is desirable for a learning algorithm to be capable of acquiring knowledge from new data. Such a learning process is referred to as incremen tal learning [3]. In general, it is suggested that an incremen tal learning algorithm should enable the ensemble to use any new training data to further improve its performance, and preserve previously learned knowledge without access to the previous data. This could involve the ensemble having to accommodate new classes of data that are introduced with the new data [4] [5].

3.1 The Basic Concepts of Negative Correlation Learning

The order of the negative correlation learning is to encourage differently individual networks of the different individual networks ensemble study learn to train different parts in the data ,in order to study the whole training gathering better for the neural network ensemble . The difference between the negative correlation learning and the other methods of neural network ensemble is that , the way to train individual networks in other method is an independent or in- order way; while the way in the negative correlation learning is to induce a relevant punishment item for training these individual network simultaneously through the error function of the individual network of the neural network ensemble. That is to say, the purpose of every individual network's training is to make the result of the whole neural network ensemble best.

Given the training data set $D = \{(\vec{X}_1, d(1)),..., (\vec{X}_n, d(N))\}$,N stands for the sample size,where $\vec{X}_i \in R^p$ is the p-dimensional training pattern,we consider estimating d by forming an neural network ensemble whose output is a simple averaging of outputs F_i of a set of neural networks.All the individual networks in the ensemble are trained on the same training data set D

$$F(n) = \frac{1}{M} \sum_{i=1}^{M} F_i(n) \tag{4}$$

Where $F_i(n)$ is the output of individual network i on the n th training pattern $x(n)$, $F(n)$ is the output of the neural network ensemble on the n th training pattern,and M is the number of individual network in the neural network ensemble.

The idea of negative correlation learning is to introduce a correlation penalty term into the error function of each individual network so that the individual network can be trained simultaneously and interactively.The error function E_i for individual i on the training data set D in negative correlation learning is defined by

$$E_i = \frac{1}{N} \sum_{n=1}^{N} \left(\frac{1}{2} (F_i(n) - d(n))^2 + \lambda p_i(n) \right) \qquad (5)$$

Where N is the number of training patterns, $E_i(n)$ is the value of the error function of individual networks i at presentation of the n th training pattern,and $d(n)$ is the desired output of nth training pattern. In the right of the formula, the first item is the experience error function for individual networks i .The second is the item of relevance punishment. p_i stands for the function of the relevance punishment item of individual networks i . By minimizing p ,every individual network Error is nega-tive correlated with all the rest of the networks of individual errors, adjusting the punishment power through the reference $0 \le \lambda \le 1$. The form of the punishment function of $p_i(n)$ on the sample n is:

$$p_i(n) = (F_i(n) - F(n)) \sum_{j \ne i} (F_j(n) - F(n)) \qquad (6)$$

$$\frac{\partial E_i(n)}{\partial F_i(n)} = F_i(n) - d(n) - \lambda (F_i(n) - F(n)) \qquad (7)$$

Observing formula (4), (5) , (6) ,and (7), we can get:

(1) During the training process,all the individual network interact with each other through their penalty terms in the error function.Each network F_i minimises not only the difference between $F_i(n)$ and $d(n)$,but also the difference be-tween $F(n)$ and $d(n)$. That is ,negative correlation learning considers error what all other neural network have learned while training an neural network.

(2) For $\lambda = 0$,there are no individual network are just training independently using BP.That is, independent training using BP for the individual networks is a special case of negative correlation learning.

(3) For $\lambda = 1$,from formula (7) we get

$$\frac{\partial E_i(n)}{\partial F_i(n)} = F(n) - d(n) \qquad (8)$$

The error function of the neural network ensemble on sample n can be defined as

$$E_{ens}(n) = \frac{1}{2} \left(\frac{1}{M} \sum_{i=1}^{M} F_i(n) - d(n) \right)^2 \qquad (9)$$

$$\frac{\partial E_{ens}(n)}{\partial F_i(n)} = \frac{1}{M}(F(n) - d(n)) \tag{10}$$

Observing formula (8)and(10),we can get:

$$\frac{\partial E_i(n)}{\partial F_i(n)} \propto \frac{\partial E_{ens}(n)}{\partial F_i(n)} \tag{11}$$

The minimisation of the error function of the ensemble is achieved by minimising the error functions of the individual networks.Form this point of view,negative orrelation learning provides a novel way to decompose the learning task of the ensemble into a number of subtasks for different individual networks.

3.2 Deviation - Variance - A Compromise between the Covariance

Mean-Squared Error (is abbreviated as MSE) can be used for weighing the generalization performance of neural network and neural network ensemble.
The mean-squared error formula of the neural network that is widely known to all:

$$E_{mse} = E_D\left((E_D[d \mid x] - F(x,D))^2\right)$$
$$= (E_D[F(x,D)] - E_D[d \mid x])^2 + (E_D[F(x,D)] - E_D[F(x,D)])^2 \tag{12}$$

The formula (12) indicates, the mean-square error can be shown as the sum of deviation item and the variance item. The best way to obtain smaller deviation and smaller variance is to try hard to understand the priori information of the goal quation. The observation of deviation and variance is useful to explain the following practices : go to look for the accurate priori knowledge of the form of solution; make use of training samples as much as possible; it is essential to study the match situation of algorithms and designated question. The mean-squared error formula of neural network ensemble is similar to the mean-squared error formula of the neural network:

$$E_{mse} = E_D[(E_D[d \mid x] - F(x,D))^2]$$
$$E_{mse} = E_D[(E_D[d \mid x] - F(x,D))^2]$$
$$+ E_D[\frac{1}{M^2}\sum_{i=1}^{M}\sum_{i \neq j}(F_i(x,D) - E_D[F_i(x,D)]) \times (F_j(x,D) - E_D[F_j(x,D)])] \tag{13}$$

In the right of the formula (13), the first item is reflected the deviation of the neural network ensemble, the second is reflected the variance, and the third is reflected the covariance of the neural network ensemble . The negative correlation learning can make the generalization performance of the neural network ensemble better through adjusting λ to keep the balance of deviation, variance and covariance.

3.3 Improved Negative Correlation Learning

In the primitive negative correlation learning, the training algorithm of every individual network in the neural network ensemble is the standard BP algorithm. Because of the inherent characteristic of standard BP algorithm, the shortcoming is slow restraint for individual networks. The algorithm with impulse BP makes the renewing weigh in No.n time partly depend on the renewing weigh in No.n-1 time in order to search for the result with long step and accelerate the restraint.

In this paper, combining   the algorithm with impulse BP , the author provides an improved negative correlation learning for the study in batches of the neural network ensemble.

Sept 1. Begin;

Sept 2. Create neural networks of number M a single-unit output of BP as individual networks in neural network ensemble of number M , BPN_i stands for individual network i ;

Sept 3. Initialize the weigh value of all individual networks into small value at random;

Sept 4. Before meeting the condition of stopping: D-training for every training sample $(\overrightarrow{x,t})$,do:

(1) For every individual Network BPN_i ,do:Enter BPN_i into sample $\overrightarrow{x}$, and calculate the output o_u of every unit in BPN_i ;

(2) Calculate $o_{total} = \dfrac{1}{M} \sum\limits_{k=1}^{M} o_k$, o_k stands for the BPN_i output of individual network of No. k;

(3) For every BPN_i of individual networks, do:

a. For the output of every unit k in BPN_i ,calculate the error item $\delta_k \leftarrow (1-\lambda)f_k(d_k-o_k)+\lambda(d_k-o_{total})$, f_k stands for the derivation of the activation function of unit k, λ stands for the punishment factor;

b. For every hidden unit h in BPN_i ,calculate the error item $\delta_h \leftarrow f_h \sum\limits_{j \in Downstream\,(h)} \delta_j w_{jh}$ .Downstream (h) stands for the output units gathering containing unit h in the direct input. w_{jh} is the weigh value associated with the input of No.h in unint j.

(4) About every individual network BPN_i , calculate the renewed value $\Delta w_{mn}(i)$ of every hidden- layer node and output node according the current sample. For example, the current training sample is the first sample in this turn, so $\Delta w_{mn}(i) = \eta\,\delta_m x_{mn}$,otherwise, $\Delta w_{mn}(i) = \eta\,\delta_m x_{mn} + \Delta w_{mn}(i)$.

In the formula, $\Delta w_{mn}(i)$ stands for the renewed part of weigh value between node n to m in the training turn of No.i, x_{mn} stands for the input from node n to unit m , η is the study rate;Renew every weigh value of the network,in the formula $w_{mn} = w_{mn} + \Delta w_{mn}(i) + \alpha\Delta w_{mn}(i-1)$, α is the impulse factor ,Goto 4;

Sept 5. End.

4 Conclusion

In this paper, the author introduces the basic conception of the negative correlation learning of the neural network ensemble,and analyses deviation, variance,a compromise between the covariance. Besides,the author provides an improved negative correlation learning, combined by the negative correlation learning and the study algorithms with impulse. Although there are some improvement in the study of the negative correlation learning of the neural network ensemble in the paper, much work are still waiting for complete in the study. For example,when selecting the proper punishment factor,the neural network ensemble can obtain very good generalization performance. But the selection of punishment factor often depends on experience parameters. It is the coming mission that how to select the proper punishment factor quickly.

Acknowledgments. This work was supported by Natural Science Foundation of Hubei Province under Grant 2007ABA183.

References

1. Hornik, K.M., Stinchcombe, M., Multiayer, H.W.: Feedforward Networks Are Universal Approximators. Neural Networks 2(2), 359–366 (2002)
2. Liu, Y., Yao, X., Higuchi, T.: Evolutionary Ensembles with Negative Correlation Learning. IEEE Transactions on Evolutionary Computation 4(4), 380–387 (2000)
3. Rumelhar, D.E., Hinton, G.E., Williams, R.J.: Learning internal representations by error propagation. In: Rumlhart, D.E., Mcclell, J.L. (eds.), vol. 1(1), pp. 318–362. MIT Press, USA (2001)
4. Yao, X., Liu, Y.: Making use of population information in evolutionary artificial neural networks. IEEE Transactions on Systems,Man and Cybernetics, Part B: Cybernetics 4(28), 417–425 (1998)
5. Cooper, L.N.: Hybrid neural network architectures: Equilibrium systems that pay attention. In: Mamone, R.J., Zeevi, Y.Y. (eds.) Neural Network: Theory and Applications, pp. 81–96. Acaddemic Press, CA (1991)
6. Liu, Y., Yao, X.: Simultaneous training of negatively correlated neural networks in an ensemble. IEEE Transactions on Systems 29(6), 297–310 (1999)
7. Brown, G.: Diversity in Neural Network Ensembles, PhD thesis, School of Computer Science. University of Birmingham (2004)

A Discrete PSO for Multi-objective Optimization in VLSI Floorplanning

Jinzhu Chen[1], Guolong Chen[1,2,*], and Wenzhong Guo[1]

[1] College of Mathematics and Computer Science, Fuzhou University,
Fuzhou, 350002, China
chenjinzhu@yahoo.cn
[2] Key Laboratory of Discrete Mathematics with Application of Ministry of
Education, Fuzhou, 350002, China

Abstract. Floorplanning is a critical step in the physical design of Very Large Scale Integrated (VLSI) circuits. Its main target is optimizing the layout area and interconnection wire length of chips, which can be transformed into a Multi-objective Optimization Problem (MOP). In this paper, we propose a discrete Particle Swarm Optimization (PSO) algorithm for MOP which could take many key objectives into consideration and give a good compromise between them. The experiments on MCNC benchmarks show that the proposed algorithm is effective, and gives out many optional results for user's choice according to partialness, which can not be finished by traditional methods.

Keywords: discrete PSO, MOP, floorplanning.

1 Introduction

With the development of deep sub micrometer technologies, the complexity of Very Large Scale Integrated (VLSI) circuits design increases drastically [1]. As an important stage in the VLSI physical design cycle, floorplanning deals with the positions, shapes and orientations of circuit modules and makes sure no two of them overlap. It commonly aims at minimize the layout area and interconnection wire length simultaneous [2]. Floorplanning has been proved to be NP-hard [9]. For years many algorithms have been developed applying stochastic search methods, such as simulated annealing and genetic algorithms, however, only a few of them work explicitly on multiple objectives optimization[3]. Literatures[4,5,6] used the weighted sum approach to minimize the area and wire length simultaneously. This approach always has a difficulty to assign the weights, and may results in undesirable bias towards a particular objective.

As a population-based evolutionary algorithm, Particle Swarm Optimization (PSO) was introduced by Eberhart and Kennedy in 1995 [7]. It is inspired by the flocking behavior of birds, in which the flight of each individual is influenced by its own experience and its companions'. PSO seems particularly suitable for

---

* Corresponding Author.

Z. Cai et al. (Eds.): ISICA 2009, LNCS 5821, pp. 400–410, 2009.

multi-objective optimization mainly because of its high speed of convergence that the algorithm presents for single-objective [8]. However, the development of multi-objective PSO algorithms(MO-PSOs) is still in the preliminary stage [10]. In this paper, we propose a discrete PSO algorithm to solve the multi-objective optimization in floorplanning. The objective is to minimize the layout area and total interconnection wire length simultaneously. The particle is encoded into an integer sequence in which each number stands for some module. A set of non-dominance solutions is maintained while iterating. To decide the global best, a fitness with phenotype sharing is defined, thus a non-dominance solution with lower neighborhood density would be selected [11].

The rest of the paper is organized as follows. Section 2 gives a brief intro-duction to the floorplanning problem. Section 3 describes the mechanism of PSO. Section 4 depicts proposed algorithm for floorplanning in detail. Section 5 summarizes the results obtained on the MCNC benchmarks. Section 6 offers concluding remarks followed by acknowledgements.

2   Problem Description

2.1   Data Structure

VLSI floorplan is to arrange the modules on a chip and the set of modules can be represented as $S = \{M_1, M_2, \ldots, M_N\}$, where N is the number of the modules and M_i $(i=1,2,\ldots,N)$ represents the i-th module. There are two different kinds of modules:

1. Hard module. The hard module's shape is fixed, and is denoted as (W, H), where W is the width while H is the height of the module.
2. Soft module. Soft module's area is also fixed, but the ratio of width/height is included in a given range. It can be denoted as (S, L, U), where S represents the area, L and U the lower and upper boundary of the width/height ratio.

2.2   Floorplan Structure

There are two layout structures in floorplan, namely, slicing and non-slicing floorplan. Slicing structure can be divided into two parts with recursive method. The recursive process ends when each part holds a single module.

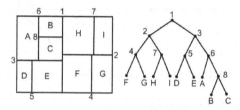

Fig. 1. Slicing floorplan and its slicing tree

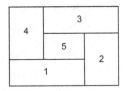

Fig. 2. Non-slicing floorplan

Figure 1 shows a slicing floorplan and its corresponding slicing-tree respectively. The number in the figures denotes the division line and the letter denotes the subregions divided. Figure 2 shows a non-slicing floorplan.

3   Particle Swarm Optimization

PSO is initialized with a population of random solutions of the objective function. The individuals in the population are called as particles. The updates of the particles are accomplished according to the following equations. Equation (1) calculates a new velocity for each particle (potential solution) based on its previous velocity (v_{id}^{t-1}) and the personal best location (p_{id}, or $pBest$) which the particle has achieved so far and the global best location (p_{gd}, or $gBest$) of the population in history. Equation (2) updates i-th particle's position in solution hyperspace.

$$v_{id}^t = w \times v_{id}^{t-1} + c_1 r_1 (p_{id} - x_{id}^{t-1}) + c_2 r_2 (p_{gd} - x_{id}^{t-1}) \tag{1}$$

$$x_{id}^t = x_{id}^{t-1} + v_{id}^t \tag{2}$$

where t is the iteration index, d is the number of dimensions (variables), w is the inertia weight, c_1 and c_2 are two positive constants, called acceleration constants, r_1 and r_2 are two random numbers within the range [0,1]. A constant, V_{max} is often used to limit the velocities of the particles and improve the resolutions of the search space.

According to (1) and (2), the first part of (1) represents the previous velocity, which provides the necessary momentum for particles to roam across the search space. The second part, known as the cognitive component, represents the personal thinking of each particle. The cognitive component encourages the particles to move toward their own best positions found so far. The third part is known as social component, which represents the collaborative effect of the particles, in finding the global optimal solution[12]. The social component always pulls the particle toward the global best particle found so far.

4   Discrete PSO for Multi-objective Floorplanning

4.1   Floorplan Representation

The slicing floorplan based on the floorplan representations can only solve the planning problems with limited scope. On the contrary, the non-slicing floorplan is much more general, and can describe any type of packing in the practice applications. Due to this reason, many researchers focus on the non-slicing floorplan representations.

In recent years, many important representations of non-slicing floorplan have been proposed: Corner Block List (CBL) representation [13]; Sequence Pair (SP) representation [14]; Bounded Slicing Grid (BSG) representation [15]; O-tree representation [4]; Transitive Closure Graph (TCG) representation [5], etc. Literature [2] introduces integer coding representation in the format of $\langle V_1, V_2, \ldots, V_i, \ldots, V_n \rangle$, where $1 \leq V_i \leq n$, $V_i = j$ and it denotes that the i-th module is placed at j-th position. Then a heuristic operator is deployed to adjust the modules while taking both their shapes and directions into consideration. Literature [16] adopts the integer coding representation proposed in [2], and modifies the heuristic adjustment method. In this paper, the representation is similar to that in [2], but it only contains the order of modeling, does not include the information of shape and direction of the modules. As a result, the modified representation can work with a much more complicated modeling method to perform the floorplanning. In addition, the shape and direction of the modules need to be encoded to convert the linear modules seriation into a two-dimensional floorplanning. Considering hard modules and soft modules, the coding representation can be divided into two parts:

1. Hard module. The shapes of the modules are fixed while their directions are undetermined. Let α_j and β_j denote the alternate direction and order of the module M_i: α represents the relative long edge of M_i which is placed in horizontality and β in verticality correspondingly, j is the order of module M_i.

2. Soft module. In practice, the shapes of soft modules don't vary arbitrarily, some candidate ratios of width/height, such as 0. 5, 1. 0, 1. 5, ... will be given for choice[9]. So alphabets A, B, C, ...can be used to denote the order of coding: 'A' denotes the first one , 'B' the second one, etc. For example,suppose one soft module has three ratios 0.5, 1, 2, and can be coded by A, B, C. thus A_i denotes that current module is module i and it adopts the first ratio 0.5.

Therefore, as to the sequence $< \alpha_4, \beta_1, A_3, B_2 >$, it represents that the order of the modules is M_4, M_1, M_3, M_2 where M_1, M_4 are hard modules, M_2, M_3 are soft modules, M_3 adopts the first ratio and M_2 adopts the second ratio.

4.2   Heuristic-Based Layout Decoder

During the decoding process, the layout of modules as specified by a floorplanning is determined from a sequence. Let code x stands for the module sequence, and some rules are needed to convert modules sequence to two-dimensional floorplanning. Each particle x is converted into module sequence according to the rules listed below:

1. Place the corresponding module of first element in x to the left bottom.
2. Place the other modules in the order of left to right.

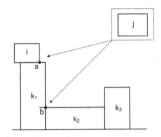

Fig. 3. Rules to place modules

3. If the module to be placed is overlapped with the assumed width, the algorithm just starts a new line above the current one.
4. If the area usage proportion in the last line is less than 50%, the assumed width should be increased to integrate the last line into the previous several lines. That is, the assumed width is increased by $s_n / \sum_{i=1}^{n-1} h_i$; if the area usage proportion in the last line exceeds 50%, the assumed width should be narrowed to fill the last line with some modules placed in the previous several lines. That is, the assumed width should be decreased by $s_n^* / \sum_{i=1}^{n} h_i$. Where S_n denotes the area of the last line, and S_n^* is the area not be placed yet in the last line, and h_i is the height of the i-th line.

One special constraint should be added to Rule 2. That is, if the module to be placed can be shifted a little right to reduce the height of floorplanning when placing modules from left to right, the algorithm just places the module in the lower place. For example, in Fig.3, if module j is to be placed in the order left to right, it should be placed at point a. But this arrangement is not suitable because placing module at point b could make its height lower. Considering the constraint mentioned above, module j should be placed at point b.

4.3   Optimization Objectives

In this paper, the layout area $f(x)$ can be written as follows:

$$f(x) = W(x) \times H(x) \tag{3}$$

where $W(x)$ is the floorplanning width of the corresponding particle x, and $H(x)$ is the floorplanning height of x.

Half-perimeter wire length (HPWL) is computed for all the nets to estimate the total wire length required. The HPWL is extensively employed because its calculation is relatively simple and accurate [17]. It is equal to the weighted sum of half-perimeters of the bounding boxes that encompass the modules incident on each net. Therefore, the wire length can be determined as follows.

$$L = x_{\max} - x_{\min} + y_{\max} - y_{\min} \tag{4}$$

where x_{max} and x_{min} are the maximum and minimum x-coordinate of the HPWL bounding box of the net, respectively. y_{max} and y_{min} are the maximum and minimum y-coordinate of the HPWL bounding box of the net, respectively. Thus considering a floorplanning problem with m nets, its layout comes out to be A, its total wire length is

$$t(A) = \sum_{i=1}^{m} L(i) \qquad (5)$$

4.4 Discrete PSO

The proposed discrete PSO algorithm incorporates the crossover and mutation operators in Genetic Algorithm (GA) to deal with the modules sequences.

The notion of mutation operator is incorporated into the first part of (1).

$$A_i^t = F_1(X_i^{t-1}, w) = \begin{cases} F_1(X_i^{t-1}) & r_1 < w \\ X_i^{t-1} & r_1 \geq w \end{cases} \qquad (6)$$

where F_1 indicates the mutation operator with the probability w, and r_1 is random number.

The second part and the third part of (1) adopt the notion of crossover operator.

$$B_i^t = F_2(A_i^t, c_1) = \begin{cases} F_2(A_i^t) & r_2 < c_1 \\ A_i^t & r_2 \geq c_1 \end{cases} \qquad (7)$$

$$X_i^t = F_3(B_i^t, c_2) = \begin{cases} F_3(B_i^t) & r_3 < c_2 \\ B_i^t & r_3 \geq c_2 \end{cases} \qquad (8)$$

where F_2, F_3 indicate the crossover operator with the probability as c_1, c_2, respectively. r_2 and r_3 are two random numbers.

Then we can get the following equation.

$$X_i^t = F_3(F_2(F_1(X_i^{t-1}, w), c_1), c_2) \qquad (9)$$

4.5 Multi-objective Approach

For multi-objective optimization, we adopt the concept of dominance to compare solutions. The personal best position can be use to store non-dominated solutions generated in the past. While iterating, a set of non-dominated solutions is maintained, and a global best should be selected from this set. Thus to make a decision, a selection method is necessary, which should promote the swarm flying towards the true pareto front and distributing along the front as uniformly as possible.

The fitness function defined in [11] is applied, in which a particle is evaluated by both pareto dominance and neighborhood density. For a global best, a non-dominated solution with lower fitness value is selected. In particular, if several solutions have the same fitness value, we choose a random one. The detail of the fitness function is given below.

Definition 1. *As to particle x_i and x_j, the distance of the k-th objective is*

$$f_k d_{ij} = |f_k(x_i) - f_k(x_j)| \qquad (10)$$

Therefore, the objective distance of particle x_i and x_j is given as

$$f d_{ij} = f_1 d_{ij} + f_2 d_{ij} + \ldots + f_m d_{ij} \qquad (11)$$

where m is the dimension of the objective.

Definition 2. *The number which particle x_i is dominated is defined as*

$$D(i) = \sum_{j=1}^{p} nd(i,j) \qquad (12)$$

where p is the size of neighborhood, and nd(i,j) is one if i-th particle dominates j-th particle and zero otherwise.

Definition 3. *For a given $f d_{ij}$, the sharing function is defined as*

$$sh(f d_{ij}) = \begin{cases} 1 & if \ \ f d_{ij} \leq \sigma \\ 0 & otherwise \end{cases} \qquad (13)$$

where σ is sharing parameter, m is the dimension of the objective.

Definition 4. *The neighbor density measure of i-th particle is defined as*

$$N(i) = \sum_{j=1}^{p} sh(f d_{ij}) \qquad (14)$$

where p denotes the size of neighborhood.

Definition 5. *Given a N(i) and D(i), the fitness function of i-th particle is*

$$F(i) = (1 + D(i))^{\alpha} \times (1 + N(i))^{\beta} \qquad (15)$$

where α and β are nonlinear parameters.

4.6 Algorithm Description

The details of algorithm are described as follows:

Step 1: Load modules data and initial the parameters of the PSO algorithm (such as population size, generations, etc.).

Step 2: Initialize population, calculate the layout area and wire length, and fitness value of each particle.

Step 3: Set the *pBest* of each particle and select the non-dominated solutions.

Step 4: Adjust the position and velocity of each particle according to (6)-(9).

Step 5: Calculate the layout area and wire length, and fitness value of each particle.

Step 6: Update *pBest* of each particle and the non-dominated solutions.

Step 7: If termination condition is satisfied, the algorithm stops; otherwise, go to step 4.

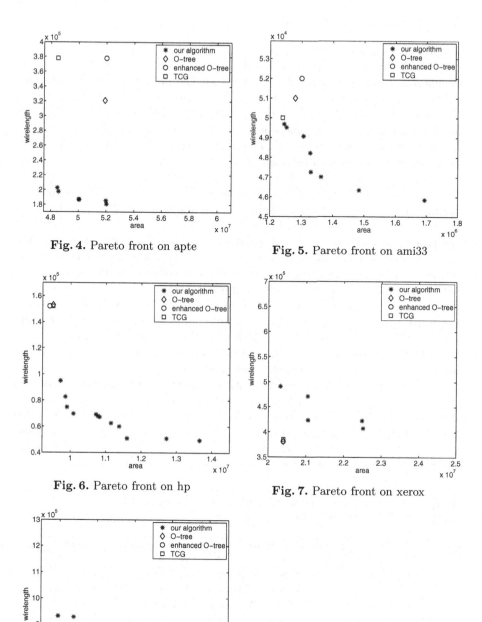

Fig. 4. Pareto front on apte

Fig. 5. Pareto front on ami33

Fig. 6. Pareto front on hp

Fig. 7. Pareto front on xerox

Fig. 8. Pareto front on ami49

5   Experimental Results

The algorithm was implemented as a MATLAB program running on a computer with 2.00 GHz CPU and 2.00 Gb RAM. The experiments were tested on MCNC benchmarks. The parameters for the PSO algorithm were set to the following values: w decreased linearly from 0.9 to 0.4, c_1 decreased linearly from 0.82 to 0.5, and c_2 increased linearly from 0.4 to 0.83. Population size was set as 100, and maximum number of generations was 5000. The nonlinear parameters in fitness function α and β were set to be 3 and 1, respectively. The algorithm has been run 10 times on each problem.

In order to validate algorithm, we compare it with O-tree [4], enchanced O-tree [6] and TCG [5]. All the three algorithms applied weighted sum approach to optimize the objectives (equal weights to area and wire length), thus they only gave out one solution for a run. Fig. 4-8 show the pareto fronts obtained and the compared results. It can be seen that the solutions distribute uniformly along the pareto fronts, and the two objectives are in conflict, as any improvement in one objective causes deterioration in the other. In terms of wire length, our algorithm outperforms all the other methods on apte, hp and ami33, but is a little worse on xerox and ami49. In terms of area, we obtain multiple solutions which are not worse than the compared results on apte, ami33, xerox and ami49. For hp, the area results are a little bigger which gives the high wire length savings.

To have a clearer view, we choose two solutions for each benchmark, which are close to the compared results, and show the comparison in Table 1. The algorithm is able to obtain better solutions on apte and competitive solutions on ami33. For hp, the remarkable shorter wire length results are obtained at the cost of small increase in area. For ami49, the area results are smaller than that in O-tree and enhanced O-tree. Although the results obtained are a little worse in some cases, our algorithm is able to provide multiple layout schemes for floorplanning while other three algorithms only give out one solution.

Table 1. Comparison among our algorithm, O-tree, enhanced O-tree and TCG(A = area(mm^2), W = wire length(mm))

Algorithm	apte		xerox		hp		ami33		ami49	
	A	W	A	W	A	W	A	W	A	W
Our algorithm	48.4	202	20.3	490	9.7	95	1.24	49.6	38.8	886
	48.5	195	21.0	423	9.8	82	1.25	49.5	39.3	855
O-tree	51.9	321	20.4	381	9.5	153	1.28	51	39.6	689
enhanced O-tree	52.0	321	20.4	381	9.4	152	1.30	52	39.9	703
TCG	48.5	378	20.4	385	9.5	152	1.24	50	38.2	663

6   Conclusions

In the paper, we describe a discrete PSO algorithm for multi-objective floorplanning. It is easy to implement and can be extended for problems with more than two objectives. The experiment results on MCNC benchmarks show that the approach is able to obtain a well distributing pareto front, and provide multiple layout schemes for users. In some cases, the results obtained are not so competitive compared with results in other literatures. It is probably due to the fact that discrete PSO is usually easy to fall in to local optimum, and the settings of some parameters need further study. Therefore, future work will focus on enhancing the efficiency of the proposed DPSO.

Acknowledgments. This work supported by the National Basic Research Program of China under Grant No. 2006CB805904, the National Natural Science Foundation of China under Grant No. 10871221, the Key Project of Fujian Provincial Natural Science Foundation of China under Grant No. A0820002, Fujian Provincial Natural Science Foundation of China under Grant No. 2009J01284, the project development foundation of Education Committee of Fujian province under Grand No. JA08011.

References

1. Kang, L., Juebang, Y., Yongbing, Y.: Configuration of floorplan and placement algorithm using horizontal and vertical contour based on single sequence. In: International conference on Communications, Circuits and Systems, pp. 1171–1174 (2008)
2. Gwee, B.H., Lim, M.H.: A GA with heuristic based decode for IC floorplanning. Integration, the VLSI Journal 28(2), 157–172 (1999)
3. Fernando, P., Katkoori, S.: An Elitist Non-Dominated Sorting Based Genetic Algorithm for Simultaneous Area and Wirelength Minimization in VLSI Floorplanning. In: 21st International Conference on VLSI Design, pp. 337–342 (2008)
4. Guo, P.N., Cheng, C.K., Yoshimura, T.: An O-tree representation of non-slicing floorplan and its applications. In: Proceedings of the 36th ACM/IEEE conference on Design automation conference, New Orleans, Louisiana, United States, pp. 268–273 (1999)
5. Lin, J.M., Chang, Y.W.: TCG:A transitive closure gragh-based representation for non-slicing floorplans. In: Proc. DAC, pp. 764–769 (2001)
6. Pang, Y., Cheng, C.K., Yoshimura, T.: An enhanced perturbing algorithm for floorplan design using the O-tree representation. In: The Proceedings of ACM International Physical Design Symposia, pp. 168–173 (2000)
7. Kennedy, J., Eberhart, R.: Particle swarm optimization. In: IEEE Int. Conf. Neural Networks, vol. 4, pp. 1942–1948 (1995)
8. Coello, C.A.C., Pulido, G.T., Lechuga, M.S.: Handling Multiple Objectives With Particle Swarm Optimization. IEEE Trans. on Evol. Comput. 8, 256–279 (2004)
9. Garey, M.R., Johnson, D.S.: Computers and Intractability, San Francisco (1979)
10. Minyou, C., Chuansheng, W., Peter, F.: An evolutionary particle swarm algorithm for multi-objective optimisation. In: Proceedings of 7th World congress on Intellgent Control and Automation, pp. 3269–3274 (2008)
11. Wenzhong, G., Guolong, C., Min, H., Shuili, C.: A discrete particle swarm optimization algorithm for the multiobjective permutation flowshop sequencing problem. In: Proceedings of the second international conference of Fuzzy Information and Engineering, pp. 323–331 (2007)

12. Ratnaweera, A., Halgamuge, S.K.: Self-Organizing Hierarchical Particle Swarm Optimizer With Time-Varying Acceleration Coefficients. IEEE Transactions on Evolutionary Computation 8(3), 240–255 (2004)

13. Hong, X., Huang, G., Cai, Y., Gu, J., Dong, S., Cheng, C.K., Gu, J.: Corner Block List:An effective and efficient topological representation of non-slicing floorplan. In: Proc. ICCAD, pp. 8–12 (2000)

14. Murata, H., Fujiyoshi, K., Nakatake, S., Kajitani, Y.: VLSI Module Placement Based on Rectangle-Packing by the Sequence-Pair. IEEE Trans. on CAD 15(12), 1518–1524 (1996)

15. Nakatake, S., Fujiyoshi, K., Murata, H., Kajitani, Y.: Module Packing Based on the BSG-Structure and IC Layout Applications. IEEE Trans. on CAD 17(6), 519–530 (1998)

16. Wang, X.G., Yao, L.S., Gan, J.R.: VLSI Floorplanning Method Based on Genetic Algorithms. Chinese Journal of Semiconductors 23(3), 330–335 (2002)

17. Chaomin, L., Anjos, M.F., Vannelli, A.: A nonlinear optimization methodology for VLSI fixed-outline floorplannin. J. Comb. Optim. 16, 378–401 (2008)

Applying Chaotic Particle Swarm Optimization to the Template Matching Problem

Chunho Wu[1], Na Dong[2], Waihung Ip[1], Zengqiang Chen[2], and Kaileung Yung[1]

[1] Department of Industrial and Systems Engineering (ISE)
The Hong Kong Polytechnic University, Hung Hom, Kln, Hong Kong
[2] Department of Automation, Nankai Unversity, Tianjin, 300071, China
jack.wu@polyu.edu.hk, dongna1110@hotmail.com,
mfwhip@inet.polyu.edu.hk, chenzq@nankai.edu.cn,
mfklyung@inet.polyu.edu.hk

Abstract. An improved particle swarm optimization algorithm, CSPSO (Chaotic Species-based particle swarm optimization), is proposed for solving the template matching problem. Template matching is one of the image comparison techniques widely applied to component existence checking in the printed circuit board (PCB) and electronics assembly industries. The proposed approach adopts the special nonlinear characteristic and ergodicity of chaos to enrich the search ability of the species-based particle swarm optimization (SPSO). To test its performance, the proposed CSPSO-based approach is compared with SPSO-based approach using two experimental studies. The CSPSO-based approach is proven to be superior to the original SPSO-based one in term of efficiency.

Keywords: Chaotic Particle Swarm Optimization, Template Matching, PCB Manufacture.

1 Introduction

Template matching has been widely used in solving object locating and recognizing problems. This technique, especially in two dimensional image domains, has various applications, such as object recognition, object tracking and stereo correspondence. Templates can either be extracted by exemplar images [1, 2, 3] or created from models [4, 5, 6]. Template matching techniques can be classified based on the features used, for example, edge pixels [7], intensity patches [8] and wavelets coefficients [9, 10]. In general, template matching requires similarity measures between the features of a template and the window of the captured image. Among several matching methods, Normalized Cross-Correlation (NCC) has been widely used as the similarity measurement [11, 12]. It reduces the sensitivity to captured images when compared with classical image subtraction and hence improves the robustness of the matching process. However, the evaluation of the correlation is computationally expensive because of the search for the closest captured image pixel of each template pixel. Sliding a template over the captured image in a pixel-by-pixel fashion is inefficient,

Z. Cai et al. (Eds.): ISICA 2009, LNCS 5821, pp. 411–421, 2009.

especially in a multiple template matching problem. In order to speed up the template matching process, Species-based Particle Swarm Optimization (SPSO) has been adopted to enhance the efficiency of the multiple template matching problem in a printed circuit board (PCB) inspection task [13].

For PCB inspection, a number of inspection approaches with various capabilities and benefits have been proposed [3, 13-15]. Recently, evolutionary methods have been adopted to solve the template matching problem in PCB inspection. The Genetic Algorithm (GA) based template matching approach has been proposed by Crispin et al. and Li et al. in 2006 [3, 15]. The matching process has been improved, however, the computation resource required by GA was still high. In 2008, a PSO based template matching algorithm was proposed [13]. Due to its simplicity, compared with GA, the run time has been greatly reduced with less parameter adjustment. Although the PSO based solution has been successfully demonstrated, a premature phenomenon can be observed due to its dependence on initial parameters and random initialization. In this paper, an improved SPSO template matching algorithm, incorporating chaos theory, is proposed. Chaos is a kind of behavior of certain dynamical systems, and it is complex and highly sensitive to initial conditions. Chaotic motion does not follow any regular pattern but is deterministic. Most importantly, every state is visited one time only. Due to its unique ergodicity, embedding chaos in PSO can improve the searching ability [16]. This paper describes a chaotic SPSO template matching method. The improved algorithm in the chosen cases provides an obvious enhancement in terms of speed.

In order to make the paper self contained, section 2 describes normalized cross-correlation. Section 3 introduced why the template matching problem is formulated as a multimodal optimization problem. In section 4, the CSPSO is discussed. Section 5 shows the tests of the proposed the CSPSO template matching method. The test results and comparison are included. Finally conclusions are drawn in Section 6.

2 Template Matching Using Cross-Correlation

Using cross-correlation for template matching is motivated by the idea of distance measure, which is the squared Euclidean distance.

$$d_{I,t}^2(u,v) = \sum_{x,y} [I(x,y) - t(x-u, y-v)]^2 \tag{1}$$

where I is the source image and the total sum is over x, y under the template, t, located at u, v. In the expansion of d^2:

$$d_{I,t}^2(u,v) = \sum_{x,y} [I^2(x,y) - 2I(x,y)t(x-u, y-v) + t^2(x-u, y-v)] \tag{2}$$

The term $\sum (t^2(x-u, y-v)$ is constant, and if the term $\sum I^2(x,y)$ is approximately constant, then the cross-correlation term can be expressed by:

$$C(u,v) = \sum_{x,y}[I(x,y)t(x-u,y-v)] \tag{3}$$

where C is a similarity measure between the window of the source image and the sub-image (template). However, several shortages can be found when applying Equation (3) for template matching. For example, the equation is variant to changes in image amplitude, the image energy $\sum I^2(x,y)$ cannot vary with position, and the range of C is dependent on the size of the template. Thus, normalizing the image and feature vectors to a unit length overcomes the disadvantages:

$$NCC(x,y) = \frac{\sum_{x,y}[I(x,y) - \overline{I}_{u,v}][t(x-u,y-v) - \overline{t}]}{\{\sum_{x,y}[I(x,y) - \overline{I}_{u,v}]^2 \sum_{x,y}t[x-u,y-v) - \overline{t}]^2\}^{1/2}} \tag{4}$$

where $\overline{t}$ is the mean grey-level intensity of the template and $\overline{I}_{u,v}$ is the mean grey-level intensity of the captured image in the region coincident with the template. NCC is the Normalized Cross-Correlation. In multiple template matching, at each point (x, y), the NCC_M value refers to the maximum of a set of NCC values which are calculated using corresponding templates. For example, at (x, y), NCC_1 is computed using template 1 and NCC_2, obtained using template 2 respectively. k is the number of templates. The NCC_M value at a particular location can be obtained by:

$$NCC_M(x,y) = \max\{NCC_1(x,y), NCC_2(x,y), \ldots\ldots, NCC_k(x,y)\} \tag{5}$$

where,

$$NCC_k(x,y) = \frac{\sum_{x,y}[I(x,y) - \overline{I}_{u,v}][t(x-u,y-v) - \overline{t}]}{\{\sum_{x,y}[I(x,y) - \overline{I}_{u,v}]^2 \sum_{x,y}t[x-u,y-v) - \overline{t}]^2\}^{1/2}}.$$

3   Reason for Formulating a Multimodal Optimization Problem

Although one can directly apply the multiple template matching technique for multiple objects detection, it is not efficient. Since the obtaining of one NCC value at each pixel needs repeated calculation of a set of NCC values to select the maximum, it is exceedingly time consuming. In the multiple template matching problem, the computational complexity, O, for an given image of size $W \times L$ and a total of b objects is $(W \bullet L)^b$. For a test image (Figure 3), the complexity is around $(712 \bullet 612)^6$, which is approximately 6.8×10^{33}. In order to get an optimal solution with a shorter computational time, an efficient search method which can track multi-peaks (multiple NCC_M) becomes essential.

Multimodal optimization, used to locate all the peaks, has been extensively studied by many researchers [17, 18]. It is a fact that formulating the multiple template matching problem as a multimodal optimization problem is a successful method [13].

4 Chaotic SPSO for Template Matching

Since the paper presents a version of a combined evolutionary search method for template matching, a brief literature review on SPSO is included. The CSPSO will then be introduced to solve the template matching problem.

4.1 Species-Based PSO (SPSO)

A PSO algorithm is an optimization technique which maintains a population of individuals, namely particles, where each particle is guided by the social interaction in order to reach the most promising area of the search space. The particles start at a random initial position in a multi-dimensional search space and search for the minimum or maximum of a given objective function by flying through the search space. The movement of i-th particle, x_i, depends on its velocity, v_i, and the location where the personal best position so far, $p_i = (p_{i1}, p_{i2}, \ldots p_{id})$, has already been found, or the neighborhood best position, $lbest_i = (lbest_{i1}, lbest_{i2}, \ldots lbest_{id})$. When a particle's neighborhood is defined as the whole swarm, the PSO is called the global version, otherwise it is a local one. Equation (6) updates the velocity of each particle, whereas equation (7) updates each particle's position in the search space, and c_1, c_2 are cognitive coefficients and φ_1, φ_2 are two uniform random numbers from $U(0, 1)$ [19].

$$v_{id} = w \cdot v_{id} + c_1 \cdot \varphi_1 \cdot (p_{id} - x_{id}) + c_2 \cdot \varphi_2 \cdot (lbest_{id} - x_{id}) \tag{6}$$

$$x_{id} = x_{id} + v_{id} \tag{7}$$

The standard PSO, however, fails to locate multiple optima since the principle of PSO uses the best-fit particle in the whole swarm or a fitter particle chosen from its neighborhood to guide the whole swarm to converge to a single optimum. Li (2004) proposed a SPSO which enables the particles to search for multiple optima simultaneously to overcome the deficiency found in the standard PSO [20]. The notion of species in the SPSO can be represented by a group of particles that share common attributes based on some similarity measure, and it is measured in term of a distance. The smaller the distance, the more similar they are. The centre of a species is a species seed which is the best-fit individual in the species, and all the particles in the species are confined within a circle of radius r_s.

4.2 Chaotic SPSO (CSPSO)

Chaotic dynamics is incorporated into the SPSO, so that the search behavior can be enhanced. Comparing the tent map with the logistic map, the tent map shows the outstanding advantages and higher iterative speed [21] which is more suitable for the uniform distribution function in the interval [0, 1]. In this paper, chaos variables are generated using the tent map for initialization. The tent map is defined by the following formula:

$$z_{n+1} = \mu\left(1-2\left|z_n - 0.5\right|\right), 0 \le z_0 \le 1 \ , \ n = 0,1,2,\cdots \tag{8}$$

where $\mu \in [0,1]$ is a bifurcation parameter.

When $\mu = 1$, the tent map exhibits entirely chaotic dynamics and ergodicity in the interval [0, 1]. Figure 1 shows the distribution of two chaos sequences after 1500 iterations with the initial point ($x_{10} = 0.231$, $x_{20} = 0.356$) in a 2D space. Each point can be described by (x_{1j}, x_{2j}), $j = 1, 2, \ldots, 1500$.

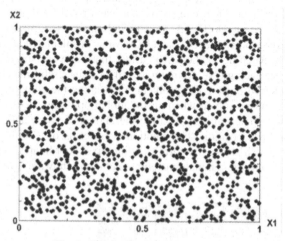

Fig. 1. Distribution of chaos variables

The tent-map chaotic dynamics is used to initialize the particle swarm in the SPSO. Firstly, the tent map, $\mu = 1$, is used to generate the chaos variables and update (8), and gives:

$$z_j^{(i+1)} = \mu\left(1-2\left|z_j^{(i)} - 0.5\right|\right) \ j = 1,2,\cdots,P \tag{9}$$

where z_j denotes the j-th chaos variable, and i denotes the chaos iteration number. Set $i = 0$ and generate P chaos variables by (9) and let $i = 1, 2, \ldots,$ m and generate the initial swarm. Then, the above chaos variable $z_j^{(i)}$ will be mapped into the search range of the decision variable:

$$x_{ij} = x_{\min,j} + z_j^{(i)}\left(x_{\max,j} - x_{\min,j}\right), \ j = 1,2,\cdots,P \tag{10}$$

The chaotic-initialized particle swarm, X_i, can be obtained by:

$$X_i = (x_{i1}, x_{i2}, \cdots, x_{iP}) \ i = 1, 2, \cdots, m \tag{11}$$

4.3   CSPSO for Template Matching

When the template matching method is adopted, objects can be matched with one template. If the multiple-template matching method is used, multiple objects can be matched with the corresponding template. Both require a NCC value space of a captured image, for example, the test image (Figure 2), with 382 pixels x 362 pixels. Every NCC value is calculated exhaustively at each pixel by the template matching approach. Another test image (Figure 3), with 762 pixels x 612 pixels, has been tested in previous research studies [3, 13]. Each NCC value is calculated at each pixel by the multiple-template matching method. It is a fact that there are six global optima and many local optima. Each global optimum identifies a successful matching of the template and the preferred object. The problems of locating the component and locating multiple resistors can be solved when all the global optimum are detected. Applying the CSPSO, each particle, initialized within the 2D search space and encoded in float format, represents one position. The solution is in terms of a rounded value of the particle location, which shows the corresponding pixel coordinates. The flow chart of the CSPSO-based multiple-template matching method is shown in Figure 4.

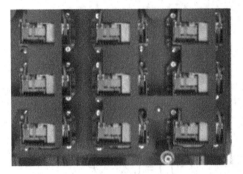

Fig. 2. The test image of the main board and the component template

Fig. 3. The test image of the printed circuit board (PCB) and the resistor templates

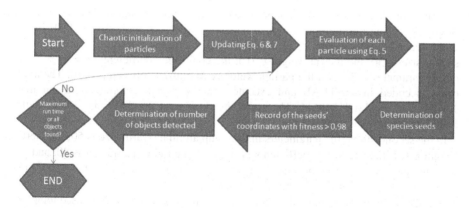

Fig. 4. The flow 0063hart of the CSPSO-based multiple-template matching

5   Experiments and Results

In order to reveal the improved performance of the proposed CSPSO-based template matching method, two experimental studies have been conducted. In the first study,

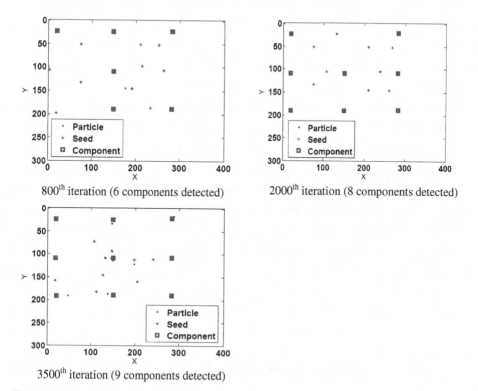

Fig. 5. The snap-shots of the CSPSO-based template matching process of the main board (1st Study)

the template matching process is done based on the captured image of the main board (Figure 2). Then, the multiple-template matching process is done for the PCB image in the second study (Figure 3). In the first study, the parameters in the setup are: the swarm size is 50, the inertia weight is 0.5, the cognitive coefficients $c_1 = c_2 = 2$, the radius parameter is 30, and the particle velocity initializes between [−6, 6]. The algorithm is coded in MATLAB and executed on a personal computer with an Intel 1.6GHz CPU and a 1G RAM. The searching process at the 800th, the 2000th & the 3500th iteration is shown in Figure 5.

In the second study, the parameters in the setup are: the swarm size is 50, the inertia weight is 0.5, the cognitive coefficients $c_1 = c_2 = 2$, the radius parameter is 80, and the particle velocity initializes between [−4, 4]. The searching process at the 3500th, the 5000th & the 6800th iteration is shown in Figure 6.

In order to show the improved performance of the proposed CSPSO-based template matching method, comparisons of the above studies have been done using the CSPSO-based approach and the SPSO-based approach. For both methods, the parameter settings in each study are identical in order to maintain a fair comparison. The results are shown in Tables 1 to 4.

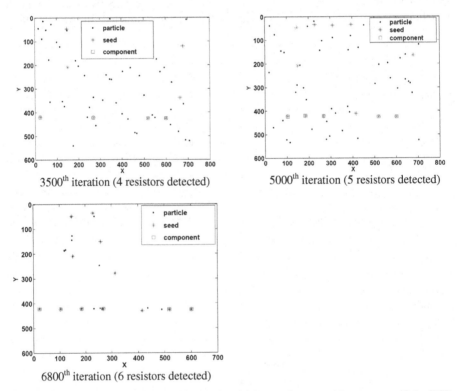

3500th iteration (4 resistors detected)

5000th iteration (5 resistors detected)

6800th iteration (6 resistors detected)

Fig. 6. The snap-shots of the CSPSO-based multiple-template matching process of the PCB (2nd Study)

Table 1. Comparison of CSPSO template matching method with SPSO template matching method in the 1st Study

Algorithm	Min. Run Time (s)	Max. Run Time (s)	Successful Rate* (%)	Time (Mean of 30 runs and Std. err.)
SPSO	1.3440	3.8600	100	2.32 ±0.95
CSPSO	0.4530	2.9690	100	1.96 ±0.80

* Successful rate means how many times that all components can be successfully detected out of 30 runs.

Table 2. Number of components detected successfully within 3 sec. in the 1st Study

Algorithm	Min. detected components	Max. detected components	Detected components (Mean of 30 runs and Std. err.)
SPSO	6	9	7.40 ±0.95
CSPSO	9	9	9.00 ±0.00

Table 3. Comparison of CSPSO multiple-template matching method with SPSO multiple-template matching method in the 2nd Study

Algorithm	Min. Run Time (s)	Max. Run Time (s)	Successful Rate* (%)	Time (Mean and Std. err.)
SPSO	13.6250	53.3600	100	32.39 ±14.48
CSPSO	11.2970	32.8440	100	20.26 ±6.64

* Successful rate means how many times that all resistors can be successfully detected out of 30 runs.

Table 4. Number of components detected successfully within 40 sec. in the 2nd Study

Algorithm	Min. detected resistors	Max. detected resistors	Detected resistors (Mean of 30 runs and Std. err.)
SPSO	2	6	5.13 ± 1.37
CSPSO	6	6	6.00 ± 0.00

According to the comparisons, the proposed CSPSO-based approach has advantages over the SPSO-based approach. Although both approaches have 100% successful rate in locating all components, the CSPSO-based approach has a better efficiency than the SPSO-based approach in terms of averaged, maximum and minimum run time (Table 1). In the three-second-constrained test, the SPSO-based approach could not detect all nine components in all runs, unlike the CSPSO-based approach (Table 2). Similar phenomena can be observed in the results of the 2nd study (Tables 3 and 4). The CSPSO-based approach guarantees to detect all components within the time constraints which can be considered as the processing time upper limits for the inspection tasks. The multiple-template matching process has been improved over 35% using the CSPSO-based approach, in terms of averaged run time.

6 Conclusions

In this research, a chaotic species-based particle swarm optimizer is proposed for improving template matching problems. It is applied to solve the components and resistors detection problem based on the template matching and multiple-template matching techniques, and experimental results have been obtained. The results showed that the proposed CSPSO-based approach successfully located all the targets in all runs, and with a higher efficiency. In addition, the standard errors of the averaged run time in both experimental studies were reduced using the proposed approach. It is a clear fact that the CSPSO-based approach can improve the template matching process in both efficiency and stability. In the future, the CSPSO-based approach will be applied to other template matching problems, in a larger scale. There is also a need to investigate how to best choose the species radius of the CSPSO multiple-template method, for example, by looking for a method to choose the species radius adaptively during the matching process.

Acknowledgments. The authors wish to thank the Research Committee and the Department of the Industrial and Systems Engineering of the Hong Kong Polytechnic University for support in this research work (G-YG44). Our gratitude is also extended to the support in part by the Natural Science Foundation of China Under Grant 60774088, the Program for New Century Excellent Talents in Universities of China (NCET), the Science & Technology Research Key Project of Education Ministry of China Under Grant 107024, and the Application Base and Frontier Technology Research Project of Tianjin of China under 08JCZDJC21900.

References

1. Gavrila, D.M.: Pedestrian Detection from a Moving Vehicle. In: 6th European Conf. on Computer Vision, vol. II, pp. 37–49. Springer, Heidelberg (2000)
2. Toyama, K., Blake, A.: Probabilistic Tracking in a Metric Space. In: 8th IEEE International Conference on Computer Vision, vol. II, pp. 50–57. IEEE Press, New York (2001)
3. Crispin, A.J., Rankov, V.: Automated Inspection of PCB Components Using a Genetic Algorithm Template-matching Approach. Int. J. Adv. Manuf. Tech. 35, 293–300 (2007)
4. Athitsos, V., Sclaroff, S.: An Appearance-based Framework for 3D Hand Shape Classification and Camera Viewpoint Estimation. In: IEEE Conf. on FGR, pp. 45–50. IEEE Press, New York (2002)
5. Shakhnarovich, G., Viola, P., Darrell, T.: Fast Pose Estimation with Parameter-sensitive Hashing. In: 9th IEEE Int. Conf. on Computer Vision, vol. II, pp. 750–757. IEEE Press, New York (2003)
6. Stenger, B., Thayananthan, A., Torr, P.H.S., Cipolla, R.: Filtering Using a Tree-based Estimator. In: 9th IEEE Int. Conf. on Computer Vision, vol. II, pp. 1063–1070. IEEE Press, New York (2003)
7. Olson, C.F., Huttenlocher, D.P.: Automatic Target Recognition by Matching Oriented Edge Pixels. IEEE T. Image Process. 6(1), 103–113 (1997)
8. Borenstein, E., Ullman, S.: Class-specific, Top-down Segmentation. In: 7th European Conf. on Computer Vision, vol. I, pp. 109–122. Springer, Heidelberg (2002)

9. Triesch, J., Von der Malsburg, C.: A System for Person-independent Hand Posture Recognition Against Complex Backgrounds. IEEE T. Pattern Analysis and Machine Intell. 23(12), 1449–1453 (2001)
10. Hewer, G., Kenney, C., Hanson, G., Wei, K., Peterson, L.: Detection of Small Objects Using Adaptive Wavelet-based Template Matching. In: SPIE Proceedings of Signal and data processing of small targets, vol. 3809, pp. 95–106. SPIE, Bellingham (1999)
11. Krattenthaler, W., Mayer, K.J., Zeiler, M.: Point Correlation: A Reduced-cost Template Matching Technique. In: 1st IEEE Int. Conf. on Image Processing, vol. I, pp. 208–212. IEEE Press, New York (1994)
12. Rosenfeld, A., Vanderburg, G.J.: Coarse-Fine Template Matching. IEEE T. Sys., Man and Cyb. 7, 104–197 (1977)
13. Wang, D.Z., Wu, C.H., Ip, A., Chan, C.Y., Wang, D.W.: Fast Multi-template Matching Using a Particle Swarm Optimization Algorithm for PCB Inspection. In: Giacobini, M., Brabazon, A., Cagnoni, S., Di Caro, G.A., Drechsler, R., Ekárt, A., Esparcia-Alcázar, A.I., Farooq, M., Fink, A., McCormack, J., O'Neill, M., Romero, J., Rothlauf, F., Squillero, G., Uyar, A.Ş., Yang, S. (eds.) EvoWorkshops 2008. LNCS, vol. 4974, pp. 365–370. Springer, Heidelberg (2008)
14. Moganti, M., Ercal, F., Dagli, C.H., Tsunekawa, S.: Automated PCB Inspection Algorithms: a Survey. Comput. Vis. Image Underst. 63(2), 287–313 (1996)
15. Li, D., Yu, C.F.: The Application of Genetic Algorithm in Detecting Printed Circuit Board Components. Journal of Fudan University (Natural Science) 45(4), 452–456 (2006)
16. Liu, B., Wang, L., Jin, Y.H., Tang, F., Huang, D.X.: Improved Particle Swarm Optimization Combined with Chaos. Chaos Soliton Fract. 25, 1261–1271 (2005)
17. Beasle, D., Bull, D.R., Martin, R.R.: A Sequential Nitche Technique for Multimodal Function. Evol. Comput. 1(2), 101–125 (1993)
18. Ling, Q., Wu, G., Wang, Q.: Restricted Evolution Based Multimodal Function Optimization in Holographic Grating Design. In: IEEE Congress on Evolutionary Computation 2005, pp. 789–794. IEEE Press, München (2005)
19. Kennedy, J., Eberhart, R.: Swarm Intelligence. Morgan Kaufmann Academic Press, San Francisco (2001)
20. Li, X.: Adaptively Choosing Neighbourhood Bests Using Species in a Particle Swarm Optimizer for Multimodal Function Optimization. In: Deb, K., et al. (eds.) GECCO 2004. LNCS, vol. 3102, pp. 105–116. Springer, Heidelberg (2004)
21. Zhang, H., Shen, J.H., Zhang, T.N., Li, Y.: An Improved Chaotic Particle Swarm Optimization and Its Application in Investment. In: International Symposium on Computational Intelligence and Design, vol. 1, pp. 124–128 (2008)

Cellular PSO: A PSO for Dynamic Environments

Ali B. Hashemi and M.R. Meybodi

Computer Engineering and Information Technology Department,
Amirkabir University of Technology, Tehran, Iran
{a_hashemi,mmeybodi}@aut.ac.ir

Abstract. Many optimization problems in real world are dynamic in the sense that the global optimum value and the shape of fitness function may change with time. The task for the optimization algorithm in these environments is to find global optima quickly after the change in environment is detected. In this paper, we propose a new hybrid model of particle swarm optimization and cellular automata which addresses this issue. The main idea behind our approach is to utilized local interactions in cellular automata and split the population of particles into different groups across cells of cellular automata. Each group tries to find an optimum locally which results in finding the global optima. Experimental results show that cellular PSO outperforms mQSO, a well known PSO model in literature, both in accuracy and complexity in a dynamic environment where peaks change in width and height quickly or there are many peaks.

Keywords: Dynamic environments, Particle swarm optimization, Cellular Automata.

1 Introduction

In the real world, many applications are non-stationary problems which need to not only finding the global optimal solution but also keeping trace of its change. Particle swarm optimization algorithms (PSO) have gained popularity in recent years. PSO is a population-based method, a variant of evolutionary algorithms with moving towards the target rather than evolution, through the search space. The basic idea behind this approach is iterative ameliorating of global participant's perception of the target by exchanging local information among them. However due to the static context of PSO usage, some issues arise when using them in dynamic environments. These challenges lie in two aspects: outdated memory due to changing environment and diversity loss due to convergence. Of these two the diversity loss is by far more serious. It has been demonstrated that the time taken for a partially converged swarm to re-diversify, find the shifted peak, and then re-converge is quite deleterious to the performance of PSO [1].

   In this paper we address diversity loss problem in adapting PSO to dynamic environments and propose a variant of multi swarm method to solve it. To this aim, embedded cellular automata are utilized to maintain diversity of particles and to scatter them over the search space. Particles in each cell of cellular automata search for a local optimum and broadcast the best solutions to neighborhood. Comparing the best

Z. Cai et al. (Eds.): ISICA 2009, LNCS 5821, pp. 422–433, 2009.

results found in neighboring cells and the best position in their cell, particles in a cell sets their direction towards the best solution found in their neighborhood and their best personal experience. However in moving towards dynamic optimum, preserving particle density in each cell below a threshold is of great concern. Hence upon arriving in a cell, a portion of particles may be reinitialized to keep particle density below this threshold. This mechanism makes the swarms spread out over the highest multiple peaks across the environment, meanwhile helps convergence onto a local optimum in a short time. Extensive experiments show that the proposed cellular PSO results less offline error than mQSO[2] a well known PSO model in literature, in environments which have many peaks or width and height of the peaks change very fast.

The rest of this paper is organized as follows: Section 2 provides a brief introduction on PSO and an overview of the previous works on adapting PSO into dynamic environments. Section 3 introduces cellular automata as the foundations of our approach following by detailed specification of the proposed algorithm in section 4. Section 5 gives out the experimental results of the proposed model along with its comparison to best results gained in previous works. Finally in section 6 we conclude our paper.

2 Related Work

2.1 Particle Swarm Optimization

The particle swarm optimization (PSO) algorithm is introduced by Kennedy and Eberhart [3] based on the social behavior metaphor. The fundament for the development of PSO is hypothesis that a potential solution to an optimization problem is treated as a bird without quality and volume, which is called a particle, flying through a D-dimensional space, adjusting its position in search space according to its own experience and its neighbors.

In PSO, the ith particle is represented as $p_i = (p_{i1}, p_{i2}, \ldots, p_{iD})$ in the D-dimensional space. The velocity for particle i is represented as $V_i = (v_{i1}, v_{i2}, \ldots, v_{iD})$, which is usually clamped to a maximum velocity V_{max}, specified by the user. In each time step t, the particles calculate their new velocity then update their position according to eq. (1) and eq. (2) respectively.

$$v_i(t+1) = v_i(t) + c_1 r_1 \left(p_i^{best} - p_i(t) \right) + c_2 r_2 \left(lbest - p_i(t) \right) \tag{1}$$

$$p_i(t+1) = p_i(t) + v_i(t+1) \tag{2}$$

Where c_1 and c_2 are positive acceleration constants used to scale the contribution of cognitive and social components respectively. r_1 and r_2 are uniform random variables in range [0,1]. p_i^{best} is the best personal position of particle i which has been visited during the lifetime of the particle. $lbest$ is the local best position that is the best position of all neighboring particles of particle i.

2.2 PSO in Dynamic Environment

The application of PSO to dynamic problems has been explored in various literatures. In this section we provide a brief overview of the most relevant works which shapes foundations of our approach through addressing diversity loss in dynamic optimization problems.

The main idea behind multi-swarms approaches is to divide swarms into sub groups and place them on the best peaks found so far, while letting some particles explore for new peaks. Following this idea, Blackwell and Branke [2, 4] has suggested dividing the whole population into several sub swarms incorporating three concepts, namely quantum particles, exclusion and anti-convergence. Quantum particles appear at random positions around the sub-swarm best ensuring a close chase of moving peaks. Exclusion operator regarding local interaction between swarms, upon falling their distance beneath a minimum threshold, reinitializes one with the aim of keeping diversity at a desired level. Moreover taking into account the possibly of existing more peaks than swarms, it is necessary to keep constantly patrolling for new and better peaks. To this end anti-convergence operator has been proposed.

In [5], Blackwell et. al. introduced two variants of the canonical method in [6] addressing self adaptation problem. One starting with a single swarm and adding additional swarms as needed regarding a predefined number of total particles, the other fixing overall number of particles and dynamically distributes particles to swarms, usually starting with many swarms, slowly converging to the required number of swarms to cover all peaks. In both methods, by reducing the number of permanent quantum particles and converting all neutral particles to quantum particles for one iteration only after a change, convergence speed towards local peaks by maximizing its use of neutral particles has been increased.

Lung and Dumitrescu used two collaborating populations of equal size to avoid premature convergence and to efficiently trace the moving optimum [7]. One is responsible for preserving the diversity of the search by using crowding differential evolutionary algorithm while the other keeps track of global optimum with a PSO algorithm. The collaboration mechanism is applied whenever a change is detected in the search space, or if the best individual in second population is too close to the best solution. The search of the second population is restarted by re-initializing it with the positions of individuals in the first population.

In [8] Li and Yang proposed a multi-swarm method which maintains the diversity through the run. To meet this end two type of swarms are used: a parent swarm which maintains the diversity and detects the promising search area in the whole search space using a fast evolutionary programming algorithm, and a group of child swarms which explore the local area for the local optima found by the parent using a fast PSO algorithm. This mechanism makes the child swarms spread out over the highest multiple peaks, as many as possible, and guarantees to converge to a local optimum in a short time.

Du and Li [9] suggest dividing particles into two parts, of which the first uses a standard PSO enhanced a Gaussian local search and the second uses differential mutation acting as a patrol team around first to extend the search area of algorithm, and catch up with the moving optimum. The introduced strategies in these two parts, respectively enhances the convergence ability of the algorithm and avoids being trapped into the local optimum.

3 Cellular Automata

Cellular automata are mathematical models for systems consisting of large number of simple identical components with local interactions in which space and time are discrete. It is called cellular because it is made up of cells like points in a lattice or like squares of checker boards, and it is called automata because it follows a simple rule[10]. Informally, a d-dimensional CA consists of a d-dimensional lattice of identical cells. The simple components act together to produce complicated patterns of behavior. Each cell can assume a state from a finite set of states. The cells update their states synchronously on discrete steps according to a local rule. The new state of each cell depends on the previous states of a set of cells, including the cell itself, and constitutes its neighborhood (Figure 1). The state of all cells in the lattice is described by a configuration. A configuration can be described as the state of the whole lattice. The rule and the initial configuration of the CA specify the evolution of CA that tells how each configuration is changed in one step. Cellular automata perform complex computations with a high degree of efficiency and robustness. They are especially suitable for modeling natural systems that can be described as massive collections of simple objects interacting locally with each other [11, 12].

 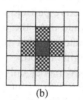

(a)   (b)

Fig. 1. Neighborhood in a 2-D cellular automata: a. Moore neighborhood b. von Neumann Neighborhood

4 Proposed Model

In previous multi-swarm methods [2, 5, 8] in order to prevent sitting of two or more swarm on a peak, every pair of swarms have to calculate their distance so that if they were too close, the worse swarm reinitialize. In the proposed model we omit the burden of exhaustive distance calculations by cellular automata into the search space as shown in Fig 2. Hence, we call our model "Cellular PSO". Although the term "Cellular PSO" was first used in [13], it was used as a synonym of a local best PSO with a Von Neumann neighborhood.

In our model, D-dimensional cellular automata with C^D equal cells are used in a D-dimensional environment. Therefore, a particle in search space can be assigned to one cell in cellular automata. This concept is used to preserve diversity in the search space. We define *particle density* of a cell c at time t, $\rho_c(t)$ to be the number of particles which are positioned in boundaries of cell c at the specified time t. By keeping

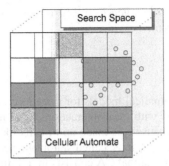

Fig. 2. Embedding cellular automata in a 2-D Search Space

the particle density of all cells bellow a specified threshold θ, we prevent all particles from converging to one cell. Therefore, only a portion of all particles can investigate a sub-space while there are particles available to search other parts of the space. Moreover, when particle density of cell i rise up beyond the acceptable threshold θ, some of the particles in cell i are randomly selected to be reinitialized in the cellular automata as follows.

First, status of a selected particle is changed to *inactive*. Then a randomly selected cell is assigned as destination of the particle. Distance of current cell and the destination cell is calculated and is set as the hop count for the selected particle. Afterwards at the next iteration, neighbors of cell i read this particle's information as part of state of cell i and add this inactive particle to their state while decreasing the particle's hop counter. This will continue until the destination cell receives this particle as part of one of its neighbors' state. At this time, particle will be activated and will begin searching in the new neighborhood.

Moreover, the proposed model only uses local interaction between cells of cellular automata (*lbest* PSO model) to maintain better diversity among the cells. *lbest*$_i$ for all particles in cell i is defined the best position found in neighborhood of cell i, including cell i.

In the proposed model, state of cell i is consists of following information.

1. Best position found in cell i. (*cbest*$_i$)
2. Best position found in cell i and neighborhood of cell i since last environment change. (*lbest*$_i$)
3. Information of all particles currently exists in cell i, including particle position, velocity, state, destination, and hop count. Where particle state can be active or inactive. When a particle is inactive it does no function evaluation. Particle's destination and hop count are only meaningful for an inactive particle which is headed to another cell as mentioned above.

A change is detected by monitoring of *lbest* as in [14, 15]. After detecting an environment change, memory of all cell including *cbest*$_i$ and *lbest*$_i$ and all particles' history is reset.

At the beginning, N particles are initialized into cellular automata randomly. Then at iteration t cell i updates its state according to its current state and it neighboring cells' with the following rule.

1. *lbest*$_i$ is updated by reading state of its neighbors, e.g. cell j, according to *update lbest* procedure in Fig. 3.

```
Procedure updatelbest
begin
    for All cell j, cell_j is a neighbour of cell i do
        if  f(lbest_i) < f(cbest_j) then
            lbest_i← cbest_j
        end if
        for all p_k∈ P_j do
        if (p_k is inactive) then
          p_k.hop ← p_k.hop-1;
        endif
        if (p_k.hop > 0) then
          add p_k to P_i
        else if ( p_k.hop == 0 and p_k.dst=i) then
          activate p_k
          add p_k to P_i
        endif
        endfor
    endfor
end
```

Fig. 3. Update *lbest_i*

```
Procedure updateParticles
begin
  for all active particles p_j then
    update particle velocity according to eq. 3
    update particle position according to eq. 2
    if  cellof(p_j(t+1) ≠ i then
        deactivate p_j
        p_j.dst← cellof(p_j(t+1)
        p_j.hop← distance(i, p_j.dst)
        p_j.initialize← false
    end if
  end for
end
```

Fig. 4. Update particle procedure for cell *i*

2. All particles p_k in cell i updates their velocity according to eq. (3)

$$v_k(t+1) = w\, v_k(t) + c_1 r_1 \left(pbest_k - p_k(t) \right) + c_2 r_2 \left(lbest_i - p_k(t) \right) \qquad (3)$$

3. Particle's next position is calculated by eq. (2). If p_k is leaving cell i to one of its neighbors e.g. cell j where $i \neq j$, then cell c_i will set the state of particle p_k to inactive. Then at time $t+1$ when cell j receives state of cell i, it will activate particle p_k and will add it to its state. (Fig. 4)

4. After updating position of all particles, cell i checks its particle density. If the particle density in cell i, $\rho_i(t)$, is above the specified threshold θ, some particles should scatter among the cellular automata. Therefore, θ-$\rho_i(t)$ particles in cell i are randomly selected to be reinitialized in cellular automata as mentioned above. This will decrease particle density below the threshold θ while increasing diversity of particles in search space. (Fig. 5)

```
Procedure ParticleDensityControl
begin
    if ρᵢ> θ then
        R←select θ-ρᵢ(t)  particles randomly;
        for all particle pᵢ∈R do
            pᵢ(t+1).statue ← inactive
            pᵢ(t+1).destinationCell ← a random cell of CA
            pᵢ(t+1).hop ←distance of pᵢ(t+1).destinationCell,c
            pᵢ(t+1).init ← true
        end for
    end if
end
```

Fig. 5. Density control procedure for cell i

5   Experimental Study

5.1   Dynamic Test Function

Branke [16] introduced a dynamic benchmark problem, called moving peaks benchmark problem. In this problem, there are some peaks in a multi-dimensional space, where the height, width and position of each peak change during the environment change. This function is widely used as a benchmark for dynamic environments in literature [8, 17].

The default parameter setting of MPB used in the experiments is presented in Table 1. In MPB, shift length (s) is the radius of peak movement after an environment change. m is the number of peaks. f is the frequency of environment change as number of fitness evaluations. H and W denote range of height and width of peaks which will change after a change in environment by *height severity* and width *severity* respectively. I is the initial heights for all peaks. Parameter A denotes minimum and maximum value on all dimensions.

For evaluating the efficiency of the algorithms, we use the offline error measure, the average deviation of the best individual from the optimum in all iterations.

Table 1. Parameters of Moving Peaks Benchmark

Parameter	Value
number of peaks m	10
f	every 5000 evaluations
height severity	7.0
width severity	1.0
peak shape	cone
shift length s	{0.0}
number of dimensions D	5
A	[0, 100]
H	[30.0, 70.0]
W	[1, 12]
I	50.0

5.2 Experimental Settings

In this study we have tested our proposed model on MPB and compared the results with mQSO [2]. In [2] Blackwell and Brank have shown that mQSO results less offline error than standard PSO with re-initialization [15] and Hierarchical Swarms [18]. Therefore we omit the results of those algorithms and only compare cellular PSO with mQSO 10(5+5^q) and mQSO10 (10+0^q) which have the parameters reported in [2] ($r_{excel}=31.5$, $r_{conv}=0.0$).

For Cellular PSO (CPSO), based on the previous experimental work[19], the acceleration constants C_1 and C_2 were both set to 1.496180, and the inertia weight w was 0.729844. We set maximum velocity for a particle equal to the neighborhood distance on the cellular automata. Hence, a particle will not move further than neighboring cells. The size of swarm has been set to 100 particles for all the experiments respectively. In cellular PSO, cellular automata with 10^D cells in a D-Dimensional space have been used. In the cellular automata neighborhood has been defined as Moore neighborhood with a neighborhood of 1 cell for D=2,3, and 2 cells for D=4,5. Moreover, the maximum allowed particle density (θ), was set equally in all cells to 10 particles per cell.

5.3 Experimental Results

Average offline error and 95% confidence interval in 100 runs for different frequency of environment change and different number of peaks for both CPSO, mQSO 10(5+5^q), and mQSO 10(10+0^q) algorithms are presented in Table 2 -Table 7. For each environment, offline error of the all algorithms have been compares statistically (with error 0.05) and the result(s) of the algorithm(s) performing significantly better than others is printed in bold.

In the fastest changing environment, where the peaks change every 500 iterations (Table 2), cellular PSO performs significantly better than mQSO for different number of peaks. This superiority also exists in the environment here the peaks change every 1000 iterations (Table 3), for different number of peaks but for the 10 peaks environment in which there is no significant difference between offline error for CPSO and mQSO $10(5+5^q)$.

By decreasing the dynamicity of the environment (increasing f), a trend in difference of CPSO and mQSO can be seen in which CPSO breaks out to perform the same as or even worse than mQSO $10(5+5^q)$ where the number of peaks is around 10 (Table 3 through Table 6). This trend, which can be due to specific tuning of mQSO $10(5+5^q)$ for 10 peaks environments [2], is describe as follows.

The trend begins in environment with f=1000 (Table 3) where CPSO performs significantly better than mQSO $10(5+5^q)$ for all number of peaks but the 10 peaks environment where there is just no significant difference between offline error of CPSO and mQSO $10(5+5^q)$. This pattern expands in the environment with f=2500 (Table 4) where not only for the environments with 30 or less peaks CPSO and mQSO $10(5+5^q)$ do not have any significant difference in offline error, but also for the 10 peaks environment mQSO $10(5+5^q)$ results significantly less offline error than CPSO. Almost the same pattern repeats for the environment with f=5000 (Table 5), but with not only mQSO $10(5+5^q)$ performs better than CPSO in the 10 peaks environment but also it expands this superiority for the single peak environment. The increasing trend can be better seen in the least changing tested environment where f=10000 (Table 6) in which CPSO can only compete with mQSO $10(5+5^q)$, in terms of offline error, for environments which have 30 peaks or more.

Furthermore, for environments that positions of the peaks also change with s=1 (Table 7 and Table 8), CPSO still outperforms mQSO in low dimensional highly dynamic environments (D=2 and f=500) or when the environment has few peaks. But when either the dimension or number of peaks increases, mQSO $10(5+5^q)$ performs significantly better than cellular PSO.

Although introducing new parameters in cellular PSO, e.g. size of cellular automata and particle density threshold, might be considered a drawback for the proposed model, the experimental results that cellular PSO can outperform mQSO[2] in various environments without changing value of its the parameters.

Table 2. Offline error for different number of peaks (f=500 and s=0)

m	CPSO	mQSO $10(10+0^q)$	mQSO $10(5+5^q)$
1	**9.78±0.79**	35.22±3.10	24.97±2.61
5	**1.91±0.18**	5.83±0.86	3.91±0.56
10	**1.44±0.13**	2.56±0.17	1.89±0.17
20	**2.40±0.06**	3.39±0.05	2.94±0.04
30	**2.90±0.08**	3.84±0.05	3.50±0.05
40	**3.12±0.07**	4.09±0.05	3.81±0.05
50	**3.31±0.08**	4.29±0.05	3.92±0.05
100	**3.57±0.06**	4.59±0.04	4.31±0.05
200	**3.75±0.07**	4.72±0.05	4.45±0.05

Table 3. Offline error for different number of peaks (f=1000 and s=0)

m	CPSO	mQSO 10(10+0^q)	mQSO 10(5+5^q)
1	**7.37±0.53**	14.56±1.49	12.25±1.42
5	**1.56±0.17**	3.18±0.43	2.68±0.23
10	1.33±0.11	1.77±0.09	**1.29±0.07**
20	**2.22±0.08**	2.64±0.05	2.46±0.06
30	**2.74±0.08**	3.20±0.05	3.05±0.06
40	**2.89±0.08**	3.42±0.05	3.36±0.06
50	**2.98±0.07**	3.58±0.06	3.45±0.06
100	**3.27±0.08**	3.95±0.06	3.78±0.06
200	**3.43±0.08**	4.03±0.06	3.92±0.07

Table 4. Offline error for different number of peaks (f=2500 and s=0)

m	CPSO	mQSO 10(10+0^q)	mQSO 10(5+5^q)
1	6.10±0.55	6.49±0.59	**5.43±0.58**
5	**1.17±0.18**	1.87±0.21	**1.38±0.11**
10	1.08±0.09	1.48±0.10	**0.90±0.06**
20	**2.19±0.11**	2.39±0.07	**2.21±0.08**
30	**2.62±0.11**	2.87±0.09	**2.71±0.08**
40	**2.77±0.12**	3.07±0.08	2.92±0.08
50	**2.94±0.09**	3.28±0.08	3.20±0.10
100	**3.08±0.10**	3.66±0.09	3.56±0.09
200	**3.22±0.11**	3.77±0.10	3.66±0.10

Table 5. Offline error for different number of peaks (f=5000 and s=0)

m	CPSO	mQSO 10(10+0^q)	mQSO 10(5+5^q)
1	5.23±0.47	3.36±0.31	**2.92±0.30**
5	**1.09±0.22**	1.25±0.13	**0.97±0.08**
10	1.14±0.13	1.54±0.13	**0.85±0.08**
20	**2.20±0.12**	2.23±0.11	**2.09±0.12**
30	**2.67±0.13**	2.67±0.10	**2.62±0.13**
40	**2.70±0.13**	2.98±0.13	2.99±0.13
50	**2.77±0.13**	3.13±0.13	3.02±0.13
100	**2.97±0.14**	3.58±0.13	3.41±0.14
200	**3.14±0.12**	3.52±0.11	3.48±0.13

Table 6. Offline error for different number of peaks (f=10000 and s=0)

m	CPSO	mQSO 10(10+0^q)	mQSO 10(5+5^q)
1	4.18±0.39	**1.59±0.16**	**1.49±0.15**
5	0.85±0.16	0.67±0.10	**0.53±0.06**
10	1.10±0.18	0.90±0.08	**0.57±0.07**
20	2.26±0.18	**1.98±0.09**	**1.86±0.11**
30	**2.57±0.17**	**2.49±0.11**	**2.48±0.13**
40	**2.72±0.18**	2.88±0.12	**2.87±0.13**
50	**2.89±0.16**	3.05±0.12	**2.89±0.13**
100	**2.90±0.16**	3.28±0.13	3.27±0.13
200	**3.17±0.17**	3.68±0.13	**3.34±0.13**

Table 7. Offline error for *CPSO* for different number of peaks and dimensions, f =500 and s=1

m＼D	2	3	4	5
1	4.58±0.16	7.43±0.33	9.23±0.34	11.41±0.68
5	3.45±0.10	4.40±0.15	6.43±0.19	6.83±0.18
10	3.42±0.06	4.29±0.08	6.34±0.12	6.81±0.17
20	3.44±0.03	5.11±0.05	6.50±0.08	7.73±0.07
30	3.42±0.03	5.46±0.07	6.78±0.06	8.39±0.11
40	3.35±0.03	5.65±0.07	6.89±0.05	8.64±0.11
50	3.29±0.03	5.63±0.07	6.96±0.05	8.63±0.11
100	3.03±0.02	5.41±0.05	6.87±0.05	8.93±0.12
200	2.76±0.01	5.00±0.04	6.61±0.04	8.68±0.11

Table 8. Offline error for *mQSO10(5+5^q)* for different number of peaks and dimensions, f =500 and, s=1

m＼D	2	3	4	5
1	9.01±0.24	17.43±1.98	22.81±3.20	28.38±1.89
5	5.15±0.12	6.96±0.45	7.57±0.57	8.80±0.45
10	4.63±0.06	5.59±0.20	5.50±0.21	5.74±0.08
20	4.36±0.03	5.27±0.07	6.01±0.06	6.80±0.04
30	4.18±0.03	5.37±0.07	6.49±0.07	7.28±0.04
40	4.04±0.02	5.49±0.06	6.66±0.08	7.52±0.04
50	3.92±0.02	5.48±0.07	6.82±0.06	7.67±0.04
100	3.51±0.01	5.21±0.05	6.92±0.04	7.92±0.04
200	3.09±0.01	4.73±0.04	6.76±0.04	7.91±0.04

6   Conclusions

In this paper, we have proposed a new particle swarm optimization algorithm called cellular PSO which tackles dynamic environments. Cellular PSO combines the power of particle swarm optimization with cellular automata concepts by embedding cellular automata into the search space and keeping particle density in each cell bellow a specified threshold. With local information exchange between cells, particles in each neighborhood look for a peak together.

Compared to other well known approaches, our proposed model results more accurate solutions in highly dynamic environments, modeled by MPB[16], where peaks change in width and height. Moreover, in the environments where positions of the peaks also change, cellular PSO results less offline error than mQSO where either number of dimensions or number of peaks are small. In addition, experimental results show that this superiority can be achieved without changing value of parameters of cellular PSO. Furthermore, cellular PSO requires less computational effort since unlike mQSO [2] it does not need to compute distance of every pair of swarms on every iteration.

References

1. Blackwell, T.M.: Particle Swarms and Population Diversity. Soft Computing - A Fusion of Foundations, Methodologies and Applications 9, 793–802 (2005)
2. Blackwell, T., Branke, J.: Multiswarms, Exclusion, and Anti-Convergence in Dynamic Environments. IEEE Transactions on Evolutionary Computation 10, 459–472 (2006)
3. Kennedy, J., Eberhart, R.C.: Particle Swarm Optimization. In: IEEE International Conference on Neural Networks, Piscataway, NJ, vol. IV, pp. 1942–1948 (1995)
4. Blackwell, T., Branke, J.: Multi-Swarm Optimization in Dynamic Environments. Applications of Evolutionary Computing, 489–500 (2004)
5. Blackwell, T., Branke, J., Li, X.: Particle Swarms for Dynamic Optimization Problems. Swarm Intelligence, 193–217 (2008)
6. Blackwell, T.: Particle Swarm Optimization in Dynamic Environments. In: Evolutionary Computatation in Dynamic and Uncertain Environments, pp. 29–49 (2007)
7. Lung, R.I., Dumitrescu, D.: A Collaborative Model for Tracking Optima in Dynamic Environments. In: IEEE Congress on Evolutionary Computation, pp. 564–567 (2007)
8. Li, C., Yang, S.: Fast Multi-Swarm Optimization for Dynamic Optimization Problems. In: Fourth International Conference on Natural Computation, Jinan, Shandong, China, vol. 7, pp. 624–628 (2008)
9. Du, W., Li, B.: Multi-Strategy Ensemble Particle Swarm Optimization for Dynamic Optimization. Information Sciences: an International Journal 178, 3096–3109 (2008)
10. Fredkin, E.: Digital Mechanics: An Informational Process Based on Reversible Universal Cellular Automata. Physica D45, 254–270 (1990)
11. Mitchell, M.: Computation in Cellular Automata: A Selected Review. In: Gramss, T., Bornholdt, S., Gross, M., Mitchell, M., Pellizzari, T. (eds.) Nonstandard Computation, pp. 95–140 (1996)
12. Wolfram, S., Packard, N.H.: Two-Dimensional Cellular Automata. Journal of Statistical Physics 38, 901–946 (1985)
13. Waintraub, M., Pereira, C.M.N.A., Schirru, R.: The Cellular Particle Swarm Optimization Algorithm. In: International Nuclear Atlantic Conference, Santos, SP, Brazil (2007)
14. Carlisle, A., Dozier, G.: Adapting Particle Swarm Optimization to Dynamic Environments. In: International Conference on Artificial Intelligence, Las Vegas, NV, USA, vol. 1, pp. 429–434 (2000)
15. Hu, X., Eberhart, R.C.: Adaptive Particle Swarm Optimization: Detection and Response to Dynamic Systems. In: IEEE Congress on Evolutionary Computation, Honolulu, HI, USA, vol. 2, pp. 1666–1670 (2002)
16. Branke, J.: Memory Enhanced Evolutionary Algorithms for Changing Optimization Problems. In: 1999 Congress on Evolutionary Computation, Washington D.C., USA, vol. 3, pp. 1875–1882 (1999)
17. Moser, I.: All Currently Known Publications on Approaches Which Solve the Moving Peaks Problem. Swinburne University of Technology, Melbourne (2007)
18. Janson, S., Middendorf, M.: A Hierarchical Particle Swarm Optimizer for Dynamic Optimization Problems. Applications of Evolutionary Computing, 513–524 (2004)
19. van den Bergh, F.: An Analysis of Particle Swarm Optimizers. Department of Computer Science, PhD. University of Pretoria, Pretoria, South Africa (2002)

Constrained Layout Optimization Based on Adaptive Particle Swarm Optimizer[*]

Kaiyou Lei

Faculty of Computer & Information Science, Southwest University, Chongqing, 400715, China
lky@swu.edu.cn

Abstract. The layout design with dynamic performance constraints belong to NP-hard problem in mathematics, optimized with the general particle swarm optimization (PSO), to slow down convergence and easy trap in local optima. This paper, taking the layout problem of satellite cabins as background, proposed an adaptive particle swarm optimizer with a excellent search performance, which employs a dynamic inertia factor, a dynamic graph plane radius and a set of dynamic search operator of space and velocity, to plan large-scale space global search and refined local search as a whole in optimization process, and to quicken convergence speed, avoid premature problem, economize computational expenses, and obtain global optimum. The experiment on the proposed algorithm and its comparison with other published methods on constrained layout examples demonstrate that the revised algorithm is feasible and efficient.

Keywords: particle swarm optimization; premature problem; constrained layout optimization; dynamic performance constraints.

1 Introduction

In recent years, a more complex layout problem is attracting a lot of attention, such as the layout design of engineering machine, spacecraft, ship, etc. Solving these kinds of problems need to consider some additional dynamic performance constraints, for instance, inertia, equilibrium, stability, vibration, etc. They are called as layout problem with behavioral constraints (constrained layout). Constrained layout belonged to NP-hard problem, which has not been well resolved till now. One effective way to solve the problem is to explore new algorithms. Recently, with the development of computational intelligent methods, for instance, the genetic algorithm, especially the evolutionary algorithms have demonstrated their superiority in the combinatorial optimization problem[1,2,3].

As a newly developed population-based computational intelligence algorithm, Particle Swarm Optimization (PSO) was originated as a simulation of simplified social model of birds in a flock [4]. The PSO algorithm is easy to implement and has been proven very competitive in large variety of global optimization problems

---

[*] The work is supported by Key Project of Chinese Ministry of Education (104262).

Z. Cai et al. (Eds.): ISICA 2009, LNCS 5821, pp. 434–442, 2009.

and application areas compared to conventional methods and other meta-heuristics [5]. Since PSO introduction, numerous variations of the basic its algorithm have been developed in the literature to avoid the premature problem and speed up the convergence process, which are the most important two topics in the research of stochastic search methods. To make search more effective, there are many approaches suggested by researchers to solve the problems, such as variety mutation and select a single inertia weight value methods, etc, but these methods have some weakness in common, they usually can not give attention to both global search and local search, preferably, so to trap local optima, especially in complex constrained layout problems [6, 7, 8].

In this paper, an adaptive particle swarm optimizer with a better search performance is designed, which employ multi-adaptive strategies to plan large-scale space global search and refined local search as a whole according to the specialties of constrained layout problems, and to quicken convergence speed, avoid premature problem, economize computational expenses, and obtain global optimum. We tested the proposed algorithm and compared it with other published methods on constrained layout examples. The experimental results demonstrated that this revised algorithm can rapidly converge at high quality solutions.

2   Mathematical Model and PSO

Mathematical Model. Taking the layout problem of satellite cabins as an example, the principle can be described as follows [3]: There is a two-dimension rotating circular table (called graph plane) with radius R and n dishes (called graph units) with uniform thickness, each of which has a radius r_i and mass m_i $(i=1, 2,..., n)$, are installed on the graph plane as shown in Fig.1. Suppose that the frictional resistance is infinite. Find the position of each graph unit such that the graph units highly concentrate on the center of the graph plane and satisfy the following constraints:

(1) There is no interference between any two graph units.
(2) No part of any graph unit protrudes out the graph plane.
(3) The deviation from dynamic-balancing for the system should not exceed a permissible value $[\delta_j]$.

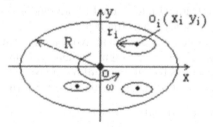

Fig. 1. layout pattern of graph units

Suppose that the center of the graph plane is origin o of the Cartesian system, the graph plane and graph units are just in plane xoy, the thickness of the graph units is ignored, and x_i, y_i are the coordinates of the center o_i of the graph unit i, which is its mass center also. The mathematical model for optimization of the problem can be formulated as follows:

$$\text{Find } X = [x_i, y_i]^T, \quad i \in I, I = 1,2,3,\cdots,n \tag{1}$$

$$min \ F(X) = max \left\{ \sqrt{(x_i^2 + y_i^2)} + r_i \right\}$$

s . t .

$$f_1(X) = r_i + r_j - \sqrt{(x_i - x_j)^2 + (y_i - y_j)^2} \le 0, i \ne j; i, j \in I \tag{2}$$

$$f_2(X) = \sqrt{(x_i^2 + y_i^2)} + r_i - R \le 0, \quad i \in I \tag{3}$$

$$f_3(X) = \sqrt{\left(\sum_{i=1}^{n} m_i x_i\right)^2 + \left(\sum_{i=1}^{n} m_i y_i\right)^2} - [\delta_j] \le 0, i \in I \tag{4}$$

PSO Algorithm. In the original PSO formulae, particle i is denoted as $Xi= (xi1, xi2,...,xiD)$, which represents a potential solution to a problem in D-dimensional space. Each particle maintains a memory of its previous best position Pbest, and a velocity along each dimension, represented as $Vi=(vi1,vi2,...,viD)$. At each iteration, the position of the particle with the best fitness in the search space, designated as gbest, and the P vector of the current particle are combined to adjust the velocity along each dimension, and that velocity is then used to compute a new position for the particle.

In the standard PSO, the velocity and position of particle i at $(t+1)$th iteration are updated as follows:

$$v_{id}^{t+1} = w * v_{id}^{t} + c_1 * r_1 * \left(p_{id}^{t} - x_{id}^{t}\right) + c_2 * r_2 * \left(p_{gd}^{t} - x_{id}^{t}\right) \tag{5}$$

$$x_{id}^{t+1} = x_{id}^{t} + v_{id}^{t+1} \tag{6}$$

Constants c1 and c2 are learning rates; r1and r2 are random numbers uniformly distributed in the interval [0, 1]; w is an inertia factor.

To speed up the convergence process and avoid the premature problem, Shi proposed the PSO with linearly decrease weight method [9]. Suppose wmax is the maximum of inertia weight, wmin is the minimum of inertia weight, run is current iteration times, runmax is the total iteration times, inertia weight is formulated as:

$$w = wmax - (wmax - wmin) * (ran / ranmax). \tag{7}$$

3 Adaptive Particle Swarm Optimizer

Due to the complexity of a great deal local and global optima, PSO is revised by four adaptive strategies to adapt the constrained layout optimization.

3.1 Improved Inertia Factor *w*

The *w* has the capability to automatically harmonize global search abilities and local search abilities, avoid premature and gain rapid convergence to global optimum. First of all, larger *w* can enhance global search abilities of PSO, so to explore large-scale search space and rapidly locate the approximate position of global optimum, smaller *w* can enhance local search abilities of PSO, particles slow down and deploy refined local search, secondly, the more difficult the optimization problems are, the more fortified the global search abilities need, once located the approximate position of global optimum, the refined local search will further be strengthen to get global optimum.

According to the conclusions above, we used (8) as new inertia weight decline curve for PSO [10].

$$w = w\ max* \ exp\left(- \ 30 * \left(run \ / \ run \ max \right)^\wedge 30\right) \tag{8}$$

3.2 Dynamic Radius Expanding Strategy

In (3), the graph plane radius R is constant, which will influence the fitness value computation and the result of search. In the search process, the more smallness the R is, the more convergence graph units are, and the algorithm quicken convergence speed, economize computational expenses. Evidently, taking the lesser radius to replace the R, the optima are searched in smaller area. But the lesser radius is kept in all search time, (2) and (3) will not be satisfy, so the lesser radius is expanded along with the search process, in this wise, the topological space is searched from smallness to bigness, the algorithm will get the lesser layout radius as well as harmony for (1), (2), (3) and (4). Suppose the lesser radius is R', which is constructed as:

$$R' = R * \left(1 - 0.3 * exp\left(- 40 * \left(run \ / \ run \ max \right)^\wedge 3\right)\right) \tag{9}$$

3.3 Dynamic Search Space Strategy

Considering that all particles gather gradually to the current best region along with the run of the algorithm, the search space, which is becomingly reduced, is propitious to quicken convergence. Because of curtailment of the flight range, the global optima may be lost, synchronously, the capability of the algorithm, which breached the local optima, is debased [9, 10]. Therefore, the improved algorithm not only reduces the search space to quicken convergence, but also avoids the premature problem, thus an adaptive reducing and expanding strategy of search space are designed. In the end of each cycle, the algorithm figures out the global optimum of swarm, if the current optimum is better last one, reduce search space, or else expand search space, in the same breath, randomly initialize the speed and position of each particle. Suppose *zmax'* and *zmin'* are the current range of search space of the swarm, *zmax* and *zmin* are the initial range of search space of the swarm, respectively, the computed equation is defined as:

$$IF \ p_{gd}^t > p_{gd}^{t-1} \quad z\,max' = zmax - zman' / ran\,max \quad z\,min' = -z\,max'$$
$$else \quad zmax' = zmax + z\,max' / ran\,max \quad z\,min' = -z\,max' \quad (10)$$

3.4 Dynamic Search Velocity Strategy

To cooperate above strategy, adaptive reducing and expanding strategy of search velocity are designed. In addition, the range of velocity affects the convergence precision and speed of algorithm strongly [9, 10]. Suppose $vmax$ and $vmin$ are the range of search velocity of each particle, the computed equation is defined as:

$$IF \quad p_{gd}^t > p_{gd}^t \quad vmax = vmax + |zmax'| / ran\,max \quad vmin = -vmax$$
$$else \quad vmax = vmax - |zmax'| / ran\,max \quad vmin = -vmax \quad (11)$$

3.5 Algorithm Designing and Flow

PSO, which is modified by the above methods, has the excellent search performance to optimize constrained layout problem, the design of the algorithm is as follows:

All particles are coded based on the rectangular plane axis system. Considering that the shortest periphery envelope circle radius is the optimization criterion based on the above constraint conditions for our problem, the fitness function and the penalty function, which are constructed in our algorithm, respectively, can be defined as:

$$\phi(X) = F(X) + \sum_{i=1}^{3} \lambda_i f_i(X) u_i(f_i), \ u_i(f_i) = \begin{cases} 0 & f_i(X) \le 0 \\ 1 & f_i(X) > 0 \end{cases}, i \in I \quad (12)$$

where λ_i ($\lambda_1=1, \lambda_2=1, \lambda_3=0.01$) is the penalty factor.

The flow of the algorithm is as follows:

Step1. Set parameters of the algorithm;

Step2. Randomly initialize the speed and position of each particle;

Step3. Evaluate the fitness of each particle using (12) and determine the initial values of the individual and global best positions: p_{id}^t, p_{gd}^t;

Step4. Update velocity and position using (5), (6) and (8);

Step5. Evaluate the fitness using (12) and determine the current values of the individual and global best positions: p_{id}^t, p_{gd}^t;

Step6. Check the p_{gd}^t, p_{gd}^{t-1}, adaptive reducing and expanding the range of search space and velocity using (10) and (11);

Step7. Loop to Step 4 and repeat until a given maximum iteration number is attained or the convergence criterion is satisfied.

4 Computational Experiments

Taking the literature [2], [3] as examples, we tested our algorithm, the comparison of statistical results are shown in Tab.1 and Tab.2, respectively.

Parameters used in our algorithm are set to be: $c_1=c_2=2$, $wmax=0.55$, $runmax=2000$. The running environment is: MATLAB7.1, Pentium IV 2GHz CPU, 256MRAM, Win XPOS.

Example1. Seven graph units are contained in the layout problem. The radius of a graph plane is R=50mm. The allowing value of static non-equilibrium J is $[\delta_J]=3.4$g*mm. The result is in Table 1 and the geometric layout is shown in Figure 4 (the particle size is 50).

Table 1. Comparison of experimental results of example 1

(a) Datum and layout results of example 1

number	Graph units		Literature [2] result		Literature [3] result		Our result	
	r(mm)	m(g)	x(mm)	y(mm)	x (mm)	y(mm)	x(mm)	y(mm)
1	10.0	100.00	-12.883	17.020	14.367	16.453	-2.124	-0.396
2	11.0	121.00	8.8472	19.773	-18.521	-9.560	5.306	-20.137
3	12.0	144.00	0.662	0.000	2.113	-19.730	19.809	-2.138
4	11.5	132.00	-8.379	-19.430	19.874	-4.340	8.609	18.521
5	9.5	90.25	-1.743	0.503	-19.271	11.241	-14.951	-16.662
6	8.5	72.25	12.368	-18.989	-3.940	22.157	-22.151	-0.091
7	10.5	110.25	-21.639	-1.799	-0.946	2.824	-13.323	16.776

(b) The performance comparison of layout results of example 1

Computational algorithm	The least circle radiusincluded all graph units (mm)	Static non-equilibrium (g.mm)	Interference	Computational time(s)
Literature [1]	32.837	0.102000	0	1735
Literature [2]	32.662	0.029000	0	1002
Literature [3]	31.985	0.018200	0	1002
Our	31.924	0.000014	0	427

(c) The comparison of layout results of example 1 based on 40 times algorithm running

The least Circle radius (mm)	Times		The least Circle radius (mm)	Times	
	Literature [3]algorithm	Our algorithm		Literature [3]algorithm	Our algorithm
≤32.3	10	18	(32.9,33.1]	2	1
(32.3,32.5]	16	12	(33.1,33.3]	2	1
(32.5,32.7]	5	4	>33.3	3	0
(32.7,32.9]	2	4			

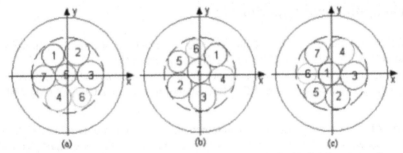

(a) Literature [2] layout result (b) Literature [3] layout result (c) Our layout result

Fig. 2. The geometry layout of example 1

Example 2. Forty graph units are contained in the layout problem. The radius of a graph plane is R=880 mm. The allowing value of static non-equilibrium J is $[\delta_J]$=20g*mm. The result is inTable2 and the geometric layout is shown in Figure3 (the particle size is 100).

Table 2. Comparison of experimental results of example 2

(a)Datum and layout results of example 2

number	Graph units		Literature [8] layout result		Our layout result	
	r(mm)	m(g)	x(mm)	y(mm)	x(mm)	y(mm)
1	106	11	192.971	0	-406.913	509.203
2	112	12	-69.924	0	-133.026	353.611
3	98	9	13.034	-478.285	-652.724	-119.745
4	105	11	-291.748	21.066	-208.031	-394.883
5	93	8	343.517	-351.055	-56.032	-262.519
6	103	10	-251.1434	674.025	355.418	294.143
7	82	6	95.268	-252.899	306.078	-43.401
8	93	8	-619.634	-421.032	-8.460	676.766
9	117	13	725.062	0	-193.583	574.468
10	81	6	127.487	175.174	137.983	-35.444
11	89	7	358.251	-104.181	-559.517	-387.886
12	92	8	694.612	-206.946	-446.045	-246.870
13	109	11	-151.494	-350.475	-437.198	176.132
14	104	10	-486.096	278.028	222.554	129.841
15	115	13	-406.944	-378.282	56.175	479.052
16	110	12	-531.396	27.583	-219.852	149.187
17	114	12	-281.428	-570.129	150.121	-230.622
18	89	7	535.186	-82.365	269.361	465.973
19	82	6	349.187	-668.540	-274.170	-219.527
20	120	14	494.958	-527.668	10.145	-465.729
21	108	11	-696.916	236.466	-557.408	356.793
22	86	7	-43.153	196.294	195.358	624.570
23	93	8	-143.066	-725.316	-54.318	-669.958
24	100	10	-433.688	-159.158	-40.402	-69.055
25	102	10	-741.858	0.000	-7.734	133.495
26	106	11	292.820	431.997	599.694	-278.410

Table 2. (*Continued*)

number	Graph units		Literature [8] layout result		Our layout result	
	r(mm)	*m*(g)	*x*(mm)	y(mm)	x(mm)	y(mm)
27	111	12	-540.511	495.023	-248.828	-607.028
28	107	11	154.296	-671.681	431.355	-503.252
29	109	11	-317.971	463.365	-649.609	117.956
30	91	8	41.295	-271.016	638.328	90.684
31	111	12	103.622	538.523	-442.274	-43.810
32	91	8	215.467	-213.844	672.381	-88.260
33	101	10	540.248	306.466	480.829	-105.474
34	91	8	58.125	341.687	-231.328	-51.749
35	108	11	-235.120	227.217	438.638	99.378
36	114	12	510.413	520.918	371.393	-290.542
37	118	13	-29.219	725.331	576.449	303.176
38	85	7	300.625	240.313	162.079	309.374
39	87	7	234.066	-494.031	-396.209	-454.664
40	98	9	411.043	119.080	226.556	-494.041

(b) The performance comparison of layout results of example 2

Computational algorithm	The least circle radius (mm)	Static non-equilibrium (g.mm)	Interference	Computational time(s)
Literature [1]	870.331	0.006000	0	1358
Literature [2]	874.830	11.395000	0	1656
Literature [3]	843.940	0.003895	0	2523
Our algorithm	769.819	0.000325	0	1724

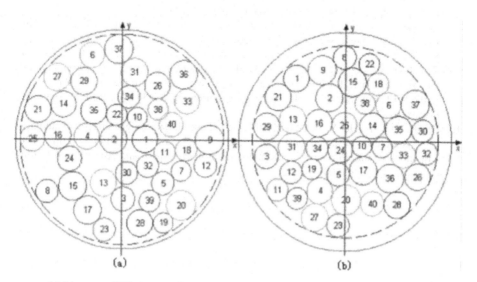

(a) Literature [3] layout result   (b) Our layout result

Fig. 3. The geometry layout of example 2

5 Conclusions

From table 1 table2, we can deduce that: PSO with four improved adaptive strategies harmonized the large-scale space global search abilities and the refined local search abilities much thoroughly, which has rapid convergence and can avoid premature, synchronously. The effectiveness of the algorithm is validated for the constrained layout of the NP-hard problems; the algorithm outperformed the known best ones in the in quality of solutions and the running time. In addition, the parameters of *wmax*, *zmax*, *vmax* and *R'* are chose by human experience, which has the certain blemish. How to choose the rather parameters are one of the future works.

References

1. Teng, H.F., Shoulin, S., Wenhai, G., et al.: Layout optimization for the dishes installed on rotating table. Science in China (Series A) 37(10), 1272–1280 (1994)
2. Fei, T., Hongfei, T.: A modified genetic algorithm and its application to layout optimization. Journal of Software 10(10), 1096–1102 (1999) (in Chinese)
3. Ning, L., Fei, L., Debao, S.: A study on the particle swarm optimization with mutation operator constrained layout optimization. Chinese Journal of Computers 27(7), 8897–9039 (2004) (in Chinese)
4. Kennedy, J., Eberhart, R.C.: Particle swarm optimization. In: Proc. of IEEE Int'l Conf. Neural Networks, pp. 1942–1948. IEEE Computer Press, Indianapolis (1995)
5. Eberhart, R.C., Kennedy, J.: A new optimizer using particles swarm theory. In: Sixth International Symposium on Micro Machine and Human Science, pp. 39–43. IEEE Service Center, Piscataway (1995)
6. Angeline, P.J.: Using selection to improve particle swarm optimization. In: Proc. IJCNN 1999, pp. 84–89. IEEE Computer Press, Indianapolis (1999)
7. Jianchao, Z., Zhihua, C.: A guaranteed global conver- gence particle swarm optimizer. Journal of computer research and development 4(8), 1334–1338 (2004) (in Chinese)
8. Shi, Y., Eberhart, R.C.: A modified particle swarm optimizer. In: Proc. of the IEEE Con. Evolutionary Computation, pp. 69–73. IEEE Computer Press, Piscataway (1998)
9. Shi, Y.H., Eberhart, R.C.: Empirical study of particle swarm optimization. In: Proceedings of the IEEE Congress on Evolutionary Computation, pp. 1945–1950. IEEE Press Center, Piscataway (1999)
10. Lei, K., Qiu, Y., He, Y.: A new adaptive well-chosen inertia weight strategy to automatically harmonize global and local search ability in particle swarm optimization. In: 1st International Symposium on Systems and Control in Aerospace and Astronautics, Harbin, China, pp. 342–346 (2006)

Multi-swarm Particle Swarm Optimizer with Cauchy Mutation for Dynamic Optimization Problems

Chengyu Hu[1,2], Xiangning Wu[2], Yongji Wang[1], and Fuqiang Xie[1]

[1] Department of Control Science and Engineering, Huazhong University of Science & Technology, Wuhan, China 430074
wangyjch@mail.hust.edu.cn, xiefuqiang@mail.hust.edu.cn
[2] School of Computer, China University of Geosciences, Wuhan, China 430074
huchengyu@cug.edu.cn, wxning@cug.edu.cn

Abstract. Many real-world problems are dynamic, requiring an optimization algorithm which is able to continuously track a changing optimum over time. This paper presents a new variant of Particle Swarm Optimization (PSO) specifically designed to work well in dynamic environments. The main idea is to divide the population of particles into a set of interacting swarms. These swarms interact locally by dynamic regrouping and dispersing. Cauchy mutation is applied to the global best particle when the swarm detects the environment of the change. The dynamic function (proposed by Morrison and De Jong) is used to test the performance of the proposed algorithm. The comparison of the numerical experimental results with those of other variant PSO illustrates that the proposed algorithm is an excellent alternative to track dynamically changing optima.

Keywords: multiple swarms, Cauchy mutation, dynamic optimization.

1 Introduction

Over these years, most research in evolutionary computation focuses on static optimization problems [1, 2]. However, many real-world problems are dynamic optimization problems (DOPs), where changes occur over time. This requires optimization algorithms to not only find the optimal solution in a short time but also track the optimal solution in a dynamic environment.

It has been argued [3] that evolutionary algorithms (EAs) may be a particularly suitable candidate for this type of problems, and over the past decade, a large number of EA variants for dynamic optimization problems have been proposed. Recently, the application of PSO to dynamic problems has also been explored [4-10].

Similar to EAs, PSO is a population-based technique, inspired from observing the social behaviors of flock of birds, a swarm of bees, or a school of fish and so on. Although that PSO has been proved as an efficient optimization algorithm for static functions, it is not adaptive to dynamic optimization. This is due to the following

Z. Cai et al. (Eds.): ISICA 2009, LNCS 5821, pp. 443–453, 2009.
© Springer-Verlag Berlin Heidelberg 2009

reasons [4]: outdated memory, diversity loss and particles can not detect the change. Of these three difficulties, the diversity loss is by far more serious [10].

Various adaptations to PSO have been suggested to tackle the difficulties mentioned above, such as recalculating, re-randomizing, maintaining the diversity over time and multiple swarms or populations scheme and so on. In all of the approaches, multiple swarms or populations scheme has been proved to be beneficial. Blackwell and Branke [10] first introduced a version of a multi-swarm PSO, which aim to maintain a multitude of swarms on different peaks. Parrott and Li [9, 12] developed a speciation PSO, which could track multiple optima simultaneously with multiple swarms.

This paper introduces a new dynamic multi-swarm method. Dynamic multiple swarms mean the neighborhood topology of the sub-swarms are changing by regrouping and dispersing. Cauchy mutation is also applied to generate the new positions of the particles, which can balance the loss of diversity and the preservation of information from previous search. Experimental results demonstrate that our proposed algorithm performs well in dynamic optimization problems.

The rest of the paper is structured as follows: Section II provides background information on dynamic environments and PSO. Section III introduces dynamic multiple swarm optimizer with Cauchy mutation. Section IV discusses the experimental setup, problems used in experiments, performance measurements specific to dynamic environments, and analyses experimental results. Section V concludes the paper, summarizing the observations. Topics for further research are also mentioned in this section.

2 Background

In this section, we will first provide a more formal introduction to dynamic optimization and measures to deal with DOPs, then PSO are discussed.

2.1 Dynamic Optimization

In contrast to static optimization, the goal in dynamic optimization is not only to reach the optimum but also to track its trajectory as closely as possible in the search space over time. A dynamic optimization problem can be described as:

$$f(\vec{x},t) \rightarrow \min, \vec{x} \in R^N, t \in T \tag{1}$$

The objective function f depends on both the solution vector $\vec{x}$ and time t.

Many literature assume that the time of a change in the environment is known to the algorithm, or can be detected, e.g., by a reevaluation of the objective function at one or several of the attractors [7]. In this paper, our main focus is the effective mechanism to respond to the change of environment. These approaches can be grouped into one of the following categories:

1) Recalculate the fitness value of each particle. The problem of outdated memory is usually solved by either simply setting each particle's memory position to its current position , or by reevaluating every memory position [5]. These approaches are

sensitive to the position of the new optimum; too close to the old one will be beneficial to find the optimum quickly.

2) Re-randomize a portion of the swarm, ranging from 10% to 100% of the particle
[7]. Because changes in many real world problems are usually smooth so that it is
often beneficial for PSO to make use of the useful information from previous search.
However, It is difficult to determine a useful amount of diversity: Too much will
resemble restart, while too little doesn't solve the problem of convergence.

3) Use memory to recall useful information from past generation [4]. This idea
seems especially useful when the optimum repeatedly returns to previous locations.

4) Maintain diversity throughout the run [4]. The diversity of the swarm is always
maintained before or after any change. In this way, the algorithm can easily adapt to
the changes since individuals are widely spread in the search space. The probability to
find the solutions to the new problem becomes higher.

2.2 Particle Swarm Optimization Algorithm

As has already been explained in the introduction, particles move through the search
space driven by attraction of their personal best found solution so far, and the best
found solution in the neighborhood.

In a PSO algorithm, each particle is a candidate solution equivalent to a point in a
D-dimensional space, so the ith particle can be represented as $\vec{x}_i$, each particle "flies"
through the search space, depending on two important factors: $\vec{p}_i$, the best position the
current particle has found so far; and $\vec{p}_g$, the global best position identified from the
entire population (or within a neighborhood).

In the beginning, particle positions and velocities are generated randomly. The algorithm then proceeds iteratively, updating all velocities and then all particles update
their positions and velocities using the following equations (2), (3).

$$\vec{V}_i = \chi * (\vec{V}_i + c_1 * r1 * (\vec{p_g} - \vec{x_i}) + c_2 * r2 * (\vec{p_i} - \vec{x_i})) \tag{2}$$

$$\overrightarrow{x_{i+1}} = \overrightarrow{x_i} + \vec{v}_i \tag{3}$$

Where $c1, c2$ represent the cognitive ans social parameters, respectively. $r1$ and $r2$
are random numbers uniformly distributed in [0, 1].

$$\chi = \frac{2}{c - 2 + \sqrt{c^2 - 4c}} \tag{4}$$

Here, $c = c1 + c2 > 4$ and is commonly set to 4.1, $c1 = c2 = 2.05$, and the constant
multiplier χ is approximately 0.7298.

3 Dynamic Multiple Swarm Optimizer with Cauchy Mutation

Although the dynamic multi-swarm particle swarm optimizer performs quite well for
multimodel problems [11], it is not applicable to DOPs. Some other measures must be
made up in the dynamic environment. Our proposed algorithm---dynamic multiple

swarms optimization with Cauchy mutation (DMS-PSO-CM) has the following characters to deal with dynamic problems.

1) Small Sized Swarms

As the [11] showed that a comparatively smaller population size enhances to optimize for most multi-modal problems, a population with three to five particles can achieve satisfactory results. For dynamic multi-swarm optimizer which with small neighborhoods performs better on complex problems. Another advantage is that small size swarm reduces the number of fitness evaluations, thus make the whole swarm could cope with the changing environment rapidly and flexibly. Hence, for the DMS-PSO-CM, small neighborhoods are used again. We divide the whole population into small sized swarms; each swarm makes a local search in the search space.

2) Disperse while sub-swarms are too close

Since the small sized swarms are searching using their own best historical information, they are easy to converge to local optimum, sometimes on different peaks, or on the same peak. In this case, we use dispersing mechanism to prevent the sub-swarms from converging to one local optimum. So every L generations, we will calculate the distances from the location of the global best particle to the other particles'. Here L is called dispersing period. According to the distances, we divide the all the sub-swarms into two categories, 70% of the particles nearby the global best particle and 30% of particles far away from the global best particle. Then the 70% of sub-swarms will update their positions in the opposite direction as the following equation as the following equation (5), thus avoid "having all the eggs in one basket".

$$\overrightarrow{x_{i+1}} = \overrightarrow{x_i} - \overrightarrow{v_i} \tag{5}$$

3) Randomly Regrouping

As all the sub-swarms evolve alone, if we keep the neighborhood structures unchanged, then there will be no information exchanged among the swarms, and it will be a co-evolutionary PSO with these swarms searching in parallel. In order to avoid this situation, a randomized regrouping schedule is introduced. Every R generations, the population is regrouped randomly and starts searching using a new configuration of small swarms. Here R is called regrouping period. In this way, the good information obtained by each swarm is exchanged among the swarms. Simultaneously the diversity of the population is increased. The new neighborhood structure has more freedom when compared with the classical neighborhood structure.

4) Cauchy mutation after detect the change of environment

Hu and Eberhart [7] list a number of these methods which involve randomization of the entire, or part of, the swarm. He point out that randomization implies loss of information gathered so far, it hard to decide the amount of swarm to re-randomize.

Gaussian mutation if often used to jump out of the local optimum, at the same time, it could preserve the information from the previous search. Xin Yao [16] suggested Cauchy mutation can perform better than Gaussian mutation. He also made a theoretical analysis for the first time on the relationship between the distance to the global optimum and the search step size, and the relationship between the search step size and the probability of finding a near optimum.

So in the paper, we decide to use Cauchy mutation to jump out the previous optimum if the change of environment happened, and at the same time, to keep the useful information. The Cauchy mutation is shown in the formula (6):

$$mut(\vec{p}_g) = \vec{p}_g + \lambda * C(0,1) \tag{6}$$

$\vec{p}_g$ is the global best particle's position found so far before the change of the environment, $C(0,1)$ is the Standard Cauchy distribution. It's good exactly from experience obtained in some experiments that $\lambda = 0.1*(Xmax-Xmin)$. Here Xmax and Xmin is the boundary of the search space.

When the swarm detected the change, we could use Cauchy mutation to generate the particles' positions, where a portion of the particles are around the best position searched before, others may be further to search in a wide fitness landscapes. As is known that most real-world problems, the changes are most rather smooth and, thus, we can transfer the knowledge from past by Cauchy mutation with the mean $\vec{p}_g$ and step size λ .

The pseudo code of DMS-PSO-CM is as following:

```
m: Each swarm's population size
n: Swarms' number
L: Dispersing period;
R: Regrouping period
Max_gen: Max generations, stop criterion

1: Initialize m*n particles (position and velocity)
2: Divide the population into n swarms randomly, with m
      particles in each swarm.
3:  For i=1: Max_gen
4:      Update each swarm using local version PSO
5:      If (the change of environment= =1)
6:          Cauchy mutation;
7:      End

8:      if mod (i, L) = =0
9:          Calculate the distances between global best
              particle and other particles;
10:             Disperse 70% of the particles nearby the
              gbest;
11:     End

12:     If mod (i, R) = =0,
              Regroup the swarms randomly;
13:     End
14:  End
```

4 Experimental Study

To investigate the new proposed algorithm's ability to track the location of moving optimum, performances of three PSO models are compared over a range of different dynamic environments. Apart from the new proposed DMS-PSO-CM, a standard PSO model (SPSO) and a randomized PSO variant (PSO-R50) are included, which is with 50% of the particles reinitialized when a change occurs.

4.1 Dynamic Test Function

The fitness landscape generated by DF1 [14] is made of a series of cones. For a 2-dimensional problem, the static evaluation function in DF1 is defined as (7):

$$f(X,Y) = \max_{i=1,N}\{H_i - R_i\sqrt{(X-X_i)^2 + (Y-Y_i)^2}\} \tag{7}$$

Where N denotes the number of cones in the environment, each cone is independently specified by its location (X_i,Y_i), where $X_i,Y_i \in [-1,1]$. Its height is H_i and slope is R_i. these cones are blended using the max function.

A range of dynamic changes on the landscape can be produced by using a one-dimensional, nonlinear logistics function (8) that has simple bifurcation transitions to progressively more complex behaviors:

$$S_i = A * S_{i-1} * (1 - S_{i-1}) \tag{8}$$

With $A = 1.2$, DF1 generates a small constant $S_i = 0.1667$. If $A = 3.3$ is chosen, a pair of large different $S_i \in \{0.8236, 0.4794\}$ is generated. $A = 3.99$ produces a sequence of chaotic S values. Fig.1. shows the changing landscapes.

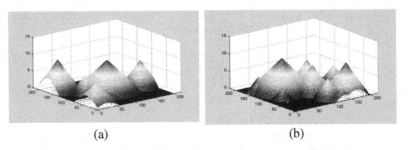

(a)　　　　　　　　　(b)

Fig. 1. The changing fitness landscapes generated by DF1, before and after the movement of location of the peaks. (a) Before (b) After.

4.2 Experimental Setting

1) DF1 settings
For the purpose of comparing the performance of DMS-PSO-CM with others SPSO and PSO-R50, the parameters of DF1 are that : The number of peaks N=15, the height of cones $Hi\in[1,10]$, the slope of cones $Ri\in [8,20]$, the dimension of the problem is 2.

The peaks make a step change at different frequencies $\Delta g \in \{10,50,100\}$, that is, applying a step move to the peaks at every 10, 50 and 100 generations respectively.

2) PSO setting

For all the three algorithms, we use an initial swarm population of 30, which are randomly generated for each variable in the range [-1, 1], we set both $c1$ and $c2$ to 2.05, and $\chi=0.7298$. For our new proposed algorithm, we divide the swarm population into 10 sub-swarms; each swarm's population size is 3. When $\Delta g \in \{50,100\}$, we set dispersing period $R=10$, as $\Delta g = 10$, we set regrouping period $R=5$. The dispersing period L is 5 for different Δg.

4.3 Performance Measurement and Results

The DF1 is an artificial maximization problem, so the exact position of the global optimum in the search space is already known. We use the track error to measure the performance, which means the average distance in the search space between the optimum and the best known solution before the change of the environments. The error is shown in equation (9).

$$error_{avg} = \frac{\sum_{l=1}^{run\_num} (\sum_{j=1}^{T} Dist / T)}{run\_num} \tag{9}$$

Where run_num is times that every algorithm runs, and T is times of the change of the environment, $Dist$ is the distance from the highest peak's location to the best particle's position before the change of the environment, the smaller this $error_{avg}$ is, the fitter the particle is considered to be, and the better the PSO variant's ability in tracking the highest peak. All the results for 40 runs are list in Table 1.

Table 1. Comparison results on DF1 with different Δg and A for three PSO models

Δg	A	SPSO	PSO-R50	DMS-PSO-CM
10	1.2	**0.1489**	0.6081	0.4546
	3.3	**0.4310**	0.6146	0.4472
	3. 99	**0.416**	0.5777	0.4284
50	1.2	0.1658	0.2107	**0.0497**
	3.3	0.3163	0.2544	**0.0874**
	3. 99	0.341	0.4149	**0.128**
100	1.2	0.1579	0.1606	**0.0363**
	3.3	0.4097	0.2159	**0.0755**
	3. 99	0.412	0.3489	**0.1078**

Morrison [15] showed that a representative performance measurement in a dynamic environment should reflect algorithm performance "across the entire range of landscape dynamics". So we use the mean tracking error (MTE) to measures the performance. MTE means the average distance in the search space between the optimum and the best known solution at the end of each generation, as shown figure2-4 with the settings: $A \in \{1.2, 3.3, 3.99\}$ and $\Delta g \in \{10, 50, 100\}$.

In figure2-4, the horizontal axis is the best particle's distance to the goal every generation; the vertical axis is the generations. From the figures, we could compare the tracking performance of the three algorithms at each generation.

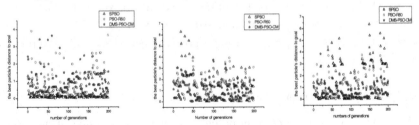

Fig. 2. g=10, A=1.2, 3.3 and 3.99. The left figure A=1.2, means small const step size changed; the middle figure A=3.3, means two large steps size changed; the right figure A=3.99, means chaotically changing step size.

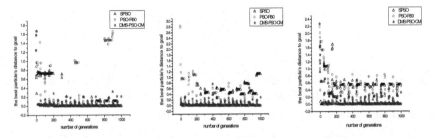

Fig. 3. g=50, A=1.2, 3.3 and 3.99. The left figure A=1.2, means small const step size changed; the middle figure A=3.3, means two large steps size changed; the right figure A=3.99, means chaotically changing step size.

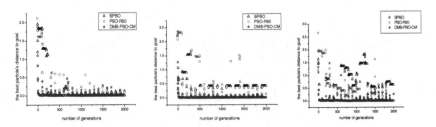

Fig. 4. g=100, A=1.2, 3.3 and 3.99. The left figure A=1.2, means small const step size changed; the middle figure A=3.3, means two large steps size changed; the right figure A=3.99, means chaotically changing step size.

Black hollow triangle, red circle, blue star in the above figures show the distance from the best particle's position to the highest peak for three PSO variants at each generation , the higher of the triangle, circle and star, the further from the goal.

As the Fig.2 shows, as the $\Delta g = 10$, all of the three algorithms behave similar under this rapidly changing circumstance, the SPSO perform better because it does not converge during so less generations, at the same time, it could make a quick response to the change of the environment.

Fig.3 shows, as the $\Delta g = 50$, SPSO is easily trapped into the optimum, thus lead to the loss of diversity, and then perform badly when next optimization occur. From the left figure to right figure, we could see that, the change of the environment becomes more complex with the A increases, thus all of the algorithms tend to deviate the trajectory of the highest peak. In each figure, we can see that DMS-PSO-CM behaved well.

When $\Delta g = 100$, means that all the algorithms have a longer time to adapt and track the optimum. The Fig.4 shows DMS-PSO-CM still behaves excellently as has expected.

4.4 Analysis of Empirical Data

In general, we can conclude from Table 1 and Fig2-4 that the performance of the three PSO variant deteriorate as Δg becomes smaller and A becomes larger. This also shows the difficulty of optimization problems has increased.

For the SPSO, it has not the mechanism to cope with the changed environment, so it converge quickly to a local optimum when the frequency of update Δg is larger, it could not jump out of the local optimum because of the loss of the diversity. On the contrary, when Δg is 10, it perform better.

For the PSO-R50, it is not sensitive to step size factor A, for different $A \in \{1.2, 3.3, 3.99\}$, the performances vary little as Δg is fixed. We found that the update frequency Δg decides the ability of these re-randomized methods although the results have an insignificant difference. Maybe the re-randomizing leads to the increase of the swarm diversity drastically. But as soon as possible, the swarm loses the diversity again.

For our proposed DMS-PSO-CM, it performs well as has expected especially with $\Delta g \in \{50, 100\}$. The first reason that DMS-PSO-CM performs well is Cauchy mutation involved. Although re-randomize all of the particles' positions, it's not like the PSO-R50 model. Re-randomization in PSO-R50 is uniform mutation actually; the swarm will lost the previous information and has to restart a new search. But for the Cauchy mutation we proposed, most of the new generated particle positions are around the previous best particle. Controlling the step size λ can guarantee the new generated swarm nearby the highest peak. The second reason is that the multiple swarms could dynamically change the neighbor topology by regrouping. The information among the sub-swarms can communicate quickly, so the algorithm could balance exploration and exploitation. The last reason is that the dispersing mechanism can prevent all sub-swarms from converging to the same peak. So our proposed algorithm can perform well in complex dynamic environment.

For an in-depth study of all of the three algorithms' capability in maintaining diversity, we use the diversity measurement to analyze the three algorithms. We just see the cases $\Delta g = 50, A = 3.3$ and $\Delta g = 100, A = 3.99$ for simple, other cases are similar. The diversity measure is defined in equation (10):

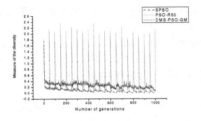
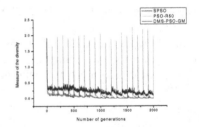

Fig. 5. g=50, A=3.3, the diversity measure curve

Fig. 6. g=100, A=3.99, the diversity measurecurve

$$Diversity(S) = \frac{1}{|S|.|L|} \sum_{i=1}^{|s|} \sqrt{\sum_{j=1}^{N} (p_{ij} - \overline{p_j})} \qquad (10)$$

Where |S| is the whole swarm size, |L| the max radius of the search space, N is the dimension of the problem, p_{ij} is the ith particle and jth dimension, $\overline{p_j}$ is the average value of the jth dimension.

Fig.5 and Fig.6 display the measure of the diversity each generation. For SPSO (red line), it lost the diversity at the first change of the environment, so the whole swarm is lack of diversity through the run because recalculating the fitness does not enhance the diversity of the swarm. But for the PSO-R50 (green line), severely change of the diversity leads to the loss of the information from past.

DMS-PSO-CM can preserve the diversity through the run, so it's not surprised that it performs better than other algorithms.

5   Conclusion and Future Work

The aim of this paper was to examine dynamic multiple swarm with Cauchy mutation for dynamic optimization. Experiments with the SPSO, PSO-R50 and proposed algorithm were run on DF1 with three different update frequencies $\Delta g \in \{10, 50, 100\}$ and step size factor $A \in \{1.2, 3.3, 3.99\}$. Experimental results have shown that Cauchy mutation, dynamic regrouping and dispersing mechanism are beneficial to track the moving peak.

Further research would involve an in-depth study of high dimension dynamic problems. For the large scale problems in static environment, it is difficult to be optimized because of "the curse of dimension", so how to quickly track the optimum for high dimension problem will be a challenge.

Acknowledgements

This work is supported in part by National Natural Science Foundation of China under Grant No. 60674105, No. 60873107.

References

1. Parsopoulos, K., Vrahatis, M.: Recent approaches to global optimization problems through particle swarm optimization. Natural Comput. 1(2–3), 235–306 (2002)
2. Clerc, M., Kennedy, J.: The particle swarm—explosion, stability, and convergence in a multidimensional complex space. IEEE Transaction on Evolutionary Computation 6(1), 58–73 (2002)
3. Blackwell, T., Branke, J.: Multi-swarm optimization in dynamic environments. In: Raidl, G.R., Cagnoni, S., Branke, J., Corne, D.W., Drechsler, R., Jin, Y., Johnson, C.G., Machado, P., Marchiori, E., Rothlauf, F., Smith, G.D., Squillero, G. (eds.) EvoWorkshops 2004. LNCS, vol. 3005, pp. 489–500. Springer, Heidelberg (2004)
4. Jin, Y., Branke, J.: Evolutionary optimization in uncertain environments-a survey. IEEE Transactions on Evolutionary Computation 9(3), 303–317 (2005)
5. Carlisle, A., Dozier, G.: Adapting particle swarm optimization to dynamic environments. In: Proceedings of International Conference on Artificial Intelligence (ICAI 2000), Las Vegas, Nevada, USA, pp. 429–434 (2000)
6. Eberhart, R.C., Shi, Y.: Tracking and optimizing dynamic systems with particle swarms. In: Proceedings of the IEEE congress on Evolutionary Computation (CEC 2001), Seoul, Korea, pp. 94–97 (2001)
7. Hu, X., Eberhart, R.: Adaptive particle swarm optimization: Detection and response to dynamic systems. In: Proc. Congr. Evol. Comput., pp. 1666–1670 (2002)
8. Blackwell, T.M., Bentley, P.: Don't push me! Collision-avoiding swarms. In: Proc. Congr. Evol. Comput., pp. 1691–1696 (2002)
9. Parrott, D., Li, X.: A particle swarm model for tracking multiple peaks in a dynamic environment using speciation. In: Proc. Congr. Evol. Comput., pp. 98–103 (2004)
10. Blackwell, T., Branke, J.: Multiswarms, Exclusion, and Anti-Convergence in Dynamic Environments. IEEE Transactions on Evolutionary Computation 10(4), 459–472 (2006)
11. Liang, J.J., Suganthan, P.N.: Dynamic Multi-Swarm Particle Swarm Optimizer. In: Proc. of IEEE Int. Swarm Intelligence Symposium, pp. 124–129 (2005)
12. Parrott, D., Li, X.: Adaptively choosing neighborhood bests using species in a particle swarm optimizer for multimodal function optimization. In: Deb, K., et al. (eds.) GECCO 2004. LNCS, vol. 3102, pp. 105–116. Springer, Heidelberg (2004)
13. Riget, J., Vestertrom, J.S.: A Diversity-Guided Particle Swarm Optimizer–the ARPSO, Technical Report No 2002-02, Dept. of Computer Science. University of Aarhus, EVALife (2002)
14. Morrison, R., De Jong, K.: A test problem generator for nonstationary environments. In: Proceedings of the 1999 Congress on Evolutionary Computation, 1999. CEC 1999, vol. 3, pp. 2047–2053 (1999)
15. Morrison, R.W.: Performance Measurement in Dynamic Environments. In: Barry, A.M. (ed.) Proc. GECCO 2003: Workshops, Genetic and Evolutionary ComputationConference, pp. 99–102. AAAI Press, Menlo Park (2003)
16. yao, X., Xu, Y.: Recent advances in evolutionary computation. J. computer. Sci.& technol. 21(11-18) (2006)

Optimization of the Damping of the Rectangular 3-D Braided Composite Based on PSO Algorithm

Ke Zhang

School of Mechanical and Automation Engineering,
Shanghai Institute of Technology
120 Caobao Road, 200235 Shanghai, China
zkwy2004@126.com

Abstract. Three-dimensional (3-D) braided composite, a new type composite, has the better performance designable characteristic. This paper describes the damping analysis of the hollow-rectangular-section three-dimensional braided composite made by 2-step method with a consideration of the wide application of hollow-rectangular-section three-dimensional braided composite in engineering. Then, it proposes the mathematical models for optimization of the damping of the three-dimensional braided composite. The objective functions are based on the specific damping capacity of the composite, and the design variables are the braiding parameters and sectional geometrical size of the composite. The results of numeral examples show that the better damping characteristic could be obtained by using optimal design with particle swarm optimization (PSO) algorithm, contenting the determinate restriction. The method proposed here is useful for the design and engineering application of the kind of member.

Keywords: Composite, optimization, particle swarm optimization.

1 Introduction

With the development of fibre architecture and textile manufacturing technology, textile composites are being widely used in advanced structures in aviation, aerospace, automobile and marine industries [1]. Textile composite technology by preforming is an application of textile processes to produce structured fabrics, known as performs. The preform is then impregnated with a selected matrix material and consolidated into the permanent shape. Three-dimensional (3-D) braiding method which was invented in 1980s offers a new opportunity in the development of advanced composite technology. The integrated fibre network provides stiffness and strength in the thickness direction, thus reducing the potential of interlaminated failure, which often occurs in conventional laminated composites. Other distinct benefits of 3-D textile composites include the potential of automated processing from preform fabrication to matrix infiltration and their near-net-shape forming capability, resulting in reduced machining, fastening, and scrap rate [2]. The direct formation of the structural shapes eliminates the need for cutting fibres to form joints, splices, or overlaps with the

Z. Cai et al. (Eds.): ISICA 2009, LNCS 5821, pp. 454–465, 2009.

associated local strength loss, and simplifies the laborious hand lay-up composite manufacturing process.

In comparing with two dimensional composite laminates, a key property of the new innovative 3-D braided composite is its ability to reinforced composites in the thickness direction. Braiding with continuous fibres or yarns can place 3-D reinforcements in monocoque structural composites, it includes multi-directional fibre bundle which interconnect layers. Since the braiding procedure dictates the yarn structure in the preform and the yarn structure dictates the properties of the composite, designing the braiding procedure to yield the desired structural shape that is endowed with the desired properties is an important element in textile composite technology [3]. Thus, it is feasible to design the textile structural composites with considerable flexibility in performance based upon a wide variety of preform geometries and structure parameter.

Particle Swarm Optimization (PSO) is an evolutionary computation technique developed by Dr. Eberhart and Dr. Kennedy in 1995 [4][5], inspired by social behavior of bird flocking or fish schooling. Compared to GA, the advantages of PSO are that it is easy to implement and there are few parameters to adjust. In recent years, there have been a lot of reported works focused on the PSO which has been applied widely in the function optimization, artificial neural network training, pattern recognition, fuzzy control and some other fields [6][7] in where GA can be applied.

In this paper, considering wide application of hollow-rectangular-section 3-D braided composite in engineering, the stiffness and damping analysis of the hollow-rectangular-section 3-D braided composite made by 2-step method were performed. Then, optimization designs of the damping for the 3-D braided composite were proposed by using a hybrid algorithm based on PSO algorithm. The calculation results of the example are obtained herein.

2 3-D Braided Composite Description

The 3-D braided fibre construction is produced by a braiding technique which interlaces and orients the yarns by an orthogonal shedding motion, followed by a compacting motion in the braided direction. The basic fibre structure of 2-step 3-D braided composite is five-direction texture. An idealized unit cell structure is constructed based upon the fibre bundles oriented in four body diagonal directions in a rectangular parallelepiped and one axial direction along x-axis which is shown schematically in Fig.1 [8][9]. The yarn orientation angles (α, β) are so-called braided angle. From the geometry of a unit cell associated with particular fibre architecture, different systems of yarn can identified whose fibre orientations are defined by their respective interior angle α and cross sectional angle β, as previously show in Fig.1. According to requirement of braid technology, the range of α and β are commonly between 20°and 60°. In Fig.1, geometric parameters of cross section of composite are b_1, b_2, h_1, and h_2 respectively.

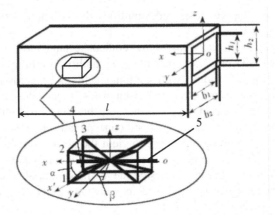

Fig. 1. The unit cell structure of a 3-D braided composite

3   The Stiffness Properties of 3-D Braided Composite

A model for grain system interruption has been closen wherein the stiffness for each system of yarns are superimposed proportionately according to contributing volume of five yarn system to determine the stiffness of the composite. Let volume percent of fibre of the composite be V_f, where volume percent of axial yarn system and braiding yarn system are V_{fa} and V_{fb}. So, volume fraction of axial yarn system is equal to V_{fa}/V_f, and volume fraction of each system of braiding yarn is equal to $V_{fb}/(4V_f)$. Assuming each system of yarn can be represented by a comparable unidirectional lamina with an elastic matrix defined as C and a coordinate transformation matrix as T, the elastic stiffness matrix Q of this yarn system in the longitudinal direction of the composite can be expressed as $Q = TCT^T$.

Here, we ignore approximately the effect of stress components σ_y, σ_z and τ_{yz}, and only consider the effect of σ_x, τ_{zx} and τ_{xy}.

According to the definition of internal force, we can find axial force, bending, torque and cross shear for 3-D braided composite N_x, M_x, M_{xy}, Q_x. Then, the constitutive relation of axial yarn system can be gotten [10]

$$[N] = [K]_5[\varepsilon], \tag{1}$$

where $\qquad [N] = [N_x M_x M_{xy} Q_x]^T \qquad , \qquad [\varepsilon] = \left[\varepsilon_x^0 k_x k_{xy} \gamma_{xz}^0\right]^T \qquad ,$

$[K]_5 = diag[(b_2 h_2 - b_1 h_1)C_{11}, \ (b_2 h_2{}^3 - b_1 h_1{}^3)C_{11}/12, \ 0, \ (b_2 h_2 - b_1 h_1)C_{66}]$.

From stress-displacement relationship,

$$\begin{cases} \sigma_x = (Q_{11} - Q_{14}Q_{41}/Q_{44})(\varepsilon_x^0 + zk_x) + (Q_{15} - Q_{14}Q_{45}/Q_{44})\gamma_{xz}^0 \\ \quad + (Q_{16} - Q_{14}Q_{46}/Q_{44})zk_{xy} \\ \tau_{xy} = (Q_{61} - Q_{64}Q_{41}/Q_{44})(\varepsilon_x^0 + zk_x) + (Q_{65} - Q_{64}Q_{45}/Q_{44})\gamma_{xz}^0 \\ \quad + (Q_{66} - Q_{64}Q_{46}/Q_{44})zk_{xy} \\ \tau_{zx} = (Q_{51} - Q_{54}Q_{41}/Q_{44})(\varepsilon_x^0 + zk_x) + (Q_{55} - Q_{54}Q_{45}/Q_{44})\gamma_{xz}^0 \\ \quad + (Q_{56} - Q_{54}Q_{46}/Q_{44})zk_{xy} \end{cases}, \qquad (2)$$

the constitutive relations of braiding yarn for 3-D braided composite are gotten as follows [11]

$$[N]_i = [K]_i[\varepsilon]_i \qquad (i = 1,2,3,4). \qquad (3)$$

Where $[N]_i = \begin{bmatrix} N_x & M_x & M_{xy} & Q_x \end{bmatrix}_i^T$, $[\varepsilon]_i = \begin{bmatrix} \varepsilon_x^0 & k_x & k_{xy} & \gamma_{xz}^0 \end{bmatrix}_i^T$,

$$[K]_i = \begin{bmatrix} K_{11} & 0 & 0 & K_{14} \\ 0 & K_{22} & K_{23} & 0 \\ 0 & K_{32} & K_{33} & 0 \\ K_{41} & 0 & 0 & K_{44} \end{bmatrix},$$

where K_{11}, K_{22}, K_{33} and K_{44} are tensile, flexural, torsional and shear stiffness coefficient respectively, the others are the coupling stiffness coefficient.

By stiffness matrix of each system, according to composition principle of composite mechanics, we can obtain general stiffness matrix of 3-D composite:

$$[K] = \sum_{i=1}^{5} \lambda_i[K]_i, \qquad (4)$$

where $\lambda_i = V_{f_i}/V_f$.

4   The Damping Properties of 3-D Braided Composite

4.1   Damping Model of Element

By definition, specific damping capacity can be expressed as

$$\Psi = \Delta U/U_m, \qquad (5)$$

where ΔU is dissipation energy in anyone stress cycle, U_m is maximum strain energy in the cycle.

Adams and Bacon had presented cell damping model of laminated composite in reference [12], they think that per unit area dissipation energy of each layer can be broken down into three component relate to direct strain, thus

$$\Delta U = \Delta U_x + \Delta U_y + \Delta U_{xy}. \tag{6}$$

Considering the influence of transverse shear deformation, reference [13] has modified equation (6). In equation (7), they added to two terms dissipation energy resulted by transverse shearing strain, namely

$$\Delta U = \Delta U_x + \Delta U_y + \Delta U_{xy} + \Delta U_{yz} + \Delta U_{xz}. \tag{7}$$

As before, 2-step 3-D braided composite can be regard as superimpose of five unidirectional fibre system, and each yarn system is not in same plane. Thus, unit energy dissipation of each system should break down into six components,

$$\Delta U = \Delta U_{x'} + \Delta U_{y'} + \Delta U_{z'} + \Delta U_{x'y'} + \Delta U_{y'z'} + \Delta U_{x'z'}. \tag{8}$$

Where $x'y'z'$ is fibre coordinate system of each system.

4.2 Damping Capacity Calculation of 3-D Braided Composite

Hereinafter, suppose composite only have the action of bending moment M_x. We have

$$\varepsilon_x = M_x z / k_{22}$$
$$\varepsilon_y = \varepsilon_z = \gamma_{xz} = \gamma_{xy} = 0 \tag{9}$$
$$\gamma_{yz} = Q_{41} M_x Z / (Q_{44} k_{22}).$$

(1) Dissipation energy of axial yarn system
By constitutive relation of unidirectional fibre composite and equation (9), dissipation energy of axial yarn system is as follows :

$$\Delta U_5 = 2 \int_0^{l/2} \left[2 \left(\int_0^{h_1/2} \frac{(b_2 - b_1)}{2} \Psi_L \sigma_x \varepsilon_x dz + \int_{h_1/2}^{h_2/2} \frac{b_2}{2} \Psi_L \sigma_x \varepsilon_x dz \right) \right] dx$$
$$= [(b_2 h_2{}^3 - b_1 h_1{}^3) c_{11}^5 \Psi_L / (12 k_{22}^2)] \int_0^{l/2} M_x^2 dx \tag{10}$$

where c_{11}^5 is elastic constant of axial yarn system, Ψ_L is specific damping capacity of unidirectional fibre composite.

(2) Dissipation energy of braiding yarn system
By conversion relation between strain $[\varepsilon_{x'}]$ of each braiding yarn system in fibre coordinate system $x'y'z'$ and strain $[\varepsilon_x]$ in composite coordinate system xyz, and equation (10), we can obtain

$$\begin{cases} \varepsilon_{x'} = (l_1^2 - Q_{41}m_1n_1 / Q_{44})M_x z / k_{22} \\ \varepsilon_{y'} = (l_2^2 - Q_{41}m_2n_2 / Q_{44})M_x z / k_{22} \\ \varepsilon_{z'} = (l_3^2 - Q_{41}m_3n_3 / Q_{44})M_x z / k_{22} \\ \gamma_{x'y'} = [2l_1l_2Q_{44} - Q_{41}(m_1n_2 + m_2n_1)]M_x z / (Q_{44}k_{22}) \\ \gamma_{y'z'} = [2l_2l_3Q_{44} - Q_{41}(m_2n_3 + m_3n_2)]M_x z / (Q_{44}k_{22}) \\ \gamma_{x'z'} = [2l_1l_3Q_{44} - Q_{41}(m_1n_3 + m_3n_1)]M_x z / (Q_{44}k_{22}) \end{cases} \tag{11}$$

Thus, each component in equation (8) can be expressed as follows

$$\begin{cases} \Delta U_{x'} = 2\int_0^{l/2}\left[2(\int_0^{h_1/2}\frac{b_2-b_1}{2}\Psi_L\sigma_{x'}\varepsilon_{x'}dz + \int_{h/2}^{h_2/2}\frac{b_2}{2}\Psi_L\sigma_{x'}\varepsilon_{x'}dz)\right]dx \\ \Delta U_{y'} = 2\int_0^{l/2}\left[2(\int_0^{h_1/2}\frac{b_2-b_1}{2}\Psi_T\sigma_{y'}\varepsilon_{y'}dz + \int_{h_1/2}^{h_2/2}\frac{b_2}{2}\Psi_T\sigma_{y'}\varepsilon_{y'}dz)\right]dx \\ \Delta U_{z'} = 2\int_0^{l/2}\left[2(\int_0^{h_1/2}\frac{b_2-b_1}{2}\Psi_T\sigma_{z'}\varepsilon_{z'}dz + \int_{h_1/2}^{h_2/2}\frac{b_2}{2}\Psi_T\sigma_{z'}\varepsilon_{z'}dz)\right]dx \\ \Delta U_{x'y'} = 2\int_0^{l/2}\left[2(\int_0^{h_1/2}\frac{b_2-b_1}{2}\Psi_{LT}\tau_{x'y'}\gamma_{x'y'}dz + \int_{h_1/2}^{h_2/2}\frac{b_2}{2}\Psi_{LT}\tau_{x'y'}\gamma_{x'y'}dz)\right]dx \\ \Delta U_{y'z'} = 2\int_0^{l/2}\left[2(\int_0^{h_1/2}\frac{b_2-b_1}{2}\Psi_{TT}\tau_{y'z'}\gamma_{y'z'}dz + \int_{h_1/2}^{h_2/2}\frac{b_2}{2}\Psi_{TT}\tau_{y'z'}\gamma_{y'z'}dz)\right]dx \\ \Delta U_{x'z'} = 2\int_0^{l/2}\left[2(\int_0^{h_1/2}\frac{b_2-b_1}{2}\Psi_{LT}\tau_{x'z'}\gamma_{x'z'}dz + \int_{h_1/2}^{h_2/2}\frac{b_2}{2}\Psi_{LT}\tau_{x'z'}\gamma_{x'z'}dz)\right]dx \end{cases} \tag{12}$$

where $\Psi_L, \Psi_T, \Psi_{LT}$ and Ψ_{TT} are specific damping capacity of unidirectional fibre composite of transverse isotropy, and they can be confirmed by experiment or be chosen from interrelated data. Substituting equation (11) into equation (12) and carrying out integral, we have

$$\Delta U_{x'} = \Delta W_{x'}\int_0^{l/2} M_x^2 \,d x,$$

$$\Delta U_{y'} = \Delta W_{y'}\int_0^{l/2} M_x^2 \,d x,$$

$$\Delta U_{z'} = \Delta W_{z'}\int_0^{l/2} M_x^2 \,d x,$$

$$\Delta U_{x'y'} = \Delta W_{x'y'}\int_0^{l/2} M_x^2 \,d x, \tag{13}$$

$$\Delta U_{y'z'} = \Delta W_{y'z'}\int_0^{l/2} M_x^2 \,d x,$$

$$\Delta U_{x'z'} = \Delta W_{x'z'}\int_0^{l/2} M_x^2 \,d x,$$

Where,

$$\Delta W_{x'} = [(b_2 h_2^{\ 3} - b_1 h_1^{\ 3}) \Psi_L / (12 k_{22}^2)](c_{11} A^2 + c_{12} AB + c_{13} AC),$$

$$\Delta W_{y'} = [(b_2 h_2^{\ 3} - b_1 h_1^{\ 3}) \Psi_T / (12 k_{22}^2)](c_{22} B^2 + c_{12} AB + c_{23} BC),$$

$$\Delta W_{z'} = [(b_2 h_2^{\ 3} - b_1 h_1^{\ 3}) \Psi_T / (12 k_{22}^2)](c_{33} C^2 + c_{13} AC + c_{23} BC),$$

$$\Delta W_{x'y'} = (b_2 h_2^{\ 3} - b_1 h_1^{\ 3}) \Psi_{LT} c_{66} [2 l_1 l_2 - Q_{41}(m_1 n_2 + m_2 n_1)/Q_{44}]^2 / (12 k_{22}^2),$$

$$\Delta W_{y'z'} = (b_2 h_2^{\ 3} - b_1 h_1^{\ 3}) \Psi_{TT} c_{44} [2 l_2 l_3 - Q_{41}(m_2 n_3 + m_3 n_3)/Q_{44}]^2 / (12 k_{22}^2),$$

$$\Delta W_{x'z'} = (b_2 h_2^{\ 3} - b_1 h_1^{\ 3}) \Psi_{LT} c_{55} [2 l_1 l_3 - Q_{41}(m_1 n_3 + m_3 n_1)/Q_{44}]^2 / (12 k_{22}^2),$$

$$A = l_1^2 - Q_{41} m_1 n_1 / Q_{44}, \quad B = l_2^2 - Q_{41} m_2 n_2 / Q_{44}, \quad C = l_3^2 - Q_{41} m_3 n_3 / Q_{44}.$$

Where l_i, m_i and n_i are direction cosine between fibre coordinate system and composite coordinate system, c_{ij} is elastic constant of unidirectional fibre composite.

4.3 Specific Damping Capacity of 3-D Braided Composite

General dissipation energy of composite is the superimpose by dissipation energy of each system according to volume fraction :

$$\Delta U = V_{f_a} \Delta U_5 + (V_{f_b} / 4) \sum_{k=1}^{4} \Delta U_k$$

$$= \left[\frac{V_{f_a} (b_2 h_2^{\ 3} - b_1 h_1^{\ 3}) C_{11}^5 \Psi_L}{12 k_{22}^2} + \frac{V_{f_b}}{4} \sum_{k=1}^{4} \Delta W_k \right] \int_0^{l/2} M_x^2 dx. \tag{14}$$

And maximum strain energy of composite is as

$$U_m = \int_0^{l/2} M_x k_x dx = \frac{1}{k_{22}} \int_0^{l/2} M_x^2 dx. \tag{15}$$

Therefore, specific damping capacity of the composite can be obtained as follows

$$\Psi = k_{22} \left[\frac{V_{f_a} (b_2 h_2^{\ 3} - b_1 h_1^{\ 3}) c_{11}^5 \Psi_L}{12 k_{22}^2} + \frac{V_{f_b}}{4} \sum_{k=1}^{4} \Delta W_k \right]. \tag{16}$$

5 Optimization Model of 3-D Braided Composite

We choose specific damping capacity (also keep one eyes on some stiffness coefficient simultaneously) as maximum optimization objective function, structure parameter of materials (α, β) and geometric parameter of section (b_1, b_2, h_1, h_2) as design variables, constraint condition are numeric area of structure parameters of materials on technological requirements and some requirement of stiffness. Here, we design three optimization models as follows,

Model 1:

$$f=\max(\Psi)$$
$$\text{s.t.}\quad \alpha_{\min} \leq \alpha \leq \alpha_{\max}, \beta_{\min} \leq \beta \leq \beta_{\max}$$
$$(h_2/b_2)_{\min} \leq (h_2/b_2) \leq (h_2/b_2)_{\max}$$
$$(b_1/b_2)_{\min} \leq (b_1/b_2) \leq (b_1/b_2)_{\max} \tag{17}$$
$$(h_1/h_2)_{\min} \leq (h_1/h_2) \leq (h_1/h_2)_{\max}$$
$$V_{f\min} \leq V_f \leq V_{f\max}$$

Model 2:

$$f=\max \Psi$$
$$\text{s.t.}\quad K_{ii} \geq K_{ii\min}$$
$$\alpha_{\min} \leq \alpha \leq \alpha_{\max}, \beta_{\min} \leq \beta \leq \beta_{\max}$$
$$(h_2/b_2)_{\min} \leq (h_2/b_2) \leq (h_2/b_2)_{\max}$$
$$(b_1/b_2)_{\min} \leq (b_1/b_2) \leq (b_1/b_2)_{\max} \tag{18}$$
$$(h_1/h_2)_{\min} \leq (h_1/h_2) \leq (h_1/h_2)_{\max}$$
$$V_{f\min} \leq V_f \leq V_{f\max}$$

Model 3:

$$f=\max \left(\eta_5\Psi + \sum_{i=1}^{4}\eta_i K_{ii}\right)$$
$$\text{s.t.}\quad \alpha_{\min} \leq \alpha \leq \alpha_{\max}, \beta_{\min} \leq \beta \leq \beta_{\max}$$
$$(h_2/b_2)_{\min} \leq (h_2/b_2) \leq (h_2/b_2)_{\max}$$
$$(b_1/b_2)_{\min} \leq (b_1/b_2) \leq (b_1/b_2)_{\max} \tag{19}$$
$$(h_1/h_2)_{\min} \leq (h_1/h_2) \leq (h_1/h_2)_{\max}$$
$$V_{f\min} \leq V_f \leq V_{f\max}$$

Where $\sum_{i=1}^{5}\eta_i = 1$, η_1 to η_5 are respectively weight coefficients for specific damping capacity and flexural stiffness coefficient in the unitive objective function. Of course, we also obtain other optimization model according to practical requirement. For the non-linear optimization design problem, optimization solution can be obtained expediently by using the facilities of the particle swarm optimization (PSO) algorithm.

6 Hybrid Optimization Algorithm

PSO simulate social behavior, in which a population of individuals exists. These individuals (also called "particles") are "evolved" by cooperation and competition among the individuals themselves through generations [14, 15]. In PSO, each potential solution is assigned a randomized velocity, are "flown" through the problem space. Each particle adjusts its flying according to its own flying experience and its companions' flying experience. The ith particle is represented as $X_i = (x_{i1}, x_{i2}, \ldots, x_{iD})$. Each particle is treated as a point in a D-dimensional space. The best previous position (the best fitness value is called *pBest*) of any particle is recorded and represented as $P_i = (p_{i1}, p_{i2}, \ldots, p_{id})$. Anther "best" value (called *gBest*) is recorded by all the particles in the population.

This location is represented as $P_g = (p_{g1}, p_{g2}, \ldots, p_{gD})$. At each time step, the rate of the position changing velocity (accelerating) for the ith particle is represented as $V_i = (v_{i1}, v_{i2}, \ldots, v_{iD})$. Each particle moves toward its *pBest* and *gBest* locations. The performance of each particle is measured according to a fitness function, which is related to the problem to be solved. The particles are manipulated according to the following equation:

$$v_{id} = w \cdot v_{id} + c_1 \cdot rand(\ ) \cdot (p_{id} - x_{id})$$
$$+ c_2 \cdot Rand(\ ) \cdot (p_{gd} - x_{id}) \qquad , \qquad (20)$$

$$x_{id} = x_{id} + v_{id} , \qquad (21)$$

where c_1 and c_2 in equation (20) are two positive constants, which represent the weighting of the stochastic acceleration terms that pull each particle toward *pBest* and *gBest* positions. Low values allow particles to roam far from the target regions before being tugged back. On the other hand, high values cause abrupt movement toward, or past, target regions. Proper values of c_1 and c_2 can quicken convergence. *rand(\ )* and *Rand(\ )* are two random functions in the range [0, 1]. The use of the inertia weight w provides a balance between global and local exploration, and results in less iteration to find an optimal solution.

6.1 Parameters Setting

Main parameters of PSO are set as follows.

(1) The inertia parameter
The inertial parameter w is introduced to control the impact of the previous history of velocities on current velocity. A larger inertia weight facilitates global optimization while smaller inertia weight facilitates local optimization. In this paper, the inertia weight ranges in a decreasing way in an adaptive way. The inertia weight is obtained by the following equation:

$$W = W_{max} - \frac{W_{max} - W_{min}}{Iter} \cdot iter . \qquad (22)$$

Where W_{max} is the maximum value of W, W_{min} is the minimum value of W, *Iter* is the maximum iteration number of PSO, and *iter* is current iteration number of PSO.

(2) The parameters c_1 and c_2
The acceleration constants c_1 and c_2 control the maximum step size the particle can do, they are set to 2 according to experiences of other researchers.

6.2 Search Algorithm Hybridization

Being a global search method, the PSO algorithm is expected to give its best results if it is augmented with a local search method that is responsible for fine search. The PSO algorithm is hybridized with a gradient based search. The "candidate" solution found by the PSO algorithm at each iteration step is used as an initial solution to commence a gradient-based search using "fmincon" function in MATLAB [16], which based on the interior-reflective Newton method. The "fmincon" function can solve the constraint problem here.

6.3 Hybrid Optimization Algorithm

The procedure of hybrid optimization algorithm is shown as follows.

Step1. Initialize V and X of each particle.

Step2. Calculate the fitness of each particle.

Step3. If the fitness value is better than the best fitness value (*pBest*) in history, set current value as the new *pBest*.

Step4. Choose the particle with the best fitness value of all the particles as the *gBest* .

Step5. Calculate particle velocity according equation (20), update particle position according equation (21).

Step6. Let the above solution as an initial solution, and carry out a gradient-based search using "fmincon" function in MATLAB Optimization Toolbox.

Step7. When the number of maximum iterations or minimum error criteria is attained, the particle with the best fitness value in X is the approximate solution and STOP; otherwise let *iter=iter+1* and turn to Step 2. Where *iter* denotes the current iteration number.

Particles' velocities on each dimension are clamped to a maximum velocity v_{max}, If the sum of accelerations would cause the velocity on that dimension to exceed v_{max}, which is a parameter specified by the user. Then the velocity on that dimension is limited to v_{max}.

7 Numerical Examples

In order to test the validity of the proposed optimization design procedure, numerical examples have been preformed. Suppose axial yarn system and braiding yarn system of 3-D braided composite be homogeneous carbon fiber, where performance of component material are: $E_{f1} = 258.2$GPa, $E_{f2} = 18.2$ GPa, $G_{f21} = 36.7$ GPa, $\mu_{f21} = 0.25$, $E_m = 3.4$ GPa, $G_m = 1.26$ GPa, $\mu_m = 0.35$, $\Psi_L = 0.0045$, $\Psi_T = 0.0422$, $\Psi_{LT} = 0.0705$, $\Psi_{TT} = 0.0421$ [11]. The performance of unidirectional composite for each system can be calculated by performance of component material according to mesomechanics. The perimeter of rectangular cross section is equal to 0.08m, and length of the composite is 0.5m.

Here, we choose common constraint condition: $\alpha_{min} = 20°$, $\alpha_{max} = 60°$, $\beta_{min} = 20°$, $\beta_{max} = 60°$, $V_{f\,min} = 0.3$, $V_{f\,max} = 0.7$, $(h_2/b_2)_{min} = 0.33$, $(h_2/b_2)_{max} = 3$,

$(b_1 / b_2)_{min} = 0.2$, $(b_1 / b_2)_{max} = 0.8$, $(h_1 / h_2)_{min} = 0.2$, $(h_1 / h_2)_{max} = 0.8$. Three examples are performed as follows.

(1) Example 1:
According to optimization Model (1), maximum of damping Ψ can be calculated by using hybrid optimization algorithm presented, and the optimization results are shown in Table 1.

(2) Example 2:
Choose constraint condition $K_{22min} = 2 \times 10^{-5}$GPa. We can obtain maximum of damping Ψ according to optimization Model (2), and the optimization results are shown in Table 1.

(3) Example 3:
Let $\eta_1 = \eta_3 = \eta_4 = 0$, and $\eta_2 = \eta_5 = 0.5$. Having eliminated difference of order of magnitude for Ψ and K_{22}, the optimization results according to optimization Model (3) are shown in Table 1.

As shown in Table 1, the damping of hollow-rectangular-section 3-D braided composite can be improved observably by optimization design for structure parameter of materials and geometric parameter of section.

From the optimization results of Example 1, if only make a search for maximizing specific damping capacity of composite, damping characteristic of the hollow-rectangular-section 3-D braided composite can be improved obviously . But it may influence on flexural stiffness of composite (result in a few reducing), thus optimization Model (1) exists any limitation and shortage. The optimization results of Example 2 show that optimal damping characteristic can be obtained under ensure flexural strength required of composite. The optimization results of Example 3 show that both of damping and flexural strength may attain better maximum at the same time. The optimization effects denote that the optimization models are propitious to engineering application

Table 1. The results of preliminary design and optimization design

	α	β	h_2 / b_2	b_1 / b_2	h_1 / h_2	Ψ	K_{22} (GPa·m^2)
Preliminary design	20°	20°	1.0	0.5	0.5	0.0031	2.7×10^{-5}
	20°	20°	1.0	0.5	0.5	0.0031	2.7×10^{-5}
	20°	20°	1.0	0.5	0.5	0.0031	2.7×10^{-5}
Optimal design	35°	53°	1.01	0.3	0.3	0.0118	1.6×10^{-6}
	31°	50°	0.45	0.26	0.26	0.0109	1.8×10^{-5}
	26°	48°	1.35	0.2	0.2	0.0051	4.38×10^{-6}

8 Conclusions

In this paper, the mathematical model for optimization of the damping of hollow-rectangular-section 3-D braided composite was proposed. The results of numeral examples show that the better damping characteristic could be obtained by using optimal design, contenting the determinate restriction. The method proposed here is useful for the design and engineering application of the kind of member.

References

1. Huang, G.: Modern Textile Composites. Chinese Textile Press, Beijing (2000)
2. Zheng, X.T., Ye, T.Q.: Microstructure Analysis of 4-Step Three-Dimensional Braided Composite. Chinese Journal of Aeronautics 16(3), 142–149 (2003)
3. Wang, Y.Q., Wang, A.S.D.: On the Topological Yarn Structure of 3-D Rectangular and Tubular Braided Preforma. Composites Science and Technology 51, 575–583 (1994)
4. Eberhart, R., Kennedy, J.: A New Optimizer Using Particle Swarm Theory. In: The Sixth International Symposium on Micro Machine and Human Science, pp. 39–43 (1995)
5. Kennedy, J., Eberhart, R.: Particle Swarm Optimization. In: IEEE International Conference on Neural Networks, pp. 1942–1948. IEEE Press, New York (2001)
6. Eberhart, R., Shi, Y.: Tracking and Optimizing Dynamic Systems with Particle Swarms. In: IEEE Congress on Evolutionary Computation, pp. 94–97. IEEE Press, New York (2001)
7. Trelea, I.C.: The Particle Swarm Optimization Algorithm: Convergence Analysis and Parameter Selection. Information Processing Letters 6, 317–325 (2003)
8. Yang, J.M.: Fiber Inclination Model of Three-dimensional Textile Structural Composites. Journal of Composite Materials 20, 472–480 (1986)
9. Li, W., Hammad, M., EI-Shiekh, A.: Structural Analysis of 3-D Braided Preforms for Composites, Part 1:Two-Step Preforms. J. Text. Inst. 81(4), 515–537 (1990)
10. Cai, G.W., Liao, D.X.: The Stiffness Coefficients of Rectangular Cross Section Beams with 2-step Three-dimensional Braided Composite Beam. Journal of Huazhong University of Science and Technology 24(12), 26–28 (1996)
11. Cai, G.W., Zhou, X.H., Liao, D.X.: Analysis of the Stiffness and Damping of the 4-step Three Dimensional Braided Composite Links. Journal of Mechanical Strength 21(1), 18–23 (1999)
12. Adams, R.D., Bacon, D.G.C.: Effect of Orientation and Laminated Geometry on the Dynamic Properties of CFRP. J. Composite Materials 7(10), 402–406 (1973)
13. Lin, D.X., Ni, R.G., Adams, R.D.: Prediction and Measurement of the Vibrational Damping Parameters of Carbon and Glass Fibre-Reinforced Plastics Plates. Journal of Composite Material 18(3), 132–151 (1984)
14. Kennedy, J., Eberhart, R.C., Shi, Y.: Swarm Intelligence. Morgan Kaufmann, San Mateo (2001)
15. Clerc, M., Kennedy, J.: The Particle Swarm-explosion Stability and Convergence in a Multidimensional Complex Space. IEEE Transaction on Evolutionary Computation 6(1), 58–73 (2002)
16. Grace, A.: Optimization Toolbox for Use with MATLAB, User's Guide. Math Works Inc. (1994)

Parallel Hybrid Particle Swarm Optimization and Applications in Geotechnical Engineering

Youliang Zhang[1], Domenico Gallipoli[2], and Charles Augarde[3]

[1] State Key Laboratory for GeoMechanics and Deep Underground Engineering, China University of Mining & Technology , Xuzhou, 221008, P.R. China
ylzhang@whrsm.ac.cn
[2] Department of Civil Engineering, University of Glasgow, Glasgow G12 8LT, UK
gallipoli@civil.gla.ac.uk
[3] School of Engineering, Durham University, South Road, Durham DH1 3LE, UK
Charles.augarde@dur.ac.uk

Abstract. A novel parallel hybrid particle swarm optimization algorithm named hmPSO is presented. The new algorithm combines particle swarm optimization (PSO) with a local search method which aims to accelerate the rate of convergence. The PSO provides initial guesses to the local search method and the local search accelerates PSO with its solutions. The hybrid global optimization algorithm adjusts its searching space through the local search results. Parallelization is based on the client-server model, which is ideal for asynchronous distributed computations. The server, the center of data exchange, manages requests and coordinates the time-consuming objective function computations undertaken by individual clients which locate in separate processors. A case study in geotechnical engineering demonstrates the effectiveness and efficiency of the proposed algorithm.

Keywords: particle swarm optimization, asynchronous parallel computation, server-client model, hmPSO.

1 Introduction

Global optimization algorithms are important tools for parameter identification in geotechnical engineering. However, due to the lack of analytical solutions for most geotechnical problems, evaluation of the objective function $f(\mathbf{x})$ during optimization is usually achieved by performing numerical (e.g. finite element) simulations of the relevant boundary value problem. This approach, which is often referred to as "simulation-based optimization" might produce multi-modal forms of the objective function due to numerical fluctuations and is generally computationally expensive.

Particle Swarm Optimization (PSO) proposed by Eberhart and Kennedy [1, 2] is a new evolutionary algorithm inspired by social behavior of bird flocks. Recently, PSO has been receiving increasing attention due to its effectiveness, efficiency, and simplicity in achieving global optimization. In particular, PSO is capable of capturing the global optimum for a wide range of multi-modal problems (i.e. those problems where the objective function might have many local minima). However, for some complex

Z. Cai et al. (Eds.): ISICA 2009, LNCS 5821, pp. 466–475, 2009.

problems, PSO could suffer from premature convergence towards a suboptimal solution, just like other evolutionary algorithms. Another weakness of PSO is the slow rate of convergence, especially in the later stage of the search [3, 4].

A modified parallel PSO is here proposed to address shortfalls such as premature identification of suboptimal solutions, slow convergence rate and high computational costs. In particular, a hybridization technique is introduced where a local search is run in parallel with the main PSO algorithm to carry out quick and efficient explorations around the current optimum at a much lower computational cost. The search space for the PSO algorithm is centered on the latest solution from the local search routine and is progressively narrowed as the algorithm progresses. Hybridization of a global optimization method such as PSO with a local search method has proved to be very effective in solving a range of problems [5-7]. In addition, an asynchronous parallel version of the hybrid PSO algorithm is here proposed to reduce computational time. The main parts of the method were presented in a previous paper [8]. The implementation details and an application to a typical geotechnical problem are instead the focus of this paper.

2 Parallel Hybrid Particle Swarm Optimization

PSO is advantageous for global exploration of the search space while local search methods offer fast convergence rates when good starting points are provided. The hybrid PSO algorithm presented here aims to combine the strengths from both these approaches. The proposed parallel hybrid PSO algorithm consists of the basic PSO, a local search method and an asynchronous parallel strategy. The Message Passing Interface (MPI) [9] is chosen as the parallel programming library.

2.1 Basic PSO

The PSO algorithm was proposed as a population-based stochastic global optimization method by Kennedy & Eberhart [1, 2]. The population, which is called "swarm" in PSO, is made up of "particles". The ith particle has such properties as fitness f_i, position $\mathbf{x}_i$, and velocity $\mathbf{v}_i$. The PSO starts by initializing the particle positions $\mathbf{x}_i$ and velocities $\mathbf{v}_i$ and computes the corresponding fitness f_i. Then particles "fly" across the search space, which means that a series of iteration is performed where, for each iteration, the fitness of all particles is updated according to the following rules

$$\mathbf{v}_i^{k+1} = w^k \mathbf{v}_i^k + c_1 r_1 \left(\mathbf{P}_i - \mathbf{x}_i \right) + c_2 r_2 \left(\mathbf{P}_g - \mathbf{x}_i \right) . \tag{1}$$

$$\mathbf{x}_i^{k+1} = \mathbf{x}_i^k + \mathbf{v}_i^{k+1} . \tag{2}$$

where the superscripts $k, k+1$ are iteration numbers; r_1 and r_2 are two random factors in the interval [0,1]; w_k is the inertia weight and c_1 and c_2 are constants representing the "cognitive" and "social" components of knowledge, respectively. Each particle remembers its best position (cognitive knowledge), which is denoted as $\mathbf{P}_i$. In addition, knowledge of the best position ever achieved across the whole swarm, which is denoted as $\mathbf{P_g}$, is shared between particles (social knowledge). Updating rules drive particles towards the optimal region and, as the algorithm progresses, all particles tend to group around the global optimum until a solution is finally found.

2.2   Local Search Method

Local search methods are a class of methods that hunt for the optimum solution in the vicinity of a given set of starting points. The particular choice of these starting points strongly affects the efficiency of the local search. The Nelder-Mead simplex algorithm [10] is used herein mainly due to its simplicity and conformity with PSO. Both Nelder-Mead and PSO methods require only evaluation of the objective function at given points in the search space and no gradient information is needed, which makes the two methods easy to combine. The simplex method needs $n + 1$ points as starting points, where n is the number of unknown parameters to be determined.

2.3   Asynchronous Parallel Hybrid PSO

The objective of the hybrid method described here is to make best use of the strengths of the global and the local search methods. PSO is powerful for global exploration of the search space while the Nelder-Mead simplex algorithm is efficient for local exploration. The combination of the two methods is achieved by taking the $n+1$ best solutions from the PSO algorithm as starting points of the Nelder-Mead simplex algorithm. The solution from the local search is then fed back into the PSO as a candidate global optimum. At the same time, a sub-swarm is allocated to explore a smaller region centered on the solution obtained from the local search. In the proposed algorithm, which is named hmPSO (hybrid moving-boundary Particle Swarm Optimization), the whole swarm is therefore divided into two sub-swarms. The first "global" sub-swarm searches in the original space while the second "local" sub-swarm searches in a smaller space that is continuously updated to coincide with the region around the latest solution from the local search.

In the parallel implementation of the hmPSO algorithm each particle is assigned to a different processor. Parallelization can be achieved by using either a synchronous or asynchronous, model. In the synchronous model, PSO moves to the next iteration only when all particles have completed their current iteration, i.e. when all particles have terminated the numerical simulation corresponding to their current position in the search space. A drawback of the synchronous model is that the slowest particle determines the speed of the algorithm and, in non-linear simulation-based optimization, the computational time can vary significantly between particles. In contrast, in the asynchronous model, each particle moves to the next iteration immediately after it finishes the current one without having to wait for other particles. This feature is particularly advantageous when load unbalances between particles are very large as no processor remains idle while other processors are busy. The use of the asynchronous model is also essential in distributed parallel computing where computing power of different processors vary significantly due to hardware configurations.

The client-server model is adopted for the implementation of the asynchronous model as shown in Fig. 1. The client-server model consists of three parts: the server, the particle clients and the local search clients. The server resides on one processor, which is the centre for data sharing and system management. The server stores and sorts the best positions of individual particles and updates the swarm's best position. The clients are instead responsible for undertaking the actual numerical simulations corresponding to the current position of their respective particles and for running the Nelder-Mead simplex local searches. Each client communicates with the server, and there is no communication between particle clients. There is only one local search client when a serial local search algorithm is used. Otherwise, if a parallel local search algorithm is employed, there is more than one local search client. In this case a master-slave model is adopted for the parallel local search where the master of the local search group coordinates and manages computations undertaken by the slaves. When a master-slave model is adopted, the server only communicates with the master of the local search group. The number of clients depends on the dimension of the problem and the specific algorithm used.

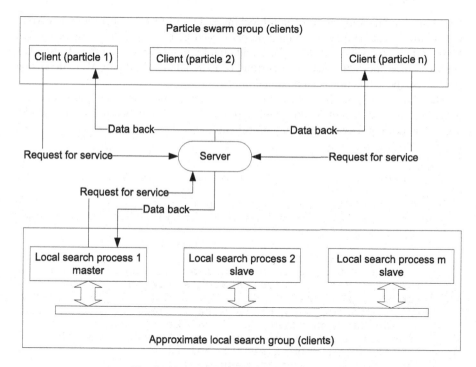

Fig. 1. Client-server model for parallel hmPS

The client's responsibility is to perform the actual numerical simulations for evaluating the objective function and to undertake the local searches. The server's responsibility is to store and manage data shared by clients, listen to clients' queries for information or data, process the queries and return data or commands back to the clients. The server is also in charge of termination of all clients on receipt of stop information either from the local search client or from a particle client. It is obvious that different processors run different programs using different data, so the paradigm of the parallel hmPSO is MPMD (Multiple Programs Multiple Data).

3   Parallel Implementation of hmPSO

Non-blocking MPI communication functions such as MPI_Isend, MPI_Irecv, and MPI_Test are used for the implementation of the asynchronous parallel hmPSO. By using non-blocking communication which allows both communications and computations to proceed concurrently, the performance of the parallel program can be improved. For example, MPI_Isend starts a send operation then returns immediately without waiting for the communication to complete. Similarly, MPI_Irecv starts a receive operation and returns before the data has been received. The structure for a communication overlapping with a computation is,

> MPI_Isend
> Do some computation
> MPI_Test

Checking for the completion of non-blocking send and receive operations is carried out by MPI_Test. This check should be performed before any data being exchanged between processors is used. MPI_Test waits until a non-blocking communication has finished but it does not block the algorithm so to avoid any deadlock. More details on how to use these functions can be found in [9].

The three parts of the algorithm, i.e. the server program, the particle client program, and the Nelder-Mead simplex program, are listed below. In the parallel algorithm, each processor hosts only one client.

```
parallel hmPSO  (program resides on the server)
   repeat
   MPI_Irecv (receiving data from all clients )
   MPI_Test
   switch according to client data/request
     if ( data is particle best solution )
        update swarm best
        send swarm best back to the particle
        If (FES>startFES)
        send starting points to clients of local search
     else if ( data is local search solution )
        update swarm best
        sort particles by their best fitness
        send starting points to local search
        restart a sub-swarm search on a smaller search
space based on the local search solution
     else if ( data is stop message )
        send stop message to all clients
        terminate server
     end if
     check stopping criterion
     if (stopping criterion is met )
        send stop message to all clients
        terminate server
     end if
   }while ( stopping criterion is not met )
```

The server program keeps on receiving data or requests from all clients, and responds accordingly. The server also stores the best position of the whole swarm and the best positions of individual particles. The swarm best position is sent back to particle clients when a request is made.

After sorting the best positions of individual particles, the top $n+1$ particles are taken as the starting points for the Nelder-Mead simplex local search. After termination of the Nelder-Mead simplex local search, a sub-swarm is allocated to explore a smaller search space centered on the solution from the local search. The server is also in charge of the termination of all clients by sending a stop message.

```
parallel hmPSO  (program resides on particle clients)
   initialize position x_i
   initialize velocity v_i
   evaluate objective function f(x_i)
   update particle best P_i
   MPI_Isend (send particle best P_i to server)
   repeat
      MPI_Irecv (receive data/command from server )
      MPI_Test
      update velocity v_i
      update position x_i
      evaluate objective function f(x_i)
      switch according to the received data from service
         if ( data is stop message )
            terminate this client process
         else if ( data is swarm best position P_g )
            update P_g for this particle
         else if ( data is to restart sub-swarm)
            reset particle's new search space
            initialize position x_i
            initialize velocity v_i
         end if
      check stopping criterion
      if (stopping criterion is met )
         send stop message to the server
      else
         MPI_Isend (send particle best P_i to server )
      end if
   }while ( stopping criterion is not met )
```

Particle clients update their respective positions and velocity by performing the relevant numerical simulation and evaluate the objective function. These are the most computationally expensive operations of the whole optimization process. The particles receive the swarm best position P_g from the server and, after completing the numerical simulation, return the particle best position P_i to the server. When the convergence criterion is met, the clients are commanded by the server to terminate their processes.

```
parallel hmPSO  (program resides on local search client)
   MPI_Irecv (receive data/command from server )
```

```
MPI_Test
repeat
  switch according to the received data from service
      if ( data is stop message )
         terminate this client process
      else if ( data is on starting points )
         perform a local search
      end if
  check stopping criterion
  if (stopping criterion is met )
      send stop message to the server
  else
      MPI_Isend (send local search solution to server )
  end if
}while ( stopping criterion is not met )
```

The local search client starts a new run of the Nelder-Mead simplex algorithm as soon as it receives a fresh set of $n+1$ starting points from the server. The solution from the local search is then sent back to the server to update the current best position of the whole swarm. When the convergence criterion is met, the local search client sends a message to the server.

4 Applications to Geotechnical Engineering

The above parallel hmPSO algorithm is here used for selecting parameter values in the Barcelona Basic Model (BBM) [11] based on the results from pressuremeter tests. BBM .is one of the best known constitutive models for unsaturated soils and is formulated in terms of 9 independent parameters. In this work, however, only a sub-set of 6 parameter values is determined. This follows a sensitivity analysis that has shown the dominant influence of these 6 parameters in governing the soil response during simulations of pressuremeter tests.

Pressuremeter testing is a widely used in-situ technique for characterizing soil properties. The technique consists in the application of an increasing pressure to the walls of a cylindrical borehole while measuring the corresponding radial strains. Cavity expansion curves showing applied pressure versus radial expansion are then analyzed to infer soil properties. Due to the nonlinearity of BBM, no closed-form analytical solution exists to predict soil behaviour during a pressuremeter test and, hence finite element simulations are here used.

In order to validate the proposed algorithm, three simulated constant suction pressuremeter tests corresponding to a known set of parameter values in BBM (see Fig. 2) were taken as the "experimental" data. The optimization algorithm was then tested to check whether the same set of parameter values could be found. The objective function is given in Eq. 3 and is defined in such a way that the three pressuremeter tests at different suctions have to be simultaneously matched

$$f = \sqrt{\sum_{i=1}^{N} \left(\varepsilon_{c,i}^{s} - \varepsilon_{c,i}^{m} \right)^2} \ . \tag{3}$$

where $(\varepsilon^s_{c,i} - \varepsilon^m_{c,i})$ is the difference between the "experimental" and simulated cavity strains at the same value of cavity pressure, and N is the total number of "experimental" points on the three curves.

The range of parameter values defining the entire 6-dimensional search space are given in Table 1. The optimum solution in this search space is $\mathbf{x}$=(M, k, κ, r, β, p^c)=(0.9, 0.5, 0.025, 1.5, 1.0e-5Pa^{-1}, 2.0e6Pa), corresponding to the set of BBM parameter values used to generate the curves shown in Fig. 2. The other three BBM parameters that were not included in the optimization process were taken equal to (G, λ(0), po*)=(3.0e+3 kPa, 0.13, 9.18 kPa) in all simulations. Readers can refer to [11] for the physical meaning of the individual model parameters.

Pressuremeter tests were simulated by a 2D axisymmetric FE model using eight-noded quadrilateral elements with pore water pressure and pore air pressure on the corner nodes. The cavity pressure was applied incrementally in steps of 10 kPa.

In the PSO algorithm, the swarm size was 35, the constants c_1 and c_2 were both taken equal to 2.0, the convergence tolerance for the objective function was equal to 1.0e-5 and the inertia weight w_k decreased linearly with the number of iterations from 0.9 to 0.4.

The parallel computer "Hamilton" was used for the analysis. This is a Linux cluster hosted at Durham University consisting of 96 dual-processor dual-core Opteron 2.2 GHz nodes with 8 GBytes of memory and a Myrinet fast interconnect for running MPI code, and 135 dual-processor Opteron 2 GHz nodes with 4 GBytes of memory and a Gigabit interconnect. The system has 3.5 Terabytes of disk storage. The operating system is SuSE Linux 10.0 (64-bit).

Table 1. BBM parameters and their ranges

parameter	Minimum value	Maximum value
M	0.1	1.4
k	0.1	0.7
κ	0.01	0.1
r	1.05	1.8
β	1.0e-6 kPa^{-1}	1.0e-4 kPa^{-1}
p^c	1.0e4 kPa	1.0e7 kPa

Results show that the algorithm was capable to find the target 6 parameter values with very high accuracy. The optimum parameter values were found at the end of a local search and it took 4 local searches to converge to the solution. As an example, the first 7 rows in Table 2 show the initial values at the 7 corners of the simplex for the last local search while the bottom row shows the final optimum solution. The hmPSO algorithm took a total number of 34884 objective function evaluations to converge towards the solution. This corresponded to a computational time of 191.6 hours for the asynchronous parallel implementation. The average time of a single objective function evaluation is 122.2 seconds. So it can be estimated that if a serial algorithm is used, the computation time could be over 1184.2 hours. This confirms the advantage of using a parallel implementation rather than a serial one.

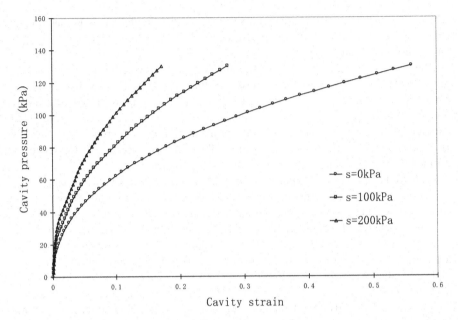

Fig. 2. Curves generated by the chosen parameter set

Table 2. Results from the last local search

objective function value	M	k	κ	r	β(kPa⁻¹)	p_c (kPa)
2.71E-05	9.00E-01	5.00E-01	2.50E-02	1.50E+00	9.99E-06	2.01E+06
3.04E-03	9.14E-01	4.54E-01	2.12E-02	1.32E+00	1.14E-05	1.62E+06
3.22E-03	9.14E-01	4.56E-01	2.14E-02	1.33E+00	1.17E-05	1.59E+06
3.24E-03	9.13E-01	4.53E-01	2.16E-02	1.32E+00	1.13E-05	1.61E+06
3.38E-03	9.11E-01	4.54E-01	2.12E-02	1.33E+00	1.12E-05	1.90E+06
3.41E-03	9.17E-01	4.54E-01	2.18E-02	1.32E+00	1.12E-05	1.30E+06
3.54E-03	9.12E-01	4.54E-01	2.18E-02	1.33E+00	1.14E-05	1.68E+06
2.0618E-06	9.00E-01	5.00E-01	2.50E-02	1.50E+00	1.00E-05	2.00E+06

5   Conclusions

The paper presents the implementation and application of a parallel hybrid moving-boundary Particle Swarm Optimization algorithm (hmPSO). The algorithm originates from the hybridization of the basic particle swarm optimization algorithm with a Nelder-Mead simplex local search. A client-server model is used for the asynchronous parallel implementation of the algorithm. Using the proposed methodology, 6 parameter values of a nonlinear constitutive unsaturated soil model were simultaneously identified by means of back analysis of pressuremeter tests. Computational time was reduced significantly by parallelization of the algorithm on the computer cluster "Hamilton" at Durham University, UK.

Acknowledgements

The authors gratefully acknowledge support from U.K. EPSRC (grant ref. EP/C526627/1) and State Key Laboratory for GeoMechanics and Deep Underground Engineering (grant SKLGDUE08003X).

References

1. Kennedy, J., Eberhart, R.: Particle swarm optimization. In: IEEE, NeuralNetworks Council Staff, IEEE Neural Networks Council (eds.) Proc. IEEE International Conference on Neural Networks, pp. 1942–1948. IEEE, Los Alamitos (1995)
2. Eberhart, R., Kennedy, J.: A new optimizer using particle swarm theory. In: Proceedings of the Sixth International Symposium on Micro Machine and Human Science, Nagoya Japan, pp. 39–43 (1995)
3. Xie, X., Zhang, W., Yang, Z.: A dissipative particle swarm optimization. In: Proceedings of the 2002 Congress on Evolutionary Computation (CEC 2002), Hawaii, USA, pp. 1456–1461 (2002)
4. Zhang, W., Liu, M., Clerc, Y.: An adaptive pso algorithm for reactive power optimization. In: Sixth international conference on advances in power system control, operation and management (APSCOM) Hong Kong, China, pp. 302–307 (2003)
5. Renders, J., Flasse, S.: Hybrid methods using genetic algorithms for global optimization. IEEE Trans. Syst. Man Cybern. B Cybern. 26(2), 243–258 (1996)
6. Yen, R., Liao, J., Lee, B., Randolph, D.: A hybrid approach to modeling metabolic systems using a genetic algorithm and Simplex method. IEEE Transactions on Systems, Man and Cybernetics Part-B 28(2), 173–191 (1998)
7. Fan, S., Liang, Y., Zahara, E.: Hybrid simplex search and particle swarm optimization for the global optimization of multimodal functions. Engineering Optimization 36, 401–418 (2004)
8. Zhang, Y., Gallipoli, D., Augarde, C.E.: Simulation-based calibration of geotechnical parameters using parallel hybrid moving boundary particle swarm optimization. Computers and Geotechnics 36(4), 604–615 (2009)
9. Snir, M., Otto, S., Huss-Lederman, S., Walker, D., Dongarra, J.: MPI: The Complete Reference. MIT Press, Cambridge (1996)
10. Nelder, J., Mead, R.: A simplex method for function minimization. The Computer Journal 7, 308–313 (1965)
11. Alonso, E.E., Gens, A., Josa, A.: A constitutive model for partially saturated soils. Géotechnique 40(3), 405–430 (1990)

Storage-Based Intrusion Detection Using Artificial Immune Technique

Yunliang Chen[1,2], Jianzhong Huang[1,*], Changsheng Xie[1], and Yunfu Fang[1]

[1] Wuhan National Laboratory for Optoelectronics, Huazhong University of Science
and Technology, Wuhan, Hubei, P.R. China. 430074
Phone: +86-27-87792283; Fax: +86-27-87543686
husthjz@sina.com
[2] School of computer science , China University of Geosciences, Wuhan, Hubei,
P.R. China. 430074

Abstract. Storage-based intrusion detection systems (SIDS) allow storage systems to watch for suspicious activity. This paper presents a novel storage- based intrusion detection scheme to monitor the user's activities with the artificial immune technique. Compared with the previous SIDS prototype, the SIDS using artificial immune technique can recognize a strange suspicious behavior. Before simulation, a set of appropriate parameters of algorithm are fitted according to the mean convergence speed and detection efficiency. The simulation shows the proposed scheme can reach higher detection rate and lower false alarm rate than the previous ones.

Keywords: network security, intrusion detection, artificial immune technique.

1 Introduction

Intrusion detection systems (IDS) have been developed over the years [1], with most falling into two schools: network-based or host-based. Network IDS (NIDS) are usually embedded in sniffers or firewalls, scanning traffic to, from, and within a network environment for attack signatures and suspicious traffic [2]. Host-based IDS (HIDS) are fully or partially embedded within each host's OS. They examine local information (such as system calls [3]) for signs of intrusion or suspicious behavior. Many environments employ multiple IDSs, each watching activity from its own vantage point.

There are also some other intruder actions [4] are quite visible at the storage interface. Examples include manipulating system utilities (e.g., to add backdoors or Trojan horses), tampering with audit log contents (e.g., to eliminate evidence), and resetting attributes (e.g., to hide changes). Therefore the storage system is another interesting vantage point for intrusion detection. By that, a storage server sees all changes to persistent data, allowing it to watch for suspicious changes and issue alerts about the corresponding client systems. Furthermore, like NIDS, S IDS must be

---

* Corresponding author.

Z. Cai et al. (Eds.): ISICA 2009, LNCS 5821, pp. 476–486, 2009.

compromise-independent of the host OS, meaning that it cannot be disabled by an intruder who only successfully gets past a host's OS-level protection.

The storage-based IDS monitor leverages the isolation provided by a file server and independently identifies possible symptoms of infections in disk states. Note that it completely rely on the pre-defined rule set to detect anomalous integrity violation. As a result, it is not able to detect unseen intrusions unless the rule set is updated by the administrator.

This paper proposes a novel intrusion detection scheme to monitor the unusual user activities using Artificial Immune System (AIS). AIS has been applied to many fields such as data mining [5], fault detection [6], pattern recognition [7] and anomaly detection [8][9] as a new computational paradigm in Artificial Intelligence. That is, AIS can be applied to storage-based intrusion detection and computer security [10].

The remainder of this paper is organized as follows. Section 2 gives a short overview of related works. Section 3 describes the details the design of the storage intrusion detection. Then, some results of the fitness test and simulation test are given in Section 4, along with some analysis of the results. Section 5 discusses three different weighting schemes used in our SSA model . Finally, we summarize the paper in section 6.

2 Related Works

2.1 Storage-Based Intrusion Detection

Storage-based intrusion detection enables storage devices to examine the requests they service for suspicious client behavior [4]. Although the world view that a storage server sees is incomplete, two features combine to make it a well positioned platform for enhancing intrusion detection efforts. First, we stress that, storage devices are independent of host OSes, they can continue to look for intrusions after the initial compromise, whereas a host-based IDS can be disabled by the intruder. Second, since most computer systems rely heavily on persistent storage for their operation, many intruder actions will cause storage activity that can be captured and analyzed [16].

2.2 Intrusion Detection Using AIS

Discrimination between Self and Non-self is one of the major mechanisms in the biological immune system, and the negative selection is a process to filter out the self reactive lymphocytes within the thymus. Inspired by the negative selection principle, Dr. Forrest proposed a Negative Selection Algorithm (NSA) [11]. The basic idea of NSA is to generate a set of detectors in the complementary space and use such detectors to classify the unseen data. In general, the NSA includes the following steps:

1.   Define self as a set S of elements of length L in space U;
2.   Generate a set D of detectors, so that each fails to match any element in S;
3.   Monitor S for changes by continually matching the detectors in D against S.

Where self set S and Non-self set N form the space U, i.e. $U = S \cup N$ and $S \cap N = \emptyset$.

Stibor et al. [12] described an intrusion detection approach, i.e. the real-valued negative selection algorithm, which employs variable-sized detectors. It has been observed
that the immune system performs intrusion detection partly by a negative selection
process, where the self reactive lymphocytes are eliminated, ensuring that all potential
antigens are recognizable. In order to improve the intrusion detection, Dr. Gonzalez
studied different representation schemes for the NSA, including hyper-rectangles,
fuzzy rules, and hyper-spheres, and proposed four different detection generation algorithms: Real-valued Negative Selection (RNS), Negative Selection with Detection
Rules (NSDR), Randomized Real-valued Negative Selection (RRNS), and Negative
Selection with Fuzzy Detection Rules (NSFDR) [13].

3 Storage-Based Intrusion Detecting System

3.1 Immune Model for Metadata

In large-scale storage system, it is difficult to detect all the anomaly of data because
the data volume is enormous. Since metadata is the data that describes other data, i.e.
data about data, we can find out the change of data by monitoring the metadata. This
method can reduce the computation and design complexity of detection system. Here
we consult the storage immune model [14] and propose a simplified immune model
for storage metadata, as shown in Figure 1.

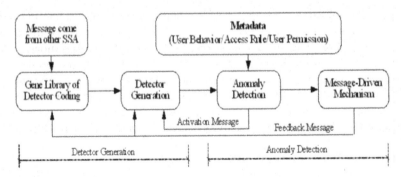

Fig. 1. Immune Model of Storage Metadata

The above storage immune model imitates the biological immune, where the resource immune model is known as SSA which constitutes the overall framework of
storage security sub-system. Variant SSAs can cooperate to accomplish the intrusion
detection. The above immune model shows that the immune process mainly consists
of two stages: detector generation and intrusion detection.

3.2 Architecture

The workflow of the storage intrusion detection is detailed as follows:

1) collect a batch of normal behavior and build an abnormal behavior antibody gene
   library using a particular negative selection algorithm;

2) intercept the access sequence and construct a specific antigen sequence by transforming the relevant access behavior which is consonant with the format of access control mode, as shown is Figure 3;

3) 3)judge the antigen sequence by matching with the antibody sequence taken from the antibody gene library, and assign a value (i.e. score) to the corresponding access behavior, then modify the weight value of the matched antibody;

4) periodically update the abnormal behavior antibody gene library, eliminating the useless antibody and adding the new antibody.

The workflow is shown in Figure 2. Using the potential mechanism of studying and forgetting, it is possible for the storage intrusion detection system to recognize both the legal access behavior and increasingly changing anomaly behavior.

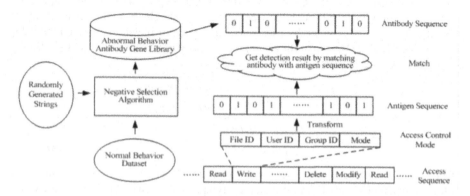

Fig. 2. Workflow of Storage Intrusion Detection

3.3 Detailed Design

3.3.1 Access Metadata

User access activity includes successful, failed, and attempted operations, e.g. login, read, write, create, modify, update, etc. As mentioned above, we can intercept the storage activity then construct the user access behavior.

Assume that each file/folder has the following format of access control mode, as shown in Figure 3, which denotes that the file FileID allows the user UserID belonged to group GroupID has certain access permission. The access control modes of all files/folders are transformed into the training dataset (i.e. abnormal behavior antibody gene library) according to certain format. When a user accesses a file/folder, the file system can obtain such access information as user name, group identifier, and access mode. The access information can also be organized into the format as showed in Figure 4. Then such information can be transformed into the continuous data format, acting as the testing data (i.e. antigen sequence). Finally one can use the techniques or algorithms of AIS to perform the intrusion detection.

File ID	User ID	Group ID	Access Mode
File/Folder Identifier	User Identifier	Group Identifier	Read/Write/Delete/Modify/...

Fig. 3. Format of Access Control Mode

If the complementary space aims at the continuous data, the NSA is referred to as real-valued negative selection algorithm (RNS), which operates on a unitary hypercube [12].

3.3.2 Weights

In a SSA model, Each antigen sequence retains two pieces of weight information and also a man-made threshold is given:

1) total_illegal_matched: Used to weigh the illegal degree of an antigen sequence
2) total_action_matched: Used to weigh how we can believe total_illegall_matched
3) threshold: given by user, one action legal or illegal determined the value "score" indicates the final illegal degree of one antigen sequence, we use a Bayesian weighting scheme:

$$\text{Bayes score} = \frac{\Sigma_{matching\ lymphocytes}\frac{illegal\_matched}{action\_matched}}{\Sigma_{matching\ lymphocytes}\frac{illegal\_matched}{action\_matched}+\Sigma_{matching\ lymphocytes}1-\frac{illegal\_matched}{action\_matched}} \quad (1)$$

there are also another ways ,such as "straight sum", which is simply a sum of the illegal_ matched values from all matching lymphocytes. "Weighted average", which is the sum of the illegal_matched values from all matching lymphocytes divided by the sum of all the action_matched values from all matching lymphocytes. They can be seen as follows:

$$\text{Straight sum} = \underset{matching\ \ lymphocytes}{\Sigma}\ illegal\_matched \quad (2)$$

$$\text{Weighted average} = \frac{\Sigma_{matching\ lymphocytes}\ illegal\_matched}{\Sigma_{matching\ lymphocytes}\ action\_matched} \quad (3)$$

4 Experiments

4.1 Dataset

During the simulation, how to obtain the training dataset and the testing dataset? Firstly, define a set of access control mode, and transform all items of the access control mode into a 32 bit hexadecimal number using particular hashing function,

Table 1. Actions of several intruder toolkits

Name	Name	Name	Name	Name
Ramen	lion	FreeBSD	FK 0.4	Sun rootkit
Taskigt	SK 1.3a	ASMD	Advanced Rootkit	Darkside 0.2.3
Knark 0.59	Flea	Dica	t0rn	lrk5
Adore	Ohara	TK 6.66		

e.g. MD5, normalize all the hexadecimal data and partition them into 2-D dataset, acting as the training self dataset. Here each item of the 2-D dataset denotes the coordinate of a point.

As to the testing dataset, we examined eighteen intrusion tools (table 1) designed to be run on compromised systems. All were downloaded from public websites, most of them from Packet Storm [15]. Twelve of the tools operate by running various binaries on the host system and overwriting existing binaries to continue gaining control. The other six insert code into the operating system kernel.

4.2 Fitting Tests

There are some key factors in the SSA model: length of abnormal storage activity, R, which is often a fixed value; length of antibody item, N; initial number of antibody, M, length of detecting window, W, sliding speed of detection window, T; detection rate, DR. We carried out the fitting test 1000 times for each parameter combination, using 10 sets of antigen data. The fitting results are shown in Table 2.

From Table 2, we see that the larger population the higher detection rate, because the population size affects the number of matching operation to a certain extent. Thus we set the parameter M to 600 in the following simulation.

Table 2. Fitting results of each SSA parameter combination

Antibody Data Group	R	N	M	W	T	Mean Detecting Rate
1	3	9	400	12	3	0.925626
2	3	9	500	12	4	0.910774
3	3	12	500	15	5	0.772282
4	3	9	500	9	3	0.914664
5	3	6	500	12	5	0.893253
6	3	9	500	12	3	0.939475
7	3	6	600	12	3	0.991019
8	3	12	500	12	4	0.812898
9	3	6	500	10	3	0.988115
10	3	9	600	12	3	0.955160

We can get the following judgments from Table 2:

1) the length of antibody item, N, has a marked effect on the detection rate;2) the detection rate validates the feasibility of AIS-based storage intrusion detection scheme; 3) both length (i.e. W) and sliding speed (i.e. T) of detection window have an obvious impact on the fitness of algorithm, 4) the population size of antibody, M, also affects the detection rate of SSA, the larger of population the higher detection rate.

4.3 Simulation Tests

There are two key metrics of the system performance, i.e. detection rate and false alarm rate. Given the true positive (TP), true negative (TN), false positive (FP) and false negative (FN), then the detection rate is equal to TP/(TP+FN), and the false alarm rate is calculated as FP/(FP+TN).With the method described in Section 4.1, we can construct a set of training dataset and synthesize a set of testing dataset. After using the V-detector algorithm, we got some simulation results as shown in Figure 4 and Figure5 respectively.

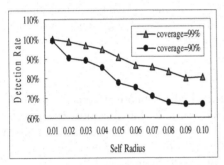 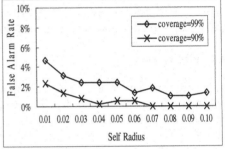

Fig. 4. Detection Rate   **Fig. 5.** False Alarm Rate

The simulation results show that:

1) the smaller self radius would result in the higher detection rate, as shown in Figure 4;
2) the proposed storage intrusion detection system can reach a rather high detection rate, e.g. approximate 90% when self radius is 0.05 and coverage is 99%;
3) the detector coverage can affect the accuracy of detection, as shown in Figure 4 and Figure 5;
4) the false alarm rate is generally less than 5%, see Figure 5.

SIDS have the same performance in isomerous architecture in terms of detection rate and false alarm rate. The most famous SIDS prototype is designed by CMU was presented in [16]. It describes a number of specific warning signs visible at the storage interface. Examination of 18 real intrusion tools (the same as we adopt) revealed that most (15) can be detected based on their changes to stored files. In one false alarm case was a configuration file on the system changed by a local user.

We can get the average score of detection rate and average false alarm rate.

Table 3.show that the proposed scheme SIDS(AIS) can reach higher detection rate and lower false alarm rate than SIDS(CMU). Only SIDS(CMU) administrator pre-informs the admin console of updated files before they are distributed to machines, the SIDS(CMU) can verify that desired updates happen correctly and the alert can be suppressed. On the other hand, two features combine to make it a well positioned platform for enhancing our SIDS(AIS) performance. Firstly, SIDS(AIS) periodically update the abnormal behavior antibody gene library, eliminating the useless antibody and adding the new antibody. Secondly, Alerts are generated and sent immediately when a detection rule is triggered in a SSA. The information of the alert is feeded back to each SSA in a network system. The weights of the rule will be updated.

Table 3. The evaluation of SIDS(AIS) and SIDS(CMU)

Prototype Evaluation	SIDS(AIS)	SIDS(CMU)
Detection rate	90% - 99%	83.3%
False alarm rate.	Less than 5%	Less than 5.5%

5 Discussion

As described in Section 3.3.4, three different weighting schemes have been used in the SSA model. The aim is to find a scoring system where the weights of illegal activity and the weights of legal activity can be separated easily with a threshold. Ideally, everything above this threshold would be illegal, everything below would be legal, but realistically there will be some outlying activities that get sorted into the wrong category.

Each of the three systems produces a very different pattern of scores when applied to the storage activity. Figures 6, 7 and 8 show these scores for one instance of the baseline test.

Figure 6 shows the pattern of the straight sum scoring system. In this graph, you can see that there is little clear division between the illegal and the legal activity. Note that there is a large spike of illegal and smaller spike of legal at the bottom end of the range – these represent activity for which few or no lymphocytes matched. The average best threshold is at score 2608, with an false alarm rate of 20.11%. So effectively the straight sum is not distinguishing any messages.

Figure 7 shows the pattern of the Bayesian scoring system. This bowl-shaped distribution shows mostly the illegal at the top of the score range, and mostly the legal at the bottom of the range. The average best threshold is at 0.62 and the average false alarm rate is 3.88%.

Figure 8 shows the pattern of the Weighted Average scoring system. The scores of the illegal and the legal are somewhat distinct, falling in two bell-curves that partially overlap at the edges. The average best threshold was 0.56, with an average false alarm rate of 4.26%.

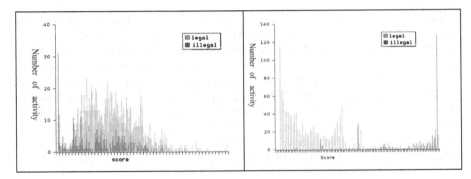

Fig. 6. Straight Sum Score Distribution   **Fig. 7.** Bayes Score Distribution

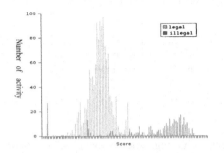

Table 4. Average threshold values

Scoring System	Threshold	false alarm rate
Straight Sum	2608	20.11%
Bayes	0.62	3.88%
Weighted Average	0.56	4.26

Fig. 8. Weighted Average scoring system

The SSA assigns scores to every storage activity, but it is the threshold that determines which scores result in an illegal classification and which results in a legal classification. As one would probably imagine, finding a good threshold for the straight sum scores was nearly impossible, as the illegal and the legal scores are thoroughly intermingled. As shown in Table 4, The Bayes scores and weighted average proved more effective in determining the two-class classification.

6 Conclusions

A storage IDS watches system activity from a new viewpoint, which immediately exposes some common intruder actions. The use of AIS in intrusion detection is an attractive idea for two reasons: first, the biological immune provides a high-level protection from pathogens; second, current security techniques cannot deal with the increasingly complex computer threat. It is hoped that biologically inspired approaches, e.g. AIS, will be able to meet such challenges.

This paper proposes a novel storage intrusion detection scheme to monitor the user access activities using the AIS technique. After analysis, the AIS model can be successfully adapted to the storage intrusion detection, and the detection system can recognize both the legal access behaviors and various anomaly behaviors. The simulation result reveals that the proposed scheme can reach relatively high detection rate and low false alarm rate, so the storage intrusion detection will strengthen the early warning of network storage system.

Acknowledgments. This paper is supported by the National Natural Science Foundation of China under the Grant NO. 60603074, and National 973 Great Research Project under Grant NO. 2004CB318203.

References

1. Axelsson, S.: Research in intrusion-detection systems: a survey. Technical report 98–17. Department of Computer Engineering, Chalmers University of Technology (December 1998)
2. NFR Security (August 2002), http://www.nfr.net/
3. Forrest, S., Hofmeyr, S.A., Somayaji, A., Longstaff, T.A.: A sense of self for UNIX processes. In: IEEE Symposium on Security and Privacy, pp. 120–128. IEEE, Los Alamitos (1996)
4. Scambray, J., McClure, S., Kurtz, G.: Hacking exposed: network security secrets & solutions. Osborne/McGraw- Hill, New York (2001)
5. Knight, T., Timmis, J.A.: A multi-layered immune inspired approach to data mining. In: Proceedings of the 4th International Conference on Recent Advances in Soft Computing, pp. 266–271 (2002)
6. Bradley, D., Tyrrell, A.: Immunotronics: Hardware fault tolerance inspired by the immune system. In: Miller, J.F., Thompson, A., Thompson, P., Fogarty, T.C. (eds.) ICES 2000. LNCS, vol. 1801, pp. 11–20. Springer, Heidelberg (2000)
7. Dasgupta, D., Yu, S., Majumdar, N.S.: MILA - Multilevel Immune Learning Algorithm. In: Cantú-Paz, E., Foster, J.A., Deb, K., Davis, L., Roy, R., O'Reilly, U.-M., Beyer, H.-G., Kendall, G., Wilson, S.W., Harman, M., Wegener, J., Dasgupta, D., Potter, M.A., Schultz, A., Dowsland, K.A., Jonoska, N., Miller, J., Standish, R.K. (eds.) GECCO 2003. LNCS, vol. 2723, pp. 183–194. Springer, Heidelberg (2003)
8. Chao, D., Forrest, S.: Information Immune Systems. In: Proceedings of the 1st International Conference on Artificial Immune Systems (ICARIS 2002), vol. 1, pp. 132–140 (2002)
9. Dasgupta, D., Forrest, S.: An Anomaly Detection Algorithm Inspired by the Immune System. In: Artificial Immune System and Their Applications, pp. 262–277. Springer, Heidelberg (1999)
10. Forrest, S., Hofmeyr, S.A., Somayaji, A.: Computer Immunology. Communications of the ACM 40(10), 88–96 (1997)
11. Forrest, S., Perelson, A.S., Allen, L., et al.: Self-Nonself Discrimination in a Computer. In: Proceedings of the 1994 IEEE Symposium on Security and Privacy. Los Alamitos, CA, pp. 202–212 (1994)
12. Stibor, T., Timmis, J., Eckert, C.: A Comparative Study of Real-Valued Negative Selection to Statistical Anomaly Detection Techniques. In: Jacob, C., Pilat, M.L., Bentley, P.J., Timmis, J.I. (eds.) ICARIS 2005. LNCS, vol. 3627, pp. 262–275. Springer, Heidelberg (2005)

13. Gonzalez, F.A.: A study of artificial immune systems applied to anomaly detection. PhD Dissertation, the University of Memphis (2003)
14. Huang, J.Z., Xie, C.S., Zhang, C.F., et al.: Security Framework for Networked Storage System based on Artificial Immune System. In: Proceeding of 5th MIPPR. Proc. SPIE, vol. 6790, 67903Q (2007)
15. Ko, C., Ruschitzka, M., Levitt, K.: Execution monitoring of security-critical programs in distributed systems: a specification-based approach. In: IEEE Symposium on Security and Privacy, pp. 175–187. IEEE, Los Alamitos (1997)
16. Adam, G., John, D.: Storage-based Intrusion Detection: Watching storage activity for suspicious behavior. In: Proceedings of the 12th USENIX Security Symposium, pp. 182–196 (2003)

A New Method for Optimal Configuration of Weapon System

Dechao Zhou, Shiyan Sun, and Qiang Wang

Electronic School, Naval University of Engineering, Wuhan,
430033 Hubei, China
ssy9751119@163.com

Abstract. This paper put forward a new method for Optimal Configuration of Weapon System (OCWS). It combines PROMETHEE II with Correspond analysis and projects the decision space on the two-dimensional principal component plane, in which R-type principal component refers to each attribute, and Q-type principal component means each alternative. This makes it possible to show the properties, such as comparability or otherness between different alternatives, the importance or conflict between different attributes and the sensitivity of compromised solution, more simply and conveniently, intuitionally. Therefore, it proves an excellent visual method for OCWS.

Keywords: Correspond analysis, PROMETHEE II, weapon system, Optimal Configuration.

1 Introduction

OCWS is to optimize the configuration schemes of the weapon system to get an optimal synthetic target. The variables of this kind are discrete which belong to classical Multi-Attribute Decision Making (MADA) problems. The main point of the problem is to order the alternatives and choose the best after estimation. Paper [2] has constructed a theoretical architecture for optimal configuration method of naval gun weapon system. In this paper, we combines PROMETHEE II [3] and Correspond analysis[4], projects the decision space on the two-dimensional principal component space, and optimizes the configuration schemes of the weapon system in a visual method. In this way we can make the properties of decision making systems simply and intuitionally shown and forms a visual method convenient for decision-maker to calculate and analysis.

2 Decision Matrix Standardization

PROMETHEE I, introduced by Brans in 1984, is a valued outranking method based on outranking relation. PROMETHEE I puts forward the conception of priority function to replace concordance test of ELECTRE, by which it overcomes the shortcomings of neglecting the gap information of parameter values and too many parameters to be set subjectively. PROMETHEE II is the improvement of PROMETHEE, while

Z. Cai et al. (Eds.): ISICA 2009, LNCS 5821, pp. 487–493, 2009.

PROMETHEE I can only get the partial sequence of the alternatives set. And PRO-METHEE II defines "net flow" to get the full sequence of the alternatives set.

Let alternatives set $X = \{x_1, x_2, \cdots, x_m\}$,attribute vector Y_i of alternative x_i , and $Y_i = \{ y_{i1}, \ldots, y_{in} \}$,define f_j as target function, $y_{ij} = f_j (x_i)$,the attribute value of each alternative can be displayed as a table (or to say "decision matrix").Define $w = (w_1, \cdots w_j, \cdots, w_n)$ as the weight matrix of attributes. Defines $p_j(x_i, x_k)$ as attribute indices of x_i relative to x_k , $0 \le p_j(x_i, x_k) \le 1$ .From $p_j(x_i, x_k)$ we can get priority index of x_i relative to x_k ,

$$\pi(x_i, x_k) = \frac{\sum\limits_{j=1}^{n} w_j p_j(x_i, x_k)}{\sum\limits_{j=1}^{n} w_j} \qquad (1)$$

Define the in-flow and out-flow of each alternative as:

$$\begin{aligned} \phi^+(x_i) &= \sum_{x \in X} \pi(x_i, x) \\ \phi^-(x_i) &= \sum_{x \in X} \pi(x, x_i) \end{aligned} \qquad (2)$$

Define net-flow as:

$$\phi(x_i) = \phi^+(x_i) - \phi^-(x_i) \qquad (3)$$

PROMETHEE I sorts the alternatives set according to the value of $\phi(x_i)$.
Here we define:

$$\phi_j(x_i) = \frac{1}{n-1} \sum_{x \in X} \{ p_j(x_i, x) - p_j(x, x_i) \} \qquad (4)$$

As we know:

$$-1 \le \phi_j(x) \le 1$$

$$\sum_{j=1}^{n} w_j \phi_j(x) = \phi(x) \qquad (5)$$

$$\sum_{i=1}^{m} \phi_j(x_i) = 0$$

Thus we can get standard decision matrix without dimensions

$$
\Phi = \begin{bmatrix}
\phi_1(x_1) & \cdots & \phi_j(x_1) & \cdots & \phi_n(x_1) \\
\phi_1(x_2) & & \phi_j(x_2) & & \phi_n(x_2) \\
\vdots & & & & \\
\phi_1(x_i) & \cdots & \phi_j(x_i) & \cdots & \phi_n(x_i) \\
\phi_1(x_m) & \cdots & \phi_j(x_m) & \cdots & \phi_n(x_m)
\end{bmatrix} = \begin{bmatrix}
x_1 \\
x_2 \\
\vdots \\
x_i \\
\vdots \\
x_m
\end{bmatrix}
\tag{6}
$$

$x_1, x_2 \ldots, x_i, \ldots, x_m$ are alternative points of alternatives set on the decision space R^n.

3 A New Method for OCWS

There have been many discussions on MADM analysis with the method of statistic multivariate analysis [5-6]. This method has strong visual abilities, but hasn't been applied to MADM or OCWS domestically. This paper puts forward a visual way to solve such problems using Correspond analysis.

3.1 Correspond Analysis

Why didn't use main-element analysis in this paper? Because in practical problems, besides getting the main element (main-element of R-type) of variables (attributes), we also hope to get the main elements of samples (main-element of Q-type) considering samples (alternatives) as variables, that is to get the main elements both of variables and samples at the same time. The process of analyzing the main elements of variables and sampling correspondingly is called Correspond analysis.

As for standard Decision Matrix Φ, covariance of attributes is m-order matrix, covariance of alternatives is n-order matrix, the nonzero of the two covariance matrixes are different, to solve the problem, we transform Φ to Z, make ZZ^T and $Z^T Z$ have the same eigenvalues and their eigenvectors are closely related, so it is convenient to solve it. Main elements of R-type and Q-type of the same eigenvalues can be marked on the same axis. So with the distributing points map both of attribute and alternative marked on the same coordinate system, we can intuitively get the properties of each alternative, which is also the strongpoint and essence of.

3.2 Building Two-Dimensional Analysis Space

In Correspond analysis, if the main elements of attribute and alternative are get, matrix Z can be seen as original matrix, and then can mark the main elements of each attribute and alternatives on the same flat. For example, if main element of a certain attribute is u, v, main element of alternative must be u', v', so a plane right-angel reference frame can be built with u (superposed with u') as horizontal axis and v (superposed with v') as vertical axis.

3.3 Representation of Attribute

Representation of attribute is relative to main element analysis of R-type. Let $A = ZZ^T$, and row element of A is sample, column element Of A is variable. Main element analysis of R-type is to analyze main element of A.

Suppose $(u'(j), v'(j))$ is the main element value of attribute j, Let $\hat{\gamma}_j = (u'(j), v'(j)) = (u'_j, v'_j)$.

(1) Length of $\hat{\gamma}_j$, $\|\hat{\gamma}_j\| = (u'(j), v'(j))$, reflect the importance degree of attribute j on alternative evaluation. The longer of $\hat{\gamma}_j$, the more importance of attribute j is, vice versa.

(2) Angels among $\hat{\gamma}_j$ reflect the conflict degree among attributes. The more degree of the angel, the more conflict there is, vice versa.

(3) Weight Vector:

$$w = \sum_{j=1}^{n} w_j e_j = (w_1, \cdots w_j, \cdots, w_n) \tag{7}$$

Related unit vector:

$$e = \frac{1}{\sqrt{\sum_{j=1}^{n} w_j^2}} \sum_{j=1}^{n} w_j e_j \tag{8}$$

Define decision axis of PROMETHEE II as:

$$\hat{\pi} = \frac{1}{\sqrt{\sum_{j=1}^{n} w_j^2}} \sum_{j=1}^{n} w_j \hat{\gamma}_j \tag{9}$$

$\hat{\pi}$ is the projection of e on plane (u, v), the angel between $\hat{\pi}$ and $\hat{\gamma}_j$ indicates whether attribute j is of the same direction with "net flow".

3.4 Representation of Alternative

Representation of alternative is relative to main element analysis of Q-type. Let $B = Z^T Z$, and row element of B is alternative, column element of B is attributive. Main element analysis Q-type is to analyze main element of B.

Put the attribute values of alternative i into u and v, get two main element value (u_i, v_i). Then let $\hat{x} = (u_i, v_i)$. $\hat{x}_r$ is close to $\hat{x}_s$ in distance on (u, v), which indicates each branch of alternative x_r and x_s is close in value on matrix Φ an is of little difference on general evaluation. $\hat{x}_i$ is close to $\hat{\gamma}_j$ indicate x_i is of better efficiency value on attribute j.

4   A Case on Naval Gun Weapon System

Take a certain naval gun weapon system as example, Let attribute set as

$$Y = \{y_1, y_2, \cdots, y_6\} \tag{10}$$

y_1 —efficiency attribute, y_2 —cost attribute, y_3 —risk attribute, y_4 —applicability attribute; y_5 —compatibility attribute; y_6 —life force attribute. Weight vector $w = (w_1, w_2, \cdots, w_6)$, $w_k (k = 1,2,\cdots,6)$ is the weight of attribute k, Let $w_k = 1/6$. Standardize each attribute to get Fig. 1:

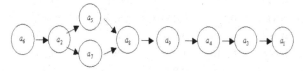

Fig. 1. Sorting Result

Use the method provided in this paper, the result denoted by figure is as follows:

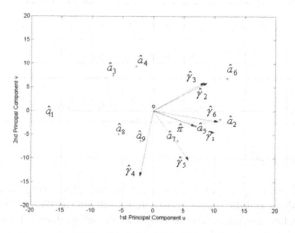

Fig. 2. Figure Show

In Fig.2, we can get these information: the length of each $\hat{\gamma}_j$ is quite near, indicating the importance of each attribute is quite the same; the degree of the angle between $\hat{\gamma}_2$ and $\hat{\gamma}_3$ is small, indicating the conflict between attributes of cost (y2) and risk (y3) is not big, while the degree of the angles between $\hat{\gamma}_2$, $\hat{\gamma}_3$ and $\hat{\gamma}_4$ is large, indicating the conflict between attributes of (y_2, y_3) and (y_4) is big; $\hat{a}_3, \hat{a}_4$ and $\hat{a}_1$ have a long distance away the (u,v), indicating alternatives x_3, x_4 and x_1 are bad and should dropped; $\hat{a}_5$ is near to original point and be of the same direction of decision axis, indicating x_5 is the best alternative. In a word, the visual method put forward by this paper have quite the same result with PROMETHEE II, but it can describe the practical problem more comprehensively and make it easy to understand.

Standardize each attribute to get these values in Table 1.

Table 1. Standardized Attribute Value

				attribute value		
alternative	Efficiency y_1	Cost y_2	Risk y_3	applicability y_4	compatibility y_5	life force y_6
	0.4	0.14	0.1	0.13	0.08	0.15
1	0.39	0.579	0.667	0.699	0.100	0.230
2	0.948	0.691	0.734	0.601	0.931	1.000
3	0.647	0.757	0.779	0.526	0.132	0.331
4	0.285	0.844	0.838	0.429	0.200	0.500
5	0.995	0.918	1.000	0.988	0.268	0.669
6	1.000	1.000	0.895	0.100	0.400	0.900
7	0.929	0.969	0.703	0.712	0.880	0.904
8	0.81	0.644	0.705	0.677	0.924	0.39
9	0.928	0.630	0.706	0.674	1.000	0.45

Sort out alternative set with ROMETHEE II, and get these results in Table 2.

Table 2. Results

	1	2	3	4	5	6	7	8	9
Φ	-5.667	3.667	-3.333	-2.333	4.000	2.667	2.667	1.333	-0.333

5 Conclusions

The method that proposed in this paper can intuitively denote the importance degree of each attribute and the relative position of each alternative, making it convenient to select the better alternative and to drop the worse, so decision makers can comprehend the optimization problem more deeply. However, this method belongs to sample principal component analysis. So, it's more applicable to those problems with relatively larger alternatives set, otherwise selecting or dropping a alternative will exert great influence on the analysis result.

References

1. Qiu, Z.M.: Analysis On Naval Gun Weapon System. National Defense Industry Press, Beijing (1999)
2. Qiu, Z.M.: On Criteria and attribute sets of Naval Gun Weapon System configuration. Water Weapons 3, 46–51 (2002)

3. Brans, J.P., Vincke, Ph., Mareschal, B.: How to select and rank projects: The PROME-THEE Method. European Journal of Operational Research 26, 228–238 (1986)
4. Yuan, Z.F., Zhou, J.Y.: Statistic Multivariate Analysis. Science Press, Beijing (1982)
5. OR research group: Static Theory and Method of Multi-Criteriav Comprehensive Evaluation. Zhengzhou Aviation Industry Management Transaction 6, 1–2 (1991)
6. Wen, X., Xu, J.C.: Multi-Criteria Comprehensive Evaluation Using Multianalysis. Zhengzhou Aviation Industry Management Transaction 3, 61–65 (1991)

A Secure Routing Algorithm for MANET

Shudong Shi

College of Computer Science & Technology, Hubei Normal University
Huangshi, Hubei, China, 435002
shudshi@163.com

Abstract. Mobile ad hoc networking (MANET) bring great challenges in security due to its high dynamics, link vulnerability and complete decentralization. With routing being a critical aspect for MANETs, existing routing protocols however are not sufficient for security requirements. In this paper, we present a route discovery algorithm that mitigates the detrimental effects of malicious behavior, as to provide correct connectivity information. Our algorithm guarantees that fabricated, compromised, or replayed route replies would either be rejected or never reach back the querying node. Furthermore, the algorithm responsiveness is safeguarded under different types of attacks that exploit the routing algorithm itself. The sole requirement of the proposed scheme is the existence of a security association between the node initiating the query and the sought destination. Specifically, no assumption is made regarding the intermediate nodes, which may exhibit arbitrary and malicious behavior. The scheme is robust in the presence of a number of non-colluding nodes, and provides accurate routing information in a timely manner.

Keywords: security, Routing Algorithms, Mobile Ad hoc Networks.

1 Introduction

Ad hoc networks are a new paradigm of wireless communication for mobile nodes. Mobile ad hoc networking (MANET) has become an exciting and important technology in recent years because of the rapid proliferation of wireless devices. Providing adequate security measures for MANET is a challenging task. First, wireless communications are easy to intercept and difficult to contain. Next to this it is easy to actively insert or modify wireless messages. This means that unprotected wireless networks are open to a wide range of attacks, including node impersonation, message injection, loss of confidentiality, etc. Secondly, in many situations the nodes may be left unattended in a hostile environment. This enables adversaries to capture them and physically attack them. Proper precautions (tamper resistance) are required to prevent attackers from extracting secret information from them. Even with these precautions, we cannot exclude that a fraction of the nodes may become compromised. This enables attacks launched from within the network. Thirdly, the dynamic topology and the absence of a supporting infrastructure renders most of the existing cryptographic algorithms useless as they were not developed for this dynamic environment. Any security solution with a static configuration would not suffice. Security mechanisms

Z. Cai et al. (Eds.): ISICA 2009, LNCS 5821, pp. 494–499, 2009.

should be able to adapt on-the-fly to these changes in topology. Fourthly, many wireless nodes will have a limited energy resource (battery, solar panel, etc.). This is particularly true in the case of ad hoc sensor networks. Security solutions should be designed with this limited energy budget in mind. Finally, an ad hoc network may consist of thousands of nodes. Security mechanisms should be scalable to handle such a large network.

The widely accepted technique in the MANET context of route discovery based on broadcasting query packets is the basis of our algorithm. More specifically, as query packets traverse the network, the relaying intermediate nodes append their identifier (e.g., IP address) in the query packet header. When one or more queries arrive at the sought destination, replies that contain the accumulated routes are returned to the querying node; the source then may use one or more of these routes to forward its data. Reliance on this basic route query broadcasting mechanism allows our proposed here Secure Routing Protocol (SRP) to be applied as an extension of a multitude of existing routing algorithms. In particular, the Dynamic Source Routing (DSR) [1] and the IERP [2] of the Zone Routing Protocol (ZRP) [3] framework are two algorithms that can be extended in a natural way to incorporate SRP. Furthermore, other protocols such as ABR [4] for example, could be combined with SRP with minimal modifications to achieve the security goals of the SRP protocol.

2 Proof of the Protocol Correctness with BAN Logic

The basic notation used below is provided here, as in [5,6]. X and Y are formulas, P and Q are principals, K is a shared secret and C is a statement.

- $P \triangleleft X$: P is told formula X.
- $P \ni X$: P possesses or is capable of possessing formula X.
- $P \mid\sim X$: P once conveyed formula X.
- $P \models\# (X)$: P believes or is entitled to believe that formula X is fresh.
- $P \models\varphi (X)$: P believes or is entitled to believe that formula X is recognizable, that is, P has certain expectations about the contents of X before actually receiving it.
- $P \models P \overset{k}{\longleftrightarrow} Q$: P believes or is entitled to believe that K is a suitable secret for P and Q.
- (X,Y): conjunction of two formulas; it is treated as a set with properties of associativity and commutativity.
- $*X$: Not-originated-here formula property. If P is told X (see below), it can distinguish it did not previously convey X in the current run..
- $H(X)$: a one-way function of X
- C_1, C_2: conjunction of two statements, treated as a set with properties of associativity and commutativity.
- $P \models C$: P believes or is entitled to believe that statement C holds.
- The horizontal line separating two statements or conjunctions of statements signifies that the upper statement implies the lower one.

For example,

$$P \overline{\lhd} (X,Y) \mathbin{|}\hspace{-0.2em}\sim P \overline{\lhd} X$$

_reads: P being told a formula implies P being told each of the formula's concatenated components.

The analysis follows the methodology of [6]. Based on a set of assumptions, the current beliefs of the participating principals are derived from their initial beliefs and possessions. The algorithm is abstracted as the exchange of two messages, a route request and a route reply. The messages are transmitted over a public channel; i.e., a sequence of intermediate nodes that may cause any impairment. The idealized form (i.e., the algorithm with parts of the messages that do not contribute to the participants' beliefs omitted) is shown in Fig. 1.

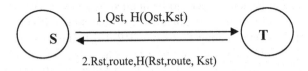

Fig. 1. Idealized SRP: the protocol viewed as an exchange of two messages, without the fields that do not contribute to the participants' beliefs

Qst is the route request and H is the Message Authentication Code (MAC) function. The relevant fields of Qst are the sequence number Qseq, and the source and destination node addresses. As for the route reply, denoted as Rst, the Qseq field binds Rab to the corresponding Qst, and route is the actual route along which T returns the reply.

The initial assumptions are:

(i) $S \ni Kst, S \models S \xleftrightarrow{\ Kst\ } T$,
    $S \ni Nst, S \models \#(Nst)$.

The sender possesses the shared key and it believes it is used for mutual proofs of identity between S and T. It possesses Nst, the newly generated sequence number, and believes that Nst has not been used before.

(ii) $T \ni Kst, T \models S \xleftrightarrow{\ Kst\ } T, T \ni N^p_{st}$

The receiver also trusts the shared secret, possesses the set of sequence numbers seen in the past and believes they were once uttered by S ($T \overline{\lhd} N^p_{st}, T \models S \mathbin{|}\hspace{-0.2em}\sim N^p_{st}$). If the message (1) is the first transmission from S to T (within the lifetime of the SA) the set of past sequence numbers is merely the Q_{seq} initialized at the SA establishment. Otherwise, the SA state justifies such a belief, which is our basis hypothesis. Moreover, S and T believe they are able to recognize Q_{ST} and R_{ST}, respectively.

(iii) $S \models *(R_{ST}, H(R_{ST}, K_{ST}))$,
    $T \models *(Q_{ST}, H(Q_{ST}, K_{ST}))$

For message (1), we have:

(iv) $T \vartriangleleft^{\overline{}} *(Q_{ST}, H(Q_{ST}, K_{ST})) \vdash$

$\quad T \vartriangleleft^{\overline{}} (Q_{ST}, H(Q_{ST}, K_{ST}))$

and

$\quad T \vartriangleleft^{\overline{}} (Q_{ST}, H(Q_{ST}, K_{ST})) \vdash$

$\quad T \ni (Q_{ST}, H(Q_{ST}, K_{ST}))$

i.e., T sees a packet with the "not-originate-here" property, that is, it can distinguish, acting as a receiver, whether it has previously transmitted the packet in the current run.

(v) $T \ni (Q_{ST}, H(Q_{ST}, K_{ST})) \vdash$

$\quad T \ni Q_{ST}, T \ni H(Q_{ST}, K_{ST})$

$\quad T \ni (Q_{Seq}, Q_{id}) \vdash T \ni Q_{seq}$

Similarly to (v), we infer that T possesses the rest of the fields of Qst. From (i) and (v), We get:

(vi) $T \models \#(Q_{seq})$,

(vii) $T \vartriangleleft^{\overline{}} H(Q_{ST}, K_{ST}), T \ni (Q_{ST}, K_{ST}),$

$\quad T \models S \xleftrightarrow{K_{st}} T, T \models \#(Q_{st}, K_{st})) \vdash$

$\quad T \models S \mid \sim (Q_{st}, K_{st}), T \models S \mid \sim H(Q_{st}, K_{st})$

This signifies the belief that both the packet payload and the MAC originate from S. Along with freshness (vi), we have the sought goal satisfied. We should note that the last inference does not imply that the sender revealed the shared key. In fact, the confirmation is independent of this issue. Moreover, we have assumed that none of the two principals compromises the shared secret by exposing it.

Similarly, for message (2), we get:

(viii) $S \ni (Rst, H(Rst, Kst)) \vdash$

$\quad S \ni Rst, S \ni H(Rst, Kst))$

$\quad S \ni (Qseq, Qid, route) \vdash S \ni Qseq$

(ix) $S \models \#(Qseq) \vdash S \models \#(Qseq, route)$

And finally

(x) $S \vartriangleleft^{\overline{}} H(R_{ST}, K_{ST}), S \ni (R_{ST}, K_{ST}),$

$\quad S \models S \xleftrightarrow{K_{st}} T, S \models \#(Rst, Kst)) \vdash$

$\quad S \models T \mid \sim (Rst, Kst), S \models T \mid \sim H(Rst, Kst)$

Accordingly, S believes that the entire route reply datagram originates from T and is fresh and, trivially, that T has constructed route, i.e., the source-route of the reply packet. The assumption of the non-colluding nodes implies that there is no alternative way for the route reply to arrive, but the one defined in the source-route. Moreover, the reply is the path along which the route request had propagated, which implies that the reply content had not been manipulated prior to its construction by T. Thus, its arrival at S implies that the corresponding connectivity information is correct.

By updating the state at both ends, we can repeat the above reasoning to conclude that, if the source increments Qseq and does not repeat it within the lifetime of a SA, the sought goals are achieved, including the preservation of message integrity. In a very similar manner, this conclusion can be reached for the case of replies generated by intermediate nodes, under the assumption that the route suffix will be correct.

3 Discussion

An interesting characteristic of the proposed algorithm is that it is essentially immune to IP spoofing. Any intermediate node may use any arbitrary IP address when queried but, as shown by the previous discussion, the algorithm is capable of capturing the correct and current connectivity snapshot. However, in practice, neighbor discovery that maintains information on the binding of the Medium Access Control and IP addresses of nodes can strengthen the algorithm.

Nevertheless, the issue of fair utilization of the network resources and possible ways to dismay nodes from broadcasting at the highest possible rate is beyond the scope of the security of routing algorithms. For example, a malicious node could simply use IP broadcast instead of the route discovery querying mechanism. It is important though to defend nodes from attacks that exploit the algorithm itself, and SRP provides protection against clogging DoS attacks. The replay protection at the end nodes, the use of the computationally inexpensive HMAC and the avoidance, in general, of any cryptographic validation by intermediate nodes are such features. These features are complemented by the scheme that regulates the propagation of queries. As a thought for future work, it would be interesting to investigate whether the use of soft state at intermediate nodes would further contribute to the algorithm efficiency in a non-benign environment.

Moreover, it is important that the application of SRP does not severely affect the efficiency of the basis algorithm under benign conditions. On one hand, in the same MANET subnet, nodes that implement SRP can co-exist with nodes that do not. In the absence of adversaries, the only overhead would be imposed on the nodes executing SRP. On the other hand, possible optimizations incorporated into the basics algorithm can retain the effectiveness of the algorithm in conjunction with SRP; an example is route shortening [1] that can be applied during the query propagation phase, based on knowledge of an active route. Finally, the fixed transmission overhead of 24 (or 27) bytes per control packet becomes less significant as wireless network speeds increase to above the current state-of-the-art of 11Mbps.

As shown above, the basic form of SRP that requires the propagation of queries to the destination is robust to malicious behavior. It is noteworthy that this statement remains true, in the absence of collusion, even if the destination node attempted to provide false replies. On the other hand, the provision of replies from intermediate nodes can achieve the same level of assurance only if a trusted node is assumed to provide a correct route segment.

4 Conclusions

In this paper, we proposed an efficient secure routing algorithm for mobile ad hoc networks that guarantees the discovery of correct connectivity information over an unknown network, in the presence of malicious nodes. The algorithm introduces a set of features, such as the requirement that the query verifiably arrives at the destination, the explicit binding of network and routing layer functionality, the consequent verifiable return of the query response over the reverse of the query propagation route, the acceptance of route error messages only when generated by nodes on the actual route, the query/reply identification by a dual identifier, the replay protection of the source and destination nodes and the regulation of the query propagation.

The resultant algorithm is capable of operating without the existence of an on-line certification authority or the complete knowledge of keys of all network nodes. Its sole requirement is that any two nodes that wish to communicate securely can simply establish a priori a shared secret, to be used by their routing algorithm modules. Moreover, the correctness of the algorithm is retained irrespective of any permanent binding of nodes to IP addresses, a feature of increased importance for the open, dynamic, and cooperative MANET environments.

Acknowledgements

This paper is supported by the Hubei Provincial Natural Science Foundation of China under Grant No.2006ABA056; the importance project fund of the education department of Hubei Province, China under Grant No. D20092203; the plan for Scientific and technological innovation team of excellent young and middle- aged in institute of high learning of Hubei province in P.R. China under Grant No. T200806.

References

[1] Johnson, D.B., et al.: The Dynamic Source Routing Protocol for Mobile Ad Hoc Networks, Internet Draft, March 2. IETF MANET Working Group (2001)
[2] Haas, Z.J., Perlman, M., Samar, P.: The Interzone Routing Protocol (IERP) for Ad Hoc Networks, June 1. IETF MANET Working Group (2001), draft-ietf-manetzone-ierp-01.txt
[3] Haas, Z.J., Perlman, M.: The Performance of Query Control Schemes of the Zone Routing Protocol. IEEE/ACM Transactions on Networking 9(4), 427–438 (2001)
[4] Toh, C.K.: Associativity-Based Routing for Ad-Hoc Mobile Networks. Wireless Personal Communications 4(2), 1–36 (2007)
[5] Gong, L., Needham, R., Yahalom, R.: Reasoning about Belief in Cryptographic Protocols. In: Proceedings of the 2000 IEEE Symposium on Research in Security and Privacy, pp. 234–248. IEEE Computer Society Press, Los Alamitos (2000)
[6] Burrows, M., Abadi, M., Needham, R.: A Logic of Authentication. In: Proceedings of the 12th ACM Symposium on Operating Systems Principles, Arizona (December 2006); ACM Operating System Review 23(5), 1-13 (December 2006); Full version: DEC SRC Report No 39, CA (February 2006)

Detection and Defense of Identity Attacks in P2P Network

Chuiwei Lu[*]

Computer School, HuangShi Institute of Technology
435003 HuangShi, China
Lcwzm@mail.hust.edu.cn

Abstract. Opening property of P2P network allows nodes to freely join P2P network and to create identity at no cost. Utilizing the loopholes, malicious nodes can create a number of identities in a short time, which will exhaust the identifiers resources and damage the operation of P2P network. The paper proposes a conundrum verification scheme which enables the node to join P2P network and creates identity more difficult. Moreover, it also puts forward a detection and elimination scheme, which can help P2P network to detect identity attackers promptly and eliminate them. Simulation experiments demonstrate that with the combination of the two schemes, P2P network can prevent identity attack effectively.

Keywords: P2P, Identify attack, Network security, Intrusion detection.

1 Introduction

P2P network is an application-level network connecting any number of nodes, and every P2P node represents an instance of an overlay participant. Each P2P node is randomly assigned an Id uniformly in a large identifier space. Sharing data is assigned unique identifiers called keys from the same space. If the local node has no direct physical knowledge of remote nodes, it perceives them only as informational abstractions that we call *identities*. The system must ensure that distinct identities refer to distinct nodes, otherwise, when the local node selects a subset of identities to redundantly perform a remote operation, it can be duped into selecting a single remote node multiple times, thereby defeating the redundancy. The attacks which disrupt the performance of P2P network through forging multiple identities is called as identify attack.

The Identity attack is general in overlay network, however, since the attack can be launched by a single malicious node, and affects routing, lookup or store operation. The famous identity attacks are *Sybil* attack [1] and *Eclipse* attack [2] In the Sybil attack, a malicious node can generates a large number of identities and uses them together to disrupt normal operation. In the Eclipse attack, a malicious node tries to organize to disproportionately populate routing tables in target nodes to disrupt routing work of P2P network. The two attacks all can intercept route request and result in the occurrence of identity attack. Reference [3] proposed an Identity Theft Protection

---

[*] Supported by Science Fund of Education Committee of Hubei Province, No: B20083004.

Z. Cai et al. (Eds.): ISICA 2009, LNCS 5821, pp. 500–507, 2009.

mechanism in Structured Overlays, in which a client node finds self-certifying proofs to verify the existence of their desired destinations. Nodes periodically push signed proofs of their existence out to a random subset of network nodes. Reference [4] an identifier authentication mechanism called *random visitor*, in which a randomly chosen delegate carries some credential that can prove sincerity, ownership, and moderate exclusiveness of a node. Reference [5] proposed a self-registration scheme which binds identifier to the IP address. If a node is trying to join the network, then it should verify its identity to multiple nodes. Singh et al. [6] proposed bounding indegree and outdegree of P2P node within threshold. Because the identity attack will cause the in or out degree relatively higher than the ordinary nodes, nodes should select their neighbor such that the node degree do not exceed the threshold.

In this paper, we proposed a conundrum verification scheme, which raise the difficulty of joining P2P network and creation of node identity for every node. Furthermore, we also presented a detection and elimination scheme, which can find identify attackers in due time and eliminate them. Simultaneously using the two schemes in P2P safety strategy, P2P network can obtain well defense effect to identity attack, which has been verified in latter experiments.

2 The Framework

Our research is based on structured P2P network with hiberarchy. The entire P2P network is divided up many regions, and a super node manages a region which includes a lot of guard nodes and popular nodes. The nodes with powerful performance and long online time are selected as super nodes or spare super nodes of current region. When current super node is failed or leave the P2P network, a spare super node will be selected as new super node in due time, which is propitious to the stability of P2P network. A popular node can become guard node based on its voluntary joining. The super node collects the suspicious message in its region and launch proper measurements through periodically communicating with its guard nodes. This monitor scheme is not only effective to identify attack, but also effective to other threats, such as worm propagation, DDos attack and so on. Our schemes are composed of two part content shown as follow.

1) That new node join the P2P network must pay a certain price, for example, to solve a mathematical problem, which can effectively inhibit the speed of forging identifiers of malicious node, and gain more time for system detection and defense.

2) Super node utilizes guard nodes to obtain the number of identifiers of normal nodes and to verify the validity of these identifiers. Lastly, super node will judge whether the detected node is an identity attacker based on the statistics result. If abnormal events have been found, the super node would send alarms to all the nodes in its region and impose the suspicious node exit the P2P network.

3 Conundrum Verification to New Node and New Identify

Due to a node needn't pay any price when it join P2P network and create identity. Utilizing the loopholes, the attackers can join the P2P network at discretion and easily create a large amount of identities in short time, which will deplete the resources such as identifier address space and network connections. Consequently, the stability and efficiency of P2P network is crippled seriously. Therefore, in our detection and defense scheme, the primary strategy is to ask for a node must pay a certain cost when it join P2P network or create a new identity, which can effectively inhibit the speed of forging identifiers of malicious node in initial phrase. For example, when applying for a QQ account, users must fill a randomly generated string, know as verification code. The code must be artificially filled, which can prevent attackers apply for a large number of QQ account by automatic-fill-machine software. Based on the elicitation of the example, we can introduce analogous mechanism when nodes join the P2P network or create identities. The mechanism will make malicious nodes pay tremendous cost if they launch identify attack, and effectively inhibit the speed of forging identities at the beginning. Our detail scheme is: when a node will join or create identifier, super nodes or guard nodes produce a random conundrum to it. Only after the node give the correct answer and pass the verification, its application would be accepted by P2P network. Our scheme keeps to the following principles.

1) System needn't pay too much cost to create a conundrum and verify its results.

2) To solve the conundrum must pay biggish cost, but the cost can be adjusted by P2P system.

3) The solution of conundrum only can be finished by software.

4) The node can't predict or conjecture the conundrum and its answer.

5) Each new node will receive a same type of conundrum, but its content is random and different.

6) That a large number of nodes work together is also no help to solve the conundrum, which means there isn't parallelism in the solution scheme of the conundrum.

7) Whenever the node adds a new identifier, it must solve a new conundrum.

There are many schemes[7,8] satisfy above-mentioned principle. In this paper, taking the advantage of these schemes and improving them, we propose a new scheme which based on the Security Hash Algorithm *SHA-1*.The conundrum produced by our scheme is that require node to decrypt Hash value with an appointed size. Due to Hash function is a single-direction and single-mapping encryption function, to resolve the conundrum can but use exhaustion method, which make the node pay biggish cost. However, it is easily to verify the correctness of answer for the P2P system. Those properties are well satisfied to our requirement.

When a node joins P2P network or creates a new identity, P2P system will send it a randomly-generated big integer and a difficulty modulus d. The node must calculate the conundrum with following formula.

$$SHA-1\big((I+ID)\bmod 2 + R\big) = \underbrace{000\cdots00}_{d\ bits}\ M \tag{1}$$

Where *ID* denote the node's identifier (represent with binary), *R* denote the answer need to solve, *M* is a random binary integer. *d* denote the number of prefix 0 in Hash value which needs to calculate, the number indicate the difficulty degree to solve the conundrum. After R has been calculated, it and 000...000M will be together sent back to the node that gives the conundrum. Based on the two parameters, P2P network can easily judge the correctness of answer. The detail algorithm of security verification is shown as follow.

```
1) IF node a asks for joining P2P Network or
creating a new identifier.
2) Then Super node or guard node generate a big
integer I(I>107) and a difficulty modulus d
(1≤d≤160), and send them to node a.
3)a calculates SHA-1((I+ID) mod 2+R) with exhaustion
method, until the number of prefix 0 in Hash value
equal d, at the same time, R is numerated.
4) Node a send R and 000...000M together back to the
node that gives the conundrum.
5) IF the answer is right, the verification is
passed, super node accepts all the requests of a
6) Else super node will reject all the requests of a
```

The value of difficulty modulus d can be set according to actual needs. d has an enormous impact on the speed of solving conundrum. When the number of prefix 0 of $SHA\text{-}1((I+ID)\ mod\ 2+R)$ achieve to d, R is numerated, and the conundrum is also solved. The relationship between calculation times x and d is approximate to an exponential function. If the Hash result is composed of n binary digits, its sample space size is 2^n. We assume that the probability of numerating correct R equal 0.9 through only calculating half sample space, then, the relationship between x and d could be approximately expressed by following formula.

$$\left(1 - \frac{2^{n-d}}{2^{n-1}}\right)^x = 0.9 \tag{2}$$

Transforming formula 2, we can get a more explicit formula shown as follow

$$x = \frac{\lg 0.9}{\lg(1 - 2^{1-d})} \tag{3}$$

As shown in the Formula 3, with the increase of d, the calculation times x will increase in an enormous speed, which mean that calculation difficulty is also rapidly increase. When $d = 27$, calculation times x equal 7070624. If $d = 160$, i.e. the maximum encryption length of $SHA\text{-}1$ algorithm, that is equivalent to completely decrypt $SHA\text{-}1$ algorithm, and it is impossible to realize under current computer level and decryption algorithm. Therefore, through setting an appropriate difficulty modulus d, it is not only greatly raise the cost of creating a large numbers of identifiers in a short time, which can effectively inhibit the spread of identity attack, but also enable most nodes don't consume too many resources to calculate answer.

4 Detection and Elimination to Identity Attacker

After new node has joined P2P network, it have chance to forge many identifiers. Therefore, a periodical detection and elimination mechanism must be established to deal with the attack. Our detection method of identity attack is based on cryptography [9]. When super node S wants to verify the authenticity of identifier T_{id} of goal node T, it will generate a function V_s filled with identity and IP address of S and T. Then S send V_s to a random guard node which fulfill the final identity verification in indirectly. To effectively verify identity of node, we adopt the method that binds identity with its IP address. Through virtual server technology in P2P network that make a physical node can own several identities, we set a threshold δ for number of identity. The node that own the identities exceed the δ is regard as identity attack node.

$$V_s = Enc\left(R_s, R_T, S_{id} - IP_s, T_{id} - IP_T \mid K_s\right) \qquad (4)$$

Where R_s and R_T are random character string generated by node S and node T respectively; S_{id}–IP_s and T_{id}–IP_T are the identity–IP address pair of S and T respectively; K_s is an IBC related credential used by IBC mechanism [10], and it is produced by node T and back to node S with encrypting. Enc is the abbreviation of encrypting function.

Where V_s is a encrypted value of R_s, R_T and S_{id}–IP_s, T_{id}–IP_T, and the encrypted key is concatenated value saf. In our scheme, only node T knows the really value of R_s limited by the IBC authentication mechanism. V_s is delivered to detected node T by a random guard node such as g, and node T must do some manipulation to V_s to prove his legal identity. When node T receives V_s, it should respond within threshold time t_v. If node T fails to manipulate V_s or not respond in due time to the super node S, then the node T is regard as identity forger such as Sybil or Eclipse attack.

Due to the P2P network is a dynamic overlay network so that the identifier of each node or their IP address is often changes, in our scheme, we bind identity of node with its IP address, which construct an ID−IP pair that is used to present exclusive of node identity in P2P network. The ID−IP pair is also become an important parameter ID-P in our scheme. For a node T, this parameter is ID-P_T that is produced by following function.

$$ID - P_T = F_H\left(R_s, R_T, G_{id}, T_{id} - T_{ip}\right) \qquad (5)$$

In the formula 5, parameter ID-P_T is the globally unique identifier of node T; F_H is Hash function; R_s and R_T are random character string generated by node S and node T respectively; T_{id}–T_{ip} is the ID−IP pair of node T; G_{id} is the IP address of guard node that is used to detect node T.

When super node S is ready to verify the identifier of node T, it needs to verify ID-P_T and count the number of identifier of T through a random guard node G. Regarding guard node might fail or leave the network, we select three guard nodes to simultaneously execute the verification task. Follow algorithm show our verification scheme in detail.

1) S obtain the IP address of T based on ID_T
2) S send Query message Enc $(R_s, S_{id}-S_{ip}, T_{id} \mid K_s)$ to T
3) T create $ID-P_T=F_H(R_s, R_T, S_{id}, T_{id}-T_{ip} \mid K_T)$ and send it to S
4) S create key data: $V_s= Enc (R_s, R_T, S_{id}-IP_s, T_{id}-T_{ip} \mid K_s)$
5) S random select three guard nodes G_i, G_j, G_f from guard node Set, then signs the V_s with its ID-IP pair
6) S encrypt V_s by ID-IP pair of G_i, G_j, G_f respectively, and send the result to G_i, G_j, G_f respectively
7) G_i, G_j, G_f decrypt V_s with their identity respectively and verify the signature of S
8) **IF** signature verification is passed, G_i, G_j, G_f sign V_s with their ID-IP pair and encrypts it with ID_T, and send them to node T respectively
9) **Else** verify command is discarded and verification scheme terminate
10) T decrypt the three verification message and get V_s respectively to verify, and then make echo message $Enc (F_H (R_s+1, G_{id}, T_{id}-T_{ip}) \mid K_T)$ to S
11) So long as one echo message is received and pass the verification by S in due time, S will count the number i of ID with same IP address
12) **IF** $i <•$ **then** T is regard as a normal node
13) **Else** T is regard as "bad" node. S will reclaim its all forged IDs to impose T to leave P2P network, and broadcast its IP address in the region using identity attack alarm, which will prevent spread of identity attack

5 Simulation Experiments

Simulation experiments were carried out at a PC with P4 3.0 GHz and 2G memory. Operating System was Fedora Linux 9.0, and simulation software employed P2Psim3.5. The overall number of nodes is 10^5 and regions are 10^2. Each region had 100 guard nodes at the beginning.

We have designed two simulation experiments, both using Chord protocol. The first experiment simulates the quantity changes of overall forging identifiers after adopting the conundrum verification mechanism. As the Fig.1 show, in this experiment the proportion of malicious nodes are fixed at 15%. The second experiment simulate the quantity changes of overall identify attackers after adopting the detection and elimination mechanism. As the figure 2 shows, in this experiment the initial quantity of malicious nodes is 10^4.

As is Fig.1 shown, when not using the conundrum verification mechanism, the number of forging identifiers take on rapid growth trend with no holdback, which consume most of identifier space in short time. After adopting the conundrum verification mechanism, the number of forged identifiers take on slow growth trend, which mean that the mechanism has greatly raised the cost of forging identifiers and effectively inhibited the spread of the identify attack. Meanwhile, we also find

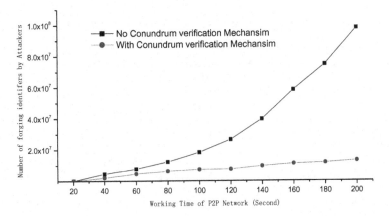

Fig. 1. Performance of conundrum verification mechanism

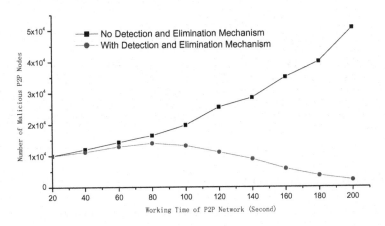

Fig. 2. Performance of detection and elimination mechanism

conundrum verification mechanism could not completely prevent the actions of forging identifiers. Because as long as there are time, malicious nodes could forge identifiers, but forging speed is very low. With the time increase, the accumulative quantity of forging identifiers is still enough to harm the work of P2P network.

As the Fig.2 shows, when not using the detection and elimination mechanism, the number of malicious nodes takes on rapid growth trend, and exceeds the number of normal nodes in short time, which seriously damage the work of P2P network. After using the detection and elimination mechanism, the number of malicious nodes takes on increase trend at beginning, subsequently, decline rapidly. This is because P2P network must cost some time to detect identify attacker. During this time the number of malicious nodes still has the opportunity to grow, but once P2P system finds the trace of identify attacker and execute elimination measures, more and more malicious nodes will be removed from the P2P network, so number of malicious rapidly decline in latter.

Through comprehensive analysis of two experiments, we find that only together using conundrum verification mechanism and detection and elimination mechanism, the P2P network can effectively defense and inhabit identify attack. There isn't good effect only to use one of the two mechanisms.

6 Conclusion

P2P systems often rely on redundancy to diminish their dependence on potentially malicious peers. If distinct identities for remote nodes are not established either by an explicit certification authority or by an implicit one, these systems are susceptible to identity attacks, in which a small number of nodes counterfeit multiple identities so as to compromise a disproportionate share of the system. The paper has proposed two schemes, conundrum verification scheme and detection and elimination scheme, to resist identify attack. Those schemes heavily raise the difficulty of joining P2P network and creating new identity, and enable P2P network easily detect and eliminate identify attackers. Simulation experiments also demonstrate: a combination of these two schemes is effective method to defense and inhabit identify attack.

References

1. Douceur, J.: The Sybil attack. In: Proc. of IPTPS, Cambridge, MA, USA, pp. 251–260 (2002)
2. Singh, A., et al.: Defending against eclipse attacks on overlay networks. In: Proc. SIGOPS, Leuven, Belgium (2004)
3. Ganesh, L., Zhao, B.Y.: Identity theft protection in structured overlays. In: Proc. of NPSec, Boston, MA (2005)
4. Gu, J., Nah, J., et al.: Random Visitor: A Defense Against Identity Attacks in P2P Overlay Networks. In: Lee, J.K., Yi, O., Yung, M. (eds.) WISA 2006. LNCS, vol. 4298, pp. 282–296. Springer, Heidelberg (2007)
5. Dinger, J., Hartenstein, H.: Defending the Sybil attack in p2p networks: Taxonomy, challenges, and a proposal for self-registration. In: Proc. of ARES, pp. 756–763 (2006)
6. Singh, A., Castro, M., et al.: Defending against eclipse attacks on overlay networks. In: Proc. of SIGOPS, Leuven, Belgium (2004)
7. Wang, P., et al.: Research and Prevent Sybil Attack in P2P Networks. In: Microelectronics and Computer, pp. 162–165 (2004)
8. Sependar, D., et al.: The Eigen Trust Algorithm for Reputation Management in P2P Networks. ACM 1-58113-680-6 (2003)
9. Boneh, D., Franklin, M.: Identity-based encryption from the well pairing. SIAM J. Computer 32, 586–615 (2004)
10. Martin, L.: Identity-based encryption: A closer look. ISSA Journal, 22–24 (2005)

License Plate Multi-DSP and Multi-FPGA Design and Realization in Highway Toll System

Guoqiang Xu and Mei Xie

University of Electronic Science and Technology of China, ZhongShan Institute, China
xiaoqiang2426@163.com, mxie@uestc.edu.cn

Abstract. License Plate Recognition is an important component of Modern highway toll systems. This paper presents an embedded technology-based License Plate Recognition System. The system uses a multi-processor technology, with three DSP and two FPGA included. Through a multi-block high-speed processor application, the accuracy of recognition system will be at a very high level. The greatest advantage of DSP and FPGA System lies in its structure flexibility, high universality and fitting in the modular design. Therefore, it can achieve highly efficient three sets of algorithm and real-time control. At the same time, its development process can be carried out in parallel.

Keywords: License Plate Recognition DSP FPGA.

1 Introduction

In modern society, involving motor vehicle traffic analysis, management of motor vehicle driving violations, as well as automatic toll collection highway Intelligent Traffic Management (ITM) system has become increasingly important. This paper is based on the license plate information, presenting an embedded system of highway toll without car-stopping, and in this system, three DSP (TMS320C6713B) and two FPGA (Cyclone EP1C12Q240C8) are used,TMS320C6713B is TI's 32-bit high-performance floating-point DSP. With maximum operating frequency 300MHZ, the implementation ability of 240MIPS and 180MFLOPS.It is very suitable for the highway toll collection system to identify the license plate with a lot of image processing data. It has a high-performance 32-bit external memory interface (EMIF), can provide seamless connectivity with Synchronous / asynchronous memory, such as: SRAM, SDRAM, SBSRAM, Flash, being Compatible with 8/16/32 bit external memory bus. At the same time, with a lot of integrated on-chip peripherals, including, PLL, CLK, EDMA, MCBSP, I2C, HPI, and so on. FPGA logic cell array uses LCA (Logic Cell Array) of such a new concept, including the internal CLB (Configurable Logic Block), IOB (Input Output Block),as well as Interconnect. User can reconfigure FPGA internal logic module, so as to realize the expected logic. Three DSP are used as main processors, and on the other hand, two FPGA are used as auxiliary processors. Independent three-way image recognition algorithm is parallel working, and this design can acquire very high speed and excellent accuracy rate. In order to

Z. Cai et al. (Eds.): ISICA 2009, LNCS 5821, pp. 508–516, 2009.

communicate well and establish two parallel bus interface, HPI is connected with FPGA, with EMIF connected with DSP.

2 Hardware Design

Fig 1 shows the design process of this system.

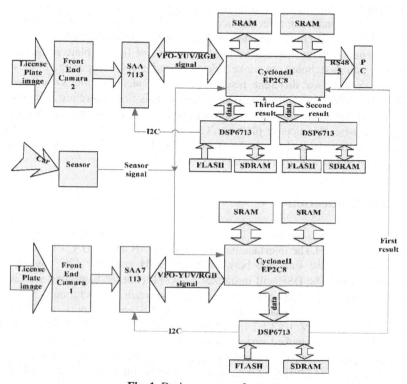

Fig. 1. Design process of system

Because of the requirement of high recognition rate and real-time acquisition of image processing, as well as transferring of the result, of course, the system should take more strict consideration on time. With reference to the experience of traditional License Plate Recognition, meeting the actual needs of intelligent traffic management, the design structure of this system can be summarized as following aspects:

(1) Sense coil trigger FPGA to acquire three-way digital video signal.
(2) Dedicated front-end simulation of the use of road surveillance cameras (dual) to acquire Image.
(3) Analog signal change into digital signal.
(4) After pre-processing the video signal by FPGA, transfer the image to or temporarily registered in SRAM.

(5) Three DSP deal with three-way image data, and transfer the result to FPGA to compare.

(6) At the end, transfer the last result to PC via interface 485 which is designed by FPGA.

The system consists of dual-DSP + FPGA and single dual-DSP + FPGA board to complete the three-way joint algorithm. The first camera corresponds to the single DSP system, because it has only one way signal. The second camera corresponds to the dual DSP system, because it requires two acquisitions of the image, equivalent to two-way signal. Finally, transfer the license plate data which is recognized by single DSP to FPGA in dual-DSP system to compare and determine the result.

Under general circumstances, the fist four frames of license plate images will be transferred into first board, to make relevant handle and comparing. If these two processors output two different results, automatic identification system will be allowed to deal with the following image frames. This time, there are three kinds of results, if two results are same, this result will be the final one as input to the auto-toll system, otherwise, this license plate can't be recognized, will be stopped manually. Through the comparison of the dual-processor, this design will enjoy an advantage of high recognition rate and high recognition speed.

3 Image Acquisition

A pickup camera takes the analog license plate image information and sends it to the A/D chip SAA7113H.The interface between SAA7113H and FPGA is shown in fig2, which also shows the interface between SAA7113H and DSP I2C bus including SCL0 and SDAT0.The DSP will initializes SAA7113H at the beginning via I2C bus. The RTS1 and RTS0 ports are configured as the vertical synchronous signal and horizontal synchronous signal which are sent to VS and HS port of FPGA. The Standard ITU 656 YUV 4 : 2 : 2 format (8-bit) data of license plate can be obtained on the VPO bus. Line-locked system clock frequencies of 24.576 MHz output from the LLCLK port is linked to the CLK port of the FPGA. This clock is used to synchronize the VPO [7:0] 8 bit data. Real-time status information output (RTCO) is also used for debugging.

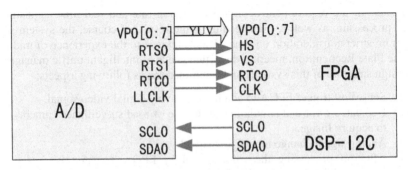

Fig. 2. The interface of SAA7113H with FPGA and DSPI2C

4   License Plate Image Processing

Of course, it is essential to make image pre-processing, since then, the system will position plate features, and do feature segmentation, so as to make further identify. Three sets of image recognition algorithm are transferred into DSP, and then, they will run effectively in the DSP, and can assure real-time processing. License Plate characteristics will be naturally divided into two parts, certainty and uncertainty. The license plate information of the certainty part will have the chance to be recognized, otherwise, the system will wait for the result of auxiliary identification to decide. Fig 3 shows the connection of relative interfaces between the DSP and FPGA. In order to communicate effectively between DSP and FPGA, it establishes two parallel bus interfaces.

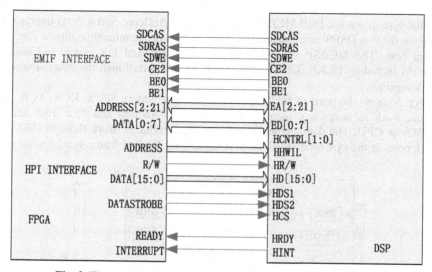

Fig. 3. The connection of relative interfaces between DSP and FPGA

Fig 4 shows FPGA programming structure, including flowing six parts: A/D, double FIFO, control core, UART, SRAM interface, DSP interface.

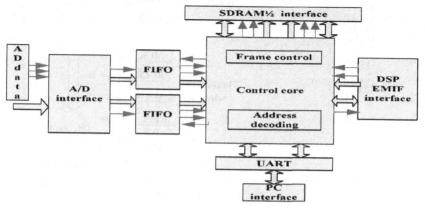

Fig. 4. FPGA programming structure

Through A/D, digital signal will be received correctly, the input signals including horizontal synchronization signals, vertical synchronization signals, synchronization clock from A / D device, image data. Double FIFO is used as buffer, at the same time, the control core make ping-pong operation on FIFO, and double high speed SRAM are used to memory continuous data flow between FPGA, A/D and DSP, with UART part responsible for system and peripheral devices (such as the PC) communication, Control Core responsible for all of the operation, as well as Ping-Pong control to ensure uninterrupted data flow.

5 Data Transmission Interface

In this system we use DSP MCBSP (Multi-channel Buffered Serial Port) interface to achieve the two DSPS' communication. MCBSP is a programmable multiple function serial port. The MCBSP data channel including DR and DX ports, and control channel including CLKX, CLKR FSX, FSR, CLKS ports finish the communication work together.

Fig. 5 shows the ports of MCBSP. The registers including SPCR, RCR, XCR, and so on, work as temporary memory to store the instruction and data from and to EDMA or CPU. The data channel completes data exchange work through DR1 and DX1 ports at the synchronous clock port CLKR, CLKS and frame synchronous port

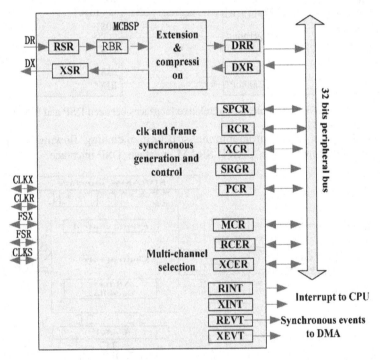

Fig. 5. Ports of MCBSP

FSX, FSR. The license plate recognition result can be compared by the three DSPS. All the data are transmitted through the 32bit peripheral bus which is connected to the CPU and EDMA. It is important to transmit data from our system to external terminal, because in computer it is easy to test our recognition arithmetic and observe the quality of the captured image. In this system both DSP and FPGA are connected to the PC for debugging and verification. MAX3232 and I2C through MCBSP are used for communication between the system and external process terminal such as PC. In addition, RS485 module is arranged through FPGA to connect the terminal device.

Here, it is a typical method to use FPGA to be a control chip of video image acquisition and system processing, DSP to be a computing core. A stable, real-time, high-speed front-end image acquisition and Memory module is an important part of this kind of image processing system. Here, the system uses ping-pang Conversion idea which is widely used in FPGA design, to keep Continuous transmission of high speed information flow. At the same time, it takes full advantage of synchronous finite state machine (FSM) to produce precise timing sequence, to control all internal operation in system.

6 Simulation Results

Fig. 6 and fig. 7 show two circuit boards which are needed in this system, the first is single DSP plus single FPGA, the other is two DSP plus single FPGA. Because of the complicated interfaces of this system, when making system simulation, we should make functional simulation for various modules at first. Only without mistake in functional simulation, can we make joint simulation of various modules, of course, including functional simulation, after-comprehension simulation, timing sequence simulation, through SignalTapII of Quartus II and SignalProbe to test whether or not the program can run stably and accurately in the circuit.

Fig. 6. Single DSP plus single FPGA circuit board

Fig. 7. Two DSP plus single FPGA circuit board

After the entire system platform has been built, we load algorithm into FLASH, so the system can work without computer, absolutely depending on these processors. In order to make the system recognition result can be watched, we install an LCD screen, connected with MCBSP. Fig. 8 shows the recognition result of a license plate.

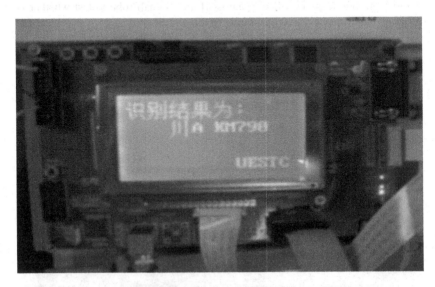

Fig. 8. Recognition result of a license plate

Fig. 9 and fig. 10 show simulation diagrams of data flow of ping-pang control.

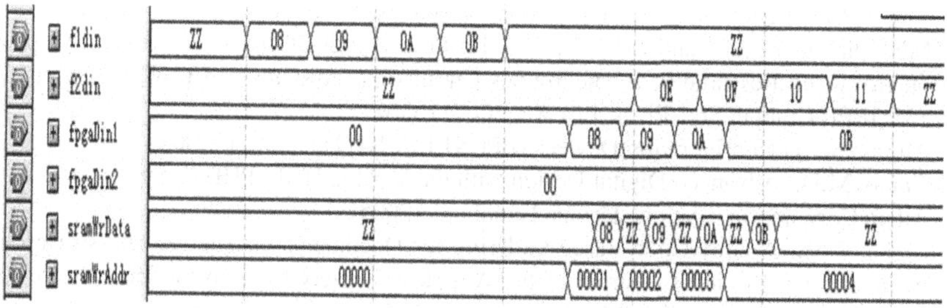

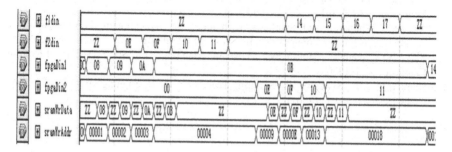

Fig. 9. Data flow diagram of ping-pang control (1)

Fig. 10. data flow diagram of ping-pang control (2)

7 Conclusion

The main innovation of this system is utilizing three sets of algorithm which are not relevant with each other to improve the recognition rate, and using three DSP plus two FPGA hardware platform of parallel processing to promote the recognition speed, so as to design a high recognition rate, a high recognition speed, convenient-installation Embedded License Plate Recognition System(ELPRS). Through testing under MATLAB environment, error rate of a set of license plate recognition algorithm is as high as 7%, but, with three sets of license plate recognition algorithm working together, which becomes only 0.35%, and at the same time, the parallel processing time is 0.8S, at most 1S.SO, in terms of recognition rate and recognition speed, there is some advantages in this system.

References

1. Dally, W.J., Poulton, J.W.: Digital Systems Engineering, pp. 460–520. Cambridge University Press, Cambridge (1998)
2. Texas Instruments Inc. TLV320AIC23B Stereo Audio CODEC,8-to 96-kHz, With Integrated Headphone Amplifier (2004)

3. Hauck, S.: Asynchronous Design Methodologies: An Overview. Proc of the IEEE 83(1), 69293 (1995)
4. Van, B.K., Bink, A.: Single2Track Handshake Signaling with Application to Micropipelines and Handshake Circuits. In: Proceedings of 2nd International Symposium on Advanced Research in Asynchronous Circuits and Systems (ASYNC 1996), pp. 122–133. IEEE Comput Soc. Press, Los Alamitos (1996)
5. Altera.: Serial Configuration Devices (EPCS1,EPCS4) Data Sheet (2003)
6. Ciletti, M.D.: Advanced Digital Design with the Verilog HDL. PHE (2005)
7. Altera Corporation. Cyclone Device Handbook (2005)
8. Losee, R.M.: A Gray Code Based Ordering for Documents on Shelves Classification for Browsing and Retrieval. Journal of the American Society for Information Science 43(4), 3122322 (1992)
9. Tang, T.C.: Experimental Studies of Metastability Behaviors of Sub-Micron CMOS ASIC Flip Flops. In: Proceedings of Fourth Annual IEEE International ASIC Conference and Exhibit, p. 7-4/1-4. IEEE, NewYork (1991)
10. Jose, S.: Simulation and Synthesis Techniques for Aynchronous FIFO Design with Asynchronous Pointer Comparisons. In: SNUG-2002 (2002)
11. Zhu, Y., Shengli: Multi-Clock Domain Handling in SoC Design. Electronic Engineer 29(11) (2003)
12. Cummings, C.E.: Synthesis and Scripting Techniques for D -esigning Multi-Asynchronous Clock Designs. SNUG (2001)

QoS Routing Algorithm for Wireless Multimedia Sensor Networks

Wushi Dong[1], Zongwu Ke[1], Niansheng Chen[1], and Qiang Sun[1,2]

[1] School of Computer Science, Hubei Normal University, Huangshi 435002, China
[2] Electronic and Information School, Shanghai Dianji University, Shanghai, 200240, China
hschenns@163.com

Abstract. As a novel information acquiring and processing technology, compared to other traditional sensor networks, wireless multimedia sensor networks pay more attention to the information-intensive data (e.g. audio, video, image). Potential applications of wireless multimedia sensor networks span a wide spectrum from military to industrial, from commercial to environmental monitoring. This paper discusses QoS routing problem model with multiple QoS constraints, which may deal with the delay, delay jitter and bandwidth, and presents QoS routing algorithm with multiple constraints based on genetic algorithm, and gives the algorithm idiographic flow. Simulating results show that higher routing successful ratio and faster convergence is achieved in the algorithm.

Keywords: wireless multimedia sensor networks, QoS routing algorithm, genetic algorithm.

1 Introduction

Wireless multimedia sensor network as a special form of wireless sensor network has become an object paid more attention by researchers[1,2].WMSN transmits real-time images, audio, video and other multimedia information. As for the requirement of multimedia information transmission, it somewhat needs Qos guarantees[3]. Qos-sensitive is an important feature of WMSN .Qos routing technology needs to be solved in the study of WMSN application .Qos routing technology mainly requires to calculate the feasible path under the multi-constrained condition ,and also to optimize the many possibly existing paths. While solving (optimizing) the feasible path under the multi-constrained condition belongs to NP-complete problem[4],the common solution to the problem is heuristic algorithm and genetic algorithm etc.

Qos of WMSN is mainly embodied in audio and video quality, network delay, network power consumption, coverage, service duration and the dealing of media information etc, but WMSN has to consider its speciality of resource-constrained, variable channel capacity, cross-layer union among different function, the flow of non-uniform distribution and the energy balance which makes it face more challenge for providing Qos guarantee. Ref.[5] presents a WMSN routing algorithm with known

Z. Cai et al. (Eds.): ISICA 2009, LNCS 5821, pp. 517–524, 2009.

energy based on the genetic algorithm, which uses the energy as fitness function to evaluate each path and makes of traditional genetic algorithm to optimize the path of energy at best .This method adopts the scheme with coding of the same length, uses each node of the next hop as a gene and uses the tradition single-point crossover .Its disadvantage is that it makes the invalid path. Ref.[6] proposes routing protocol of WMSN with known energy, which uses the genetic algorithm to provide delay bound and energy confinement for Qos routing.

This paper uses the genetic algorithm to design and realize the Qos routing algorithm of WMSN. It makes use of random walk to generate the initial population, encodes as the given path and provides the process of algorithm realization. Simulating shown that the algorithm has the characteristic of fast convergence and high rate of routing success.

2 Description of Network Model and Routing Problem

This article assumes that WMSN is a Mesh network structure .Network consists of a cluster and a number of nodes. Sensor nodes can be multimedia sensor node and others simple data (such as temperature etc) node. Any node in network has at least more than one neighbor node. That is to say, WMSN can be expressed as $G = (V, E)$, where V is the set of sensor nodes and E is the set of duplex links corresponding with nodes. If r is the communication radius of sensor node, $d(v_1, v_2)$ stands for the distance between the two nodes ($v_1, v_2 \in V$). when $d(v_1, v_2) \leq r$,there is a two-way link existing between v_1, v_2, which is expressed as $e(v_1, v_2) \in E$. Information required for genetic routing algorithm is collected by the nodes of Mesh without energy restriction . Node pool finish the genetic algorithm and pass the optimal paths to all sensor nodes.

In WMSN ,different applications demand different Qos requirements .Specifically, it needs to provide the different Qos guarantee for real-time application, application with delay constraint, and the application with loss rate constraint or without. This paper discusses Qos routing problem of continuous media. Namely ,look for a path to content multiple QoS constraints on the basis of rational use of energy in sensor nodes .

Definition 1: In WMSN $G = (V, E)$. T stands for the path sets from source node $s \in V$ to the cluster node $d \in V$. $E(t)$ is the edge set of $t \in T$, its Qos parameters can be described as follows :

(1) $bandwidth(t) = \min\{bandwidth(e(v_i, v_j)), \quad e(v_i, v_j) \in E(t)\}$.

(2) $delay(t) = \sum\limits_{e(v_i, v_j) \in E(t)} deley(e(v_i, v_j))$.

(3) $delay\_jitter = \sum\limits_{e(v_i, v_j) \in E(t)} delay\_jitter(e(v_i, v_j))$.

Definition 2: The Qos routing problem of WMSN: In WMSN $G = (V, E)$,needs to find a path $t^* \in T$ to satisfy the follow Qos requests and optimal conditions.

(1) $bandwidth(t^*) \geq B_{\min}$.

(2) $delay(t^*) \le D_{\max}$.

(3) $delay\_jitter(t^*) \le J_{\max}$.

(4) $\cos t(t^*)$ is minimum.

$B_{\min}$, $D_{\max}$ and $J_{\max}$ separately stands for lower limit bandwidth, upper limit delay and upper limit delay-jitter of the end-to-end QoS constraints. The $\cos t(t^*)$ is the cost of path, the times of path hop is used as the cost. The formula (4) brings a kind of optimization target, in order to find the shortest path which can meet multiple QoS constraints.

3 Qos Routing Algorithm Based on Genetic Algorithm

Genetic algorithm imitates the mechanism of choices and the genetic in the natural biological evolution process and forms an optimized search algorithm. The general operating process of genetic algorithm consists of encoding, production of initial population, the determination of fitness function, method of selection, crossover operation and mutation operation etc.

3.1 Encoding

Given network $G = (V, E)$ and a routing request adopts random walk to find a random path from the source node to the destination node. The path method used to encode, a chromosome can be expressed as $C = \{g_1, g_2, \cdots g_i, \cdots g_n \mid g_i \in V\}$, among which g_i is expressed by the node number, the path from node 11 to node 10 is express as $\{11,38,15,28,10\}$.

3.2 Fitness Function

The optimize aim of routing algorithm is to find the shortest path to meet the Qos multi-constraints, so the fitness function of using to evaluate path can be defined as:

$$f = \begin{cases} \dfrac{1}{\cos t(t)}, & bandwidth(t) \ge B_{\min} \wedge delay(t) \le D_{\max} \wedge delay\_jitter(t) \le J_{\max} \\ \dfrac{\varepsilon}{\cos t(t)}, & others \end{cases}$$

The ε is positive numbers far smaller than 1,inorder to let the path which cannot meet the demand of Qos has the few chances to participate in cross operation, especially in initial population where there is no path to meet the Qos demands can make the algorithm not stagnate. Obviously, the shorter the path which satisfies the Qos constraint is, the larger the fitness is ,thus the path in line with the optimize condition is ensured at the next generation.

3.3 Crossover Operation

The process of crossover operation is as follows: first of all, select several numbers of pairs of chromosomes randomly, compare two chromosomes and find all the same genes (ie nodes), select one form these genes randomly as a crossover point, from which all genes can be exchanged. eg: Gene 28 is used as the crossover point between chromosome (11.13.15.28.10.25) and chromosome (43.22.28.21.7.29.30),next generation can be (11.13.15.28.21.7.29.30) and (43.22.28.10.23).

3.4 Mutation

The process of mutation: first of all, select a chromosome randomly and also find a node k randomly, add all nodes before k to the offspring, and then starts with k,the destination node is defined as the final node, and uses random walk to method to find a random path,which doesn`t contain all the nodes before k,and add this path to the back path offspring. This method can avoid generating illegal path and at the same time can ensure the diversity of population.

3.5 Algorithm Description

The flow of Qos routing algorithm based on the genetic algorithm is as follow.

Step 1: Make use of the random walk method to generate the initial population.
Step 2: Calculate the the fitness value of initial population.
Step 3: While (termination condition not satisfied) do
  {select some parts of chromosome from the father`s population to implement crossover operation.
  Implement mutation.
  Calculate the fitness value of all individuals.
  Combine the father`s individual and the offspring`s individual
  Implement the roulette selection to generate new population.}

The cycle of termination condition in algorithm uses the same path ratio, when the new population in the same path is beyond a certain percentage, the cycle exists.

4 Simulation Experiments

In order to evaluate and measure the performance of QoS routing, it can be defined as follows:

Definition 3: Success of routing rate: Assume that the fitness of path found in algorithm is near zero,it shows that path found cannot meet the demand of Qos and the route fails.Then the ratio between average times of finding paths to meet the demands of Qos and the implementation times of algorithm.

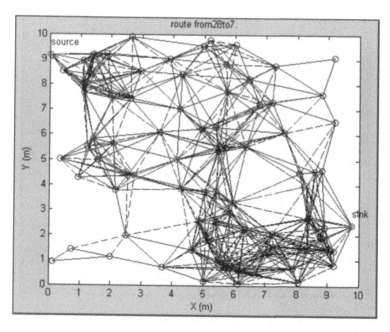

Fig. 1. The network topology with 87 nodes randomly in the range of 10x10

Definition 4: The average fitness of the population: the average of all the individual fitness in population.

Definition 5: The best fitness value of the population: the maximum of all the individual fitness in population.

Simulation experiment uses Waxman[7] network model and network bandwidth, link delay and delay jitter to randomly generate.

Fig.1. is in the range of 10x10, with 87 nodes of Waxman model, the source node is defined as 28, the cluster node as 7, the network bandwidth is a random number in [1,10], link delay is a random number in [10,30], the link delay jitter is a random number [0.01,0.1]; genetic algorithm parameters are to set as follows: crossover probability is 0.7, mutation probability is 0.05 , the number initial population is 20; at the same time assume that the demand for QoS is $B_{min} = 2$, $D_{max} = 130$, $J_{max} = 1$.

Fig.2. is a sketch map of algorithm astringency. seen from the diagram , there are no paths to meet the demand of the Qos in the initial population at the initial iteration, but the algorithm does not stagnate, when the iteration times 22 the path in population starts with meeting the QoS constrain. Since then the average fitness of population converges on the best fitness of the population rapidly. From the simulation experiment it can be seen that the basic genetic routing algorithm has good adaptability and the algorithm is convergent.

Fig.3. and Fig.4., respectively, show the relationship between the crossover probability, the average iteration times and the rate of routing success in the QoS routing algorithm. Compare two simulation results and we will find that when the

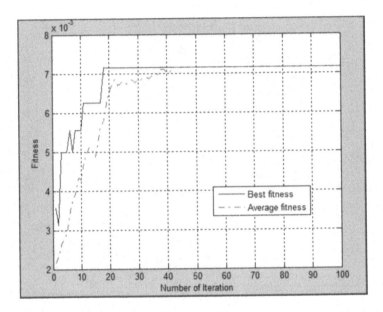

Fig. 2. The diagram of algorithm convergence

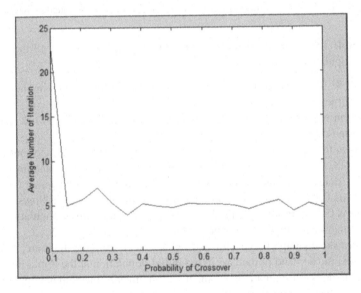

Fig. 3. The relationship between the crossover probability and the average iteration times

crossover probability is very small, such as crossover probability less than 0.2, the average number of iteration times is large , that is to say the convergence is slow, and at the same time the ratio routing failure is larger. From theoretical analysis, we can see that when the crossover probability is small, and because the probability to generate the new individuals is smaller, which makes the probability to generate high-quality individuals in population get smaller, it results in slow convergence of algorithm, and easily leads the algorithm to be too premature to converge on the path to meet the QoS requirements; when the crossover probability is too large, such as greater than 0.95, the speed of convergence slows down. From theoretical analysis, we will see when crossover probability is too large, it is easy to ruin the good individual in population so as to result in lower convergence rate.

In addition, through repeated experiments, it is found that because of the basic genetic algorithm with a lot of randomness, such as the quality of the initial population etc, the best convergence rate corresponding to the crossover probability is uncertain. Generally adopting the experience value in the choice of crossover probability brings a certain amount of difficulty for the application, and meanwhile the basic genetic algorithm does not consider node energy problem.

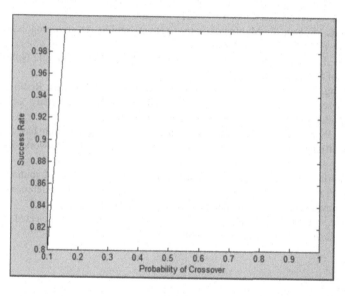

Fig. 4. The relationship between the crossover probability and the rate of routing success

5   Conclusion

This paper aims at describing the bandwidth, delay and delay jitter of the multi-constrained QoS routing problem model for the wireless multimedia sensor network which has a Mesh and based on the basic genetic algorithm it can effectively solve the NP problem, and puts forward a multi-constrained QoS routing algorithm, give the specific implementation flow of the algorithm, and verifies it through simulation experiments on the algorithm convergence and the rate of routing success. But as for characteristic of wireless multimedia sensor network, how we consider the multi-constrained Qos unicast and multicast routing problem which has energy confinement mechanism needs us to study further.

Acknowledgements

The work was supported by the plan for scientific and technological innovation team of excellent young and middle-aged in institute of high learning of Hubei Province in P.R. China (Grant No:T200806), The young research project of Hubei Province Department of education in P.R.China(Grant NO: Q20082203) and Shanghai scientific research funds for selection and training of outstanding young teachers in institute of high learning (Grant No: sdj-07011).

References

[1] Akyildiz, I.F., Melodia, T., Chowdhury, K.R.: A survey on wireless multimedia sensor networks. Computer Networks 51(4), 921–960 (2007)

[2] HuaDong, M., Dan, T.: Multimedia sensor network and its research progresses. Journal of Software 17(9), 2013–2028 (2006)

[3] La-Yuan, L., Chun-Lin, L.: A Multicast Routing Protocol with Multiple QoS Constraints. Journal of Software 15(02), 286–291 (2004)

[4] Niansheng, C., Layuan, L., Wushi, D.: A Widest-bandwidth Multicast Routing of Multiple QoS Based on Ad Hoc Networks. Journal of Wuhan University of Technology (Transportation Science & Engineering) 29(4), 499–502 (2005)

[5] Bari, A., Wazed, S., Jaekel, A., Bandyopadhyay, S.: A genetic algorithm based approach for energy efficient routing in two-tiered sensor networks. Ad Hoc Networks 7(4), 665–676 (2009)

[6] Pourkabirian, A., Haghighat, A.T.: Energy-aware, delay-constrained routing in wireless sensor networks through genetic algorithm. In: 15th International Conference on Software, Telecommunications & Computer Networks, pp. 37–41 (2007)

[7] Waxman, B.M.: Routing of multipoint connections. Selected Areas in Communications 6(9), 1617–1622 (1988)

Realization of Fingerprint Identification on DSP

Huaibin Shi and Mei Xie

University of Electronic Science and Technology of China Zhongshan Institute, China
shb0527@126.com, mxie@uestc.edu.cn

Abstract. Along with the rapid development of biometric identification techniques, the fingerprint identification is becoming a significant subject. Automated fingerprint identification is a method to identify a person based on his fingerprint physiological characteristics. This paper presents an automatic fingerprint capture and preprocessing system with a fixed point DSP, TMS320VC5510A and a fingerprint sensor, FPC1011C. This system supplies two types of power: 1) wall adapter power, which can automatically switch from the wall adapter power to the battery in case of power-fail or brownout conditions, and 2) battery . With the interactive module , keyboard and the LCD in this system, the algorithm can run smoothly to realize the fingerprint processing.

Keywords: DSP, Fingerprint Identification, Automatically power switch.

1 Introduction

Biometric Identification Technology is the use of human physiological characteristics (such as fingerprint, iris, face and DNA) or behavioral characteristics (gait, costumed keystroke) to identify and verify identity. Because the object it distinguishes has the characteristic of stability (long-term invariable), uniqueness (different individual, different fingerprint), the universality. And the characteristics has essential connect with the recognition individual, which are not easy to forge and counterfeit Fingerprint identification technology, with the advantages of conveniently collect, high quality image, high precision algorithm and low cost development, has been the main biometric verify technology.

In this paper, the system is developed under such background. The system is an embedded fingerprint recognition system based on DSP.

2 System Hardware Structure

The system this paper presents used TMS320VC5510A [1] as the hardware platform. The DSP and FLASH, SDRAM, the fingerprint sensor, LCD and keyboards constructed the embedded fingerprint recognition system. The system hardware structure diagram is shown in Figure1:

Z. Cai et al. (Eds.): ISICA 2009, LNCS 5821, pp. 525–532, 2009.
© Springer-Verlag Berlin Heidelberg 2009

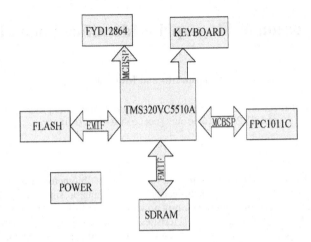

Fig. 1. The hardware structure diagram of the fingerprint recognition system

2.1 DSP Control Module

The system's primary CPU is a high-performance, low-power and 16 bit fixed-point DSP. Its core voltage is 1.6V, clock rate 160/200MHz may be selected, the 24kBytes instruction cache, 320kBytes on-chip RAM,32kBytes on-chip ROM, the external addressable space is 8M×16bit,32bit the external memory interface[2] (EMIF), may with glueless interface to synchronized/asynchronous memories such as FLASH, SDRAM, SRRAM, SBSRAM, the size of which maybe 8bit,16bit or 32bit. Meanwhile It has rich peripherals, for example: Multichannel buffered serial port [3] (MCBSP), DMA controller, Timer, parallel enhanced host port (EHPI), general purpose I/O pins (GPIO) as well as digital phase-locked loop (DPLL) and so on. The fingerprint recognition system this paper presents put FLASH and SDRAM on the EMIF bus, which is facilitated to read and write the data and the program.

2.2 Power Management Module

As an embedded system, on one hand it can be used at the fixed place with the wall adapter source, on the other hand it must can be used as the portable device with the battery source. To meet this demands, and meanwhile to avoid the conditions of power-fail or brownout, this system designs the two types of power. Generally, we used the wall adapter source. But in case of power-fail or brownout the system can automatically switch to the battery. To realize this function we used the chipTPS3600D50 [4] to monitor and transform the power.

In case of a brownout or power failure, it may be necessary to keep a processor running. If a backup battery is installed at VBAT, the devices automatically connect the processor to backup power when VDD fails. The supply voltage which connects with VDD is 5V, and the battery is 6V. In order to allow the backup battery to have a higher voltage than VDD, this chip will not connect VBAT to VDD when VBAT is greater than VDD.VBAT only connect to VOUT (through a 2- Ω switch), when VOUT falls below 4.5V and VBAT is greater than VDD. When VDD recovers,

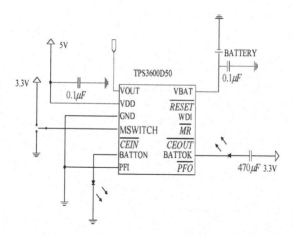

Fig. 2. Power automatically switchover module

switchover is deferred either until VDD crosses VBAT, or when VDD rises above the threshold 4.5V.

2.3 Fingerprint Sensor Module

Generally speaking, the fingerprint senor we used is based on the optical technology, or the semiconductor silicon technology or the radio frequency technology. In which semiconductor silicon technology is using the semiconductor silicon capacity effect to make the senor. The silicon sensor becomes a capacity's pole plate; the finger is another pole plate. It makes use of the silicon sensor's electricity tolerance between fingerprint line keel and the valley, and then it forms 8bit the gradation image.

The fingerprint sensor FPC1011C [5] this system used is one kind of electric capacity type surface attire fingerprint sensor. FPC1011C is a new leading-edge capacitive fingerprint sensor, based on the Certus Sensor Platform. It offers several strong advantages; acknowledged high image quality, 256 gray scale values in every single pixel and especially, the reflective capacitive measurement method enables the use of a thick protective surface coating, preventing the user from directly touching the CMOS circuitry. At the same time, FPC1011C is protected against ESD well above 15 kV and the everyday wear-and-tear. FPC1011C is interfaced through a flexible printed circuit (8-pin) and therefore easy to integrate into a system using standard low-cost connectors. Its working voltage is 2.5V or 3.3V (when the working voltage is 3.3V, the power loss is 50mW). The active sensing area can be set by values of the XSHIFT and YSHIFT registers, and its max image size is 152×200 pixels. Meanwhile the start position when it begins to collect the fingerprint can be changed by set the SENSEX and SENSEY registers. And during the read operation, 8 pixels are captured every time. The concrete connection diagram is shown in figure 3.

In this system, the working voltage of the fingerprint is 3.3V. The communication between the DSP and the senor is realized by SPI protocol. The senor interfaced with DSP'Mcbap, and the DSP works as the master. The baud rate is set to 1MHz.

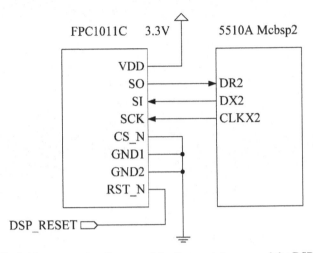

Fig. 3. The connection diagram of the fingerprint senor and the DSP

2.4 External Memory Module

In this system, the DSP has on-chip ROM 32kBytes, DARAM 64kBytes, and SARAM 256kBytes. But during the fingerprint capture, process and store, the quantity of data is so big that the on-chip memory space can't meet the need of the memory. As a result, we must use the external memory. The DSP's external addressable space is 8M×16bit, and the space can be controlled by setting the values of the EMIF registers. This system used the chip of Micron Corporation's 32 MT48LC2M32B2TG [6] to expand the memory space. It is a Synchronization dynamic random access memory (short as SDRAM). Its internal configuration is 2 Meg×32 (512k×32×4banks). So the size of the SDRAM is 8Mbytes. When the clock rate is 200MHz its setup time and maintains the time respectively is 1.5ns and 1ns. Its cycle time is only 5ns.The SDRAM is configured on DSP CE2 space. The start address is 0x800000H.

However, we configured the SDRAM to expand the external memory, but there also exist a problem that the data stored in the SDRAM will be lost when in case of power failure or reset. At the same moment, the system need solidify the program in the memory to make sure that when power-up the system can work normally. To solve this problem we must introduce one kind of non- volatility memory. So FLASH which is the EPROM in nature is a very good solution to this question. What this system uses is SST39VF1602 [7], in which the memory is organized as 1M×16bit. It can also work at the low power consumption(the typical value is work at 5MHz), the standby current and the automatic low current are 3 μ A, and the fast read access time is.70ns. It supports the erase mode such as: sector erase, block erase, chip erase. The connection diagram is shown in figure 4.

In this system we use the block erase mode and put the FLASH and the SDRAM on the EMIF bus to control the read and write access to the FLASH and the SDRAM.

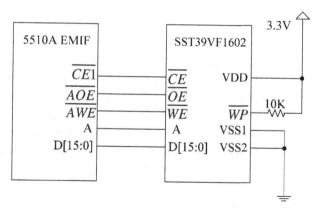

Fig. 4. The connection diagram of the FLASH and the DSP

2.5 Interactive Module

As a portable fingerprint recognition system, the man-machine interaction is a very essential function. In this system, keyboards and the liquid crystal display are used to realize the man-machine interaction. The keyboards trigger hardware interrupt to realize the functions of fingerprint capture, fingerprint registration and fingerprint match. In each interrupt the LCD will demonstration the corresponding content.

The liquid crystal we used is FYD12864-0402B . The max number of the Chinese character the LCD can demonstrate is 4Colx8Line.The LCD can also realize the graphical display. It has 4/8bit mode, parallel/serial interface, to support the SPI protocol. This system takes DSP as the SPI master, through to the Mcbsp register's configuration to realize the communication between the DSP and the LCD. Because what the LCD only need to do is to receive the command and the character. There are only two wires between the DSP and the LCD.

The clock rate and the frame length, the transmission speed can also be controlled by setting the Specific register of the Mcbsp. The figure 5 shown below is the clock timings. In the timings we can see, the DSP must sent five high levels to synchronize the LCD and itself. The RW and the RS can determine whether the data or the instructions can be transmitted. When the RW and RS are set as "00" (binary), the instructions are transmitted to the LCD. And when they are "11" (binary), the data is transmitted. As shown in the timings, the 8 bit data or instructions are repackaged into 16 bit. The 8bits are divided into two parts, the first four bits and the latter four bits. Then it adds 0000(binary) to tail of the first and the latter four bits to construct the 8bits. So the transmission frame length of the Mcbsp is set to 24bit. When transmitting, the "BF" bit must be read first to ensure that the former instruction has implemented. In this system, the transmission speed is set at 115207bit/s. At the speed, it can communicate with the DSP properly. It also can show the content on real time and meet the need of the system.

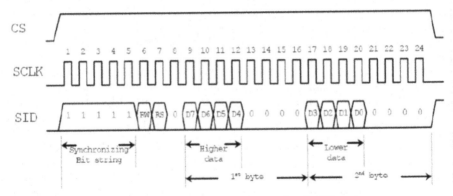

Fig. 5. The LCD transmission clock timings in SPI mode

3 Software Module

In this system, the main program is developed on the DSP, so we used the embedded real time operation system DSP/BIOS and the CCS to realize the program's design and debug. DSP/BIOS is a scalable real-time kernel. It is designed to be used by applications that require real-time scheduling and synchronization, host-to target communication, or real-time instrumentation. The DSP/BIOS provide preemptive multi-threading, hardware abstraction, real-time analysis, and configuration tools. Application programs use DSP/BIOS by making calls to the API. All DSP/BIOS modules provide C-callable interfaces. In addition, some of the API modules contain optimized assembly language macros. Most C-callable interfaces can also be called from assembly language, provided that C calling conventions are followed.

In the system, we must package the fingerprint identification algorithm into the C functions. That means the C functions must can be run in the DSP board without the PC. And the in the immigration, the variable must has the defined address. The global

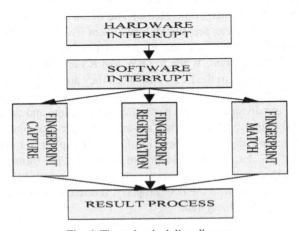

Fig. 6. The task scheduling diagram

variable and the global functions must be packaged in a head files to make sure that the functions can be call in the main functions. The algorithm can be scheduled as the corresponding task. The task schedule is defined in the DSP/BIOS. The task can be trigger by the hardware interrupt. Meanwhile the code can be optimized by the assemble language [8] to speed the code process. The driver program is based on the CSL [9], which is the function library the DSP itself owned. When we used the CSL, we can just call for the API functions in the library to realize the driver's developed. .

In this paper the keyboard triggers the hardware interrupt, and the hardware interrupt call for the corresponding software interrupt to realize the capture, the registration and the match. In each task, the fingerprint is processed in the following steps: fingerprint image input, image division, image enhancement, image binarization, Image refinement and character extract. The following figure 6 is the task scheduling diagram.

4 Conclusions

The fingerprint identification system based on DSP this paper designed has the characteristics such as: the small size, the low power consumption, the fast speed, the higher recognition rate. The board has provided a good platform for the fingerprint recognition algorithm. To test the performance of the system hundreds of images of the fingerprint are tested. As shown by the test, the time of extracting the fingerprint is more than 1 second; the match process is less than 1 second. The all time is no more than two seconds. The average FAR [10] (the false accept rate) is about 0.18%, and the FRR (the false rejection rate) is about 2.79%.

The system in this paper is used the automatically power switch device to ensure that it can be used as the portable device. Meanwhile, the keyboard makes the operation easier; the LCD makes the result easier to look at. The image of the fingerprint is about 3k bytes, so it has enough space to store the image. It can satisfy the need of the real time fingerprint process completely. And the system has the huge marketing potential.

References

1. Texas Instruments, TMS320VC5510/5510A Fixed-Point Digital Signal Processors SPRS076O (June 2000) – (revised September 2007)
2. Texas Instruments, TMS320VC5510 DSP External Memory Interface (EMIF) Reference Guide SPRU590 (August 2004)
3. Texas Instruments, TMS320VC5501/5502/5503/5507/5509/5510 DSP Multichannel Buffered Serial Port (McBSP) Reference Guide SPRU592E (April 2005)
4. Texas Instruments, TPS3600D20, TPS3600D25, TPS3600D33, TPS3600D50, Battery-Backup Supervisors For Low-Power Processors Slvs336 (December 2000) -(revised April 2001)
5. FPC1011C Area Sensor Package Product Specification
6. MICRON, MT48LC2M32B2TG-6

7. SST, 16 Mbit / 32 Mbit / 64 Mbit (x16) Multi-Purpose Flash Plus SST39VF1601 / SST39VF3201 / SST39VF6401 SST39VF1602 / SST39VF3202 / SST39VF6402
8. Texas Instruments, TMS320C55x Assembly Language Tools User's Guid Literature Number: SPRU280G (March 2003)
9. Texas Instruments, TMS320C55x Chip Support LibraryAPI Reference Guide SPRU433J (September 2004)
10. Ruili, J., Jing, F.: VC5509A Based Fingerprint Identification. In: Preprocessing System ICSP 2008 Proceedings, pp. 2859–2863

Localization Algorithm of Beacon-Free Node in WSN Based on Probability

Bing Hu[1], Hongsheng Li[2], and Sumin Liu[1]

[1] Wuhan University of Technology, Mechanism and Automation, Wuhan, China
[2] Wuhan University of Technology, Department of Automation, Wuhan, China

Abstract. The localization technology based on beacon-free node can significantly reduce the network cost when it takes into account the configuration constraints and cost factors of wireless sensor network as well as satisfies the lower hardware requirements. This inspires the wireless sensor network node localization studies. With an analysis of the beacon nodes and beacon-free node localization algorithm, this paper puts forward the localization algorithm of wireless sensor network beacon-free node probability-based. Simulation results show that the algorithm, at no additional hardware, will reduce the computation overhead and improve the localization accuracy and that has good adaptability.

Keywords: wireless sensor networks, beacon node, node localization, probability.

1 Introduction

Node localization technology is one of the main supporting technologies of wireless sensor networks, and it is a very important research direction in wireless sensor networks research areas. Localization is a mechanism that for a group of network nodes with unknown location, we determine the location of those nodes by measuring or estimating the distance among them or hops, or using the exchange of information between nodes.

According to whether or not to use the beacon nodes in the process of localization, we have two localization algorithms: localization algorithm based on beacon node and algorithms based on beacon-free node. Localization method based on beacon nodes mainly use the location information of a small number of known nodes in the sensor networks to obtain the location information of other unknown nodes (called unknown nodes).We can get beacon node location information by the way of being pre-configured, or GPS, etc. while the remaining unknown nodes can calculate its own location information from the location information of the beacon nodes.

As a result of the limited energy and size of nodes, the large number of nodes, non-line-of-sight problems caused by obstructions in the localization method based on beacon node, node localization does not use GPS way in general. If determine the beacon node location information through the way of being pre-configured, the mobility of the networks will be reduced, and it need deploy a large number of beacon nodes to reduce the Localization error in practical applications.

Z. Cai et al. (Eds.): ISICA 2009, LNCS 5821, pp. 533–540, 2009.

Taking into account the configuration constraints and cost factors of wireless sensor network, we put forward some location algorithms based on non-beacon node in the literature[1]-[3].That is, do not use beacon nodes to achieve the node Localization technology. With the development of communication technology and node computing power, location method based on the non-beacon node may be the future of wireless sensor network node localization studies.

Localization technology based on beacon-free node can significantly reduce the network cost, and it need low hardware requirements. But the Localization accuracy is minimum. So, how to make a compromise between Localization accuracy and hardware requirements and make full use of the advantages of different Localization technology to promote the application of wireless sensor networks will be one of the issues that need to be resolved in node Localization technology research. In this paper, based on the problems that may exist in the application of the non-beacon node Localization technology, we put forward the probability-based wireless sensor network localization algorithm without beacon nodes.

2   Related Work

2.1   Localization Algorithm Based on Beacon Node

Localization algorithm based on beacon node takes beacon nodes as a positioning reference point; each node will generate the overall absolute coordinate system after localization in order to achieve the absolute positioning of the entire network. At present, the vast majority of node positioning algorithms are such algorithm, such as Centroid algorithm, DV-Hop algorithm, Amorphous algorithm, APIT algorithm and so on. Adopts RSSI (received signal strength indicator) and TDOA (Time Difference on arrival) Ranging technology in the literature 4.RSSI subjects to channel environmental impact largely, and TDOA requires the network-intensive deployment. Adopt AOA (angle of arival) Ranging Technology in the literature 5.AOA not only is affected by the external environment, but also required additional hardware, such as antenna array. And calls for higher on the node size and power consumption. Propose an outdoor localization algorithm only based on network connectivity in literature 6. The central idea of this algorithm is that the required positioning of node will take the geometry centroid of all the beacon nodes that within the scope of its communication as its estimated location. A localization algorithm was proposed in literature 7, which first obtained the network average hop distance as well as hops of to be located nodes and anchor nodes. Then according to the two numerical values to calculate the distance between to be located nodes and anchor nodes.

Terrain algorithm is based on ABC algorithm that is unrelated to beacon nodes. First of all broadcast information from each beacon nodes, and the unknown nodes will use triangulation method to obtain their locations after they receive the distance information of three or more than three different beacon nodes. Robust Position algorithm proposed in literature [10] is composed of two parts: the initial phase and the refinement phase. In initial stage, we make use of Hop-Terrain algorithm (variant of Terrain algorithm) to provide the initial location estimation of each node. And this method has better fault tolerance to ranging error. The introduction of confidence level in refinement phase is used to improve the accuracy of position estimation. Bergamo put forward the scheme that uses the two beacon nodes to locate [11]. The two fixed location beacon nodes broadcast information to the whole network, and the rest unknown nodes that are in motion make their own locations according to the received signal strength.

2.2 Localization Algorithm Based on Beacon-Free Node

Localization algorithm based on beacon-free node only concerned about the relative positions of nodes. The procession of localization does not need beacon-free nodes. Every node takes itself as the reference point, and takes its neighboring nodes into the coordinate system. Then the adjacent coordinate systems convert and merger by turns and finally coming into being the overall relative coordinate system. Localization algorithm based on beacon-free node which has been proposed recently mainly includes AFL algorithm [1], ABC algorithm [2] and KPS algorithms [3].

(1) AFL (Anchor Free Localization) algorithm has been applied in the famous Cricket positioning systems. The algorithm has two steps. The first step is to gain a non-folding layout which close to the actual layout structure by using a heuristic principle. If the network map shows a center radiation structure, the approximation effect is more effective. The second step is to correct and balance the local optimal solution by adopting the optimization algorithm based on particle - spring model to ensure that the energy in new location is less than that in the original location. The greatest feature of AFL is that it never given a local optimal solution. Simulation results show that: a simple particle - spring algorithm, the initial position estimation will make a greater impact on it. And when network average connectivity is higher than 7, AFL algorithm will have a better localization result; the subsequent non-folding approach of AFL has better fault tolerance than increasing approach in ranging error.

ABC (Assumption Based Coordinates) algorithm calculates one unknown point coordinates at a time with the order of the nodes connections have set up. The coordinates of all nodes can be got under ideal circumstances, especially if the location accuracy is not high enough; ABC algorithm is very conducive to reducing the localization error. When without a reliable method of measuring, ABC algorithms improve the accuracy of local localization. But the accumulation of errors caused by the increasing beacon-free node localization program does not solve the overall localization accuracy.

KPS (deployment Knowledge-based Positioning System) algorithm is such an algorithm which based on pre-configured knowledge and the configuration probability distribution. This algorithm introduces two concepts: configuration point and the probability distribution function (probability distribution function, PDF). Configuration point is the location of the determined point which is in the node group when deploying the nodes; and the probability distribution function expresses the probability distribution that is obeyed by each group nodes after the sensor nodes configuration.

In the above-mentioned three kinds of beacon-free node localization algorithm, AFL algorithm is fully distributed, only requires a relatively small number of communications and simple calculation, and has good scalability and robustness. ABC algorithm can be realized easily, but the localization accuracy is poor.

3 Localization Algorithm of Beacon-Free Node Probability-Based (BFNP)

According to the central limit theorem in probability theory, we know that a large number of random variables we encountered in the practice are subject to Gaussian distribution. Suppose there are N sensor nodes in some region, and existing some pre-configured mechanism to make each node can find its neighbor nodes through wireless communication and to estimate the distance of them, or identify the number of neighbors. The each pair of neighbor relationship has a corresponding network graph G = (N, L). Here N is a collection of the vertexes, L is a collection of edges. For any one point $m_i, m_j \in N$ which is the vertex of graph G, so $r_{ij} \in L$, r_{ij} is the distance between vertex mi and vertex mj, d_{ij} is the true distance. Localization algorithm based on beacon-free node is that, given the distance measured values of all the neighbors r_{ij}, calculate the coordinates of each node B_i, and to make it be consistent with ranging results. That is, for $\forall e \in G$, to make $\left\| B_j - B_i \right\| = d_{ij}$. We will analysis detailed in the following part that how to achieve the Localization of the unknown nodes through the node configuration Likelihood Function and adjacent nodes ranging likelihood function.

3.1 Node Configuration Likelihood Function

Suppose we configure m configuration nodes in advance, its coordinate can be expressed as (x_i, y_i), $i = 1,2,3......m$, and (x_i, y_i) is known and stored in the memory of node. And then deploy and throw all the nodes randomly. According to Central Limit Theorem of probability theory, the arbitrary deployed configuration node k has the same probability function with configuration node, and they are all subject to two-dimensional Gaussian distribution. The probability density of this distribution can be expressed as following:

$$f_k^i (x, y \mid k \in N) = \frac{1}{2\pi\sigma^2} e^{-\left[(x - x_i)^2 + (y - y_i)^2 \right] / 2\sigma^2} \tag{1}$$

Here, the parameter σ is the variance of X and Y, x_i and y_i is the mathematical expectation of random variable X and Y respectively.

Let the coordinate of the configuration node m_i is v_{di}, its physical location exists in the vicinity of v_{di} in some probability. According to the probability theory, the likelihood function of physical location v_i is the conditional probability density function of v_{di} under the conditions of v_i. We called this function as the likelihood function of node configuration. That is:

$$L(v) = \prod_{i=1}^{n} f_k^i (x, y; v) \tag{2}$$

3.2 Likelihood Function of Adjacent Nodes Ranging

Suppose that the unknown node m_j can receive the information packet of the configured node m_i, the distance between two nodes can be estimated by RSSI. Let the location of the unknown node is $m_j = (x_j, x_j)$, $\hat{d}_{ij}$ expresses the estimated distance between m_i and m_j. $p(\theta)$ expresses the distribution probability of arbitrary node that is located in the communication range of the unknown node m_j.

The expression for $p(\theta)$ derived in literature [3] is:

$$p(\theta) = \left(\frac{1}{2\pi\Omega^2} e^{-z^2/2\Omega^2} \right) \bullet \pi R^2 \tag{3}$$

Here, $\Omega = 6.328R^2/\sigma^2 + \sigma$. The distributing probability around the unknown node m_j of the configuration node m_i is:

$$f(x = m_i, \theta) = C_m^a (p(\theta))^a (1 - p(\theta))^{m-a} \tag{4}$$

Here, m is the number of the configuration nodes, a is the number of the configuration nodes that are around the unknown nodes. By virtue of the estimated location v_{ij} and $\hat{d}_{ij}$ of the configuration node m_i, the likelihood function of actual distance d_{ij} can be estimated approximately, and then the adjacent nodes ranging likelihood function as follows:

$$L(d) = \prod_{i=1}^{n} f(\theta; d) \tag{5}$$

3.3 Location Algorithm Steps

The idea of Localization algorithm of beacon-free node probability-based is:(1) There are m sensor nodes in a certain region, we configure m configuration nodes in advance, its coordinate can be expressed as (x_i, y_i), and (x_i, y_i) is known and stored in the memory of node. (2) And then throw and deploy all the nodes randomly, the arbitrary node after deployment all obeys the two-dimensional Gaussian distribution. (3) After nodes being deployed, the distance between the unknown node and its neighbor nodes can be measured through the RSSI in the communication framework, and use the maximum likelihood estimation method to calculate the distance. (4) Finally, the node gets three distances, so it can locate its own.

4   Simulation Results Analysis

4.1   Estimate Error Analysis

Firstly, we assess the estimate error under different positioning factors. Assume that the deployment area is square with the size of 100m × 100m.Here m means the number of configuration nodes, R means transmission distance. Choose $\sigma = 10$. Then sensor networks are generated randomly on the base of the node configuration model. The simulation results are shown in Figure 1.

Fig.1 (a) shows the relationship between estimate error and m when R = 10m, 20m, 30m. From the Figure we can see clearly that the estimate error reduce as the value of m increases. Fig.1 (b) shows the relationship between estimate error and R when m = 100,200,300. Figure analysis shows that the error will reduce increase as the value of R increase.

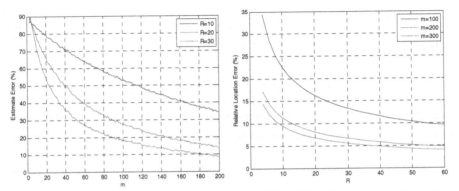

a) The relationship between estimate error and m   b) The relationship between estimate error and R

Fig. 1. Estimate error under different factors

The two simulation results show that there will be more sensors can be found, i.e. providing these activities nodes much observation with the density of WSN increase. Thus, more accurate results can generate by using this algorithm.

4.2   Analysis of Localization Accuracy

KPS algorithm and BFNP algorithm proposed in this paper has been simulated, from Figure 2 we can see that localization error of configuration point can quickly converge to the 4% -10%, when the configuration node localization error is 5%, the localization accuracy of the unknown nodes can improve 2%-10%.

From the above experiment we can see that when the R or m is larger, using the localization algorithm of this paper can provide node localization accuracy. Such precision can satisfy the majority of application needs in sensor network; therefore the result of this localization algorithm is desirable.

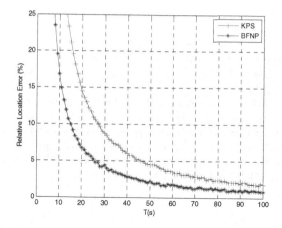

Fig. 2. Configuration node localization accuracy simulation map

5 Conclusion

This paper has analyzed and compared the beacon node algorithm and beacon-free node algorithm in sensor network. In cognizance of some aspects of disadvantages of existing beacon-free node localization algorithm, we put forward the localization algorithm of wireless sensor network beacon-free node probability-based according to the probability distribution of nodes deployment and likelihood function of adjacent nodes ranging. Simulation shows that the algorithm will reduce the computation and communication expenses in sensor network and improve the localization accuracy and has better adaptability.

References

1. Nissanka, B., Priyantha, H.B.: Anchor-free distributed localization in sensor networks. R. Technical Report 892, MIT Laboratory for Computer Science. 462—469 (2003)
2. Savarese, C., Rabaey, J.M., Beutel, J.: Locationing in distributed Ad-Hoc wireless sensor networks. In: Piscataway, C. (ed.) Proc. of 2001 IEEE Int'1 Conf Acoustics, Speech and Signal Processing(ICASSP 2001), NJ, USA, pp. 2037–2040 (2001)
3. Fang, L., Du, V., Ning, P.: A beacon-less location discovery scheme for wireless sensor networks. In: IEEE Conference on Computer Communications (INFOCOM), pp. 1632–1638 (2005)
4. Bahl, P., Padmanabhan, V.N.: RADAR An in-building RF-based user location and tracking system. In: Proceedings of the IEEE INFOCOM, pp. 775–784 (2000)
5. Niculescu, D., Nath, B.: Ad Hoc positioning system(APS)using AOA.C. In: Proceedings of the 22nd Annual Joint Conference of the IEEE Computer and Communications Societies (INFOCOM 2003), pp. 1734–1743. IEEE Computer and Communications Societies, San Francisco (2003)
6. Bulusu, N., Heidemann, J., Estrin, D.: GPS-less Low cost Outdoor Localization for Very Small Devices. C. IEEE Personal Communications, 28–34 (2002)

7. iculescu, D., Nath, B.: Ad hoe Positioning System. In: GLOBECOM (2001)
8. Tian, H., Chengdu, H., Blum, M.: Range-free Localization Schemes in Large Scale Sensor Networks. In: Proceedings of the 9th Annual International Conference on Mobile Computing and Networking M0BIC0M 2003 (2003)
9. Capkun, S., Hamdi, M., Hubaux, J.P.: GPS-free positioning in mobile Ad-Hoc networks. Cluster Computing Journal 5, 157–167 (2002)
10. Savarese, C., Rabay, J., Langendoen, K.: Robust positioning algorithms for distributed Ad-Hoc wireless sensor networks. In: Ellis, C.S. (ed.) Proceedings of the USENIX Technical Annual Conference Monterey, pp. 317–327. USENIX Press, CA,USA (2002)
11. Bergamo, P., Mazzini, G.: Localization in sensor networks with fading and mobility. In: 13th IEEE International Symposium on Personal Indoor and Mobile Radio Communications (IEEE PIMRC 2002), pp. 750–754 (2002)

The Method of Knowledge Processing in Intelligent Design System of Products

Lingling Li, Jingzheng Liu, Zhigang Li, and Jungang Zhou

Electrical apparatus institute, Hebei University of Technology, 300130 Tianjin, China
haohaohao@eyou.com, loojz@126.com, zgli@hebut.edu.cn,
jungang1983@126.com

Abstract. In all intelligent systems, knowledge is the cornerstone of the construction of system. This paper discusses a number of ways of the knowledge expression, such as rule, processing, semantic network, nonspecification logic ,as well as the organization, management and acquisition of knowledge. With the electrical apparatus products as an example, the paper proposes the approach of designing object knowledge, including forward and reverse mixed reasoning mechanism and rule based reasoning(RBR) method under the fuzzy mechanism. It also presents the establishment of an intelligent model of knowledge processing and evaluation method for projects of product conceptual design.

Keywords: knowledge processing, system reasoning, RBR.

1 Introduction

With the information age is coming, the life circle of products is becoming shorter and shorter, and shows diversified, personalized features, so the ability of rapid development of manufacturing new products is challenged for the enterprises. This century the core of economic competitiveness is based on knowledge of new products in the market. Therefore, utilizing AI (Artificial Intelligence, AI) technique to solve logic processing automation problems in the designing field, on the basis of the realization of innovative design, has become a powerful measure for enterprises to develop.

Knowledge processing, including that the expression, organization, management, utilization, acquisition of knowledge and so on. Among them, the knowledge expression is not only the foundation but also one of cores of AI research. The utilization and acquisition of knowledge are related to system reasoning and machine larning respectively; the organization and management of knowledge are both related to the knowledge expression and reasoning. Appropriate methods of organization and management are benefit to the maintenance of the knowledge database and improve the efficiency of reasoning. In this paper, the purpose is product innovation and studying knowledge expression, organization and management problems.

Z. Cai et al. (Eds.): ISICA 2009, LNCS 5821, pp. 541–551, 2009.

2 The Organization, Expression, Management, and Acquisition of Knowledge

2.1 The Organization and Expression of Knowledge

Different from the ordinary program that embeds knowledge and algorithm being used to solve the problem, the knowledge in our expert system is divided into three levels, namely data, knowledge database and control strategy. The knowledge relevant to solving problem in the applied field is organized into an independent entity—knowledge database that is an important resource of the system's intelligence. The control strategy is usually expressed as some kind of reasoning strategy to deal with the knowledge in database, which is independent of knowledge database. The operation of the system begins from knowledge database to reach conclusion with the control of reasoning.

Organizing and expressing of the knowledge rationally is the key factor to manifest the system's intelligence. The knowledge dealing with designing electrical apparatus is very large and complicated, including not only the knowledge relevant to designing goal but also the knowledge relevant to designing procedure. The different knowledge is used for different goal, some are used for planning the procedure of designing electrical apparatus and some are used directly for designing the part of electrical apparatus. One of the features of our system is to express meta knowledge obviously and managed by groups. The meta knowledge groups include the group to select designing methods, the group to determine designing procedure, the group to divide the job into sub-jobs, the group to revise the design and the group to evaluate the design.

2.2 Some Basic Methods of Knowledge Expression

"Knowledge expression" is often refer to "adopting based symbolized formal language in the expression knowledge in computer". There are many knowledge in electrical design field,including division of product types,mechanical structure,design experience,example,formula and so on of each subclass,for expessing those knowledge sufficiently,in this paper semantic network, production rule, nonspecification logic and process are mixed used to make the knowledge database posses multiple knowledge expression structure.

Semantic Network of Knowledge Expression. Hierarchical diversication of product types and hierarchical decomposition product components and accessory can be expressed by semantic network, as Fig. 1 showed.

Note represents object and the descriptions of the object.the object is not only refer to physical entity(such as relay, electromagnetic relay, clap assembling type electromagnetic relay); the descriping part can be also abstract entities or abstract category(such as description of relay Characters); the descriping part offers the additional information of the object(such as : application field of relay); Arc is used to join the object and the desciping part. A-KIND-OF(AKO)is used to join individual class and the parent class; IS-A joins an example or an individual class to a nomal class; HAS-A is used to join an object and a part of it.

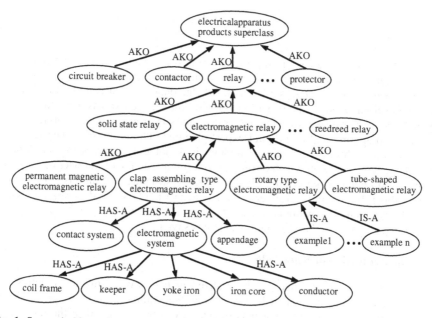

Fig. 1. Semantic Network expression composed of classification of electric apparatus product and their components

The Expression Method of Knowledge Production Rule and Nonspecification Logic. The knowledge of design of electric apparatus product including two species -- -certainty and uncertainty,for managing the knowledge and the testing of consistency and integrity better, a unified rule is set on the expression form of "rule class" knowledge ,its structure is the quadruple as bellowed:

$$\text{Rule= (rule name, rule premise, rule conclusion, rule reliability).} \qquad (1)$$

This is an expression method of designing rule mixed with "production rule" and "nonspecification logic", it rewrites by the normal way of production expression method form: "if rule premise then rule conclusion".

The Process Expression of Knowledge. There are many formals in the electronic apparatus design, this kind of knowledge can be expressed by "process", it can be described as the quadruple bellowed:

$$\text{Process = (process name, excitation condition, operation, return).} \qquad (2)$$

If the "excitation condition" is satisfied, this process will be activatingd; "operation" refers to calculation process, which is similar as a process of subprogram; the result is returned to the superior program that calls this process.

2.3 The Management of Knowledge Database

The content of knowledge database is divided into several independent files according to different problems that are going to be deal with. Each of the file is divided into multi-level sub-files according to the class and function of knowledge it includes, and several rules, frames or process are included in the lowest level files. All files and sub-files are expressed by frames. The name of the top level frame is knowledge database and its slot name is second level frame; the names of second frame are file names and their slot names are third level frames; etc. Rule and process entities are the slot values of lowest frame. The names of lowest frame are the names of rule and process. In this way, created is a large knowledge database that is under the direction by metalevel knowledge , be of various kind of knowledge expressions and managed by multi level frames ,a knowledge integrated entity is produced that combines digital scientific computing and non-digital expert planning. The knowledge database managed by frame shows a feature of module, it is not only express various kind of knowledge adequately but also convenient to test consistency of knowledge, or maintenance and update of knowledge; In addition, the structure of frame is very suitable to describing the hierarchical inheritance character of "class" used in object-oriented technology which is convenient to classify knowledge, in this way efficiency of reasoning machine is raised and system resource is saved.

2.4 The Acqusition of Knowledge

The acquisition of knowledge can be realized in two ways ---manual inputing and machine self-learning, no matter by which way the acquired knowledge get, it should not in contradiction with the demands of integrity constraint fixed in the knowledge database.integrity constraint of knowledge is a process of the coordination and balance among knowledge entity under meta reasoning function controlled, including testing of consistency and redundancy of knowledge. For example, as a certain rule that just matched from machine reasoning if the premises are the same but the conclusions are different, besides the reliability of new conclusion is lager than the former one, then refresh the old rule to ensure the consistency of the knowledge. If the premise and conclusion of the new rule is same with the old one, but the reliability of the new rule is lager than the old one, then only refresh the value of the reliability; if the conclusion set of the old rule is the subset of new one, then the system will replace the new one with the old one according to the redundancy testing rule, in order to reduce the redundancy degree. The supervision of knowledge object and the using method by metalevel reasoning function make the system have the self-teaching ability.

3 Processing Method of Designing Object Knowledge

3.1 Forward and Reverse Mixed Reasoning Mechanism of the System

Forward and reverse mixed reasoning conduction mainly represent in the using of feature model. Take an example of designing a relay, the user put the designing goal parameters into the system, such as output circuit's rated current, rated voltage, contacting resistance and overload current or voltage as well as control circuit's rated power, acting power, rated voltage, acting voltage and releasing voltage etc. The parameters to be determined are that of core, yoke, winding etc. So, it is typically backward reasoning chain. The system takes forward reasoning in the inner, because the system will analyze and check some functions (such as dynamic and static characteristic) using relevant rule and procedure entities once a primary scheme is determined according to designing goal. In this way, the system optimizes and adjusts design parameters. The whole process equals the reasoning process from fact to goal that is a typically forward reasoning chain.

Feature model is an important "media" to cast the designing question P from the parameter domain to domain,functional domain,behavior district.In one hand ,for a customer ,the design requirements usually are described by a group of numerical type technical index(technical attribute),so P is mainly related to parameter domain;on the other hand, as mentioned before, feature model is organized and managed according to hierarchical diversion of products types. The Fig.1 shows that the types of electrical apparatus products is classified according to the structure of subclass product based on function decomposition.Therefore all layers of feature model not only related to the domain itself, but also decompose domain layer by layer, by particle size from big to small.In the mean time ,because some kind of product fuction, information of behavior property and information of numerical type technical attribute are incuded in feature model.So association can be built among parameter domain , domain,functional domain and behavior district by using feature model.

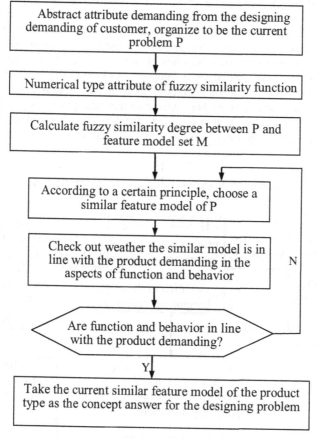

Fig. 2. The procedure of figuring out the concept answer of the designing problem by using feature model

Simply speaking,the function of feature model is to build a mapping from parameter domain to domain,functional domain and behavior district.This mapping leads system in a solving of design problem in the product conceptual design stage.

The method and procedure of using feature model to slove conceptual solution of design problem is as Fig. 2 showed. This procedure can be descriped step by step as bellowed:

Step 1:definging all the fuzzy similarity function related to all the technical attributes in the design problem P and feature model set M, calculate fuzzy similarity degree of them.then stand on parameter domain,take maximum similarity principle or hreshold principle to match out preliminarily the most similar feature model of P.

Step 2:check out whether the the most similar feature model of P matched out preliminarily can satisfy requirments from two aspects---function attribute and behavior attribute.If the answer is yes then this feature model is the structure designing answer of P in the procdure of concept designing stage;if the answer is no,then take other feature model to check out the fuction and behavior according to calculated value of the fuzzy similarty degree.

Step1 is the forward reasoning, taking product attribute proposed by user's requirements as the initial evidence to the process of solving design problems, and based on this reasoning, a preliminary assumption is proposed, namely: in the aspect of the technical attributes, the most similar to this characteristic of the model is conceptual design solutions. Step2 is the reverse reasoning, checking out the preliminary matched model, which is most similar to the characteristics of functional, behavioral attributes, that is, trying to find evidence to support the assumption. As long as the result of forward reasoning is exactly the reverse to find evidence, then the reasoning is successful. Because of forward and reverse reasoning both appear in the conceptual design of products to solve the problem,Therefore, with reference to the direction of reasoning, the system is being used, forward and backward reasoning,as Fig. 3 showed.

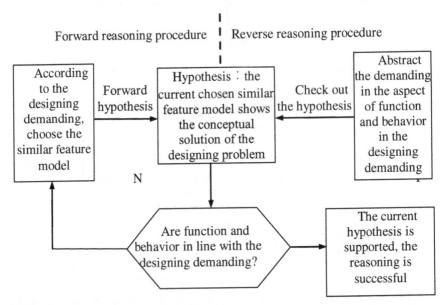

Fig. 3. The forward and backward reasoning in product conceptual designing procedure

3.2 The Reasoning Method Based Rule under the Fuzzy Mechanism

Rule based reasoning(RBR) is the most widely used reasoning method in the expert system, it is the method that from of the known knowledge object expands to the new one by a certain strategy. In most of time product design is a question solving process with certainty and uncertainty, it is not only including accurate quantization reasoning but also including fuzzy discrimination by using the experience knowledge. The advantage of RBR system is that it can deal very well with the experience knowledge described by symbols and the processing knowledge aimed at numerical calculation,in favor of combine of the symbols reasoning and numerical calculation.

The Fuzzy Rule Reasoning Model. The form of fuzzy rule R is often the one below:

$$R : \text{if } A \text{ then } B \text{ with } CF_R$$

In the form A is the precondition of rule called antecedent of rule; B is the conclusion part of rule called consequent; $CF_R \in (0,1.0]$ is deterministic function of precondition A and conclusion B , it reflects the influence degree of B when A is the true rule R so it is called "rule confidence" or "rule strength". In the deterministic rules $CF_R = 1.0$.

By using rule R, conclusion can be obtained from the known fact. A and B in R can be express in the accurate way and the fuzzy way; in the same way, A' in the practical reasoning can be accurate or fuzzy. In the CBR of product design , A' is often fuzzy, namely A' is only the fuzzy fact approximate to A . The fuzzy degree of A' to A is called "fact credibility", denoted as $CF_{A/A'}$ in this paper.

RBR under fuzzy mechanism can be described as:

Rule: if A then B ; rule credibility CF_R

Fact: if A' is exited now; fact credibility $CF_{A/A'}$

Conclusion: B' is tenable; concultion credibility $CF_{B/B'}$

Among them, conclusion credibility $CF_{B/B'}$ shows the approximate degree between conclusion B' and rule consequent B .By the fuzzy rule reasoning above, expansion from the known object to the new one is accomplished. In this system, fuzzy RBR is used to choose one rule to carry out from many rules that matched, namely conflict resolution is processing among rule set.

For describing better, the reasoning structure is established for fuzzy RBR as bellowed:

$$
\begin{array}{l}
A \to B, \ CF_R \\
A', \ CF_{A/A'} \\
\hline
B', \ CF_{B/B'} = CF_R \otimes CF_{A/A'}
\end{array}
\qquad (3)
$$

In the formula above $\otimes$ is adjoint operation of " $\to$ ". In this paper the definition is:

$$CF_{B/B'} = CF_R \otimes CF_{A/A'} = CF_R \times CF_{A/A'} . \qquad (4)$$

Fuzziness of conclusion B' is spreaded by the fact credibility though the implicative relations above.

Rule antecedent A and consequent B both have the possibility of including several sub-sentence, the number of them are set as n and m respectively, described as $A = \{A_1, A_2, ..., A_n\}$, $B = \{B_1, B_2, ..., B_m\}$. Rule in this paper: For every rule , logical operator of each sub-sentences in rule's antecedent set A and consequent set B are both "and" or both "or", two of them can not be used mixed in A and B. If the mixed utilization is existed in the product design rule, then it must be separated into two or several rules when setting rule set, in order to the testing of consistency and reluctance of knowledge.

No matter the logic relationship of sub-sentences of B is "and" or "or", credibility $CF_{B/B'}$ of B' all calculated as the formal above, and:

$$CF_{B/B'} = CF_{B_1/B_1'} = ... = CF_{B_m/B_m'}. \tag{5}$$

In the formula $CF_{B/B'}$ is the credibility of the conclusion sub-sentence B_j' ($j = 1,2,...,m$).

If the sub-sentences of A are independent with each other and combine together with the logic relationship "and", namely $A = A_1 \wedge A_2 \wedge ... \wedge A_n$.

Set: credibility $CF_{A_i/A_i'}$ is the sub fact $A_i'(i = 1,2,...,n)$ of fuzzy fact A', then:

$$CF_{A/A'} = \bigwedge_{i=1}^{n} \{CF_{A_i/A_i'}\}. \tag{6}$$

Namely choose the smallest one for the fact credibility $CF_{A/A'}$ among the set $\{CF_{A_i/A_i'} | i = 1,2,...,n\}$.

If the sub-sentences of A are independent with each other and combine together with the logic relationship "or", namely: $A = A_1 \vee A_2 \vee ... \vee A_n$, then:

$$CF_{A/A'} = \bigvee_{i=1}^{n} \{CF_{A/A_i'}\}. \tag{7}$$

Formla (7) can be used as a basis for judging confliction of rule set. A best suitable one can be chosen among them, if many rules are matched that are packaging in the product object model, namely: the rule with the biggest conclusion credibility $CF_{B/B'}$.

Matching Example of Design Rule. There are three rules when make sure the free path of keeper S_1 in electromagnetic relay design:

R1: If vibration grade acceleration of relay application place is more than 10g, or vibration frequency is above 500HZ, then $S_1 > 0.30$mm, rule credibility $CF_{R1} = 0.95$.

R2: If vibration grade acceleration is from 5g to 10g, or vibration frequency is from 200HZ to 500HZ, then $S_1 > 0.15$mm, rule credibility $CF_{R2} = 0.95$.

R3: If vibration grade acceleration is below 5g, or vibration frequency is below 200HZ, then $S_1 > 0.05$mm, rule credibility $CF_{R3} = 0.95$.

Here,"g" in rule is acceleration of gravity . Appearance that antecedent of the above three rules can be all described as the form " $A = A_1 \vee A_2$ ".

Known: the design conditions that users input are "vibration grade acceleration is 10g, vibration frequency is 600HZ". This known condition is the objective fact A' used for fuzzy reasoning. Here A' is given in the accurate form.

For explaining question better, in this paper $Z = \{z_1, z_2\} = \{$vibration grade acceleration, vibration frequency$\}$, the attribution set is set up, and x_1, x_2 is represent for the value of z_1 and z_2 respectively.

If membership function $r_1(x_1), r_2(x_1), r_3(x_1)$ of attribution z_1 can be set up in the universe (10g, ∞),[5g, 10g],(0, 5g), then three membership degree of fuzzy set above about 10g can be solved, membership degree are $r_1(x_1)\big|_{x_1=10g}$, $r_2(x_1)\big|_{x_1=10g}$, $r_3(x_1)\big|_{x_1=10g}$ respectively; in the same way, if membership function $r_1^*(x_2), r_2^*(x_2)$, $r_3^*(x_2)$ of attribution z_2 can be set up in the universe (500HZ, ∞)、 [200HZ, 500HZ]、 (0, 200HZ) then three membership degree of fuzzy set above about 600HZ can be solved, membership degree are $r_1^*(x_2)\big|_{x_2=600HZ}$, , $r_3^*(x_2)\big|_{x_2=600HZ}$ respectively.

In the process of matching R_1, $r_1(x_1)\big|_{x_1=10g}$ and $r_1^*(x_2)\big|_{x_2=600HZ}$ is equal to credibility $CF_{A_i/A_i'}$ of the sub fact $A_i'(i=1,2)$,it is set as $CF_{A_i/A_i'}(R_1)$ for distinguishing from the related contents in R_2, R_3 .

In the same way: $r_2(x_1)\big|_{x_1=10g} = CF_{A_1/A_1'}(R_2)$;

$r_2^*(x_2)\big|_{x_2=600HZ} = CF_{A_2/A_2'}(R_2)$;

$r_3(x_1)\big|_{x_1=10g} = CF_{A_1/A_1'}(R_3)$;

$r_3^*(x_2)\big|_{x_2=600HZ} = CF_{A_2/A_2'}(R_3)$

Set: given $r_1(x_1)\big|_{x_1=10g} = 0.5; r_1^*(x_2)\big|_{x_2=600HZ} = 0.8;$

$r_2(x_1)\big|_{x_1=10g} = 0.5; r_2^*(x_2)\big|_{x_2=600HZ} = 0.2;$

$r_3(x_1)\big|_{x_1=10g} = 0.1; r_3^*(x_2)\big|_{x_2=600HZ} = 0$

Then:for R_1 ,conclusion credibility $CF_{B/B'}(R_1) = CF_{R_1} \times CF_{A/A'}(R_1) = 0.95 \times \max\{0.5, 0.8\} = 0.76$.

For R_2, $CF_{B/B'}(R_2) = CF_{R_2} \times CF_{A/A'}(R_2) = 0.95 \times \max\{0.5, 0.2\} = 0.19$;

For R_3 , $CF_{B/B'}(R_3) = CF_{R_3} \times CF_{A/A'}(R_3) = 0.95 \times \max\{0.1, 0\} = 0.095$

According to "Decision Strategies of rule set confliction" in the paper, if R_1 matches successfully, the system executes $S_1 > 0.30mm$, which is used to design the free path S_1 of relay keeper.

If A' is given with fuzzy form, the fuzzy set of attributes z_1 and z_2 should be established respectively according to A' , then the fact credibility $CF_{A/A'}$ should be calculated with the closeness degree of these two fuzzy set. Principle of choosing algorithm and rule of conclusion credibility is as the same of above one.

4   The Evaluation Model of the Electrical Apparatus Designs

The evaluation of the electrical apparatus designs can be classified into three aspects, function, and cost and technology feasibility. The function deals with technical parameters raised by user, also taking relay as an example, the items to be evaluated are: static characteristics, dynamic characteristics, work limit temperature and work mechanical shocking etc. In special environment, there are some special requirements such as anti-salt or anti-fog and so on. The cost corresponds to manufacturing costs, such as material and labor etc. The technology feasibility corresponds to the manufacturing equipments and the working conditions, etc. It also includes throughput and assembly ability.

The evaluating scores C_i of electrical apparatus design about function, cost and feasibility can be gotten according to following formula,

$$C_i = \sum_{j=1}^{n} u_j C_{ij} \ , i = 1,2,3 \ . \tag{8}$$

Where, n is the number of items being evaluated, $u_j (j = 1,2,...,n)$ is weight factor given by expert, C_{ij} is the score of the j sub-item of the i item being evaluated.

So, total score of every design scheme $c = \sum_{i=1}^{3} v_i C_i$, here v_i is the weight factor that experts give to function, cost and feasibility respectively. The user can revise and optimize the design scheme according to evaluations after getting C_i and C. The system set a threshold ρ of C and will choose the scheme with $C \geq \rho$ and maximum of C as final scheme without the user's interfering. For all items to be evaluated, if $C \leq \rho$, the system will design again until finding a scheme with $C \geq \rho$.

5   Conclusion

In this paper, aiming to different types of knowledge used in electrical apparatus design, a combination of knowledge expression such as:rules, process, semantic networks,nonspecification logic are used to build a knowledge database,to make knowledge system have the structure of a number of knowledge expression and multi-system architecture. In the aspect of reasoning in the system control strategy, forward and backward mixed reasoning method is used to make system reasoning under control; intelligent knowledge process model is established.

Acknowledgement. This work was supported by the National Natural Science Foundation (No. 60771069) and the Hebei Province Natural Science Foundation (No. F2007000115 and No. 602069).

References

[1] Sánchez, A.M., Patricio, M.A., García, J., Molina, J.M.: Expert Systems with Applications. 36(8), 10995 (2009)
[2] Park, M., Kang, B., Jin, S.J., Luo, S.: Expert Systems with Applications. 36(3), 7242 (2009)
[3] Lingling, L., Zhigang, L., Chunlai, Z., et al.: Control & Automation. 27(2), 187 (2007)
[4] Li, J.-p., Yu, J.-x.: TIAN Jia Ship Engineering 31(1), 47 (2009)
[5] Lin, Y., Chun-xia, L., et al.: Journal of Computer Applications. 27(3), 765 (2007)
[6] Xiangjun, Z., Changlin, G.: Chinese Journal of Mechanical Engineering. 37(2), 8 (2001)
[7] Zhaohui, G., Zhigang, L., Jianna, W.: Relay. 33(16), 10 (2005)
[8] Muhui, L., Jie, Z., Zhengwei, B.: Journal of Fujian Normal University. 25(1), 120 (2009)

Author Index